SOUTH-WESTERN
CENGAGE Learning·

OM, 2012–2013
David A. Collier, James R. Evans

Executive Vice President, LRS Solutions
  Strategy & Design: Jonathan Hulbert

Sr. Vice President, Learning Acquisitions &
  Solutions Planning: Jack W. Calhoun

Editorial Director, Business &
  Economics: Erin Joyner

Publisher: Joe Sabatino

Publisher/Director, 4LTR Press: Neil Marquardt

Sr. Acquisitions Editor: Charles McCormick, Jr.

Development Editor: Margaret Kubale

Product Development Manager, 4LTR Press:
  Steven Joos

Team Assistant, 4LTR Press: Brian Storck

Sr. Content Project Manager: Colleen A. Farmer

Media Editor: Chris Valentine

Manufacturing Planner: Ron Montgomery

Manufacturing Frontlist Buyer: Amanda Klapper

Production House: S4Carlisle Publishing
  Services

Sr. Art Director: Stacy Jenkins Shirley

Cover and Internal Designer: Red Hanger Design

Cover Image: shutterstock images/Chris Rawlins

Sr. Rights Specialist, Text and Photo: John Hill

For product information and technology assistance, contact us at
Cengage Learning Customer & Sales Support, 1-800-354-9706

For permission to use material from this text or product,
submit all requests online at **cengage.com/permissions**
Further permissions questions can be emailed to
permissionrequest@cengage.com

ExamView® is a registered trademark of eInstruction Corp. Windows is a registered trademark of the Microsoft Corporation used herein under license. Macintosh and Power Macintosh are registered trademarks of Apple Computer, Inc. used herein under license.

Cengage Learning WebTutor™ is a trademark of Cengage Learning.

Microsoft Excel® is a registered trademark of Microsoft Corporation. © 2013 Microsoft.

Library of Congress Control Number: 2012941910

Student Edition Package
ISBN-13: 978-1-133-37242-4
ISBN-10: 1-133-37242-2

Student Edition (book only)
ISBN-13: 978-1-133-37241-7
ISBN-10: 1-133-37241-4

South-Western Cengage Learning
5191 Natorp Boulevard
Mason, OH 45040
USA

Cengage Learning products are represented in Canada by Nelson Education, Ltd.

For your course and learning solutions, visit **www.cengage.com**

Purchase any of our products at your local college store or at our preferred online store **www.cengagebrain.com**

Printed in the United States of America
1 2 3 4 5 6 7 16 15 14 13 12

Brief Contents

Supplementary Chapters (online)

Contents

© Matt Antonino/Shutterstock.com

© iStockphoto.com/Daniel Cooper

© Simone Vanden Berg/Shutterstock.com

© Michael Dwyer/Alamy

© kali9/iStockphoto.com

© Mario Ruiz/Time Life Pictures/Getty Images

GOODS, SERVICES, AND OPERATIONS MANAGEMENT

 want to be a director of a museum like this one day," Carol said to her mom as they walked through Chicago Museum of Science and Industry. Carol's family had just finished a tour of the 1944 German submarine known as the U-505 that was captured during World War II. They had spent the day learning about coal mines, the science of the human body, Dr. Seuss, and much more. As they walked past the museum offices, Carol noticed a directory of eight departments:

- Business Operations
- Facilities
- Food Service
- Exhibit Maintenance
- Guest Call Center
- Guest Operations
- Information Services
- Protective Services

She asked, "Dad, why does a museum need all these? All I see are the exhibits!"

learning outcomes

After studying this chapter you should be able to:

1-1 **Explain the concept and importance of operations management.**

1-2 **Describe what operations managers do.**

1-3 **Explain the differences between goods and services.**

1-4 **Describe a customer benefit package.**

1-5 **Explain the role of processes in OM and identify three general types of processes.**

1-6 **Summarize the historical development of OM.**

1-7 **Describe current challenges facing OM.**

What do **you** think?

Can you provide examples of the type of work activities and decisions that are made in each of these eight departments at the Chicago Museum of Science and Industry?

AfriPics.com/Alamy Limited

1-1 Operations Management

Operations management (OM) *is the science and art of ensuring that goods and services are created and delivered successfully to customers.* OM includes the *design of* goods, services, and the processes that create them; the day-to-day *management* of those processes; and the continual *improvement* of these goods, services, and processes. Why is OM important? To answer this, we might first ask the question: What makes a company successful? In 1887, William Cooper Procter, grandson of the founder of Procter & Gamble, told his employees, "The first job we have is to turn out quality merchandise that consumers will buy and keep on buying. If we produce it efficiently and economically, we will earn a profit, in which you will share." Procter's statement—which is still as relevant today as it was over 100 years ago—addresses three issues that are at the core of operations management: *efficiency, cost,* and *quality.* Efficiency (a measure of how well resources are used in creating outputs), the cost of operations, and the quality of the goods and services that create customer satisfaction all contribute to profitability, and ultimately, the long-run success of a company. A company cannot be successful without people who understand how these concepts relate to each other, which is the essence of OM, and can apply OM principles effectively in making decisions.

> **Operations management (OM)** is the science and art of ensuring that goods and services are created and delivered successfully to customers.

▼ *A variety of departments, including Security, Exhibit Maintenance, and Guest Operations, are required to keep a museum running smoothly.*

The opening description of Chicago's Museum of Science and Industry suggests that the way in which goods and services, and the processes that create and support them, are designed and managed can make the difference between a delightful or unhappy customer experience. That is what OM is all about! Operations management is the only function by which managers can directly affect the value provided to all stakeholders—customers, employees, investors, and society.

The eight departments at Chicago's Museum of Science and Industry highlight the importance of OM in designing and managing the museum. Each of these departments uses one or more processes to create customer value and ensure efficient operations. The guest call center, for example, must design processes to handle a wide variety of customer inquiries, forecast call volume, determine the number (capacity) of customer service representatives (CSRs) to have on duty by time of day, schedule them, design their jobs, and train them to deliver superior customer experiences. In fact, the museum does all of the activities described in the box "What Do Operations Managers Do?"

1-2 OM in the Workplace

any people who are considered "operations managers" have titles such as chief operating officer, hotel or restaurant manager, vice president of manufacturing, customer service manager, plant manager, field service manager, or supply chain manager. The concepts and methods of OM can be used in any job, regardless of the functional area of business or industry, to better create value for internal customers (within the organization) and for external customers (outside the organization). OM principles are used in accounting, human resources management, legal work, financial activities, marketing, environmental management, and every type of service activity. Thus, everyone should understand OM and be

What Do Operations Managers Do?

Some of the key activities that operations managers perform include the following:

- *Forecasting: Predict the future demand for raw materials, finished goods, and services.*
- *Supply Chain Management: Manage the flow of materials, information, people, and money from suppliers to customers.*
- *Facility Layout and Design: Determine the best configuration of machines, storage, offices, and departments to provide the highest levels of efficiency and customer satisfaction.*
- *Technology Selection: Use technology to improve productivity and respond faster to customers.*
- *Quality Management: Ensure that goods, services, and processes will meet customer expectations and requirements.*
- *Purchasing: Coordinate the acquisition of materials, supplies, and services.*
- *Resource and Capacity Management: Ensure that the right amount of resources (labor, equipment, materials, and information) is available when needed.*
- *Process Design: Select the right equipment, information, and work methods to produce high-quality goods and services efficiently.*
- *Job Design: Decide the best way to assign people to work tasks and job responsibilities.*
- *Service Encounter Design: Determine the best types of interactions between service providers and customers, and how to recover from service upsets.*
- *Scheduling: Determine when resources such as employees and equipment should be assigned to work.*
- *Sustainability: Decide the best way to manage the risks associated with products and operations to preserve resources for future generations.*

able to apply its tools and concepts. Following are some examples of how our former students (who were not OM majors!) are using OM in their jobs.

The concepts and methods of OM can be used in any job, regardless of the functional area of business or industry.

SMART TRASH CONTAINERS & OPERATIONS

A new solar-powered trash container on a Florida public road not only compacts the trash but also sends an e-mail for pickup when full. One side of the container is for recycling and the other for trash. Regular trash containers must be picked up several times a week. Each 300-pound solar-powered trash container costs about $3,800 but reduces the overall carbon footprint by lowering transportation costs, in addition to offering the environmental benefits of recycling. Compacting the trash also results in less pickups. The covered containers also protect animals from foraging through the trash and harming themselves and the environment. Cash-strapped cities such as Philadelphia and Chicago have bought hundreds of these "smart trash containers."

This smart and new way of collecting trash and recycling has a major impact on the operation of this government service (see box "What Do Operations Managers Do?"). First, there is less need to forecast when the containers are full, and better quality because the containers don't overflow and contaminate the surroundings. In addition, less trucks (resources) are required for the total trash collection system, jobs and processes are streamlined and more efficient, the scheduling of trucks (called vehicle routing) is more efficient and reduces total miles travelled, and the trash collection system is more sustainable in preserving resources for future generations.

Richard Graulich/ZUMA Press/Newscom

Source: "Jupiter's new solar-powered trash bins already having effect across Florida," *The Palm Beach Post News*, October 24, 2011, http://www.palmbeachpost.com/news/jupiters-new-solar-powered-trash-bins-already-having-1929714.html.

- **Scheduling:** Production schedules are created to ensure that enough product is available for both retail and wholesale customers, taking into account such factors as current inventory and soap production capacity.

- **Quality management:** Each product is inspected and must conform to the highest quality standards. If a product does not conform to standard (for example, wrong color, improper packaging, improper labeling, improper weight, size, or shape), then it is removed from inventory to determine where the process broke down and to initiate corrective action.

Without an understanding of OM, the company would never have gotten off the ground!

Tom James is a senior software developer for a small software development company that creates sales proposal automation software. Tom uses OM skills in dealing with quality and customer service issues related to the software products he is involved in developing. He is also extensively involved in project management activities related to the development process, including identifying tasks, assigning developers to tasks, estimating the time and cost to complete projects, and studying the variance between the estimated and actual time it took to complete the project. He is also involved in continuous improvement projects; for example, he seeks to reduce development time and increase the efficiency of the development team. Tom was an information technology and management major in college.

Brooke Wilson is a process manager for JPMorgan Chase in the credit card division. After several years working as an operations analyst, he was promoted to a production supervisor position overseeing "plastic card production." Among his OM-related activities are the following:

- **Planning and budgeting:** Representing the plastic card production area in all meetings, developing annual budgets and staffing plans, and watching

Soap Box Soap Company (soapboxsoapco.com) manufactures and sells natural soaps and body products. The company was created as an entrepreneurial venture by Shelly Decker and her sister. Shelly was an accounting and information systems major in college, but she is involved in using OM skills every day:

- **Process design:** When a new product is to be introduced, the best way to produce it must be determined. This involves charting the detailed steps needed to make the product.

- **Inventory management:** Inventory is tightly controlled to keep cost down and to avoid production that isn't needed. Inventory is taken every four weeks and adjusted in the inventory management system accordingly.

technology that might affect the production of plastic credit cards.

- **Inventory management:** Overseeing the management of inventory for items such as plastic blank cards; inserts such as advertisements; envelopes, postage, and credit card rules and disclosure inserts.
- **Scheduling and capacity:** Daily to annual scheduling of all resources (equipment, people, inventory) necessary to issue new credit cards and reissue cards that are up for renewal, replace old or damaged cards, as well as cards that are stolen.
- **Quality:** Embossing the card with accurate customer information and quickly getting the card in the hands of the customer.

Brooke was an accounting major in college.

1-3 Understanding Goods and Services

Companies design, produce, and deliver a wide variety of goods and services that consumers purchase. *A good is a physical product that you can see, touch, or possibly consume.* Examples of goods include cell phones, appliances, food, flowers, soap, airplanes, furniture, coal, lumber, personal computers, paper, and industrial machines. *A durable good is one that does not quickly wear out and typically lasts at least three years.* Vehicles, dishwashers, and furniture are some examples. *A nondurable good is one that is no longer useful once it's used, or lasts for less than three years.* Examples are toothpaste, software, clothing and shoes, and food. Goods-producing firms are found in industries such as manufacturing, farming, forestry, mining, construction, and fishing.

A service is any primary or complementary activity that does not directly produce a physical product. Services represent the nongoods part of a transaction between a buyer (customer) and seller (supplier).[1] Service-providing firms are found in industries such as banking, lodging, education, health care, and government.

The services they provide might be a mortgage loan, a comfortable and safe place to sleep, a college degree, a medical procedure, or police and fire protection.

Designing and managing operations in a goods-producing firm is quite different from that in a service organization. Thus, it is important to understand the nature of goods and services, and particularly the differences between them.

Goods and services share many similarities. They are driven by customers and provide value and satisfaction to customers who purchase and use them. They can be standardized for the mass market or customized to individual needs. They are created and provided to customers by some type of process involving people and technology. Services that do not involve significant interaction with customers (for example, credit card processing) can be managed much the same as goods in a factory, using proven principles of OM that have been refined over the years. Nevertheless, some very significant differences exist between goods and services that make the management of service-providing organizations different from goods-producing organizations and create different demands on the operations function.[2]

1. **Goods are tangible, whereas services are intangible.** Goods are consumed, but services are experienced. Goods-producing industries rely on

Stephen Coburn/Shutterstock

Dmitriy Shironosov/Shutterstock

> A **good** is a physical product that you can see, touch, or possibly consume.
>
> A **durable good** is one that does not quickly wear out and typically lasts at least three years.
>
> A **nondurable good** is one that is no longer useful once it's used, or lasts for less than three years.
>
> A **service** is any primary or complementary activity that does not directly produce a physical product.

Andersen Ross/Getty Images

In addition, the customer and service provider often co-produce a service, meaning that they work together to create and simultaneously consume the service, as would be the case between a bank teller and a customer to complete a financial transaction.

This characteristic has interesting implications for operations. For example, it might be possible to off-load some work to the customer by encouraging self-service (supermarkets, cafeterias, libraries) and self-cleanup (fast-food restaurants, campgrounds, vacation home rentals). The higher the customer participation, the more uncertainty the firm has with respect to service time, capacity, scheduling, quality performance, and operating cost.

A service encounter is an interaction between the customer and the service provider. Some examples of service encounters are making a hotel reservation, asking a grocery store employee where to find the pickles, or making a purchase on a Web site. Service encounters consist of one or more **moments of truth**—*any episodes, transactions, or experiences in which a customer comes into contact with any aspect of the delivery system, however remote, and thereby has an opportunity to form an impression.*[4] A moment of truth might be a gracious welcome by an employee at the hotel check-in counter, a grocery store employee who seems too impatient to help, or trying to navigate a confusing Web site. Customers judge the value of a service and form perceptions through service encounters. Therefore, employees who interact directly with customers, such as airline flight attendants, customer service representatives, and bank tellers, need to understand the importance of service encounters. Also, those who design Web sites and telephone menus that customers use in service encounters must also understand how they may influence customer perceptions.

machines and "hard technology" to perform work. Goods can be moved, stored, and repaired, and generally require physical skills and expertise during production. Customers can often try them before buying. Services, on the other hand, make more use of information systems and other "soft technology," require strong behavioral skills, and are often difficult to describe and demonstrate. A senior executive of the Hilton Corporation stated, "We sell time. You can't put a hotel room on the shelf."[3]

2. **Customers participate in many service processes, activities, and transactions.** Many services require that the customer be present either physically, on a telephone, or online for service to commence.

A **service encounter** is an interaction between the customer and the service provider.

Moments of truth are episodes, transactions, or experiences in which a customer comes into contact with any aspect of the delivery system, however remote, and thereby has an opportunity to form an impression.

3. **The demand for services is more difficult to predict than the demand for goods.** Customer arrival rates

and demand patterns for such service delivery systems as banks, airlines, supermarkets, call centers, and courts are very difficult to forecast. The demand for services is time-dependent, especially over the short term (by hour or day). This places many pressures on service firm managers to adequately plan staffing levels and capacity.

4. **Services cannot be stored as physical inventory.** In goods-producing firms, inventory can be used to decouple customer demand from the production process or between stages of the production process and ensure constant availability despite fluctuations in demand. Service firms do not have physical inventory to absorb such fluctuations in demand. For service delivery systems, availability depends on the system's capacity. For example, a hospital must have an adequate supply of beds for the purpose of meeting unanticipated patient demand, and a float pool of nurses when things get very busy. Once an airline seat, a hotel room, or an hour of a lawyer's day are gone, there is no way to recapture the lost revenue.

5. **Service management skills are paramount to a successful service encounter.** Service providers require service management skills such as knowledge and technical expertise (operations), cross-selling other products and services (marketing), and good human interaction skills (human resources). **Service management** *integrates marketing, human resources, and operations functions to plan, create, and deliver goods and services, and their associated service encounters.* OM principles are useful in designing service encounters and supporting marketing objectives.

6. **Service facilities typically need to be in close proximity to the customer.** When customers must physically interact with a service facility—for example, post offices, hotels, and branch banks—they must be in a location convenient to customers. A manufacturing facility, on the other hand, can be located on the other side of the globe, as long as goods are delivered to customers in a timely fashion. In today's Internet age and with evolving service technologies, "proximity" need not be the same as location; many services are only a few mouse clicks away.

7. **Patents do not protect services.** A patent on a physical good or software code can provide protection from competitors. The intangible nature of a service makes it more difficult to keep a competitor from copying a business concept, facility layout, or service encounter design. For example,

restaurant chains are quick to copy new menu items or drive-through concepts.

These differences between goods and services have important implications to all areas of an organization, and especially to operations. These are summarized in Exhibit 1.1. Some are obvious, whereas others are more subtle. By understanding them, organizations can better select the appropriate mix of goods and services to meet customer needs and create the most effective operating systems to produce and deliver those goods and services.

1-4 Customer Benefit Packages

many goods and services are "bundled" in a certain way to provide value to customers. This not only enhances what customers receive, but can also differentiate the product from competitors. Such a bundle is often called a customer benefit package. *A* **customer benefit package (CBP)** *is a clearly defined set of tangible (goods-content) and intangible (service-content) features that the customer recognizes, pays for, uses, or experiences.* The CBP is a way to conceptualize and visualize goods and services by thinking broadly about how goods and services are bundled and configured together.

A CBP consists of a primary good or service, coupled with peripheral goods and/or services, and sometimes variants. *A* **primary good or service** *is the "core" offering that attracts customers and responds to their basic needs.* For example, the primary service of a personal checking account is convenient financial transactions. **Peripheral goods or services** *are*

Service management integrates marketing, human resources, and operations functions to plan, create, and deliver goods and services, and their associated service encounters.

A **customer benefit package (CBP)** is a clearly defined set of tangible (goods-content) and intangible (service-content) features that the customer recognizes, pays for, uses, or experiences.

A **primary good or service** is the "core" offering that attracts customers and responds to their basic needs.

Peripheral goods or services are those that are not essential to the primary good or service, but enhance it.

Exhibit 1.1 *How Goods and Services Affect Operations Management Activities*

OM Activity	Goods	Services
Forecasting	Forecasts involve longer-term time horizons. Goods-producing firms can use physical inventory as a buffer to mitigate forecast errors. Forecasts can be aggregated over larger time frames (e.g., months or weeks).	Forecast horizons generally are shorter, and forecasts are more variable and time-dependent. Forecasting must often be done on a daily or hourly basis, or sometimes even more frequently.
Facility Location	Goods-producing facilities can be located close to raw materials, suppliers, labor, or customers/markets.	Service facilities must be located close to customers/markets for convenience and speed of service.
Facility Layout and Design	Factories and warehouses can be designed for efficiency because few, if any, customers are present.	The facility must be designed for good customer interaction and movement through the facility and its processes.
Technology	Goods-producing facilities use various types of automation to produce, package, and ship physical goods.	Service facilities tend to rely more on information-based hardware and software.
Quality	Goods-producing firms can define clear, physical, and measurable quality standards and capture measurements using various physical devices.	Quality measurements must account for customer's perception of service quality and often must be gathered through surveys or personal contact.
Inventory/ Capacity	Goods-producing firms use physical inventory such as raw materials and finished goods as a buffer for fluctuations in demand.	Service capacity such as equipment or employees is the substitute for physical inventory.
Process Design	Because customers have no participation or involvement in goods-producing processes, the processes can be more mechanistic and controllable.	Customers usually participate extensively in service creation and delivery (sometimes called co-production), requiring more flexibility and adaptation to special circumstances.
Job/Service Encounter Design	Goods-producing employees require strong technical and production skills.	Service employees need more behavioral and service management skills.
Scheduling	Scheduling revolves around the movement and location of materials, parts, and subassemblies and when to assign resources (i.e., employees, equipment) to accomplish the work most efficiently.	Scheduling focuses on when to assign employees and equipment (i.e., service capacity) to accomplish the work most efficiently without the benefit of physical inventory.
Supply Chain Management	Goods-producing firms focus mainly on the physical flow of goods, often in a global network, with the goal of maximizing customer satisfaction and profit, and minimizing delivery time, costs, and environmental impact.	Service-providing firms focus mainly on the flow of people, information, and services, often in a global network, with the goal of maximizing customer satisfaction and profit, and minimizing delivery time, costs, and environmental impact.

A similar classification of OM activities in terms of high/low customer contact was first proposed in the classic article: Chase, R. B., "Where does the customer fit in a service operation?" *Harvard Business Review,* November–December 1978, p. 139.

those that are not essential to the primary good or service, but enhance it. A personal checking account might be supported and enhanced by such peripheral goods as a printed monthly account statement, designer checks and checkbooks, a special credit card, and such peripheral services as a customer service hot line and online bill payment. It is interesting to note that today, many business-to-business manufacturers, such as custom machining or metal fabricators, think of their core offering as service—providing customized design assistance and on-time delivery—with the actual good as peripheral. Finally, *a variant is a CBP feature that departs from the standard CBP and is normally location- or firm-specific.*

A CBP can easily be expressed in a graphical fashion as shown in Exhibit 1.2. The CBP attributes and features (described in the circles) are chosen by management to fulfill certain customer wants and needs. For

A variant is a CBP feature that departs from the standard CBP and is normally location- or firm-specific.

Exhibit 1.2 *A CBP Example for Purchasing a Vehicle*

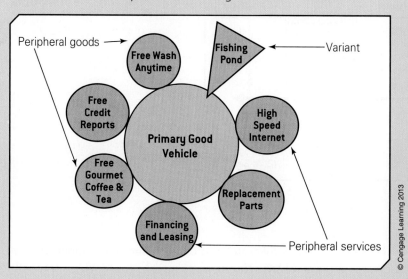

Peripheral goods →

Free Wash Anytime

Fishing Pond ← Variant

Free Credit Reports

Primary Good Vehicle

High Speed Internet

Free Gourmet Coffee & Tea

Replacement Parts

Financing and Leasing

→ Peripheral services

© Cengage Learning 2013

needs. For example, if a customer need is to ensure the safety of their valuables in a hotel, a CBP feature that management might select is a room safe. Thus, you would not put "safety of valuables" on a CBP diagram, but rather "room safe." A CBP diagram should reflect on the features management selects to fulfill certain customer wants and needs.

The size of the circles in the CBP framework can signify the relative importance of each good and service. In some cases, goods and services content in a CBP framework will be approximately equal. For example, McDonald's (food and fast service) and IBM (computers and customer solutions) might argue that their primary goods and services are of equal importance, so a graphical representation would show two equal-sized and overlapping circles as the center of the CBP.

Verizon, for example, buys an iPhone from Apple for about $600 and sells it to customers for $200. Verizon subsidizes each phone to make sales and capture customers with its service contracts. Verizon tries to make up the short-term loss on the physical good by the long-term gains on the service fees. Cell phones are good examples of how goods and services are bundled together for long-term profits.[5]

example, financing and leasing, which are peripheral services, meet the customer's wants and needs of personal financial security. In fact, if two vehicles have similar prices and quality levels, then the leasing program may be the key to which vehicle the customer buys. Vehicle replacement parts, a peripheral good, meet the customer's wants and needs of fast service and safety. A variant might be a fishing pond where kids can fish while parents shop for vehicles.

When defining a CBP, don't confuse the features determined by management with customers' wants and

D–Ozeri/iStockphoto

Buying More Than a Car

People usually think that when they buy a new car, they are simply purchasing the vehicle. Far from it. Most automobiles, for example, bundle a good, the automobile, with many peripheral services. Such services might include the sales process, customized leasing, insurance, warranty programs, loaner cars when a major service or repair is needed, free car washes at the dealership, opportunities to attend a manufacturer's driving school, monthly newsletters sent by e-mail, and Web-based scheduling of oil changes and other service requirements. Such bundling is described by the customer benefit package framework.[6]

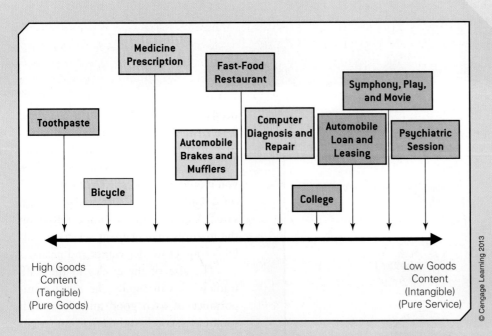

Exhibit 1.3
Examples of Goods and Service Content

© Cengage Learning 2013

Finally, we may bundle a group of CBPs together. One example would be a combined land-cruise vacation to Alaska, which might consist of a bundle of CBPs such as the travel agency that books the package and optional land excursions from the ship; the land-tour operator that handles hotels, transportation, and baggage handling; and the cruise line that provides air travel, meals, and entertainment. Bundled CBPs raise some interesting issues about pricing strategies and partnerships among firms. For example, a firm might actually be able to charge a premium price for the bundled CBPs than if purchased separately, or alliances between hotels and airlines provide discounted vacation packages that are less expensive than if booked separately.

In most cases, many "goods" and "services" that we normally think of have a mixture of both goods and service content. Exhibit 1.3 illustrates a continuum of goods and service content with several examples. Toothpaste, for instance, is high in goods content, but when you purchase it, you are also purchasing some services, such as a telephone call center to field customer questions and complaints. Similarly, a bicycle might seem like a pure good, but it often includes such services as safety instruction and maintenance. At the other extreme in Exhibit 1.3 are psychiatric services, which are much higher in service content, but might include goods such as a

> A **process** is a sequence of activities that is intended to create a certain result.

bill, books, and medical brochures that support the service. Attending a symphony, play, or movie is essentially a pure service, but may include program brochures and ticket stubs that offer discounts at local restaurants as peripheral goods.

1-5 Processes

each good or service in the customer benefit package requires a process to create and deliver it to customers.

A **process** *is a sequence of activities that is intended to create a certain result*, such as a physical good, a service, or information. A practical definition, according to AT&T, is that a process is how work creates value for customers.[7] Processes are the means by which goods and services are produced and delivered. For example, think of a car wash. A car wash process might consist of the following steps: check the car in, perform the wash, inspect the results, notify the customer that the car is finished, quickly deliver the car back to the customer, and pay the bill. In designing such a process, operations managers need to consider the process goals, such as speed of service, a clean car, no vehicle damage, and the quality of all service encounters. OM managers would ask questions such as: Should the car be cleaned inside as well as outside? How long should a customer be

Biztainment—(Huh?)

Why would someone pay, for example, to crush grapes with her feet? Might it be that the process of doing this is as valuable to the customer as the outcome itself? Entertainment is the act of providing hospitality, escapism, fun, excitement, and/or relaxation to people as they go about their daily work and personal activities. The addition of entertainment to an organization's customer benefit package provides unique opportunities for companies to increase customer satisfaction and grow revenue. **Biztainment** *is the practice of adding entertainment content to a bundle of goods and services in order to gain competitive advantage. The old business model of just selling and servicing a physical vehicle is gone. For example, a BMW automobile dealership in Fort Myers, Florida, opened a new 52,000-square-foot facility that offers a putting green, private work areas, a movie theater, wireless Internet access, massage chairs, a golf simulator, and a café, so that customers have multiple entertainment options during their visits.*

Biztainment can be applied in both manufacturing and service settings. Consider the following examples:

- *Manufacturing—old and new factory tours, showrooms, customer training and education courses, virtual tours, short films on how things are made, driving schools, history lessons on the design and development of a physical good*

- *Retail—shopping malls, simulators, product demonstrations, climbing walls, music, games, contests, holiday decorations and walk-around characters, blogs, interactive store designs, aquariums, movie theaters, makeovers*

- *Restaurants—toys, themes, contests, games, characters, playgrounds, live music*

- *Agriculture—pick-your-own food, mazes, make-your-own wine, grape-stomping, petting zoos, farm tours*

- *Lodging—kids' spas, health clubs, casinos, cable television, arcades, massage, wireless Internet, arts and crafts classes, pools, family games, wildlife, miniature golf*

- *Telecommunications—picture mail, text and video messaging, music and TV downloads, cool ring tones, designer phones, iPhone "apps"*

Some organizations that use entertainment as a means of enhancing the firm's image and increasing sales that you might be familiar with are the Hard Rock Café, Chuck E. Cheese, and Benihana of Tokyo restaurants; cable TV shows like How It's Made; *the Las Vegas Treasure Island casino/hotel pirate battle; and so on. The data show the value of biztainment. For example, Build-A-Bear Workshop boasts an average of $600 per square foot in annual revenue, double the U.S. mall average, and Holiday Inns found that hotels with holidomes have a 20 percent higher occupancy rate and room rates that are, on average, $28 higher.[8]*

expected to wait? What types of chemicals should be used to clean the car? What training should the employees who wash the cars and interact with the customer have?

Key processes in business typically include

1. **value creation processes**, focused on producing or delivering an organization's primary goods or services, such as filling and shipping a customer's

ZUMA Press/Newscom

order, assembling a dishwasher, or providing a home mortgage;

2. **support processes**, such as purchasing materials and supplies used in manufacturing, managing inventory, installation, health benefits, technology acquisition, day care on-site services, and research and development; and

3. **general management processes**, including accounting and information systems, human resource management, and marketing.

It is important to realize that nearly every major activity within an organization involves a process that crosses traditional organizational boundaries. For example, an order fulfilment process might involve a salesperson placing the order; a marketing representative entering it on the company's computer system; a credit check by finance; picking, packaging, and shipping by distribution and logistics personnel; invoicing by finance; and installation by field service engineers. Thus, a process does not necessarily

PAL'S SUDDEN SERVICE: BEST-IN-CLASS OPERATIONS MANAGEMENT

Pal's Sudden Service is a small chain of mostly drive-through quick-service restaurants located in northeast Tennessee and southwest Virginia. Pal's competes against major national chains and outperforms all of them by focusing on important customer requirements such as speed, accuracy, friendly service, correct ingredients and amounts, proper food temperature, and safety. Pal's uses extensive market research to fully understand customer requirements: convenience; ease of driving in and out; easy-to-read menus; simple, accurate order-system; fast service; wholesome food; and reasonable price. To create value, Pal's has developed a unique ability to effectively integrate production and service into its operations. Pal's has learned to apply world-class management principles and best-in-class processes in a customer-driven approach to business excellence that causes other companies to emulate its systems. Every process is flowcharted and analyzed for opportunities for error, and then mistake-proofed if at all possible. Entry-level employees—mostly high school students in their first jobs—receive 120 hours of training on precise work procedures and process standards in unique self-teaching, classroom, and on-the-

job settings, and reinforced by a "Caught Doing Good" program that provides recognition for meeting quality standards and high-performance expectations. In such performance measures as complaints, profitability, employee turnover, safety, and productivity, Pal's has a significant advantage over its competition.

Courtesy of Pal's Sudden Service

---

reside within a department or traditional management function.

All organizations have networks of processes that create value for customers (called *value chains*, which we explore in Chapter 2). For example, Pal's Sudden Service (see the box above) begins with raw materials and suppliers providing items such as meat, lettuce, tomatoes, buns, and packaging; uses intermediate processes for order taking, cooking, and final assembly; and ends with order delivery and, hopefully, happy customers.

1-6 OM: A History of Change and Challenge

In the last century, operations management has undergone more changes than any other functional area of business and is the most important factor in competitiveness. That is one of the reasons why every business student needs a basic understanding of the field. Exhibit 1.4 is a chronology of major themes that have changed the scope and direction of operations management over the last

half century. To better understand the challenges facing modern business and the role of OM in meeting them, let us briefly trace the history and evolution of these themes.

1-6a A Focus on Efficiency

Contemporary OM has its roots in the Industrial Revolution that occurred during the late 18th and early 19th centuries in England. Until that time, goods had been produced in small shops by artisans and their apprentices without the aid of mechanical equipment. During the Industrial Revolution, however, many new inventions came into being that allowed goods to be manufactured with greater ease and speed. The inventions reduced the need for individual artisans and led to the development of modern factories.

As international trade grew in the 1960s, the emphasis on operations efficiency and cost reduction increased. Many companies moved their factories to low-wage countries. Managers became enamored with computers, robots, and other forms of technology. Although advanced technology continues to revolutionize

Exhibit 1.4 *Seven Eras of Operations Management*

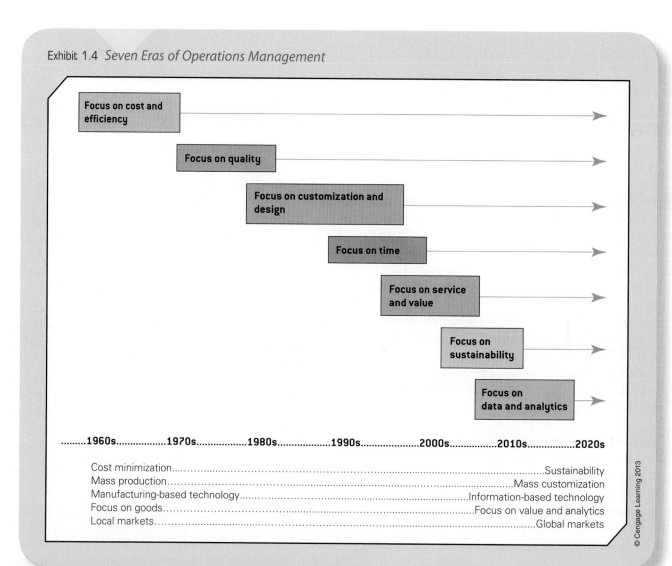

Focus on cost and efficiency						
	Focus on quality					
		Focus on customization and design				
			Focus on time			
				Focus on service and value		
					Focus on sustainability	
						Focus on data and analytics

.........1960s.................1970s.................1980s.................1990s.................2000s.................2010s.................2020s

Cost minimization	Sustainability
Mass production	Mass customization
Manufacturing-based technology	Information-based technology
Focus on goods	Focus on value and analytics
Local markets	Global markets

© Cengage Learning 2013

Chad Ehlers/Getty Images

and improve production, in the 1960s and 1970s technology was viewed primarily as a method of reducing costs, and distracted managers from the important goal of improving the quality of goods and services and the processes that create them. American business was soon to face a rude awakening.

Today, about 90 percent of the jobs in the U.S. economy are in service-providing processes.

1-6b The Quality Revolution

As Japan was rebuilding from the devastation of World War II, two U.S. consultants, W. Edwards Deming and Joseph Juran, were sought extensively by Japanese industry. Deming and Juran told Japanese executives that continual improvement of quality would open world markets, free up capacity, and improve their economy. The Japanese eagerly embraced that message. They embarked on a massive effort to train the workforce, using statistical tools developed at Western Electric and other innovative management tools to identify causes of quality problems and fix them. They made steady progress in reducing defects and paid careful attention to what consumers wanted. Those efforts continued at a relentless pace until, by the mid 1970s, the world discovered that Japanese goods had fewer defects, were more reliable, and better met consumer needs than American goods. As a result, Japanese firms captured major shares of world markets in many different industries such as automobiles and electronics. Thereafter, quality became an obsession with top managers of nearly every major company and its impact continues to be seen today. In 1987 the U.S. government established the Malcolm Baldrige Award to focus national attention on quality.

1-6c Customization and Design

As the goals of low cost and high product quality became "givens," companies began to emphasize innovative designs and product features to gain a competitive edge. Quality meant much more than simply defect reduction; quality meant offering consumers new and innovative products that not only met their expectations, but also surprised and delighted them. Inflexible mass-production methods that produced high volumes of standardized goods and services using unskilled or semiskilled workers and expensive single-purpose equipment, though very efficient and cost-effective, were inadequate for the new goals of increased good and service variety and continual product improvement. The operating system had to change.

New types of operating systems emerged that enabled companies to manufacture goods and services better, cheaper, and faster than their competitors, while facilitating innovation and increasing variety. The Internet began to help companies customize their goods and services for global markets.

1-6d Time-Based Competition

Companies that do not respond quickly to changing customer needs will lose out to competitors that do. An example of quick response is the production of the custom-designed Motorola pager, which is completed within 80 minutes and often can be delivered to the customer the same day. As information technology matured, time became an important source of competitive advantage. Quick response is achieved by continually improving and reengineering processes—that is, fundamentally rethinking and redesigning processes to achieve dramatic improvements in cost, quality, speed, and service. That task includes developing products faster than competitors, speeding ordering and delivering processes, rapidly responding to changes in customers' needs, and improving the flow of paperwork.

1-6e The Service Revolution

While the goods-producing industries were getting all the attention in the business community, the popular press, and in business school curricula, service industries were quietly growing and creating many new jobs in the U.S. economy. In 1955, about 50 percent of the U.S. workforce was employed in goods-producing industries and 50 percent in service-providing industries. Today, about four of every five U.S. jobs are in services.

Exhibit 1.5 documents the structure of the U.S. economy and where people work. This aggregate mix between goods-producing and service-providing jobs is 81.8 percent service and 18.2 percent goods. There are many interesting industry comparisons in Exhibit 1.5, but let's point out just a few. Manufacturing, for example, accounts for 11.6 percent of total U.S. employment, or about 1 in 10 jobs. Today, state and local government jobs are 11.9 percent of total jobs, that is, about the same percent as manufacturing. Many other countries, such as France and the United Kingdom, also have a high percentage of total jobs in the service sector. Where are you going to work?

Exhibit 1.5 *U.S. Employment by Major Industry*

U.S. Industry	Percent of Total Employment
Goods-Producing Sector	
Construction	4.1%
Agriculture	2.2
Mining	0.3
Fishing, Forestry, Hunting, and Misc.	0.1
Manufacturing	11.6
Durable Goods*	7.0
Nondurable Goods**	4.6
Total	18.2%
Service-Providing Sector	
Transportation	3.0%
Communication and Public Utilities	1.7
Wholesale Trade	4.5
Finance, Insurance, and Real Estate	5.2
Agricultural Services	0.7
Hotels and Lodging	1.5
Personal Services	1.0
Business Services	8.0
Auto Repair and Parking	1.1
Motion Pictures	0.5
Amusement and Recreation Services	1.4
Health Services	8.6
Legal Services	0.8
Education Services	2.2
Child Care and Other Services	2.6
Membership Organizations	2.1
Museums and Zoological Gardens	0.1
Engineering, Architectural, and Management Services	3.1
Retail Trade and Services	15.7
Federal Government Services	1.6
State and Local Government Services	11.9
Miscellaneous Services	4.6
Total	81.8%
Grand Total	**100.0%**

Source: United States Bureau of Labor Statistics.

*Durable goods are items such as instruments, vehicles, aircraft, computer and office equipment, machinery, furniture, glass, metals, and appliances.

**Nondurable goods are items such as textiles, apparel, paper, food, coal, oil, leather, plastics, chemicals, and books.

In addition, estimates are that at least 50 percent of the jobs in goods-producing industries are service- and information-related, such as human resources management, accounting, financial, legal, advertising, purchasing, engineering, and so on. Thus, today, about 90 percent of the jobs in the U.S. economy are in service-providing processes [81.8 + (.5)(18.2%) = 90.9%]. This means that if you are employed in the United States, you will most likely work in a service- or information-related field. Because of these statistics, a principal emphasis in this book is on services—either in service-providing industries such as health care and banking or understanding how services complement the sale of goods in goods-producing industries such as machine tools and computers.

1-6f Sustainability

In today's world, sustainability has become one of the most important issues that organizations face, and it is placing increased pressure on all goods-producing and service-providing organizations worldwide. **Sustainability** *refers to an organization's ability to strategically address current business needs and successfully develop a long-term strategy that embraces opportunities and manages risk for all products, systems, supply chains, and processes to preserve resources for future generations.* Sustainability can be viewed from three perspectives: environmental, social, and economic.

- **Environmental sustainability** *is an organization's commitment to the long-term quality of our environment.* Environmental sustainability is important because environmental concerns are placing increased pressure on all goods-producing and service-providing organizations across the globe.

- **Social sustainability** *is an organization's commitment to maintain healthy communities and a society that improves the quality of life.* Social sustainability is important because every organization must

Sustainability refers to an organization's ability to strategically address current business needs and successfully develop a long-term strategy that embraces opportunities and manages risk for all products, systems, supply chains, and processes to preserve resources for future generations.

Environmental sustainability is an organization's commitment to the long-term quality of our environment.

Social sustainability is an organization's commitment to maintain healthy communities and a society that improves the quality of life.

protect the health and well-being of all stakeholders and their respective communities, treat all stakeholders fairly, and provide them with essential services.

- **Economic sustainability** *is an organization's commitment to address current business needs and economic vitality, and to have the agility and strategic management to prepare successfully for future business, markets, and operating environments.* Economic sustainability is important because staying in business for the long term, expanding markets, and providing jobs are vital to national economies.

Economic sustainability is an organization's commitment to address current business needs and economic vitality, and to have the agility and strategic management to prepare successfully for future business, markets, and operating environments.

Business analytics is a process of transforming data into actions through analysis and insights in the context of organizational decision making and problem solving.

NY Daily News via Getty Images

Exhibit 1.6 *Examples of Sustainability Practices*

Environmental Sustainability
- **Waste management**: Reduce waste and manage recycling efforts
- **Energy optimization**: Reduce consumption during peak energy demand times
- **Transportation optimization**: Design efficient vehicles and routes to save fuel
- **Technology upgrades**: Develop improvements to save energy and clean and reuse water in manufacturing processes
- **Air quality**: Reduce greenhouse gas emissions
- **Sustainable product design**: Design goods whose parts can be recycled or safely disposed of

Social Sustainability
- **Product safety**: Ensure consumer safety in using goods and services
- **Workforce health and safety**: Ensure a healthy and safe work environment
- **Ethics and governance**: Ensure compliance with legal and regulatory requirements and transparency in management decisions
- **Community**: Improve the quality of life through industry–community partnerships

Economic Sustainability
- **Performance excellence**: Build a high-performing organization with a capable leadership and workforce
- **Financial management**: Make sound financial plans to ensure long-term organizational survival
- **Resource management**: Acquire and manage all resources effectively and efficiently
- **Emergency preparedness**: Have plans in place for business, environmental, and social emergencies

© Cengage Learning 2013

These three dimensions of sustainability are often referred to as the "triple bottom line." Sustainability represents a broad and, to many, a new paradigm for organizational performance. OM plays a vital role in helping organizations accomplish these goals. Exhibit 1.6 provides examples of business practices that support these three dimensions. Operations management plays an important role in all three of these sustainability perspectives. We will discuss the role that OM has in achieving sustainability in more detail in the next chapter and throughout the book.

1-6g Data and Analytics

Today, all organizations have access to an enormous amount of data and information. In OM, data are used to evaluate operations performance, quality, order accuracy, customer satisfaction, delivery, cost, environmental compliance, and many other areas of the business. Leveraging such data is fast becoming a necessity in creating competitive advantage. A new discipline has emerged in recent years called business analytics. **Business analytics** *is a process of transforming data into actions through analysis and insights in the context of organizational decision making and problem solving.*[9] Business analytics is used to understand past and current performance (descriptive analytics), predict the future by detecting patterns and relationships in data (predictive analytics), and identify the best decisions (prescriptive analytics).

The supplementary chapters available on the CourseMate Web site that accompanies this book provide an introduction to some key analytical techniques used in OM. With this book we also provide a unique set of Microsoft Excel spreadsheet templates that we will present throughout the text to facilitate the use of analytic techniques. The templates are found on worksheets in *OM4 Spreadsheet Templates* on the

Table 1.1 *Summary of Excel Spreadsheet Templates*

Template	Chapter Reference	Description
Break-Even	2	Computes a break-even point and optimal outsourcing decision
VLC	3	Computes the value of a loyal customer (VLC)
Taguchi	6	Computes the Taguchi loss function and economic tolerance
Little's Law	7	Computes flowtime, throughput, or work-in-process using Little's Law
Location Analysis	9	Computes total costs to determine least cost location for production
Center of Gravity	9	Finds and plots the center of gravity
Capacity	10	Computes capacity measures
Moving Average	11	Calculates and plots moving average forecasts
Exponential Smoothing	11	Calculates and plots exponential smoothing forecasts
ABC	12	Conducts ABC inventory analysis
EOQ	12	Finds the economic order quantity and plots the cost functions
FQS Safety Stock	12	Computes safety stock and reorder point for fixed-quantity inventory systems
FPS Safety Stock	12	Computes safety stock and reorder point for fixed-period inventory systems
Single-Period Inventory	12	Finds the optimal ordering quantity for a single-period inventory systems with uniform or normal demand
Agg. Plan–Level	13	Evaluates aggregate planning using a level production strategy
Agg. Plan–Chase	13	Evaluates aggregate planning using a chase production strategy
Aggregate Planning	13	General Template for Aggregate Planning
Sequencing	14	Computes flowtime, lateness, and tradiness for job sequencing problems
Six Sigma	14	Computes DPU, dpmo, and sigma level
Pareto	15	Finds and plots a Pareto distribution
x-Bar and R-Chart	16	Plots an x-bar and R-chart for quality control
p-Chart	16	Plots a p-chart for quality control
c-Chart	16	Plots a c-chart for quality control
Process Capability	16	Computes process capability measures and a frequency distribution and histogram
Work Measurement	Supplementary Chapter A	Calculates normal and standard times for work measurement studies
Learning Curve	Supplementary Chapter A	Computes the time to produce the first 100 units for a learning curve
Single-Server Queue	Supplementary Chapter B	Calculates measures for a single-server queue
Multiple-Server Queue	Supplementary Chapter B	Calculates measures for a multiple-server queue
Queue Simulation	Supplementary Chapter D	Performs a single-server queuing simulation for discrete arrival and service time distributions
Inventory Simulation	Supplementary Chapter D	Performs a fixed-quantity inventory simulation
Decision Analysis	Supplementary Chapter E	Computes decision strategies for payoff tables for both minimize and maximize objectives

CourseMate Web site. Table 1.1 summarizes where the templates are best used.

1-7 Current Challenges in OM

M is continually changing, and all managers need to stay abreast of the challenges that will define the future workplace. Among these are technology, globalization, changing customer expectations, a changing workforce, the loss of manufacturing jobs in Western nations, and building sustainability as part of an organization's corporate responsibility.

- Technology has been one of the most important influences on the growth and development of OM. Applications in design and manufacturing as well as the use of information technology in services have provided the ability to develop innovative products and more effectively manage and control extremely complex operations. As technology continues to evolve, OM needs to find ways to leverage and exploit it.

- Globalization has changed the way companies do business and must manage their operations. With advances in communications and transportation, we have passed from the era of huge regional factories with large labor forces and tight community ties to an era of the "borderless marketplace." Value chains now span across many continents.

The "Great Disconnect" of U.S. Manufacturing

The biggest manufacturing challenges in the United States today are the loss of manufacturing jobs and simultaneously a labor shortage of high-tech production skills. One survey from the Manpower Group calls this situation the "Great Disconnect." Although U.S. unemployment is high, 52 percent of U.S. employers say they cannot find qualified talent to fill their jobs.

While simple work tasks get automated or sent overseas, and the U.S. workforce ages and begins to retire, high-tech jobs in the United States go unfilled. Today's manufacturers are seeking workers who can combine skills ranging from computers to hydraulics and pneumatics to operate, maintain, and troubleshoot equipment.

What are U.S. companies doing to meet these challenges? MAG Industrial Automation in Kentucky, for example, reinstituted an apprenticeship program to develop skilled field service technicians. GE Aviation, which has invested $34 million in advanced manufacturing systems since 2007, is piloting teams of 10 to 20 workers who assume responsibility for all operations in their areas. Others are partnering with local governments and educational institutions to train new workers.[10]

Operations managers must continue to find better ways to manage and improve global value chains to compete against those of competitors.

- Consumers' expectations continually rise. They demand an increasing variety of high-quality goods with new and improved features that are delivered faster than ever—along with outstanding service and support. OM faces the challenge of ensuring that these multidimensional and often conflicting expectations are met.

- Today's workers demand increasing levels of empowerment and more meaningful work than in the past. This requires continual learning, new decision-making skills, more diversity, and better performance management. OM must be able to incorporate these new dimensions into job designs and daily management.

Ian McKinnell/Getty Images

- Despite more than a half-century of intense focus on quality, it continues to be a challenge, even for the best of companies, as we have witnessed with Toyota's numerous recalls. Despite significant advances, organizations cannot take quality for granted and must continue to focus on it when designing goods and services, operations, and management systems.

- To compete in today's environment, manufacturers must stay ahead of consumers' needs by increasing product innovation, speeding up time-to-market, and operating highly effective global supply chains. However, many emerging concepts, such as sustainability and green manufacturing, genetic engineering, nanotechnology, new methods of energy generation, and robotic medical equipment, provide new and exciting opportunities for revitalizing manufacturing through OM.[11]

Discussion Questions

1. Explain how operations management activities affect customer experiences described in the Museum of Science and Industry anecdote at the beginning of this chapter. What "moments of truth" would a customer encounter?

2. Explain why a bank teller, nurse, or flight attendant must have *service management* skills. How do the required skills differ for someone working in a factory? What are the implications for hiring criteria and training?

3. Why is process thinking important in operations management? Thinking of yourself as an "operations manager" for your education, how could process thinking improve your performance as a student?

4. Do you think you will be working in manufacturing or services when you graduate? What do you think will be the role of manufacturing in the U.S. economy in the future?

5. Select one of the OM challenges and investigate it in more detail. Be ready to present what you found to the class in at most a 10-minute presentation.

Problems and Activities

1. Describe a customer experience you have personally encountered where the good or service or both were unsatisfactory (for example, defective product, errors, mistakes, poor service, service upsets, and so on). How might the organization have handled it better and how could operations management have helped?

2. Interview a manager at a local company about the work he or she performs. Identify (a) the aspects of the job that relate to OM (as in the OM activities in the box "What Do Operations Managers Do?") and (b) an example of primary, support, and general management processes.

3. Evaluate how the activities described in the box "What Do Operations Managers Do?" can be applied to a student organization or fraternity to improve its effectiveness.

4. Review the box for Pal's Sudden Service and find Pal's Web site. Based on this information, describe all of the OM activities that occur in a typical day at Pal's.

5. Interview a working friend or family member as to how he or she uses operations management principles on the job and write a short paper summarizing your findings (maximum two pages).

6. Choose one of the following services and explain, using specific examples, how each of the ways that services differ from manufactured goods applies.

   a. a family practice medical office

   b. a fire department

   c. a restaurant

   d. an automobile repair shop

7. Provide some examples similar to those in Exhibit 1.3, and explain the degree of goods and services content for these examples.

8. Draw the customer benefit package (CBP) for one of the items in the following list and explain how your CBP provides value to the customer. Make a list of a few example processes that you think would be necessary to create and deliver each good or service in the CBP you selected and briefly describe issues that must be considered in designing these processes.

   • a trip to Disney World

   • a new personal computer

   • a credit card

   • a fast-food restaurant

   • a wireless mobile telephone

   • a one-night stay in a hotel

9. One of our students, who had worked for Taco Bell, related a story of how his particular store developed a "60-second, 10-pack club" as an improvement initiative and training tool. The goal was to make a 10-pack of tacos in a minute or less, each made and wrapped correctly, and the total within 1 ounce of the correct weight. Employees received recognition and free meals for a day. Employees strove to become a part of this club and, more important, service times dropped dramatically. Techniques similar to those used to improve the taco-making process were used to improve other products. Explain how this anecdote relates to process thinking. What would the employees have to do to become a part of the club?

10. Research and write a short one-page paper that describes two new examples of how organizations are using biztainment to gain competitive advantage.

11. Search the Web for an organization that has defined its sustainability strategy and policy, and give examples of how the organization is implementing it. Write a paper describing what you found (maximum of two typed pages).

12. Describe new ways for how your college or university can apply the sustainability practices in Exhibit 1.6. Summarize your results in a short paper.

13. Research and write a short paper on job opportunities related to sustainability.

14. Research and write a short paper describing how business analytics have been applied to problems and decisions in operations management. Use the information in the box "What Do Operations Managers Do?" to help your search process.

15. Search recent articles in your local newspaper and business magazines such as *Fortune, Business Week, Fast Company,* and so on and identify OM concepts and issues that are discussed. How do these fit into the classification in the box "What Do Operations Managers Do?" in this chapter?

Zappos Case Study

Zappos (www.zappos.com) is a Las Vegas–based on-line retailer that has been cited in *Fortune's* list of the Best Companies to Work For and *Fast Company's* list of the world's most innovative companies. In fact, its remarkable success resulted in Zappos being bought by Amazon for $850 million in 2009. Zappos was founded in San Francisco in 1999 and moved to Las Vegas for the cheap real estate and abundant call center workers. The company sells a large variety of shoes from nearly every major manufacturer and has expanded its offerings to handbags, apparel, sunglasses, watches, and electronics. Despite the crippling economic downturn, sales jumped almost 20 percent in 2008, passing the $1 billion mark two years ahead of schedule.

The company's first core value is "Deliver WOW through service," which is obvious if you've ever ordered from Zappos. It provides free shipping in both directions on all purchases. It often gives customers surprise upgrades for faster shipping. And it has a 365-day return policy. In 2003, Zappos made a decision about customer service: it views any expense that enhances the customer experience as a marketing cost because it generates more repeat customers through word of mouth. CEO Tony Hsieh

Zappos provides free shipping in both directions on all purchases.

Ethan Miller/Staff/Getty Images

never outsourced his call center because he considers the function too important to be sent to India. Job one for these front-liners is to delight callers. Unlike most inbound telemarketers, they don't work from a script. They're trained to encourage callers to order more than one size or color, because shipping is free in both directions, and to refer shoppers to competitors when a product is out of stock. Most important, though, they're implored to use their imaginations. Which means that a customer having a tough day might find flowers on his or her doorstep the next morning. One Minnesota customer complained that her boots had begun leaking after almost a year of use. Not only did the Zappos customer service representative send out a new pair—in spite of a policy that only unworn shoes are returnable—but she also told the customer to keep the old ones, and mailed a hand-written thank-you.[12] Over 95 percent of Zappo's transactions take place over the Web, so each actual customer phone call is a special opportunity. "They may only call once in their life, but that is our chance to wow them," Hsieh says.

Zappos uses a sophisticated computer system known as *Genghis* to manage its operations. This includes an order entry, purchasing, warehouse management, inventory, shipping, and e-commerce system. It tracks inventory so closely that customers can check online how many pairs of size 12 Clarks Desert boots are available in the color sand. For employees, it automatically sends daily e-mail reminders to call a customer back, coordinates the warehouse robot system, and produces reports that can specifically assess the impact on margins of putting a particular item on sale.

Free shipping has become a customer expectation. Research has found that online customers abandon their virtual shopping carts up to 75 percent of the time at the end of their order entry process when they can't get free shipping. Other online retailers have copied the free-shipping policies of Zappos. L.L. Bean, for example, now provides free shipping and free returns with no minimum order amount.

Case Questions for Discussion

1. Draw and describe the customer benefit package that Zappos provides. Identify and describe one primary value creation, one support, and one general management process you might encounter at Zappos.

2. Explain the role of service encounters and service management skills at Zappos. How does Zappos create superior customer experiences?

3. Describe how any three of the OM activities in the box "What Do Operations Managers Do?" impact the management of both the goods that Zappos sells and the services that it provides.

4. Explain how this case illustrates each of the seven major differences between goods-producing and service-providing businesses.

VALUE CHAINS

pple has mastered the art of blending physical goods with services to create value for its customers. Think iPod + iTunes, iPhone/iPad + apps, Apple stores + Genius Bar; well, you get the picture. Managing all operations involved from the creation of goods and services through their delivery to the customer and postsale services—which we call the value chain—is one of Apple's core competencies. "Operations expertise is as big an asset for Apple as product innovation or marketing," says Mike Fawkes, the former supply chain chief at Hewlett-Packard. "They've taken operational excellence to a level never seen before." Apple controls every piece of the value chain. For example, managers and engineers often work at supplier and manufacturer sites to refine their operations, and designers work with suppliers to create new tooling equipment. When the iPad 2 debuted, Apple employees monitored every handoff point—suppliers, production, loading dock, airport, truck depot, and distribution center—to make sure each unit was accounted for and of the highest quality. Apple's retail stores give it a final operational advantage. The company can track demand by the store and by the hour, and adjust production forecasts daily. If it becomes clear a given part will run out, teams are deployed and given approval to spend millions of dollars on extra equipment to get around the bottleneck. Apple's significant profit margins are in large part due to this focus on operational excellence in its value chain.[1]

learning outcomes

After studying this chapter you should be able to:

2-1 **Explain the concept of value and how it can be increased.**

2-2 **Describe a value chain and the two major perspectives that characterize it.**

2-3 **Explain outsourcing and vertical integration in value chains.**

2-4 **Explain offshoring and issues that managers must consider in offshoring decisions.**

2-5 **Identify important issues associated with value chains in a global business environment.**

2-6 **Describe how sustainability plays an important role in value chains.**

What do you think?

Cite some other examples in which digital content has been combined with a physical good. How do you see the digital revolution changing the nature of physical goods in the future?

Chris Hackett/Getty Images

The creation of customer value depends on an effective system of linked facilities and processes and the ability to manage them effectively. Apple, for example, manages a large global network of suppliers in countries such as Malaysia and Indonesia, and factories in the United States, China, and other countries to produce its physical goods, which must be coordinated with the development and production of software and other digital content, retail sales, and service and support. As the opening anecdote suggests, coordinating these goods-producing and service-providing processes can be challenging.

The set of activities involved in providing goods and services to customers is called a value chain, and helps to characterize the scope of operations management activities. *A value chain is a network of facilities and processes that describes the flow of materials, finished goods, services, information, and financial transactions from suppliers, through the facilities and processes that create goods and services, and those that deliver them to the* *customer.* Value chains involve all major functions in an organization. This includes not only operations, but also purchasing, marketing and sales, human resource management, finance and accounting, information systems and technology, distribution, and service and support.

Many organizations use the terms "value chain" and "supply chain" interchangeably; however, we differentiate these two terms in this book. *A **supply chain** is the portion of the value chain that focuses primarily on the*

> A **value chain** is a network of facilities and processes that describes the flow of materials, finished goods, services, information, and financial transactions from suppliers, through the facilities and processes that create goods and services, and those that deliver them to the customer.
>
> A **supply chain** is the portion of the value chain that focuses primarily on the physical movement of goods and materials, and supporting flows of information and financial transactions through the supply, production, and distribution processes.

▼ *Apple can track demand by the store and by the hour, and adjust production forecasts daily.*

physical movement of goods and materials, and supporting flows of information and financial transactions through the supply, production, and distribution processes. A value chain is broader in scope than a supply chain and is easier to apply to service-providing organizations as well as to goods-producing firms. We will focus on supply chains in Chapter 9.

It is important for you to understand how operations management influences the design and management of value chains. Today's organizations face difficult decisions in balancing cost, quality, service, and sustainability objectives to create value for their customers and stakeholders, and in coordinating the many activities that take place within value chains. Modern firms increasingly deliver goods and services to multiple markets and operate in a global business environment. As a result, many companies have reconfigured their value chains and moved some operations out of the United States to keep costs competitive, remain profitable, and improve customer service. As one chief financial officer wrote in a *CFO Magazine* survey, "You cannot compete globally unless you use global resources."[2] Thus, we emphasize the importance of understanding the global business environment and local culture, and their impact on value chain design and operations.

The complexity of value chains and global operations adds significant pressures to achieve environmental, social, and economic sustainability—concepts we introduced in the previous chapter. Apple, for example, in its *2010 Progress Report on Supplier Responsibility*, stated:

Apple is committed to ensuring the highest standards of social responsibility throughout our supply base. The companies we do business with must provide safe working conditions, treat workers with dignity and respect, and use environmentally responsible

manufacturing processes wherever Apple products are made.

Apple also created a Supplier Code of Conduct that outlines a comprehensive set of expectations covering labor and human rights, health and safety, the environment, ethics, and management systems. These include such practices as prevention of underage labor, prevention of chemical exposure, waste management, and protection of intellectual property. Thus, effective management of value chains should include a commitment to sustainability.

2-1 The Concept of Value

today's consumers demand innovative products, high quality, quick response, impeccable service, and low prices; in short, they want value in every purchase or experience. One of the most important points that we can emphasize in this book is that the underlying purpose of every organization is to provide value to its customers and stakeholders.

Value *is the perception of the benefits associated with a good, service, or bundle of goods and services (i.e., the customer benefit package) in relation to what buyers are willing to pay for them.* The decision to purchase a good or service or a customer benefit package is based on an assessment by the customer of the perceived benefits in relation to its price. The customer's cumulative judgment of the perceived benefits leads to either satisfaction or dissatisfaction. One of the simplest functional forms of value is:

$$\text{Value} = \frac{\text{Perceived benefits}}{\text{Price (cost) to the customer}}$$

> **Value** is the perception of the benefits associated with a good, service, or bundle of goods and services (i.e., the customer benefit package) in relation to what buyers are willing to pay for them.

The underlying purpose of every organization is to provide value to its customers and stakeholders.

JERZY DABROWSKI/DPA/Landov

If the value ratio is high, the good or service is perceived favorably by customers, and the organization providing it is more likely to be successful.

A competitively dominant customer experience is often called a **value proposition.**[3] The economist Adam Smith, in his 1776 book *The Wealth of Nations*, recognized that economic exchange is based on the production of goods that acquire value during design and manufacturing processes. However, he also noted that "real value" is represented by "value in-use"; that is, a good such as a cell phone provides value only when used, and thus reflects the importance of services in a value proposition. The focus on value has forced many traditional goods-producing companies to add services and, increasingly, digital content to their customer benefit packages. If the quality or features of goods cannot be improved at a reasonable cost and prices cannot be lowered, then enhanced or additional services may provide better total value to customers.

The integration of services in manufacturing was recognized some time ago. "In the same way that service businesses were managed and organized around manufacturing models during the industrial economy, we can expect that manufacturing businesses will be managed and organized around service models in this new economy."[4] A goods-producing company can no longer be viewed as simply a factory that churns out physical goods, because customer perceptions of goods are influenced highly by such facilitating services as financing and leasing, shipping and installation, maintenance and repair, and technical support and consulting. Today we see digital content, such as Web sites, streaming videos, social networks, and e-mail newsletters, becoming an important aspect of a company's value proposition. Coordinating the operational capability to design and deliver an integrated customer benefit package of physical and digital goods and services is the essence of operations management.

Understanding the integration of goods and services and customer benefit packages is fundamental to how managers view their business, strategy, and value chains. Some important questions that operations managers must consider are: What do customers buy from us? Do all value chains create and deliver services (sometimes through physical goods)? How does one value chain compete against another? The answers aren't easy, but they can make the difference in creating true customer value and a sustainable competitive advantage for the firm.

2-2 Value Chain Paradigms and Perspectives

We will describe a value chain from two different perspectives: an input-output framework and a pre- and postproduction services framework. Examples using actual companies will be used to illustrate these. It is important to recognize that each of these frameworks incorporates *both* goods and services into the value chain.

2-2a Value Chains: An Input-Output Perspective

As shown in Exhibit 2.1, a value chain can be depicted as a "cradle-to-grave" input-output model of the operations function. The value chain begins with suppliers who provide inputs to a goods-producing or service-providing process or network of processes. Suppliers might be retail stores, distributors, employment agencies, dealers, financing and leasing agents, information and Internet companies, field maintenance

A competitively dominant customer experience is often called a **value proposition.**

Darren Baker/Shutterstock.com

and repair services, architectural and engineering design firms, and contractors, as well as manufacturers of materials and components. The inputs they provide might be physical goods such as automobile engines or microprocessors provided to an assembly plant; meat, fish, and vegetables provided to a restaurant; trained employees provided to organizations by universities and technical schools; or information such as market research or a medical diagnosis.

Inputs are transformed into value-added goods and services through processes that are supported by such resources as equipment and facilities, labor, money,

and information. Note that what is being transformed can be almost anything—for instance, people in a hospital, a physical good in an oil refinery, information in an e-publishing business, or a mixture of people, physical goods, and information. Value chain processes include the three types we defined in Chapter 1: value-creation processes (those that directly create and deliver goods and services), support processes (those "behind the scenes," but which support value-creation processes), and general management processes (those that are needed for efficient and effective business performance). At a hospital, for example, value-creation processes such as surgery and drug administration are used to transform sick people into healthy ones, whereas support processes such as lab testing and purchasing help to ensure that surgery and drug administration accomplish their goals. Finally, the value chain outputs—goods and services—are delivered or provided to customers and targeted market segments. Some examples of value chains that illustrate the elements in Exhibit 2.1 are shown in Exhibit 2.2. The success of the entire value chain depends on how it is designed and managed. This includes measuring performance (which we address in the next chapter) and using the feedback from measurements to improve all aspects of the value chain.

Exhibit 2.1 *An Input-Output Perspective of a Value Chain*

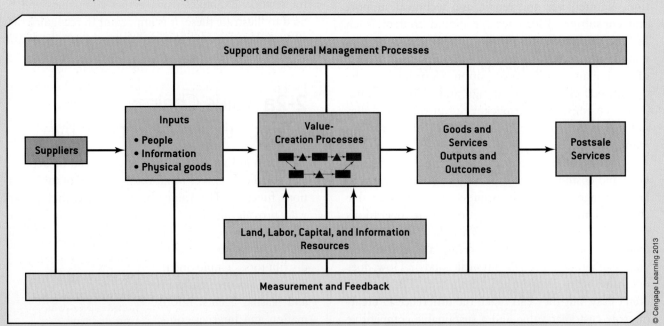

© Cengage Learning 2013

Organization	Suppliers	Inputs	Transformation Process	Outputs	Customers and Market Segments
Auto assembly plant	Engine plant Tires Frame Axles Paint Seats	Labor Energy Auto parts Specifications	Welding Machining Assembly Painting	Automobiles Trucks	Economy Luxury Rental Trucking Ambulance Police
Hospital	Pharmaceutical companies Equipment suppliers Food suppliers Organ donors Medical suppliers	Patients Beds Staff Drugs Diagnostic equipment Knowledge	Admissions Lab testing Doctor diagnosis Food service Surgery Schedules Drug administration Rehabilitation	Healthy people Lab results Accurate bills Community health education	Heart clinics Pediatrics Emergency and trauma services Ambulatory services Medical specialties and hospital wards
State Government	Highway and building contractors Employment agencies Food suppliers Equipment suppliers Other governments	Labor Energy Information Trash Crimes Disputes Sick people Low-income people	Health care benefits Food stamps Legal services Prisons Trash removal Park services License services Police services Tax services	Good use of tax-payers' monies Safety net Security Reallocate taxes Clean, safe, and fun parks	Disabled people Low-income people Criminals and prisons Corporate taxes Boat licenses Building inspections Weekend vacationers Child custody services Legal court services

2-2b The Value Chain at Buhrke Industries, Inc.

To illustrate the input-output perspective of a value chain, we highlight Buhrke Industries Inc., located in Arlington Heights, Illinois, which provides stamped metal parts to many industries, including automotive, appliance, computer, electronics, hardware, housewares, power tools, medical, and telecommunications. A simplified view of Buhrke's value chain is shown in Exhibit 2.3.

Buhrke's objective is to be a customer's best total-value producer with on-time delivery, fewer rejects, and high-quality stampings. However, the company goes beyond manufacturing goods; it prides itself in providing the best service available as part of its customer value chain. Service is more than delivering a product on time. It's also partnering with customers by providing personalized service for fast, accurate response; customized engineering designs to meet customer needs;

preventive maintenance systems to ensure high machine uptime; experienced, highly trained, long-term employees; and troubleshooting by a knowledgeable sales staff.

Suppliers and other value chain inputs include people, information, and physical goods—for example, engineering blueprints and specifications, rolled steel, factory equipment and lubricants, pallets and boxes, employment agencies, inbound shipping, and outside training and industrial marketing firms. Value-creation processes include tooling, inspection, production, finishing, and sometimes assembly into a complete subassembly. Outputs include the stamped metal parts and postsale service outcomes such as out-in-the-field consulting and troubleshooting by company employees. General management processes coordinate processes, often in different functional areas, while support processes include hiring, medical benefits, and accounting. As many as 100 processes are required for Buhrke to perform its work and create value for its customers.

Exhibit 2.3 *The Value Chain at Buhrke Industries*

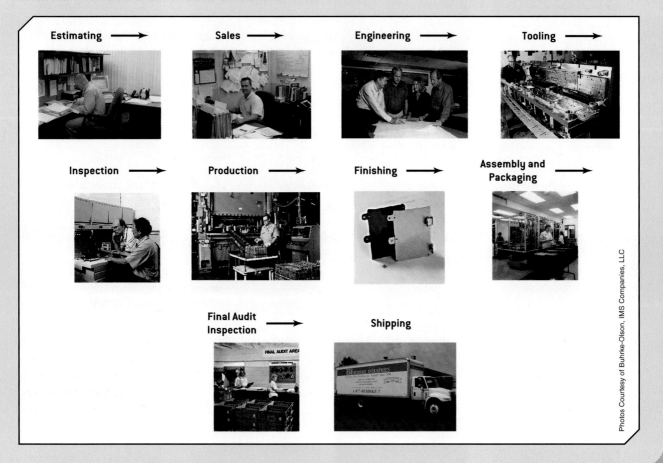

Photos Courtesy of Buhrke-Olson, IMS Companies, LLC

The major stages of Buhrke's value chain shown in Exhibit 2.3 begin with a customer request for a quotation. The estimating department processes such job parameters as specifications, metals, finishing or packaging services, the presses that will be used to run the job, and customer deadlines in developing a quote. Next, a sales engineer is assigned to monitor each stamping job from start to finish, so the customer may have the convenience of a single point of contact. Sales engineers work closely with the engineering staff to convey customer needs. Engineers then design the best tooling for the job, using computer-assisted design processes to ensure precise designs and timely completion. After a tool is designed and built, it is maintained in an on-site tool room. Burhke's toolmakers have decades of experience constructing tools for metal stamping, and they are put on a strict maintenance regimen to ensure long life and consistent stampings.

Production of the metal parts is accomplished on a full range of presses, from 15 tons to 200 tons, with speeds of up to 1,500 parts per minute. Inspection of raw materials (inputs), work-in-process, and finished products (outputs) helps ensure zero defects. The company provides a full range of secondary and finishing operations, from heat-treating to powder coating to tapping, to add value to customers. Customers do not need to ship stampings elsewhere or arrange for another service provider to finish the job.

At the customer's request, Buhrke will assemble the stampings with other components to deliver a complete subassembly. Buhrke will even procure parts for assembly, such as plastics that the company does not manufacture. Buhrke is also able to package finished stampings or subassemblies. Before stampings are boxed up and shipped (and even after the incoming inspection and in-process audits), Buhrke provides a final audit inspection. Finally, Buhrke offers the convenience of shipping the finished product where and when customers want. For further information and video tours of the plant, visit www.buhrke.com.

2-2c Value Chains: Pre- and Postproduction Services Perspective

A second view of the value chain can be described from the pre- and postservice perspective as shown in Exhibit 2.4. Pre- and postproduction services complete the ownership cycle for the good or service. Preproduction services include customized and team-oriented product design, consulting services, contract negotiations, product and service guarantees, customer financing to help purchase the product, training customers to use and maintain the product, purchasing and supplier services, and other types of front-end services. The focus here is on "gaining a customer."

Postproduction services include on-site installation or application services, maintenance and repair in the field, servicing loans and financing, warranty and claim services, warehouse and inventory management for your company and sometimes for your customers, training, telephone service centers, transportation delivery services, postsale visits to the customer's facility

by knowledgeable sales and technical-support people, recycling and remanufacturing initiatives, and other back-end services. The focus here is on "keeping the customer."

This view of the value chain emphasizes the notion that service is a critical component of traditional manufacturing processes. Preproduction services for Ford Motor Company include engineering design, supplier, sales, and leasing processes, and postproduction

Exhibit 2.4 *Pre- and Postservice View of the Value Chain*

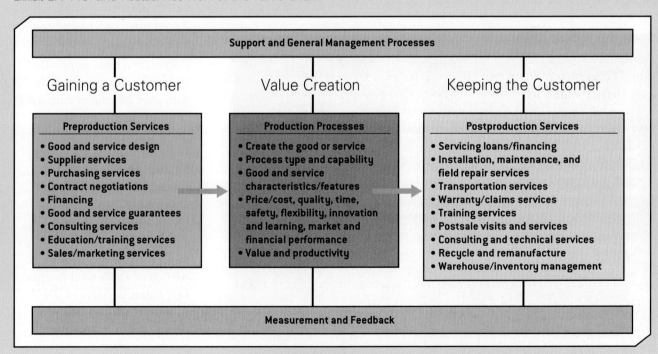

Support and General Management Processes

Gaining a Customer   Value Creation   Keeping the Customer

Preproduction Services
- Good and service design
- Supplier services
- Purchasing services
- Contract negotiations
- Financing
- Good and service guarantees
- Consulting services
- Education/training services
- Sales/marketing services

Production Processes
- Create the good or service
- Process type and capability
- Good and service characteristics/features
- Price/cost, quality, time, safety, flexibility, innovation and learning, market and financial performance
- Value and productivity

Postproduction Services
- Servicing loans/financing
- Installation, maintenance, and field repair services
- Transportation services
- Warranty/claims services
- Training services
- Postsale visits and services
- Consulting and technical services
- Recycle and remanufacture
- Warehouse/inventory management

Measurement and Feedback

© Cengage Learning 2013

services include financing, maintenance and repair, warranty and claims, and customer education and training programs. Service is a key differentiating factor in the eyes of customers for many manufacturing firms. Ford Motor Company is continuing to develop a competitive strategy where "service is the centerpiece of their global strategy." Note that the Buhrke Industries, Inc. value chain can also be defined using the pre- and postservice perspectives. Both perspectives enhance management's understanding of where and how they create value for customers. Automobile companies such as Ford Motor Company might use the pre- and postservice model to highlight service processes, and associated customer service encounters and experiences.

2-2d The Value Chain at Dell, Inc.

To illustrate the pre- and postproduction services perspective of a value chain, we highlight Dell, Inc. Dell's value-creation processes focus on designing and assembling highly customized personal computers, servers, workstations, and peripherals, which it sells directly to customers as well as through traditional stores such as Best Buy. In addition, it also provides customer value through consulting to global corporate and consumer markets in such areas as mobile computing, software, and technology management. For example, Dell works with 96 percent of the Fortune 500 companies on issues such as global networking, storage, servers, and mobile and cloud computing. With Dell's consulting expertise, ABNAMRO,

an international bank, reduced energy consumption by 20 percent globally, improved its licensing processes, and is working toward reducing the environmental impact of its entire IT system to carbon neutral.[5] These consulting services have much higher margins than the production and distribution of hardware.

However, Dell's value chain extends far beyond its hardware and consulting activities. Pre- and post-production services are as vital to Dell's value chain as its value-creation processes. Exhibit 2.5 depicts Dell's value chain from the perspective of the model shown in Exhibit 2.4. Customers buy the entire customer benefit package, not just the manufactured goods. For example, Dell's financing options or online training services often are the order winner.

Preproduction services, many of which are information-intensive, include the following:

- *Customer benefit package design and configuration*—Dell offers a variety of models and configurations to meet the needs of different markets (for example, home, business, and education) and price points, all of which can be customized to individual and company specifications. Many peripheral goods are available, including preloaded software, printers, digital cameras, and other products. Dell systems use a "Green by Design" approach to all goods and services design. Peripheral services include technical support and advice for configuring the right system, financing, warranty options such as next-day onsite repair, and even rapid ordering of consumable supplies.

- *Corporate partnerships*—Dell has established partnerships with over 200 major corporate clients. Using secure, customized intranet sites called Premier Pages, the clients' employees can order preauthorized Dell products online, usually at a discount.

- *Customer financing*—Business, education, and government customers represent a substantial portion of Dell's total revenue. Dell Financial Services (DFS) was established to help such organizations finance their purchases, often an order winner in developing economies.

NESTLÉ: SELLING MORE THAN COFFEE

Pre- and postproduction services also represent huge opportunities to increase revenue and provide new sources of income. For example, Nestlé once defined its business from a physical-good viewpoint as "selling coffee machines." Using service management thinking, Nestlé redefined its business from a service perspective where the coffee machine is more of a peripheral good. Nestlé decided to lease coffee machines and provide daily replenishment of the coffee and maintenance of the machines for a contracted service fee. This "primary leasing service" was offered to organizations that sold more than 50 cups of coffee per day. The results were greatly increased coffee sales, new revenue opportunities, and much stronger profits. Of course, Nestlé's service vision of its business required a completely new service and logistical value chain capability. Moreover, the difficulty of providing this service to thousands of organizations (sites) in a geographical region is a barrier to entry for competitors and a challenge for Nestlé.

Exhibit 2.5 *A Value Chain Model of Dell, Inc.*

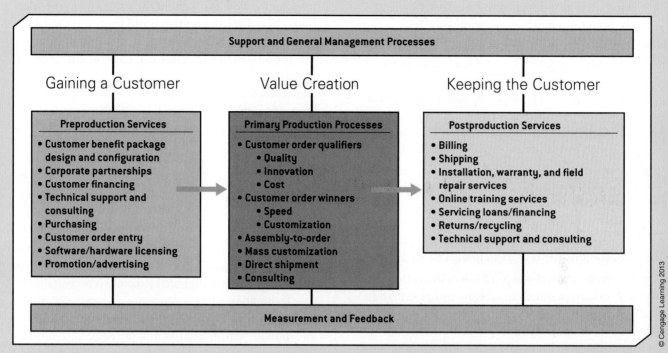

Support and General Management Processes

Gaining a Customer | Value Creation | Keeping the Customer

Preproduction Services
- Customer benefit package design and configuration
- Corporate partnerships
- Customer financing
- Technical support and consulting
- Purchasing
- Customer order entry
- Software/hardware licensing
- Promotion/advertising

Primary Production Processes
- Customer order qualifiers
  - Quality
  - Innovation
  - Cost
- Customer order winners
  - Speed
  - Customization
- Assembly-to-order
- Mass customization
- Direct shipment
- Consulting

Postproduction Services
- Billing
- Shipping
- Installation, warranty, and field repair services
- Online training services
- Servicing loans/financing
- Returns/recycling
- Technical support and consulting

Measurement and Feedback

© Cengage Learning 2013

- *Technical support and consulting*—Dell's technical support call centers handle thousands of calls a day from corporate and individual customers. Customer calls involve presale questions as well as postdelivery questions. Therefore, technical support is both a pre-and postproduction global service.

- *Customer order entry*—Dell's online ordering capability gives customers the power to design and configure their customer benefit package any way they want it by selecting the specific hardware and software options, peripherals, service contracts, financing, and so on.

- *Software and hardware licensing*—Dell equipment comes fully loaded with the latest software from suppliers such as Microsoft.

- *Promotion/Advertising*—Dell offers numerous special deals and promotions on its Web site, such as free or upgraded peripheral options, free shipping, or an instant rebate.

Postproduction services, which focus on "keeping the customer," include the following:

- *Billing*—Dell's Premier Pages customers are billed electronically. Individual customer purchases are

Bloomberg via Getty Image

charged to credit cards. Once the equipment is paid for, the operating system generates supplier and Dell factory production orders, shipping information, and bills.

- *Installation, warranty, and field repair services*— Dell offers limited warranty, consulting, and repair service on a prepaid contract basis for individual and corporate clients.

- *Online training services*—Dell provides or refers customers to online training programs. Dell's online instructions are very clear, with examples and frequently-asked-question links. For major business and government clients, customized training software is also designed to meet specific client needs and can be accessed worldwide.

- *Servicing loans/financing*—Dell's Premier Pages helps key clients manage and track equipment purchases, contracts, and leasing agreements online. Customers who lease through Dell Financial Services can use these pages to obtain new lease quotes, place lease orders, access credit reports, and track leased assets throughout their life cycles.

- *Returns/Recycling*—With millions of obsolete computers, Dell provides detailed instructions for returning old equipment to Dell's Recycling and Asset Recovery Services to either donate them or to have them recycled and disposed of in an environmentally safe way, even if it isn't a Dell brand.

- *Technical support*—In addition to live technical support, Dell embeds diagnostic equipment and software into its equipment before it leaves the factory, making it possible to run many equipment and software checks and make fixes online.

As we see, the value chain for Dell, Inc. includes many services that extend far beyond a physical-goods-focused value chain paradigm.

2-3 Value Chain Decisions

Organizations face numerous decisions in designing and configuring their value chains. Looking back at Exhibits 2.1 and 2.3, we see that these decisions must include the number, type, and location of manufacturing plants, distribution centers, retail stores, repair facilities, and customer service or technical support centers; the choice of technology and processes to make goods and deliver services; ways of managing information flow throughout the value chain; the selection of suppliers and partners; and the integration of all the pieces into an effective and efficient system.

The **operational structure** *of a value chain is the configuration of resources, such as suppliers, factories, warehouses, distributors, technical support centers, engineering design and sales offices, and communication links.* Different management skills are required for different operational structures. For example, Walmart's value chain, though very large, is focused on purchasing and distribution, and is controlled from a centralized location in Bentonville, Arkansas. In contrast, General Electric's value chain, which encompasses such diverse businesses as medical imaging, jet engines, appliances, and electrical power generation, are all quite different. Each business is a profit center with its own unique market and operating conditions. Consequently, the operational structure is decentralized.

Technology enables processes and value chains to lower the cost of goods and services, speed delivery, and provide customization where required. Examples include rental car transponders to speed checkout and check-in, computer-driven machines to produce manufactured parts, geographic and wireless information systems to locate vehicles and inventory, and electronic patient medical records.

2-3a Outsourcing and Vertical Integration

One of the most important strategic decisions a firm can make about its value chain is whether to vertically integrate or outsource key business processes and functions. **Vertical integration** *refers to the process of acquiring and consolidating elements of a value chain to achieve more control.* Some firms might consolidate all processes for a specific product or product line in a single facility; for example, Henry Ford's early factories did everything from steelmaking to final assembly. Although such a strategy provides more control, it adds more complexity to managing the value chain. In contrast, today's automobile production is characterized by a complex network of suppliers. Decentralizing value chain activities lessens the control that a firm has over cost, quality, and other important business metrics, and often leads to higher levels of risk.

Companies must decide whether to integrate backward (acquiring suppliers) or forward (acquiring distributors), or both. **Backward integration** *refers*

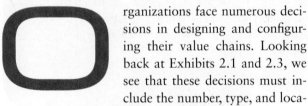

The **operational structure** of a value chain is the configuration of resources, such as suppliers, factories, warehouses, distributors, technical support centers, engineering design and sales offices, and communication links.

Vertical integration refers to the process of acquiring and consolidating elements of a value chain to achieve more control.

Backward integration refers to acquiring capabilities toward suppliers.

to acquiring capabilities toward suppliers, whereas **forward integration** *refers to acquiring capabilities toward distribution or even customers.* Large companies such as Motorola, Siemens, and Sony have the resources to build facilities in foreign countries and develop a high level of vertical integration. Their objective is to own or control most, if not all, of the supply chain. Many large chemical manufacturers, for example, such as DuPont, British Petroleum, Haimen Jiangbin, and GFS Chemicals, are buying raw material suppliers and integrating backward. At the same time, chemical companies in industrial countries are acquiring smaller and more profitable specialty manufacturers of chemicals and advanced materials, a form of forward integration.

Outsourcing *is the process of having suppliers provide goods and services that were previously provided internally.* Outsourcing is the opposite of vertical integration in the sense that the organization is shedding (not acquiring) a part of its organization. The organization that outsources does not have ownership of the outsourced process or function. Some large U.S. banks and airlines, for example, have outsourced their telephone call service centers to third-party suppliers within or outside the United States.

The United States has experienced three waves of outsourcing:

- The first wave involved the exodus of *goods producing jobs* from the United States in many industries several decades ago. Companies relied on foreign factories for the production of computer components, electronics, and many other goods. Gibson Guitars, for example, produces its Epiphone line in Korea.

- The second wave involved *simple service work*, such as standard credit card processing, billing, keying information into computers, and writing simple software programs. Accenture, for example, has information technology and bookkeeping operations in Costa Rica.

- The third, and current wave, involves *skilled knowledge work*, such as engineering design, graphic artists, architectural plans, call center customer service representatives, and computer chip design. For example, Fluor Corporation of Aliso Viejo, California, uses engineers and draftspeople in the Philippines, Poland, and India to develop detailed blueprints and specs for industrial construction and improvement projects.[6]

Bettmann/CORBIS

2-3b The Economics of Outsourcing

The decision on whether to outsource is usually based on economics, and break-even analysis can be used to provide insight into the best decision.

If a company decides to make a part, it typically incurs fixed costs associated with purchasing equipment or setting up a production line. Fixed costs do not vary with volume and often include costs of a building, buying or leasing equipment, and administrative costs. However, the variable cost per unit will be less if the work is outsourced to some external supplier. Variable costs are a function of the quantity produced and might include labor, transportation, and materials costs.

Define

VC_1 = Variable cost/unit if produced

VC_2 = Variable cost/unit (i.e., purchase price/unit) if outsourced

FC = fixed costs associated with producing the part

Q = Quantity produced (volume)

Forward integration refers to acquiring capabilities toward distribution or even customers.

Outsourcing is the process of having suppliers provide goods and services that were previously provided internally.

Then

$$\text{Total cost of production} = (VC_1)Q + FC$$
$$\text{Total cost of outsourcing} = (VC_2)Q$$

If we set these costs equal to each other, we obtain

$$(VC_2)Q = (VC_1)Q + FC$$
$$(VC_2)Q - (VC_1)Q = FC$$
$$(VC_2 - VC_1)Q = FC$$

The break-even quantity is found by solving for Q:

$$Q^* = \frac{FC}{VC_2 - VC_1} \qquad [2.1]$$

Solved Problem

Suppose that a manufacturer needs to produce a custom aluminum housing for a special customer order. Because it currently does not have the equipment necessary to make the housing, it would have to acquire machines and tooling at a fixed cost (net of salvage value after the project is completed) of $250,000. The variable cost of production is estimated to be $20 per unit. The company can outsource the housing to a metal fabricator at a cost of $35 per unit. The customer order is for 12,000 units. What should it do?

Solution

VC_1 = Variable cost/unit if produced = $20
VC_2 = Variable cost/unit if outsourced = $35
FC = fixed costs associated with producing the part = $250,000
Q = quantity produced

Using Equation 2.1, we obtain

$$Q^* = \frac{250,000}{(35-20)} = 16,667$$

In this case, because the customer order is only for 12,000 units, which is less than the break-even point (Q^*), the least-cost decision is to outsource the component.

Exhibit 2.6 shows the results of using the Excel Break-Even template to compute the costs and find the optimal decision. The Excel Goal Seek tool may be used to find the break-even point. Select Goal Seek from the appropriate Excel menu and a small dialog box will appear. In the "Set Cell" field, enter B15 (or simply click on this cell); in the "To Value" field, enter 0; and in the "By changing cell" field, enter B4 (or again, simply click on the cell). When you click OK, Excel will find the production volume in cell B4 that results in a cost difference of 0 in cell B15. This is the break-even point.

Whenever the anticipated volume is greater than Q^*, the firm should produce the part in-house; otherwise it is best to outsource.

2-3c Value Chain Integration

For complex value chains that incorporate numerous suppliers, facilities, and outsourced processes, firms need an approach to coordinate and manage information, physical goods, and services among all the players in the value chain. **Value chain integration** *is the process of managing information, physical goods, and services to ensure their availability at the right place, at the right time, at the right cost, at the right quantity, and with the highest attention to quality.* (A focus solely on coordinating the physical flow of materials to ensure that the right parts are available at various stages of the supply chain, such as manufacturing and assembly plants, is commonly called *supply chain integration*.) For goods-producing firms it requires consolidating information systems among suppliers, factories, distributors, and

Value chain integration is the process of managing information, physical goods, and services to ensure their availability at the right place, at the right time, at the right cost, at the right quantity, and with the highest attention to quality.

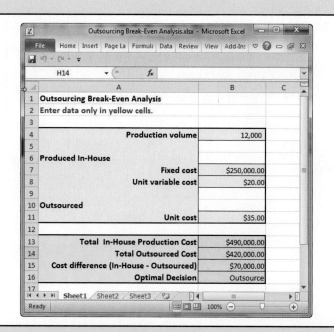

customers; managing the supply chain and scheduling factories; and studying new ways to use technology.

Value chain integration includes improving internal processes for the client as well as external processes that tie together suppliers, manufacturers, distributors, and customers. Other benefits are lower total value chain costs to the client, reduced inventory obsolescence, better global communication among all parties, access to new technologies, and better customer service. Some firms, such as Walmart, manage value chain integration themselves. Others make use of third-party "system integrators" such as Exel (www.exel.com) to manage the process. Exel manages value chain activities across industries and geographic regions to reduce costs, accelerate product movement, and allow manufacturers and retailers to focus on their core business. Exel is able to deliver services and solutions such as consulting, e-commerce, transport, global freight, warehousing, home delivery, labeling, and co-packing, on a local, regional, or global basis.

Value chain integration in services—where value is in the form of low prices, convenience, and access to special time-sensitive deals and travel packages—takes many forms. For example, third-party integrators for the leisure and travel industry value chains include Orbitz, Expedia, Priceline, and Travelocity. They manage information to make these value chains more efficient and create value for their customers. Many financial services use information networks provided by third-party information technology integrators such as AT&T, Sprint, IBM, and Verizon to coordinate their value chains. Hospitals also use third-party integrators for both their information and physical goods, such as managing patient billing and hospital inventories.

 **2-4 Offshoring**

a s we discussed at the beginning of this chapter, offshoring represents one of the most controversial topics in business today. **Offshoring** *is the building, acquiring, or moving of process capabilities from a domestic location to another country location while maintaining ownership and control.*

Offshoring decisions involve determining what value creation, support, and/or general management

> **Offshoring** is the building, acquiring, or moving of process capabilities from a domestic location to another country location while maintaining ownership and control.

ALLEN-EDMONDS SHOE CORPORATION: NOT EVERYONE OFFSHORES

At a time when more than 98 percent of all shoes sold in the United States are made in other countries, Allen-Edmonds Shoe Corp. is a lonely holdout against offshoring. Moving to China could have saved the company as much as 60 percent. However, John Stollenwerk, chief executive, will not compromise on quality, and believes that Allen-Edmonds can make better shoes and serve customers faster in the United States. An experiment in producing one model in Portugal resulted in lining that wasn't quite right and stitching that wasn't as fine. Stollenwerk noted "We could take out a few stitches and you'd never notice it—and then we could take out a few more. Pretty soon you've cheapened the product, and you don't stand for what you're about."[7] Instead, Allen-Edmonds invested more than $1 million to completely overhaul its manufacturing process into a leaner and more efficient system that could reduce the cost of each pair of shoes by 5 percent. One year after implementing its new production processes, productivity was up 30 percent, damages were down 14 percent, and order fulfillment neared 100 percent, enabling the company to serve customers better than ever.[8]

processes should move to other countries. For example, a company might move a soda-bottling factory from the United States to India. The company benefits from lower wages, avoiding country trade tariffs, and access to local markets and customers. However, such a decision does not compromise the company's product development or other proprietary activities. At the other extreme, a high-tech company might establish a facility in China that develops, engineers, and manufactures new products. Such a decision might leave it vulnerable to protecting trade secrets.

Some global trade experts recommend keeping some primary processes or key parts of a manufacturing process out of foreign lands to protect the firm's core competencies. We can pose four possible scenarios. In the first scenario, all key processes remain in the home country, even though the firm sells its products overseas. An example would be Harley-Davidson. The second scenario represents a low degree of offshoring in which some noncritical support processes are moved overseas. Examples would be Microsoft and American Express. A third scenario is for a company to offshore many of its primary as well as support processes while keeping its management processes consolidated at the corporate headquarters, such as Coca-Cola and FedEx. Finally, true global multinational firms, such as Procter & Gamble and Honda, locate all of their key processes across the globe for more effective coordination and local management. The global alignments, of course, may change over time.

The decision to offshore or outsource involves a variety of economic and noneconomic issues. Exhibit 2.7 summarizes the key issues in these decisions.

When many manufacturers began outsourcing to Asia in the early 1990s, they were focused strictly on low labor cost. But outsourcing can create numerous problems. For instance, the logistics of shipping from Asia can be complex. Travel expenses for executives and other employees needed to teach or monitor operations can mount up. Quality is more difficult to control, as is enforcing intellectual property rights. When all these factors are considered, some argue that the total cost of production in the United States is actually cheaper. As a result, many firms are "reshoring"—bringing operations back to the United States.[9]

> The decision to offshore or outsource involves a variety of economic and noneconomic issues.

 ## 2-5 Value Chains in a Global Business Environment

although not every organization operates in the global business environment, modern technology and distribution have made it feasible and attractive for both

Exhibit 2.7 *Things to Consider When Making Offshore Decisions*

Economic reasons

Low labor costs
Lower import duties and fees
Lower capital costs
Grow global market share
Avoid national currency fluctuations
Preempt competitors from entering global market(s)
Hire worldwide skills and knowledge workers
Build robust value chain networks for global markets
Build relationships with government officials
The negative impact and media attention on remaining employees
Potential loss of intellectual property
Lose control of key processes
Develop secure sources of supply and reduce risks
Build relationships with suppliers
Avoid environmental regulations and laws
Possible political instability in offshore country
Lack of communication and/or technical skills
Learn foreign markets and cultures

Noneconomic reasons

© Cengage Learning 2013

large and small companies to develop value chains that span international boundaries. *A* **multinational enterprise** *is an organization that sources, markets, and produces its goods and services in several countries to minimize costs, and to maximize profit, customer satisfaction, and social welfare.* Examples of multinational enterprises include British Petroleum, General Electric, United Parcel Service, Siemens, Procter & Gamble, Toyota, and the International Red Cross. Their value chains provide the capability to source, market, create, and deliver their goods and services to customers worldwide.

Multinational enterprises operate complex value chains that challenge operations managers. Some issues that operations managers must confront in a global business environment include (1) how to design a value chain to meet the slower growth of industrialized countries and more rapid growth of emerging economies; (2) where to locate manufacturing and distribution facilities around the globe to capitalize on value chain efficiencies and improve customer value; (3) what performance metrics to use in making critical value chain decisions; and (4) how to decide if partnerships should be developed with competitors to share engineering, manufacturing, or distribution technology and knowledge.

A **multinational enterprise** is an organization that sources, markets, and produces its goods and services in several countries to minimize costs, and to maximize profit, customer satisfaction, and social welfare.

To gain a better understanding of value chains in a global context, we present a case study of Rocky Brands, Inc. next.

2-5a A Global Value Chain: Rocky Brands, Inc.

Rocky Brands, Inc. (www.rockyboots.com) headquartered in Nelsonville, Ohio, manufactures rugged leather work boots and shoes. Timberland, Wolverine, and Rocky are popular brand names for this shoe market segment. Rocky began making boots in 1932 as the William Brooks Shoe Company. In the 1960s, Rocky boots and shoes were 100 percent "Made in America." In 1960, more than 95 percent of all shoes sold in America were made in America.

After 70 years in Nelsonville, the main factory closed in 2002. At that time, local labor costs were about $11 per hour without benefits, whereas in Puerto Rico, the hourly rate was $6; in the Dominican Republic, $1.25; and in China, 40 cents. The unemployed U.S. factory workers had a hard time finding other jobs. Some ended up as greeters at retail stores, collecting scrap metal, doing lawn work, and other odd jobs. The Union of Needle Trades, Industrial, and Textile Employees, Local 146, closed its doors. "Company medical insurance ran out in February 2003. Since 1972, the U.S. Department of Labor reports, 235,000 U.S. shoe jobs have been lost. It is very difficult for these displaced employees to retrain themselves in today's job market.

Today, Rocky Brands, Inc. headquarters remains in Nelsonville along with a warehouse, but all manufacturing is now done overseas at locations such as Moca, Puerto Rico, and La Vega, Dominican Republic. The company made the move to offshore manufacturing much later than its competitors, Wolverine, Dexter, and Timberland, which moved their factories offshore 20 to 30 years ago. However, Rocky Brands, Inc. has successfully transitioned to a global operation. Rocky's global value chain is shown in Exhibit 2.8. A pair of premium Rocky work, hunting, or western boots may reflect components and labor from as many as five countries before landing on a store shelf. The principal characteristics of this global value chain are described as follows:

1. Leather is produced in Australia and then shipped to the Dominican Republic.

2. Outsoles are purchased in China and shipped to Puerto Rico.

3. Gore-Tex fabric waterproofing materials are made in the United States.

4. Shoe uppers are cut and stitched in the Dominican Republic, and then shipped to Puerto Rico.

5. Final shoe assembly is done at the Puerto Rico factory.

6. The finished boots are packed and shipped to the warehouse in Nelsonville, Ohio.

Customer orders are filled and shipped to individual stores and contract customers from Nelsonville. The challenges continue for Rocky Brands, Inc., which must compete against larger competitors. Rocky profit margins are only about 2 percent on sales of over $100 million, whereas Timberland sales top $1 billion with a 9 percent profit margin. Meanwhile, the price of boots continues to decline from roughly $95 a pair to $85 and is heading toward $75. The grandson of the founder of Rocky Brands, Inc. said, "We've got to get there, or we're not going to be able to compete."[10]

Exhibit 2.8 *Rocky Brands, Inc. Value Chain*

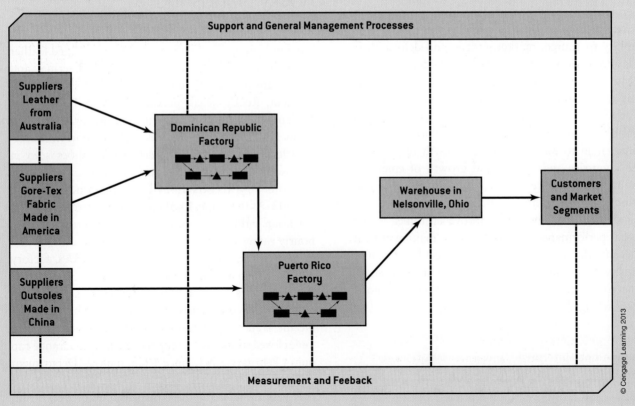

2-5b Issues in Global Value Chain Decisions

Complex global value chains are more difficult to manage than small domestic value chains. Some of the many issues include the following:

- Global value chains face higher levels of risk and uncertainty, requiring more inventory and day-to-day monitoring to prevent product shortages. Workforce disruptions such as labor strikes and government turmoil in foreign countries can create inventory shortages and disrupting surges in orders.

- Transportation is more complex in global value chains. For example, tracing global shipments normally involves more than one mode of transportation and foreign company. Even a natural disaster can create havoc in a global supply chain (see the box about the Japanese earthquake).

- The transportation infrastructure may vary considerably in foreign countries. The coast of China, for example, enjoys much better transportation, distribution, and retail infrastructures than the vast interior of the country.

- Global purchasing can be a difficult process to manage when sources of supply, regional economies, and even governments change. Daily changes in international currencies necessitate careful planning and in the case of commodities, consideration of futures contracts.

- International purchasing can lead to disputes and legal challenges relating to such things as price fixing, nongreen practices, and quality defects. International quality, cost, and delivery disputes have few legal options, and therefore it is imperative that global supplier relationships are well established.

- To extend the firm's value chain to other nations requires an understanding of national cultures and practices. For example, because Chinese words are pictures, the Chinese think more in terms of holistic thoughts and process information emphasizing the big picture over details. Americans think sequentially, focus on details, and individualistically. They break complex situations into a series of smaller issues such as delivery dates, price, and quantity. Such differences can cause confusion, or at worst, ill-will among the constituents.[11]

- Privatizing companies and property is another form of major change in global trade and regulatory issues. Eastern European nations, China, Brazil, and Russia are other countries initiating private ownership of assets such as land, equipment, and businesses. This privatization movement also helps improve the efficiency and effectiveness of global supply chains.

- The pre-planning, response, and recovery from natural or man-made disasters, often called *disaster or emergency management,* is another important part of value chain management. When disasters occur, such as earthquakes, tsunamis, volcanoes, chemical spills, droughts, airplane crashes, or terrorist attacks, organizations or governments worldwide must respond. An organization or government's response to a disaster is only as good as its value chain operations and logistic (supply chain) capability (see the boxes on Japanese earthquake and the Iceland volcano).

In making global value chain decisions, managers must ask and answer some difficult questions.[12] For example, why go global? Is it to sell products and services to the local market, to export products to other markets, or to source materials, components, labor, or knowledge? Do customers require a presence in these markets? What are different global customer and market segments? Are there key competitors in these regions? Which functions (sales, engineering, manufacturing, purchasing, finance, etc.) need to be present in the region? What is the best way to organize our presence in the region (facilities, joint ventures, alliances, licensing arrangements, etc.)? How will we enter the region? How long will it take to be operational? Who will do the globalization work in our company? How much travel are they willing to do, and for how long? Are core staff willing to relocate? Do local suppliers and governments support sustainability initiatives? What is

The Japanese Earthquake Disrupts Global Value Chains

On March 11, 2011, a devastating earthquake and tsunami in Japan caused ripples among global supply chains, particularly in the automotive industry. As Japan is an important source for automotive parts, graphic chips, and other high-tech components, the disaster caused General Motors to shut down a Louisiana factory that makes pickup trucks. North American Toyota plants experienced shortages of 150 critical parts and reduced operations to 30 percent of normal capacity. Companies scrambled to find suppliers in other countries such as China, Taiwan, and South Korea. Subsequently, Toyota announced that it was working to create a robust supply chain that would recover within two weeks in the event of a similar disaster.[13]

our disaster management plan? Clearly, a global value chain strategy places numerous demands on operations as well as other functions and their employees, and requires effective planning and execution.

2-6 Sustainable Value Chains

eading organizations are paying increased attention to the sustainability of their environmental, social, and economic systems, and the design and management of value chains can have a significant impact on these. Sustainability is vital to long-term business survival. It not only improves the organization's perception among consumers, but it also improves the bottom line through reduced costs. In addition, sustainable practices can lead to

increased revenues. For example, organizations that emit greenhouse gases, such as factories and electrical utilities, may one day buy and sell carbon credits in a commodities-type stock market. In addition, many

customers favor products and services that are designed and produced in a sustainable way.

OM plays a critical role in achieving environmental, social, and economic sustainability because the protection of the environment, workforce and community health and safety, and costs and profits are strongly driven by an organization's operations, as well as the life cycles of its products. Every time a good, service, process, or value chain is created or redesigned, OM is involved.

2-6a Green Operations and Vocabulary

The terms *green operations*, *green manufacturing*, and *green practices* are often used to describe sustainability activities that involve operations and the value chain.

The emergence of green thinking has also introduced a new set of vocabulary for managers; see the accompanying box for some examples.

Sustainable environmental practices have caught on with some of the biggest and most powerful companies in the world such as Walmart, McDonald's, Hewlett-Packard, Ritz-Carlton, Nike, and many others. Walmart, for example, has set ambitious goals to operate solely on renewable energy, create zero waste, and sell goods and services that conserve resources. It also plans to require more than 60,000 suppliers by 2015 to source 95 percent of its production from factories receiving one of the retailer's two highest rankings in environmental and social audits. Many small firms have invested in energy efficiency programs, including alternative energy sources, hybrid or alternative fuel vehicles, and employee incentives to cut back on driving and find better routes and traffic patterns.[14]

Green Vocabulary

Biodegradable: *Capable of decomposing naturally within a relatively short period of time.*

Carbon Footprint: *An estimate of how much carbon dioxide an entity (e.g., a person, physical good, service, manufacturing facility, packaging, vehicle, office building) produces and releases into the atmosphere.*

Carbon Neutral: *Reducing energy use and compensating for the amount of carbon dioxide an entity generates through either obtaining energy from renewable sources or 0% setting.*

Carbon Offsets: *Credits earned for activities that help balance carbon dioxide (CO_2) emissions, such as planting trees.*

Environmental Accounting: *An approach to accounting that refers to the modification of standard accounting methods to incorporate the use or depletion of natural resources; sometimes referred to as "green accounting," "resource accounting," or "integrated economic and environmental accounting."*

Passive Solar: *This refers to capitalizing on the warmth and light of the sun with simple strategies instead of complex technologies, such as the use of windows and heat-absorbing and/or reflective materials as opposed to heating and cooling systems.*

Photovoltaics: *A solar power technology that uses cells, panels, or arrays to convert light from the sun directly into electricity.*

Rapidly Renewable Materials: *Resources that can be rapidly replenished as they are used, such as some woods, grasses, and cork.*

Solar Thermal Panel: *A device that collects energy from the sun and converts it into heat for domestic water systems and/or space-heating systems.*

Sustainable Architecture: *A general term that describes environmentally conscious design of structures such as roads, buildings, dams, and airports that minimizes the negative environmental impact of these structures by enhancing efficiency and moderation in the use of materials, energy, and development space.*

Zero-Carbon Buildings: *Buildings that produce no emissions of carbon dioxide from any of their systems and appliances.*

Zero-Energy Buildings: *These structures incorporate systems to both generate and conserve energy, so net energy consumption over a period of a year is zero.*

Source: Green Glossary, American Hotel & Lodging Association, March 5, 2010, http://www.ahla.com/Green.aspx?id=25034.

OM Tools for Sustainability

Many organizations have been using OM tools and principles in sustainability efforts. These tools—such as lean thinking, kaizen, Six Sigma, and value stream mapping—will be described in other chapters of this book. The results speak for themselves. For example, Baxter Healthcare Corporation, a manufacturer of medical products, implemented sustainability tools that helped the company double in size while keeping total waste generation close to 1996 levels. One application expects to save 170,000 gallons of water per day. Lockheed Martin Corporation, a defense contractor, applied OM tools to its chemical and waste-management activities, reducing chemical inventories and eliminating the chemical warehouse and obsolescence of chemicals in inventory. The 3M Company reduced volatile air emissions by 25 percent and waste by 20 percent, and improved energy efficiency by 20 percent. 3M has been using "Pollution Prevention Pays" projects since 1975 to prevent pollution in its products and manufacturing processes rather than after the products are created.[15]

Many OM practices can improve environmental sustainability in value chains. These include designing goods and services using recyclable and environmentally friendly materials, remanufacturing, designing facilities and using equipment that conserves energy, using electronic media and technology to reduce paper and fuel, using transportation modes that minimize costs and carbon output, and cleaning and reusing water used for manufacturing.

Discussion Questions

1. Provide an example where you have compared a good or service by its value and compared with perceived benefits and price. How did your assessment of value lead to a purchase or nonpurchase decision?

2. What implications have the three waves of outsourcing had on the U.S. economy?

3. One study that focused on the impact of China trade on the U.S. textile industry noted that 19 U.S. textile factories were closed and 26,000 jobs were lost in 2004 and 2005. If these factories had not closed, it would have cost U.S. consumers $6 billion more in higher textile prices. Assuming these facts are true, offer an argument for or against offshoring U.S. jobs.

4. Explain why it is important for operations managers to understand the local culture and practices of the countries in which a firm does business. What are some of the potential consequences if they don't?

5. Explain Apple's value proposition and why it can charge more than competitors for similar products.

Problems and Activities

Note: an asterisk denotes problems for which a spreadsheet template on the CourseMate Web site may be used.

1. What is the best way to increase value the most, given the following information for one customer?

   Base Case: Perceived benefits = $50 and Price = $10.00

   Improvement Option A: Perceived benefits = $65 and Price = $13.00

   Improvement Option B: Perceived benefits = $65 and Price = $12.50

   Improvement Option C: Perceived benefits = $60 and Price = $12.50

2. Describe a value chain based upon your work experience, summer job, or experience as a

customer. Sketch a picture of it (as best you can). List suppliers, inputs, resources, outputs, customers, and target markets in a format similar to that in Exhibit 2.1, or use a pre- and postproduction paradigm similar to that in Exhibit 2.3.

3. Research current articles relating to offshoring or outsourcing and focus on business, operations, and political issues. Summarize your findings in a one- to two-page typed paper.

4. Research and write a short paper on companies that have recently reshored their operations back to the United States or another host country.

5. Select two organizations and provide examples of their value chains using the framework in Exhibit 2.2.

6.* Marine International manufactures an aquarium pump and is trying to decide whether to produce the filter system in-house or sign an outsourcing contract with Bayfront Manufacturing to make the filter system. Marine's expertise is producing the pumps itself, but it is considering producing the filter systems also. To establish a filter system production area at Marine International, the fixed costs is $370,000 per year, and it estimates the variable cost of production in-house at $11.27 per filter system. If Marine outsources the production of the filter system to Bayfront, Bayfront will charge Marine $25 per filter system. Should Marine International outsource the production of the filter system to Bayfront if marine sells 25,000 pumps a year?

7.* A firm is evaluating the alternative of manufacturing a part that is currently being outsourced from a supplier. The relevant information is as follows:

For in-house manufacturing:

   Annual fixed cost = $100,000

   Variable cost per part = $140

For purchasing from supplier:

   Purchase price per part = $160

Using this information, determine the break-even quantity for which the firm would be indifferent between manufacturing the part in-house or outsourcing it.

8.* Refer to the information provided in question 7 to answer the following:

   a. If demand is forecast to be 5,500 parts, should the firm make the part in-house or purchase it from a supplier?

   b. The marketing department forecasts that the upcoming year's demand will be 5,500 parts. A new supplier offers to make the parts for $156 each. Should the company accept the offer?

   c. What is the maximum price per part the manufacturer should be willing to pay to the supplier if the forecast is 5,500 parts, using the information in the original problem (question 7)?

9.* A university currently has a recycling program for paper waste. The fixed cost of running this program is $8,000 per year. The variable cost for picking up and disposing of each ton of recyclable paper is $40. If the work is outsourced to a recycling company, the cost would be $70 per ton.

   a. Find the break-even point.

   b. If the university recycles 200 tons each year, what should it do?

10. Research and find a value chain integrator in a goods- or service-focused value chain and write a short paper (maximum of two typed pages) on how it does its job within the supply chain. What value does the integrator bring to the supply chain and its suppliers and customers?

11. Summarize the key issues that managers face with global value chains in comparison with domestic value chains. What must an organization do to address these issues?

12. Research and find an organization that has a disaster or emergency readiness plan and write a short paper (maximum of two typed pages) on the topic. Focus your discussion on value chain operations and logistic (supply-chain) capability. Cite your sources.

13. Research and find a good or service with a quantifiable carbon footprint. Write a short paper (maximum of two typed pages) on the topic, and if possible, how the carbon footprint was computed. Cite your sources.

14. Research and find a good or service that is biodegradable or carbon neutral. Be prepared to present your findings to the class in a short two- to five-minute discussion.

15. Research any topic discussed in this chapter and write a box feature similar to those in the book about what you found. Develop a creative title, cite your sources, and explain to the class what lessons can be learned from the box (maximum of two typed pages).

"I'm going to Bookmaster to buy a book," Drew yelled as he walked out of his apartment. "I'll be back in about one hour," he continued, as his roommate lay on the sofa after a hard night of partying. As he drove to the bookstore he caught a red stoplight at the first highway intersection. He always hated this intersection because the light took four minutes to complete a cycle. After seven traffic lights he arrived at the store parking lot only to find a city bus blocking the driveway entrance, so he parked on the street and walked about 1,000 feet to the store entrance. There he encountered a lady in a wheelchair exiting the store so he patiently held the doors open for her and her friend. After his 25-minute ordeal to get to the store, he went up to the information booth, waited until the current customer completed her query, and then asked the customer relations associate (CRA), if they had the book. After a quick search on the store's computer Millie said, "Yes, we have copies. The book is $39.95."

"I'll take you to the book," Millie said with a smile. Upon wandering the aisles of books she came to the shelf where the book should be residing. But after a careful search, the book was missing. The store computer said they had two copies but they were not on the shelf as expected. After an extended search only one Bookmaster store across town had this book.

"Do you want to drive over there and get it," she asked again with a smile, "or would you like me to order it for you? It only takes a couple of days to get the book over to this store." "No, I don't want to drive over to that store—it's 15 miles away," Drew said with a sigh. (Pause) As he began to walk out of the store Millie asked, "Why don't I check to see if an eBook exists?" After examining the computer Millie said, "Yes, this book is in digital form. It costs $19.95 as an eBook." "Thanks, Millie, I'll go back home and see if I can download it to my computer. I don't have an iPad

Kindle and iPad designs impose various restrictions on their use.

David Levenson/Alamy

or Kindle reader yet—they're too expensive," Drew said as he began the difficult journey back to his apartment.

Kindle and iPad designs impose various restrictions on their use. For example, Apple's hardware and software locks purchased media to Apple's platform; Apple's development model requires a non-disclosure agreement and the centralized approval process for apps. Of particular concern is the ability for Apple to remotely disable or delete apps, media, or data on the iPad at will. Another tough issue is who owns and controls the digital rights to digital content such as eBooks, music, apps, movies, and games. The creators of digital content are concerned about diminished or no royalties due to piracy of their work.

Case Questions for Discussion

1. Draw the "bricks-and-mortar" process stages of the value chain by which hard-copy books are created, produced, distributed, and sold in retail stores. How does each player in the value chain make money? (You can use the exhibits in this chapter to help you identify major stages in the value chain.)

2. Draw the process stages for creating and downloading an eBook today. How does each player in this new electronic/digital value chain make money?

3. Compare and contrast value chain design and structure in the previous two questions from customer and management viewpoints. What are the advantages and disadvantages to each value chain design?

4. What is the role of operations in each of these value chain designs and structures?

5. What other criteria and issues are important in critiquing these two different value chain designs?

4LTR Press solutions are designed for today's learners through the continuous feedback of students like you. Tell us what you think about **OM4** and help us improve the learning experience for future students.

YOUR FEEDBACK MATTERS.

Complete the Speak Up survey in CourseMate at www.cengagebrain.com

 Follow us at www.facebook.com/4ltrpress

MEASURING PERFORMANCE IN OPERATIONS

 magine entering the cockpit of a modern jet airplane and seeing only a single instrument there.[1] How would you feel about boarding the plane after the following conversation with the pilot?

Passenger: *I'm surprised to see you operating the plane with only a single instrument. What does it measure?*

Pilot: *Airspeed. I'm really working on airspeed this flight.*

Passenger: *That's good. Airspeed certainly seems important. But what about altitude? Wouldn't an altimeter be helpful?*

Pilot: *I worked on altitude for the last few flights and I've gotten pretty good on it. Now I have to concentrate on proper airspeed.*

Passenger: *But I notice you don't even have a fuel gauge. Wouldn't that be useful?*

Pilot: *You're right; fuel is significant, but I can't concentrate on doing too many things well at the same time. So on this flight I'm focusing on airspeed. Once I get to be excellent at airspeed, as well as altitude, I intend to concentrate on fuel consumption on the next set of flights.*

learning outcomes

After studying this chapter you should be able to:

3-1   **Describe the types of measures used for decision making.**

3-2   **Explain the use of analytics in OM and how internal and external measures are related.**

3-3   **Explain how to design a good performance measurement system.**

3-4   **Describe four models of organizational performance.**

What do you think?

What measures do you think a company should use to evaluate its company's goods or services? Provide some examples.

Matt Antonino/Shutterstock.com

Measurement *is the act of quantifying the performance of organizational units, goods and services, processes, people, and other business activities.* Measurement provides an objective basis for making decisions. The theme of the opening anecdote is about the wisdom of using a single measure to fly the airplane. Would you fly in such a plane? Concentrating on only one measure at a time is not a good idea. World-class organizations normally use between 3 to 10 performance measures per process depending on the complexity of goods and services, number of market segments, competitive pressures, and opportunities for failure.

Good measures provide a "scorecard" of performance, help identify performance gaps, and make accomplishments visible to the workforce, the stock market, and other stakeholders. For example, the ground-operations area of American Airlines is concerned primarily with the service passengers receive at airports.[2] The ground-operations area routinely measures several factors that customers have noted are important, such as waiting time at the ticket counter, time to opening the cabin door after gate arrival, bag-delivery time, and cabin cleanliness. Knowing that one is doing a good job—or a better job than before—is a powerful motivator for most workers. However, the wrong kind of performance measure can be dangerous. The popular phrase, "How you are measured is how you perform," can destroy good intentions.

> **Measurement** is the act of quantifying the performance of organizational units, goods and services, processes, people, and other business activities.

▼ *I can't concentrate on doing too many things well at the same time, so on this flight I'm focusing on airspeed.*

Regien Paassen/Shutterstock

3-1 Types of Performance Measures

Organizational performance measures can be classified into several important categories:

- Financial
- Customer and market
- Quality
- Time
- Flexibility
- Innovation and learning
- Productivity and operational efficiency
- Sustainability

Within each of these categories are organizational-level measures that are of interest primarily to senior managers, as well as more specific measures that are used by operations managers. Some of them are summarized in Exhibit 3.1.

3-1a Financial Measures

Financial measures, such as cost and revenue, often take top priority in for-profit organizations. For example, the banking industry monitors closely the costs associated with checking account transactions. Internet banking is being promoted because it has a distinct cost advantage: the estimated transaction costs typically are 1 percent of branch bank transaction costs. Traditional financial measures that companies use include revenue, return on investment, operating profit, pretax profit margin, asset utilization, growth, revenue from new goods and services, earnings per share, and other liquidity measures. Non-profit organizations, such as the Red Cross, churches, and government agencies, focus more on minimizing costs and maximizing value to their target markets, customers,

---

Exhibit 3.1 *The Scope of Business and Operations Performance Measurement*

Performance Measurement Category	Typical Organizational-Level Performance Measures	Typical Operational-Level Performance Measures
Financial	Revenue and profit Return on assets Earnings per share	Labor and material costs Cost of quality Budget variance
Customer and market	Customer satisfaction Customer retention Market share	Customer claims and complaints Type of warranty failure/upset Sales forecast accuracy
Quality	Customer ratings of goods and services Product recalls	Defects/unit or errors/opportunity Service representative courtesy
Time	Speed Reliability	Flow processing or cycle time Percent of time meeting promised due date
Flexibility	Design flexibility Volume flexibility	Number of engineering changes Assembly-line changeover time
Innovation and learning	New product development rates Employee satisfaction Employee turnover	Number of patent applications Number of improvement suggestions implemented Percent of workers trained on statistical process control
Productivity and operational efficiency	Labor productivity Equipment utilization	Manufacturing yield Order fulfillment time
Sustainability	Environmental and regulatory compliance Product-related litigation Financial audits	Toxic waste discharge rate Workplace safety violations Percent of employees with emergency preparedness training

Measures of customer satisfaction reveal areas that need improvement and show whether changes actually result in improvement. A **customer-satisfaction measurement system** *provides a company with customer ratings of specific goods and service features and indicates the relationship between those ratings and the customer's likely future buying behavior.* It tracks trends and reveals patterns of customer behavior from which the company can predict future customer needs and wants. It also tracks and analyzes complaints and other measures of dissatisfaction. At Federal Express, for instance, customers are asked to rate everything from billing to the performance of couriers, package condition, tracking and tracing capabilities, complaint handling, and helpfulness of employees. A restaurant might rate food appearance, taste, temperature, and portions, as well as cleanliness, staff friendliness, attentiveness, and perception of value.

Marketplace performance indicators could include market share, measures of business growth, new product and geographic markets entered, and percentage of new product sales, as appropriate. For example, in a commodity market in which Cargill Kitchen Solutions competes (making various egg products for restaurants and schools from raw eggs), its performance drivers include the U.S. share of market and total pounds of egg products sold. In the highly competitive semiconductor industry, ST-Microelectronics looks not only at sales growth, but also at differentiated product sales.

and society. Monitoring cost and adherence to budgets are important factors in their operational success.

3-1b Customer and Market Measures

You have probably completed customer satisfaction surveys at a restaurant or after an Internet purchase, or perhaps you have lodged a complaint. Through customer and market feedback, an organization learns how satisfied its customers and stakeholders are with its goods and services and performance. Other customer-focused performance measures include customer retention, gains and losses of customers and customer accounts, customer complaints, warranty claims, measures of perceived value, loyalty, positive referral, and customer relationship building.

3-1c Quality

Quality *measures the degree to which the output of a process meets customer requirements.* Quality applies to both goods and services. **Goods quality** *relates to the physical performance and characteristics of a good.* Goods quality is generally measured using instruments, technology, and data-collection processes. For example,

A **customer-satisfaction measurement system** provides a company with customer ratings of specific goods and service features and indicates the relationship between those ratings and the customer's likely future buying behavior.

Quality measures the degree to which the output of a process meets customer requirements.

Goods quality relates to the physical performance and characteristics of a good.

the dimensions and weight of a good such as a laptop computer, its storage capacity, battery life, and actual speed are easy to measure. **Service quality** *is consistently meeting or exceeding customer expectations (external focus) and service-delivery system performance (internal focus) for all service encounters.* Many companies, including Amazon.com, Federal Express, and Nordstrom, have worked hard to provide superior service quality to their customers. Measuring service quality is paramount in such organizations.

Service-quality measures are based primarily on human perceptions of service collected from customer surveys, focus groups, and interviews. Research has shown that customers use five key dimensions to assess service quality:[4]

1. *Tangibles*—Physical facilities, uniforms, equipment, vehicles, and appearance of employees (i.e., the physical evidence).

2. *Reliability*—Ability to perform the promised service dependably and accurately.

3. *Responsiveness*—Willingness to help customers and provide prompt recovery to service upsets.

4. *Assurance*—Knowledge and courtesy of the service providers, and their ability to inspire trust and confidence in customers.

5. *Empathy*—Caring attitude and individualized attention provided to customers.

These five dimensions help form the basis for quality measurement in service organizations. Note that all but the first pertain to behavioral characteristics at the service encounter level, which are more difficult to measure than physical and technical characteristics.

Every service encounter provides an opportunity for error. *Errors in service creation and delivery are sometimes called* **service upsets** *or* **service failures.** Service measures should be linked closely to customer satisfaction so that they form the basis for improvement efforts. For example, a restaurant manager might keep track of the number and type of incorrect orders or measure the time from customer order to delivery.

3-1d Time

Time relates to two types of performance measures—the *speed* of doing something (such as the time to process a customer's mortgage application) and the *variability* of the process. Speed can lead to a significant competitive advantage. Progressive Insurance, for example, boasts that it settles auto-insurance claims before competitors know there has been an accident![5] Speed is usually measured in clock time, whereas variability is usually measured by quantifying the variance around average performance or targets. A useful measure is **processing time**—*the time it takes to perform some task.* For example, to make a pizza, a worker needs to roll out the dough, spread the sauce, and add the toppings, which might take three minutes. **Queue time** *is a fancy word for* **wait time**—*the time spent waiting.*

An important aspect of measuring time is the variance around the average time, as unanticipated variability is what often leads to an unhappy customer experience.

Service quality is consistently meeting or exceeding customer expectations (external focus) and service-delivery system performance (internal focus) for all service encounters.

Errors in service creation and delivery are sometimes called **service upsets** or **service failures.**

Processing time is the time it takes to perform some task.

Queue time is a fancy word for **wait time**—the time spent waiting.

Corbis (RF)/Photolibrary

Variability is usually measured by statistics such as the standard deviation or mean absolute deviation. For example, suppose that one company takes 10 days to process a new life insurance application plus or minus 1 day, while another takes 10 days plus or minus 5 days. Which life insurance process will give the best service to its customers? Which firm would you rather do business with?

3-1e Flexibility

Flexibility *is the ability to adapt quickly and effectively to changing requirements.* Because customer needs and the competitive landscape often change rapidly, operations managers must design value chains that are highly flexible. Flexibility can relate either to adapting to changing customer needs or to the volume of demand. **Goods and service design flexibility** *is the ability to develop a wide range of customized goods or services*

to meet different or changing customer needs. Examples of design flexibility include Dell's ability to provide a wide range of customized computer hardware to accommodate home users, small businesses, and large company's server needs, or a health club's ability to customize an individual client's workout or provide cardio rehabilitation classes for heart patients. Such flexibility requires a highly adaptable operations capability. Design flexibility is often evaluated by such measures as the rate of new product development or the percent of a firm's product mix that has been developed over the past three years.

> **Flexibility** is the ability to adapt quickly and effectively to changing requirements.
>
> **Goods and service design flexibility** is the ability to develop a wide range of customized goods or services to meet different or changing customer needs.

Edyta Pawlowska/Shutterstock

Volume flexibility *is the ability to respond quickly to changes in the volume and type of demand.* This might mean rapid changeover from one product to another as the demand for certain goods increases or decreases, or the ability to produce a wide range of volumes as demand fluctuates. A hospital may have intensive-care nurses on standby in case of a dramatic increase in patient demand because of an accident or be able to borrow specialized diagnostic equipment from other hospitals when needed. Measures of volume flexibility would include the time required to change machine set-ups or the time required to "ramp up" to an increased production volume in response to surges in sales.

3-1f Innovation and Learning

Innovation *refers to the ability to create new and unique goods and services that delight customers and create competitive advantage.* Many goods and services are innovative when they first appear—think of the iPhone. However, competitors quickly catch up (for example, Google's Android operating system and the latest Droid phones); thus, innovation needs to be a constant process for many companies and must be measured and assessed. **Learning** *refers to creating, acquiring, and transferring knowledge, and modifying the behavior of employees in response to internal and external change.* For instance, when something goes wrong in one office or division, can the organization ensure that the mistake is not repeated again and does not occur in other offices or divisions? The importance of innovation and learning is well stated by Bill Gates, who said, "Microsoft is always two years away from failure."

Measures of innovation and learning focus on an organization's people and infrastructure. Key measures might

CB2/ZOB WENN Photos/Newscom

include intellectual asset growth, patent applications, the number of "best practices" implemented within the organization, and the percentage of new products developed over the past few years in the product portfolio. Of particular importance are measures associated with an organization's human resource capabilities. These can relate to employee training and skills development, satisfaction, and work-system performance and effectiveness. Examples include absenteeism, turnover, employee satisfaction, training hours per employee, training effectiveness, and measures of improvement in job effectiveness. For instance, The Ritz-Carlton Hotel Company tracks percent turnover very closely, as this measure is a key indicator of employee satisfaction and the effectiveness of its selection and training processes.

Volume flexibility is the ability to respond quickly to changes in the volume and type of demand.

Innovation refers to the ability to create new and unique goods and services that delight customers and create competitive advantage.

Learning refers to creating, acquiring, and transferring knowledge, and modifying the behavior of employees in response to internal and external change.

H&M: Flexibility and Fashion

One example of building flexibility into operations is the Stockholm-based fashion retailer Hennes & Mauritz (H&M). Whereas traditional clothing retailers design their products at least six months in advance of the selling season, H&M can rush items into stores in as little as three weeks. By monitoring consumer trends and identifying hot-selling items, its designers immediately start to sketch new styles, which are then developed by pattern makers, often using employees as live models. Designs are sent electronically to factories in Europe and Asia that can handle the jobs quickly, and in less than two months, most H&M stores will have the new styles in stock.[6]

Source: Used with permission of Bloomberg L.P. Copyright © 2012. All rights reserved.

3-1g Productivity and Operational Efficiency

Productivity *is the ratio of the output of a process to the input.* As output increases for a constant level of input, or as the amount of input decreases for a constant level of output, productivity increases. Thus, a productivity measure describes how well the resources of an organization are being used to produce output.

$$\text{Productivity} = \frac{\text{Quantity of Output}}{\text{Quantity of Input}} \qquad [3.1]$$

The measures used for the quantity of output and quantity of input in Equation 3.1 need not be expressed in the same units.

Examples of productivity measures include units produced per labor hour, airline revenue per passenger mile, hotel revenue per full time employee, meals served per labor dollar, and the number of students per

Drazen Vukelic/iStockphoto

teacher. Productivity measures are often used to track trends over time.

Operational efficiency *is the ability to provide goods and services to customers with minimum waste and maximum utilization of resources.* Some measures of operational efficiency might include the time it takes to fulfill orders, times to set up machinery and equipment, times to change from one product to another on an assembly line, manufacturing yields, and supply-chain performance, to name just a few.

3-1h Sustainability

The **triple bottom line (TBL or 3BL)** *refers to the measurement of environmental, social, and economic sustainability.* Environmental regulations usually require organizations to measure and report compliance, but many companies go beyond what is minimally required. Organizations track numerous environmental measures such as energy consumption, recycling and other resource conservation activities, air emissions, solid and hazardous waste rates, and so on. Social sustainability measures include consumer and workplace safety, community relations, and corporate ethics and governance. Measuring consumer and workplace safety is vital to all organizations, as the well-being of their customers and employees should be a major concern. Federal and state agencies such as the Occupational Safety and Health Administration (OSHA) require organizations to track and report safety indicators, such as reportable accidents. Examples of safety-related performance measures include

Solved Problem

Consider a division of Miller Chemicals that produces water purification crystals for swimming pools. The major inputs used in the production process are labor, raw materials, and energy. For Year 1, labor costs are $180,000; raw materials cost $30,000; and energy costs amount to $5,000. Labor costs for Year 2 are $350,000; raw materials cost $40,000; and energy costs amount to $6,000. Miller Chemicals produced 100,000 pounds of crystals in Year 1 and 150,000 pounds of crystals in Year 2.

Solution

Using Equation 3.1, we have for Year 1:

$$\text{Productivity} = \frac{\text{Quantity of Output}}{\text{Quantity of Input}}$$
$$= \frac{100,000}{(\$180,000 + \$30,000 + \$5,000)}$$
$$= 0.465 \text{ lb/dollar}$$

For Year 2 we have:

$$\text{Productivity} = \frac{\text{Quantity of Output}}{\text{Quantity of Input}}$$
$$= \frac{150,000}{(\$350,000 + \$40,000 + \$6,000)}$$
$$= 0.379 \text{ lb/dollar}$$

We see that productivity has declined in the past year.

Productivity is the ratio of the output of a process to the input.

Operational efficiency is the ability to provide goods and services to customers with minimum waste and maximum utilization of resources.

The **triple bottom line (TBL or 3BL)** refers to the measurement of environmental, social, and economic sustainability.

accident rates, the parts per million of toxic chemicals in a public water supply, or the security in a hotel room. Other social sustainability measures would be the number of ethical violations and community service hours. Finally, economic sustainability measures might include financial audit results, regulatory compliance, legal or governmental sanctions, donations to civic groups, fines for environmental violations, and measures of accomplishment of strategic initiatives, such as the percentage of action plans and project milestones completed on time.

3-2 Analytics in Operations Management

as we noted in Chapter 1, business analytics is helping operations managers to analyze data more effectively and make better decisions. Typical applications of business analytics include visualizing data using charts to examine performance trends; calculating basic statistical measures such as means, proportions, and standard deviations; comparing results relative to other business units, competitors, or best-in-class benchmarks; and using correlation and regression analyses to help understand relationships among different measures. For example, Pal's Sudden Service uses an automated data collection, integration, and analysis system, SysDine, to generate store-level and companywide reports on sales, customer count, product mix, ideal food and material cost, and turnover rates, and also has an automated correlation routine available for analyzing key data to support organizational performance reviews and strategic planning. As a result, Pal's is able to identify how changes in one performance area affect all other areas, make accurate performance projections, and understand

> The quantitative modeling of cause-and-effect relationships between external and internal performance criteria is called **interlinking**.

how to optimize its management system. Understanding the cause-and-effect linkages between key measures of performance is an important application of analytics.

3-2a Linking Internal and External Measures

Managers must understand the cause-and-effect linkages between key measures of performance. These relationships often explain the impact of (internal) operational performance on external results, such as profitability, market share, or customer satisfaction. For example, how do goods- and service-quality improvements impact revenue growth? How do improvements in complaint handling affect customer retention? How do increases or decreases in employee satisfaction affect customer satisfaction? How do changes in customer satisfaction affect costs and revenues?

The quantitative modeling of cause-and-effect relationships between external and internal performance criteria is called **interlinking**.[7] Interlinking tries to quantify the performance relationships between all parts of the value chain—the processes ("how"), goods and services outputs ("what"), and customer experiences and outcomes ("why"). With interlinking models, managers can objectively make internal decisions that impact external outcomes, for example, determining the effects of adding resources or changing the operating system to reduce waiting time, and thereby increase customer satisfaction (see Exhibit 3.2).

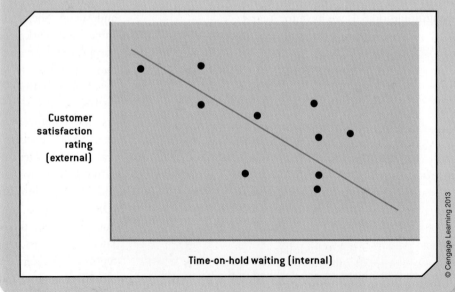

Exhibit 3.2 *Interlinking Internal and External Performance Measures*

Customer satisfaction rating (external)

Time-on-hold waiting (internal)

© Cengage Learning 2013

Analytics for Managing Sports Teams

Professional and amateur sports are just beginning to take advantage of today's analytical methods and software capabilities in order to evaluate performance and return on investment. In basketball, for example, the "box score" documents traditional performance metrics such as points, field goal percentage, fouls, blocked shots, assists, steals, turnovers, minutes played, and offensive and defensive rebounds. Analytics in the form of shot charts, rebound charts, play-by-play data, and motion-capture video and analysis is used to supplement traditional data. Today, the critical question is how to effectively analyze such data in order to maximize performance and owners' returns for minimal cost.

The popular book and film Moneyball has demonstrated the use of analytics in sports management to the average sports fan. The book, published in 2003 before analytics became a buzzword in business, profiles how the Oakland Athletics baseball team used analytics to build a competitive team even with a limited budget, and compete with better-funded teams such as the New York Yankees, which spent nearly three times as much on player personnel. To promote the use of analytics in sports management, the Massachusetts Institute of Technology hosts the annual MIT Sloan Sports Analytics Conference that has been attended by students from over 150 different schools and representatives from over 50 professional sports teams.

3-2b The Value of a Loyal Customer

Many organizations lose customers because of poor goods quality or service performance. This is often the result of operations managers failing to consider the economic impact of lost customers when they cut service staff or downgrade product designs. Likewise, many organizations do not understand the economic value of potential new customers when evaluating proposed goods or service improvements on a strict economic basis. Thus, they need an understanding of how customer satisfaction and loyalty affect the bottom line. One way to do this is to compute the economic value that good customers provide.

*The **value of a loyal customer (VLC)** quantifies the total revenue or profit each target market customer generates over the buyer's life cycle.* Understanding the effects of operational decisions on revenue and customer retention can help organizations more appropriately use their resources. Goods-producing and service-providing organizations both benefit from understanding the value of a loyal customer performance relationship. When one considers the fact that it costs three to five times more to acquire a new customer than keep an existing customer, it is clear why customer retention is often the focus of top management improvement initiatives and strategies.

The **value of a loyal customer (VLC)** quantifies the total revenue or profit each target market customer generates over the buyer's life cycle.

We will walk through an example of computing the average value of a loyal customer. Suppose that a computer manufacturer estimates that its annual customer retention rate is 80 percent, which means that 20 percent of customers who purchase a computer will not buy from it again (we call this the *customer defection rate* $= 1 -$ customer retention rate). Assume that fixed costs are 35 percent and the manufacturer makes a before-tax profit margin of 10 percent. Therefore, the incremental contribution to profit and overhead is 45 percent. We also assume that customers buy a new computer every two years or 0.5 times per year at an average cost of $1,000.

On an annual basis, the average contribution to profit and overhead of a new customer is ($1,000)(0.45)(0.5) = $225 (the multiplier of 0.5 takes into account that customers purchase a new machine every two years). If 20 percent of customers do not return each year, then, on average, the buying life of a customer is five years (1/0.2 = 5). Therefore, the average value of a loyal customer over his or her average buying life is ($225 per year)(5 years) = $1,125.

Now suppose that the customer defection rate can be reduced to 10 percent by improving operations and/or employee service management skills. In this case, the average buying life doubles and the average value of a loyal customer increases to ($225 per year)(10 years) = $2,250. If goods and service improvements can also lead to a market share increase of 10,000 customers, the total contribution to profit and overhead would be $22,500,000 = ($1,000)(0.45)(0.5)(10)(10,000).

We can summarize the logic of these calculations with the following equation:

$$VLC = (P)(CM)(RF)(BLC) \qquad [3.2]$$

where P = the revenue per unit

CM = contribution margin to profit and overhead expressed as a fraction (i.e., 0.45, 0.5, and so on).

RF = repurchase frequency = number of purchases per year.

BLC = buyer's life cycle, computed as 1/defection rate, expressed as a fraction (1/0.2 = 5 years, 1/0.1 = 10 years, and so on).

By multiplying the VLC times the absolute number of customers gained or lost, the total market value can be found.

Operations managers can influence the VLC by increasing the contribution margin through reducing operating costs, increasing repurchase frequency by better customer service, and reducing customer defection rates by creating and delivering consistently excellent system performance. Process managers can use the

Solved Problem

What is the value of a loyal customer (VLC) in the small contractor target market segment who buys an electric drill on average every four years or 0.25 years for $100, when the gross margin on the drill averages 50 percent, and the customer retention rate is 60 percent? What if the customer retention rate increases to 80 percent? What is a 1 percent change in market share worth to the manufacturer if it represents 100,000 customers? What do you conclude?

Solution

If customer retention rate is 60 percent, the average customer defection rate = (1 − customer retention rate). Thus, the customer defection rate is 40 percent, or 0.4. The average buyer's life cycle is 1/0.4 = 2.5 years. The repurchase frequency is every four years, or 0.25 (1/4). Therefore,

VLC = (P)(RF)(CM)(BLC) = ($100)(0.25)(0.50)(1/0.4) = $31.25

The value of a 1 percent change in market share
= (100,000 customers)($31.25/customer/year)
= $3,125,000

If the customer retention rate is 80 percent, the average customer defection rate is 0.2, and the average buyer's life cycle is 1/0.2 = 5 years. Then,
VLC = (P)(RF)(CM)(BLC) = ($100)(0.25)(0.50)(1/.2) = $62.50

Thus, the value of a 1 percent change in market share
= (100,000 customers)($62.50/customer/year)
= $6,250,000

The economics are clear. If customer retention can be increased from 60 to 80 percent through better value chain performance, the economic payoff is doubled.

Exhibit 3.3 *Excel VLC Template*

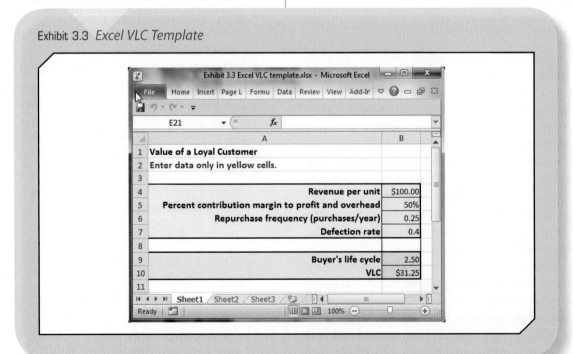

VLC numbers to help justify improvement initiatives in job and process design, capacity and scheduling, and facility design.

Exhibit 3.3 shows the calculations for the base case using the Excel VLC template available on the Course-Mate Web site. The template can be used to compute the impact of different "what-if?" assumptions in this example.

3-3 Designing Measurement Systems in Operations

What makes a good performance measurement system for operations? Many organizations define specific criteria for selecting and deleting performance measures from the organization's information system. IBM Rochester, for example, asks the following questions:

- Does the measurement support our mission?
- Will the measurement be used to manage change?
- Is it important to our customers?
- Is it effective in measuring performance?
- Is it effective in forecasting results?
- Is it easy to understand/simple?
- Are the data easy/cost-efficient to collect?
- Does the measurement have validity, integrity, and timeliness?
- Does the measurement have an owner?

Good performance measures are actionable. **Actionable measures** *provide the basis for decisions at the level at which they are applied*—the value chain, organization, process, department, workstation, job, and service encounter. They should be meaningful to the user, timely, and reflect how the organization generates value to customers. Performance measures should support, not conflict with, customer requirements. For example, customers expect a timely response when calling a customer support number. A common operational measure is the number of rings until the call is picked up. If a company performs well on this measure, but puts the customer on hold or in a never-ending menu, then a conflict clearly exists.

3-4 Models of Organizational Performance

Four models of organizational performance—the Baldrige Performance Excellence framework, the balanced scorecard, the value chain model, and the Service-Profit Chain—provide popular frameworks for thinking about designing, monitoring, and evaluating performance. The first two models provide more of a "big picture" of organizational performance, whereas the last two provide more detailed frameworks for operations managers. Although OM focuses on execution and delivery of goods and services to customers, it is important to understand these "big-picture" models of organizational performance because operations managers must communicate with all functional areas. In addition, understanding these models helps you to better appreciate the interdisciplinary nature of an organization's performance system, the role that operations plays, and why operations managers need interdisciplinary skills.

3-4a Malcolm Baldrige Performance Excellence Framework

The Baldrige Performance Excellence program, formerly known as the Malcolm Baldrige National Quality Award Program, was created to help stimulate American organizations to improve quality, productivity, and overall competitiveness, and to encourage the development of high-performance management practices through innovation, learning, and sharing of best practices. Organizations can receive awards in manufacturing, small business, service, education, health care, and not-for-profit categories. Baldrige recipients show exceptional results that outperform those of their competitors and peers. The program's Web site at www.nist.gov/baldrige/ provides a wealth of current information about the award, the performance criteria, award recipients, and other aspects of the program.

Although the award itself receives the most attention, the primary purpose of the program is to provide

Actionable measures provide the basis for decisions at the level at which they are applied.

USA.gov

Criteria for Performance Excellence. The criteria are designed to provide a framework for managing an organization to achieve outstanding results. The seven categories are:

1. *Leadership*: This category addresses how senior leaders' personal actions guide and sustain the organization, the organization's governance system, and approaches for fulfilling ethical, legal, and societal responsibilities, as well as supporting key communities.

2. *Strategic Planning*: This category focuses on how an organization develops strategic objectives and action plans, how they are deployed and changed if circumstances require, and how progress is measured.

3. *Customer Focus*: This category addresses how an organization engages its customers for long-term marketplace success, builds a customer-focused culture, listens to the voice of its customers, and uses this information to improve and identify opportunities for innovation.

4. *Measurement, Analysis, and Knowledge Management*: This category focuses on how an organization selects, gathers, analyzes,

a framework for performance excellence through self-assessment to understand an organization's strengths and weaknesses, thereby setting priorities for improvement. This framework is shown in Exhibit 3.4, and defines the

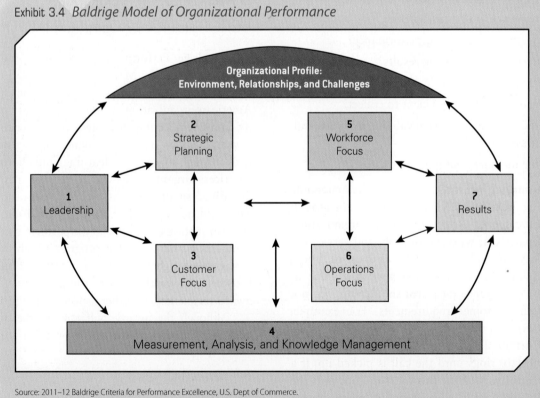

Exhibit 3.4 *Baldrige Model of Organizational Performance*

Source: 2011–12 Baldrige Criteria for Performance Excellence, U.S. Dept of Commerce.

manages, and improves its data, information, and knowledge assets; how it manages its information technology; and how it reviews data and uses the results to improve its performance.

5. *Workforce Focus*: This category addresses how an organization engages, manages, and develops its workforce to utilize its full potential in alignment with the organization's overall mission, strategy, and action plans; assesses workforce capability and capacity needs; and builds a workforce environment conducive to high performance.

6. *Operations Focus*: This category addresses how an organization designs, manages, and improves its work systems and work processes to deliver customer value, achieve organizational success and sustainability, and prepare for emergencies.

7. *Results*: This category examines an organization's performance and improvement in key business areas—product and process outcomes, customer-focused outcomes, workforce-focused outcomes, leadership and governance outcomes, and financial and market outcomes.

In essence, the criteria framework represents a macro-level interlinking model that relates management practices to business results. For example, if senior managers understand their customers and lead the strategic planning process effectively (Categories 1, 2, and 3), and then translate plans into actions through the workforce and operations (Categories 5 and 6), then positive business results (Category 7) should follow. Category 4 provides the foundation for measuring and assessing results and continual improvements. Some simplify the theory of the Baldrige Award by saying that "leadership drives the system that creates results."

3-4b The Balanced Scorecard

Robert Kaplan and David Norton of the Harvard Business School, in response to the limitations of traditional accounting measures, popularized the notion of the *balanced scorecard*, which was first developed at Analog Devices. Its purpose is "to translate strategy into measures that uniquely communicate your vision to the organization." Their version of the balanced scorecard, as shown in Exhibit 3.5, consists of four performance perspectives:

- *Financial Perspective*: Measures the ultimate value that the business provides to its shareholders. This includes profitability, revenue growth, stock price, cash flows, return on investment, economic value added (EVA), and shareholder value.

- *Customer Perspective*: Focuses on customer wants and needs and satisfaction as well as market share and growth in market share. This includes safety, service levels, satisfaction ratings, delivery reliability, number of cooperative customer–company design initiatives, value of a loyal customer, customer retention, percent of sale from new goods and services, and frequency of repeat business.

- *Innovation and Learning Perspective*: Directs attention to the basis of a future success—the organization's people and infrastructure. Key measures might include intellectual and research assets, time to develop new goods and services, number of improvement suggestions per employee, employee satisfaction, market innovation, training hours per employee, hiring process effectiveness, revenue per employee, and skills development.

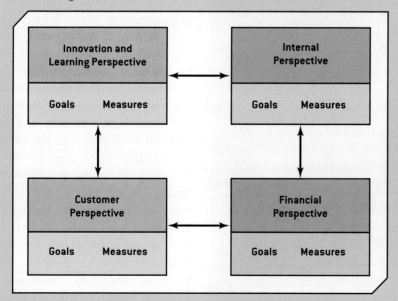

Exhibit 3.5 *The Balanced Scorecard Performance Categories and Linkages*

Source: R. S. Kaplan and D. P. Norton, "The Balanced Scorecard—Measures That Drive Performance," *Harvard Business Review*, January–February 1992, p. 72. Copyright © 1992 by the Harvard Business School Publishing Corporation. Reprinted by permission.

- *Internal Perspective:* Focuses attention on the performance of the key internal processes that drive the business. This includes such measures as goods- and service- quality levels, productivity, flow time, design and demand flexibility, asset utilization, safety, environmental quality, rework, and cost.

The internal perspective is most meaningful to operations managers, as they deal with the day-to-day decisions that revolve around creating and delivering goods and services. As noted in Chapter 1, the internal perspective includes all types of internal processes: value-creation processes, support processes, and general management or business processes.

The balanced scorecard is designed to be linked to an organization's strategy. The linkages between corporate and operations strategy and associated performance measures (called *competitive priorities*) are discussed in Chapter 4. Top management's job is to guide the organization, make trade-offs among these four performance categories, and set future directions.

3-4c The Value Chain Model

A third way of viewing performance measurement is through the value chain concept itself. Of the four models of organizational performance presented in this chapter, the value chain model is probably the dominant model, especially for operations managers. Exhibit 3.6 shows the value chain structure and suggests some typical measures that managers would use to evaluate performance at each point in the value chain.

Suppliers provide goods and services inputs to the value chain that are used in the creation and delivery of value chain outputs. Measuring supplier performance is critical to managing a value chain. Typical supplier performance measures include quality of the inputs provided, price, delivery reliability, and service measures such as rates of problem resolution. Good supplier-based performance data are also the basis for cooperative partnerships between suppliers and their customers.

Operations managers have the primary responsibility to design and manage the processes and associated resources that create value for customers. Process data can reflect defect and error rates of intermediate operations, and also efficiency measures such as cost, flow time, delivery variability, productivity, schedule performance, equipment downtime, preventive maintenance activity, rates of problem resolution, energy and equipment efficiency, and raw material usage. For example, Motorola measures nearly every process in the company, including engineering design, order entry, manufacturing, human resources, purchasing, accounting, and marketing, for improvements in error rates and flow times. One of its key business objectives is to reduce total organizational flow time—the time from the point a customer expresses a need until the customer pays the company for the good or service.

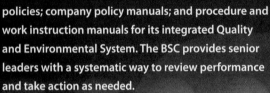

PRO-TEC COATING COMPANY: KEEPING PERFORMANCE IN BALANCE

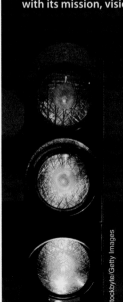

PRO-TEC Coating Company, a joint venture between United States Steel Corporation and Kobe Steel Ltd. of Japan, is the industry leader in advanced high-strength steel coating and ultra-high-strength steel coating. PRO-TEC uses a balanced-scorecard (BSC) approach to help align the company's six key success factors (KSFs)—associate quality of life, customer service, technical innovation and product development, system reliability, good citizenship, and long-term viability—with its mission, vision, and values; its quality, safety, and environmental policies; company policy manuals; and procedure and work instruction manuals for its integrated Quality and Environmental System. The BSC provides senior leaders with a systematic way to review performance and take action as needed.

The BSC uses a stoplight color-coded designation (green, yellow, red) that reflects the actual performance (good, marginal, or at-risk) against short-term targets. The at-risk BSC measures require action, and are reviewed at monthly plant management meetings. The BSC is also used for managing daily operations. For example, measures for safety and health, such as completion of housekeeping and quarterly safety audit items, mobile equipment inspections, and the weekly safety binder sign-off, are reviewed each Monday.[8]

Stockbyte/Getty Images

Measuring goods and service outputs and outcomes tell a company whether its processes are providing the levels of quality and service that customers expect. Organizations measure outputs and outcomes using measures such as unit cost, defects per million opportunities, and lead time. Through customer and market information, an organization learns how satisfied its customers and stakeholders are with its goods and services and performance and how best to configure the goods and services (i.e., customer benefit packages). Measures of customer satisfaction and retention reveal areas that need improvement, and show whether changes actually result in improvement.

Measurement and feedback provide the means of coordinating the value chain's physical and information flows, and for assessing whether the organization

Exhibit 3.6 *Examples of Value Chain Performance Measurements*

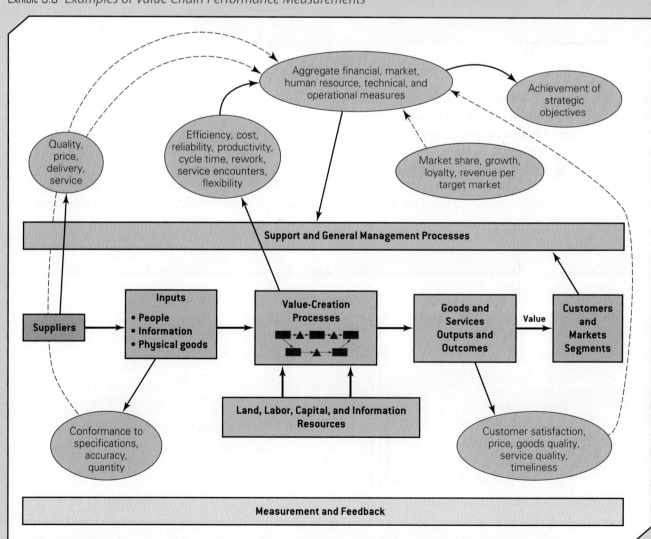

Richard B. Levine/Ambient Images/Glow Images

immediately at General Electric factories and production is scheduled to real-time sales data. Fewer resources are needed to achieve performance goals when "information replaces assets." That is, inventories are reduced, flow times are shorter, quality is better, and costs are lower.

3-4d The Service-Profit Chain

The Service-Profit Chain (SPC) was first proposed in a 1994 *Harvard Business Review* article and is most applicable to service environments.[9] Exhibit 3.7 is one representation of the SPC, and many variations of this model have been proposed in academic and practitioner articles. Many companies, such as Citibank, General Electric, Intuit, Southwest Airlines, Taco Bell, Harrah's Entertainment, and Xerox, have used this model of organizational performance. The theory of the Service-Profit Chain is that employees, through the service-delivery system, create customer value and drive

is achieving its strategic objectives. This is similar to the role of Category 4 (Measurement, Analysis, and Knowledge Management) in the Malcolm Baldrige framework. One objective of timely information sharing is to reduce or replace assets (employees, inventory, trucks, buildings, etc.) with smart and timely performance information. For example, General Electric sells lightbulbs in Walmart stores; these sales are recorded

Exhibit 3.7 *The Service-Profit Chain Model*

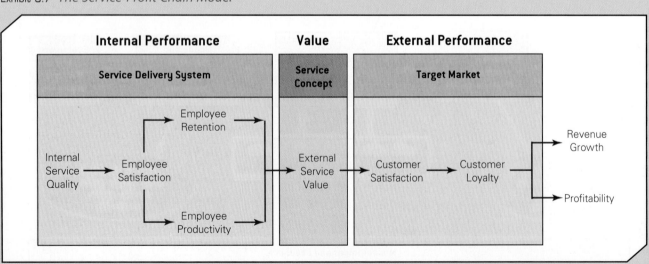

Adapted from J. L. Heskett, T. O. Jones, G. W. Loveman, W. E. Sasser, Jr., and L. A. Schlesinger, "Putting the Service-Profit Chain to Work," *Harvard Business Review*, March–April 1994, pp. 164–174. Copyright © 1994 by the Harvard Business School Publishing Corporation. Reprinted by permission.

profitability. As J. W. Marriott, the founder of Marriott Hotels, said long ago, "Happy employees create happy customers."

The model is based on a set of cause-and-effect linkages between internal and external performance, and in this fashion, defines the key performance measurements on which service-based firms should focus. Because much of the value created in service processes is at the service-encounter level, the Service-Profit Chain focuses on employees or service providers.

Healthy, motivated, well-trained, and loyal employees demonstrate higher levels of satisfaction that result in higher retention and productivity. This leads to higher levels of external service value to customers. External service value is created by service providers mainly at the service-encounter level. Buyers of services focus on outcomes, results, and experiences. Ultimately, good value creates higher customer satisfaction and loyalty, which in turn leads to higher revenue growth and profitability.

Discussion Questions

1. What types of performance measurements might be used to evaluate a fraternity or student organization?

2. What information would you need to fully answer the questions that IBM Rochester uses for selecting measures and indicators that are listed in Section 3 of this chapter? Where would you get this information?

3. Discuss some analytical or graphical approaches that organizations can use for analyzing performance data based on your experience and previous coursework.

4. Under which perspective of the balanced scorecard would you classify each of the following measurements?
   a. On-time delivery to customers
   b. Time to develop the next generation of products
   c. Manufacturing yield
   d. Engineering efficiency
   e. Quarterly sales growth
   f. Percentage of products that equal 70 percent of sales
   g. Cash flow
   h. Number of customer partnerships
   i. Increase in market share
   j. Unit cost of products

5. When the value of a loyal customer (VLC) market segment is high, should these customers be given premium goods and services for premium prices? If the VLC is low, should they be given less service? Explain.

Problems and Activities

Note: an asterisk denotes problems for which a spreadsheet template on the CourseMate Web site may be used.

1. Interview managers at a local company to identify the key business measures (financial, market, supplier, employee, process, information, innovation, etc.) for that company. What quality indicators does that company measure? What cause-and-effect (interlinking) performance relationships would be of interest to the organization?

2. Each day, FedEx processes approximately 85,000 shipments. Suppose that FedEx identified the following numbers of errors during a five-day week (see the "FedEx: Measuring Service Performance" box): These values are hypothetical and do not reflect FedEx actual performance.

Complaints reopened: 143

Damaged packages: 18

International: 96

Invoice adjustments: 282

Late pickup stops: 409

Lost packages: 2

Missed proof of delivery: 76

Right date late: 751

Traces: 42

Wrong day late: 28

Compute the Service Quality Indicator by finding the weighted sum of errors as a percentage of total shipments and subtracting from 100 percent. How might such an index be used in other organizations, such as a hotel or automobile service facility?

3. Research and write a short paper on how some organization (you choose the organization) applies the five dimensions of service quality.

4. A major airline is attempting to evaluate the effect of recent changes it has made in scheduling flights between New York City and Los Angeles. Data available are as follows:

	Number of Flights	Number of Passengers
Month prior to schedule change	18	8,335
Month after schedule change	24	12,472

Using passengers per flight as a productivity indicator, comment on the apparent effect of the schedule change.

5. Revenue or costs per passenger mile are two key performance measures in the airline industry. Research their use in this industry and prepare a one-page paper summarizing how they are used and why they are so important.

6. A hamburger factory produces 40,000 hamburgers each week. The equipment used costs $5,000 and will remain productive for four years. The labor cost per year is $9,500.

   a. What is the productivity measure of "units of output per dollar of input" averaged over the four-year period?

   b. The company has the option of purchasing $10,000 equipment, with an operating life of five years. It would reduce labor costs to $6,000 per year. Should it consider purchasing this equipment (using productivity arguments alone)?

7. A fast-food restaurant has a drive-through window and during peak lunch times can handle a maximum of 50 cars per hour with one person taking orders, assembling them, and acting as cashier. The average sale per order is $8.00. A proposal has been made to add two workers and divide the tasks among the three. One will take orders, the second will assemble them, and the third will act as cashier. With this system, it is estimated that 90 cars per hour can be serviced. Use productivity arguments to recommend whether or not to change the current system.

8. A key hospital outcome measure of clinical performance is length of stay (LOS)—that is, the number of days a patient is hospitalized. For patients at one hospital with acute myocardial infarction (heart attack), the length of stay over the past four years has consistently decreased. The hospital also has data for various treatment options, such as the percentage of patients who received aspirin upon arrival and cardiac medication for left ventricular systolic dysfunction (LVSD). The data are as follows:

Year	Average LOS	Aspirin on Arrival	LVSD Medication
2007	4.55 days	95%	89%
2008	4.33 days	98%	93%
2009	4.12 days	99%	97%
2010	4.02 days	100%	99%

Develop a graphical interlinking model by drawing charts (using Excel if possible) showing the LOS as a function of the other variables. What does the model tell you?

9. Customers call a call center to make room reservations for a small chain of 42 motels located throughout the southwestern part of the United States. Business analytics is used to determine how and if the following performance metrics are related: time by quarter, average time on hold (seconds) before a customer reaches a company customer service representative, percent of time the customer inquiry is solved the first time (called first-pass quality), and customer satisfaction with the overall call center experience. The company has collected the following data:

Quarter	Average Hold Time	Percent Solved First Time	Overall Customer Satisfaction
Q1	22 seconds	82%	96%
Q2	34 seconds	80%	92%
Q3	44 seconds	88%	82%
Q5	67 seconds	85%	84%
Q6	38 seconds	85%	90%
Q7	70 seconds	76%	80%
Q8	86 seconds	73%	81%

Develop a graphical interlinking model by drawing charts (using Excel if possible) showing two key relationships among the four variables. What do your two models tell you? Bonus Question: How many ways can these four variables be compared on an X-versus-Y graph?

10.* What is the average value of a loyal customer (VLC) in a target market segment if the average purchase price is $75 per visit, the frequency of repurchase is six times per year, the contribution margin is 10 percent, and the average customer defection rate is 25 percent?

11.* Using the base case data in question 10, analyze how the value of a loyal customer (VLC) will change if the average customer defection rate varies between 15 and 40 percent (in increments of 5 percent) and the frequency of repurchase varies between three and nine times per year (in increments of one year). Sketch graphs (or use Excel charts) to illustrate the impact of these assumptions on the VLC.

12.* What is the average defection rate for grocery store shoppers in a local area of a large city if customers spend $60 per visit, customers shop 52 weeks per year, the grocery store has a 12 percent gross margin, and the value of a loyal customer is estimated at $2,750 per year?

13. Research and write a short paper on how sports analytics is used by some professional team (you select the team).

14. Go to the Baldrige Web site and find the links to the most recent award recipients. Review one of the application summaries and describe the types of performance measures that these companies use.

15. The balanced scorecard was originally developed by Arthur M. Schneiderman at Analog Devices. Visit his Web site, www.schneiderman.com, and read the articles to answer the following questions:

   a. How was the first balanced scorecard developed?

   b. What steps should an organization follow to build a good balanced scorecard?

   c. Why do balanced scorecards sometimes fail?

BankUSA: Credit Card Division Case Study

BankUSA operates in 20 states and provides a full range of financial services for individuals and business. The credit card division is a profit center that has experienced a 20 percent annual growth rate over the last five years. The credit card division processes two types of credit (bank) cards. One type is for traditional card issuers such as savings and loan banks, credit unions, small banks without credit card processing capability, selected private-label firms such as a retail chain, and BankUSA's own credit cards. This "individual customer" market segment involves about 15,000,000 cardholders. These credit card services include producing and mailing the plastic credit cards to customers, preparing and distributing monthly statements to customers via the Internet or by mail, handling all customer requests such as stop payments and customer complaints, and preparation and distribution of summary reports to all internal and external customers.

The second major category of credit card customers includes major brokers and corporations such as IBM, Dean Witter, State Farm Insurance, and Merrill Lynch.

BankUSA's individual customer market segment involves about 15,000,000 cardholders.

Diego Cervo/Shutterstock.com

These corporate customers use all the services of traditional card issuers but also usually have direct electronic access to their account files and desire a cash management type service. Although there are less than 3,000,000 cards issued, the dollar volume of transactions processed is about equal to that of the traditional individual card issuers.

"Our internal operational measures seem to be good," Ms. Juanita Sutherland, the president of BankUSA's credit card division stated, "but the customer perceives our performance as poor based on marketing's recent customer survey. So, what's going on here? Can anyone at this meeting explain to me this mismatch between these two different sources of information? Is it an important problem or not?"

Mr. H. C. Morris, the vice president of operations, quickly responded, "Juanita, one reason there's a mismatch is that operations doesn't have a say in the customer survey's design or performance criteria. We don't ask the same questions or use the same criteria!"

"Wait a minute, H. C.! We often ask you operations folks for input into our customer survey design but the job usually gets shuttled to your newest MBA who doesn't have enough company knowledge to truly help us out," stated Mr. Bill Barlow, the corporate vice president of marketing, as he leaned forward on the conference room table.

"O.K.," Ms. Sutherland interjected, "I want you two to work on this issue and tell me in one week what to do. I've got another appointment so I must leave now, but you two have got to work together and figure this thing out. I'm worried that we are losing customers!"

At a subsequent meeting between Mr. Morris and Mr. Barlow and their respective operations and marketing staffs, the following comments were made:

- "Reports are routed to over 1,200 institutions (i.e., card issuers), some electronically and others by mail. We don't have total control over providing accurate and timely report distribution because we must depend on other banks for certain detailed information such as debt notices and various transportation modes such as airborne courier service."

- "The trends in the marketing customer survey are helpful to everyone, but the performance criteria simply do not match up well between marketing and operations."

- "Who cares about averages? If a client bank or corporate customer gets a quarterly performance report from us and it says we are meeting 99.2 percent of our service requirements but they are getting bad service, then they wonder how important a customer they are to us."

- "Plastic card turnaround performance is very good based on the marketing survey data, but the wording of the customer survey questions on plastic card turnaround time is vague."

- "Operations people think they know what constitutes excellent service, but how can they be sure?"

- "You'll never get marketing to let us help them design 'their' customer survey," said an angry operations supervisor. "Their marketing questions and what really happens are two different things."

- "We need a consistent numerical basis for knowing how well process performance matches up with external performance. My sample of data (see Exhibit 3.8) is a place to start."

- "Multiple sites and too many services complicate the analysis of what our basic problem is."

- "If your backroom operational performance measures really do the job, who cares about matching marketing and operations performance information? The backroom is a cost center, not a profit center!"

The meeting ended with a lot of arguing but not much progress. Both functional areas were protecting their "turf." How would you address Ms. Sutherland's questions?

Case Questions for Discussion

1. What are the major problems facing the credit card division?

2. What steps are required to develop a good internal and external performance and information system?

3. How should internal and external performance data be related? Are these data related? What do graphs and/or statistical data analysis tell you, if anything? (Use the data in Exhibit 3.8 to help answer these questions.)

4. Is the real service level what is measured internally or externally? Explain your reasoning.

5. What are your final recommendations?

Month	Customer Satisfaction Percent (%)	New Applicant Processing Time (Days)	Plastic Production Turnaround Time (Days)
1	85.0	1.7	1.005
2	83.8	1.8	1.007
3	82.6	1.4	1.208
4	84.6	1.8	0.906
5	83.3	1.6	1.057
6	83.7	1.5	1.099
7	84.0	1.2	0.755
8	84.5	1.3	1.208
9	83.3	1.7	0.906
10	84.6	1.1	1.087
11	84.2	1.3	0.884
12	85.0	1.1	0.987
13	84.6	0.9	0.755
14	85.8	1.0	1.102
15	85.1	0.9	0.782

Exhibit 3.8 *Sample Internal and External Credit Card Division Performance Data (This spreadsheet is available in the OM4 Data Workbook on the CourseMate Web site.)*

© Cengage Learning 2013

THE IN-CROWD

Share your 4LTR Press story on Facebook at www.facebook.com/4ltrpress for a chance to win.

To learn more about the In-Crowd opportunity 'like' us on Facebook.

OPERATIONS STRATEGY

many durable products, such as cell phones, televisions, and refrigerators, contain hazardous materials and cannot be easily reused or recycled. As a result, organizations need to rethink strategically the environmental challenges that result from obsolete durable goods. Cell phones, for example, become obsolete quickly as a result of manufacturers making rapid improvements in design and service providers offering new incentives. The value chain is complex, and includes original equipment manufacturers (OEMs), retailers, service providers, remanufacturers, recyclers, and waste-management companies. Some new strategies that have been suggested include:

- Creating better designs that focus on ease of disassembly and lower costs for refurbishing and recycling. This might include modular designs that make it easier to reuse parts rather than have to recycle them, or recover valuable materials more easily.
- Incorporating refurbishing and recycling activities into manufacturers' value chains. As many as 130 million phones are retired each year, with significant waste and environmental implications.
- Creating more secondary markets for refurbished phones. This can increase profits by enticing users of voice-only phones to upgrade to data plans if the prices of the phones can be reduced.
- Developing new processes to collect and refurbish old phones. For example, ReCellular Inc. has partnered with Verizon, Motorola, Walmart, and others, but still it only captures 5 percent of retired phones, suggesting that the cell phone value chain has not matured.[1]

learning outcomes

After studying this chapter you should be able to:

4-1   **Explain how organizations seek to gain competitive advantage.**

4-2   **Explain approaches for understanding customer wants and needs.**

4-3   **Describe how customers evaluate goods and services.**

4-4   **Explain the five key competitive priorities.**

4-5   **Explain the role of OM, sustainability, and operations in strategic planning.**

4-6   **Describe Hill's framework for operations strategy.**

What do you think?

Which of the following strategies do you think is best for major cell phone providers?

- *Refurbish all phones and sell in developing countries.*
- *Disassemble and recycle domestically 100 percent of all metals and plastics.*
- *Let other firms and third-party organizations, but not major cell phone providers, recycle phones.*

Jim West/Alamy

4-1 Gaining Competitive Advantage

Competitive advantage *denotes a firm's ability to achieve market and financial superiority over its competitors.* In the long run, a sustainable competitive advantage provides above-average performance and is essential to survival of the business. Creating a competitive advantage requires a fundamental understanding of two things. First, management must understand customer needs and expectations—and how the value chain can best meet these through the design and delivery of attractive customer benefit packages. Second, management must build and leverage operational capabilities to support desired competitive priorities.

Every organization has a myriad of choices in deciding where to focus its efforts—for example, on low cost, high quality, quick response, or flexibility and customization—and in designing its operations to support its chosen strategy. The opening scenario suggests that cell phone manufacturers and service providers have many strategic choices in designing and operating their domestic and global value chains. These choices should be driven by the most important customer needs and expectations. In particular, what happens in operations—on the front lines and on the factory floor—must support the strategic direction the firm has chosen.

Any change in a firm's customer benefit package, targeted markets, or strategic direction typically has significant consequences for the entire value chain and for operations.

> **Competitive advantage** denotes a firm's ability to achieve market and financial superiority over its competitors.

MICHAEL REYNOLDS/EPA/Newscom

▼ *As many as 130 million cell phones are retired each year, having significant waste and environmental implications.*

Although it may be difficult to change the *structure* of the value chain, operations managers have considerable freedom in determining what components of the value chain to emphasize, in selecting technology and processes, in making human resource policy choices, and in making other relevant decisions to support the firm's strategic emphasis.

4-2 Understanding Customer Wants and Needs

because the fundamental purpose of an organization is to provide goods and services of value to customers, it is important to first understand customer desires, and also to understand how customers evaluate goods and services. However, a company usually cannot satisfy all customers with the same goods and services. Often, customers must be segmented into several natural groups, each with unique wants and needs. These segments might be based on buying behavior, geography, demographics, sales volume, profitability, or expected levels of service. By understanding differences among such segments, a company can design the most appropriate customer benefit packages, competitive strategies, and processes to create the goods and services to meet the unique needs of each segment.

To correctly identify what customers expect requires being "close to the customer." There are many ways to do this, such as having employees visit and talk to customers, having managers talk to customers, and doing formal marketing research. Marriott Corporation, for example, requires top managers to annually work a full day or more in the hotels as bellhops, waiters, bartenders, front-desk service providers, and so on, to gain a true understanding of customer wants and needs, and the types of issues that their hotel service providers must face in serving the customer. Good marketing research includes such techniques as focus groups, salesperson and employee feedback, complaint analysis, on-the-spot interviews with customers, videotaped service encounters, mystery shoppers, telephone hotlines, Internet monitoring, and customer surveys.

Basic customer expectations are generally considered the minimum performance level required to stay in business and are often called **order qualifiers.** For example, a radio and driver-side air bag are generally expected by all customers for an automobile; for a hotel, customers expect that the room will be safe and clean. The unexpected features that surprise, entertain, and delight customers by going beyond the expected often make the difference in closing a sale. **Order winners** *are goods and service features and performance characteristics that differentiate one customer benefit package from another, and win the customer's business.* Collision avoidance systems or a voice-activated music system in an automobile, for example, or free Internet and gaming devices in a hotel, can be order winners. Over time, however, order winners eventually become order qualifiers as customers begin to expect them. Thus, to stay competitive, companies must continually innovate and improve their customer benefit packages.

Basic customer expectations are generally considered the minimum performance level required to stay in business and are often called **order qualifiers.**

Order winners are goods and service features and performance characteristics that differentiate one customer benefit package from another, and win the customer's business.

PAPA JOHN'S: FOCUS ON THE ORDER WINNER

John Schnatter, founder of Papa John's Pizza, described how he got started in the pizza business and identified Papa John's key competitive priority as now reflected in the slogan "Better ingredients, better pizza, Papa John's." In 1983, John's father hired him to run a bar he co-owned that was nearly bankrupt. Thinking back to his college days when he had a dream of starting a pizza business (where he came up with the name, menu, and recipes), he believed if they could sell $5 pizzas and 50-cent beer, they'd make a fortune. So he installed a pizza oven and began selling Papa John's pizza. He realized early on that Domino's had the speed, Little Caesars had the price, and Pizza Hut had variety, and yet they made up only 35 percent or 40 percent of the market. He didn't understand why pizzas with better ingredients didn't win every time. He thought if you had a national chain that acted like an independent as far as qual-

AP Photo/Patti Longmire

ity, then you'd have the best of all worlds. The bar was like a laboratory where they would try things out. He tried pasta, fried zucchini, and salads as well as sit-down service. But the customers told him early on, "We like your pizza delivered—you're a delivery chain." So he focused on the pizza. Papa John's strategy is to provide a high-quality product (the order winner) with efficient delivery in a competitive market (the order qualifier).[2]

Listen to Your Customers—Creatively!

At IDEO, one of the world's leading design firms (which designed Apple's first mouse, standup toothpaste tubes, and the Palm V), design doesn't begin with a far-out concept or a cool drawing. It begins with a deep understanding of the people who might use whatever product or service eventually emerges from its work, drawing from anthropology, psychology, biomechanics, and other disciplines. When former Disney executive Paul Pressler assumed the CEO position at

AP Photo/Akron Beacon Journal, Lew Stamp

Gap, he met with each of Gap's top 50 executives, asking them such standard questions as "What about Gap do you want to preserve and why?" "What about Gap do you want to change and why?" and so on. But he also added one of his own: "What is your most important tool for figuring out what the consumer wants?" Some companies use unconventional and innovative approaches to understand customers. Texas Instruments created a simulated classroom to understand how mathematics teachers use calculators; and a manager at Levi Strauss used to talk with teens who were lined up to buy rock concert tickets. The president of Chick-fil-A spends at least one day each year behind the counter, as do all of the company's employees, and has camped out overnight with customers at store openings. At Whirlpool, when customers rate a competitor's product higher in satisfaction surveys, engineers take it apart to find out why. The company also has hundreds of consumers fiddle with computer-simulated products while engineers record the users' reactions on videotape.[3]

4-3 Evaluating Goods and Services

research suggests that customers use three types of attributes in evaluating the quality of goods and services: search, experience, and credence.[4] **Search attributes** *are those that a customer can determine prior to purchasing the goods and/or services.* These attributes include things like color, price, freshness, style, fit, feel, hardness, and smell. **Experience attributes** *are those that can be discerned only after purchase or during consumption or use.* Examples of these attributes are friendliness, taste, wearability, safety, fun, and customer satisfaction. **Credence attributes** *are any aspects of a good or service that the customer must believe in, but cannot personally evaluate even after purchase and consumption.* Examples include the expertise of a surgeon or mechanic, the knowledge of a tax advisor, or the accuracy of tax preparation software.

This classification has several important implications for operations. For example, the most important search and experience attributes should be evaluated during design, measured during manufacturing, and drive key operational controls to ensure that they are built into the good with high quality. Credence attributes stem from the nature of services, the design of the service system, and the training and expertise of the service providers.

These three evaluation criteria form an evaluation continuum from easy to difficult, as shown in Exhibit 4.1. This model suggests that goods are easier to evaluate than services, and that goods are high in search qualities, whereas services are high in experience and credence attributes. Of course, goods and services are usually combined and configured in unique ways, making for an even more complex customer evaluation process. Customers evaluate services in ways that are often different from goods. A few ways are summarized below along with significant issues that affect operations.

- Customers seek and rely more on information from personal sources than from nonpersonal sources when evaluating services prior to purchase. Operations must ensure that accurate information is available, and that experiences with prior services and service providers result in positive experiences and customer satisfaction.

- Customers perceive greater risks when buying services than when buying goods. Because services are intangible, customers cannot look at or touch them prior to the purchase decision. They experience the service only when they actually go through the process. This is why many are hesitant to use online banking or bill-paying.

Dissatisfaction with services is often the result of customers' inability to properly perform or co-produce their part of the service. A wrong order placed on the

---

Search attributes are those that a customer can determine prior to purchasing the goods and/or services.

Experience attributes are those that can be discerned only after purchase or during consumption or use.

Credence attributes are any aspects of a good or service that the customer must believe in, but cannot personally evaluate even after purchase and consumption.

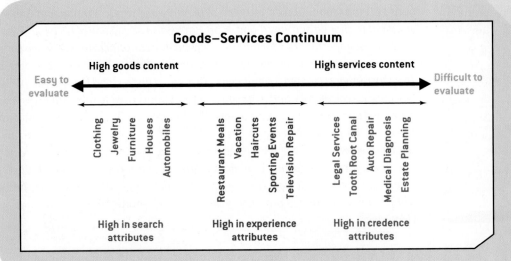

Goods–Services Continuum

High goods content ← → High services content

Easy to evaluate ←———————————————————→ Difficult to evaluate

High in search attributes	High in experience attributes	High in credence attributes
Clothing, Jewelry, Furniture, Houses, Automobiles	Restaurant Meals, Vacation, Haircuts, Sporting Events, Television Repair	Legal Services, Tooth Root Canal, Auto Repair, Medical Diagnosis, Estate Planning

Exhibit 4.1 *How Customers Evaluate Goods and Services*

Source: Adapted from V. A. Zeithamel, "How Consumer Evaluation Processes Differ Between Goods and Services," in J. H. Donnelly and W. R. George, eds., *Marketing in Services,* published by the American Marketing Association, Chicago, 1981, pp. 186–199. Reprinted with permission from the American Marketing Association.

Internet can be the result of customer error despite all efforts on the part of the company to provide clear instructions. The design of services must be sensitive to the need to educate customers on their role in the service process.

These insights help to explain why it is more difficult to design services and service processes than goods and manufacturing operations.

4-4 Competitive Priorities

Competitive priorities *represent the strategic emphasis that a firm places on certain performance measures and operational capabilities within a value chain.* Understanding competitive priorities and their relationships with customer benefit packages provides a basis for designing the processes that create and deliver goods and services. Every organization is concerned with building and sustaining a competitive advantage in its markets. A strong competitive advantage is driven by customer needs and aligns the organization's resources with its business opportunities. A strong competitive advantage is difficult to copy, often because of a firm's culture, habits, or sunk costs.

Competitive advantage can be achieved in different ways, such as outperforming competitors on price or quality, responding quickly to changing customer needs in designing goods and services, or providing rapid design or delivery. In general, organizations can compete on five key competitive priorities:

1. Cost
2. Quality
3. Time
4. Flexibility
5. Innovation

All of these competitive priorities are vital to success. For example, no firm today can sacrifice quality simply to reduce costs, or emphasize flexibility to the extent that it would make its goods and services unaffordable. However, organizations generally make trade-offs among these competitive priorities and focus their efforts along one or two key dimensions. For example, Dell Computer manufactures PCs (1) configured to customer specifications, (2) with high goods quality, and (3) tries to deliver them quickly to customers. However, they are not always the least-expensive machines available, and customers must wait longer to get a Dell computer as opposed to picking one off the shelf at a retail store. Hence, high goods quality and flexibility are top competitive priorities at Dell, whereas cost and delivery time are of somewhat lesser importance.

4-4a Cost

Many firms, such as Walmart, gain competitive advantage by establishing themselves as the low-cost leader in an industry. These firms handle high volumes of goods and services and achieve their competitive advantage through low prices. Although prices are generally set outside the realm of operations, low prices cannot be achieved without strict attention to cost and the design and management

Competitive priorities represent the strategic emphasis that a firm places on certain performance measures and operational capabilities within a value chain.

Southwest Airlines: Competing with Low Cost

The only major U.S. airline that has been continuously profitable over the last several decades is Southwest Airlines. Other airlines have had to collectively reduce costs by $18.6 billion, or 29 percent of their total operating expenses, to operate at the same level (cost per mile) as Southwest. The high-cost airlines such as United and American face enormous pressure from low-fare carriers such as Southwest Airlines. Mr. Roach, a long-time industry consultant, says "The industry really is at a point where survival is in question." In recent years, airlines have reduced capacity, cut routes, and increased fees for peripheral services like baggage and food. We have also seen mergers, such as between Delta and Northwest, and between United and Continental, to reduce system-wide costs.[5]

David Osborn/Alamy

of operations. General Electric, for example, discovered that 75 percent of its manufacturing costs is determined by design. Costs accumulate through the value chain, and include the costs of raw materials and purchased parts, direct manufacturing cost, distribution, postsale services, and all supporting processes. Through good design and by chipping away at costs, operations managers help to support a firm's strategy to be a low-price leader. They emphasize achieving economies of scale and finding cost advantages from all sources in the value chain.

Low cost can result from high productivity and high-capacity utilization. More important, improvements in quality lead to improvements in productivity, which in turn lead to lower costs. Thus a strategy of continuous improvement is essential to achieve a low-cost competitive advantage.

4-4b Quality

The role of quality in achieving competitive advantage was demonstrated by several research studies.[6] Researchers have found that

- Businesses offering premium-quality goods usually have large market shares and were early entrants into their markets.
- Quality is positively and significantly related to a higher return on investment for almost all kinds of market situations.
- A strategy of quality improvement usually leads to increased market share, but at a cost in terms of reduced short-run profitability.
- Producers of high-quality goods can usually charge premium prices.

Exhibit 4.2 summarizes the impact of quality on profitability. The value of a good or service in the marketplace is influenced by the quality of its design. Improvements in performance, features, and reliability will differentiate the good or service from its competitors, improve a firm's quality reputation, and improve the perceived value of the customer benefit package. This allows the company to command higher prices and achieve an increased market share. This, in turn, leads to increased revenues that offset the added costs of improved design. Improved conformance in production leads to lower manufacturing and service costs through savings in rework, scrap, and warranty expenses. The net effect of improved quality of design and conformance is increased profits.

Operations managers deal with quality issues on a daily basis; these include ensuring that goods are produced defect-free, or that service is delivered flawlessly.

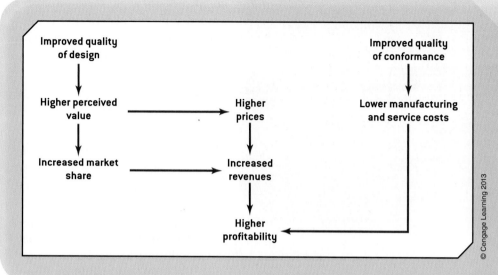

Exhibit 4.2 *Interlinking Quality and Profitability Performance*

Improved quality of design → Higher perceived value → Higher prices

Higher perceived value → Increased market share

Increased market share → Increased revenues

Higher prices → Increased revenues

Increased revenues → Higher profitability

Improved quality of conformance → Lower manufacturing and service costs → Higher profitability

© Cengage Learning 2013

In many industries, strategies often lead to trade-offs between quality and cost; some company strategies are willing to sacrifice quality in order to develop a low-cost advantage. Such was the case with new automobile startups, especially with Hyundai Motor Co. However, goods quality has evolved over the years and now is generally considered to be an order qualifier. Operations managers deal with quality issues on a daily basis; these include ensuring that goods are produced defect-free, or that service is delivered flawlessly. In the long run, it is the design of goods and service processes that ultimately defines the quality of outputs and outcomes.

4-4c Time

In today's society, time is perhaps the most important source of competitive advantage (see the box on Your Cell Phone Becomes your Wallet). Customers demand quick response, short waiting times, and consistency in performance. Many firms, such as CNN, FedEx, and Walmart, know how to use time as a competitive weapon to create and deliver superior goods and services.

Speeding up work processes improves customer response. Deliveries

Mike Flippo/Shutterstock.com

can be made faster, and more often on time. However, time reductions in processes and value chains can only be accomplished by streamlining and simplifying them to eliminate non-value-added steps such as rework and waiting time. This forces improvements in quality by reducing the opportunity for mistakes and errors. By reducing non-value-added steps, costs are reduced as well. Thus, time reductions often drive simultaneous improvements in quality, cost, and productivity. Designing processes and using technology efficiently to improve speed and time reliability are some of the most important activities for operations managers.

4-4d Flexibility

Success in globally competitive markets requires both design and demand flexibility. In the automobile industry, for example, new models are constantly being developed. Companies that can exploit flexibility by building several different vehicles on the same assembly line at one time, enabling them to switch output as demand shifts, will be able to sell profitably at lower volumes. The Spanish clothing company Inditex (which owns the well-known brand Zara) uses

companies to align their activities around differentiated customer segments and design goods, services, and operations around flexibility.

4-4e Innovation

Innovation *is the discovery and practical application or commercialization of a device, method, or idea that differs from existing norms.* Over the years, innovations in goods (such as telephones, automobiles, computers, optical fiber, satellites, and cell phones) and services (self-service, all-suite hotels, health maintenance organizations, and Internet banking) have improved the overall quality of life. Within business organizations, innovations in manufacturing equipment (computer-aided design, robots and automation, and smart tags) and management practices (customer satisfaction surveys, quantitative decision models, and the Malcolm Baldrige criteria) have allowed organizations to be more efficient and better meet customers' needs.

Many firms, such as Apple, focus on research and development for innovation as a core component of their strategy. Such firms are on the leading edge of product technology, and their ability to innovate and introduce new products is a critical success factor.

in-house pattern-cutting operations and subcontracts labor-intensive sewing to smaller regional facilities. Most other fashion retailers outsource these operations to Asia to reduce labor costs, resulting in slow supply chains that require the designers to make early style and volume commitments. Intidex's supply chain allows it to copy ideas from fashion leaders in Paris and Milan and quickly change styles to capitalize on the hottest trends.

Flexibility is manifest in mass-customization strategies that are becoming increasingly prevalent today. **Mass customization** *is being able to make whatever goods and services the customer wants, at any volume, at any time for anybody, and for a global organization, from any place in the world.*[8] Some examples include Sign-tic company signs that are uniquely designed for each customer from a standard base sign structure; business consulting; Levi's jeans that are cut to exact measurements; personal Web pages; estate planning; Motorola pagers customized in different colors, sizes, and shapes; personal weight-training programs; and modular furniture that customers can configure to their unique needs and tastes. Customer involvement might occur at the design (as in the case of custom signs), fabrication (Levi's jeans), assembly (Motorola pagers), or postproduction (customer-assembled modular furniture) stages of the value chain. Mass customization requires

Mass customization is being able to make whatever goods and services the customer wants, at any volume, at any time for anybody, and for a global organization, from any place in the world.

Innovation is the discovery and practical application or commercialization of a device, method, or idea that differs from existing norms.

Nata Pupo/Shutterstock.com

Product performance, not price, is the major selling feature. When competition enters the market and profit margins fall, these companies often drop out of the market while continuing to introduce innovative new products. These companies focus on outstanding product research, design, and development; high product quality; and the ability to modify production facilities to produce new products frequently.

4-5 OM and Strategic Planning

he direction an organization takes and the competitive priorities it chooses are driven by its strategy. The concept of strategy has different meanings to different people. **Strategy** *is a pattern or plan that integrates an organization's major goals, policies, and action sequences into a cohesive whole.*[9] Basically, a strategy is the approach by which an organization seeks to develop the capabilities required for achieving its competitive advantage. Effective strategies develop around a few key competitive priorities, such as low cost or fast service time, which provide a focus for the entire organization and exploit an organization's **core competencies,** *which are the strengths that are unique to that organization.* Such strengths might be a particularly skilled or creative workforce, customer relationship management, clever bundling of goods and services, strong supply chain networks, extraordinary service, green goods and services, marketing expertise, or the ability to rapidly develop new products or change production-output rates.

Strategic planning is the process of determining long-term goals, policies, and plans for an organization. The objective of strategic planning is to build

> **Strategy** is a pattern or plan that integrates an organization's major goals, policies, and action sequences into a cohesive whole.
>
> **Core competencies** are the strengths that are unique to an organization.

Solved Problem

Define the customer benefit package (CBP) for a health club, recreation center, or gymnasium you frequent. (Check out the Web site of your favorite club, center, or gym for more information.) Use this information to help describe the organization's strategic mission, strategy, competitive priorities, and how it wins customers.

One example is depicted below.

Mission: The mission of our health club is to offer many pathways to a healthy living style and body.

Strategy: We strive to provide our customers with superior:

- ways to improve and maintain the health and well-being of the body and mind.
- friendly professional staff that care about them.
- clean facilities, equipment, uniforms, parking lot, food service, and the like.
- customer convenience (location, food, communication, schedules, etc.).

Competitive Priorities: #1 Priority: Many pathways to healthy living and a healthy body (design flexibility); #2 Priority: Friendly, professional staff and service encounters (service quality); #3 Priority: Everything is super-clean (goods, facility, and environmental quality); #4 Priority: Customer convenience in all respects (time); and #5 Priority: Price (cost).

How to win customers? Providing a full-service health club with superior service, staff, and facilities. (Although you would not see this in company literature, this health club provides premium service at premium prices.)

Remember that each primary or peripheral good or service in the customer benefit package requires a process to create and deliver it to customers, and therefore OM skills are needed.

a position that is so strong in selected ways that the organization can achieve its goals despite unforeseeable external forces that may arise. Strategy is the result of a series of hierarchical decisions about goals, directions, and resources; thus, most large organizations have three levels of strategy: corporate, business, and functional. At the top level, *corporate strategy* is necessary to define the businesses in which the corporation will participate and develop plans for the acquisition and allocation of resources among those businesses. The businesses in which the firm will participate are often called strategic business units (SBUs), and are usually defined as families of goods or services having similar characteristics or methods of creation. For small organizations, the corporate and business strategies frequently are the same.

The second level of strategy is generally called *business strategy*, and defines the focus for SBUs. The major decisions involve which markets to pursue and how best to compete in those markets—that is, what competitive priorities the firm should pursue.

Finally, the third level of strategy is *functional strategies*, the means by which business strategies are accomplished. A functional strategy is the set of decisions that each functional area (marketing, finance, operations, research and development, engineering, and so on) develops to support its particular business strategy.

Our particular focus will be on *operations strategy*—how an organization's processes are designed and organized to produce the type of goods and services to support the corporate and business strategies.

4-5a Operations Strategy

An **operations strategy** *defines how an organization will execute its chosen business strategies.* Developing an operations strategy involves translating competitive priorities into operational capabilities by making a variety of choices and trade-offs for design and operating decisions. That is, operating decisions must be aligned with achieving the desired competitive priorities. For example, Progressive automobile insurance has developed a competitive advantage around superior customer service. To accomplish this, its operating decisions have included on-the-spot claims processing at accident sites; "Total Loss Concierge" service to help customers with unrepairable vehicles get a replacement vehicle; and the industry's first Web 2.0 site with easier navigation, customization, and video content.

An **operations strategy** defines how an organization will execute its chosen business strategies.

What kind of an operations strategy might a company like Pal's Sudden Service (see Chapter 1) have? Consider the operations management implications of key elements of the company's vision: *To be the preferred quick-service restaurant in our market achieving the largest market share by providing*

1. *The quickest, friendliest, most accurate service available.* To achieve quick and accurate service, Pal's needs highly standardized processes. The staff at each Pal's facility is organized into process teams along the order-taking, processing, packaging, and order-completion line. The process layout is designed so that raw materials enter through a delivery door and are worked forward through the store with one process serving the next. Employees must have clearly defined roles and responsibilities, understanding of all operating and service procedures and quality standards, and job flexibility through cross-training to be able to respond to volume cycles and unplanned reassignments to work activities. To ensure friendly service, Pal's uses specific performance criteria to evaluate and select employees who demonstrate the aptitude, talents, and characteristics to meet performance standards; invests heavily in training; and pays close attention to employee satisfaction.

2. *A focused menu that delights customers.* Employees must understand their customers' likes and dislikes of their products and services as well as those of their competitors. Operations must address such questions as: What capabilities will we need to support a new menu offering? Do our suppliers have the capacity to support this new offering? Is the appropriate technology available?

3. *Daily excellence in product, service, and systems execution.* Successful day-to-day operations require employees to effectively apply Pal's On-Line Quality Control process, consisting of four simple steps: standardize the method or process, use the method, study the results, and take control. Each employee is thoroughly trained and coached on precise work procedures and process standards, focusing on developing a visual reference to verify product quality.

4. *Clean, organized, sanitary facilities.* Pal's focuses on prevention—eliminating all possible causes of accidents—first, then finding and eliminating causes of actual incidents. In-house health and safety inspections are conducted monthly using the Food and Drug Administration (FDA) Food Service

Sanitation Ordinance. Results are compiled and distributed to all stores within 24 hours, with any identified improvements applied in each store.

5. *Exceptional value.* Through methods of listening and learning from customers and studies of industry standards and best practices, Pal's has designed the following items into its operations: convenient locations with easy ingress and egress, long hours of operation (6:00 a.m. to 10:00 p.m.), easy-to-read 3-D menus, direct fact-to-face access to order taker and cashier/order deliverer, fresh food (cooked hot dogs are discarded after 10 minutes if not purchased), a 20-second delivery target, and a Web site for contacting corporate office and stores. Pal's selects suppliers carefully to ensure not only product quality and on-time delivery, but also the best price for the volume level purchased. Overall supply chain costs are minimized by maintaining only a few, long-term core suppliers.

From this discussion of Pal's Sudden Service, it is clear that how operations are designed and implemented can have a dramatic effect on business performance and achievement of the strategy. Therefore, operations require close coordination with functional strategies in other areas of the firm, such as marketing and finance.

4-5b Sustainability and Operations Strategy

Sustainability is defined in previous chapters using three dimensions—environmental, social, and economic sustainability. Stakeholders such as the community, green advocacy groups, and the government drive environmental sustainability. Social sustainability is driven by ethics and human ideals of protecting the planet and its people for the well-being of future generations. Economic sustainability is driven by shareholders such as pension funds and insurance companies. Therefore, sustainability is an organizational strategy—it is broader than a competitive priority. Sustainability requires major changes in the culture of the organization (see box on General Electric).

Many companies, such as Dell, Kaiser Permanente, and Nike, view sustainability as a corporate strategy. A majority of global consumers believes that it is their responsibility to contribute to a better environment and would pay more for brands that support this aim. Likewise, retailers and manufacturers are demanding greener

FREE WHEELCHAIR MISSION— A STRATEGY OF SOCIAL SUSTAINABILITY

Social sustainability, sometimes called ethical sustainability, is driven by ethics and human ideals of protecting the planet and its people for the well-being of future generations. It begins with a vision of the business and a strategy. Donald Schoendorfer, an entrepreneur and founder of Free Wheelchair Mission (FWM), travelled to many developing countries and noticed family and friends carrying disabled people because they could not afford to buy a wheelchair. Some 100 million people worldwide face this situation. He researched this problem but found no solution.

Mr. Schoendorfer, who held more than 50 patents in the medical industry, decided to make a simple and inexpensive but rugged wheelchair using commonly available components such as plastic patio furniture for the seat, old wheelchair frames, and used mountain bike parts and tires. The cost of the first wheelchair was $28 and it could be shipped anywhere in the world for about $41. The chairs are manufactured in China and shipped to some of the most remote regions in the world in ocean-going containers. Once they arrive at the port, carefully-selected distribution partners assume financial, logistical, and distribution control of the chairs for local qualified beneficiaries. They have shipped hundreds of thousands of these wheelchairs, achieving the goal "to lift someone up off the ground and change a life forever.[10]

products and supply chains. In 2007, Walmart Stores Inc. announced that it would transition toward selling only concentrated laundry detergents, which use much less water and therefore require less packaging and space for transport and storage. Every major supplier in the detergent industry was involved. Government actions are also driving these initiatives. The 2009 U.S. stimulus package earmarked $70 billion for the development of renewable and efficient energy technologies and manufacturing. The European Union has set targets for reducing emissions to 20 percent of 1990 levels by 2020.

Companies that have embraced sustainability pursue this strategy throughout their operations. For example, computer maker Dell Inc. has announced that it is committed to becoming "the greenest technology company on the planet." Such a strategy often requires considerable innovation in value chains, operations design, and day-to-day management. For example, Dell launched a program called Design for the Environment that seeks to minimize adverse impacts on the environment by controlling raw material acquisition, manufacturing processes, and distribution programs while linking green policies with consumer use and disposal. This framework encourages Dell's product designers to consider the full product life cycle, and it provides them with a platform for collaborating with suppliers, supply chain experts, and external recycling experts and other downstream partners to help them fully understand the environmental implications of their design decisions.[11]

4-6 A Framework for Operations Strategy

a useful framework for strategy development that ties corporate and marketing strategy to operations strategy was proposed by Professor Terry Hill at Templeton College, Oxford University, and is shown in Exhibit 4.3.[12] It was originally designed for goods-producing organizations; however, it can also be applied to service-providing firms. This framework defines the essential elements of an effective operations strategy in the last two columns—*operations design choices and building the right infrastructure.*

Operations design choices *are the decisions management must make as to what type of process structure is best suited to produce goods or create services.* It typically

Operations design choices are the decisions management must make as to what type of process structure is best suited to produce goods or create services.

Infrastructure focuses on the nonprocess features and capabilities of the organization and includes the workforce, operating plans and control systems, quality control, organizational structure, compensation systems, learning and innovation systems, and support services.

GENERAL ELECTRIC: GREEN STARTS AT THE TOP

Jeffrey Immelt, the CEO of General Electric, proposed a green business strategy and plan to his 35 top executives in 2004, and they voted against it. Immelt refused to take no for an answer and overruled his executives. The result of his efforts is now defined in GE's highly successful Ecomagination initiative. Ecomagination (http://ge.ecomagination.com) is a business strategy designed to drive innovation and the growth of profitable environmental solutions while engaging stakeholders. GE invests in innovation through its R&D efforts and outside venture capital investments. The resulting goods and services enable GE and its customers to reduce emissions while generating revenue from their sale. Combining profits and energy savings, GE continues to invest in environmental solutions, perpetuating the cycle. Specific green and measurable targets have been established by year. For example, GE's greenhouse gas (GHG) target set in 2008 has been exceeded by 30 percent.

Roman Sotola/Shutterstock.com

Exhibit 4.3 *Hill's Strategy Development Framework*

Corporate Objectives	Marketing Strategy	How Do Goods and Services Qualify and Win Orders in the Marketplace?	Operations Strategy	
			Operations Design Choices	Infrastructure
• Growth • Economic sustainability (survival)[+] • Profit • Return on investment • Other market and financial measures • Social (welfare) sustainability[+] • Environmental sustainability[+]	• Goods and services markets and segments • Range • Mix • Volumes • Standardization versus customization • Level of innovation • Leader versus follower alternatives	• Safety • Price (cost) • Range • Flexibility • Demand • Goods and service design • Quality • Service • Goods • Environment • Social (community) • Brand image • Delivery • Speed • Variability • Technical support • Pre- and postservice support	• Type of processes and alternative designs • Supply chain integration and outsourcing • Technology • Capacity and facilities (size, timing, location) • Inventory • Trade-off analysis	• Workforce • Operating plans and control system(s) • Quality control • Organizational structure • Compensation system • Learning and innovation systems • Support services

[+]Note: We have added sustainability criteria to Professor Hill's original framework.

Sources: T. Hill, *Manufacturing Strategy: Text and Cases*, 3rd ed., Burr Ridge, IL: McGraw-Hill, 2000, p. 32; T. Hill, *Operations Management: Strategic Context and Managerial Analysis*, 2nd ed., Prigrame MacMillan, 2005, p. 50. Reprinted with permission from the McGraw-Hill Companies.

addresses six key areas—types of processes, value chain integration and outsourcing, technology, capacity and facilities, inventory and service capacity, and trade-offs among these decisions.

Infrastructure *focuses on the nonprocess features and capabilities of the organization and includes the workforce, operating plans and control systems, quality control, organizational structure, compensation systems, learning and innovation systems, and support services*. The infrastructure must support process choice and provide managers with accurate and timely information to make good decisions. These decisions lie at the core of organizational effectiveness, and suggest that the integrative nature of operations management is one of the most important aspects of success. Operations design and infrastructure criteria and decisions in Prof. Hill's strategy framework define the value chain that supports environmental, social, and economic sustainability.

A key feature of this framework is the link between operations and corporate and marketing strategies. Clearly, it is counterproductive to design a customer benefit package and an operations system to produce and deliver it, and then discover that these plans will

not achieve corporate and marketing objectives. This linkage is described by the four major decision loops illustrated in Exhibit 4.4. Decision loop #1 (shown in red) ties together corporate strategy—which establishes the organization's direction and boundaries—and marketing strategy—which evaluates customer wants and needs and targets market segments.

The output of red loop #1 is the input for green loop #2. Decision loop #2 (green) describes how operations evaluates the implications of competitive priorities in terms of process choice and infrastructure. The key decisions are "Do we have the process capability to achieve the corporate and marketing objectives per target market segment? Are our processes capable of consistently achieving order-winner performance in each market segment?"

Decision loop #3 (blue) lies within the operations function of the organization and involves determining if process choice decisions and capabilities are consistent with infrastructure decisions and capabilities. The fourth decision loop (yellow loop #4) represents operations' input into the corporate and marketing strategy. Corporate decision makers ultimately decide how to allocate resources to achieve corporate objectives.

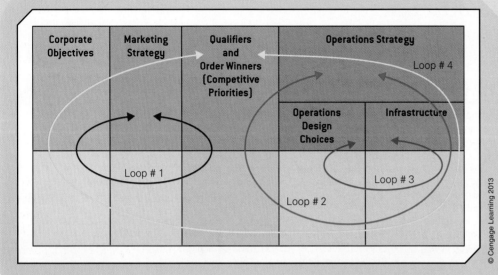

Corporate Objectives	Marketing Strategy	Qualifiers and Order Winners (Competitive Priorities)	Operations Strategy	
				Loop # 4
			Operations Design Choices	Infrastructure
	Loop # 1			Loop # 3
		Loop # 2		

© Cengage Learning 2013

4-6a Operations Strategy at McDonald's

McDonald's Corporation is the world's leading food-service retailer, with sales of almost $23 billion in more than 32,000 restaurants in 117 countries, employing 1.6 million people.[13] The company's vision provides the basis for its strategy:

McDonald's vision is to be the world's best quick-service restaurant experience. Being the best means providing outstanding quality, service, cleanliness, and value, so that we make every customer in every restaurant smile. To achieve our vision, we focus on three worldwide strategies:

1. **Be the Best Employer**
   Be the best employer for our people in each community around the world.

2. **Deliver Operational Excellence**
   Deliver operational excellence to our customers in each of our restaurants.

3. **Achieve Enduring Profitable Growth**
   Achieve enduring profitable growth by expanding the brand and leveraging the strengths of the McDonald's system through innovation and technology.

McDonald's also defines its "Values in Action" policies, program, and practices, which is basically "doing the right thing." In its Corporate Responsibility Report, it defines the following four sustainability initiatives:

- *Build a sustainable McDonald's that involves all facets of our business.* For example, McDonald's is developing an environmental scorecard that drives greater awareness of resource use (energy, water, air emission, and waste), with the ultimate goal of reducing the environmental impact of its supply chains.

- *Commit to a three-pronged approach—reduce, reuse, and recycle.* For example, 82 percent of McDonald's packaging is made from renewable materials. In some global markets, McDonald's delivery trucks use their own reprocessed cooking oil for fuel.

- *Strive to provide eco-friendly workplaces and restaurants.* Better recycling efforts have diverted over 58 percent of waste normally targeted for a landfill to other recycling uses. Green facilities have been built in countries such as Brazil, Germany, and France.

- *Work with suppliers and outside experts to continuously improve purchasing decisions and evaluation of supplier performance regarding animal welfare.* Animal welfare scorecards and supplier audits in addition to better designs of animal-handling facilities are two examples of this initiative.

McDonald's also actively participates in social media platforms to share information about its sustainability policies and initiatives.

What is the CBP that McDonald's offers? Exhibit 4.5 shows the CBP, in which goods and service content (food and fast service) are equally important to the primary mission, and are supported by peripheral goods and services.

Exhibit 4.6 illustrates how Hill's strategy framework can be applied to McDonald's. One corporate objective is profitable growth. The marketing strategy to support profitable growth consists of adding both company-owned and franchised McDonald's and Partner Brand restaurants. McDonald's is committed to franchising as a key strategy to grow and leverage value chain capabilities. Over 75 percent of McDonald's restaurants worldwide are owned and operated by independent businesspeople—franchisees.

The core competency to profitable growth is maintaining low-cost and fast service. To support this strategy, McDonald's has many operational decisions to make, such as: Does it adopt an assembly-line approach to process design? Does it standardize store design to make process flow, training, and performance evaluation consistent among stores? Does it standardize equipment and job design work activities? The french fryer equipment and procedure are a good example of standardizing equipment design. There is "only one way to make french fries" in 32,000 stores

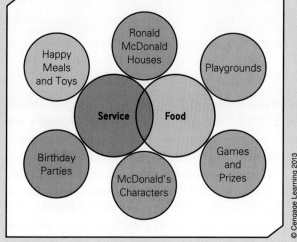

Brand X Pictures/Jupiter Images

worldwide, and this contributes to consistent goods quality, fast service, and a standardized training program. Likewise, ordering by the numbers and digital printouts of customer orders in the drive-through improves order accuracy and speed of service. Of course, the entire human resource function is built around the needs of the McDonald's value chain and operating systems. McDonald's has been identified as one of the best places to work by *Fortune* and *The American Economic Review*. Examples of supportive infrastructure include good hiring criteria, recognition and reward programs, training, and promotion criteria.

⌈The ultimate objective of operational excellence is satisfied customers. Operational excellence includes the value chain, process, equipment, and job efficiencies, as well as superior people-related performance—all focused to support the service-encounter level.⌋

A second corporate objective is *operational excellence*. The ultimate objective of operational excellence is satisfied customers. Operational excellence includes value chain, process, equipment, and job efficiencies, as well as superior people-related performance—all focused to support the service-encounter level. McDonald's strategy is to deliver exceptional customer experiences through a combination of great-tasting food, outstanding service, being a good place to work, profitable growth, and consistent value. McDonald's service goals also include extended or 24-hour service to make McDonald's the most convenient food-service choice for customers. To put sparkle in McDonald's service, initiatives include training for the unexpected and keeping it simple.

A third corporate objective is leveraging innovation and technology capabilities. In the United States,

Exhibit 4.5 *McDonald's Customer Benefit Package*

Happy Meals and Toys

Ronald McDonald Houses

Playgrounds

Service

Food

Birthday Parties

McDonald's Characters

Games and Prizes

© Cengage Learning 2013

Exhibit 4.6 *Applying the Hill's Strategy Development Framework to McDonald's*

Corporate Objective Examples	Marketing Strategy Examples	How Do Goods and Services Qualify and Win Orders in the Marketplace?	Operations Strategy	
			Operating Design Choice Examples	Infrastructure Examples
Profitable Growth	Add worldwide 1,000 McDonald's restaurants using company-owned and franchised stores	Competitive priorities tie the corporate and marketing strategies to the operational strategy ⟷	• Flow shop process design • Standardized store design • Equipment design • Job design • Order-taking process • Capacity and facility size, location, and clusters	• Hiring process and criteria • First job training • Recognition and rewards • Training for the unexpected • Keeping it simple • Manager trainee program • Coaching and counseling • Teamwork • e-mail capabilities
Operational Excellence	Ideal store location, best training and employee well-being programs	• #1 Low prices • #2 Quick service (delivery speed) • #3 High service quality	• Global value chain coordination • Suppliers • Resource scheduling • Inventory placement and control • Distribution centers • Standardized operational and job procedures	• Operating plans and control system(s) • Shift management • Supplier relations and negotiation • Equipment maintenance • Online network capability • Distribution centers
Leverage Strengths through Innovation and Technology	Develop new food items, store and food mix Tie demand analysis to promotions	⟷ • #4 High goods quality	• Store equipment technology • Value chain information systems to tie stores, distribution centers, and suppliers together • New food products	• Quality control • Laboratory testing • Organizational structure • Compensation systems • Online network capability
Diversity	Long-standing commitment to a diverse workforce	• #5 Demand flexibility	• Training and franchising • Process performance • Career paths	• Learning and innovation systems • Hamburger University
Sustainability	Values in Action policies and initiatives	• #6 Brand image ⟷	• Greener supply chains • Recycling processes • Reduce energy use • Animal welfare	• Greener buildings • Ronald McDonald House • Mobile health centers • Youth camps

© Cengage Learning 2013

McDonald's has 40 distribution centers to support more than 12,000 restaurants and about 350 suppliers. More than 2,000 safety and quality checks surround McDonald's food as it moves through its supply chains (from farms to restaurants). Information technology is used to coordinate the activities of McDonald's value chain.

Another corporate objective is developing and maintaining a diverse workforce. Diversity at McDonald's means understanding, recognizing, and valuing the differences that make each person unique. Hamburger University, located in Oak Brook, Illinois, has trained over 275,000 managers in 22 different languages and also manages 10 international training centers in places such as Australia, England, Japan, and Germany.

McDonald's supports its social responsibility objective with over 200 Ronald McDonald House Charities. Social responsibility activities also include funding immunization programs for 1 million African children, Olympic youth camps, disaster relief, and sponsored mobile health centers in underserved areas. Other corporate objectives not shown in Exhibit 4.6 include a high return on investment, exploring nontraditional locations for stores, and commitment to the environment.

Competitive priorities are derived from McDonald's vision statement and strategy. The ranking in Exhibit 4.6 reflects their importance. The competitive priorities tie the corporate and marketing strategies to the operations strategy. The competitive priorities provide direction on key operations-strategy issues listed in the last two columns of Exhibit 4.6.

PRNewsFoto/McDonald's Corporation

Discussion Questions

1. Select a business with which you are familiar and identify examples of customers using search, experience, and credence quality to evaluate the good or service. You might also look up the businesses on the Internet or visit the library.

2. Select a business with which you are familiar and identify examples of order qualifiers and winners. You might also look up the businesses on the Internet or visit the library.

3. Explain the interlinking model of quality and profitability (Exhibit 4.2). How does it connect to business and operations strategy? Can you provide any examples of goods and services that support and add credibility to this model?

4. Is it possible for a world-class organization to achieve superiority in all five major competitive priorities—price (cost), quality, time, flexibility, and innovation? Explain your reasoning. Provide examples pro or con.

5. Why is sustainability a strategy and not a competitive priority? Explain your reasoning.

Problems and Activities

1. Research and write a short paper (two pages maximum) about your cell phone provider. What are its mission, strategy, and competitive priorities? How is sustainability incorporated into its strategy, value chain, and operations?

2. What might the competitive advantage be for each of the following companies?
   a. eBay
   b. Southwest Airlines
   c. Starbucks
   d. Apple
   e Facebook

3. Choose an organization with which you are famili... that falls into *one* of the following categorie...
   - sporting goods store
   - haircut salon
   - college bar or restaurant
   - pizza business
   - a sports team
   - wireless telephone

Define the firm's strategic mission, strategy, and competitive priorities. What are the order qualifiers and winners? What would operations have to be good at to make this a successful business or organization?

4. Research and explain the logic behind the statement, "General Electric discovered that 75 percent of its manufacturing costs is determined by design."

5. How does a package-delivery service such as UPS or FedEx use the competitive priority of "time" to its competitive advantage? Research, then explain and provide examples in a short paper (maximum of two typed pages).

6. How does Walmart use the competitive priority of "cost" to its competitive advantage? Research, then explain and provide examples in a short paper (maximum of two typed pages).

7. How does Procter & Gamble use the competitive priority of "quality" to its competitive advantage? Research, then explain and provide examples in a short paper (maximum of two typed pages).

8. How does your cell phone provider use the competitive priority of "flexibility" to its competitive advantage? Research, then explain and provide examples in a short paper (maximum of two typed pages).

9. How does General Electric use the competitive priority of "innovation" to its competitive advantage? Research, then explain and provide examples in a short paper (maximum of two typed pages).

10. Explore the Web sites for several competing companies on the Fortune 500 list. Based on the information you find, on which competitive priorities do these firms appear to focus? What can you say about their operations strategies (either explicit or implied)? Report your findings in a short paper (maximum of two typed pages).

11. Research and write a short paper on a company that has a clear strategy based on social and ethical sustainability.

12. Apply Hill's strategy framework to one of the companies in question 2. This will require research to identify corporate objectives and competitive priorities. See the McDonald's example in the chapter for guidance, and make sure that you emphasize OM concepts, capabilities, and execution. Report your findings in a short paper (maximum of two typed pages).

13. Identify two competing organizations (for example, AT&T and Sprint, TaylorMade and Callaway golf club manufacturers, or Starbucks and McDonald's). Explain the differences in their missions, strategies, and competitive priorities, and how their operations strategies might differ. Use the Internet or business magazines to research the information you need. Report your findings in a short paper (maximum of two typed pages).

14. Research Apple and define its strategic mission, vision, corporate strategy, competitive priorities, and operations strategy. What can you say about Apple's strategy and practices regarding sustainability? You might use the Internet or visit the library. Report your findings in a short paper (maximum of two typed pages).

15. Using the information about Pal's Sudden Service provided in this chapter, apply Hill's generic strategy framework in a manner similar to the McDonald's example. How do the strategies of Pal's and McDonald's appear to differ? What differences exist in their operations strategies and decisions? Report your findings in a short paper (maximum of two typed pages).

Sustainable Lawn Care Case Study

"Chris, we make the highest-quality grass seed and fertilizer in the world. Our brands are known everywhere!" stated Caroline Ebelhar, the vice president of manufacturing for The Lawn Care Company. "Yeah! But the customer doesn't have a Ph.D. in organic chem[istr]y to understand the difference between our grass [seed] and fertilizer compared to those of our competi[tors. W]e need to also be in the lawn-care application [b]usiness, and not just the manufacturer of super[ior pro]ducts," responded Chris Kilbourne, the vice [president of] marketing, as he walked out of Caroline's

office. This ongoing debate among Lawn Care's senior management team had not been resolved but the chief executive officer, Mr. Steven Marion, had been listening very closely. A major strategic decision would soon have to be made.

The Lawn Care Company, a fertilizer and grass seed manufacturer with sales of almost $1 billion, sold some of its products directly to parks and golf courses. Customer service in this goods-producing company was historically very narrowly defined as providing "the right product to the right customer at the right time." Once these goods were delivered to the customer's premises and the customer signed the shipping documents, Lawn Care's job was done. For many park and golf course customers, a local subcontractor or the customers themselves applied the fertilizer and seed. These application personnel often did the job incorrectly using inappropriate equipment and methods. The relationship among these non-Lawn Care application service personnel, The Lawn Care Company, and the customer also was not always ideal.

When claims were made against The Lawn Care Company because of damaged lawns or polluted lakes and streams, the question then became one of who was at fault. Did the quality of the physical product or the way it was applied cause the damage? Either way, the customers' lawns or waterways were in poor shape, and in some cases, the golf courses lost substantial revenue if a green or hole was severely damaged or not playable. One claim filed by a green advocacy group focused on a fish kill in a stream near a golf course.

One of Lawn Care's competitors began an application service for parks and golf courses that routinely applied the fertilizer and grass seed for its primary customers. This competitor bundled the application service to the primary goods, fertilizer and grass seed, and charged a higher price for this service. The competitor delivered and applied the fertilizer on the same day to avoid the liability of storing toxic fertilizer outside on the golf course or park grounds. The competitor learned the application business in

The competitor bundled application service to the primary goods—fertilizer and grass seed.

the parks and golf course target market segment and was beginning to explore expanding into the residential lawn-care application service target market. The Lawn Care Company sold the "highest-quality physical products" in the industry but it was not currently in either the professional park and golf course or the residential "application service" lawn-care market segments. The Lawn Care Company considered its value chain to end once it delivered its products to the job site or non-Lawn Care application service. The competitor sold the customer "a beautiful lawn with a promise of no hassles." To the competitor, this included an application service bundled to grass seed and fertilizer.

Case Questions for Discussion

1. Define Lawn Care's current strategic mission, strategy, competitive priorities, value chain, and how it wins customers. What are the order qualifiers and winners? Draw the major stages in its value chain without an application service.

2. What problems, if any, do you see with Lawn Care's current strategy, vision, customer benefit package and value chain design, and pre- and postservices?

3. Redo questions (1) and (2) and provide a new or revised strategy and associated customer benefit package and value chain that is more appropriate for today's marketplace. What does operations have to be good at to successfully execute your revised strategy?

4. What are your final recommendations?

TECHNOLOGY AND OPERATIONS MANAGEMENT

ord Motor Company and Toyota, an unlikely couple, recently agreed to jointly develop the next generation of gas–electric hybrid systems for pickup trucks and sport utility vehicles (SUVs). Toyota has built more hybrids than Ford, but it produces no hybrid pickup trucks, whereas Ford has been a leader in first-generation hybrids for SUVs. Their partnership includes swapping patents, research and development, joint supplier qualification and sourcing, and building the next-generation global supply chain that supports hybrids and ultimately electric vehicles. Software development is also a major part of this joint venture, as Ford's Volt, for example, contains over 10 million lines of code. Other supply chain participants are contributing to building the supply chain necessary for electric vehicles. Cracker Barrel, for example, is installing electric vehicle chargers in 24 of its restaurants.

learning outcomes

After studying this chapter you should be able to:

5-1 **Describe different types of technology and their role in manufacturing and service operations.**

5-2 **Explain how manufacturing and service technology and analytics strengthen the value chain.**

5-3 **Explain the benefits and challenges of using technology.**

5-4 **Describe key technology decisions.**

What do you think?

In what ways has technology benefited your life and work as a student?

AP Photo/Mark Lennihan

Technology—both physical and information—has dramatically changed how work is accomplished in every industry—from mining to manufacturing to education to health care. Technology is the enabler that makes today's service and manufacturing systems operate productively and meet customer needs better than ever. Most of you probably cannot imagine living in a world without personal computers, the Internet, or wireless communications. We are sure that people in the early 1900s felt the same way about the steam engine, as did your parents and grandparents about the automobile and radio.

Technological innovation in goods, services, manufacturing, and service delivery is a competitive necessity. Jack Welch, retired CEO of General Electric, for example, pushed GE to become a leader among traditional old-economy companies in embracing the Internet after noticing his wife Christmas shopping on the Web. "I realized that if I didn't watch it, I would retire as a Neanderthal," he was reported as saying, "So I just started reading everything I could about it." He began by pairing 1,000 Web-savvy mentors with senior people to get his top teams up to Internet speed quickly.[1]

5-1 Understanding Technology in Operations

We may categorize technology into two basic groups. **Hard technology** *refers to equipment and devices that perform a variety of tasks in the creation and delivery of goods and services.* Some examples of hard technology are computers, microprocessors, optical switches, satellites, sensors, robots, automated

▼ Ford Motor Company and Toyota, an unlikely couple, announced their agreement to work jointly on hybrid pickup trucks and SUVs.

machines, bar-code scanners, and radio frequency identification (RFID) tags.

RFID tags are the modern successor to bar codes. RFID tags are tiny computer chips that can be placed on shipping containers, individual products, credit cards, prescription medicines, passports, livestock, and even people. They transmit radio signals to identify locations and track movements throughout the supply chain. They have many applications in both manufacturing and service industries. Retail, defense, transportation, and health care have begun requiring their suppliers to implement this technology. RFID can bring visibility and enhanced security to the handling and transportation of materials, baggage, and other cargo. RFID can help to identify genuine products from counterfeit knock-offs, thus helping to lower overall product and operational costs.[2] They have also been used to monitor residents in assisted living buildings and track the movements of doctors, nurses, and equipment in hospital emergency rooms.

Soft technology *refers to the application of the Internet, computer software, and information systems to provide data, information, and analysis and to facilitate the accomplishment of creating and delivering goods and services.* Some examples are database systems, artificial intelligence programs, and voice-recognition software. Both types are essential to modern organizations (see the box about Amazon.com later in this chapter). As described in the introduction to this chapter, the hybrid and ultimately the electric vehicle are good examples of integrating hard and soft technology.

Information technology provides the ability to integrate all parts of the value chain through better management of data and information. This leads to more effective strategic and operational decisions to design better customer benefit packages that support customers' wants and needs, achieve competitive priorities, and improve the design and operation of all processes in the value chain.

Increasingly, both hard and soft technology are being integrated across the organization, allowing managers to make better decisions and share information across the value chain. Such systems, often called integrated operating systems (IOSs), include computer integrated manufacturing systems (CIMs), enterprise resource planning (ERP) systems, and customer relationship management (CRM) systems, all of which use technology to create better and more customized goods and services and deliver them faster at lower prices. We will discuss these systems in the following sections.

5-1a Manufacturing Technology

Although high-tech, automated manufacturing processes receive a lot of media attention, much of the technology used in small- and medium-sized manufacturing enterprises around the world is still quite basic. The accompanying boxes that highlight making jigsaw puzzles and motorcycle gears illustrate how technology is used and integrated into manufacturing operations. Clearly, there are worlds of differences in the technology used for making puzzles and gears. However, from an operations management standpoint, all organizations face common issues regarding technology:

- The right technology must be selected for the goods that are produced.
- Process resources, such as machines and employees, must be set up and configured in a logical fashion to support production efficiency.
- Labor must be trained to operate the equipment.
- Process performance must be continually improved.
- Work must be scheduled to meet shipping commitments/customer promise dates.
- Quality must be ensured.

Hard technology refers to equipment and devices that perform a variety of tasks in the creation and delivery of goods and services.

Soft technology refers to the application of the Internet, computer software, and information systems to provide data, information, and analysis and to facilitate the accomplishment of creating and delivering goods and services.

Mr.Zach/Shutterstock.com

bar code + RFID chip

Drescher Paper Box: Making Jigsaw Puzzles

Drescher Paper Box in Buffalo, New York, formed in 1867, manufactures high-quality laminated cardboard jigsaw puzzles and board games and assembles them for retail stores. Drescher also produces cotton-filled jewelry boxes, candy boxes, business card boxes, and custom-made industrial boxes. Manufacturing jigsaw puzzles consists of three major steps: making the puzzle pieces, making the puzzle boxes, and final assembly. A printed picture is cut to size and laminated on a thick puzzleboard backing. Large presses are used to cut the puzzle into pieces, which are then bagged. The box-making process begins with blank cardboard. Boxes are scored and cut, then laminated with printed graphics. In the final assembly process, the puzzles are boxed and shrink-wrapped for shipment.

Drescher Paper Box, Inc.

5-1b Computer-Integrated Manufacturing Systems (CIMSs)

Much of the technology used in manufacturing today is automated and linked with information technology. **Computer-integrated manufacturing systems (CIMSs)** *represent the union of hardware, software, database management, and communications to automate and control production activities, from planning and design to manufacturing and distribution.* CIMSs include many hard and soft technologies with a wide variety of acronyms, vendors, and applications and are essential to productivity and efficiency in modern manufacturing.

The roots of CIMSs began with **numerical control (NC)** *machine tools, which enable the machinist's skills to be duplicated by a programmable device (originally punched paper tape) that controls the movements of a tool used to make complex shapes.* **Computer numerical control (CNC)** *machines are NC machines whose operations are driven by a computer.*

Industrial robots were the next major advance in manufacturing automation. *A* **robot** *is a programmable machine designed to handle materials or tools in the performance of a variety of tasks.* Robots can be "taught" a large number of sequences of motions and operations and even to make certain logical decisions. Other typical applications are spray painting, machining, inspection,

and material handling. Robots are especially useful for working with hazardous materials or heavy objects; for instance, in nuclear power plants robots are used to do work in highly radioactive areas. In services, robots help doctors complete intricate brain surgery by drilling very precise holes into the skull.

Integrated manufacturing systems began to emerge with computer-aided design/computer-aided engineering (CAD/CAE) and computer-aided manufacturing (CAM) systems. **CAD/CAE** *enables engineers to design, analyze, test, simulate, and*

Computer-integrated manufacturing systems (CIMSs) represent the union of hardware, software, database management, and communications to automate and control production activities, from planning and design to manufacturing and distribution.

Numerical control (NC) machine tools enable the machinist's skills to be duplicated by a programmable device (originally punched paper tape) that controls the movements of a tool used to make complex shapes.

Computer numerical control (CNC) machines are NC machines whose operations are driven by a computer.

A **robot** is a programmable machine designed to handle materials or tools in the performance of a variety of tasks.

CAD/CAE enables engineers to design, analyze, test, simulate, and "manufacture" products before they physically exist, thus ensuring that a product can be manufactured to specifications when it is released to the shop floor.

"manufacture" products before they physically exist, thus ensuring that a product can be manufactured to specifications when it is released to the shop floor. For example, Nissan is cutting the time needed to take new cars from design to showroom in half using computer-aided design software. The Nissan Note subcompact was rolled out to the Japanese market just 10.5 months after its design was finalized, in contrast to the 20.75 months that the process used to take.[3] **CAM** *involves computer control of the manufacturing process, such as determining tool movements and cutting speeds.*

Flexible manufacturing systems (FMSs) *consist of two or more computer-controlled machines or robots linked by automated handling devices such as transfer machines, conveyors, and transport systems. Computers direct the overall sequence of operations and route the work to the appropriate machine, select and load the proper tools, and control the operations performed by the machine.* More than one item can be machined or assembled simultaneously, and many different items can be processed in random order. Honda has been a pioneer in using FMSs and robotic technology. Its competitive priorities are moving toward design and demand flexibility so it is changing operating systems and technology to support these priorities. Honda assembly plants use flexible manufacturing cells where the robots can be reprogrammed to build different models of cars.[4]

CAM involves computer control of the manufacturing process, such as determining tool movements and cutting speeds.

Flexible manufacturing systems (FMSs) consist of two or more computer-controlled machines or robots linked by automated handling devices such as transfer machines, conveyors, and transport systems. Computers direct the overall sequence of operations and route the work to the appropriate machine, select and load the proper tools, and control the operations performed by the machine.

Today, many companies have achieved complete integration of CAD/CAE, CAM, and FMSs into what we now call computer-integrated manufacturing systems (CIMSs).

5-1c Service Technology

You have undoubtedly encountered quite a bit of service technology in your own daily lives. Technology is used in many services, including downloading music, banking, automated car washes, voice recognition in telephone menus, medical procedures, hotel and airline kiosks, and entertainment such as the robots used in Disney World's Hall of Presidents and Country Bear Jamboree attractions. One innovation that is being used by Stop & Shop, a grocery chain serving New England, is a portable device called EasyShop. EasyShop is a handheld terminal that allows loyalty card shoppers to scan items as they shop and receive targeted offers. Shoppers can also place an order at the deli department, for example, and then be alerted when the order is ready.[6]

CIMS Facts

According to the National Research Council, companies with computer-integrated manufacturing system experience have been able to

- *decrease engineering design costs by up to 30 percent;*
- *increase productivity by 40 to 70 percent;*
- *increase equipment utilization by a factor of 2 to 3;*
- *reduce work-in-process and lead times by 30 to 60 percent; and*
- *improve quality by a factor of 3 to 4.*

KROGER: LEVERAGING TWO SECONDS OF SAVINGS

Bar code scanners have been used in grocery stores for many years, requiring associates to scan items manually in the checkout lanes. Using a patented technology, the national grocery chain Kroger has been testing a new innovation called Advantage Checkout, designed to save customers time as well as to save the company operating costs and labor. Customers place items on a quick-moving conveyor belt. The items enter a tunnel lined with high-powered cameras to capture images of the products and scan the bar codes, then leave the tunnel on another conveyor to be bagged. The scanner can perform the function of several traditional or self-checkout lanes, takes up less floor space, and requires fewer workers. For a process that is done thousands of times in 2,400 stores, Kroger's CFO noted, "You can really leverage two seconds of savings that way."[5]

HIGH-TECH LIBRARIES

With Internet search today, libraries may be becoming extinct. Nevertheless, many people still use them. Some libraries use bar code scanners on books to make it easier for customers to check them out, much like a modern supermarket checkout. Others are beginning to use RFID technology. RFID scanners installed in counters at the checkout can identify and check out multiple books faster than using bar codes, and customers are often not aware of it when their receipt is printed. RFID technology is also helping to ensure that books are placed correctly on shelves. Librarians used to do this manually and it took a lot of time. Such systems increase productivity, and allow staff to spend more time answering questions helping their customers.

Other service technologies are used behind the scenes in hotels, airlines, hospitals, and retail stores to facilitate service experiences. To speed order entry for pizza delivery, for instance, many firms use a touch-sensitive computer screen that is linked to a customer database. When a repeat customer calls, the employee need only ask for the customer's phone number to bring up the customer's name, address, and delivery directions (for a new customer, the information need only be entered once). The employee is able to address the customer immediately by name, enhancing the perception of service quality, and then enter the order quickly on the touch-sensitive screen to print for the kitchen, eliminating errors due to misreading of handwritten orders.[7]

Perhaps the most common service technology in use today involves the Internet. **E-service** *refers to using the Internet and technology to provide services that create and deliver time, place, information, entertainment, and exchange value to customers and/or support the sale of goods.* Many individuals use airline, hotel, and rental car Web sites or "one-stop" e-services like Microsoft Expedia in planning a vacation. The boxes that highlight electronic medical record (EMR) systems and library services provide some interesting examples.

5-2 Technology in Value Chains

Technology, especially the Internet and e-communications, is changing the operation, speed, and efficiency of the value chain and presents many new challenges to operations managers. In many situations, electronic transaction capability allows all parts of the value chain to immediately know and react to changes in demand and supply. This requires tighter integration of many of the components of the value chain. In some cases, technology provides the capability to eliminate parts of the traditional value chain structure and streamline operations.

> "Technology, especially the Internet and e-communications, is changing the operation, speed, and efficiency of the value chain and presents many new challenges to operations managers."

With all the new technology that has evolved, a new perspective and capability for the value chain has emerged—the *e-commerce view of the value chain* shown in Exhibit 5.1. Major e-commerce relationships include B2B—business to business, B2C—business to customer, C2C—customer to customer, G2C—government to customer, G2G—government to government, and G2B—government to business. Here, buyers and sellers are connected by bricks-and-mortar intermediaries such as logistic and transportation services and/or by information technology to share information directly. *An* **intermediary** *is any entity—real or virtual—that*

E-service refers to using the Internet and technology to provide services that create and deliver time, place, information, entertainment, and exchange value to customers and/or support the sale of goods.

An **intermediary** is any entity—real or virtual—that coordinates and shares information between buyers and sellers.

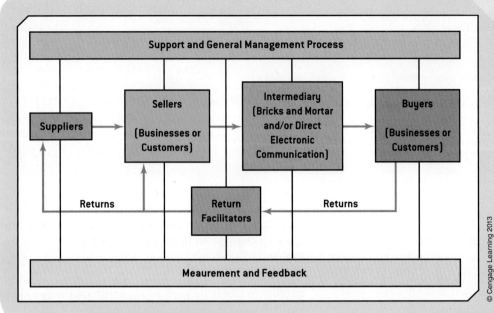

Exhibit 5.1
*E-Commerce View
of the Value Chain*

© Cengage Learning 2013

coordinates and shares information between buyers and sellers. Some firms, such as General Electric, Walmart, and Procter & Gamble, use e-commerce to communicate

Return facilitators specialize in handling all aspects of customers returning a manufactured good or delivered service and requesting their money back, repairing the manufactured good and returning it to the customer, and/or invoking the service guarantee.

directly with suppliers and retail stores, and thereby skip traditional bricks-and-mortar intermediaries. **Return facilitators** *specialize in handling all aspects of customers returning a manufactured good or delivered service and requesting their money back, repairing the manufactured good and returning it to the customer, and/or invoking the service guarantee.*

IT in Health Care

To ensure quality yet dramatically reduce costs, hospitals and health care clinics are adopting electronic medical record (EMR) systems. EMR systems record all the information generated by the health care facility and its patients in electronic form. Instead of a paper-based medical chart for each patient, the doctor uses a wireless PDA or tablet PC. EMR information also is easily integrated with other health care facility information systems, such as billing, patient scheduling, and accounting.

The benefits of an EMR system include:

- *Cost Reduction. At one medical clinic, transcription costs were reduced by 33 percent and transcription turnaround time went from seven days to one day.*

- *Revenue Enhancement. One health maintenance organization (HMO) used the Internet to contact over 600 patients who were overdue for mammograms, resulting in services that generated $670,000 in additional revenue.*

- *Improved Administrative and Support Process Efficiency. In one medical clinic, one full-time employee filed 600 to 700 patient charts per week. With the installation of EMR, these same medical records could be downloaded in 10 minutes.*

- *Improved Clinical Efficiency and Patient Care. An EMR system helps to standardize chart quality across the clinic or hospital and therefore minimizes the problems that result from poor handwriting and other inconsistencies in paper-based systems.*

AMAZON.COM: CAPITALIZING ON TECHNOLOGY

In 1995, Amazon.com began as an online bookstore, but soon diversified into other product lines such as DVDs, apparel, furniture, and toys. Amazon.com combined hard and soft technology to accomplish its early success. It built its operational capability through online order entry as well as automated warehouses and order-picking, packaging, shipping, and electronic customer payment. Today, it continues to exploit technology in its value chain. For example, Amazon Services launched a new version of Amazon WebStore (http://webstore.amazon.com), providing business customers with new capabilities, greater control, increased flexibility, and lower pricing. Amazon WebStore is a full-featured e-commerce system that enables small- to medium-sized sellers to easily design, build, and manage their multichannel e-commerce businesses using Amazon's technology. Amazon's WebStore is used by companies such as Black and Decker, Honeywell, ToyWatch, MTV, Martha Stewart, Motorola, Samsonite, and Timex. "When we launched our new Amazon WebStore, we saw an immediate lift of 40 percent in revenue and average order size," said Cal Crouch, director, e-commerce, Timex. "And on the support side, we have gained the flexibility to make most changes to content as well as brand ourselves—saving us thousands in development costs."[8]

amazon.com

© Kurt Strazdins/MCT/Newscom

Some examples of how information technology has enabled companies to build and sustain competitive advantage for e-commerce follow.

- GE Plastics (www.geplastics.com) used the Internet to completely change how plastics are designed, ordered, researched, and delivered for B2B customers. The entire GE Plastics Web site represents a value-added, information-intensive set of services—e-services—that facilitate the sale of goods—chemicals, plastics, resins, polymers, and the like. GE Polymerland (www.gepolymerland.com) allows other companies to buy, design, interact, research, and participate in a global auction service for many types of chemicals and plastics. The "buy" button reveals many value-added services, such as how to place an order, order status, shipment tracking, pricing, and inventory availability.

- FedEx has a rich history of technology innovation for its B2C value chain. It was the first to install computers in delivery vehicles, providing sophisticated automation for corporate mailing services and developing tracking capabilities and software. In 1994, it was the first to offer package-status

tracking for improved customer service via fedex.com. It also pioneered the use of wireless technology for shipping with the introduction of the Digital Assisted Dispatch System (DADS) over 25 years ago. FedEx developed the FedEx Innovation Labs, an information technology project designed to create an atmosphere of collaborative thinking around critical technologies such as advanced optics for scanning, robotics, pervasive computing, social networking, and more.[9]

- eBay (www.ebay.com) started out as a C2C value chain but quickly incorporated B2C and B2B transactions. The eBay business is built on the values of open communication and honesty, and the vast majority of buyers and sellers at eBay are reliable. eBay fights fraud using customer feedback that keeps track of the trustworthiness of its sellers using a point system and posts this information

AP Photo/Paul Sakuma

for all site members to see, as well as its own security monitoring processes. In the event a customer pays for an item and never receives it, eBay will reimburse buyers up to a dollar limit, minus processing costs. eBay provides a variety of services, such as online seminars and interactive tutorials, to help customers learn how to buy and sell on the Web site, how to search for goods or services on eBay, how to add photos of their goods or services, how to design store fronts and marketing, and so on.

Günay Mutlu/iStockphoto.com

- Federal, state, and local government value chains (i.e., G2C, G2G, and G2B) use e-commerce to provide better service for citizens, control waste and fraud, and minimize costs. Filing your taxes electronically and the direct deposit monthly Social Security checks are two examples. Food stamps are now in the form of electronic credit cards and student loan applications must be electronically filed.

5-2a Analytics in Value Chains

Business analytics plays a critical role in managing value chains, particularly for integrating and analyzing data throughout the value chain within an information systems framework. Netflix, for example, uses analytics everywhere, from marketing to operations to customer service. Netflix collects extensive data using surveys, Web site user testing, brand awareness studies, and segmentation research. It uses analytics to help decide what price to pay for the rights to distribute new DVDs.[10] Using data on customer preferences, film ratings, and comparisons with people who have similar viewing and preference histories, Netflix predicts movies that a customer is likely to enjoy and creates personalized recommendations. This information also helps to manage its film inventory by recommending older movies to balance demand for newer releases.[11]

Two key information systems that drive value chain management are enterprise resource planning (ERP) and customer relationship management (CRM). **ERP** *systems integrate all aspects of a business—accounting, customer relationship management, supply chain management, manufacturing, sales, human resources—into a unified information system and provide more timely analysis and reporting of sales, customer, inventory, manufacturing, human resource, and accounting data.* Traditionally, each department of a company, such as finance, human resources, and manufacturing, has individual information systems optimized to the needs of that department. If the sales department wants to know the status of a customer's order, for example, someone would typically have to call manufacturing or shipping. ERP combines each department's information into a single, integrated system with a common database so that departments can easily share information and communicate with each other.

ERP systems usually consist of different modules that can be implemented individually so that each department still has a level of autonomy, but they are combined into an integrated operating system. For example, when a customer's order is entered by sales, all information necessary to fulfill the order is built into

Enterprise resource planning (ERP) systems integrate all aspects of a business—accounting, customer relationship management, supply chain management, manufacturing, sales, human resources—into a unified information system and provide more timely analysis and reporting of sales, customer, inventory, manufacturing, human resource, and accounting data.

the ERP system. The finance module would have the customer's order history and credit rating; the warehouse module would have current inventory levels; and the supply chain module would have distribution and shipping information. Not only would sales be able to provide accurate information about product availability and shipping dates, but orders would get processed faster with fewer errors and delays.

Most of the subsystems of ERP systems, such as customer ordering, inventory management, and production scheduling, are *real-time transaction processing systems,* as opposed to *batched processing systems,* in which a day's entire batch of transactions was typically processed during the night. In real-time processing, information is updated continuously, allowing the impacts to be reflected immediately in all other areas of the ERP system. Some business processes, however, such as the weekly payroll, monthly accounting reports, and billing, do not need real-time processing. Two prominent vendors of ERP software are SAP (www.sap.com) and Oracle (www.oracle.com).

Customer relationship management (CRM) *is a business strategy designed to learn more about customers' wants, needs, and behaviors in order to build customer relationships and loyalty and ultimately enhance revenues and profits.* CRM exploits the vast amount of data that can be collected from consumers. For example, using a cell phone to make a voice call leaves behind data on whom you called, how long you talked, what time you called, whether your call was successful or if was dropped, your location, the promotion you may be responding to, and purchase histories.[12] Similarly, supermarkets, drug stores, and retail stores use "loyalty cards" that leave behind a digital trail of data about purchasing patterns. By better understanding these patterns and hidden relationships in data, stores can customize advertisements, promotions, coupons, and so on down to each individual customer and send targeted text messages and e-mail offers.

A typical CRM system includes market segmentation and analysis, customer service and relationship building, effective complaint resolution, cross-selling of goods and services, and pre- and postproduction processes such as preproduction order processing and postproduction field service. Of course, the value chain must be capable of delivering what the customer wants, and that is where sound operational analysis is required.

CRM helps firms gain and maintain competitive advantage by

- segmenting markets based on demographic and behavioral characteristics;

- tracking sales trends and advertising effectiveness by customer and market segment;
- identifying which customers should be the focus of targeted marketing initiatives with predicted high customer response rates;
- forecasting customer retention (and defection) rates and providing feedback as to why customers leave the company;
- identifying which transactions are likely candidates to be fraudulent;
- studying which goods and services are purchased together, and what might be good ways to bundle them (that is, the customer benefit package);
- studying and predicting what Web characteristics are most attractive to customers and how the Web site might be improved; and
- linking the previous information to competitive priorities by market segment and process and value chain performance.

In recent years, cloud computing has improved the efficiency, productivity, and cost for organizations using information technology (IT) and such systems as ERP and CRM. Many now outsource ERP, CRM, and other IT services; for instance, Netflix outsourced most of its Web technology work to Amazon.

Customer relationship management (CRM) is a business strategy designed to learn more about customers' wants, needs, and behaviors in order to build customer relationships and loyalty and ultimately enhance revenues and profits.

5-3 Benefits and Challenges of Technology

technology provides many benefits, but at the same time poses some key challenges. A summary of the benefits and challenges of technology is given in Exhibit 5.2. Can you think of others?

One of the major benefits of technology has been its impact on sustainability. In Florida, for example, Card Sound Golf Club in Key Largo had an underground sensor system installed that allowed the club to cut in half the amount of fresh water it used to flush salt out of water used to irrigate the golf course. Many other golf courses are using this advanced sensor technology to reduce water consumption and keep their golf courses green—and not just in color.[13]

Intel suggests that the microprocessor is the "ultimate invention for achieving sustainability."[14] Microprocessor-based Information and Communication Technology (ICT) provides sustainable economic, environmental, and social benefits on a national and global basis. One study cited ICT as directly responsible for contributing to two-thirds of the productivity gains in the U.S. economy between 1997 and 2002. These gains have significantly offset carbon usage, enabling more to be done, less miles traveled, and greater operational and material efficiencies. ICT is responsible for a phenomenon known as *dematerialization*, by which the same or an increased quality and quantity of goods and/or services are created using fewer natural resources. ICT has also enabled flexible work options such as telecommuting, which not only yields environmental benefits, but social benefits as well.

5-4 Technology Decisions and Implementation

managers must make good decisions about introducing and using new technology. They must understand the relative advantages and disadvantages of using technologies and their impact on the workforce. Although technology has proven quite useful in eliminating monotony and hazardous work and can help people develop new skills

Exhibit 5.2 *Example Benefits and Challenges of Adopting Technology*

Benefits	Challenges
Creates new industries and job opportunities	Higher employee skill levels required, such as information technology and service management skills
Restructures old and less productive industries	Integration of old (legacy) and new technology and systems
Integrates supply and value chain players	Job shift and displacement
Increases marketplace competitiveness and maintains the survival of the firm	Less opportunity for employee creativity and empowerment
Provides the capability to focus on smaller target market segments through mass customization	Protecting the employee's and customer's privacy and security
Improves/increases productivity, quality, customer satisfaction, speed, safety, and flexibility/customization—does more with less	Fewer human service providers, resulting in customer ownership not being assigned, nonhuman service encounters, and inability of the customer to change decisions and return goods easily
Lowers cost	Information overload
Raises world's standard of living	Global outsourcing and impact on domestic job opportunities
Monitors the environment and health of the planet	Enforcement of regulations and laws to support sustainability goals

© Cengage Learning 2013

Volvo: There's an App for That!

Volvo is partnering with Chalmers University in Sweden to develop tools that allow assembly-line workers to access instructions and manuals for operating their equipment using an iPhone or iPod Touch. The concepts are being tested at a Volvo Trucks assembly plant. One of the benefits would be consuming less paper, thus adding to environmental sustainability. Another benefit is the ability to instantly update unexpected or rapidly changing production needs, thus improving the company's agility.[15]

Solved Problem

Maling Manufacturing needs to purchase a new piece of machining equipment. The two choices are a conventional (labor-intensive) machine and an automated (computer-controlled) machine. Profitability will depend on a future unknown event—the demand volume. The following table presents an estimate of the net present value of profit over the next three years.

	Demand Volume	
Decision	Low	High
Conventional machine	($10,000)	$110,000
Automated machine	($50,000)	$145,000

Given the uncertainty associated with the demand volume, and no other information to work with, how would you make a decision?

Solution

Supplementary Chapter (SC) E describes decision criteria for addressing this situation, and Exhibit 5.3 shows the Decision Analysis Excel template from the CourseMate Web site. An aggressive, risk-taking manager would use a "maximax" criterion that would choose the decision that maximizes the maximum profit among all events (cell G9)—in this case, the automated machine. A conservative, risk-averse manager would use a "maximin" criterion that would choose the decision that will maximize the minimum possible profit among all events (cell H8)—in this case, the conventional machine. A third criterion is "minimax regret," which chooses the decision that minimizes the maximum opportunity loss (cell G17). There is no optimal decision; the decision involves determining how much risk one is willing to take.

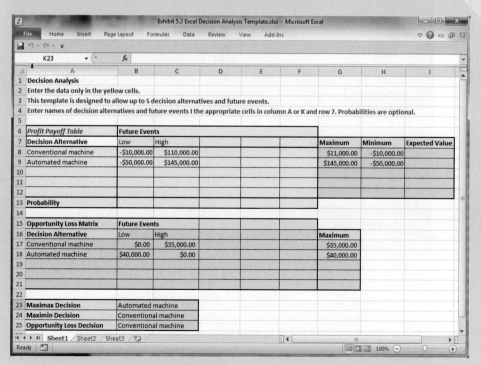

Exhibit 5.3
Portion of Excel Decision Analysis Template

and talents, it can also rob them of empowerment and creativity. The goal of the operations manager is to provide the best synthesis of technology, people, and processes; this interaction is often called the *sociotechnical system*. Designing the sociotechnical system includes making decisions about job specialization versus enlargement, employee empowerment, training, decision support systems, teams and work groups, job design, recognition and reward, career advancement, and facility and equipment layout.

A key factor that affects technology decisions is scalability. **Scalability** *is a measure of the contribution margin (revenue minus variable costs) required to deliver a good or service as the business grows and volumes increase.* Scalability is a key issue in e-commerce. **High scalability** *is the capability to serve additional customers at zero or extremely low incremental costs.* For example, Monster.com is an online job posting and placement service that is largely information-intensive. Customers can post their resumes on the Monster.com Web site and print out job advertisements and opportunities on their office or home computers at their expense. This service is highly scalable because its fixed costs are approximately 80 to 85 percent of total costs. The incremental cost to serve an additional customer is very small, yet the revenue obtained from this customer remains high. If an organization establishes a business where the incremental cost (or variable cost) to serve more customers is zero, then the firm is said to be *infinitely scalable*. Online newspapers, magazines, and encyclopedias; e-banking services; and other information-intensive businesses have the potential to be infinitely scalable.

On the other hand, **low scalability** *implies that serving additional customers requires high incremental variable costs.* Many of the dot.com

companies that failed around the year 2000 had low scalability and unsustainable demand (volumes) created by extraordinary advertising expenses and artificially low prices (see WebVan box).

Many companies do not really understand how to implement technology effectively. The risk of a technology adoption failure is high. For instance, Hershey Foods installed three software packages in the summer

---

WEBVAN: A VALUE CHAIN FAILURE

One dot.com company with a lot of potential, WebVan, focused on customers' ordering their groceries online and the company then picking up the orders in a warehouse and delivering them to the customers' homes. The idea was to support the order-pick-pack-deliver process of acquiring groceries through an e-service at the front end of the value chain and with delivery vans at the back end of the value chain. This service made several assumptions about customer wants and needs; for example, that customers have perfect knowledge of what they want when they surf the online catalogs; that customers would be home when the delivery arrived; that what the e-catalogue shows is what the customer will get; that the customer doesn't make mistakes when selecting the items; and that time-starved customers are willing to pay a high premium for home delivery. Unfortunately, this was a very high-cost process. The $30 to $40 delivery charge for complex and heterogeneous customer orders and the many opportunities for error doomed WebVan. The founders of WebVan did not clearly define their strategy and target market and properly evaluate the operational and logistical issues associated with their value chain design. WebVan designed its system with low scalability and limited growth potential.[16]

> Although technology has proven quite useful in eliminating monotony and hazardous work and can help people develop new skills and talents, it can also rob them of empowerment and creativity.

of 1999, just as retailers placed orders for Halloween candy. The software was incompatible with other systems, and candy piled up in warehouses because of missed or delayed deliveries. Such experiences are reminiscent of comparable failures of automated manufacturing technology encountered by the automobile and other industries during the 1970s. Reasons include rushing to the wrong technology, buying too much and not implementing it properly, and underestimating the time needed to make it work.

Discussion Questions

1. Describe at least one application of modern technology in each of these service industries:

   a. financial services

   b. public and government services

   c. transportation services

   d. educational services

   e. hotel and motel services

   How does your example application improve things, or does it?

2. Describe a situation where self-service and technology help create and deliver the customer benefit package to the customer. Provide examples of how such a system can cause a defect, mistake, or service upset.

3. Discuss each of these statements. What might be wrong with each of them?

   a. "We've thought about computer integration of all our manufacturing functions, but when we looked at it, we realized that the labor savings wouldn't justify the cost."

   b. "We've had these computer-controlled robots on the line for several months now, and they're great! We no longer have to reconfigure the whole line to shift to a different product. I just give the robots new instructions, and they change operations. Just wait until this run is done and I'll show you."

   c. "Each of my manufacturing departments is authorized to invest in whatever technologies are necessary to perform its function more effectively. As a result, we have state-of-the-art equipment throughout our factories—from CAD/CAM to automated materials handling to robots on the line. When we're ready to migrate to a CIM environment, we can just tie all these pieces together."

   d. "I'm glad we finally got that CAD system," the designer said, a computer-generated blueprint in hand. "I was able to draw these plans and make modifications right on the computer screen in a fraction of the time it used to take by hand." "They tell me this new computer-aided manufacturing system will do the same for me," the manufacturing engineer replied. "I'll just punch in your specs and find out."

4. Identify one low and one highly scalable organization and explain why each is so.

5. What challenges do companies face when trying to implement e-commerce business plans and strategies? What can they learn from the WebVan experience?

Problems and Activities

Note: an asterisk denotes problems for which an Excel spreadsheet template on the CourseMate Web site may be used.

1. Research and write a short paper (maximum of two typed pages) on the impact of electric cars on the three dimensions of sustainability.

2. Identify and describe (maximum of two typed pages) two apps for your cell phone or electronic reader and how they improve your productivity and quality of life.

3. Identify and describe (maximum of one typed page) a service encounter where technology helps create and deliver the service in total or in part. What hard and soft technology most likely is involved?

4. Research radio frequency identification devices (RFIDs) and provide examples of how they are or might be used to improve productivity in operations.

5. Find at least two new applications of modern technology in businesses that are not discussed in this chapter. What impacts on productivity and quality do you think these applications have had?

6. Investigate the current technology available for laptop computers, cell phones, iPods, or iPads. Select two different models and compare their features and operational characteristics, as well as the manufacturer's support and service. Briefly explain how you might advise (a) a college student majoring in art, and (b) a salesperson for a high-tech machine tool company in selecting the best device for his or her needs (maximum of two typed pages).

7. Research and write a short paper (maximum of two typed pages) about how business analytics or advances in information systems influence the use of technology and decision making in operations management.

8. Identify and describe (maximum of two typed pages) a business that uses ERP to manage its value chain (if possible, draw a picture of key elements of the value chain, such as sourcing, production, shipping, sales, billing, and so on). What benefits and challenges does ERP bring to this business?

9.* Suzy's Temporary Employee (STE) business, located in a big city, can do an online criminal background check in-house for $1.46 per search with a fixed cost of $22,000. A third-party online security firm offered to do a similar security search for $10.00 per person with an annual service contract with STE. If STE's forecast is 3,000 searches next year, should STE continue to do the search in-house or accept the third-party offer? What other criteria are important in making this decision?

10.* A manager of Paris Manufacturing, which produces computer hard drives, is planning to lease a new automated inspection system. The manager believes the new system will be more accurate than the current manual inspection process. The firm has had problems with hard drive defects in the past and the automated system should help catch these defects before the drives are shipped to the final assembly manufacturer. The relevant information follows.

Current Manual Inspection System

Annual fixed cost = $35,000

Inspection variable cost per unit = $15 per unit

New Automated Inspection System

Annual fixed cost = $165,000

Inspection variable cost per unit = $0.55 per unit

Suppose annual demand is 11,000 units. Should the firm lease the new inspection system?

11.* In problem 10, assume the cost factors given have not changed. A marketing representative of NEWSPEC, a firm that specializes in providing manual inspection processes for other firms, approached Paris Manufacturing and offered to inspect parts for $17 each with no fixed cost. It assured Paris Manufacturing that the accuracy and quality of its manual inspections would equal that of the automated inspection system. Demand for the upcoming year is forecast to be 11,000 units. Should the manufacturer accept the offer?

12.* Edwards Machine Tools needs to purchase a new machine. The basic model is slower but costs less, whereas the advanced model is faster but costs more. Profitability will depend on future demand. The following table presents an estimate of profits over the next three years.

| | Demand Volume | | |
Decision	Low	Medium	High
Basic model	$80,000	$100,000	$150,000
Advanced model	$40,000	$110,000	$220,000

Given the uncertainty associated with the demand volume, and no other information to work with, how would you make a decision? Explain your reasoning.

13.* Suppose that in problem 12, a forecasting study determines that the probabilities of demand volume are Low = 0.4, Medium = 0.1, and High = 0.5. Using the techniques in Supplementary Chapter SC E on decision analysis, determine the expected value decision. How appropriate is it to use this criterion?

14. For the information provided in problem 13, compute the expected value of perfect information (EVPI) as discussed in Supplementary Chapter SC E on decision analysis. Clearly explain how to interpret EVPI for Edwards Machine Tools.

15.* A company is considering three vendors for purchasing a CRM system, Delphi Inc., CRM International, and Murray Analytics. The costs of the system are expected to depend on the length of time required to implement the system, which depends on such factors as the amount of customization required, integration with legacy systems, resistance to change, and so on. Each vendor has different expertise in handling these things, which affect the cost. The costs (in millions of $) are shown below for short, medium, and long implementation durations. Conduct a decision analysis using the techniques in Supplementary Chapter SC E on decision analysis to evaluate the choice of a vendor. Clearly explain your recommendation.

Decision Alternative	Short	Medium	Long
Delphi Inc.	$5.00	$3.00	$6.00
CRM International	$3.00	$5.00	$5.50
Murray Analytics	$4.00	$4.50	$7.20

Bracket International—The RFID Decision Case Study

Jack Bracket, the CEO of Bracket International (BI), has grown his business to sales last year of $78 million with a cost of goods sold of $61 million. Average inventory levels are about $14 million. As a small manufacturer of steel shelving and brackets, the firm operates three small factories in Ohio, Kentucky, and South Carolina. BI's number one competitive priority is "service first," while high product quality and low cost are #2 and #3. Service at BI includes preproduction services such as customized engineering design, production services such as meeting customer promise dates and being flexible to customer-driven changes, and postproduction services such as shipping, distribution, and field service.

The Ohio and Kentucky factories are automated flow shops, whereas the South Carolina factory specializes in small custom orders and is more of a batch-processing job shop. All three factories use bar coding labels and scanning equipment to monitor and control the flow of materials. BI manually scans about 8,850 items per day at all three factories. An item may be an individual part, a roll of sheet steel, a box of 1,000 rivets, a pallet load of brackets, a box of quart oil cans, a finished shelf or bracket set ready for shipment, and so on. That is, whatever a bar code label can be stuck on is bar coded. A factory year consists of 260 days. One full-time BI employee works 2,000 hours per year with an average salary including benefits of $55,000.

Two recent sales calls have Mr. Bracket considering switching from the old bar coding system to a radio frequency identification device (RFID) system. The RFID vendors kept talking about "on-demand" operational planning and control and how their RFID and software systems could speed up the pace of BI's workflows. One RFID vendor provided the following information:

Bracket International manufactures steel shelving and brackets.

Evgeny Korshenkov/Shutterstock.com

- Bar code scan times for the sheet metal business (similar to BI) average 10 seconds per item and include employee time to find the bar code, pick up the item and/or position the item or handheld bar code reader so it can read the bar code, and in some cases physically reposition the item. Item orientation is a problem with manual bar coding.

- The 10-second bar code scan time does not include the employee walking to the bar coding spot or equipment. It is assumed that the employee is in position to scan the item. The 10 seconds does not include the time to replace a scratched or defective bar code label. Replacing a damaged bar code tag, including changes to the computer system, may take up to 5 minutes.

- All three BI factories can be fitted with RFID technology (readers, item tags, and hardware-related software) for $620,000. In addition, new supply chain operating system software that takes advantage of the faster pace of RFID information is priced for all three factories at $480,000 and includes substantial training and debugging consulting services.

- RFID scan time is estimated to be 2/100ths of a second, or basically instantaneous.

- For the sheet metal business, bar code misreads average 2 percent (i.e., 0.02) over the year of total reads, and this is estimated to reduce to 0.2 percent (i.e., 0.002) for RFID technology. The 0.2 percent is due to damaged RFID tags or occasional radio frequency interference or transmission problems. Misreads are a problem because items are lost and not recorded in BI's computer system. The vendor guessed that a single misread could cost a manufacturer on average $4 but noted this estimate could vary quite a bit.

- According to the RFID vendors, other benefits of RFID systems include readily located inventory, fewer required inventory audits, and reduced misplacements and theft. However, they did not have any information quantifying these benefits.

Bracket International recently had problems adapting quickly to changing customer requirements. BI had to deny a Wolf Furniture job order request because it could not react quickly enough to a change in job specifications and order size. Eventually, BI lost the Wolf Furniture business that averaged about $2 million per year. Another BI customer, Home Depot, keeps talking about BI needing to be more flexible because Home Depot's on-demand point-of-sale systems require frequent changes to BI orders. Home Depot is BI's top customer, so every effort needs to be made to keep Home Depot happy.

Mr. Bracket doesn't think throwing away the bar coding system that works is a good idea. The BI employees are familiar with using bar coding technology, whereas the RFID technology seems hidden from employees. He also doesn't think the return on investment (ROI) on an RFID system is compelling. So why does he feel so guilty when the RFID vendors leave his office? Is he doing the right thing or not? He has an obligation to his trusted employees to do the right thing. Should he adopt RFID based purely on strategic and/or economic benefits? He writes down several questions he needs to investigate.

Case Questions for Discussion

1. How does RFID compare to bar coding?

2. What is the economic payback in years for this possible RFID adoption? (Hint: There are two benefits that can be quantified—labor savings due to faster scan times and misread savings. Annual benefits divided by economic benefits equals payback.)

3. What are the risks of adopting a new technology too early? Too late?

4. What do you recommend Mr. Bracket do in the short and long terms? Explain your reasoning.

USE THE TOOLS.

- Rip out the Review Cards in the back of your book to study.

Or Visit CourseMate to:

- Read, search, highlight, and take notes in the Interactive eBook
- Review Flashcards (Print or Online) to master key terms
- Test yourself with Auto-Graded Quizzes
- Bring concepts to life with Games, Videos, and Animations!

Go to CourseMate for **OM4** to begin using these tools.
Access at **www.cengagebrain.com**

Complete the Speak Up survey in CourseMate at www.cengagebrain.com

f Follow us at www.facebook.com/4ltrpress

GOODS AND SERVICE DESIGN

 n developing markets such as China and India, consumers can't afford large, expensive cars, much less drive them in over-crowded population centers. Fuel efficiency as well as environmental concerns are also important, as developing nations seek to cap carbon emissions even as the number of vehicles on their streets continues to rise. But these consumers are not willing to buy inferior cars that simply cost less. Rather, like most of us, they want low-cost vehicles that are designed to meet their needs and still have high quality, reliability, and style—in other words, have value. Consumers in India, for instance, need cars that maximize passenger room because they use their autos primarily as family vehicles to drive around town; by contrast, in the West, with its better roads and routine long-distance driving, cargo capacity matters more. Indian drivers are willing to pay a bit more for cars that offer the latest in comfort, safety, and utility, but not for cars with power windows and locks or fancy sound systems. Automatic transmissions are desirable in India and China—nobody wants to keep pressing the clutch and shifting gears in the inevitable stop-and-go traffic—but powerful engines are not. Succeeding in developing markets, therefore, requires rethinking from start to finish how new cars should be designed and built. It calls for a deep understanding of the unique needs of consumers and the ability to assemble the combination of power trains, bodies, features, and options that best match those desires—at affordable prices.[1]

learning outcomes

After studying this chapter you should be able to:

6-1 **Describe the steps involved in designing goods and services.**

6-2 **Explain the concept and application of quality function deployment.**

6-3 **Describe how the Taguchi loss function, reliability, design for manufacturability, and design for sustainability are used for designing manufactured goods.**

6-4 **Explain the five elements of service-delivery system design.**

6-5 **Describe the four elements of service-encounter design.**

6-6 **Explain how goods and service design concepts are integrated at LensCrafters.**

What do you think?

How important are design and value in your purchasing decisions? Provide some examples for goods and services.

JB Reed/Bloomberg/Getty Images

Perhaps the most important strategic decision that any firm makes involves the design and development of new goods and services, and the value chain structure and processes that make and deliver them. In fact, decisions about what goods and services to offer and how to position them in the marketplace often determine the ultimate growth, profitability, and success of the firm. Every design project—a new automobile or cell phone, a new online or financial service, and even a new pizza—is a series of trade-offs: between technology and functionality, between ambition and affordability, between the desires of the people creating the object and the needs of the people using it.[2]

In today's world, the complexity of customer benefit packages requires a high level of coordination throughout the value chain. As the authors of the opening anecdote about automobile design note, design for value "involves a series of complex, varied, carefully thought-out decisions about which types of engines to use; which equipment should be standard; what safety add-ons to include; how parts and materials are engineered; and which designs are most attractive to the target customer base." At the other end of the value chain, sales and maintenance and even financing should also be examined for new ideas: Given limited dealer networks, might roving mechanics be sent around to perform regular maintenance? Could entire extended families enter into financing deals for new cars? Similar questions apply to the design of every good and service.

▼ *Fuel efficiency and environmental concerns are important in developing nations as the number of vehicles on their streets continues to rise.*

6-1 Designing Goods and Services

t o design and improve goods and services, most companies use some type of structured process. The typical goods and services development processes are shown in Exhibit 6.1. In general, the designs of both goods and services follow a similar path. The critical differences lie in the detailed product and process design phases.

Steps 1 and 2—Strategic Mission, Analysis, and Competitive Priorities

Strategic directions and competitive priorities should be consistent with and support the firm's mission and vision. These steps require a significant amount of research and innovation involving marketing, engineering, operations, and sales functions, and should involve customers, suppliers, and employees throughout the value chain. The data and information that result from this effort provide the key input for designing the final customer benefit package.

Step 3—Customer Benefit Package Design and Configuration

Clearly, firms have a large variety of possible choices in configuring a customer benefit package (CBP). For example, when buying a new vehicle an automobile dealer might include such options as leasing, free oil changes and/or maintenance, a performance driving school, free auto washes, service pickup and delivery, loaner cars, and so on.

Essentially, CBP design and configuration choices revolve around a solid understanding of customer needs and target markets, and the value that customers place on such attributes as the following:

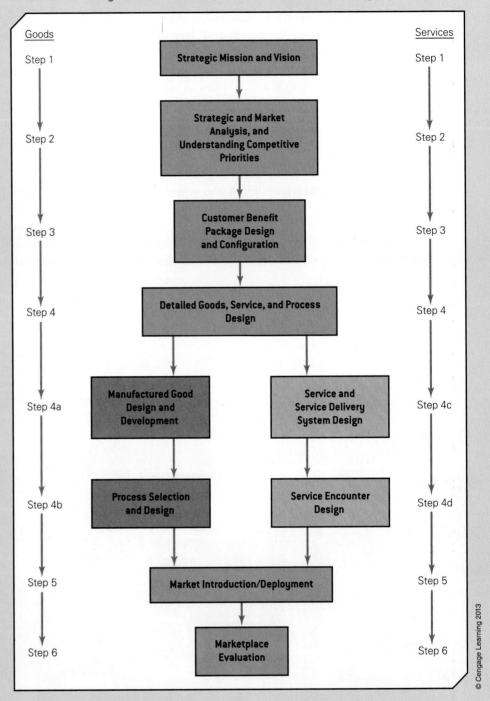

Exhibit 6.1 *An Integrated Framework for Goods and Service Design*

Goods | Services

Step 1 — Strategic Mission and Vision

Step 2 — Strategic and Market Analysis, and Understanding Competitive Priorities

Step 3 — Customer Benefit Package Design and Configuration

Step 4 — Detailed Goods, Service, and Process Design

Step 4a — Manufactured Good Design and Development | Service and Service Delivery System Design — Step 4c

Step 4b — Process Selection and Design | Service Encounter Design — Step 4d

Step 5 — Market Introduction/Deployment

Step 6 — Marketplace Evaluation

© Cengage Learning 2013

> Every design project—a new automobile or cell phone, a new online or financial service, and even a new pizza—is a series of tradeoffs: between technology and functionality, between ambition and affordability, between the desires of the people creating the object and the needs of the people using it

- **Time**—Many grocery stores now offer self-service checkout to reduce customer waiting time, and manufacturers such as Dell use the Internet to acquire customer information for more responsive product design.

- **Place**—UPS has "UPS Stores" strategically located for customer convenience that also provide packaging services; many companies offer day-care centers on-site to provide convenience to their employees.

- **Information**—Bank of America provides an Internet search capability for the best home equity loan; and a business dedicated to providing guitar music books and videos (www.ChordMelody.com) offers a telephone hot line to speak with a professional guitarist for questions on selecting the proper instructional and performance material.

- **Entertainment**—Some Dick's Sporting Goods Stores provide a rock-climbing wall for children while other family members shop; a pianist serenades shoppers at Nordstrom's department stores; and some minivans have built-in DVD players. (See the box on "Biztainment" in Chapter 1.)

- **Exchange**—Retail stores such as Best Buy allow customers to travel to the store and buy the goods, purchase goods on their Web sites and have them delivered, or purchase goods on their Web sites and have them ready to be picked up at the store.

- **Form**—For manufactured goods, form is associated with the physical characteristics of the good, and addresses the important customer need of aesthetics. An interior designer might use different methods, such as sketches, photographs, physical samples, or even computer-simulated renderings, to show how a kitchen might be transformed.

A job-seeking service such as Monster.com provides pure information value, whereas buying an automobile or going on a vacation involves all six types.

Greenland/Shutterstock.com

Step 4—Detailed Goods, Services, and Process Design

If a proposal survives the concept stage—and many do not—each good or service in the CBP, as well as the process that creates it, must be designed in more detail. This is where the designs of goods and services differ, as suggested by the alternate paths in Exhibit 6.1. The first three steps in Exhibit 6.1 are more strategic and conceptual in nature, whereas step 4 focuses on detailed design and implementation.

The design of a manufactured good focuses on its physical characteristics—dimensions, materials, color, and so on. Much of this work is done by artists and engineers to translate customer requirements into physical specifications. This is the focus of step 4a in the exhibit. The process by which the good is manufactured (that is, the configuration of machines and labor) can be designed as a separate activity (step 4b), with, of course, proper communication and coordination with the designers of the good.

> "The process by which the service is created and delivered (that is, 'produced') is, in essence, the service itself!"

The design of a service in steps 4c and 4d in Exhibit 6.1, however, cannot be done independently from the "process" by which the service is delivered. The process by which the service is created and delivered (that is, "produced") is, in essence, the service itself! For example, the steps that a desk clerk follows to check in a guest at a hotel represents the process by which the guest is served and (hopefully) experiences a sense of satisfaction. Thus, service design must be addressed from two perspectives—the service delivery system and the service encounter—as noted in steps 4c and 4d in Exhibit 6.1.

For both goods and services, this phase usually includes prototype testing. **Prototype testing** *is the process by which a model (real or simulated) is constructed to test the product's performance under actual operating conditions, as well as consumer reactions to the prototypes.* For example, at General Motors (GM), parts are designed and digitally analyzed using special software; one-third scale models are produced, assembled, and tested in a wind tunnel to evaluate the aerodynamics of automobile designs. Today, many companies use advanced technology to perform *rapid prototyping*—the process of building prototypes quickly to reduce product development cost and time-to-market. GM has a laboratory where 15 specialists take part orders from GM design centers all over the world, build them within hours, and then express ship them back, allowing designers and engineers to quickly evaluate them.[4]

> **Prototype testing** is the process by which a model (real or simulated) is constructed to test the product's performance under actual operating conditions, as well as consumer reactions to the prototypes.

Step 5—Market Introduction/Deployment

In this step, the final bundle of goods and services—the customer benefit package—is advertised, marketed, and offered to customers. For manufactured goods, this includes making the item in the factory and shipping it to warehouses or wholesale and retail stores; for services, it might include hiring and training employees or staying open an extra hour in the evening. For many services, it means building sites such as branch banks or hotels or retail stores.

Step 6—Marketplace Evaluation

The marketplace is a graveyard of missed opportunities: poorly designed goods and services and failed execution resulting from ineffective operations. The final step in

> The marketplace is a graveyard of missed opportunities: poorly designed goods and services and failed execution resulting from ineffective operations.

designing and delivering a customer benefit package is to constantly evaluate how well the goods and services are selling and what customers' reactions to them are.

6-2 Customer-Focused Design

the design of a good or service should reflect customer wants and needs, which are often termed customer requirements. *Customer requirements, as expressed in the customer's own words, are called the* **voice of the customer.** The design process must translate the voice of the customer into specific technical features that characterize a design and provide the "blueprint" for manufacturing or service delivery. Technical features are generally expressed in the language of designers and engineers; examples include the type and amount of materials, size and shape of parts, strength requirements, service procedures to follow, and employee behavior during service interactions. An effective approach for doing this is called *quality function deployment.* **Quality function deployment (QFD)** *is an approach to guide the design,*

creation, and marketing of goods and services by integrating the voice of the customer into all decisions. QFD can be applied to a specific manufactured good, service, or the entire CBP. The process is initiated with a matrix, which, because of its structure (shown in Exhibit 6.2), is often called the *House of Quality.*

Building a House of Quality begins by identifying the voice of the customer and technical features of the design and listing them in the appropriate places in the diagram. As shown in Exhibit 6.2, the voice of the customer and the technical features create a matrix structure in the center of the diagram. By evaluating how each technical feature relates to each customer requirement (using a scale such as "very strong," "strong," "weak," or "no relationship"), designers can determine how well a design reflects the actual customer requirements. This might be based on expert experience, customer surveys, or other experiments. The lack of a relationship between a customer requirement and any of the technical features would suggest that the final good or service will have

> Customer requirements, as expressed in the customer's own words, are called the **voice of the customer.**
>
> **Quality function deployment (QFD)** is an approach to guide the design, creation, and marketing of goods and services by integrating the voice of the customer into all decisions.

Example: Building a Better Pizza

A restaurant wants to develop a "signature" pizza. The voice of the customer in this case consists of four attributes. The pizza should be tasty, be healthy, be visually appealing, and should provide good value. The "technical features" that can be designed into this particular product are price, size, amount of cheese, type of additional toppings, and amount of additional toppings. The symbols in the matrix in the exhibit at the right show the relationships between each customer requirement and technical feature. For example, taste bears a moderate relationship with amount of cheese and a strong relationship with type of additional toppings. In the roof, the price and size area seem to be strongly related (as size increases, the price must increase). The competitive evaluation shows that competitors are currently weak on nutrition and value, so those attributes can become key selling points in a marketing plan if the restaurant can capitalize on them. Finally, at the bottom of the house are targets for the technical features based on an analysis of customer-importance ratings and competitive ratings. The features with asterisks are the ones to be "deployed," or emphasized, in subsequent design and production activities.

House of Quality Example for a Pizza

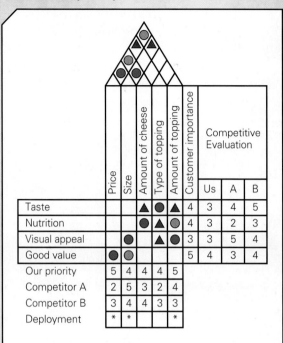

	Price	Size	Amount of cheese	Type of topping	Amount of topping	Customer importance	Us	A	B
Taste			▲	⬤	▲	4	3	4	5
Nutrition			⬤	▲	⬤	4	3	2	3
Visual appeal		⬤		▲	⬤	3	3	5	4
Good value	⬤	⬤				5	4	3	4
Our priority	5	4	4	4	5				
Competitor A	2	5	3	2	4				
Competitor B	3	4	4	3	3				
Deployment	*	*			*				

Columns 7–9 under "Competitive Evaluation."

Legend: 1=low, 5=high
⬤ Very strong relationship
⬤ Strong relationship
▲ Weak relationship

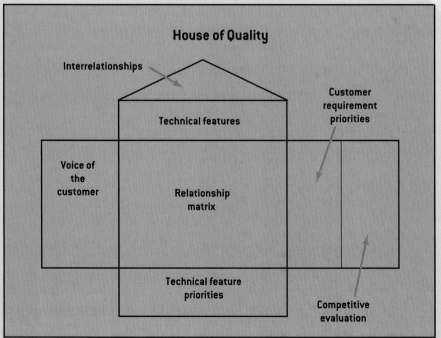

House of Quality

Interrelationships

Technical features

Customer requirement priorities

Voice of the customer

Relationship matrix

Technical feature priorities

Competitive evaluation

Exhibit 6.2
The House of Quality

difficulty in meeting customer needs. Similarly, if a technical feature does not relate to any customer requirement, it may be unnecessary in the design. The roof of the House of Quality shows the interrelationships between any pair of technical features, and these relationships help in answering questions such as "How does a change in one product characteristic affect others?" This can help refine a design and evaluate trade-offs in design decisions.

To the right of the relationship matrix is an assessment of the importance of each customer requirement and how competitors' products compare with the proposed design in terms of meeting the voice of the customer. This helps to identify key "selling points" and features that would help to differentiate the good or service from competitors' products.

The final step (bottom of the House) is to identify those technical features that have the strongest relationships to customer requirements, have poor competitive performance, or will be strong selling points. This helps to prioritize those technical features that should be "deployed," or paid the most attention to during subsequent design and production or service delivery activities. This will ensure that the voice of the customer will be maintained in subsequent detailed design, manufacturing or service, and control activities.

QFD has been used successfully by many companies, such as Mitsubishi, Toyota, Motorola, Xerox, IBM, Procter & Gamble, and AT&T. Toyota, for example, reduced startup costs by over 60 percent and product development time by one-third using QFD.

✇6-3 Designing Manufactured Goods

f or a manufactured good, such as an automobile, computer, or a textbook, design involves determining technical specifications such as dimensions, tolerances, materials, and purchased components; or choice of fonts and page layout for a textbook. This step also requires coordination with operations managers to ensure that manufacturing processes can

produce the design (step 4b of Exhibit 6.1). Many different tools and techniques are used to support product design activities; we review some of the most important ones in this section.

6-3a Tolerance Design and the Taguchi Loss Function

For most manufactured goods, design blueprints specify a target dimension (called the *nominal*), along with a range of permissible variation (called the *tolerance*), for example, 0.500 ± 0.020 cm. The nominal dimension is 0.500 cm, but may vary anywhere in the range from 0.480 to 0.520 cm. This is sometimes called the *goal-post model* (see Exhibit 6.3). Tolerance design involves determining the acceptable tolerance. Narrow tolerances improve product functionality and performance, but tend to raise manufacturing costs because they usually require higher-precision technology. Wide tolerances, on the other hand, reduce costs, but may have a negative impact on product performance. Thus, designers must consider these trade-offs, and should use sound scientific and engineering approaches to optimizing tolerances rather than simply setting them judgmentally.

Genichi Taguchi, a Japanese engineer, maintained that the traditional practice of setting design specifications is inherently flawed. The goal-post model assumes that any value within the tolerance range is acceptable, but those outside are not. In the previous example, what is the real difference between 0.479 and 0.481? Not much; the impact of either value on the performance characteristic of the product would be about the same, yet a part having the dimension of 0.481 would be acceptable while the other would not be. In reality, neither

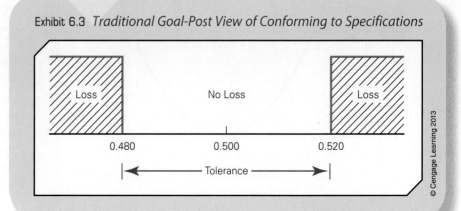

Exhibit 6.3 *Traditional Goal-Post View of Conforming to Specifications*

© Cengage Learning 2013

value is close to the nominal specification. Taguchi argued that the smaller the variation about the nominal specification, the better is the quality. In turn, products are more consistent, would fail less frequently, and thus would be less costly in the long run.

Taguchi measured quality as the variation from the target value of a design specification and then translated that variation into an economic "loss function" that expresses the cost of variation in monetary terms. This approach can be applied to both goods and services.

Taguchi proposed measuring the loss resulting from the deviation from the target by a quadratic function so that larger deviations cause increasingly larger losses. The loss function is

$$L(x) = k(x - T)^2 \qquad [6.1]$$

where

$L(x)$ is the monetary value of the loss associated with deviating from the target, T;

x is the actual value of the dimension; and

k is a constant that translates the deviation into dollars.

Exhibit 6.4 illustrates this Taguchi loss function. The constant, k, is estimated by determining the cost of repair or replacement if a certain deviation from the target occurs. The Solved Problems on pages 117 and 118

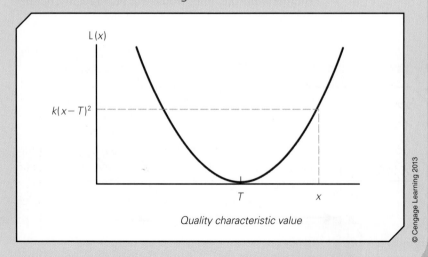

Exhibit 6.4 *Nominal-Is-Best Taguchi Loss Function*

L(x)

$k(x-T)^2$

T   x

Quality characteristic value

© Cengage Learning 2013

Automotive Gremlins

Have you even encountered mysterious noises and rattles in your engine or transmission? While some might attribute such mischievous behavior to gremlins, there is usually an engineering explanation. In transmissions, for example, which consist of many gears and other parts in a "stack-up" assembly, the lack of precision tolerances can lead to problems in performance such as gear clashes upon shifting, and eventually, premature failure. When the parts in the assembly are at the high end of the tolerance range, the stack-up becomes too tight; if they are at the low end of the tolerance range, the stack-up is too loose. In either case, drivers will notice the difference. This is why Taguchi advocated producing parts on the nominal specification with minimal variation.

show an example of the Taguchi loss function and how it can be used to set design tolerances.

6-3b Design for Reliability

Everyone expects their car to start each morning and their computer to work without crashing. **Reliability is the probability that a manufactured good, piece of equipment, or system performs its intended function for a stated period of time under specified operating conditions.** Reliability applies to services as well as manufacturing; a system could be a service process where each stage (work activity or station) is analogous to a component part in a manufactured good.

Reliability is a *probability*, that is, a value between 0 and 1. For example, a reliability of .97 indicates that, on average, 97 out of 100 times the item will perform its function for a given period of time under specified operating conditions. Often, reliability is expressed as a percentage simply to be more descriptive (97 percent reliable). Reliability can be improved by using better components or by adding redundant components. In either case, costs increase; thus, trade-offs must be made.

Many manufactured goods consist of several components that are arranged in series but are assumed to be independent of one another, as illustrated in Exhibit 6.7. If one component or process step fails, the entire system fails. If we know the individual reliability, p_j, for each component, j, we can compute the total reliability

Solved Problem

Cassette tapes are still used in some handheld recording devices and in less expensive portable musical instrument recording devices. The desired speed of a cassette tape is 1.875 inches per second. Any deviation from this value causes a change in pitch and tempo and thus poor sound quality. Suppose that adjusting the tape speed under warranty when a customer complains and returns a device costs a manufacturer $20. Based on past information, the company knows the average customer will return a device if the tape speed is off the target by at least 0.15 inch per second; in other words, when the speed is either 2.025 or 1.725. Find the Taguchi loss function.

Solution

The loss associated with a deviation of $(x - T) = 0.15$ from the target is $L(x) = 20. To find the loss function for any value of x, we substitute these values into Equation 6.1 and solve for k:

$$20 = k(0.15)^2$$
$$k = 888.9$$

and thus the loss function is

$$L(x) = 888.9(x - 1.875)^2$$

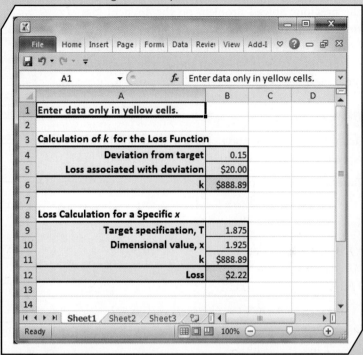

Exhibit 6.5 *Excel Taguchi Template.xlsx-Microsoft Excel*

For example, if the actual speed is 1.925 inches per second, the Taguchi loss function estimates that the economic loss will be $L(1.9) = 888.89(1.925 - 1.875)^2 = 2.22. Some, but not all, customers might perceive poor sound quality for this small of a deviation and return the product for adjustment, so the average loss is smaller. Exhibit 6.5 shows a portion of the Excel Taguchi template that can be used to perform these calculations.

of an n-component series system, R_s. If the individual reliabilities are denoted by $p_1, p_2, \ldots, p_n$ and the system reliability is denoted by R_s, then

$$R_s = (p_1)(p_2)(p_3) \ldots (p_n) \qquad [6.2]$$

Other designs consist of several parallel components that function independently of each other, as illustrated in Exhibit 6.8. The entire system will fail only if all components fail; this is an example of redundancy. The system reliability of an n-component parallel system is computed as

$$R_p = 1 - (1 - p_1)(1 - p_2)(1 - p_3) \ldots (1 - p_n) \qquad [6.3]$$

Many other systems are combinations of series and parallel components. To compute the reliability of such systems, *first* compute the reliability of the parallel components using Equation 6.3 and treat the result as a single series component; *then* use Equation 6.2 to compute the reliability of the resulting series system. These formulas can be used to help designers and engineers assess the reliability of proposed designs and optimize their performance.

Solved Problem

For the previous Solved Problem on the Taguchi loss function, suppose that a technician tests the tape speed prior to packaging and can adjust the speed to the target of 1.875 at a cost of $5. What should the economic specification limits be?

Solution

The accompanying table shows the loss associated with tape speeds from 1.725 to 2.025.

Tape Speed, x	L(x)
1.725	$20.00
1.740	$16.20
1.755	$12.80
1.770	$9.80
1.785	$7.20
1.800	$5.00
1.815	$3.20
1.830	$1.80
1.845	$0.80
1.860	$0.20
1.875	$0
1.890	$0.20
1.905	$0.80
1.920	$1.80
1.935	$3.20
1.950	$5.00
1.965	$7.20
1.980	$9.80
1.995	$12.80
2.010	$16.20
2.025	$20.00

Note that if the tape speed is less than 1.800 or greater than 1.950, the loss incurred by not adjusting the tape is greater than $5. Therefore it is more economical to

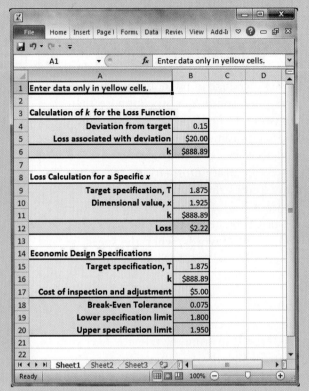

Exhibit 6.6 *Economic Design Specifications Using the Excel Taguchi Spreadsheet Template*

inspect and adjust the tape if the actual speed is outside of these limits. If the speed is greater than 1.800 or less than 1.950 (shown in red), then clearly it costs more to inspect and adjust than to simply ship the unit as is. Therefore, 1.800 and 1.950 represent the economical design specifications that the company should try to achieve. The Excel Taguchi template computes these economic specifications using a break-even analysis approach in rows 15–19, as shown in Exhibit 6.6.

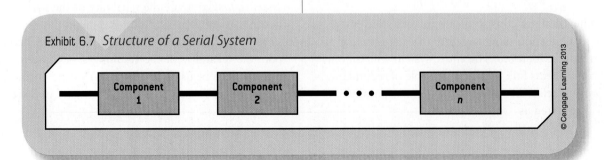

Exhibit 6.7 *Structure of a Serial System*

© Cengage Learning 2013

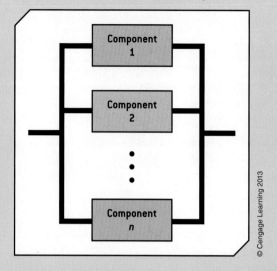

Exhibit 6.8 *Structure of a Parallel System*

© Cengage Learning 2013

6-3c Design for Manufacturability

Many aspects of product design can adversely affect manufacturability and, hence, quality. Some parts may be designed with features difficult to fabricate repeatedly or with unnecessarily tight tolerances.[5] Some parts may lack details for self-alignment or features for correct insertion. In other cases, parts so fragile or so susceptible to corrosion or contamination may be damaged in shipping or by internal handling. Sometimes a design simply has more parts than are needed to perform the desired functions, which increases the chance of assembly error.

Solved Problem

Consider a new laboratory blood analysis machine consisting of three major subassemblies: A, B, and C. The manufacturer is evaluating the preliminary design of this piece of equipment. The reliabilities of each subassembly are shown in Exhibit 6.9.

Exhibit 6.9 *Subassembly Reliabilities*

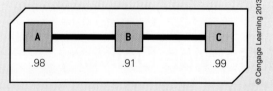

© Cengage Learning 2013

To find the reliability of the proposed product design, we note that this is a series system and use Equation 6.2:

$R_s = (.98)(.91)(.99) = .883$, or 88.3 percent

Now suppose that the original subassembly B (with a reliability of .91) is duplicated, creating a parallel (backup) path as shown in Exhibit 6.10. (Assume equipment software switches to the working subassembly B.) What is the reliability of this configuration? The reliability of the parallel system for subassembly B is $R_p = 1 - (1 - .91)(1 - .91) = 1 - .0081 = .9919$. Now we replace the parallel subsystem with its equivalent series component. We use Equation 6.2 to compute

Exhibit 6.10 *Modified Design*

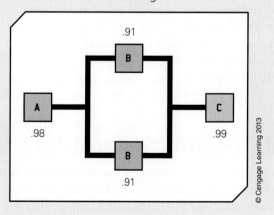

© Cengage Learning 2013

the reliability of the equipment as $R_s = (.98)(.9919)(.99) = .962$, or 96.2 percent. The reliability of the total product increases from 88.3 percent to 96.2 percent for an absolute increase of 7.9 percent.

Design for manufacturability (DFM) is the process of designing a product for efficient production at the highest level of quality.

Product simplification is the process of trying to simplify designs to reduce complexity and costs and thus improve productivity, quality, flexibility, and customer satisfaction.

Design for Environment (DfE) is the explicit consideration of environmental concerns during the design of goods, services, and processes and includes such practices as designing for recycling and disassembly.

Service-delivery system design includes facility location and layout, the servicescape, service process and job design, technology and information support systems, and organizational structure.

Thus, problems of poor design may show up as errors, poor yield, damage, or functional failure in fabrication, assembly, test, transport, and end use. **Design for manufacturability (DFM)** *is the process of designing a product for efficient production at the highest level of quality.* DFM is intended to prevent product designs that simplify assembly operations but require more complex and expensive components, designs that simplify component manufacture while complicating the assembly process, and designs that are simple and inexpensive to produce but difficult or expensive to service or support. One way of doing this is through product simplification.

Product simplification *is the process of trying to simplify designs to reduce complexity and costs and thus improve productivity, quality, flexibility, and customer satisfaction.* The simpler the design, the fewer opportunities for error, the faster the flow time, the better the chance of high process efficiency, and the more reliable the manufactured good or service process. For example, the redesign of the Cadillac Seville rear-bumper assembly reduced the number of parts by half and cut assembly time by 57 percent, to less than 8 minutes, saving the company over $450,000 annually in labor costs.[7] Because many of the eliminated parts were squeak- and rattle-causing fasteners, nuts, bolts, and screws, the change also improved the quality of the car.

6-3d Design for Sustainability

Environmental concerns are placing increased pressure on design. Pressures from environmental groups clamoring for "socially responsive" designs, states and municipalities that are running out of space for landfills, and consumers who want the most for their money have caused designers and managers to look carefully at the concept of Design for Environment.[8] **Design for Environment (DfE)** *is the explicit consideration of environmental concerns during*

PEPSI: FROM PLASTIC- TO PLANT-BASED BOTTLES

Pepsi introduced new soft-drink bottles made entirely from plant material such as switch grass, pine bark, and corn husks instead of oil-based plastic. The new bottles look, feel, and protect the drink inside exactly the same as Pepsi's current bottles. Pepsi is conducting tests of the bottles, and after it can be sure that it can successfully produce them on a large scale, Pepsi will begin to convert all of its products—billions of bottles each year—to the new design. Pepsi noted that the cost to research and design the new bottle was in the millions of dollars.[9]

---

the design of goods, services, and processes and includes such practices as designing for recycling and disassembly. Energy Star dishwashers use advanced technology to get your dishes clean while using less water and energy. For example, a dishwasher built in 1994 uses considerably more water per cycle than today's Energy-Star-certified models, and costs an extra $40 a year in electrical utility bills. In addition, an Energy Star dishwasher results in a reduction of 1,140 pounds of carbon dioxide that is released to the air due to less demand on electrical power and water plants. With millions of dishwashers on the planet, the impact is huge![10] Many products are discarded simply because the cost of maintenance or repair is too high when compared with the cost of a new item. One aspect of designing for sustainability is designing products that can easily be repaired and refurbished or otherwise salvaged for reuse.

6-4 Service-Delivery System Design

As we illustrated in Exhibit 6.1, the design of services revolves around designing the service-delivery system and service encounters. **Service-delivery system design** *includes facility location and layout, the servicescape, service process and job design, technology and information support systems, and organizational structure.*

Integrating all of these elements is necessary to design a service that provides value to customers and can create a competitive advantage. A poor choice on any one of these components, such as technology or job design, can degrade service system efficiency and effectiveness.

6-4a Facility Location and Layout

Location affects a customer's travel time and is an important competitive priority in a service business. Health clinics, rental car firms, post offices, health clubs, branch banks, libraries, hotels, emergency service facilities, retail stores, and many other types of service facilities depend on good location decisions. Starbuck's Coffee shops, for example, are ubiquitous in many cities, airports, and shopping malls. The layout of a facility affects process flow, costs, and customer perception and satisfaction.

6-4b Servicescape

The **servicescape** *is all the physical evidence a customer might use to form an impression.*[11] *The servicescape also provides the behavioral setting where service encounters take place.* People around the world, for example, recognize the servicescape of McDonald's restaurants. The building design ("golden arches"), decorative schemes and colors, playground, menu board, packaging, employee uniforms, drive-through, and so on all support McDonald's competitive priorities of speed, consistency, cleanliness, and customer service. The standardization and integration of the servicescape and service processes enhance efficiency. McDonald's servicescape helps to establish its brand image.

> McDonald's servicescape helps to establish its brand image.

A servicescape has three principal dimensions:[12]

1. *Ambient conditions*—made manifest by sight, sound, smell, touch, and temperature. These are designed into a servicescape to please the five human senses. For example, Starbucks decided to quit serving a warm breakfast in all Starbucks stores because the egg-and-cheese breakfast sandwiches were interfering with the aroma of the coffee in stores.

2. *Spatial layout and functionality*—how furniture, equipment, and office spaces are arranged. This includes building footprints and facades, streets, and

EpicStockMedia/Shutterstock.com

parking lots. A law firm would probably design various conference areas for conversations to take place in a quiet and private setting; a children's hospital would probably include safe and enclosed play areas for kids.

3. *Signs, symbols, and artifacts*—the more explicit signals that communicate an image about a firm. Examples include mission statements and diplomas on a wall, a prominently displayed company logo on company vehicles, a trophy case of awards, letterhead, and company uniforms. Luxury automobile dealers offer free food and soft drinks instead of vending machines.

The **servicescape** is all the physical evidence a customer might use to form an impression. The servicescape also provides the behavioral setting where service encounters take place.

*Some servicescapes, termed **lean servicescape environments,** are very simple.* Ticketron outlets and Federal Express drop-off kiosks would qualify as lean servicescape environments, as both provide service from one simple design. *More complicated designs and service systems are termed **elaborate servicescape environments.*** Examples include hospitals, airports, and universities.[13]

6-4c Service Process and Job Design

Service process design *is the activity of developing an efficient sequence of activities to satisfy both internal and external customer requirements.* Service process designers must concentrate on developing procedures to ensure that things are done right the first time, that interactions between customers and service providers are simple and quick, and that human error is avoided. Fast-food restaurants, for example, have carefully designed their processes for a high degree of accuracy and fast response time.[14] New hands-free intercom systems, better microphones that reduce ambient kitchen noise, and screens that display a customer's order are all focused on these requirements.

In many services, the customer and service provider co-produce the service, which makes service process and job design more uncertain and challenging. For example, customers can slow down or upset service providers and other customers at any time. Therefore, managers need to anticipate potential service upsets—including those caused by customers—and develop appropriate responses, such as providing extra capacity, training service providers on proper behavior, and empowering them to deal with problems when they occur. Superior service management training is critical for excellent service process and job design.

Lean servicescape environments provide service using simple designs (for example, Ticketron outlets or FedEx kiosks).

Elaborate servicescape environments provide service using more complicated designs and service systems (for example, hospitals, airports, and universities).

Service process design is the activity of developing an efficient sequence of activities to satisfy both internal and external customer requirements.

What Is a Service?

A service is not something that is built in a factory, shipped to a store, put on a shelf, and then taken home by a consumer. A service is a dynamic, living process. A service is performed. A service is rendered. The "raw materials" of a service are time and motion; not plastic or steel. A service cannot be stored or shipped; only the means for creating it can. A service cannot be held in one's hand or physically possessed. In short, a service is not a thing.
                                        —G. Lynn Shostack

6-4d Technology and Information Support Systems

Hard and soft technology is an important factor in designing services to ensure speed, accuracy, customization, and flexibility. Nurses, airline flight attendants, bank tellers, police, insurance claims processors, dentists, auto mechanics and service-counter personnel, engineers, hotel room maids, financial portfolio managers, purchasing buyers, and waiters are just a few examples of job designs that are highly dependent on accurate and timely information.

THE SERVICESCAPE IN BOEING'S 787 DREAMLINER CABIN

After many production delays, the new Boeing 787 Dreamliner is coming off the assembly line. The bigger passenger cabin, which was designed by Boeing's state-of-the-art Customer Experience Center, defines a new standard for an airline cabin's "servicescape." The passenger's experience begins when he or she steps into the plane through a tall and open archway with light-blue sky ceilings. Other cabin attributes include larger windows that the passenger can dim rather than tug on a shade, soothing lighting such as full-spectrum LEDs, full office

and leisure electronic capabilities per seat, larger stow bins, and music, game, and movie options. The seats in the 787 can be arranged from six to nine abreast in various configurations. Passengers can customize their service experience(s), and airline management has a great degree of flexibility in alternative cabin designs.

6-4e Organizational Structure

The performance of a service delivery system depends on how work is organized. A pure functional organization generally requires more handoffs between work activities, resulting in increased opportunities for errors and slower processing times. Because no one "owns" the processes, there is usually little incentive to make them efficient and to improve cooperation among business functions.

A process-based organization is vital to a good service design because services are generally interdisciplinary and cross-functional. For example, service upsets and mistakes that occur in the presence of the customer call for immediate responses by the service provider and often require extensive cooperation among various functions in a service process.

6-5 Service-Encounter Design

Service-encounter design *focuses on the interaction, directly or indirectly, between the service provider(s) and the customer.* It is during these points of contact with the customer that perceptions of the firm and its goods and services are created. Service–encounter design and job design are frequently done in iterative improvement cycles.

The principal elements of service-encounter design are

- customer contact behavior and skills;
- service-provider selection, development, and empowerment;
- recognition and reward; and
- service recovery and guarantees.

These elements are necessary to support excellent performance and create customer value and satisfaction.

6-5a Customer-Contact Behavior and Skills

Customer contact *refers to the physical or virtual presence of the customer in the service-delivery system during a service experience.* Customer contact is measured by the percentage of time the customer must be in the system relative to the total time it takes to provide the service. *Systems in which the percentage of customer contact is high are called* **high-contact systems;** *those in which it is low are called* **low-contact systems.**[16,17] Examples of high-contact systems are estate planning and hotel check-in; examples of low-contact systems are construction services and package sorting and distribution.

> **Service-encounter design** focuses on the interaction, directly or indirectly, between the service provider(s) and the customer.
>
> **Customer contact** refers to the physical or virtual presence of the customer in the service-delivery system during a service experience.
>
> Systems in which the percentage of customer contact is high are called **high-contact systems;** those in which it is low are called **low-contact systems.**

Where Are My Clothes?

A dry-cleaning service in Naples, Florida, is the first U.S. dry cleaner and the second in the world to have three conveyor belts with radio frequency identification devices (RFIDs) for tracking customer garments. The company has invested more than $400,000 in computers, software, and other technology, including chips that track garments every step of the way so they're rarely lost. The chips are colored-coded and removed once the garment is cleaned. In this state-of-the-art facility, shirts, dresses, and pants whiz past dry-cleaning workstations where RFID technology helps sort and route garments. Employees no longer have to worry about reading and matching up numbers on safety pin tags and carrying clothing all around the production facility. Customer clothes are much less likely to get mixed in with those of another customer. The owner says, "The equipment is on its way to paying for itself!"[5]

Many low-contact systems, such as processing an insurance policy in the backroom, can be treated much like an assembly line, whereas service-delivery systems with high customer contact are more difficult to design and control. One of the reasons for this is the variation and uncertainty that people (customers) introduce into high-contact service processes. For example, the time it takes to check a customer into a hotel can be affected by special requests (for example, a king bed or handicapped-accessible room) and questions that customers might ask the desk clerk. Low-customer-contact systems are essentially free of this type of customer-induced uncertainty, and therefore are capable of operating at higher levels of operating efficiency. High-customer-contact areas of the organization are sometimes described as the "front room or front office" and low-customer-contact areas as "back room or back office."

Customer-contact requirements *are measurable performance levels or expectations that define the quality of customer contact with representatives of an organization.* These might include such technical requirements as response time (answering the telephone within two rings), service management skills such as cross-selling other services, and/or behavioral requirements (using a customer's name whenever possible). Walt Disney Company, highly recognized for extraordinary customer service, clearly defines expected behaviors in its guidelines for guest service, which include making eye contact and smiling, greeting and welcoming every guest, seeking out guests who may need assistance, providing immediate service recovery, displaying approachable body language, focusing on the positive rather than rules and regulations, and thanking each and every guest.[18]

L.L. Bean: Service Guarantee

In 1916, Mr. L.L. Bean placed the following notice on the wall of his store—"I do not consider a sale complete until goods are worn out and customers still satisfied." Today, L.L. Bean's explicit service guarantee is "Our products are guaranteed to give 100% satisfaction in every way. Return anything purchased from us at any time if it proves otherwise. We do not want you to have anything from L.L. Bean that is not completely satisfactory." L.L. Bean continues by saying, "From kayaks to slippers, fly rods to sweaters, everything we sell at L.L. Bean is backed by the same rock solid guarantee of satisfaction. It's been that way since our founder sold his very first pair of Bean Boots in 1912. Whether you purchased your item on llbean.com, by mail, by phone or at one of our stores, visit any L.L. Bean retail store for fast and friendly service." L.L. Bean's Web site and call center give detailed instructions on returns and exchanges, including free shipping in some situations. L.L. Bean makes it as easy as possible for customers to invoke the service guarantee.[19]

6-5b Service-Provider Selection, Development, and Empowerment

Companies must carefully select customer-contact employees, train them well, and empower them to meet and exceed customer expectations. Many companies begin with the recruiting process, selecting those employees who show the ability and desire to develop good customer relationships. Major companies such as Procter & Gamble seek people with excellent interpersonal and communication skills, strong problem-solving and analytical skills, assertiveness, stress tolerance, patience and empathy, accuracy and attention to detail, and computer literacy.

Empowerment *simply means giving people authority to make decisions based on what they feel is right, to have control over their work, to take risks and learn from mistakes, and to promote change.* At The Ritz-Carlton Hotel Company, no matter what their normal duties are, employees must assist a fellow service provider who is responding to a guest's complaint or wish if such assistance is requested. Ritz-Carlton employees can spend up to $2,000 to resolve complaints with no questions asked. However, the actions of empowered employees should be guided by a common vision. That is, employees require a consistent understanding of what actions they may or should take.

Customer-contact requirements are measurable performance levels or expectations that define the quality of customer contact with representatives of an organization.

Empowerment simply means giving people authority to make decisions based on what they feel is right, to have control over their work, to take risks and learn from mistakes, and to promote change.

6-5c Recognition and Reward

After a firm hires, trains, and empowers good service providers, the next challenge is how to motivate and keep them. Research has identified key motivational factors to be recognition, advancement, achievement, and the nature of the work itself. A good compensation system can help to attract, retain, and motivate employees. Other forms of recognition, such as formal and informal employee and team recognition, preferred parking spots, free trips and extra vacation days, discounts and gift certificates, and a simple "thank you" from supervisors, are vital to achieving a high-performance workplace.

6-5d Service Guarantees and Recovery

Despite all efforts to satisfy customers, every business experiences unhappy customers. *A service upset is any problem a customer has—real or perceived—with the service-delivery system and includes terms such as service failure, error, defect, mistake, and crisis.* Service upsets can adversely affect business if not dealt with effectively.

A service guarantee is a promise to reward and compensate a customer if a service upset occurs during the service experience. Many organizations, for example, Federal Express and Disney, have well-publicized service guarantees to gain competitive advantage. An *explicit service guarantee* is in writing and included in service provider publications and advertisements. Taco Bell and Hampton Inns use explicit service guarantees to differentiate themselves from competitors. *Implicit guarantees* are not in writing but are implied in everything the service provider does. Premium service providers such as The Ritz Carlton Hotel Company and many engineering, consulting, and medical organizations use implicit service guarantees. Objectives of service guarantees include setting customer expectations prior to experiencing the service, setting employee performance expectations, reducing customer risk, allowing premium pricing, forcing operational improvement, building customer loyalty and

RESERVED PARKING Employee of the Month

Robert J. Beyers II/Shutterstock.com

brand image, and increasing sales and revenue.[20]

Service guarantees are carefully designed and offered prior to the customer experiencing the service. A good service guarantee includes determining what services to include, procedures for the customer and service provider to invoke the guarantee, and the best economic payout amount. Clearly, the best a firm can hope for is never to have to invoke a service guarantee; thus, the firm must design its processes and operational capability to minimize service upsets.

Nevertheless, service upsets occasionally occur. When this happens, companies need to recover the customer's trust and confidence. *Service recovery is the process of correcting a service upset and satisfying the customer.* Service recovery should begin immediately after a service upset occurs and when the customer is visibly upset; the longer customers wait, the angrier they might get. Service-recovery processes should be clearly documented, and employees should be trained and empowered to use them whenever necessary. Service providers need to listen carefully to determine the customer's feelings and then respond sympathetically, ensuring that the issue is understood. Then they should make every effort to resolve the problem quickly, provide a simple apology, and may offer compensation, such as free meals or discount coupons.

> A **service upset** is any problem a customer has—real or perceived—with the service-delivery system and includes terms such as *service failure, error, defect, mistake,* and *crisis.*
>
> A **service guarantee** is a promise to reward and compensate a customer if a service upset occurs during the service experience.
>
> **Service recovery** is the process of correcting a service upset and satisfying the customer.

Companies must carefully select customer-contact employees, train them well, and empower them to meet and exceed customer expectations.

◎6-6 An Integrative Case Study of LensCrafters

t o illustrate how goods and services are designed in an integrated fashion, we will study LensCrafters—a well-known provider of eyeglasses produced "in about an hour." We use the framework for goods and service design shown in Exhibit 6.1.

Steps 1 and 2—Strategic Mission, Market Analysis, and Competitive Priorities

LensCrafters (www.lenscrafters.com) is an optical chain of about 860 special service shops with on-site eyeglass production capabilities in the United States, Canada, and Puerto Rico. All resources necessary to create and deliver "one-stop-shopping" and eyeglasses "in about an hour" are available in each store.

LensCrafters' mission statement is focused on being the best by

- creating customers for life by delivering legendary customer service,
- developing and energizing associates and leaders in the world's best work place,
- crafting perfect-quality eyewear in about an hour, and
- delivering superior overall value to meet each customer's individual needs.[21]

Step 3—Customer Benefit Package Design and Configuration

Our perception of the LensCrafters customer benefit package is the integrated set of goods and services depicted in Exhibit 6.11. The primary good (eyewear) and the primary service (accurate eye exam and one-hour service) are of equal importance. Peripheral goods and

GWImages/Shutterstock.com

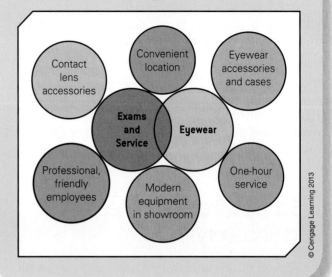

Exhibit 6.11 *One Example View of LensCrafters' Customer Benefit Package*

© Cengage Learning 2013

services encircle the primary ones to create "a total LensCrafters' experience."

Steps 4a and b—Manufactured Good Design and Process Selection

The manufacturing process is integrated into the service facility to provide rapid order response, yet not sacrifice quality. In this industry, it is unusual for customers to watch their eyeglasses being made and this "service experience" is viewed as adding value. The equipment used in the labs is the most technologically advanced equipment in the industry. The eyewear is manufactured to specifications in a clean, modern, and professionally run facility.

Other issues that LensCrafters would need to consider in designing its manufacturing processes are the following:

- How are eyeglass lenses and frames ordered? Are these materials ordered by individual stores or consolidated by region/district? How can the high quality of eyewear be ensured? What new materials are available?
- What items should be stored at the region/district warehouse and stores? What type of purchasing and inventory control systems should be used? How should supplier performance be evaluated?
- What eyewear-making equipment should be used? What is the latest technology? Which equipment is most flexible? Should the equipment be purchased or leased? How should it be maintained and by whom?
- What is the most efficient production procedure to make the goods and meet time schedules? Where should quality be checked in the manufacturing process?

Step 4c—Service-Delivery System Design

The service-delivery system, as evidenced by the location and layout, servicescape, service processes, job designs, technology, and organizational structure, is combined into an integrated service-delivery system. LensCrafters' stores are located in high-traffic areas such as shopping centers and malls within 5 to 10 miles of the target market.

A typical store layout is shown in Exhibit 6.12. The servicescape is designed to convey an impression of quality and professionalism. The store is spacious, open, clean, carpeted, with professional merchandise display areas, modern furniture in the retail area, and modern equipment in the laboratory, technicians in white lab coats, shiny machines in the lab, and bright lights throughout. The store display cases, eye examination areas, and fitting stations are in the high-contact area where customers and service providers interact frequently. Optometry degrees, certifications, and licenses hanging on the wall provide physical evidence of employees' abilities.

A greeter directs each customer to the appropriate service area as he or she enters the store. The low contact area of a LensCrafters store—the optical laboratory—is separated from the retail area by large glass panels. The optical laboratory becomes a "showroom" where the customer's perception of the total delivery process is established.

The store is a service factory. The typical service process begins when a customer makes an appointment with an optician and continues until the eyeglasses are received and paid for. Between these two events, the customer travels to the store, parks, receives a greeting from store employees, obtains an eye examination, selects frames, is measured for proper eyeglasses and frame fit, watches the eyeglasses being made in the laboratory, and receives a final fitting to make sure all is well. Information flow in the forms of prescriptions, bills, and receipts complements the physical flows of people and eyewear.

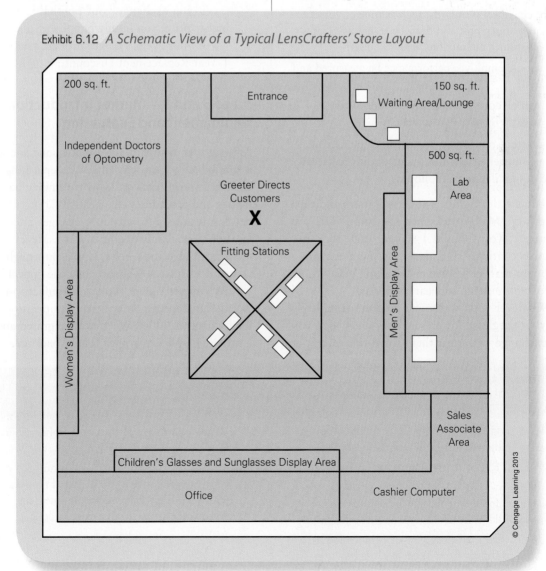

Exhibit 6.12 *A Schematic View of a Typical LensCrafters' Store Layout*

Step 4d—Service Encounter Design

Each job at LensCrafters—sales associate, lab technician, and doctor of optometry—requires both technical skills and service management skills. Associates are well trained, friendly, and knowledgeable about their jobs. The lab technicians are certified in all work tasks and processes. Many associates are cross-trained.

At the service-encounter level, key issues that managers need to consider include the following:

- What human resource management processes and systems will ensure hiring the right people, training them properly, and motivating them to provide excellent service? What recognitions and rewards should be provided?

- How are associates trained to handle service upsets and service recovery?

- What standards should be set for grooming and appearance?

- What behavioral standards, such as tone of voice, physical mannerisms, and the words that associates use in customer interactions, should be set?

- How should employee performance be measured and evaluated?

- What can be done to make the one-hour wait a positive experience for customers?

LensCrafters reinforces its customer benefit package with a comprehensive 30-day unconditional service guarantee design defined as follows:

You buy a pair of glasses at LensCrafters and then you think, "Maybe red's not my color." Or, you question, "Wow, should I have gotten the anti-reflective coating?" Or after wearing them for a while you realize, "These really aren't going to be comfortable enough to wear every day."

Whatever your reason, if you don't completely love your eyeglasses or prescription sunglasses, you can exchange or return them for a full refund at LensCrafters—no excuses, no explanations. That's what our 30-Day Unconditional Guarantee is all about—giving you peace of mind with every pair.

So how does it work? Simple. Just return your eyeglasses—in their original condition—to LensCrafters within 30 days. We'll exchange them for a new pair or refund your money. Why do we do it? Because LensCrafters stands behind each and every pair of our glasses. And we want to make sure you simply love them.

What does "Unconditional" really mean? The 30 days begins on the date you actually receive your eyeglasses.

You can return or exchange your new eyewear as many times as needed within the 30-day time period. However, the 30 days does not start over with each return or exchange.

If you exchange your purchase for a pair at a lower price, we'll refund the price difference.

If you exchange your purchase for a pair at a higher price, you'll only pay the price difference.

If your eyeglasses get broken, you can use our 1-Year Replacement Discount.[22]

Steps 5 and 6—Market Introduction/ Deployment and Evaluation

Although the company has been around for some time, it undoubtedly faces challenges in replicating its design concept in new locations. On a continuing basis, as technology and procedures change, LensCrafters will have to develop processes to introduce changes into all existing locations to maintain operational consistency and achieve its strategic objectives. For example, how might it react as competitors such as Walmart enter the optical industry?

As you see, LensCrafters, manufacturing and service design depends on a variety of operations management concepts, all of which are integrated and support a rather complex customer benefit package.

Discussion Questions

1. How might today's technology, such as the Internet, be used to understand the voice of the customer?

2. What lessons can be learned from the LaRosa's Pizzeria boxed example?

3. In building a House of Quality, what departments or functions should be involved in each step of the process?

4. Explain how the goal-post view of conforming to specifications differs from Taguchi's loss function. Would you rather buy an automobile where suppliers used the goal-post or Taguchi models? Why?

5. Propose an explicit service guarantee for an airline. Clearly explain why you included the features of your service guarantee (maximum of one page). Do you think that an airline would adopt it? Why or why not?

Problems and Activities

Note: an asterisk denotes problems for which an Excel spreadsheet template in the Premium Online Content may be used.

1. Build a House of Quality (showing only the voice of the customer, technical features, interrelationships, and relationship matrix from Exhibit 6.2) for designing and producing chocolate chip cookies. The voice of the customer consists of:

   a. Soft
   b. Fresh
   c. Bittersweet
   d. Not burned
   e. Large size
   f. Moderate price
   g. Lots of chocolate

   The technical features identified are:

   a. Baking temperature
   b. Baking time
   c. Type of chocolate
   d. Proportion of chocolate
   e. Size
   f. Shape
   g. Thickness
   h. Batch size
   i. Amount of preservatives

   Clearly explain your reasoning for your ratings of the interrelationships and relationship matrix. Can you think of other technical features that should be included to better address the voice of the customer?

2.* Suppose that the specifications for a part (in inches) are 6.00 ± 0.05, and that the Taguchi loss function is estimated to be $L(x) = 6,500 (x - T)^2$. Determine the economic loss if $x = 6.07$ inches.

3.* A quality characteristic has a design specification (in cm.) of 0.200 ± 0.020. If the actual process value of the quality characteristic exceeds the target by 0.020 on either side, the product will require a repair of $50. Find the value of k and state the Taguchi loss function. What is the economic loss associated with $x = 0.015$?

4.* For the situation in problem 3, what are the economic design specifications if the cost of inspection and adjustment is $7.50?

5.* Suppose that the design specifications for a hydraulic cylinder are 10.00 ± 0.10 centimeters, and that

the Taguchi loss function is estimated to be $L(x) = 2,400 (x - T)^2$.

   a. Determine the estimated loss for a production order if the quality characteristic under study takes on a value of 10.04 and 100 parts are produced.

   b. Assume the production process is recalibrated weekly and a new sample of cylinders after recalibration reveals an x-bar of 9.789. What action, if any, is need in this situation? Explain.

6. The service center for a brokerage company provides three functions to callers: account status, order confirmations, and stock quotes. The reliability was measured for each of these services over one month with these results: 90 percent, 70 percent and 80 percent, respectively. What is the overall reliability of the call center?

7. Two cooling fans are installed in some laptop computers. Suppose the reliability of each cooling fan is 0.99. What percent improvement in reliability does adding the second fan provide?

8. Given the following diagram, determine the total system reliability if the individual component reliabilities are: A = 0.98, B = 0.92, and C = 0.85. (Hint: Use Equations 6.2 and 6.3 and note that the reliabilities of the parallel components are different.)

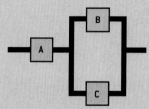

9. A simple electronic assembly consists of two components in a series configuration with reliabilities as shown in the figure below.

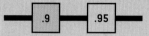

Engineers would like to increase the reliability by adding additional components in one of the two proposed designs shown in the figure on the next page (notice the difference in the diagram design with respect to being in series and parallel):

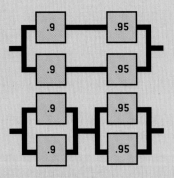

a. Find the reliability of the original design.

b. Explain how the configurations of the proposed designs differ.

c. Which proposed design has the best reliability?

10. Research and write a short paper (maximum two typed pages) illustrating an example of how a company applies concepts of Design for Environment (DfE).

11. Choose a servicescape for a business with which you are familiar and list key physical attributes of the servicescape using the three subdimensions, and discuss their impact on customer service and value. Explain how the servicescape establishes the behavioral setting for your example.

12. Select a service at your school, such as financial aid, bookstore, curriculum advising, and so on. Propose a redesign of this service and its service-delivery system. First, baseline the current service and system, and then suggest how to redesign and improve it. Make use of chapter ideas as best you can.

13. Identify a job in an organization and describe how the four elements of service-encounter design are designed and managed for this job. (The job you select could be in a professional organization such as a dentist or tax advisor, or in a routine service organization such as a hotel check-in desk clerk or airline flight attendant.)

14. When Walt Disney created the Disney empire in the 1950s, he forbid its star characters such as Mickey Mouse and Pluto to talk. Mr. Disney thought it would be too difficult to control the service encounters between customers and Disney characters, and it would ruin the "magic" of Disney. Therefore, Disney characters were trained to gesture and use only their body language to interact and entertain guests. Today, Disney is experimenting with talking characters. What are some advantages and disadvantages of talking Disney characters from a service design perspective? Research the current status of this Disney design decision and include a brief summary in your write-up (no more than two typed pages).

15. Identify a service-provider job and associated service encounters and design and write a job description for it. (Consider desired customer-contact skills and behaviors, education and training requirements, empowerment capabilities, hiring criteria, and so on.)

Tom's Auto Service Case Study

Tom's Auto Service (TAS) is a regional quick-service vehicle oil-change and lubricant-change service somewhat similar to Jiffy Lube and Tuffy Tire & Auto Service. TAS seeks to differentiate its 32 stores from competition by focusing on peripheral goods and services, the servicescape, and customer-friendly employees. The primary customer benefit package consists of friendly and professional employees who regularly interact with customers providing oil, oil filters, air filters, tires, windshield wiper blades, and lubricants. Automotive associations also certify TAS mechanical and technical personnel, and their certificates are displayed in the customer waiting room. All technical work is guaranteed for 90 days. Employees are carefully interviewed for employment, and background checks are done on technical skills and criminal history. Video on-the-job-training is required of all new hires. All employees are trained to operate the store cash register and payment software. Store managers are responsible for the overall store operations and the customer waiting lounge.

Many other peripheral goods and services define TAS's customer benefit package. For example, the customer waiting rooms include several blends of fresh coffee and tea, sodas, current magazines, Wi-Fi, and a high-definition television.

The customer waiting area is larger and more comfortable at Tom's Auto Service than at most of their competitors.

Customers receive vehicle maintenance brochures and discount coupons for their next visit. TAS also offers other services, such as cleaning the vehicle's windows outside and inside, vacuuming carpets, reviewing service history with the customer, and explaining the technical aspects of vehicle service if the customer asks or if a potential safety or mechanical problem is discovered.

The facility layout consists of four service bays, with a pit below three of the bays for draining and changing oil and lubricants. All necessary tools and equipment are provided for each bay. The customer waiting area is carpeted and larger than those of competitors, with comfortable sofas and chairs. A large glass window in the waiting area allows customers to see their vehicles being serviced in any of the bays. Employees are professionally dressed in clean blue uniforms paid for by TAS with their first names embroidered on them. To maintain a professional appearance, employees are required to wash their arms and hands after each service job.

A vehicle checklist is used to ensure completeness of the work and as a means of quality control. The standard time to complete a routine job is 18 minutes in the bay area, plus 9 minutes for customer check-in and checkout. Other work, such as changing tires, takes longer. Store managers and assistant managers are trained and empowered to approve free service if the customer is dissatisfied for any reason.

TAS surveys customers regularly as a way of understanding customer satisfaction. Results from 206 customer surveys are summarized in Exhibit 6.13. Samples of good and bad written customer comments are shown in Exhibit 6.14. These results are over the past three months for nine randomly selected stores. Store managers never know when their store may be in the corporate survey results. The corporate vice presidents of marketing, human

Exhibit 6.13 *TAS Customer Quarterly Example Survey Results* (n = 206)

Survey Questions	Average Score on 1 (worst) to 5 (best) Scale
Store Managers	
1. Store managers monitor my vehicle's maintenance and repair very well.	4.36
2. Store managers understand my individual wants and needs.	3.87
3. Store managers always go over the vehicle check sheet with me prior to paying the bill.	4.40
Standards of Performance	
4. Cleaning the vehicle windows and vacuuming are extra services that I like.	4.66
5. Knowing the vehicle history makes me feel secure that I am doing the right thing in terms of vehicle maintenance and repair.	4.43
6. My vehicle was fixed correctly (i.e., technically competent).	4.83
7. Standards of performance at TAS are clearly visible inside the store, such as employee certifications and good equipment.	4.54
8. Standards of performance at TAS are clearly advertised in the media and help me understand what to expect during vehicle service.	4.68
Employees	
9. TAS employees are really good at what they do.	4.06
10. Service personnel are polite, friendly, and clearly explain technical details if I ask.	4.01
11. When problems come up, the mechanics are always helpful in correcting and explaining the issue/problem.	3.88
Facility	
12. The facility is clean and well maintained.	4.84
13. The customer waiting area is really nice and why I come here.	4.79
Overall Experience	
14. The total time I spent in TAS was as expected.	4.59
15. My service experience during each repeat visit is of consistent high quality and meets my expectations.	3.94
16. TAS is clearly better than competitors.	4.45

Exhibit 6.14 *Five Good and Five Bad Sample TAS Customer Written Comments*

1. I come to TAS because of the outstanding vehicle technical knowledge and skills of the employees.
2. Believe it or not, I really like the coffee and enjoy reading the magazines in the waiting area.
3. The mechanics are very careful and conscientious when working on my car.
4. When I complained that there were streaks on my windows, they redid my windows and gave me a discount coupon for my next visit—real nice people.
5. Very fast and convenient service—I'll be back.
6. Store managers are super but the mechanics don't like to talk to us customers.
7. I won't come back; a mechanic kept staring at me!
8. I felt pressured to buy the air and fuel filters but they looked clean to me.
9. All the mechanics seem hurried while I was there.
10. The mechanic got grease on my fender and when I ask him to please clean it off, he shrugged and wiped it off with a cleaner.

resource management, and operations were asked to analyze these data to determine what actions might be necessary to reward or improve performance.

The VP of operations, David Margate, decided to analyze this information. A final report to the CEO was due in two weeks. To assist Mr. Margate, answer the following questions.

Case Discussion Questions

1. Define and draw the customer benefit package and state TAS's mission, strategy, and rank order of competitive priorities.

2. Identify and briefly describe the "design" features of the (a) service-delivery system and (b) service encounters.

3. Identify and briefly describe five processes TAS stores use and their relative importance.

4. Given your analysis of the survey data, what opportunities for improvement, if any, do you recommend?

5. Summarize you final recommendation to the CEO.

WHY CHOOSE?

Every 4LTR Press solution comes complete with a visually engaging textbook in addition to an interactive eBook. Go to CourseMate for **OM4** to begin using the eBook. Access at **www.cengagebrain.com**

Complete the Speak Up survey in CourseMate at **www.cengagebrain.com**

 Follow us at **www.facebook.com/4ltrpress**

PROCESS SELECTION, DESIGN, AND ANALYSIS

apanese automakers such as Toyota and Honda have used flexible manufacturing for decades. Some production lines can build six different models. Until recently, American factories were designed to produce only one. This is changing, as Ford retooled an inflexible sport utility vehicle (SUV) factory in Wayne, Michigan, to become an environmentally friendly workplace with flexible manufacturing capability. The factory will be the first facility in the world capable of building a wide range of vehicles—gas-powered, electric, hybrid, and plug-in hybrid—all on the same production line. This allows rapid change to different models as consumer wants and needs change.

To accomplish this, Ford's manufacturing team had to redesign and program most of the 696 robots to weld a variety of parts, and get them to move in additional directions, recognize panels for different vehicles, grasp each at the right points, and know exactly how to weld them. Vehicles on the line ride on "skillets" that automatically raise and lower to the ideal height

learning outcomes

After studying this chapter you should be able to:

7-1   **Describe the four types of processes used to produce goods and services.**

7-2   **Explain the logic and use of the product-process matrix.**

7-3   **Explain the logic and use of the service-positioning matrix.**

7-4   **Describe how to apply process and value stream mapping for process design.**

7-5   **Explain how to improve process designs and analyze process maps.**

7-6   **Describe how to compute resource utilization and apply Little's Law.**

What do you think?

Describe a situation that you have encountered in which a process was either well designed and enhanced your customer experience, or poorly designed and resulted in dissatisfaction.

Monkey Business Images/Shutterstock.com

at each station for the task and model. The factory's integrated stamping facility allows the stamping and welding of all large sheet metal parts on-site, and also employs an efficient, synchronous material flow in which parts and other components move in kits to each operator, providing employees with the tools they need in the sequence they will need them.

The factory is not only flexible, but environmentally friendly. The factory runs on a blend of renewable and conventional electricity. For example, it has 10 electric vehicle charging stations that recharge electric switcher trucks that transport parts between adjacent facilities, and the factory recycles everything from packing materials to water bottles.[1]

Process design is an important operational decision that affects the cost of operations, customer service, and sustainability.

Choosing appropriate processes and designing them to work effectively with each other is vital for an effective and efficient value chain and cannot be taken lightly. As the introductory example suggests, process design is an important operational decision that affects the cost of operations, customer service, and sustainability. Companies are just beginning to consider the environmental impact of their processes and those of their customers.

One example of a company that is doing this is Alfa Laval, a Swedish company that operates 27 factories and 70 service centers, and provides goods and services to the energy, food, refrigeration and cooling, water, and pharmaceutical industries in over 100 countries. Alfa Laval's corporate mission is "to optimize the performance of their customer's processes. Time and time again." For Alfa Laval, customer service is a total concept that covers everything from supplying the smallest spare part to being a lifetime performance partner.

Carbon dioxide emissions from transporting Alfa Laval's products accounted for approximately 2 percent of its total emissions. Its Global Transport Department

▼ *This factory is the first facillity in the world capable of building a wide range of vehicles—gas-powered, electric, hybrid, and plug-in hybrid—on the same production line.*

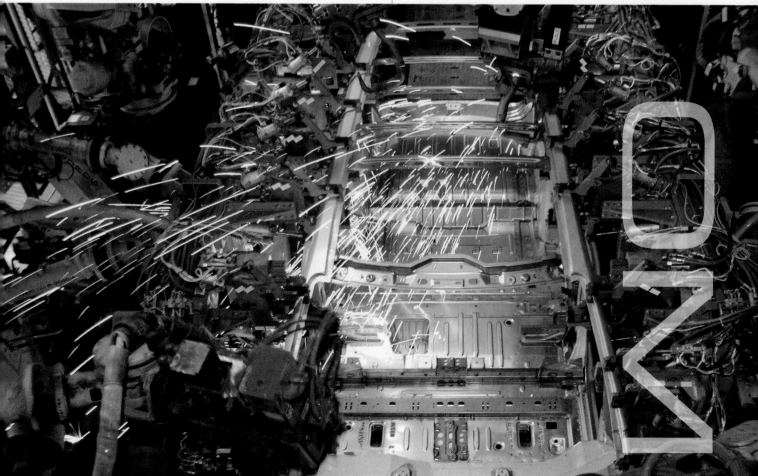

analyzed over 100,000 transactions to identify opportunities to reduce emissions by shifting from airfreight to surface (mainly ocean) transportation. The advantage of airfreight had been that the inventory levels could be minimized and a fast response to changing customer needs could be assured. However, a thorough cost-benefit analysis confirmed that increased inventory costs using surface shipping were more than outweighed by the carbon dioxide reduction and freight cost savings. The move from air to surface shipping meant redesigning and switching the ordering process for 32,000 order lines per year.

Switching to sea freight required an inventory buildup at distribution centers to ensure that delivery performance to end customers would not suffer, along with major changes to Alfa Laval's processes. A project team consisting of customer service employees, shipping and purchasing specialists, warehouse managers, controllers, IT personnel, the Global Transport

s_oleg/Shutterstock.com

Department, and external shipping forwarders combined efforts to manage the redesign. The process changes resulted in a reduction of approximately 12 percent in inventory, carbon dioxide emissions, and similar freight shipping savings.[2]

Solved Problem

Clear Water Pool Service (CWPS) provides the maintenance for over 7,000 pools in southwest Florida. In 2010, CWPS purchased vehicle routing and scheduling software and a GPS truck locator system. Before the use of the "smart system," CWPS's vans and trucks drove 1.26 million miles to service these pools on monthly and weekly appointment schedules. After one year of using the "smart system," CWPS reduced total miles driven to 1.03 million miles by using better vehicle routes from site to site, and using fewer vehicles. CWPS's vehicles average 20 miles per gallon. Unleaded gasoline has 8.91 kg (19.643 lbs) of carbon dioxide (CO_2) per gallon, and 1 metric ton equals 1,000 kilograms (kg), according to government sources.

a. Find the number of gallons of gasoline saved annually.

b. How many metric tons of CO_2 did not go into the earth's atmosphere because of CWPS using smart vehicle scheduling and locator technology?

Solution

a. By dividing number of miles saved by miles per gallon, we get the number of gallons of gasoline saved annually:

(1,260,000 − 1,030,000 miles/year)/(20 miles per gallon) = 11,500 gallons saved/year.

b. By multiplying the number of gallons saved/year by 8.91 and dividing by 1,000, we get metric tons of CO_2 released into the atmosphere:

(11,500 gallons saved/year)(8.91 kg of CO_2 per gallon)/1,000 kg CO_2 per metric ton = 102.5 metric tons of CO_2 not released into the atmosphere due to better vehicle routing and scheduling.

7-1 Process Choice Decisions

firms generally produce either in response to customer orders and demand or in anticipation of them. This leads to three major types of goods and services: custom, option-oriented, and standard.[3] **Custom**, *or* **make-to-order, goods and services** *are generally produced and delivered as one-of-a-kind or in small quantities, and are designed to meet specific customers' specifications.* Examples include ships, Internet sites, weddings, taxi service, estate plans, buildings, and surgery. Because custom goods and services are produced on demand, the customer must wait for them, often for a long time because the good or service must be designed, created, and delivered.

Option, *or* **assemble-to-order, goods and services** *are configurations of standard parts, subassemblies, or services that can be selected by customers from a limited set.* Common examples are Dell computers, Subway sandwiches, machine tools, and travel agent services. Although the customer chooses how the good or service is configured, any unique technical specifications or requirements cannot generally be accommodated.

Standard, *or* **make-to-stock, goods and services** *are made according to a fixed design, and the customer has no options from which to choose.* Appliances, shoes, sporting goods, credit cards, on-line Web-based courses, and bus service are some examples. Standard goods are made in anticipation of customer demand and stocked in inventory and therefore are usually available, although in some cases the proper color or size might be out of stock.

We note that manufacturing systems often use the terms *make-to-order, assemble-to-order,* and *make-to-stock* to describe the types of systems used to manufacture goods. The terminology is not as standardized in service industries, although the concepts are similar.

Four principal types of processes are used to produce goods and services:

1. projects
2. job shop processes
3. flow shop processes
4. continuous flow processes

Projects *are large-scale, customized initiatives that consist of many smaller tasks and activities that must be coordinated and completed to finish on time and within budget.* Some examples of projects are legal defense preparation, construction, and software development. Projects are often used for custom goods and services, and occasionally for standardized products, such as "market homes" that are built from a standard design.

Job shop processes *are organized around particular types of general-purpose equipment that are flexible and capable of customizing work for individual customers.* Job shops produce a wide variety of goods and services, often in small quantities. Thus they are often used for custom or option type products. In job shops, customer orders are generally processed in batches, and different orders may require a different sequence of processing steps and movement to different work areas.

Flow shop processes *are organized around a fixed sequence of activities and process steps, such as an assembly line, to produce a limited variety of similar goods or services.* An assembly line is a common example of a flow shop process. Many large-volume option-oriented and standard goods and services are produced in flow shop settings. Some common examples are automobiles, appliances, insurance policies, checking account statements, and hospital laboratory work. Flow shops tend to use highly productive, specialized equipment and computer software.

Continuous flow processes *create highly standardized goods or services, usually around the clock in very high volumes.* Examples of continuous flow processes are automated car washes, paper and steel mills, paint

---

Custom, or **make-to-order, goods and services** are generally produced and delivered as one-of-a-kind or in small quantities, and are designed to meet specific customers' specifications.

Option, or **assemble-to-order, goods and services** are configurations of standard parts, subassemblies, or services that can be selected by customers from a limited set.

Standard, or **make-to-stock, goods and services** are made according to a fixed design, and the customer has no options from which to choose.

Projects are large-scale, customized initiatives that consist of many smaller tasks and activities that must be coordinated and completed to finish on time and within budget.

Job shop processes are organized around particular types of general-purpose equipment that are flexible and capable of customizing work for individual customers.

Flow shop processes are organized around a fixed sequence of activities and process steps, such as an assembly line, to produce a limited variety of similar goods or services.

Continuous flow processes create highly standardized goods or services, usually around the clock in very high volumes.

So You Want a Bicycle!

Most major bicycle manufacturers—including Taiwan-based Giant, the world's largest bike maker, and Specialized Bicycles—are offering some form of "limited edition" or personalized model bikes that are produced in limited quantities, have frames signed by famous designers, come with custom paint jobs, or fit your body. The custom strategy is the latest attempt by bike makers to extract more dollars from a shrinking pool of riders. Still, bike makers were able to keep sales and profits up by adopting this limited-edition strategy. These bikes are made in small batches and are priced as high as $10,000 each. What type of process is needed to make these custom bicycles?[4]

Tatuasha/Shutterstock.com

factories, and many electronic information-intensive services such as credit card authorizations and security systems. The sequence of work tasks is very rigid and the processes use highly specialized and automated equipment that is often controlled by computers with minimal human oversight.

Exhibit 7.1 summarizes these different process types and their characteristics.

Exhibit 7.1 *Characteristics of Different Process Types*

Type of Process	Characteristics	Goods and Services Examples	Type of Product
PROJECT	One-of-a-kind	Space shuttle, cruise ships, small business tax service, consulting	
	Large scale, complex	Dams, bridges, skyscrapers	
	Resources brought to the site	Skyscrapers, weddings, consulting	
	Wide variation in specifications or tasks	Custom jewelry, surgery, Web pages	
JOB SHOP	Significant setup and/or changeover time	Automobile engines, auto body repair, major legal cases	Custom or Make-to-Order
	Low to moderate volume	Machine tools, beauty salons	
	Batching (small to large jobs)	Orders from small customers, mortgages, tourist tour groups	
	Many process routes with some repetitive steps	Shoes, hospital care, commercial loans	
	Customized design to customer's specifications	Commercial and Web-based printing	
	Many different products	Heavy equipment, financial services	
	High workforce skills	Legal services, consulting	
FLOW SHOP	Little or no setup or changeover time	Insurance policies	Option or Assemble-to-Order
	Dedicated to a small range of goods or services that are highly similar	Cafeterias, airline frequent flyer programs	
	Similar sequence of process steps	Refrigerators, stock trades	
	Moderate to high volumes	Toys, furniture, lawnmowers	
CONTINUOUS FLOW	Very high volumes in a fixed processing sequence	Gasoline, paint, memory chips, check posting	Standardized or Make-to-Stock
	Not made from discrete parts	Grain, chemicals	
	High investment in equipment and facility	Steel, paper, power-generating facilities	
	Dedicated to a small range of goods or services	Automated car wash	
	Automated movement of goods or information between process steps	Credit card authorizations, electric utilities	
	24-hour/7-day continuous operation	Steel, electronic funds transfer, broadcasting	

© Cengage Learning 2013

*A **product life cycle** is a characterization of product growth, maturity, and decline over time.* It is important to understand product life cycles because when goods and services change and mature, so must the processes and value chains that create and deliver them.

The traditional product life cycle (PLC) generally consists of four phases—*introduction, growth, maturity*, and *decline and turnaround*. A product's life cycle has important implications in terms of process design and choice. For example, new products with low sales volume might be produced in a job shop process; however, as sales grow and volumes increase, a flow shop process might be more efficient. As another example, a firm might introduce a standard product that is produced with a flow shop process, but as the market matures, the product might become more customized. In this case, a job shop process might be more advantageous. What often happens in many firms is that product strategies change, but managers do not make the necessary changes in the process to reflect the new product characteristics.

Two approaches to help understand the relationships between product characteristics for goods and services and process choice decisions are the product-process matrix and service-positioning matrix, which we introduce in the following sections.

7-2 The Product-Process Matrix

The product-process matrix was first proposed by Hayes and Wheelwright and is shown in Exhibit 7.2.[5] *The product-process matrix is a model that describes the alignment of process choice with the characteristics of the manufactured good.* The most appropriate match between type of product and type of process occurs along the diagonal in the product-process matrix. As one moves down the diagonal, the emphasis on both product and process structure shifts from low volume and high flexibility, to higher volumes and more standardization. If product and process characteristics are not well matched, the firm will be unable to achieve its competitive priorities effectively.

For example, consider a firm that manufactures only a few products with high volumes and low customization using a flow shop process structure. This process choice best matches the product characteristics. However, suppose that as time goes on and customer needs evolve, marketing and engineering functions develop more product options and add new products to the mix. This results in a larger number and variety of products to make, lower volumes, and increased customization. The firm finds itself "off the diagonal" and in the lower left-hand corner of the matrix (denoted by Position A in Exhibit 7.2). There is a mismatch between product characteristics and process choice. If the firm continues to use the flow shop process, it may find itself struggling to meet delivery promises and incur unnecessary costs because of low efficiencies.

On the other hand, by selectively and consciously positioning a business off the diagonal of the product-process matrix (often called a "positioning strategy"), a company can differentiate itself from its competitors. However, it must be careful not to get too far off the diagonal or it must have a market where high prices absorb any operational inefficiencies. For example, Rolls-Royce produces a small line of automobiles using a process similar to a job shop rather than the traditional flow shop of other automobile manufacturers. Each car requires about 900 hours of labor. For Rolls-Royce this strategy has worked, but its target market is willing to pay premium prices for premium quality and features.

> A **product life cycle** is a characterization of product growth, maturity, and decline over time.
>
> The **product-process matrix** is a model that describes the alignment of process choice with the characteristics of the manufactured good.

Exhibit 7.2
Product-Process Matrix

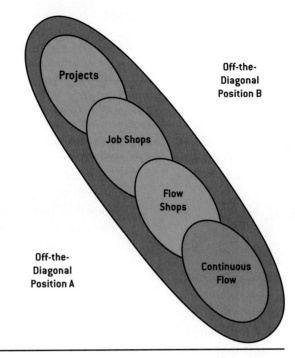

OPERATIONS
Process Choice Decision
with Example Process
Characteristics

- One-of-a-kind
- Large scale
- Complex
- Wide variation of tasks
- Resources to site

———————————

- High setup time
- Batching
- Many process routes
- Customized
- Many different products
- General high level skills

———————————

- Low/no setup time
- Highly similar products
- Dominant line flow(s)
- Specialized skills

———————————

- High investment in equipment and facility
- Not made from discrete parts
- Automated
- 24/7 continuous operation

Projects

Job Shops

Flow Shops

Continuous Flow

Off-the-Diagonal Position B

Off-the-Diagonal Position A

	Low	Moderate	High
- Demand (Volume)	Low	Moderate	High
- Degree of Customization	High	Moderate	Low
- Number/Range of Products	Low	Many/Multiple	Several
- Type of Good	Custom Make-to-Order	Options Assemble-to-Order	Standardized Make-to-Stock

MARKETING Product Characteristic/Decisions

© Cengage Learning 2013

The theory of the product-process matrix has been challenged by some who suggest that advanced manufacturing technologies may allow firms to be successful even when they position themselves off the diagonal. These new technologies provide manufacturers with the capability to be highly flexible and produce lower volumes of products in greater varieties at lower costs. Therefore, off-diagonal positioning strategies are becoming more and more viable for many organizations and allow for "mass-customization" strategies and capabilities.[6]

7-3 The Service-Positioning Matrix

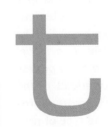

he product-process matrix does not transfer well to service businesses and processes.[7,8] The relationship between volume and process is not found in many service businesses. For example, to meet increased volume, service businesses such as retail outlets, banks, and hotels have historically added capacity in the form of new stores, branch banks, and hotels to meet demand but do not change their processes. These limitations are resolved by introducing the *service-positioning matrix*. To better understand it, we first discuss the concept of a pathway in a service-delivery system.

A **pathway** *is a unique route through a service system.* Pathways can be customer- or provider-driven, depending on the level of control that the service firm wants to ensure. Pathways can be physical in nature, as in walking around Disney World or a golf course; procedural, as in initiating a transaction via the telephone with a brokerage firm; or purely mental and virtual, as in doing an Internet search. **Customer-routed services** *are those that offer customers broad freedom to select the pathways that are best suited for their immediate needs and wants from many possible pathways through the service-delivery system.* The customer decides what path to take through the service-delivery system with only minimal guidance from management. Searching the Internet to purchase an item or visiting a park are examples.

Provider-routed services *constrain customers to follow a very small number of possible and predefined pathways through the service system.* An automatic teller machine (ATM) is an example. A limited number of pathways exist—for example, getting cash, making a deposit, checking an account balance, and moving money from one account to another. Mailing and processing a package using the U.S. Postal Service, Federal Express, or UPS is another example of a provider-routed service.

Some services fall in between these extremes. For example, consider placing a telephone order with a company such as L.L. Bean. The pathway is relatively constrained (that is, provider-routed) as the service representative first acquires the customer's name and address, takes the order and asks questions about colors and sizes, and then processes the credit card payment. However, while placing the order, customers have complete freedom in selecting the sequence in which items are ordered, asking questions, or obtaining additional information.

A **pathway** is a unique route through a service system.

Customer-routed services are those that offer customers broad freedom to select the pathways that are best suited for their immediate needs and wants from many possible pathways through the service delivery system.

Provider-routed services constrain customers to follow a very small number of possible and predefined pathways through the service system.

BECTON DICKINSON: OFF THE DIAGONAL

Becton Dickinson (BD) is the leading producer of needle devices for the medical industry. BD has been an innovator in developing new products to reduce the potential risks of health care workers' accidently sticking themselves with a contaminated needle that might carry HIV or a fatal strain of hepatitis C. As a result, the company needed to convert many of its large and older factories, which had large and inflexible manufacturing systems dedicated to low-cost production, to accommodate high-volume production of a larger variety of safe sharp products.

Spring-loaded IV catheters have 12 parts, assembled in an automated process with 48 steps carried out at incredibly fast speeds. Instead of using one long assembly line, BD's Utah plant uses a production system that makes it relatively easy to modify a product by altering or adding subassembly stations. BD's manufacturing process choice is somewhat of the diagonal of the product-process matrix, producing multiple products in high volumes in more-or-less a continuous flow pattern. A simple product design and a high degree of automation helped BD work off the product-process diagonal. This strategy helps the company to continue to hold and grow its market share in a highly competitive industry.

Exhibit 7.3 *The Service-Positioning Matrix*

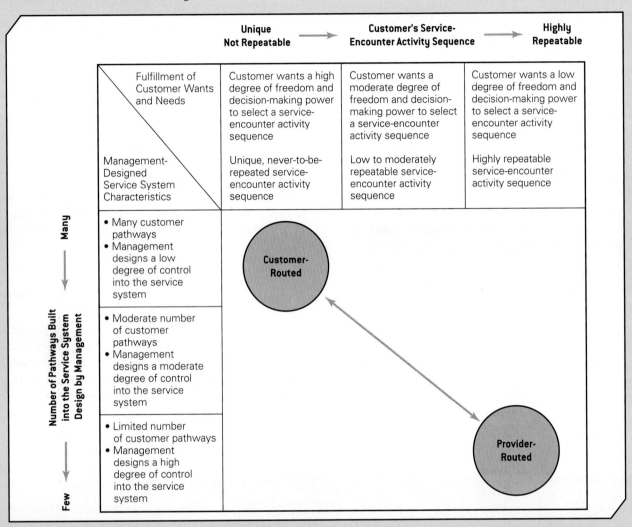

	Fulfillment of Customer Wants and Needs	Customer wants a high degree of freedom and decision-making power to select a service-encounter activity sequence	Customer wants a moderate degree of freedom and decision-making power to select a service-encounter activity sequence	Customer wants a low degree of freedom and decision-making power to select a service-encounter activity sequence
	Management-Designed Service System Characteristics	Unique, never-to-be-repeated service-encounter activity sequence	Low to moderately repeatable service-encounter activity sequence	Highly repeatable service-encounter activity sequence

Sources: Adapted from D. A. Collier and S. M. Meyer, "A Service Positioning Matrix," *International Journal of Operations and Production Management,* 18, no. 12, (1998) pp. 1123–1244. Also see D. A. Collier and S. Meyer, "An Empirical Comparison of Service Matrices," *International Journal of Operations and Production Management,* 20, no. 5–6 (2000), pp. 705–729.

Designs for customer-routed services require a solid understanding of the features that can delight customers, as well as methods to educate customers about the variety of pathways that may exist and how to select and navigate through them.

The service-positioning matrix (SPM), shown in Exhibit 7.3, is roughly analogous to the product-process matrix for manufacturing. The SPM focuses on the service encounter level and helps management design a service system that best meets the technical and behavioral needs of customers. The position along the horizontal axis is described by the sequence of service encounters. *The* **service-encounter activity sequence** *consists of all the process steps and associated service encounters necessary to complete a service transaction and fulfill a customer's wants and needs.* It depends on two things:

1. *The degree of customer discretion, freedom, and decision-making power in selecting the service-encounter activity sequence.* Customers may want the opportunity to design their own unique service-encounter activity sequence, in any order they choose.

The **service-encounter activity sequence** consists of all the process steps and associated service encounters necessary to complete a service transaction and fulfill a customer's wants and needs.

APPLE: NEW DESIGN REQUIRES NEW PROCESSES

Apple introduced a redesigned line of MacBooks in 2008 that featured precision unibody enclosures milled from an extruded block of aluminum. This not only improved rigidity and durability, but also resulted in a thinner design. However, to manufacture the new design, Apple needed to develop an entirely new process. The process starts with an extruded block of aluminum that is carved out using computer numerical control (CNC) machines, similar to processes used in the aerospace industry. The aluminum sheets are cut into blocks that undergo 13 separate milling operations. Apple uses CNC to precision-cut keyboard holes from the face of the slab, mill out the "thumbscoop" that provides enough of a recession to open the display lid, machine out complex patterns from the inside, and perforate the speaker grill holes using lasers. A portion of the front edge is milled thin enough that a laser can be used to micro-perforate the metal to allow light from the sleep indicator LED to pass through the metal. When the sleep indicator is off, the metal appears to be solid. Once the inside is precision cut, the edges are rounded and polished. The material machined from the aluminum block is collected and recycled.[9]

2. *The degree of repeatability of the service-encounter activity sequence.* Service-encounter repeatability refers to the frequency that a specific service encounter activity sequence is used by customers. Service-encounter repeatability provides a measure analogous to product volume for goods-producing firms.

The more unique the service encounter, the less repeatable it is. A high degree of repeatability encourages standardized process and equipment design and dedicated service channels and results in lower costs and improved efficiency. A low degree of repeatability encourages more customization and more flexible equipment and process designs and typically results in higher relative cost per transaction and lower efficiency.

The position along the vertical axis of the SPM reflects the number of pathways built into the service system design by management. That is, the designers or management predefine exactly how many pathways will be possible for the customer to select, ranging from one to an infinite number of pathways.

The SPM is similar to the product-process matrix in that it suggests that the nature of the customer's desired service-encounter activity sequence should lead to the most appropriate service system design and that superior performance results by generally staying along the diagonal of the matrix. Like the product-process matrix, organizations that venture too far off the diagonal create a mismatch between service system characteristics and desired activity sequence characteristics. As we move down the diagonal of the SPM, the service-encounter activity sequence becomes less unique and more repeatable with fewer pathways. Like the product-process matrix, the midrange portion of the matrix contains a broad range of intermediate design choices.

7-4 Process Design

The goal of process design is to create the right combination of equipment, labor, software, work methods, and environment to produce and deliver goods and services that satisfy both internal and external customer requirements. Process design can have a significant impact on cost (and hence profitability), flexibility (the ability to produce the right types and amounts of products as customer demand or preferences change), and the quality of the output.

We can think about work at four levels:

1. Task
2. Activity
3. Process
4. Value Chain

A **task** *is a specific unit of work required to create an output.* Examples are inserting a circuit board into an iPad subassembly or typing the address on an invoice. An **activity** *is a group of tasks needed to create and deliver an intermediate or final output.* Examples include all the tasks necessary to build an iPad, for example, connecting the battery and assembling the cover pieces; or inputting all the information correctly on an invoice, such as the items ordered, prices, discounts, and so on.

> A **task** is a specific unit of work required to create an output.
>
> An **activity** is a group of tasks needed to create and deliver an intermediate or final output.

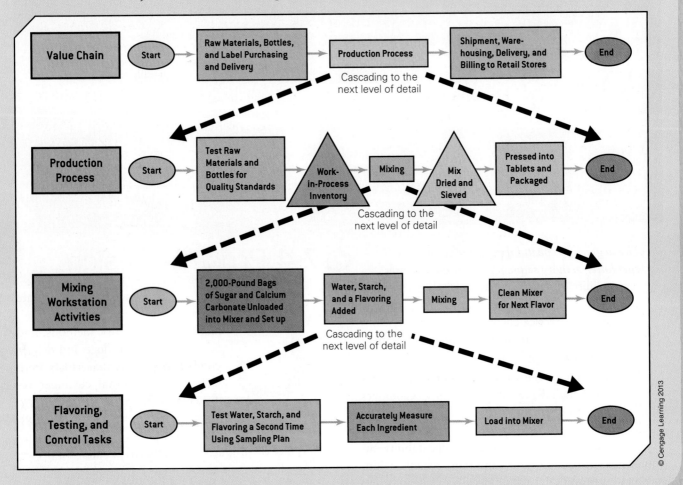

A **process** consists of a group of activities, and a **value chain** is a network of processes. Examples of processes would be moving the parts and materials for an Apple's iPad to the assembly stations, building the iPad, and packaging the unit and peripherals; or taking a customer order, filling the order, shipping it, and processing the invoice. An example of a value chain might include developing the Web site and video clips for advertising an iPad, purchasing the materials for an iPad, manufacturing and packaging the units, transporting them to warehouses and retail stores, distributing them to customers, and providing customer support, software updates, and so on.

A **process** consists of a group of activities.

A **value chain** is a network of processes.

Exhibit 7.4 shows an example for the production of antacid tablets. The value chain shows an aggregate view focused on the *goods-producing processes* (supporting services such as engineering, shipping, accounts payable, advertising, and retailing are not shown). The next level in the hierarchy of work is at the *production process* level where tablets are made. The third level focuses on the *mixing workstation (or work activities)* where the ingredients are unloaded into mixers. The mixer must be set up for each batch and cleaned for the next batch since many different flavors, such as peppermint, strawberry-banana, cherry, and mandarin orange, are produced using the same mixers. The fourth and final level in the work hierarchy is the *flavoring tasks*, which are defined as three tasks each with specific procedures, standard times per task, and labor requirements. These three tasks could be broken down into even more detail if required.

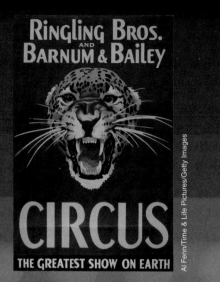

THE GREATEST SHOW ON EARTH: NO CLOWNING AROUND

The Ringling Brothers Circus was founded in 1884 by five brothers. In 1907 it acquired the Barnum & Bailey Circus, merging them in 1919 to become Ringling Brothers Barnum and Bailey Circus, promoted as *The Greatest Show on Earth*. The circus brought unique entertainment to many people, and continues to do so today.

In 1889, two of the Ringlings went to Philadelphia, where they purchased railroad cars and parade equipment that provided the basis for improving their ability to serve more cities and customers. With this new equipment and better planning, teamwork, and scheduling, the circus was no longer limited to moving only 15 to 20 miles a day. As a result, the circus greatly increased revenue. Using the railroad cars required significant changes in their process design. A typical circus train had 60 cars, 45 of them flatcars, and carried about 100 wagons. Ringling Brothers devised a system of inclined planes, called runs, and crossover plates between cars, and a system of ropes and pulleys to facilitate loading and unloading. Each team of employees was assigned certain work tasks and activities that defined a process, such as setting up a tent, purchasing food supplies for employees and animals, or selling tickets. They would often arrive in the night, set up their massive tents, bleachers, and food service, only to tear it all down several days later on their way to the next town. As John Ringling stated, "We divided the work; but stood together."[10]

⌈ "We divided the work; but stood together."

— *Mr. John Ringling, Ringling Bros. Barnum & Bailey Circus, 1907* ⌋

7-4a Process and Value Stream Mapping

Understanding process design objectives focuses on answering the question: What is the process intended to accomplish? An example process objective might be "to create and deliver the output to the customer in 48 hours." Another key question to consider is: What are the critical customer and organizational requirements that must be achieved?

Designing a goods-producing or service-providing process requires six major activities:

1. Define the purpose and objectives of the process.

2. Create a detailed process or value stream map that describes how the process is currently performed (sometimes called a current state or baseline map). Of course, if you are designing an entirely new process, this step is skipped.

3. Evaluate alternative process designs. That is, create process or value stream maps (sometimes called future state maps) that describe how the process can best achieve customer and organizational objectives.

4. Identify and define appropriate performance measures for the process.

5. Select the appropriate equipment and technology.

6. Develop an implementation plan to introduce the new or revised process design. This includes developing process performance criteria and standards to monitor and control the process.

A **process map
(flowchart)** *describes
the sequence of all pro-
cess activities and tasks
necessary to create
and deliver a desired
output or outcome.* It
documents how work
either is, or should
be, accomplished and
how the transforma-
tion process creates
value. We usually first
develop a "baseline"
map of how the cur-
rent process operates
in order to under-
stand it and identify
improvements for
redesign.

Process maps de-
lineate the boundaries
of a process. *A* **process
boundary** *is the begin-
ning or end of a process.*
The advantages of a
clearly defined process
boundary are that it
makes it easier to ob-
tain senior manage-
ment support, assign
process ownership to
individuals or teams,
identify key inter-
faces with internal or
external customers,
and identify where

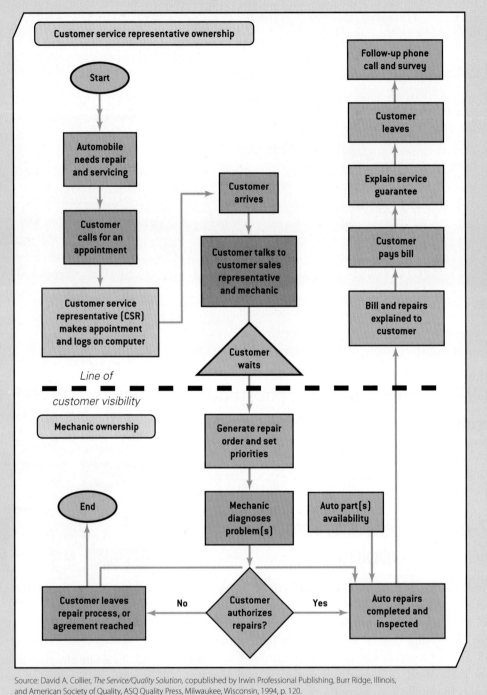

Exhibit 7.5 *Automobile Repair Flowchart*

Source: David A. Collier, *The Service/Quality Solution*, copublished by Irwin Professional Publishing, Burr Ridge, Illinois, and American Society of Quality, ASQ Quality Press, Milwaukee, Wisconsin, 1994, p. 120.

A **process map (flowchart)** describes the sequence of all process activities and tasks necessary to create and deliver a desired
output or outcome.

A **process boundary** is the beginning or end of a process.

performance measurements should be taken. Thus,
each of the levels in Exhibit 7.4 represents a process
map defining different process boundaries.

Typical symbols used for process maps are the following:

- ▬ A rectangle denotes a task or work activity.
- ▲ A triangle indicates waiting.
- ● An oval denotes the "start" or "end" of the process and defines the process boundaries.
- → An arrow denotes movement, transfer, or flow to the next task or activity.
- ⇒ A double-headed arrow denotes an input or arrival into a process.
- ◆ A diamond denotes a decision that might result in taking alternative paths.

One example flowchart is shown in Exhibit 7.5 for an automobile repair process. Process maps clearly delineate the process boundaries.

In service applications, flowcharts generally highlight the points of contact with the customer and are often called *service blueprints* or *service maps*. Such flowcharts often show the separation between the back office and the front office with a "line of customer visibility," such as the one shown in Exhibit 7.5.

Non-value-added activities, such as transferring materials between two nonadjacent workstations, waiting for service, or requiring multiple approvals for a low-cost electronic transaction, simply lengthen processing time, increase costs, and, often, increase customer frustration. Eliminating non-value-added activities in a process design is one of the most important responsibilities of operations managers. This is often accomplished using value stream mapping, a variant of more generic process mapping.

The **value stream** *refers to all value-added activities involved in designing, producing, and delivering goods and services to customers.* A value stream map (VSM) shows the process flows in a manner similar to an ordinary process map; however, the difference lies in that value stream maps highlight value-added versus non-value-added activities and include costs associated with work activities for both value- and non-value-added activities.

To illustrate this, consider a process map for the order fulfillment process in a restaurant shown in

Exhibit 7.6. From the times on the process map, the "service standard" order posting and fulfillment time is an average of 30 minutes per order (5 + 1 + 4 + 12 + 3 + 5). The restaurant's service guarantee requires that if this order posting and fulfillment time is more than 40 minutes, the customer's order is free of charge.

The chef's time is valued at $30 per hour, oven operation at $10 per hour, precooking order waiting time at $5 per hour, and postcooking order waiting time at $60 per hour. The $60 estimate reflects the cost of poor quality for a dinner waiting too long that might be delivered to the customer late (and cold!).

Exhibit 7.7 illustrates a value stream map for the order posting and fulfillment process in Exhibit 7.6. Exhibit 7.7 is one of many formats for value stream mapping. Here, non-value-added time is 33.3 percent (10/30 minutes) of the total order posting and fulfillment time, and non-value-added cost is 31.7 percent ($5.417/$17.087) of total cost. Suppose that a process improvement incorporates wireless technology to transmit food orders to the kitchen and notify the waiter when the order is ready so that the waiting time can be reduced from 10 minutes to 4 minutes on the front and back ends of the process. Hence, the total processing time is reduced from 30 to 24 minutes (a 20 percent improvement).

The **value stream** refers to all value-added activities involved in designing, producing, and delivering goods and services to customers.

Exhibit 7.6 *Restaurant Order Posting and Fulfillment Process*

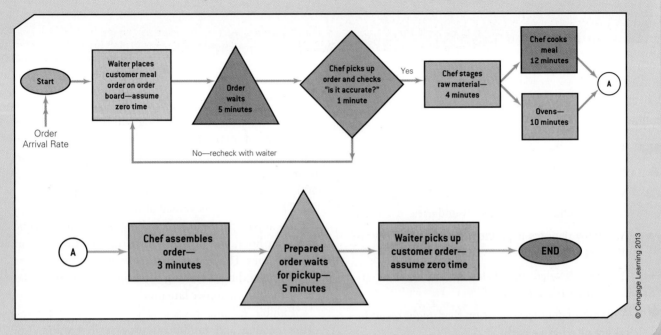

Costs are reduced by $3.25 with a 3-minute wait time reduction on the front and back ends of the process. Therefore, cost per order goes from $17.087 to $13.837 (a 19 percent improvement). Increasing the speed of this part of the restaurant delivery process may also allow for a higher seat turnover during peak demand periods and help to increase total revenue and contribute to profit and overhead.

7-5 Process Analysis and Improvement

few processes are designed from scratch. Many process design activities involve redesigning an existing process to improve performance. Management strategies to improve process designs usually focus on one or more of the following:

- *increasing revenue* by improving process efficiency in creating goods and services and delivery of the customer benefit package;

- *increasing agility* by improving flexibility and response to changes in demand and customer expectations;

- *increasing product and/or service quality* by reducing defects, mistakes, failures, or service upsets;

- *decreasing costs* through better technology or elimination of non-value-added activities;

- *decreasing process flow time* by reducing waiting time or speeding up movement through the process and value chain; and

- *decreasing the carbon footprint of the task, activity, process, and/or value chain.*

Process and value stream maps are the foundation for improvement activities. Typical questions that need to be evaluated during process analysis include the following:

- Are the steps in the process arranged in logical sequence?

- Do all steps add value? Can some steps be eliminated and should others be added in order to improve quality or operational performance? Can some be combined? Should some be reordered?

- Are capacities of each step in balance; that is, do bottlenecks exist for which customers will incur excessive waiting time?

- What skills, equipment, and tools are required at each step of the process? Should some steps be automated?

- At which points in the system (sometimes called process fail points) might errors occur that would result in customer dissatisfaction, and how might these errors be corrected?

- At which point or points in the process should performance be measured? What are appropriate measures?

- Where interaction with the customer occurs, what procedures, behaviors, and guidelines should employees follow that will present a positive image?

- What is the impact of the process on sustainability? Can we quantify the carbon footprint of the current process?

Sometimes, processes have gotten so complex that it is easier to start from a "clean sheet" rather than try to improve incrementally. **Reengineering** *has been defined as "the fundamental rethinking and radical redesign of business processes to achieve dramatic improvements in critical, contemporary measures of performance, such as cost, quality, service, and speed."*[11]

Reengineering was spawned by the revolution in information technology and involves asking basic questions about business processes: Why do we do it? Why is it done this way? Such questioning often uncovers obsolete, erroneous, or inappropriate assumptions. Radical redesign involves tossing out existing procedures and reinventing the process, not just incrementally improving it. The goal is to achieve quantum leaps in performance. All processes and functional areas participate in reengineering efforts, each requiring knowledge and skills in operations management.

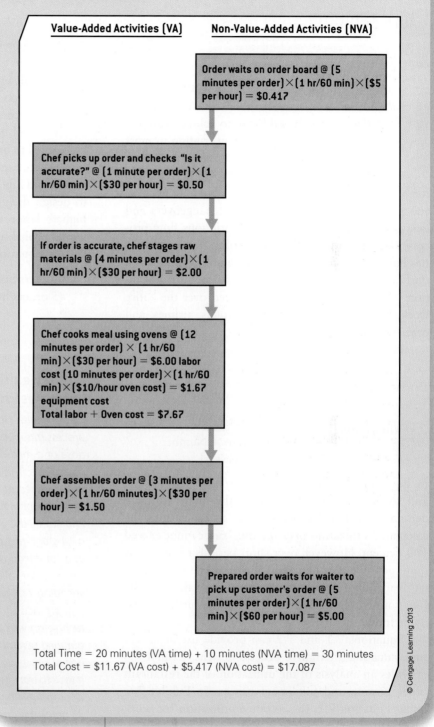

Exhibit 7.7 *Value Stream Map for Restaurant Order Posting and Fulfillment Process*

Value-Added Activities (VA)	Non-Value-Added Activities (NVA)
	Order waits on order board @ (5 minutes per order) × (1 hr/60 min) × ($5 per hour) = $0.417
Chef picks up order and checks "Is it accurate?" @ (1 minute per order) × (1 hr/60 min) × ($30 per hour) = $0.50	
If order is accurate, chef stages raw materials @ (4 minutes per order) × (1 hr/60 min) × ($30 per hour) = $2.00	
Chef cooks meal using ovens @ (12 minutes per order) × (1 hr/60 min) × ($30 per hour) = $6.00 labor cost (10 minutes per order) × (1 hr/60 min) × ($10/hour oven cost) = $1.67 equipment cost Total labor + Oven cost = $7.67	
Chef assembles order @ (3 minutes per order) × (1 hr/60 minutes) × ($30 per hour) = $1.50	
	Prepared order waits for waiter to pick up customer's order @ (5 minutes per order) × (1 hr/60 min) × ($60 per hour) = $5.00

Total Time = 20 minutes (VA time) + 10 minutes (NVA time) = 30 minutes
Total Cost = $11.67 (VA cost) + $5.417 (NVA cost) = $17.087

© Cengage Learning 2013

Reengineering has been defined as "the fundamental rethinking and radical redesign of business processes to achieve dramatic improvements in critical, contemporary measures of performance, such as cost, quality, service, and speed."

7-6 Process Design and Resource Utilization

dle machines, trucks, people, computers, warehouse space, and other resources used in a process simply drain away potential profit. **Utilization** *is the fraction of time a workstation or individual is busy over the long run.* It is difficult to achieve 100 percent utilization. For example, utilization in most job shops ranges from 65 to 90 percent. In flow shops, it might be between 80 to 95 percent, and for most continuous flow processes, above 95 percent. Job shops require frequent machine changeovers and delays, whereas flow shops and continuous flow processes keep equipment more fully utilized. Service facilities have a greater range of resource utilization. Movie theaters, for example, average 5 to 20 percent utilization when seat utilization is computed over the entire week. Similar comments apply to hotels, airlines, and other services.

Two ways of computing resource utilization are

$$\text{Utilization (U)} = \frac{\text{Resources Used}}{\text{Resources Available}} \qquad [7.1]$$

$$\text{Utilization (U)} = \frac{\text{Demand Rate}}{[\text{Service Rate} \times \text{Number of Servers}]} \qquad [7.2]$$

In Equation 7.1, the measurement base (time, units, and so on) must be the same in the numerator and denominator. For a process design to be feasible, the calculated utilization *over the long run* cannot exceed 100 percent. However, over short periods of time, it is quite possible that demand for a resource will exceed its availability. If a manager knows any three of the four variables in Equation 7.2, then the fourth can easily be found.

Equations 7.1 and 7.2 can provide useful insight for evaluating alternative process designs. Exhibit 7.8 provides an analysis of the utilization of the restaurant order posting and fulfillment process in Exhibit 7.6. Using Equation 7.2, the resource utilization for work

activity #3, assuming only one chef and two ovens, is computed as

$$\text{(20 orders/hour)}/[(5 \text{ orders/hour})$$
$$(1 \text{ chef}) = 4.0 \text{ or } 400 \text{ percent}$$

As we noted earlier, whenever the utilization is calculated to be greater than 100 percent, the work will endlessly pile up before the workstation. Therefore, this is clearly a poor process design and we need to add more resources.

A logical question to consider is how many chefs are needed to bring the utilization down below 100 percent at work activity #3? Because the chef is the most skilled and highest paid employee, it would make sense to design the process so that the chef would have the highest labor utilization rate (although 100 percent would probably not be practical). This can be found by solving Equation 7.2 as follows:

$$\text{(20 orders/hour)}/[(5 \text{ orders/hour}) (X \text{ chefs})] = 1.00$$
$$(5 \text{ orders/hour}) \times 1.00 \times X = 20 \text{ orders/hour,}$$
$$\text{or } X = 4.00 \text{ chefs}$$

Metro Health Hospital: Process Mapping Improves Pharmacy Service

Metro Health Hospital in Grand Rapids, Michigan, applied process mapping, reducing the lead time for getting the first dose of a medication to a patient in its pharmacy services operations. The lead time was measured from the time an order arrived at the pharmacy to its delivery on the appropriate hospital floor. A process improvement team carefully laid out all the process steps involved and found that it had a 14-stage process with some unnecessary steps, resulting in a total lead time of 166 minutes. During the evaluation process, the pharmacy calculated that technicians were spending 77.4 percent of their time locating products; when a pharmacist needed a technician for clinical activities, the technician was usually off searching for a drug. The team outlined several non-value-added steps in the process, only one of which was out of the pharmacy's control (i.e., the time it took to transport the ordered medication, once filled, to the appropriate floor). Overall, the pharmacy at Metro realized a 33 percent reduction in time to get medications to patients, and reduced the number of process steps from 14 to 9 simply by removing non-value-added steps. Patients have experienced a 40 percent reduction in pharmacy-related medication errors, and the severity of those errors has decreased. [12]

Utilization is the fraction of time a workstation or individual is busy over the long run.

Solved Problem

An inspection station for assembling printers receives 40 printers/hour and has two inspectors, each of whom can inspect 30 printers per hour. What is the utilization of the inspectors? What service rate would be required to have a target utilization of 85 percent?

Solution

The utilization at this inspection station is calculated to be

$$\text{Utilization} = 40/(30/2) \times 0.67 \text{ or } 67 \text{ percent.}$$

If the utilization rate is 85 percent, we can calculate the target service rate (SR) by solving Equation 7.2:

$$0.85 = 40/(SR \times 2)$$
$$1.7 \times SR = 40$$
$$SR = 23.5 \text{ printers/hour}$$

With four chefs, the resource utilizations are recomputed in Exhibit 7.9. We see that the oven is still a problem, with a calculated 167 percent utilization. To determine how many ovens to have for a 100 percent utilization, we solve the equation:

$$(20 \text{ orders/hour})/[(6 \text{ orders/hour}) (Y \text{ ovens})] = 1.00$$
$$(6 \text{ orders/hour}) \times 1.00 \times Y = 20 \text{ orders/hour,}$$
$$\text{or } Y = 3.33 \text{ chefs}$$

Rounding this up to 4, actual oven utilization would now be 83 percent (see Exhibit 7.10 for the final results).

Exhibit 7.11 shows a simplified flowchart of the order fulfillment process along with the output rates from Exhibit 7.10 that can be achieved for each work activity. *The average number of entities completed per unit time—the output rate—from a process is called* **throughput**. Throughput might be measured as parts per day,

> The average number of entities completed per unit time—the output rate—from a process is called **throughput**.

Exhibit 7.8 *Utilization Analysis of Restaurant Order Posting and Fulfillment Process*

	Work Activity #1 (Chef decides if order is accurate)	Work Activity #2 (Chef stages raw materials)	Work Activity #3 (Chef prepares side dishes)	Work Activity #4 (Oven operation)	Work Activity #5 (Chef assembles order)
Order arrival rate (given)	20 orders/hr	20 orders/hr	20 orders/hr	20 orders/hr	20 orders/hr
Time per order	1 minute	4 minutes	12 minutes	10 minutes	3 minutes
Number of resources	1 chef	1 chef	1 chef	2 ovens	1 chef
Output per time period	60 orders/hr	15 orders/hr	5 orders/hr	12 orders/hr	20 orders/hr
Resource utilization with 1 chef and 2 ovens	33%	133%	400%	167%	100%

© Cengage Learning 2013

Exhibit 7.9 *Revised Utilization Analysis of Restaurant Order Posting and Fulfillment Process (4 chefs)*

	Work Activity #1 (Chef decides if order is accurate)	Work Activity #2 (Chef stages raw materials)	Work Activity #3 (Chef prepares side dishes)	Work Activity #4 (Oven operation)	Work Activity #5 (Chef assembles order)
Resource utilization with 4 chefs and 2 ovens	8.33%	33%	100%	167%	25%

© Cengage Learning 2013

Exhibit 7.10 *Revised Utilization Analysis of Restaurant Order Posting and Fulfillment Process (4 ovens)*

	Work Activity #1 (Chef decides if order is accurate)	Work Activity #2 (Chef stages raw materials)	Work Activity #3 (Chef prepares side dishes)	Work Activity #4 (Oven operation)	Work Activity #5 (Chef assembles order)
Order arrival rate (given)	20 orders/hr	20 orders/hr	20 orders/hr	20 orders/hr	20 orders/hr
Time per order	1 minute	4 minutes	12 minutes	10 minutes	3 minutes
Number of resources	4 chefs	4 chefs	4 chefs	4 ovens	4 chefs
Output per time period	240 orders/hr	60 orders/hr	20 orders/hr	24 orders/hr	80 orders/hr
Resource utilization with 4 chefs and 4 ovens	8.33%	33%	100%	83%	25%

© Cengage Learning 2013

Exhibit 7.11 *Simplified Restaurant Fulfillment Process*

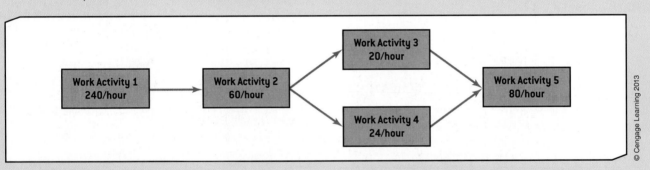

© Cengage Learning 2013

transactions per minute, or customers per hour, depending on the context.

A logical question to consider is what throughput can be achieved for the entire process. *A* **bottleneck** *is the work activity that effectively limits the throughput of the entire process.* A bottleneck is like the weakest link of a chain; the process in Exhibit 7.11 can never produce more than 20 orders/hour—the output rate of work activity #3 (assuming all five activities must be completed)! Identifying and breaking process bottlenecks is an important part of process design and improvement, and will increase the speed of the process, reduce waiting and work-in-process inventory, and use resources more efficiently.

A **bottleneck** is the work activity that effectively limits the throughput of the entire process.

7-6a Little's Law

At any moment of time, people, orders, jobs, documents, money, and other entities that flow through processes are in various stages of completion and may be waiting

Solved Problems

These solved problems illustrate the application of Little's Law and formula.

1. Suppose that a voting facility processes an average of 50 people per hour and that, on average, it takes 10 minutes for each person to complete the voting process. Using Equation 7.3, we can compute the average number of voters in process:

   $$WIP = R \times T$$
   $$= 50 \text{ voters/hr} \times (10 \text{ minutes}/60 \text{ minutes per hour})$$
   $$= 8.33 \text{ voters}$$

   Therefore, on average, we would expect to find about 8 or 9 voters inside the facility.

   Exhibit 7.12 shows the use of the Excel template Little's Law for solving this problem. The template may be used for the other solved problems here by entering the input data in the appropriate cells.

2. Suppose that the loan department of a bank takes an average of 6 days (0.2 months) to process an application and that an internal audit found that about 100 applications are in various stages of processing at any one time. Using Little's Law, we see that T = 0.2 and WIP = 100. Therefore, we can calculate the throughput of the department as

   $$R = WIP/T = 100 \text{ application}/0.2 \text{ months}$$
   $$= 500 \text{ application per month}$$

3. Suppose that a restaurant makes 400 pizzas per week, each of which uses 1/2 pound of dough, and that it typically maintains an inventory of 70 pounds of dough. In this case, R = 200 pounds per week of dough and WIP = 70 pounds. Using Little's Law, we can compute the average flow time as

   $$T = WIP/T = 70/200$$
   $$= 0.35 \text{ weeks, or about } 2\frac{1}{2} \text{ days}$$

   This information can be used to verify the freshness of the dough.

Exhibit 7.12
Spreadsheet from Excel Little's Law Template

Chuck Nacke/Alamy

Excel spreadsheet:

Exhibit 7.12 Little's Law Template.xlsx - Microsoft Excel

F14

	A	B	C	D
1	**Little's Law**			
2	**Enter any two of the three values only in the yellow cells**			
3	**and the spreadsheet will calculate the third.**			
4	Throughput (R)	50		
5	Flow time (T)	0.166667		
6	Work-in-process (WIP)			
7				
8	Throughput (R)			
9	Flow time (T)			
10	Work-in-process (WIP)	8.33		
11				
12				

Sheet1 / Sheet2 / Sheet3

Ready   100%

in queues. **Flow time,** *or* **cycle time,** *is the average time it takes to complete one cycle of a process.* It makes sense that the flow time will depend not only on the actual time to perform the tasks required but also on how many other entities are in the "work-in-process" stage.

Little's Law is a simple formula that explains the relationship among flow time (T), throughput (R), and work-in-process (WIP): [13]

$$\text{Work-in-process} = \text{Throughput} \times \text{Flow time}$$

> **Flow time,** or **cycle time,** is the average time it takes to complete one cycle of a process.

or

$$WIP = R \times T \qquad [7.3]$$

Little's Law provides a simple way of evaluating average process performance. If we know any two of the three variables, we can compute the third using Little's Law. Little's Law can be applied to many different types of manufacturing and service operations. (See the accompanying Solved Problems.)

It is important to understand that Little's Law is based on *simple averages* for all variables. Such an analysis serves as a good baseline for understanding process performance on an aggregate basis, but it does not take into account any randomness in arrivals or service times or different probability distributions.

Discussion Questions

1. What type of process—project, job shop, flow shop, and continuous flow—would most likely be used to produce the following? Explain your reasoning.
   a. Apple iPads
   b. Weddings
   c. Paper
   d. Tax preparation

2. Provide some examples of customer- and provider-routed services that you have encountered that are different from those described in this chapter. Can you identify any improvements that could be made to these processes?

3. List some common processes that you perform as a student. How can you use the knowledge from this chapter, such as identifying bottlenecks, to improve them?

4. In Section 5 we listed several questions to ask in order to identify and analyze improvements in a process. Can you think of others?

5. What sustainability issues are present in the restaurant order fulfillment process example (Exhibits 7.6 to 7.11)? What other restaurant processes need to include sustainability criteria in their design and day-to-day management?

Problems and Activities

Note: an asterisk denotes problems for which an Excel spreadsheet template in CourseMate may be used.

1. Research and find an example of a process and/or value chain improvement initiative where sustainability is included in the analysis. Write a short paper (maximum of two typed pages) describing the initiative in a manner similar to the chapter description of Alfa Laval.

2. Carbon dioxide emissions associated with a one-night stay in a hotel room are calculated at 29.53 kg of CO_2 per room day for an average hotel. If your hotel's 102 rooms are all occupied for two days

during a college football game, how much CO_2 did the guests and hotel release into the atmosphere? What work and leisure activities and processes in the hotel generate CO_2 emissions? Provide three examples and explain why these activities generate emissions.

3. Draw a flowchart for a process of interest to you, such as a quick oil-change service, a factory process you might have worked in, ordering a pizza, renting a car or truck, buying products on the Internet, or

applying for an automobile loan. Identify the points where something (people, information) waits for service or is held in work-in-process inventory, the estimated time to accomplish each activity in the process, and the total flow time. Evaluate how well the process worked and what might be done to improve it.

4. Design a process for one of the following activities:

   a. Preparing for an exam

   b. Writing a term paper

   c. Planning a vacation

5. A 40,000-seat college football stadium is used 22 times for games, concerts, and graduation ceremonies. Each event averages four hours, and assume the stadium is full for each event. The stadium is available 365 days a year from 6 a.m. to midnight. Using Equation 7.1, find the stadium (seat) utilization. Can you think of one or two other assets that have such a low resource utilization?

6. The demand for intensive care services in an urban hospital on Mondays is 14 patients per hour. Intensive care nurses can handle 3.4 patients per hour. What is the nurse (labor) utilization if four intensive care nurses are scheduled to be on duty for Monday? (Hint: Use Equation 7.2.) What are the advantages and disadvantages of this resource schedule for Mondays from the patient's and management's perspective?

7. A telephone call center uses three customer service representatives (CSRs) during the 8:30 a.m. to 9:00 a.m. time period. The standard service rate is 2.0 minutes per telephone call per CSR. Assuming a target labor utilization rate of 80 percent, how many calls can these three CSRs handle during this half-hour period?

8. What is the implied service rate at a bank teller window if customer demand is 34 customers per hour, two bank tellers are on duty, and their labor utilization is 85 percent?

9. Refer to Exhibit 7.7. Suppose that if the restaurant uses iPads to place orders and notify waiters when the customer's order is ready, the time on the order board (now an electronic order board) decreases from 5 to 1 minute, and the prepared order wait time decreases from 5 to 3 minutes. Recompute the total value-added and non-value-added time and cost for this scenario. Explain how speeding up the order and delivery process might affect customer satisfaction.

10.* A checkout line at a grocery store takes an average of 4 minutes to ring up a customer's order. On average, five customers are in the checkout line. What is the average number of customers per hour processed in the checkout line?

11.* An accounts receivable manager processes 200 checks per day with an average processing time of 15 working days. What is the average number of accounts receivable checks being processed in her office? What if, through information technology, she reduces the processing time from 15 days to 10 days to 5 days? What are the advantages and disadvantages of adopting this technology? Explain.

12.* A manufacturer's average work-in-process inventory for Part #2934 is 500 parts. The workstation produces parts at the rate of 200 parts per day. What is the average time a part spends in this workstation?

13. Marion Health Clinic sees patients on a walk-in basis only. On average, 10 patients per hour enter the clinic. All patients register at the registration window with a registration clerk (RC), which takes 3 minutes. After registration, but before being seen by a nurse practitioner (NP), the registration records clerk (RRC) pulls the patient's records from the records room, which takes 6 minutes. At his or her turn, each patient then sees an NP, who checks weight, temperature, and blood pressure. This work activity takes 5 minutes. The NP determines if the patient must see a doctor (MD) or can be handled by a physician's assistant (PA). There is one MD, one PA, one NP, one RRC, one billing clerk (BC), and one RC in the system at the current time.

   The NP sends 40 percent of the patients to the PA and 60 percent to the MD. The PA takes on average 6 minutes per patient, whereas the MD takes 15 minutes. After the patient sees the PA and/or MD, the patient pays the bill or processes insurance information with the BC, which takes 5 minutes per patient. Then the patient exits the process.

   a. Draw a process flow diagram, label everything, and place the times and percentages given in the problem on the diagram.

   b. What is the throughput in patients per hour of each stage in the process?

   c. What are the labor utilization rates for the MD, NP, PA, BC, RRC, and RC? Are these values appropriate? If not, how might you redesign the process? Where is the bottleneck?

   d. The PA often discovers that the patient should see an MD, so the patient is sent to the MD after seeing the PA 50 percent of the time. How does this change affect your answers to the preceding questions?

14. The Wilcox Student Health Center has just implemented a new computer system and service process

to "improve efficiency." The process flowchart and analysis framework is also provided. As pharmacy manager, you are concerned about waiting time and its potential impact on college students who "get no respect." All prescriptions (Rxs) go through the following process:

Assume that students arrive to drop off Rxs at a steady rate of two Rxs per minute, with an average of one Rx per student. The average number of students in process (assume waiting and being serviced) at each station is: DROP-OFF—five students, PICK-UP—three students, and PAY CASHIER—six students.

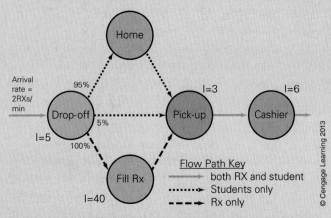

WIP = R*T	Drop Off	Fill Rx	Pick Up	Cashier	Totals
Inventory (WIP)					
Throughput Rate (R)					
Flow Time (T)					

The fill Rx station typically has 40 Rxs in process and waiting, on average. Because of this perceived long wait, 95 percent of the students decide to come back later for pick-up. They come back an average of three hours later. If the students choose to stay, each name is called as soon as the Rx is filled and the student then enters the pick-up line. Assume that the system is operating at a steady state.

a. What is the average time a student spends in the pharmacy if he or she stays to pick up the Rx?

b. How many minutes does the student spend in the pharmacy if he or she picks up the Rx three hours later (i.e., the student goes home after dropping the Rx off)?

c. What is the average time in minutes that all students spend in the pharmacy?

d. What is the average time in minutes that the Rx spends in the process? Count time from entering the drop-off line to completing payment.

15. A manufacturer of air-conditioner compressors is concerned that too much money is tied up in its value chain. Average raw material inventory is $50 million and work-in-process (WIP) production inventory is $20 million. Sales are $20 million per week and finished goods inventory averages $30 million. The average outstanding accounts receivable is $60 million. Assume 50 weeks in one year. The value chain is as follows:

Raw Material Inventory → Production (WIP) Inventory → Finished Goods → Accounts Receivable

a. What is the total flow (process) time of a throughput dollar? (Hint: Use a WIP = R × T format and table as shown in problem 14 to organize your solution.)

b. What is the average dollar inventory in the value chain?

c. Which of the major stages—raw materials, WIP, finished goods, or accounts receivable—is the best candidate for freeing up dollars for the air-conditioner manufacturer?

d. What is the target level of average accounts receivable inventory if management can reduce the time a dollar spends in accounts receivable inventory (processing and collections) by one-half by improving the accounts receivable process?

e. What else does this flow time analysis problem demonstrate?

Hopewell Hospital Pharmacy Case Study

Hopewell Hospital is trying to reduce costs yet improve patient and medical services. A hospital pharmacy, a primary process, uses two types of medications—fluids such as intravenous liquids and pharmaceuticals such as pills. The pharmacy buys drugs in bulk containers and bottles and dispenses them in smaller unit-dose amounts based on the doctor's orders. The objective of the pharmacy is to "get the right drug in the right amount to the right patient at the right time." The consequences of errors in this process range from no visible effects on patient health to allergic reactions, or in the extreme case, to death of the patient. National studies on hospital pharmacies found error rates ranging from one error per thousand to 15 errors per hundred prescriptions.

The hospital pharmacy process at Hopewell Hospital includes seven major steps:

Step 1—Receive the doctor's patient medication order via a written prescription, over the telephone, or through the hospital Internet system. This step averages 0.5 minutes per prescription and could be done by the medical technician or a legally registered pharmacist.

Hospital pharmacies are studying the prescription process to reduce errors.

Shadow216/Shutterstock.com

Step 2—Verify and validate the order through whatever means necessary. For example, if the handwriting was not legible, the doctor must be contacted to verify the medical prescription. Only a registered pharmacist can do this step, which takes from one-third of a minute to 10 minutes depending on the nature of the prescription and checking out potential problems. Because only 10 percent of prescriptions require extensive verification, the weighted average time for this step is 1.3 minutes [.9 × (1/3 minute) + .1 × (10 minutes)].

Step 3—Determine if duplicate prescriptions exist, and check the patient's allergic reaction history and current medications. This work activity averages 1.4 minutes using the hospital pharmacy's computer system. Only a registered pharmacist can perform this step.

Step 4—Establish that the drug(s) are in stock, have not expired, and are available in the requested form and quantity. Only a registered pharmacist can perform this step and it takes 1 minute.

Step 5—Prepare the prescription, including the label, and attach the proper labels to the proper bottles. Only a registered pharmacist can do this work activity and it averages 3.2 minutes.

Step 6—Store the prescription in the proper place for pickup and delivery to the patient. Only a registered pharmacist can do this step and it takes 0.8 minute.

Step 7—Prepare all charges, write notes or comments if needed, and close the patient's pharmacy record in the pharmacy computer system. This step takes 1.5 minutes and may be done by a registered pharmacist but the law does not require it.

Currently, the pharmacist always performs steps 2 to 7 for each patient's prescription and sometimes step 1. Two medical technicians are on duty at all times to receive the prescriptions, answer the telephone, receive supplies and stock shelves, deliver prescriptions through the service window, and interact with nurses and doctors as they visit the pharmacy service window. You have been called in as a consultant to improve the process and begin by considering the following case questions.

Case Questions for Discussion

1. Draw the process flowchart, including processing times and capacities per step, and total time per prescription.

2. As a baseline measure for one time period, what is the labor utilization if 30 prescriptions arrive between 8 a.m. and 9 a.m. on Monday and four or five pharmacists are on duty doing all seven steps? (You do not have the data to evaluate staffing levels by hour of the day for Monday.)

3. Clearly identify two other ways to group and divide the work among the medical technicians and pharmacists, compute labor utilizations, and discuss the advantages and disadvantages of each job and process-design option.

4. What are your final recommendations?

FACILITY AND WORK DESIGN

ytec (www.vytec.com) is a leading manufacturer of vinyl siding for homes and businesses. Vytec makes 50 different product lines (called profiles) of siding, soffits, and accessories. Each profile is typically produced in 15 colors, creating 750 stock-keeping units. The finished siding is packaged in a carton that holds 20 pieces that are usually 12 feet long. The cartons are stacked in steel racks (called beds). Each bed holds 30 to 60 cartons depending on the bed's location in the warehouse. Vytec's main warehouse is more than 200,000 square feet.

Over time, demand for each siding profile changes, and some are added and others discontinued. One problem the warehouse faces periodically is the need to redo the location and capacity of beds in the warehouse. Using basic layout principles, high-demand siding profiles are located closest to the shipping dock to minimize travel and order-picking time. Although management would like to find a permanent solution to this stock placement problem in the warehouse, the continuous changes in demand and product mix necessitate a new design every few years.[1]

learning outcomes

After studying this chapter you should be able to:

8-1 **Describe four layout patterns and when they should be used.**

8-2 **Explain how to design product layouts using assembly-line balancing.**

8-3 **Explain the concepts of process layout.**

8-4 **Describe issues related to workplace design.**

8-5 **Describe the human issues related to workplace design.**

What do you think?

Think of a facility in which you have conducted business—for instance, a restaurant, bank, or automobile dealership. How did the physical environment and layout enhance or degrade your customer experience?

Duygu Ozen/iStockphoto.com

Once processes are selected and designed, organizations must design the infrastructure to implement these processes. This is accomplished through the design of the physical facilities and work tasks that must be performed. The physical design of a factory needs to support operations as efficiently as possible, as we can see in the example about Vytec. Facility and work design are important elements of an organization's infrastructure and key strategic decisions that affect cost, productivity, responsiveness, and agility.

In both goods-producing and service-providing organizations, facility layout and work design influence the ability to meet customer wants and needs, enhance sustainability, and provide value. A poorly designed facility can lock management into a noncompetitive situation, and be very costly to correct. For many service organizations, the physical facility and workplace are vital parts of service design (see the box on green baseball parks). It can also play a significant role in creating a satisfying customer experience, particularly when customer contact is high. Facility design must be integrated with and support job and process design.

8-1 Facility Layout

facility layout *refers to the specific arrangement of physical facilities.* Facility layout studies are necessary whenever (1) a new facility is constructed; (2) there is a significant change in demand or throughput volume; (3) a new good or service is introduced to the customer benefit package; or (4) different processes, equipment, and/or technology are installed. The objectives of layout studies are to minimize delays in materials handling and customer movement, maintain flexibility, use labor and space effectively, promote high employee morale and customer satisfaction, minimize energy use and environmental impact, provide for good housekeeping and maintenance, and enhance

> **Facility layout** refers to the specific arrangement of physical facilities.

▼ *Continuous changes in demand and product mix necessitate a new design every few years.*

sales as appropriate in manufacturing and service facilities. Essentially, a good layout should support the ability of operations to accomplish its mission.

> A good layout should support the ability of operations to accomplish its mission.

Four major layout patterns are commonly used in configuring facilities: product layout, process layout, cellular layout, and fixed-position layout.

8-1a Product Layout

A product layout is an arrangement based on the sequence of operations that is performed during the manufacturing of a good or delivery of a service. Exhibit 8.1 shows a typical product layout used in winemaking. Product layouts support a smooth and logical flow where all goods or services move in a continuous path from one process stage to the next using the same sequence of work tasks and activities. You have seen a product

> A **product layout** is an arrangement based on the sequence of operations that is performed during the manufacturing of a good or delivery of a service.

Play Ball and Save the Planet

U.S. major league baseball parks are being redesigned to be eco-friendly, and their workplaces are going green, far beyond the grass in the outfield. For example, the Tampa Bay Rays team allocates free parking for carpoolers, and waterless urinals have been installed at the New York Mets' new Citi Field. The new Yankee Stadium uses energy-efficient bulbs, and avoids harsh chemicals to maintain the field. Stadium sponsors also get recognized if they fund solar panels, waterless urinals, and green food stands and restaurants in the stadium. Food services use biodegradable utensils, plates, cups, and napkins. When the Atlanta Braves play home games, about 2,000 stadium employees wear shirts with Atlanta Braves patches made from 50 percent recycled soda bottles. These shirts keep about 10,000 bottles per year out of landfills. Volunteers wearing these shirts work through the stands during games to collect plastic recyclables.[2]

Jim McIsaac/Getty Images Sport/Getty Images

layout if you have ever eaten at Subway or Chipotle; the ingredients are arranged in a specific order as you build your sandwich or burrito. Other examples include credit card processing, paper manufacturers, insurance policy processing, and automobile assembly lines.

Exhibit 8.1 *Product Layout for Wine Manufacturer*

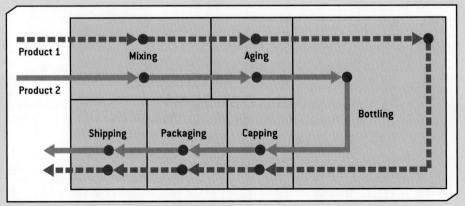

© Cengage Learning 2013

Advantages of product layouts include higher output rates, lower work-in-process inventories, less material handling, higher labor and equipment utilization, and simple planning and control systems. However, several disadvantages are associated with product layouts. For instance, a breakdown of one piece of equipment can cause the entire process to shut down. In addition, because the layout is determined by the good or service, a change in product design or the introduction of new products may require major changes in the layout; thus flexibility can be limited. Therefore, product layouts are less flexible and expensive to change. They also usually require more costly, specialized equipment. Finally, and perhaps most important, the jobs in a product-layout facility, such as those on a mass-production line, may provide little job satisfaction. This is primarily because of the high level of division of labor often required, which usually results in monotony. However, this can be avoided by cross-training and frequently rotating job responsibilities (see the box about Cargill Kitchen Solutions later in this chapter).

8-1b Process Layout

*A **process layout** consists of a functional grouping of equipment or activities that do similar work.* For example, all drill presses or fax machines may be grouped together in one department and all milling or data entry machines in another. Depending on the processing they require, tasks may be moved in different sequences among departments (see Exhibit 8.2). Job shops are an example of facilities that use process layouts because they typically handle a wide variety of customized orders. Legal offices, shoe manufacturing, jet engine turbine blades, and hospitals also use process layouts.

Compared to product layouts, process layouts provide more flexibility and generally require a lower investment in equipment. If a piece of equipment fails, it generally does not affect the entire system. Also, the diversity of jobs inherent in a process layout can lead to increased worker satisfaction. Some of the limitations of process layouts are low equipment utilization, high

material handling costs, more complicated planning and control systems, and higher worker skill requirements.

8-1c Cellular Layout

*In a **cellular layout**, the design is not according to the functional characteristics of equipment, but rather by self-contained groups of equipment (called cells) needed for producing a particular set of goods or services.* The cellular concept was developed at the Toyota Motor Company.

An example of a manufacturing cell is shown in Exhibit 8.3. In this exhibit we see a U-shaped arrangement of machines that is typical of cellular manufacturing. The cell looks similar to a product layout, but operates differently. Within the cell, materials move clockwise or counterclockwise from one operation to the next. The cell is designed to operate with one, two, or three employees, depending on the needed output during the day (Exhibit 8.3 shows how three operators might be assigned to machines). Each operator is responsible for loading the parts on the individual machine, performing the processing operation, unloading the parts, and moving them to the next operation. Working in parallel, they increase the output from the cell.

Cellular layouts facilitate the processing of families of parts with similar processing requirements. The procedure of classifying parts into such families is called *group*

A **process layout** consists of a functional grouping of equipment or activities that do similar work.

In a **cellular layout,** the design is not according to the functional characteristics of equipment, but rather by self-contained groups of equipment (called cells) needed for producing a particular set of goods or services.

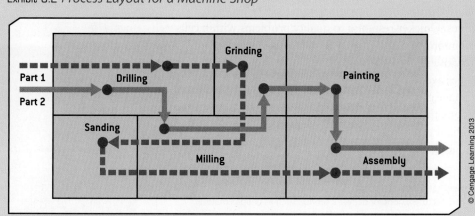

Exhibit 8.2 *Process Layout for a Machine Shop*

© Cengage Learning 2013

Exhibit 8.3 *Cellular Manufacturing Layout*

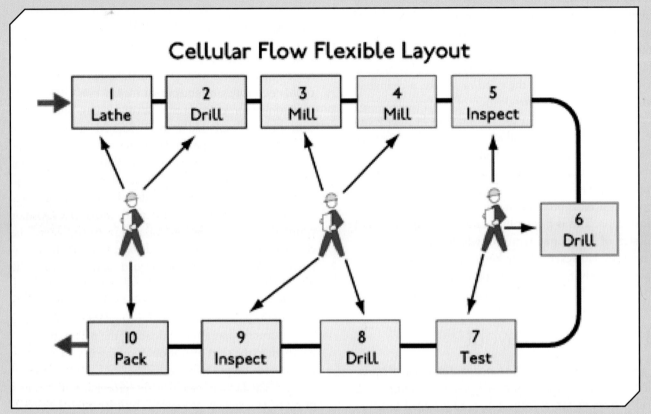

Cellular Flow Flexible Layout

| 1 Lathe | 2 Drill | 3 Mill | 4 Mill | 5 Inspect |

6 Drill

| 10 Pack | 9 Inspect | 8 Drill | 7 Test |

Source: www.nist.gov

technology. Services also group work analogous to manufacturers, such as legal (labor law, bankruptcy, divorce, etc.) or medical specialties (maternity, oncology, surgery, etc.).

Because the workflow is standardized and centrally located in a cellular layout, materials-handling requirements are reduced, enabling workers to concentrate on production rather than on moving parts between machines. Quicker response to quality problems within cells can improve the overall level of quality. Because machines are closely linked within a cell, additional floor space becomes available for other productive uses. Because workers have greater responsibility in a cellular manufacturing system, they become more aware of their contribution to the final product; this increases their morale and satisfaction and, ultimately, quality and productivity.

A **fixed-position layout** consolidates the resources necessary to manufacture a good or deliver a service, such as people, materials, and equipment, in one physical location.

8-1d Fixed-Position Layout

A **fixed-position layout** *consolidates the resources necessary to manufacture a good or deliver a service, such as people, materials, and equipment, in one physical location.*

Oleg - F/Shutterstock.com

Rather than moving work-in-process from one work center to another, it remains stationary. The production of large items such as heavy machine tools, airplanes, buildings, locomotives, and ships is usually accomplished in a fixed position layout. This fixed-position layout is synonymous with the "project" classification of processes. Service-providing firms also use fixed position layouts; examples include major hardware and software installations, sporting events, and concerts. Fixed position layouts usually require a high level of planning and control compared with other types of layouts.

Exhibit 8.4 summarizes the relative features of product, process, cellular, and fixed-position layouts. It is clear that the basic trade-off in selecting among these layout types is flexibility versus productivity.

8-1e Facility Layout in Service Organizations

Service organizations use product, process, cellular, and fixed-position layouts to organize different types of work. For example, looking back at Exhibit 6.12, which shows the typical LensCrafters facility layout, we see the customer-contact area is arranged in a process layout. In the lab area, however, where lenses are manufactured, a cellular layout is used.

In service organizations, the basic trade-off between product and process layouts concerns the degree of specialization versus flexibility. Services must consider

the volume of demand, range of the types of services offered, degree of personalization of the service, skills of employees, and cost. Those that need the ability to provide a wide variety of services to customers with differing requirements usually use a process layout. For example, libraries place reference materials, serials, and microfilms into separate areas; hospitals group services by function also, such as maternity, oncology, surgery, and X ray; and insurance companies have office layouts in which claims, underwriting, and filing are individual departments.

Service organizations that provide highly standardized services tend to use product layouts. For example, Exhibit 8.5 shows the layout of the kitchen at a small pizza restaurant that has both dine-in and delivery.

The design of service facilities requires the clever integration of layout with the servicescape and process design to support service encounters. At Victoria's Secret, the layout of a typical store is defined by different

Exhibit 8.4 *Comparison of Basic Layout Patterns*

Characteristic	Product Layout	Process Layout	Cellular Layout	Fixed-Position Layout
Demand volume	High	Low	Moderate	Very low
Equipment utilization	High	Low	High	Moderate
Automation potential	High	Moderate	High	Moderate
Setup/changover requirements	High	Moderate	Low	High
Flexibility	Low	High	Moderate	Moderate
Type of equipment	Highly specialized	General purpose	Moderate specialization	Moderate specialization

© Cengage Learning 2013

Exhibit 8.5 *Product Layout for a Pizza Kitchen*

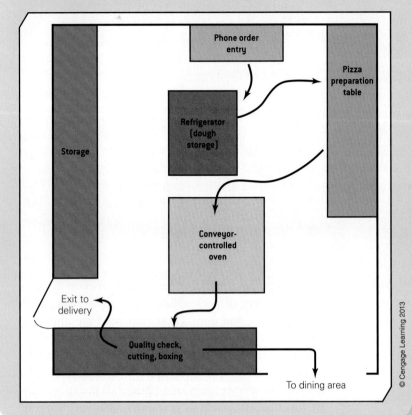

8-2 Designing Product Layouts

Product layouts in flow shops generally consist of a fixed sequence of workstations. Workstations are generally separated by buffers (queues of work-in-process) to store work waiting for processing, and are often linked by gravity conveyors (which cause parts to simply roll to the end and stop) to allow easy transfer of work. An example is shown in Exhibit 8.6. Such product layouts, however, can suffer from two sources of delay: flow-blocking delay and lack-of-work delay. **Flow blocking delay** *occurs when a work center completes a unit but cannot release it because the in-process storage at the next stage is full*. The worker must remain idle until storage space becomes available. **Lack-of-work delay** *occurs whenever one stage completes work and no units from the previous stage are awaiting processing.*

These sources of delay can be minimized by attempting to "balance" the process by designing the appropriate level of capacity at each workstation. This is often done by adding additional workstations in parallel. Product layouts might have workstations in series,

zones, each with a certain type of apparel, such as women's sleepwear, intimate apparel, and personal-care products. Display case placement in the store is carefully planned. A companion store, Victoria's Secret Perfume, which specializes in fragrances, color cosmetics, skincare, and personal accessories, is often placed next to and connected to a Victoria's Secret store to increase traffic and sales in both stores.

Flow-blocking delay
occurs when a work center completes a unit but cannot release it because the in-process storage at the next stage is full.

Lack-of-work delay
occurs whenever one stage completes work and no units from the previous stage are awaiting processing.

Exhibit 8.6 *A Typical Manufacturing Workstation Layout*

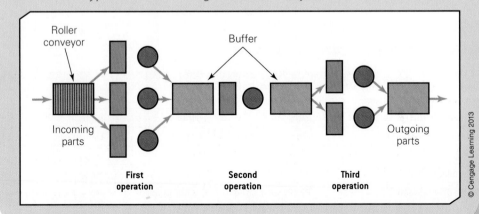

Mikhailishin Igor/ITAR-TASS /Landov

in parallel, or in a combination of both. Thus, many different configurations of workstations and buffers are possible, and it is a challenge to design the right one.

An important type of product layout is an assembly line. *An assembly line is a product layout dedicated to combining the components of a good or service that has been created previously.* Assembly lines were pioneered by Henry Ford and are vital to economic prosperity and are the backbone of many industries such as automobiles and appliances; their efficiencies lower costs and make goods and services affordable to mass markets. Assembly lines are also important in many service operations such as processing laundry, insurance policies, mail, and financial transactions.

8-2a Assembly-Line Balancing

The sequence of tasks required to assemble a product is generally dictated by its physical design. Clearly, you cannot put the cap on a ballpoint pen until the ink refill has been inserted. However, for many assemblies that consist of a large number of tasks, there are a large number of ways to group tasks together into individual workstations while still ensuring the proper sequence of work. **Assembly-line balancing** *is a technique to group tasks among workstations so that each workstation has—in*

the ideal case—the same amount of work. Assembly-line balancing focuses on organizing work efficiently in flow shops.

For example, if it took 90 seconds per unit to assemble an alarm clock and the work was divided evenly among three workstations, then each workstation would be assigned 30 seconds of work content per unit. Here, there is no idle time per workstation and the output of the first workstation immediately becomes the input to the next workstation. Technically, there is no bottleneck workstation and the flow of clocks through the assembly line is constant and continuous. In reality, this is seldom possible, so the objective is to minimize the imbalance among workstations while trying to achieve a desired output rate. A good balance results in achieving throughput necessary to meet sales commitments and minimize the cost of operations. Typically, one either minimizes the number of workstations for a given production rate or maximizes the production rate for a given number of workstations.

To begin, we need to know three types of information:

1. the set of tasks to be performed and the time required to perform each task,

2. the precedence relations among the tasks—that is, the sequence in which tasks must be performed, and

3. the desired output rate or forecast of demand for the assembly line.

The first two can be obtained from an analysis of the design specifications of a good or service. The third is

An **assembly line** is a product layout dedicated to combining the components of a good or service that has been created previously.

Assembly-line balancing is a technique to group tasks among workstations so that each workstation has—in the ideal case—the same amount of work.

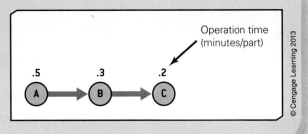

Exhibit 8.7 *A Three-Task Assembly Line*

Operation time
(minutes/part)

.5   .3   .2

A → B → C

© Cengage Learning 2013

primarily a management policy issue, because management must decide whether to produce exactly to the forecast, overproduce and hold inventory, subcontract, and so on.

To illustrate the issues associated with assembly-line balancing, let us consider an activity consisting of three tasks as shown in Exhibit 8.7. Task A is first, takes 0.5 minute, and must be completed before task B can be performed. After task B, which takes 0.3 minute, is finished, task C can be performed; it takes 0.2 minute. Because all three tasks must be performed to complete one part, the total time required to complete one part is .5 + .3 + .2 = 1.0 minute.

Suppose that one worker performs all three tasks in sequence. In an eight-hour day, he or she could produce (1 part/1.0 min)(60 minutes per hour)(8 hours per day) = 480 parts/day. Hence, the capacity of the process is 480 parts/day.

Alternatively, suppose that three workers are assigned to the line, each performing one of the three tasks. The first operator can produce 120 parts per hour, as his or her task time is 0.5 minute. Thus, a total of (1 part/0.5 min)(60 minutes per hour) (8 hours per day) = 960 parts/day could be sent to operator 2. Because the time operator 2 needs for his or her operation is only 0.3 minute, he or she could produce (1 part/0.3 min) (60 minutes per hour)(8 hours per day) = 1,600 parts/day. However, operator 2 cannot do so because the first operator has a lower production rate. The second operator will be idle some of the time waiting on components to arrive. Even though the third operator can produce (1 part/0.2 min) (60 minutes per hour) (8 hours per day) = 2,400 parts/day, we see that the maximum output of this three operator assembly line

is 960 parts per day. That is, workstation 1 performing task A is the bottleneck in the process.

A third alternative is to use two workstations. The first operator could perform operation A while the second performs operations B and C. Because each operator needs 0.5 minute to perform the assigned duties, the line is in perfect balance, and 960 parts per day can be produced. We can achieve the same output rate with two operators as we can with three, thus saving labor costs. How you group work tasks and activities into workstations is important in terms of process capacity (throughput), cost, and time to do the work.

An important concept in assembly-line balancing is the cycle time. **Cycle time** *is the interval between successive outputs coming off the assembly line.* These could be manufactured goods or service-related outcomes. In the three-operation example shown in Exhibit 8.7, if we use only one workstation, the cycle time is 1 minute/unit; that is, one completed assembly is produced every minute. If two workstations are used, as just described, the cycle time is 0.5 minute/unit. Finally, if three workstations are used, the cycle time is still 0.5 minute/unit, because task A is the bottleneck, or slowest operation. The line can produce only one assembly every 0.5 minute.

The cycle time (CT) cannot be smaller than the largest operation time, nor can it be larger than the sum of all operation times (Σt). Thus,

$$\text{Maximum operation time} \leq CT$$
$$\leq \text{Sum of operation times} \qquad [8.1]$$

This provides a range of feasible cycle times. In the example, CT must be between 0.5 and 1.0.

Cycle time is related to the output required to be produced in some period of time (R) by the following equation:

$$CT = A/R \qquad [8.2]$$

where A = available time to produce the output. R is normally the demand forecast. Thus, if we specify a required output (demand forecast), we can calculate the maximum cycle time needed to achieve it. Note that if the required cycle time is smaller than the largest task time, then the work content must be redefined by splitting some tasks into smaller elements.

For a given cycle time, we may also compute the theoretical minimum number of workstations required:

$$\text{Minimum number of workstations required}$$
$$= \text{Sum of task times/Cycle time} = \Sigma t/CT \; [8.3]$$

Solved Problem

Bass Fishing, Inc. assembles fishing reels in an assembly line using six workstations. Management wants an output rate of 300 reels per day (with a 7.5 hour workday). The sum of the task times is 8 minutes/reel.

a. What is the cycle time?

$CT = A/R = [(7.5 \text{ hours/day})(60 \text{ minutes/hour})]/ (300 \text{ reels/day}) = 450/300 = 1.5 \text{ minutes/reel}$

b. What is the assembly-line efficiency?

$\text{Efficiency} = \Sigma t /(N \times CT) = 8/(6 \times 1.5) = 88.9\%$

c. What is total idle time?

$\text{Total idle time} = (N)(CT) - \Sigma t = 6*1.5 - 8 = 1 \text{ minute/reel}$

Management is paying for 8 minutes of work and 1 minute of idle time per reel.

When this number is a fraction, the theoretical minimum number of workstations should be rounded up to the next highest integer number. For example, for a cycle time of 0.5, we would need at least 1.0/0.5 = 2 workstations.

The following equations provide additional information about the performance of an assembly line:

Total time available

$$= (\text{Number of workstations})(\text{Cycle time})$$
$$= (N)(CT) \qquad [8.4]$$
$$\text{Total idle time} = (N)(CT) - \Sigma t \qquad [8.5]$$
$$\text{Assembly-line efficiency} = \Sigma t/(N \times CT) \qquad [8.6]$$
$$\text{Balance delay} = 1 - \text{Assembly-line efficiency} \quad [8.7]$$

The total time available computed by Equation 8.4 represents the total productive capacity that management pays for. Idle time is the difference between total time available and the sum of the actual times for productive tasks as given by Equation 8.5. Assembly-line efficiency, computed by Equation 8.6, specifies the fraction of available productive capacity that is used. One minus efficiency represents the amount of idle time that results from imbalance among workstations and is called the *balance delay*, as given by Equation 8.7.

In the Solved Problem, suppose that we use seven workstations. The total time available is 7(1.5) = 10.5 minutes; the total idle time is 10.5 − 8 = 2.5 minutes; and the line efficiency is reduced to 8/10.5 = 0.76.

One objective of assembly-line balancing is to maximize the line efficiency. Note that if we use only six workstations, the total time available is 5(1.5) = 7.5 minutes. Because this is less than the sum of the task times, it would be impossible to achieve the desired output rate of 300 reels per day.

8-2b Line-Balancing Approaches

Balancing the three-task example in the previous section was quite easy to do by inspection. With a large number of tasks, the number of possible workstation configurations can be very large, making the balancing problem very complex. Decision rules, or heuristics, are used to assign tasks to workstations. Because heuristics cannot guarantee the best solution, one often applies a variety of different rules in an attempt to find a very good solution among several alternatives. For large line-balancing problems, such decision rules are incorporated into computerized algorithms and simulation models.

To illustrate a simple, yet effective, approach to balancing an assembly line, suppose that we are producing an in-line skate as shown in Exhibit 8.8. The target output rate is 360 units per week. The effective workday

Stanislav Fridkin/Shutterstock.com

(assuming one shift) is 7.2 hours, considering breaks and lunch periods. We will assume that the facility operates five days per week.

Eight tasks are required to assemble the individual parts. These, along with task times, are

1. Assemble wheels, bearings, and axle hardware (2.0 min).

2. Assemble brake housing and pad (0.2 min).

3. Complete wheel assembly (1.5 min).

4. Inspect wheel assembly (0.5 min).

5. Assemble boot (3.5 min).

6. Join boot and wheel subassemblies (1.0 min).

7. Add line and final assembly (0.2 min).

8. Perform final inspection (0.5 min).

If we use only one workstation for the entire assembly and assign all tasks to it, the cycle time is 9.4 minutes. Alternatively, if each task is assigned to a unique workstation, the cycle time is 3.5, the largest task time. Thus, feasible cycle times must be between 3.5 and 9.4 minutes. Given the target output rate of 360 units per week and operating one shift per day for five days per week, we can use Equation 8.2 to find the appropriate cycle time:

$$CT = A/R$$
$$= [(7.2 \text{ hours/shift})(60 \text{ min/hr}]/(72 \text{ units/shift})$$
$$= 6.0 \text{ minutes/unit}$$

The theoretical minimum number of workstations is found using Equation 8.3:

$$\Sigma t/CT = 9.4/6.0 = 1.57, \text{ or rounded up, is 2}$$

The eight tasks need not be performed in this exact order; however, it is important to ensure that certain precedence restrictions are met. For example, you cannot perform the wheel assembly (task 3) until both tasks 1 and 2 have been completed, but it does not matter whether task 1 or task 2 is performed first because they are independent of each other. These types of relationships are usually developed through an engineering analysis of the product. We can represent them by an arrow diagram, shown in Exhibit 8.9. The arrows indicate what tasks must precede others. Thus, the arrow pointing from tasks 1 and 2 to task 3 indicate that tasks 1 and 2 must be completed before task 3 is performed; similarly, task 3 must precede task 4. The numbers next to each task represent the task times.

This precedence network helps to visually determine whether a workstation assignment is *feasible*—that is, meets the precedence restrictions. For example, in Exhibit 8.9 we might assign tasks 1, 2, 3, and 4 to one workstation, and tasks 5, 6, 7, and 8 to a second workstation as illustrated by the shading. This is feasible because all tasks assigned to workstation 1 are completed before those assigned to workstation 2. However, we could not assign tasks 1, 2, 3, 4, and 6 to workstation 1 and tasks 5, 7, and 8 to workstation 2, because operation 5 must precede operation 6.

Exhibit 8.8 *A Typical In-Line Skate*

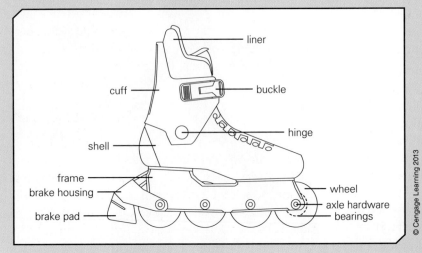

© Cengage Learning 2013

The problem is to assign the eight work activities to workstations without violating precedence or exceeding the cycle time of 6.0. Different rules may be used to assign tasks to workstations. For example, one line-balancing decision rule example is to assign the task with the *longest task time first* to a workstation if the cycle time would not be exceeded. The longest-task-time-first decision rule assigns tasks with long task times first, because shorter task times are easier to fit in the line balance later in the procedure. Another rule might be to assign the shortest task first. These rules attempt to minimize the amount of idle time at workstations, but they are heuristics and do not guarantee optimal solutions.

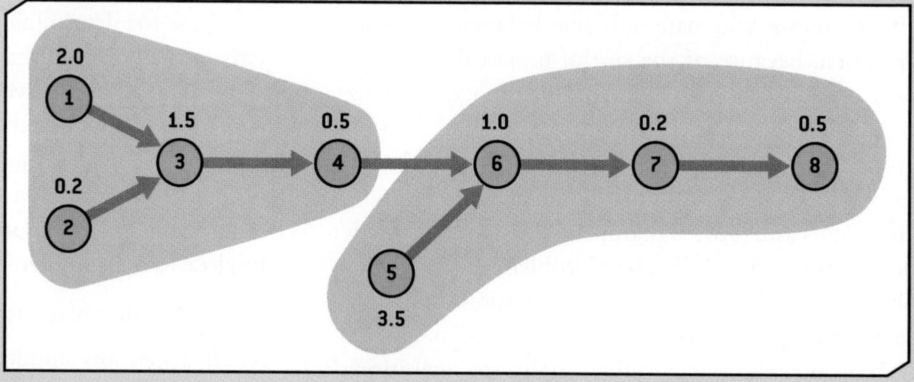

The longest-task-time rule can be formalized as follows:

1. Choose a set of "assignable tasks"—those for which all immediate predecessors have already been assigned.

2. Assign the assignable task with the *longest* task time first. Break ties by choosing the lowest task number.

3. Construct a new set of assignable candidates. If no further tasks can be assigned, move on to the next workstation. Continue in this way until all tasks have been assigned.

Let us illustrate this with an example. We will call the first workstation "A" and determine which tasks can be assigned. In this case, tasks 1, 2, and 5 are candidates, as they have no immediate predecessors. Using the decision rule—*choose the activity with the longest task time first*—we therefore assign task 5 to workstation A.

Next, we determine a new set of tasks that may be considered for assignment. At this point, we may only choose among tasks 1 and 2 (even though task 5 has been assigned, we cannot consider task 6 as a candidate because task 4 has not yet been assigned to a workstation). Note that we can assign both tasks 1 and 2 to workstation A without violating the cycle time restriction.

Exhibit 8.9 *Precedence Network and Workstation Assignment*

© Cengage Learning 2013

At this point, task 3 becomes the only candidate for assignment. Because the total time for tasks 5, 1, and 2 is 5.7 minutes, we cannot assign task 3 to workstation A without violating the cycle time restriction of 6.0 minutes. In this case, we move on to workstation B.

At workstation B, the only candidate we can assign next is task 3. Continuing, we can assign tasks 4, 6, 7, and 8 in that order and still be within the cycle time limit. Because all tasks have been assigned to a workstation, we are finished. This assembly-line balance is summarized as follows:

Workstation	Tasks	Total Time	Idle Time
A	1, 2, 5	5.7	0.3
B	3, 4, 6, 7, 8	3.7	2.3
	Total	9.4	2.6

Using Equations 8.4 to 8.6, we may compute the following:

Total time available
$$= \text{(Number of workstations)(Cycle time)}$$
$$= (N)(CT) = (2)(6) = 12 \text{ minutes}$$
Total idle time $= (N)(CT) - \Sigma t$
$$= (2)(6) - 9.4 = 2.6 \text{ minutes}$$
Assembly-line efficiency $= \Sigma t/(N \times CT)$
$$= 9.4/(2 \times 6) = 0.783 \text{ or } 78.3\%$$

In this example, efficiency is not very high because the precedence relationships constrained the possible line-balancing solutions. The target efficiency for most assembly lines is 80 percent to 90 percent, but this is highly dependent on things like the degree of automation, inspection stations, workforce skills, complexity of the assembly, and so on. One option is to redefine the work content for the assembly task in more detail if this is possible, by breaking down the tasks into smaller elements with smaller task times and rebalancing the line, hoping to achieve a higher efficiency.

In the real world, assembly-line balancing is quite complicated, because of the size of practical problems as well as constraints that mechanization or tooling place on work tasks. Also, in today's manufacturing plants, there is virtually no such thing as a single-model assembly line. In the automotive industry, many model combinations and work assignments exist. Such mixed-model assembly-line-balancing problems are considerably more difficult to solve. Simulation modeling is frequently used to obtain a "best set" of assembly-line-balancing solutions and then engineers, operations managers, and suppliers evaluate and critique these solutions to find the best design.

8-3 Designing Process Layouts

In designing process layouts, we are concerned with the arrangement of departments or work centers relative to each other. Costs associated with moving materials or the inconvenience that customers might experience in moving between physical locations are usually the principal design criteria for process layouts. In general, work centers with a large number of moves between them should be located close to one another.

Several software packages have been written expressly for designing process layouts; some include simulations of the entire factory layout. These packages have the advantage of being able to search among a much larger number of potential layouts than could possibly be done manually. Despite the capabilities of the computer, no layout program will provide optimal solutions for large, realistic problems. Like many practical solution procedures in management science, they are heuristic; that is, they can help the user to find a very good, but not necessarily the optimal, solution.

One of the most widely used facility-layout programs is CRAFT (Computerized Relative Allocation of Facilities Technique). CRAFT attempts to minimize the total materials-handling cost. The user must generate an initial layout and provide data on the volume between departments and the materials-handling costs. CRAFT uses the centroid of each department to compute distances and materials-handling costs for a particular layout. In an effort to improve the current solution, CRAFT

exchanges the location of two (in later versions, three) departments at a time and determines if the total cost has been reduced. If so, it then uses the new solution as a base for determining new potential improvements. Other programs that have been used in facilities layout are ALDEP (Automated Layout-DEsign Program) and CORELAP (COmputerized RElationship LAyout Planning). Rather than using materials-handling costs as the primary solution, the user constructs a preference table that specifies how important it is for two departments to be close to one another. These "closeness ratings" follow.

A Absolutely necessary

B Especially important

C Important

D Ordinary closeness okay

E Unimportant

F Undesirable

The computer programs attempt to optimize the total closeness rating of the layout. Computer graphics is providing a major advance in layout planning. It allows interactive design of layouts in real time and can eliminate some of the disadvantages, such as irregularly shaped departments, that often result from noninteractive computer packages.

8-4 Workplace Design

Not only is it important to effectively design the overall facility layout, but it is equally important to focus on individual workstations. A well-designed workplace should allow for maximum efficiency and effectiveness as the work task or activity is performed, and may also need to facilitate service management skills, particularly in high-contact, front-office environments.

Key questions that must be addressed at the workstation level include:

1. Who will use the workplace? Will the workstation be shared? How much space is required? Workplace designs must take into account different physical characteristics of individuals, such as differences in size, arm length, strength, and dexterity.

2. How will the work be performed? What tasks are required? How much time does each task take?

How much time is required to set up for the workday or for a particular job? How might the tasks be grouped into work activities most effectively? This includes knowing what information, equipment, items, and procedures are required for each task, work activity, and job.

3. What technology is needed? Employees may need to use a computer or have access to customer records and files, special equipment, intercoms, and other forms of technology.

4. What must the employee be able to see? Employees might need special fixtures for blueprints, test procedures, sorting paper, antiglare computer screens, and so on.

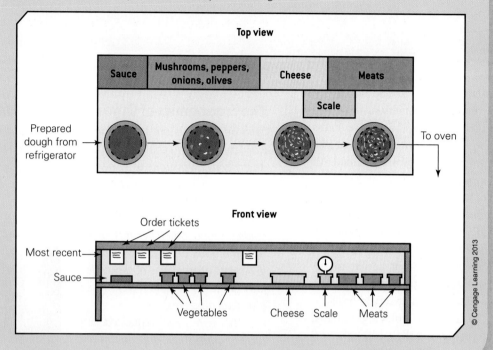

Exhibit 8.10 *Pizza-Preparation Workplace Design*

© Cengage Learning 2013

Bil Zelman/Jupiterimages

5. What must the employee be able to hear? Employees may need to communicate with others, wear a telephone headset all day, be able to listen for certain sounds during product and laboratory testing, or be able to hear warning sounds of equipment.

6. What environmental and safety issues need to be addressed? What protective clothing or gear should the employee wear?

To illustrate some of these issues, let us consider the design of the pizza-preparation table for a pizza restaurant. The objective of a design is to maximize throughput, that is, the number of pizzas that can be made; minimize errors in fulfilling customer orders; and minimize total flow time and customer waiting and delivery time. In slow-demand periods, one or two employees may make the entire pizza. During periods of high demand, such as weekends and holidays, more employees may be needed. The workplace design would need to accommodate this.

An example of a pizza-preparation workstation is shown in Exhibit 8.10. Ingredients should be put on the pizzas in the following order: sauce, vegetables (mushrooms, peppers, onions, etc.), cheese, and, finally, meat. Because cheese and meat are the highest-cost items and also greatly affect taste and customer satisfaction, the manager requires that those items be weighed to ensure that the proper amounts are included. All items are arranged in the order of assembly within easy reach of the employee and, as the front view illustrates, order tickets are hung at eye level, with the most recent orders on the left to ensure that pizzas are prepared on a first-come-first-served basis.

In office cubicles, e-mails, telephone calls, cell phones, pagers, and the like interrupt office workers so much that some companies have established "information-free zones" within the office. If you work in one of these zones, all of these interruption devices are turned off or blocked from operating so employees can focus on their work. Companies think information-free zones improve employee attention spans and productivity.

The Ergonomics of Office Chairs and Productivity

"Bad office chairs are to chiropractors what candy is to dentists," says Robert Hayden, a Georgia chiropractor. Good chair ergonomics can improve office productivity by an average of 17 percent according to a review of over 40 studies of office workers published in the Journal of Safety Research. These studies found other benefits of sitting in a good office chair, such as a lower rate of employee absences, less job-related errors, and fewer musculoskeletal problems.

The two most requested features of office chairs are comfort and adjustability. A good chair supports different body shapes and sizes with a flexible back and armrests and the seat promotes movement in all directions. People spend more time in chairs than in bed sleeping, so the office chair is an important part of the office servicescape. What type of chairs do you sit in throughout the week? Are they comfortable?[4]

Source: Sue Shellenbarger, "Does Your Chair Have Your Back?" The Wall Street Journal, September 21, 2011, pp. D1 and D4 or on web at http://online.wsj.com/article/SB10001424053111903374004576582673310637998.html

Safety is one of the most important aspects of workplace design, particularly in today's society.

8-4a Safety, Ergonomics, and the Work Environment

Safety is one of the most important aspects of workplace design, particularly in today's society. To provide safe and healthful working conditions and reduce hazards in the work environment, the Occupational Safety and Health Act (OSHA) was passed in 1970. It requires employers to furnish to each of their employees a place of employment free from recognized hazards that cause or are likely to cause death or serious physical harm. As a result of this legislation, the National Institute of Occupational Safety and Health (NIOSH) was formed to enforce standards provided by OSHA. Business and industry must abide by OSHA guidelines or face potential fines and penalties.

Safety is a function of the job, the person performing the job, and the surrounding environment. The job should be designed so that it will be highly unlikely that a worker can injure himself or herself. At the same time, the worker must be educated in the proper use

Bogdan Vasilescu/Shutterstock.com

8-4b The Human Side of Work

The physical design of a facility and the workplace can influence significantly how workers perform their jobs as well as their psychological well-being. Thus, operations managers who design jobs for individual workers need to understand how the physical environment can affect people. *A **job** is the set of tasks an individual performs.* ***Job design** involves determining the specific job tasks and responsibilities, the work environment, and the methods by which the tasks will be carried out to meet the goals of operations.*

of equipment and the methods designed for performing the job. Finally, the surrounding environment must be conducive to safety. This might include nonslip surfaces, warning signs, or buzzers.

***Ergonomics** is concerned with improving productivity and safety by designing workplaces, equipment, instruments, computers, workstations, and so on that take into account the physical capabilities of people.* The objective of ergonomics is to reduce fatigue, the cost of training, human errors, the cost of doing the job, and energy requirements while increasing accuracy, speed, reliability, and flexibility. Although ergonomics has traditionally focused on manufacturing workers and service providers, it is also important in designing the servicescape to improve customer interaction in high-contact environments.

Finally, it is important to pay serious attention to the work environment, not only in factories, but in every facility where work is performed, such as offices, restaurants, hospitals, and retail stores. A Gallup study showed that the less satisfied workers are with the physical aspects of their work environment, such as temperature, noise, or visual surroundings, the more likely they are to be dissatisfied with their jobs.[5] The study also found that workers who can personalize their workspaces to make it feel like their own were more productive and engaged in their work.

> **Ergonomics** is concerned with improving productivity and safety by designing workplaces, equipment, instruments, computers, workstations, and so on that take into account the physical capabilities of people.
>
> A **job** is the set of tasks an individual performs.
>
> **Job design** involves determining the specific job tasks and responsibilities, the work environment, and the methods by which the tasks will be carried out to meet the goals of operations.

CARGILL KITCHEN SOLUTIONS: INNOVATIVE JOB DESIGN

Cargill Kitchen Solutions manufactures and distributes more than 160 different types of egg-based food products to more than 1,200 U.S. foodservice operations such as quick-service restaurants, schools, hospitals, convenience stores, and food processors. Although production efficiency requires a product layout design in which each production department is organized into specific work or task areas, Cargill Kitchen Solutions has several innovative strategies to design its work systems to also provide a highly satisfying work environment for its employees. Workers are put on a "ramp-in" schedule when hired and only allowed to work for a specified number of hours initially. This not only provides better training and orientation to work tasks but also minimizes the potential for repetitive-stress injuries. The company uses a rotation system whereby workers rotate to another workstation every 20 minutes. This minimizes stress injuries, fights boredom, reinforces the concept of "internal customers," and provides a way of improving and reinforcing learning. Cargill Kitchen Solutions has led its industry with this workplace design approach since 1990, and OSHA standards were developed that mirror this rotation system.[6]

Two broad objectives must be satisfied in job design. One is to meet the firm's competitive priorities—cost, efficiency, flexibility, quality, and so on; the other is to make the job safe, satisfying, and motivating for the worker. Resolving conflicts between the need for technical and economic efficiency and the need for employee satisfaction is the challenge that faces operations managers in designing jobs. Clearly, efficiency improvements are needed to keep a firm competitive. However, it is also clear that any organization with a large percentage of dissatisfied employees cannot be competitive.

What is sought is a job design that provides for high levels of performance and at the same time a satisfying job and work environment.

The relationships between the technology of operations and the social/psychological aspects of work has been understood since the 1950s and is known as the *sociotechnical approach* to job design and provides useful ideas for operations managers. Sociotechnical approaches to work design provide opportunities for continual learning and personal growth for all employees. **Job enlargement** *is the horizontal expansion of the job to give the worker more variety—although not necessarily more responsibility.* Job enlargement might be accomplished, for example, by giving a production-line worker the task of building an entire product rather than a small subassembly, or by job rotation, such as rotating nurses among hospital wards or flight crews on different airline routes.

Job enrichment *is vertical expansion of job duties to give the worker more responsibility.* For instance, an assembly worker may be given the added responsibility of testing a completed assembly, so that he or she acts also as a quality inspector. A highly effective approach to job enrichment is to use teams. Some of the more common ones are:

- natural work teams, which perform entire jobs, rather than specialized, assembly-line work;
- virtual teams, in which members communicate by computer, take turns as leaders, and join and leave the team as necessary; and
- self-managed teams (SMTs), which are empowered work teams that also assume many traditional management responsibilities.

Virtual teams, in particular, have taken on increased importance in today's business world. Information technology provides the ability to assemble virtual teams of people located in different geographic locations.[7] For example, product designers and engineers in the United States can work with counterparts in Japan, transferring files at the end of each work shift to provide an almost continuous product development effort.

> **Job enlargement** is the horizontal expansion of the job to give the worker more variety—although not necessarily more responsibility.
>
> **Job enrichment** is vertical expansion of job duties to give the worker more responsibility.

Discussion Questions

1. Discuss the type of facility layout that would be most appropriate for
   a. printing books.
   b. performing hospital laboratory tests.
   c. manufacturing home furniture.
   d. a hospital.
   e. a photography studio.
   f. a library.

2. Describe the layout of a typical fast-food franchise such as McDonald's. What type of layout is it? How does it support productivity? Do different franchises (e.g., Burger King or Wendy's) have different types of layouts? Why?

3. How might sustainability issues be incorporated into the design of facilities and workplaces? Provide examples and explain your reasoning.

4. Describe the ergonomic features in the automobile that you drive most often. If it is an older model, visit a new-car showroom and contrast those features with those found in some newer models.

5. What do you think of Cargill Kitchen Solutions' 20-minute job rotation approach? Would you want to work in such an environment, or one in which you performed the same tasks all day? Why?

Problems and Activities

1. Research and write a short report (maximum of two typed pages) on green facility design, making sure that you incorporate some of the key topics in this chapter.

2. Research and write a short paper (maximum of two typed pages) illustrating how an organization uses one of the following types of facility layouts:
   • Product layout
   • Process layout
   • Cellular layout
   • Fixed-position layout

   What are the advantages and disadvantages in this organization? How does the layout affect process flows, quality, efficiency, time, and cost?

3. Visit a manufacturer or service organization and critique its facility design. What are the advantages and disadvantages? How does the layout affect process flows, customer service, efficiency, and cost?

4. Bass Fishing, Inc. assembles fishing nets with aluminum handles in an assembly line using four workstations. Management wants an output rate of 200 nets per day using a 7.5-hour work day. The sum of the task times is 6.25 minutes/net.
   a. What is the cycle time?
   b. What is assembly-line efficiency?
   c. What is total idle time?

5. Peter's Paper Clips uses a three-stage production process: cutting wire to prescribed lengths, inner bending, and outer bending. The cutting process can produce at a rate of 150 pieces per minute; inner bending, 140 pieces per minute; and outer bending, 110 pieces per minute. Determine the hourly capacity of each process stage and the number of machines needed to meet an output rate of 20,000 units per hour. How does facility layout impact your numerical analysis and process efficiency? Explain.

6. An assembly line with 30 activities is to be balanced. The total amount of time to complete all 30 activities is 42 minutes. The longest activity takes 2.4 minutes and the shortest takes 0.3 minute. The line will operate for 480 minutes per day.
   a. What are the maximum and minimum cycle times?
   b. How much daily output will be achieved by each of those cycle times?

7. In problem 6, suppose the line is balanced using 10 workstations and a finished product can be produced every 4.2 minutes.
   a. What is the production rate in units per day?
   b. What is the assembly-line efficiency?

8. A small assembly line for the assembly of power steering pumps needs to be balanced. Exhibit 8.11

is the precedence diagram. The cycle time is determined to be 1.5 minutes. How would the line be balanced by choosing the assignable task having the *longest* task time first?

9. For the assembly line described in problem 8, how would the line be balanced by choosing the assignable task having the *shortest* task time first?

10. For the in-line skate assembly example in this chapter, suppose the times for the individual operations are as follows:

Task	Time (sec.)
1	20
2	10
3	30
4	10
5	30
6	20
7	10
8	20

   Assume that inspections cannot be performed by production personnel, but only by persons from quality control. Therefore, assembly operations are separated into three groups for inspection. Design a production line to achieve an output rate of 120 per hour.

11. For the in-line skate example described in problem 10, design a production line to achieve an output rate of 90 per hour.

12. You have been asked to set up an assembly line to assemble a computer mouse. The precedence network is shown in Exhibit 8.12; task times in minutes are given in parentheses. There are 480 minutes of assembly time per shift and the company operates one shift each day. The required output rate is forecasted to be 60 units per shift.

   a. Balance the assembly line using the *longest-processing-time* rule. State the tasks associated with each workstation, total time, and idle time.

   b. What is the assembly-line efficiency?

   c. Is your assembly-line-balance solution good or bad? What criteria do you use to make this assessment? Explain.

13. Balance the assembly line in Exhibit 8.13 for (a) a shift output of 60 pieces and (b) a shift output of 40 pieces. Assume an eight-hour shift, and use the rule: choose the assignable task with the

longest processing time. Compute the line efficiency for each case.

14. List the ergonomic features of your automobile's interior and discuss any improvements that you can identify.

15. Research and write a short paper (1 page maximum) on the advantages and disadvantages of virtual teams in today's digital environment.

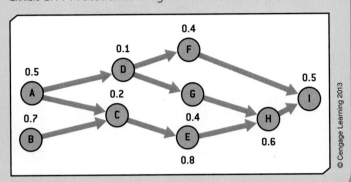

Exhibit 8.11 *Precedence Diagram for Problems 8 and 9*

© Cengage Learning 2013

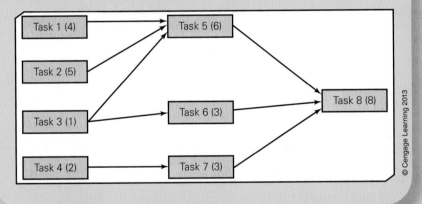

Exhibit 8.12 *Precedence Network for Problem 12*

© Cengage Learning 2013

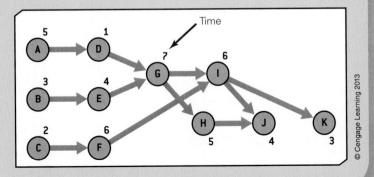

Exhibit 8.13 *Precedence Diagram for Problem 13*

© Cengage Learning 2013

BankUSA: Cash Movement Case Study

"Del, every wire transfer request is processed first-come-first-served. Some of these wires are for millions of dollars while others are under $100," said Betty Kelly, a 28-year old manager of Cash Movement (CM). She continued by saying, "I'm also concerned that all wires regardless of dollar amount go through the same quality checkpoints and whether we are staffed correctly."

Betty left her boss Del Carr's office with many related issues on her mind. As Betty sat down in her office chair, Steve Breslin, supervisor of outgoing wires, said, "Betty, last week we processed a wire for $80,000 incorrectly to Houston Oaks Bank and now they won't give it back. What should we do?" "Steve, give me the information, and I'll call the bank now," said Betty. The rest of Betty's day was spent recovering this money and discussing several personnel issues.

The Cash Movement (CM) operating unit is responsible for transferring money for BankUSA and any of its customers. Over 80 percent of all transaction requests are for individual customers, while the remaining requests are for commercial (business) customers. For example, a customer will sell stock and request that cash funds be sent to another institution such as a mutual fund, credit union, or another bank. The customer will request his or her local customer investment manager (CIM) to transfer money into or out of the account. The CIM will then request by e-mail or fax that Cash Movement process the transaction. All wires must be settled on the same day.

The average demand for outgoing wires is 306 wires per day for a 7.5-hour workday. Therefore, the cycle time for this demand rate using Equation 8.2 is computed as follows:

$$CT = A/R = [(7.5 \text{ hours/day})(60 \text{ minutes/hour})]$$
$$\div (306 \text{ wires/day})$$
$$= (450 \text{ minutes/day})/(306 \text{ wires/day})$$
$$= 1.47 \text{ minutes/wire}$$

Cash Movement employs 21 people, with 3 managers, 11 associates in outgoing wires, 2 associates in incoming wires, 3 associates in checks, and 2 associates in other areas. The average annual salary per associate is $30,000 with an additional 30 percent for benefits and overhead costs. Overhead costs include the cost of leasing/renting the building, operation of common areas such as the cafeteria and meeting rooms, utilities, insurance, and photocopy services.

Process workflow is documented in Exhibit 8.14 with 47 detailed steps consolidated into 16 logical workgroups/activities. The assembly line could be balanced using the original 47 steps if the times per step were given (they are not), but Betty thought she would begin by trying to balance the line using a more aggregate grouping of work with 16 workgroup activities. The 16 work activities are performed in a series or sequentially but how they are grouped does make a difference.

The first stage is external to the internal Cash Movement process and involves the front-room interaction between the customer (client) and the CIM. Here,

We processed a wire for $80,000 incorrectly to Houston Oaks Bank and now they won't give it back.

bullet74/Shutterstock.com

Exhibit 8.14 *Outgoing Wire Process Steps and Standard Times*

Process Steps (47 detailed steps Aggregated into 16 steps)	Workgroup Activity Number	% Work through This Stage	Processing Times per Client Transfer Request* (minutes)
Client Requests			
Steps 1 to 3 (client and customer investment manager interaction, accurate collection of process input information, submit to backroom outgoing wire process for transaction execution)		100%	16 minutes (2 to 120 minutes) This front-room step is not part of the outgoing wire backroom process so ignore it.
Logging (Begin Outgoing Wire Process)			
Steps 4 and 5 (receive request and verify)	1	100%	0.8 minute
Steps 6, 11, and back to 4 and 5 (incorrect or missing information—rework)	2	3%	10 minutes
Step 7 (confirm if >$50,000)	3	100%	0.8 minute
Steps 8 to 10 (separate into different batches and forward)	4	100%	0.1 minute
Verify the Receipt of Fax (Wire Request)			**First Quality Control Checkpoint**
(Steps 4 to 7 above)			
Direct Wire Input			
Steps 12 and 13 (receive batches and key into system—batches are variable but a typical batch is about 30 wires, which takes about 30 minutes to key into the computer)	5	100%	1 minute
Steps 14 to 16 (run remote report and tape and see if total dollar amounts match—verify)	6	100%	0.1 minute
Steps 17 to 19 (tape and remote report do not match—rework manually by checking each wire against each computer file—done by someone other than keyer)	7	3%	10 minutes
Verify the Accuracy of Wire Request			**Second Quality Control Checkpoint**
(Steps 12 to 19 above with a focus on keying the wire)	8	100%	0.5 minute
Steps 20 and 23 (receive and verify the wire's accuracy a second time in the computer—done by someone else)			

*These times are based on stopwatch time studies. The weighted average time per outgoing wire is 7.05 minutes. A total of 11 people work in this process.

an electronic transfer request can range from a few minutes to hours trying to help the customer decide what to do and may include a visit to the customer's home or office. This external work activity is not part of the internal process assembly line balance. The process begins at work activity 1 and ends at work activity 16.

A wire transfer request can "fail" in several ways with cost consequences to the bank. For example, if the wire is processed incorrectly or is not completed on time, the customer's transaction may fail. The effect of a failed transaction includes the customer being upset, customers leaving the bank forever, customers referring other friends and relatives to other banks, and the possible financial loss of processing the transaction the next business day at a new security price. BankUSA may have to compensate the customer for a failed transaction in terms of customer losses due to lost interest earnings on daily price changes plus processing fees. The average processing fee is $50 per wire. Moreover, any failed transaction must be researched and reprocessed, which constitutes "internal failure costs." Research and reprocessing costs per wire are estimated at $200. CM processes about 1,500 outgoing wires per week with about one error every two weeks. Errors happen due to CM mistakes but also are caused by other BankUSA departments, other financial institutions, and customers themselves. The information flow of this electronic funds transfer system is sometimes quite complex, with BankUSA having only partial control of the value chain.

Specific types of errors include the same wire being sent out twice, not sent out at all, sent with inaccurate information on it including dollar amount, or sent to the wrong place. No dollar amount has been assigned to each type of failure. The largest risk to Cash

Exhibit 8.14—continued *Outgoing Wire Process Steps and Standard Times*

Process Steps (47 detailed steps Aggregated into 16 steps)	Workgroup Activity Number	% Work through This Stage	Processing Times per Client Transfer Request* (minutes)
Verify the Accuracy of the Keyed Wire			**Third Quality Control Checkpoint**
(Steps 20 and 23 above with a focus on the wire in the computer)	9	100%	1 minute
Steps 24 and 28 (release the wire)	10	5%	3 minutes
Steps 25 to 27 (if wire incorrect, cancel wire, and rekey—back to step 12)	11	70%	0.1 minute
Step 29 (if CM needs to debit a customer's account, do steps 30 to 32 and batch and run tape)	12	30%	0.1 minute
Step 29 (if CM does not need to debit a customer's account, do step 33—wire is complete and paperwork filed)			
Verify the Wire Was Sent Correctly			**Fourth Quality Control Checkpoint**
(Steps 29 to 33)			
Steps 34 to 36 (taking money out of the customer's trust account and putting it in a Cash Management internal account)	13	100%	0.75 minute
Verify That Appropriate Funds Were Taken from the Customer's Account			**Fifth Quality Control Checkpoint**
(Steps 34 to 36—done by someone else)			
Step 37 (if totals on tape match totals on batch, go to steps 38 to 44)	14	97%	0.1 minute
Step 37 (if totals do not match, find the error by examining the batch of wires, then go to steps 39 to 43)	15	3%	10 minutes
Steps 45 to 47 (verify and file wire information)	16	100%	0.75 minute

*These times are based on stopwatch time studies. The weighted average time per outgoing wire is 7.05 minutes. A total of 11 people work in this process.

© Cengage Learning 2013

Movement is to send the money twice or to send it to the wrong institution. If CM catches the error the same day the wire is sent, the wire is requested to be returned that day. If a wire is sent in duplication, the receiving institution must receive permission from the customer to return the money to BankUSA. This results in lost interest and the possibility of long delays in returning the money or with BankUSA having to take legal action to get the money back. For international transaction requests that are wired with errors, the cost of getting the money back is high. These costs are potentially so high, up to several hundred thousand dollars, that five quality control steps are built into the cash management process, as shown in Exhibit 8.14. All wires, even low dollar amounts, are currently checked and rechecked to ensure completeness and accuracy.

As Betty, the manager of Cash Movement, drove home, she wondered when she would ever get the time to analyze these issues. She remembered taking a college course in operations management and studying the topic of assembly-line balancing (she majored in finance), but she wondered if this method would work for services. She decided to begin her analysis by answering the following questions.

Case Questions for Discussion

1. What is the best way to group the work represented by the 16 workgroups for an average demand of 306 outgoing wires per day? What is your line balance if peak demand is 450 wires per day? What is assembly-line efficiency for each line-balance solution?

2. How many people are needed for the outgoing wire process using assembly-line-balancing methods versus the current staffing level of 11 full-time-equivalent employees?

3. How many staff members do you need for the outgoing wire process if you eliminate all rework?

4. What are your final recommendations?

Operations Management
Part 2 Chapter 9

SUPPLY CHAIN DESIGN

any of you have probably shopped at apparel stores such as the Gap, Old Navy, or Banana Republic. Apparel supply chains typically begin at farms that grow raw materials such as cotton. Textile mills then weave the raw materials into fabrics for making T-shirts, jeans, and other clothing items. Factories then cut and sew the fabrics into finished goods, which are then transported to retail stores for sale to consumers. For clothing manufacturers, which depend on a lot of manual labor, the supply chain has significant implications for social responsibility and sustainability. The Gap is one company that takes this seriously. As they note: "Gap Inc. seeks to ensure that the people working at various points along the supply chain are treated with fairness, dignity and respect—an aspiration

learning outcomes

After studying this chapter you should be able to:

9-1   **Explain the concept of supply chain management.**

9-2   **Describe the key issues in designing supply chains.**

9-3   **Define metrics used in evaluating supply chain performance.**

9-4   **Explain important factors and decisions in locating facilities.**

9-5   **Describe the role of transportation, supplier evaluation, technology, and inventory in supply chain management.**

What do **you** think?

What percent of the clothes in your closet do you think are produced in other countries? What do you think the structure of the manufacturers' supply chains look like? Do clothing firms have a responsibility to improve work conditions and sustainability practices wherever they do business?

Sozaijiten/Datacraft/Getty Images

that is born out of the belief that each life is of equal value, whether the person is sitting behind a sewing machine at a factory that produces clothes for Gap Inc., working at one of our stores, or wearing a pair of our jeans. We know that our efforts to improve the lives of people who work on behalf of our company help us to run a more successful business. People who work a reasonable number of hours in a safe and healthy environment not only have a better quality of life, but they also tend to be more productive and deliver higher quality product than those who work in poor conditions."[1]

> The location of factories, distribution centers, and service facilities establishes the infrastructure for the supply chain and has a major impact on the profitability.

▼ *For the Gap and many other clothing manufacturers, the supply chain has significant implications for social responsibility and sustainability.*

Alfred/Sipa Pres/Newscom

We introduced the concept of a **supply chain** in Chapter 2, noting that a supply chain is a key subsystem of a value chain that focuses primarily on the physical movement of goods and materials along with supporting information through the supply, production, and distribution processes. Supply chains are all about speed and efficiency; poor supply chain performance can undermine the objectives of the firm and can easily result in loss of customers, either individual consumers or major retailers. As a firm's product lines and markets change or expand, the design or redesign of supply chains becomes a critical issue.

As companies merge and consolidate, they face many challenges and must reevaluate their supply chains and locations of facilities. The location of factories, distribution centers, and service facilities establishes the infrastructure for the supply chain and has a major impact on the profitability. In today's global business environment with emerging markets and sources of supply in Asia and other countries, identifying the best locations is not easy, but good location analysis can lead to major reductions in total supply chain costs and improvements in customer response.

9-1 Understanding Supply Chains

Every day, HP delivers 1.3 million inkjet cartridges, 110,000 printers, 75,000 personal computer systems, and 3,500 servers. The company spends about $50 billion, or about 64 percent of its revenue, on supply chain activities. Supply chain optimization "has a direct impact on customer satisfaction, stock price and profitability," says an HP senior vice president of supply chain.[2]

Distribution centers (DCs) are warehouses that act as intermediaries between factories and customers, shipping directly to customers or to retail stores where products are made available to customers.

Inventory refers to raw materials, work-in-process, or finished goods that are maintained to support production or satisfy customer demand.

The Supply Chain Operations Reference (SCOR) model is a framework for understanding the scope of supply chain management (SCM) that is based on five basic functions involved in managing a supply chain: plan, source, make, deliver, and return.

The basic purpose of a supply chain is to coordinate the flow of materials, services, and information among the elements of the supply chain to maximize customer value. The key functions generally include purchasing and procurement of materials and supplies, sales and order processing, operations, inventory and materials management, transportation and distribution, information management, finance, and customer service.

A goods-producing supply chain generally consists of suppliers, manufacturers, distributors, retailers, and customers arranged in a hierarchical structure, as illustrated in Exhibit 9.1. Raw materials and components are ordered from suppliers and must be transported to manufacturing facilities for production and assembly into finished goods. Finished goods are shipped to distributors who operate distribution centers. **Distribution centers (DCs)** *are warehouses that act as intermediaries between factories and customers, shipping directly to customers or to retail stores where products are made available to customers.* At each factory, distribution center, and retail store, inventory generally is maintained to improve the ability to meet demand quickly. **Inventory** *refers to raw materials, work in-process, or finished goods that are maintained to support production or satisfy customer demand.* As inventory levels diminish, orders are sent to the previous stage upstream in the process for replenishing stock. Orders are passed up the supply chain, fulfilled at each stage, and shipped to the next stage.

Not all supply chains have each of the stages illustrated in Exhibit 9.1. A simple supply chain might be one that supplies fresh fish at a Boston restaurant. Being close to the suppliers (fisherman), the restaurant might purchase fish directly from them daily and cut and fillet the fish directly at the restaurant. A slightly more complex supply chain for a restaurant in the Midwest might include processing and packaging by a seafood wholesaler and air transportation and delivery to the restaurant. For

The SCOR Model

*The **Supply Chain Operations Reference (SCOR) model** is a framework for understanding the scope of supply chain management (SCM) that is based on five basic functions involved in managing a supply chain: plan, source, make, deliver, and return.*[3]

1. *Plan—Developing a strategy that balances resources with requirements and establishes and communicates plans for the entire supply chain. This includes management policies and aligning the supply chain plan with financial plans.*

2. *Source—Procuring goods and services to meet planned or actual demand. This includes identifying and selecting suppliers, scheduling deliveries, authorizing payments, and managing inventory.*

3. *Make—Transforming goods and services to a finished state to meet demand. This includes production scheduling, managing work-in-process, manufacturing, testing, packaging, and product release.*

4. *Deliver—Managing orders, transportation, and distribution to provide the goods and services. This entails all order management activities from processing customer orders to routing shipments, managing goods at distribution centers, and invoicing the customer.*

5. *Return—Processing customer returns; providing maintenance, repair, and overhaul; and dealing with excess goods. This includes return authorization, receiving, verification, disposition, and replacement or credit.*

Each major player in the supply chain illustrated in Exhibit 9.1, such as a supplier or retail store, would typically manage its own supply chain using this framework, in essence, chaining together these functions within the broader supply chain.

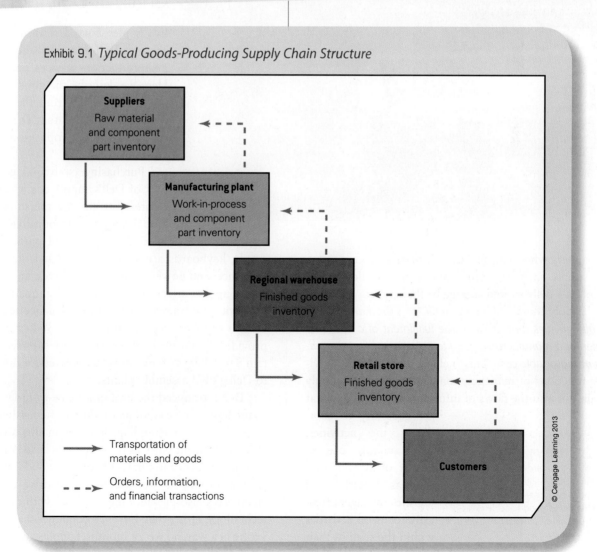

Exhibit 9.1 *Typical Goods-Producing Supply Chain Structure*

© Cengage Learning 2013

BOEING: SUPPLY CHAIN PROBLEMS HOLD BACK THE DREAMLINER

The Boeing 787 Dreamliner is a new long-range wide-body jet. The twin-engine plane is the first to make use of composite materials and is the most fuel-efficient plane in Boeing's fleet. With over 800 orders, it's also the best-selling new airplane in Boeing's history. The Dreamliner was scheduled to begin delivery in May 2008; however, Boeing had to push back the production schedule multiple times to late 2010 because of supply chain problems. Boeing outsourced about 70 percent of the production to suppliers, requiring an unprecedented amount of global supply chain coordination. Boeing's partners in Italy, Japan, and elsewhere in the United States are responsible for manufacturing much of the 787 structure, including the composite wings and composite fuselage. But they stumbled early on, and their spotty performance, coupled with parts shortages from various suppliers, slowed work on the first test plane in final assembly at Boeing's plant in Everett, Washington. That forced Boeing to delay the first flight and initial deliveries. Some of this work has been shifted back to the United States.[4]

Steven May/Alamy

consumers who want to buy fish from a grocery store, the supply chain is more complex and would include wholesale delivery and storage by the retailer.

Supply chain management (SCM) *is the management of all activities that facilitate the fulfillment of a customer order for a manufactured good to achieve satisfied customers at reasonable cost.* This includes not only the obvious functions of managing materials within the supply chain but also the flows of information and money that are necessary to coordinate the activities. The unique characteristic of SCM is that whereas material and logistics managers typically focus on activities within the span of their

> **Supply chain management (SCM)** is the management of all activities that facilitate the fulfillment of a customer order for a manufactured good to achieve satisfied customers at reasonable cost.

purchasing, manufacturing, and distribution processes, SCM requires a clear understanding of the interactions among all parts of the system. For example, supply chain managers must use forecasting and information technology to better match production levels with demand and reduce costs; tightly integrate design, development, production, delivery, and marketing; and provide more customization to meet increasingly demanding customers. As such, a supply chain is an integrated system and requires much coordination and collaboration among the various players in it.

9-1a The Supply Chain at Dell, Inc.

In Chapter 2 we described the value chain at Dell, Inc. from the pre- and postproduction services perspective. Here we describe the goods producing supply chain from the perspective of Exhibit 9.1 that Dell uses to support its value proposition of mass customization.

Purchasing (sourcing) is a vital part of Dell's supply chain, and Dell creates strong partnerships with global suppliers responsible for delivering thousands of parts. For example, keyboards are sourced in Mexico, soundcards in France, and power supplies, disk drives, and chips in Asia. Supplier selection is based on cost, quality, speed of service, and flexibility; and performance is tracked using a supplier "report card." About 30 key suppliers provide 75 percent of the parts; most suppliers maintain 8 to 10 days of inventory in multivendor hubs close to Dell global assembly plants.

Dell introduced the idea of a make-to-order supply chain design to the computer industry and has long been recognized for outstanding practices in this area. Dell pulls component parts into its factories based on actual customer orders and carries no finished goods inventory, relying on information technology to drive its supply chain. This also provides the customer with the newest technology, rather than buying a computer that has been sitting in a warehouse for months. Suppliers' component part delivery schedules must match Dell's factory assembly schedules, which in turn must be integrated with shipping schedules. Each factory worldwide is rescheduled every two hours, and at the same time updates are sent to all third-party suppliers and logistics providers.

On one end of Dell's 250,000-square-foot factory in Round Rock, Texas, purchased parts are unloaded from supplier's trucks. Most of them come from supplier's warehouses, so technically, Dell does not own the parts until they are unloaded at the factory. This helps to lower inventory holding costs, and therefore prices. The parts are loaded into bins and moved around the factory in elevated and automated conveyors. Elevators lower these parts to assembly workstations where it takes about five hours to completely assemble, burn-in, load software, and test all of it. From the time the customer orders a PC, it is often ready to ship in about one hour and may cost more to ship a Dell PC than to build it! Finished PCs are packaged and shipped immediately to individual customers or retail outlets that sell its products. Dell distributes its products to customers using standard carriers such as United Parcel Service (UPS) and Federal Express (FedEx). These outsourcing arrangements provide quality service as well as tracking capability during shipment. Because of direct shipment, Dell does not store its products in warehouses as do many other consumer goods manufacturers.

Sustainability is a key part of Dell's supply chain. *Technology Business Research* ranked Dell No. 1 in its inaugural Corporate Sustainability Index Benchmark Report. The report measures the environmental initiatives of 40 companies in the computer hardware, software, professional services, and network and telecommunications sectors. Dell also led firms in the computing sector, and scored particularly well in *renewable energy* use, *recycling,* and its integration of a *sustainability* strategy in its business. Dell sources about 35 percent of its U.S. *energy use* from green power and approximately 20 percent globally.[5]

One of its packaging practices is to use bamboo cushions that are biodegradable, nontoxic, and made of compost. "The whole process of re-thinking our packaging began back in January 2009," Mr. Campbell, senior manager of packaging, said. "We wanted to break the paradigm for polyethylene and polystyrene packaging, and we knew we didn't want something paper-based. So, we took a look at bamboo." Bamboo is a member of the grass family and grows very fast. It's strong, promotes healthy soil, has a deep root system to prevent land erosion, is widely available especially in China, and it meets high standards of sustainability.

Coordinating Dell's supply chain management system is a comprehensive information technology (IT) infrastructure (using Dell PowerEdge servers, of course!) that uses Oracle database software. The Dell SCM system must handle an enormous number of transactions and pieces of information, and includes multiple core subsystems necessary to keep operations running smoothly:

- *Configuration management*: The configuration management component manages over 1 million Dell part numbers per year across approximately 200 product families, and over 2 million bills of materials (BOMs) per year. BOMs listing component part numbers are created for manufacturing facilities to build assemblies and subassemblies for Dell products.

- *Procurement*: The procurement component manages nearly 1.8 million purchase order lines per year from more than 5,000 suppliers worldwide. To streamline the procurement process, Dell uses an automated application that includes workflow approvals and vendor communication and enables services such as defective part replacement.

- *Cost management*: The cost component runs mostly in batch mode to calculate the costs to Dell for all BOMs. These batch jobs run weekly, monthly, and quarterly, with each job aggregating total material costs.

- *Inventory*: The inventory component manages more than 3 million inventory movements daily from stockrooms to factory floors across all Dell sites, along with the corresponding 3 million messages transmitted to different systems for reporting, analysis, and factory scheduling.

- *Accounts payable*: The accounts payable component handles approximately 15,000 items per day, including payments to Dell suppliers, invoices, and receipts. Vendor information includes vendor ID number, location, negotiated terms, and contact information.[6]

9-2 Designing the Supply Chain

managers face numerous alternatives in designing a supply chain. For example, most major airlines and trucking firms operate a "hub-and-spoke" system, whereas others operate on a point-to-point basis. Some manufacturers use complex networks of distribution centers, whereas others like Dell often ship directly to customers. Supply chains should support an organization's strategy, mission, and competitive priorities. Thus, both strategic and operational perspectives must be included in supply chain design decisions.

Many supply chains use contract manufacturing. *A **contract manufacturer** is a firm that specializes in certain types of goods-producing activities, such as customized design, manufacturing, assembly, and packaging, and works under contract for end users.* Outsourcing to contract manufacturers can offer significant competitive advantages, such as access to advanced manufacturing technologies, faster product time-to-market, customization of goods in regional markets, and lower total costs resulting from economies of scale.

Many companies use **third-party logistics (3PL) providers** *that provide integrated* services that might include packaging, warehousing, inventory management, and inbound or outbound transportation. 3PLs can leverage business intelligence and analytics to create efficiencies and economies of scale in the supply chain (see the box on Greatwide Logistics Services). Zappos is a good example of using 3PLs for customer deliveries, returns, and some inbound shipping from Asian factories. Toshiba used to have repair locations across the country, while UPS warehoused its parts. UPS suggested that Toshiba move its repair technicians into UPS facilities, which resulted in a 24-hour turnaround for computer repairs. It also saved transportation costs, lowered inventories, and reduced the carbon footprint. 3PLs provide many services that help integrate and coordinate different parts of a supply chain.[8]

9-2a Efficient and Responsive Supply Chains

Supply chains can be designed from two strategic perspectives—providing high efficiency and low cost or providing agile response. **Efficient supply chains** *are designed for efficiency and low cost by minimizing inventory and maximizing efficiencies in process flow.* A focus on efficiency works best for goods and services with highly predictable demand, stable product lines with long life cycles that do not change frequently, and low contribution margins. In designing an efficient supply chain, for example, an organization would seek to balance capacity and demand, resulting in low levels of inventory; might use only a few large distribution centers (as opposed to small ones) to generate economies of scale; and use optimization models that minimize costs of routing products from factory through distribution centers to retail stores and customers. Examples of companies that run efficient supply chains are Procter & Gamble and Walmart.

On the other hand, **responsive supply chains** *focus on flexibility and responsive service and are able to react quickly to changing market demand and requirements.* A focus on flexibility and response is best when demand is unpredictable; product life cycles are short and change often because of product innovations; fast response is

---

A contract manufacturer is a firm that specializes in certain types of goods-producing activities, such as customized design, manufacturing, assembly, and packaging, and works under contract for end users.

Third-party logistics (3PL) providers provide integrated services that might include packaging, warehousing, inventory management, and transportation.

Efficient supply chains are designed for efficiency and low cost by minimizing inventory and maximizing efficiencies in process flow.

Responsive supply chains focus on flexibility and responsive service and are able to react quickly to changing market demand and requirements.

the main competitive priority; customers require customization; and contribution margins are high. Responsive supply chains have the ability to quickly respond to market changes and conditions faster than traditional supply chains; are supported by information technology that provides real-time, accurate information to managers across the supply chain; and use information to identify market changes and redirect resources to address these changes. Companies such as Apple and Nordstrom are examples of companies having responsive supply chains.

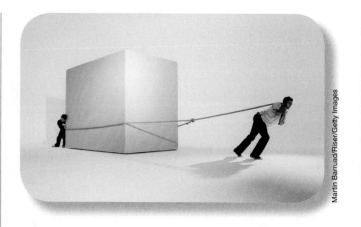

9-2b Push and Pull Systems

Two ways to configure and run a supply chain are as a push or pull system. A supply chain can be viewed from "left to right"—that is, materials, information, and goods are moved or pushed downstream from supplier to customer. *A push system produces goods in advance of customer demand using a forecast of sales and moves them through the supply chain to points of sale, where they are stored as finished-goods inventory.* Examples of push systems are "big-box" retailers such as Best Buy and department stores such as Macy's. A push system has several advantages, such as immediate availability of goods to customers and the ability to reduce transportation costs by using full-truckload shipments to move goods to distribution centers. Push systems work best when sales patterns are consistent and when there are a small number of distribution centers and products.

In contrast, viewing the supply chain from "right to left" and transferring demand to upstream processes is sometimes referred to as a *demand chain* or *pull system. A pull system produces only what is needed at upstream stages in the supply chain in response to customer demand signals from downstream stages.* Examples of pull systems are airplane manufacturers such as Boeing, and

> A **push system** produces goods in advance of customer demand using a forecast of sales and moves them through the supply chain to points of sale, where they are stored as finished-goods inventory.
>
> A **pull system** produces only what is needed at upstream stages in the supply chain in response to customer demand signals from downstream stages.

manufacturers of custom machine tools. Pull systems are more effective when there are many production facilities, many points of distribution, and a large number of products.

Many supply chains are combinations of push and pull systems. This can be seen in the simplified version of several supply chains in Exhibit 9.2. *The point in the supply chain that separates the push system from the pull*

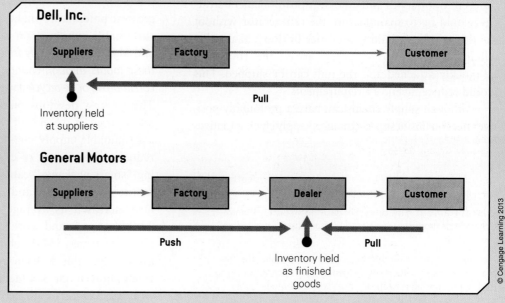

Exhibit 9.2 *Supply Chain Push-Pull Systems and Boundaries*

Dell, Inc.

Suppliers → Factory → Customer

Pull

Inventory held at suppliers

General Motors

Suppliers → Factory → Dealer → Customer

Push — Pull

Inventory held as finished goods

© Cengage Learning 2013

system is called the **push-pull boundary**. For a company like Dell, the push-pull boundary is very early in the supply chain where suppliers store inventory for frequent deliveries to Dell factories. Dell also ships directly to the customer, skipping the distributors and retailers. General Motors stores finished goods closer to the customer, at dealers. GM pushes finished goods from its factories to the dealer. Dealers might install various options to customize the automobile for the customer. Customers pull the finished goods from the dealer. Thus, the push-pull boundary for General Motors is at the dealers.

The location of the push-pull boundary can affect how responsive a supply chain is. Many firms try to push as much of the finished product as possible close to the customer to speed up response and reduce work-in-process inventory requirements. **Postponement** *is the process of delaying product customization until the product is closer to the customer at the end of the supply chain.* An example is a manufacturer of refrigerators that have different door styles and colors. A postponement strategy would be to manufacture the refrigerator without the door and maintain inventories of doors at the distribution centers. When orders arrive, the doors can be quickly attached and the unit can be shipped. This would reduce inventory requirements.

Although supply chains can have a profoundly positive effect on business performance, supply chain initiatives do not always work out as one would hope. Nike, for example, spent about $500 million on developing a global supply chain over the last couple of decades, and only now is it beginning to reap the benefits of this long and costly supply chain design and improvement initiative.

9-3 Sustainable Supply Chains

the purpose of a sustainable supply chain is to reduce costs while helping the environment. "Our data indicates that upwards of 60 to 70 percent of a company's carbon footprint is found along their supply chain," says Ms. Annie Berger, relationships director of greensupplychain.org. "We think improving supply chain performance holds the greatest potential to make a real difference."[9] *A* **green sustainable supply chain** *can be defined as the process of using environmentally friendly inputs and transforming these inputs through change agents—whose by-products can improve or be recycled within the existing environment.* This process develops outputs that can be reclaimed and re-used at the end of their life-cycle thus, creating a sustainable supply chain.[10] Something as simple as reducing the amount of cardboard or filler by designing "smart packages" can save companies money and reduce landfill waste and energy usage. For example, Dell increased its average truckload from 18,000 to 22,000 pounds and worked with UPS to optimize delivery strategies. 3M developed an innovative system to install adjustable decks in trucks. Placing pallets on two levels allowed one 3M facility to reduce the number of daily truckloads by 40 percent and allowed it to save $110,000 per year.[11]

The point in the supply chain that separates the push system from the pull system is called the **push-pull boundary.**

Postponement is the process of delaying product customization until the product is closer to the customer at the end of the supply chain.

A **green sustainable supply chain** can be defined as "the process of using environmentally friendly inputs and transforming these inputs through change agents—whose by-products can improve or be recycled within the existing environment."

SUSTAINABLE SUPPLY CHAIN PRACTICES

Companies such as UPS and FedEx move a multitude of goods using trucks, airplanes, and trains. They use a lot of fuel, and these companies are challenged not only to save high energy costs, but to reduce their carbon footprint. Customers today are more sensitive to environmental impact and are demanding better stewardship from the companies they deal with. UPS, for example, has been using low-emission rail transport since 1966 and selects the lowest-carbon route for customer shipments.[12] They also evaluate customers' supply chains for their environment impact and suggest improvements in transportation, inventory management, and shipping decisions. FedEx works with its suppliers to understand the environmental impacts of materials they use, and seeks to reduce those impacts.[13] Both UPS and FedEx often work with customers to analyze and improve their supply chains to enhance efficiency and reduce their customers' environmental footprint. These companies also exploit business analytics to improve routing their vehicles to reduce fuel consumption, and have introduced hybrid and electric vehicles in their fleets.

Daniel Cooper/iStockphoto.com

Other environmental-performance-enhancing supply chain management activities include the following:

- Substantially decreasing scrap, packaging, and material losses

- Adopting paperless practices for all information processing, such as billing and purchasing

- Lowering the training, material handling, and other extra expenses associated with hazardous materials

- Increasing revenues by converting wastes to by-products

- Reducing water and energy requirements throughout the supply chain

- Decreasing the use and waste of solvents, paints, cleaning fluids, and other chemicals through better product, process, and job design

- Selecting suppliers that support sustainability. Ms. Berger, cited earlier, suggests the following questions for original equipment manufacturers (OEMs) to ask when seeking good suppliers: Does the supplier publish an annual sustainability report? How does the OEM evaluate suppliers on sustainability performance criteria? How does the supplier ensure that its processes are free from environmentally harmful pollutants? How does the supplier plan for and handle its product's end-of life reclamation?

- Recovering valuable materials and assets through efficient product take-back and recycle programs.

9-3a Manufactured Goods Recovery and Reverse Logistics

The last bullet point in the previous section is especially important to today's focus on sustainability. Many companies are developing options to recover manufactured goods that may be discarded or otherwise unusable. This is often called *manufactured goods recovery*, and consists of one or more of the following:

- *Reuse or resell* the equipment and its various component parts directly to customers once the original manufactured good is discarded. Furniture, appliances, and clothes are examples of the reuse and resell recovery option.

- *Repair* a manufactured good by replacing broken parts so it operates as required. Personal computers, vehicle parts, and shoes are examples of physical goods that may need to be repaired.

- *Refurbish* a manufactured good by updating its looks and/or components—for example, cleaning, painting, or perhaps replacing parts that are near failure. Products may have scratches, dents, or other forms of "cosmetic damage" that do not affect the performance of the unit. Refurbished products cannot be sold as new in the United States, which is why they are relabeled as refurbished or refreshed units even if they are good-as-new. Often the equipment is returned to the manufacturer, which then fixes and certifies the unit and sells it at a discount.

- *Remanufacture a good* by completely disassembling it and repairing or replacing worn out or obsolete components and modules. Honda, for example, remanufactures vehicle steering mechanism controls for sale as dealer-authorized replacement parts with the same warranty as new parts.

- *Cannibalize* parts for use and repair of other equipment of the same kind, such as automobiles, locomotives, and airplanes. Cannibalization can normally occur only with equipment that uses interchangeable parts, such as with automobiles and airplanes.

- *Recycle* goods by disassembling them and selling the parts or scrap materials to other suppliers. Aluminum soda cans, for example, are often melted and formed into new aluminum sheets and cans.

- *Incineration or landfill disposal* of goods that are not economical to repair, refurbish, remanufacture, or recycle.

For products that are of high enough value, it is normally more cost-effective to remanufacture or refurbish the product, and convert damaged inventory into saleable goods, thus recapturing value on products that would otherwise be lost in disposition. In addition, efficiencies associated with manufactured goods recovery can yield increases in customer loyalty and retention through an enhanced public and sustainable image, boost revenue, reduce operating costs, provide customers with replaceable parts typically at lower prices than totally new parts, and improve the new customer's uptime.

Managing the flow of goods and materials from the customer backward through the supply chain to accomplish manufactured goods recovery is called reverse logistics. **Reverse logistics** *refers to managing the flow of finished goods, materials, or components that may be unusable or discarded through the supply chain from customers toward either suppliers, distributors, or manufacturers for the purpose of reuse, resale, or disposal.* This reverse flow is opposite the normal operating supply chain where the raw materials and parts are assembled into finished goods and then delivered to wholesalers, retailers, and ultimately customers. The forward supply chain normally operates independently of any reverse logistics activities, sometimes with different owners and players. Reverse logistics includes the following activities:

- *Logistics:* authorizing returns, receiving, sorting, testing, refurbishing, cannibalizing, repairing, remanufacturing, recycling, restocking, reshipping, and disposing of materials.

- *Marketing/Sales:* remarketing and selling the recovered good for reuse or resale to wholesalers and retailers.

- *Accounting/Finance:* approving warranty repairs, tracking reverse logistic revenue and costs, billing, and paying appropriate suppliers and third-party vendors.

- *Call Center Service:* managing service center calls all along the supply chain to coordinate work activities such as collecting items from many diverse sources for recovery operations.

- *Legal/Regulatory Compliance:* constantly monitoring compliance with local, state, federal, and country laws, import and export regulations including environmental, and service contract commitments.

An example of manufactured goods recovery within a reverse logistics supply chain is shown in Exhibit 9.3.

Best Buy, Sears, and Target have all used reverse logistics to find buyers for

> **Reverse logistics** refers to managing the flow of finished goods, materials, or components that may be unusable or discarded through the supply chain from customers toward either suppliers, distributors, or manufacturers for the purpose of reuse, resale, or disposal.

Exhibit 9.3 *Example of a Manufactured Goods Recovery (Reverse Logistics) Supply Chain*

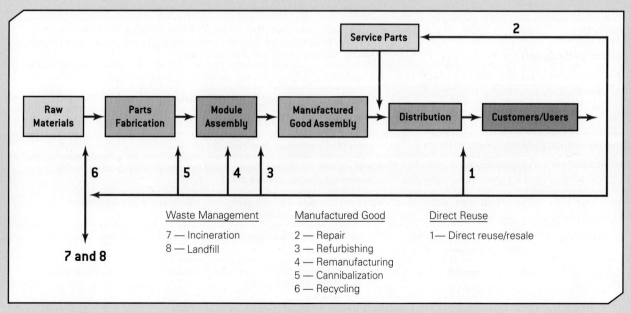

Source: "Example of a Manufactured Good Recovery (Reverse Logistics) Supply Chain," in Martijn Thierry et al., "Strategic Issues in Product Recovery Management," in *California Management Review* vol. 37, no. 2 (Winter 1995), pp. 114–135. © 1995 by the Regents of the University of California. Reprinted by permission of the University of California Press.

defective or broken or returned products that would otherwise end up in landfills. KPMG research found that companies can recover 0.3 percent of annual sales with a good reverse logistics system. Best Buy, for example, would make an extra $100 million at this 0.3 percent rate. As another example, Patagonia recaptures all of the fiber from its outdoor clothes and those of competitors as customers drop off worn duds at distribution centers or mail them in. Ninety percent of this recycled fiber is spun into new clothing and the rest is sold to a cement additive company.

OM managers must evaluate the trade-offs between adopting different recovery options for a particular physical good. For example, how does the total cost of remanufacturing compare to cannibalizing parts or subassemblies? In addition, the OM manager must consider social and environmental sustainability criteria and issues in the final analysis of manufactured goods recovery.

9-4 Measuring Supply Chain Performance

Supply chain managers use numerous metrics to evaluate performance and identify improvements to the design and operation of their supply chains. These basic metrics typically balance customer requirements as well as internal supply chain efficiencies and fall into several categories, as summarized in Exhibit 9.4.

- *Delivery reliability* is often measured by perfect order fulfillment. A "perfect order" is defined as one that is delivered meeting all customer requirements, such as delivery date, condition of goods, accuracy of items, correct invoice, and so on.

Exhibit 9.4 *Common Metrics Used to Measure Supply Chain Performance*

Metric Category	Metric	Definition
Delivery reliability	Perfect order fulfillment	The number of perfect orders divided by the total number of orders
Responsiveness	Order fulfillment lead time	The time to fill a customer's order
	Perfect delivery fulfillment	The proportion of deliveries that were not just complete but also on time
Customer-related	Customer satisfaction	Customer perception of whether customers receive what they need when they need it, as well as such intangibles as convenient time of delivery, product and service quality, helpful manuals, and after-sales support
Supply chain efficiency	Average inventory value	The total average value of all items and materials held in inventory
	Inventory turnover	How quickly goods are moving through the supply chain
	Inventory days' supply	How many days of inventory are in the supply chain or part of the supply chain?
Sustainability	Carbon dioxide emissions	The tons of CO_2 emissions generated per manufactured good or service process
	Energy reduction	How many kWh are needed before or after the change to the product, facility, equipment, process, or value chain?
Financial	Total supply chain costs	Total costs of order fulfillment, purchasing, maintaining inventory, distribution, technical support, and production
	Warranty/returns processing costs	The cost associated with repairs or restocking goods that have been returned
	Cash-to-cash conversion cycle	The average time to convert a dollar spent to acquire raw materials into a dollar collected for a finished good

© Cengage Learning 2013

> A great servicescape and facility layout can seldom overcome a poor location decision, simply because customers may not have convenient access, which is one of the most important requirements for a service facility.

- *Responsiveness* is often measured by order fulfillment lead time or by perfect delivery fulfillment. Customers today expect rapid fulfillment of orders and having promised delivery dates met.

- *Customer-related measures* focus on the ability of the supply chain to meet customer wants and needs. Customer satisfaction is often measured by a variety of attributes on a perception scale that might range from "Extremely Dissatisfied" to "Extremely Satisfied."

- *Supply chain efficiency* measures include average inventory value and inventory turnover. Average inventory value tells managers how much of the firm's assets are tied up in inventory. Inventory turnover is the ratio of the cost of goods sold divided by the average inventory value.

- *Sustainability measures* show how supply chain performance affects the environment. These might include recycle versus original product manufacturing costs, water discharge quality, carbon dioxide emissions, and energy reductions. The goal is a carbon-neutral value (supply) chain.

- *Financial measures* show how supply chain performance affects the bottom line. These might include total supply chain costs and costs of processing returns and warranties.

9-5 Location Decisions in Value Chains

The principal goal of a value (supply) chain is to provide customers with accurate and quick response to their orders at the lowest possible cost. This requires a network of facilities that are located strategically in the supply chain. Facility network and location focuses on determining the best network structure and geographical locations for facilities to maximize service and revenue and to minimize costs. These decisions can become complex, especially for a global supply chain, which must consider shipping costs between all demand and supply points in the network, fixed operating costs of each distribution and/or retail facility, revenue generation per customer location, facility labor and operating costs, and construction costs.

Larger firms have more complex location decisions; they might have to position a large number of factories and distribution centers advantageously with respect to suppliers, retail outlets, *and* each other. Rarely are these decisions made simultaneously. Typically, factories are located with respect to suppliers and a fixed set of distribution centers, or distribution centers are located with respect to a fixed set of factories and markets. A firm might also choose to locate a facility in a new geographic region not only to provide cost or service efficiencies but also to create cultural ties between the firm and the local community.

Location is also critical in service value chains. A great servicescape and facility layout can seldom

Brian Snyder/Reuters/Landov

overcome a poor location decision, simply because customers may not have convenient access, which is one of the most important requirements for a service facility. Service facilities such as post offices, branch banks, dentist offices, and fire stations typically need to be in close proximity to the customer. In many cases, the customer travels to the service facility, whereas in others, such as mobile X-ray and imaging centers or "on-call" computer repair services, the service travels to the customer.

Many service organizations operate large numbers of similar facilities. **Multisite management** *is the process of managing geographically dispersed service-providing facilities.* For example, McDonald's has over 30,000 restaurants worldwide plus hundreds of food-processing factories and distribution centers. Federal Express has over 1 million pickup and delivery sites worldwide plus hundreds of sorting and distribution facilities. Some major banks have over 5,000 branch banks plus thousands of ATM locations. Supply chains are vital to multisite management, and in each of these cases, it can be difficult to design a good supply chain.

Multisite management is the process of managing geographically dispersed service-providing facilities.

Criteria for locating these facilities differ, depending on the nature of the service. For example, service facilities that customers travel to, such as public libraries and urgent-care facilities, seek to *minimize the average or maximum distance or travel time required* from among the customer population. For those that travel to customer locations, such as fire stations, the location decision seeks to minimize response time to customers.

9-5a Critical Factors in Location Decisions

Location decisions in supply and value chains are based on both economic and noneconomic factors. For example, although the Gap, Banana Republic, and Old Navy are part of the same corporation, each firm locates its factories differently. The Gap makes its goods in Mexico to provide more agility in supplying the North American market; Old Navy sources in China to keep costs down; and Banana Republic has facilities in Italy in order to be close to fashion innovations. Exhibit 9.5 is a list of some important location factors for site selection. Economic factors include facility costs, such as

Exhibit 9.5 *Example Location Factors for Site Selection*

Location Factors	Transportation Factors	Utilities Factors	Climate, Community Environment, and Quality-of-Life Factors	State and Local Legal and Political Factors
Customer Access	Minimize distance travelled (i.e., convenience)	Fuel availability	Housing and Roads	Payroll taxes
Demand and Markets	Closeness to markets	Waste disposal	K–12 schools	Local and state tax structure
Sourcing	Closeness to sources of supply	Water supply	Climate and living conditions	Taxation climate and policies
Ability to retain labor force	Adequacy of transportation modes (air, truck, train, water)	Power supply	Universities and research facilities	Opportunity for highway advertising
Availability of adequate labor skills	Costs of transportation	Local energy costs	Community attitudes	Tax incentives and abatements
Labor rates	Visibility of the facility from the highway	Communications capability	Health care facilities	Zoning laws
Location of competitors	Parking capability	Price/cost	Property costs	Health and safety laws
Volume of traffic around location (i.e., traffic congestion)	Inbound and outbound driving time for employees and customers	Utility regulatory laws and practices	Cost of living	Regulatory agencies and policies

© Cengage Learning 2013

Solved Problem

The following data are related to the operating costs of three possible locations for Fountains Manufacturing:

	Location 1	Location 2	Location 3
Fixed costs	$165,000	$125,000	$180,000
Direct material cost per unit	$8.50	$8.40	$8.60
Direct labor cost per unit	$4.20	$3.90	$3.70
Overhead per unit	$1.20	$1.10	$1.00
Transportation cost per unit	$0.80	$1.10	$0.95

Which location would minimize the total costs, given an annual production of 50,000 units?

Solution

Compute the total cost associated with the annual production. For example, the direct material cost at location 1 is ($8.50)(50,000 units) = $425,000. These are summarized as follows:

Total Costs	Loc. 1	Loc. 2	Loc. 3
Fixed costs	$165,000	$125,000	$180,000
Direct material	$425,000	$420,000	$430,000
Direct labor	$210,000	$195,000	$185,000
Overhead	$60,000	$55,000	$50,000
Transportation	$40,000	$55,000	$47,500
Total	$900,000	$850,000	$892,500

Based on total manufacturing and distribution costs, location 2 would be best. Exhibit 9.6 shows the Excel Location Analysis template, which can be used to perform these calculations.

Exhibit 9.6 *Excel Location Analysis for Fountains Manufacturing Template*

construction, utilities, insurance, taxes, depreciation, and maintenance; operating costs, including fuel, direct labor, and administrative personnel; and transportation costs associated with moving goods and services from their origins to the final destinations or the opportunity cost of customers coming to the facility.

Economic criteria are not always the most important factors in such decisions. Sometimes location decisions are based upon strategic objectives, such as preempting competitors from entering a geographical region. New facilities also require large amounts of capital investment and, once built, cannot easily be moved. Moreover, location decisions also affect the management of operations at lower levels of the organization. For instance, if a manufacturing facility is located far from sources of raw materials, it may take a considerable amount of time to deliver an order, and there will be more uncertainty as to the actual time of delivery. Noneconomic factors in location decisions include the availability of labor, transportation services, and utilities; climate, community environment, and quality of life; and state and local legal and political factors. These must be balanced with economic factors in arriving at a location decision that meets financial as well as customer and operational needs.

9-5b Location Decision Process

Facility location is typically conducted hierarchically and involves the following four basic decisions where appropriate:

Global Location Decision

Many companies must cope with issues of global operations, such as time zones, foreign languages, international funds transfer, customs, tariffs and other trade restrictions, packaging, international monetary policy, and cultural practices. The global location decision involves evaluating the product portfolio, new market opportunities, changes in regulatory laws and procedures, production and delivery economics, sustainability, and the cost to locate in different countries. With this information, the company needs to determine whether it should locate domestically or in another country; what countries are most amenable to setting up a facility (and what countries to avoid); and how important it is to establish a local presence in other regions of the world. The decision by Mercedes-Benz to locate in Alabama was based on the fact that German labor costs were about 50 percent higher than in the southern United States; the plant also gives the company better inroads into the American market and functions as a kind of laboratory for future global manufacturing ventures.

Regional Location Decision

The regional location decision involves choosing a general region of a country, such as the northeast or south. Factors that affect the regional decision include size of the target market, the locations of major customers and sources of materials and supply; labor availability and costs; degree of unionization; land, construction, and utility costs; quality of life; and climate.

Community Location Decision

The community location decision involves selecting a specific city or community in which to locate. In addition to the factors cited previously, a company would consider managers' preferences, community services and taxes (as well as tax incentives), available transportation systems, banking services, and environmental impacts. Mercedes-Benz settled on Vance, Alabama, after considering sites in 30 different states. Alabama pledged $250 million in tax abatements and other incentives, and the local business community came up with $11 million. The community also submitted a plan for how it would help the families of German workers adjust to life in that community.

Local Site Location Decision

The site location decision involves the selection of a particular location within the chosen community. Site costs, proximity to transportation systems, utilities, payroll and local taxes, sustainability issues, and zoning restrictions are among the factors to be considered.

9-5c The Center-of-Gravity Method

Supply chain design and location decisions are quite difficult to analyze and make. Many types of quantitative models and approaches, ranging from simple to complex, can be used to facilitate these decisions. We introduce a simple quantitative approach; however, in practice, more sophisticated models are generally used.

*The **center-of-gravity method** determines the x and y coordinates (location) for a single facility.* Although it

The **center-of-gravity method** determines the x and y coordinates (location) for a single facility.

does not explicitly address customer service objectives, it can be used to assist managers in balancing cost and service objectives. The center-of-gravity method takes into account the locations of the facility and markets, demand, and transportation costs in arriving at the best location for a single facility. It would seem reasonable to find some "central" location between the goods-producing or service-providing facility and

Solved Problem

Taylor Paper Products is a producer of paper stock used in newspapers and magazines. Taylor's demand is relatively constant and thus can be forecast rather accurately. The company's two factories are located in Hamilton, Ohio, and Kingsport, Tennessee. The company distributes paper stock to four major markets: Chicago, Pittsburgh, New York, and Atlanta. The board of directors has authorized the construction of an intermediate warehouse to service those markets. Coordinates for the factories and markets are shown in Exhibit 9.6. For example, we see that location 1, Hamilton, is at the coordinate (58, 96); therefore, $X_1 = 58$ and $Y_1 = 96$. Hamilton and Kingsport produce 400 and 300 tons per month, respectively. Demand at Chicago, Pittsburgh, New York, and Atlanta is 200, 100, 300, and 100 tons per month, respectively. With that information, using Equations 9.1 and 9.2, the center of gravity coordinates are computed as follows:

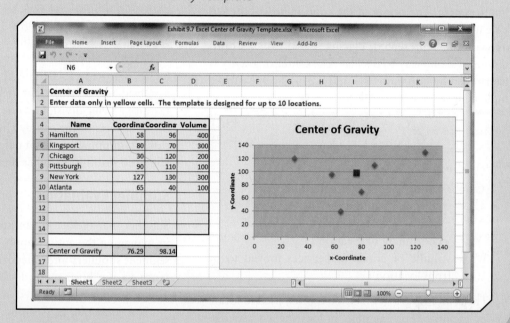

Exhibit 9.7 *Excel Center of Gravity Template*

$$C_x = \frac{58(400) + 80(300) + 30(200) + 90(100) + 127(300) + 65(100)}{400 + 300 + 200 + 100 + 300 + 100} = 76.3$$

$$C_y = \frac{96(400) + 70(300) + 120(200) + 110(100) + 130(300) + 40(100)}{400 + 300 + 200 + 100 + 300 + 100} = 98.1$$

Exhibit 9.7 shows the Excel Center of Gravity template, which can be used to find the best location. By overlaying a map on the chart, we see that the location is near the border of southern Ohio and West Virginia. Managers now can search that area for an appropriate site.

customers at which to locate the new facility. But distance alone should not be the principal criterion, as the demand (volume, transactions, and so on) from one location to another also affects the costs. To incorporate distance and demand, the center of gravity is defined as the location that minimizes the weighted distance between the facility and its supply and demand points.

The first step in the procedure is to place the locations of existing supply and demand points on a coordinate system. The origin of the coordinate system and scale used are arbitrary, as long as the relative distances are correctly represented. Placing a grid over an ordinary map is one way to do that. The center of gravity is determined by Equations 9.1 and 9.2, and can easily be implemented on a spreadsheet.

$$C_x = \Sigma X_i W_i / \Sigma W_i \qquad [9.1]$$
$$C_y = \Sigma Y_i W_i / \Sigma W_i \qquad [9.2]$$

where

C_x = x coordinate of the center of gravity
C_y = y coordinate of the center of gravity
X_i = x coordinate of location i
Y_i = y coordinate of location i
W_i = volume of goods or services moved to or from location i

The center-of-gravity method is often used to locate service facilities. For example, in locating a waste disposal facility, the location coordinates can be weighted by the average amount of waste generated from residential neighborhoods and industrial sites. Similarly, to locate a library, fire station, hospital, or post office, the population densities will define the appropriate weights in the model.

Selecting Transportation Services

The selection of transportation services is a complex decision, as varied services are available—rail, motor carrier, air, water, and pipeline. Pipelines have limited use and accessibility and are used primarily for such products as oil and natural gas. Similarly, water transportation is generally limited to transporting large quantities of bulky items—historically, raw materials such as coal, but recently, items such as furniture. Most consumer items are shipped via rail, motor carrier, and air. The critical factors in selecting a transportation mode are speed, accessibility, cost, and capability.

Many companies are moving toward third-party logistics providers. UPS Supply Chain Solutions (SCS), a subsidiary of the giant delivery company and its fastest-growing division, is one provider that is focusing on all aspects of the supply chain, including order processing, shipping, repair of defective or damaged goods, and even staffing customer service phone centers.[14]

Supplier Evaluation

Supplier management is an important support process in managing the entire supply chain. Many companies segment suppliers into categories based on their importance to the business and manage them accordingly. Today, suppliers are located in all parts of the world.

For example, at Corning, Level 1 suppliers, who provide raw materials, cases, and hardware, are deemed critical to business success and are managed by teams that include representatives from engineering, materials control, purchasing, and the supplier company. Level 2 suppliers provide specialty materials, equipment, and services and are managed by internal customers. Level 3

9-6 Other Issues in Supply Chain Management

ssues of supply chain structure and facility location represent broad strategic decisions in supply chain design. Managing a supply chain also requires numerous operational decisions, such as selecting transportation services, evaluating suppliers, managing inventory, and other issues.

> Managing a supply chain also requires numerous operational decisions, such as selecting transportation services, evaluating suppliers, managing inventory, and other issues.

suppliers provide commodity items and are centrally managed by purchasing.[15] Measurement also plays an important role in supplier management. Texas Instruments measures suppliers' quality performance by parts per million defective, percentage of on-time deliveries, and cost of ownership.[16]

Technology

Technology is playing an increasingly important role in supply chain design, and selecting the appropriate technology is critical for both planning and design of supply chains as well as execution. Some important needs in supply chain management include having accurate receipt information identifying goods that have been received, reducing the time spent in staging (between receipt and storage) at distribution centers, updating inventory records, routing customer orders for picking, generating bills of lading, and providing various managerial reports. SCM has benefited greatly from information technology, particularly bar coding and radio frequency identification (RFID) tags, to control and manage these activities. Chapter 5 discussed the use of RFID extensively; RFID has become an important technology in supply chains.

Electronic data interchange and Internet links streamline information flow between global customers and suppliers and increase the velocity of supply chains, as we illustrated with Dell. Many other firms, such as MetLife, Marriott Hotels, Victoria's Secret, General Electric, Federal Express, Dow Chemical, Enterprise Rent-A-Car, and Bank of America, have exploited technology effectively in their global supply chain designs. E-marketplaces offer many more options for sourcing materials and supplies and facilitate optimization of the supply chain globally.

Trucking companies now track their trucks via global positioning system (GPS) technology as they move across the country. In-vehicle navigational systems, vehicle location systems, emergency vehicle deployment, and traffic management are other examples of how geographical information system (GIS) and GPS are changing all industries and their value chains.

Inventory Management

An efficient distribution system can enable a company to operate with lower inventory levels, thus reducing costs, as well as providing high levels of service that create satisfied customers. Careful management of inventory is critical to supply chain time-based performance in order to respond effectively to customers.

Vendor-managed inventory (VMI) is where the vendor (a consumer goods manufacturer, for example) monitors and manages inventory for the customer (a grocery store,

> **Vendor-managed inventory (VMI)** is where the vendor (a consumer goods manufacturer, for example) monitors and manages inventory for the customer (a grocery store, for example).

WALMART: THE VALUE OF RFID

Walmart Stores, Inc. is accelerating its RFID rollout. The company requires all suppliers shipping products to its Sam's Club distribution center in DeSoto, Texas, to apply the radio tags to their pallets. If they don't, Walmart charges the suppliers $2 per pallet to do it for them. "I think everyone recognizes that it's the future of how products are going to move through the supply chain, and not just at Walmart, but everywhere," said Walmart spokesman John Simley. Dean Frew, president and chief executive of Xterprise Inc., which helps companies implement RFID systems, noted that the benefits are not only for Walmart. "There's clearly a benefit for the suppliers, ... you can't ignore the fact that if they're able to keep the shelf stocked more efficiently, in the end suppliers are going to benefit as well."[17]

for example). VMI essentially outsources the inventory management function in supply chains to suppliers. VMI allows the vendor to view inventory needs from the customer's perspective and use this information to optimize its own production operations, better control inventory and capacity, and reduce total supply chain costs. VMI also allows vendors to make production decisions using downstream customer demand data. One disadvantage of VMI is that it does not account for substitutable products from competing manufacturers and often results in higher customer inventories than necessary.

Discussion Questions

1. Describe the three types of value (supply) chain frameworks (i.e., Exhibits 2.1, 2.3, and 9.1), and state which one you like the best. Why? Explain. Justify.

2. Suppose that a company wanted to write a mission statement for its value (supply) chain. Such a mission statement might include statements about customers, suppliers, quality, delivery, cost, and sustainability. What questions might you ask a company to help develop a good mission statement? Propose an example for some industry of your choice, such as coffee, movie theater, pizza, credit card, trash/waste removal, utility, or automotive service.

3. Define the principal criteria that might be used for locating each of the following facilities:

   - hospital
   - chemical factory
   - fire station
   - coffee shop
   - regional automobile parts warehouse

4. Select a firm such as Taco Bell (www.tacobell.com), Bank of America (www.bankofamerica.com), Walmart (www.walmart.com), or another service-providing organization of interest to you and write a short analysis of location and multisite management decisions that the firm faces. What criteria do you think the firm uses?

5. Describe a value chain that creates and delivers services, such as in airlines, banking, health care, hotels, or education, and how it is becoming more green and sustainable.

Problems and Activities

Note: an asterisk denotes problems for which a spreadsheet template on the CourseMate Web site may be used.

1. Identify a manufactured good and draw its reverse logistics supply chain similar to Exhibit 9.3. Explain some of the issues in designing and managing this reverse supply chain, and whether your manufactured good participates in some or all of the eight options, such as resale, refurbishing, remanufacturing, recycling, incineration, and so on.

2. Describe a supply chain you are most familiar with and apply the SCOR model (i.e., plan, source, make, deliver, and return) to define and describe it. Draw a simple diagram of the value (supply) chain using this model and describe how it works.

3. Interview a manager for a retail store, health clinic, factory, school, emergency fire or ambulance facility, or warehouse that was recently built in your area, and ask for an explanation of the economic and noneconomic factors that helped determine this facility's location.

4. Research and write a short paper (two pages maximum) on how organizations use business analytics in supply chain design.

5.* For the location decision faced by Fountains Manufacturing in the first Solved Problem in this chapter, determine the ranges of annual production for which each location would be best. (Hint: Use break-even analysis by developing equations for the total cost at each location as a function of the annual production. You might wish to consider using a data table in the Excel template to evaluate total costs for a range of production volumes.)

6.* Cunningham Products is evaluating five possible locations to build a distribution center. Data estimated from the accounting department are provided below. The annual production is estimated to be 25,000 units.

   a. Which location provides the least cost?

   b. For what range of demand would each location be best?

Data	Location 1	Location 2	Location 3	Location 4	Location 5
Fixed costs	$80,000.00	$100,000.00	$75,000.00	$125,000.00	$110,000.00
Direct material cost/unit	$4.25	$4.30	$4.05	$4.50	$4.50
Direct labor cost/unit	$12.60	$14.40	$11.80	$15.60	$13.75
Overhead/unit	$2.00	$2.50	$1.95	$2.75	$2.10
Transportation cost/unit	$0.45	$0.60	$0.30	$0.83	$0.67

7.* Given the location information and volume of material movements from a supply point to several retail locations for Bourbon Hardware, find the optimal location for the supply point using the center-of-gravity method.

Retail Outlet	Location Coordinates x	y	Material Movements
1	20	5	2,800
2	18	15	2,500
3	3	16	1,600
4	3	4	1,100
5	10	20	2,000

8.* The Davis national drugstore chain prefers to operate one outlet in a town that has four major market segments. The number of potential customers in each segment along with the coordinates are as follows:

Market Segment	Location Coordinates x	y	Number of Customers
1	2	18	2,000
2	15	17	600
3	2	2	1,500
4	14	2	2,400

Which would be the best location by the center-of-gravity method?

9.* For the Davis drugstore chain in problem 8, suppose that after five years, half the customers from segment 4 are expected to move to segment 2. Where should the drugstore shift, assuming the same criteria are adopted?

10.* MicroFix provides computer repair service on a contract basis to customers in five sections of the city. The five sections, the number of service contracts in each section, and the x, y coordinates of each section are as follows:

Section	No. of Contracts	Coordinates x	y
Parkview	90	8.0	15
Mt. Airy	220	6.7	5.9
Valley	50	12.0	5.2
Norwood	300	15.0	6.3
Southgate	170	11.7	8.3

Use the center-of-gravity method to determine an ideal location for a service center.

11. A supply chain manager faced with choosing among four possible locations has assessed each location according to the following criteria, where the weights reflect the importance of the criteria. How can he use this information to choose a location? Can you develop a quantitative approach to do this?

Criteria	Weight	Location 1	2	3	4
Raw material availability	0.15	G	P	OK	VG
Infrastructure	0.1	OK	OK	OK	OK
Transportation costs	0.35	VG	OK	P	OK
Labor relations	0.2	G	VG	P	OK
Quality of life	0.2	G	VG	P	OK

VG = Very good

G = Good

OK = Acceptable

P = Poor

12. Research a supply chain for an organization of interest to you and draw a flowchart of its key components similar to Exhibit 9.2. Describe and explain the location of the push-pull boundary.

13. How can satellite-based global positioning systems improve the performance of supply chains in the following industries: (a) trucking, (b) farming and food distribution, (c) manufacturing, and (d) ambulance service?

14. Research and write a paper on the risks associated with global supply chains.

15. Research and write a paper on green and/or ethical supply chains similar to the box "Sneakers with a Conscience—Veja's Supply Chain." Do these supply chains incorporate all three dimensions of sustainability?

Boston Red Sox Spring Training Decision Case Study

"Whew, I'm glad the town hall meeting is over. The audience was hostile!" Tom Bourbon commented as he was escorted by a police officer to his car in the high school parking lot. The officer replied. "There were over 1,000 people in the gymnasium sir, and they were in an uproar. Let's get you out of here safely."

Tom and the other City Council members had just finished a town hall meeting open to the public to discuss four alternative locations for a new $80 million baseball stadium in Lee County, Florida. The City Council originally evaluated 16 sites and had arrived at the final four locations. The new 10,000-seat ballpark also includes practice fields, batting cages, and weight rooms. The stadium facility design and layout is to mimic the regular season Fenway Park in Boston, Massachusetts. However, the new park planned on "going green" by reducing energy consumption, allocating a carpooling parking lot close to the stadium to reduce patron traffic congestion and transportation costs and fuel use, and changing some of its work practices.

The five board members of City Council have to make a location decision in three weeks if they are to meet the contractual requirements of previous agreements. Once the stadium for spring training was complete, the Red Sox would sign a 30-year lease. Two economic impact studies indicated the stadium would

Economic impact studies indicated the stadium would generage $25 to $40 million annually to the local economy.

generate $25 to $40 million annually to the local economy and support thousands of jobs in airports, hotels, restaurants, and retail stores.

The four possible locations were described as follows:

- Site A includes 241 acres and is big enough to build a sports village, and is located next to a shopping mall (denoted as 1 in Exhibit 9.7) and within 4 miles of Florida Gulf Coast University and an 8,000-seat indoor arena for events such as hockey and basketball games in a second shopping mall (denoted as 2 in Exhibit 9.8.) The land cost to the City Council is $18 million.

- Site B includes 209 acres and is located between the two shopping malls 1 and 2. The site is about 2 miles from Florida Gulf Coast University. The land cost to the City Council is $22 million.

- Site C includes 2,000 acres of wetlands and habitat for animals. The area is within 3 miles of shopping mall 2 and Florida Gulf Coast University. The developer planned to donate 100 acres to the city, so the stadium land cost is free. The developer also offered to place 20 acres in a nature preserve for every acre that is developed for commercial purposes.

- Site D includes 106 acres located close to the airport and about 8 miles from the shopping mall 2 and Florida Gulf Coast University. The airport also includes a research park that hopes to attract high-tech industries and jobs. The land cost to the City Council is $22 million.

Exhibit 9.8 provides the coordinates in miles for the four possible locations. The populations for the five population centers are as follows: 1 (290,000), 2 (95,000), 3 (145,000), 4 (80,000), and 5 (120,000). Exhibit 9.9 summarizes the cost and judgments of the five City Council members for each site. It was thought that locating the Red Sox stadium close to the existing retail malls, restaurants, hotels, Florida Gulf Coast University, and the 8,000-seat indoor arena would create a retail and leisure service cluster where all could benefit. In the 10-month off-season for the Red Sox stadium, for example, local, regional, and national baseball clinics and tournaments could be played using this cluster of assets. Another viewpoint argued that locating the stadium next to the airport would encourage commercial development in this area, including the airport's research park.

Case Study Questions for Discussion

You just finished your college's spring semester and have been working for the City Council as a summer intern. Your major is Information Systems & Operations Management (ISOM), and you want to earn a good recommendation from your summer intern boss. Your boss asks you to build an electronic spreadsheet model

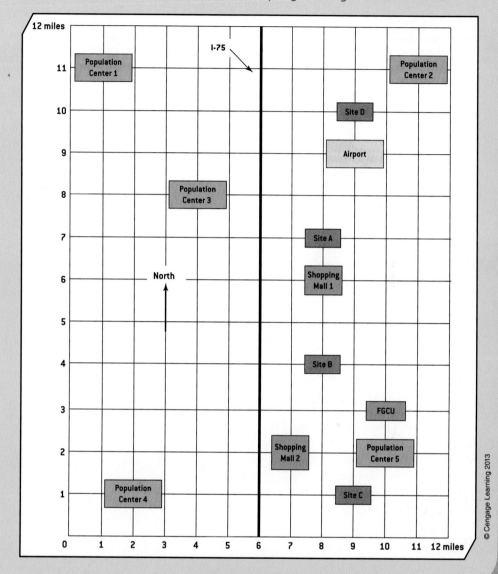

Exhibit 9.8 *Location Grid for Boston Red Sox Spring Training Stadium Finalists*

© Cengage Learning 2013

that scores, weights, and evaluates each quantitative and qualitative criterion and arrives at a summary score for each stadium site. To organize your analysis you decide to answer the following questions:

1. Using the center-of-gravity model, compute the center of gravity for the population of the county. Show all computations, explain, and justify. Based solely on this criterion, where is the best stadium location?

2. Using a weighted scoring model of your own design, what are the summary scores for each stadium site for the qualitative criteria in Exhibit 9.9? (You must

Exhibit 9.9 *Site Cost Estimates and Rankings for Boston Red Sox Spring Training Stadium Finalists*

Cost/Criteria	Site A	Site B	Site C	Site D
Stadium land cost	$18 million	$22 million	$0 million	$22 million
Additional utility cost	$1 million	$0.5 million	$3 million	$0.5 million
New road cost	$2 million	$0.5 million	$15 million	$2 million
Gain environmental group(s) endorsement	Almost	No	No	Yes
Traffic access and congestion	Good	Poor	Poor	Moderate
Utility, road, environment, and construction permits ready to go (shortest permit time)	Ready	Mostly Ready	Not Ready	Ready
Long-term economic growth and development around site (1 lowest to 5 highest/best)	4	3	4	5
Chance to preserve a huge area of the county	Moderate	Low	High	Low

decide how to scale and weight each criterion and whether to include or not include cost estimates.) Show all computations, explain, and justify.

3. How will you combine these results (your center-of gravity results, cost, and qualitative criteria analyses)? How might you compute a summary score for each site using all three criteria? Explain and justify.

4. Research and explain at least three ways a sports stadium can "go green," including at least one work practice for stadium employees. Do jobs and processes have to change too? Explain the role of OM.

5. What is your final stadium recommendation? Explain and justify.

ONE APPROACH.
70 UNIQUE SOLUTIONS.

CENGAGE
Learning™

www.cengage.com/4ltrpress

CAPACITY MANAGEMENT

 n 2011, Fortune *magazine interviewed Jeff Smisek, CEO of United Continental Holdings, Inc., the holding company created by the merger between United Airlines and Continental Airlines. In response to a question of what the recent recession taught him and the company, Mr. Smisek responded:*

> *What we learned is the importance of capacity discipline. Ours has been an industry where it's very easy to add seats, through increased frequencies, flying the aircraft longer, or taking delivery of additional aircraft. In the recession we were very disciplined in getting our capacity down, and as we saw the recovery with high fuel prices, we've been very disciplined at United and across the industry in making sure we've got the right level of capacity and not supplying overcapacity, driving down pricing.[1]*

learning outcomes

After studying this chapter you should be able to:

10-1 **Explain the concept of capacity.**

10-2 **Describe how to compute and use capacity measures.**

10-3 **Describe long-term capacity expansion strategies.**

10-4 **Describe short-term capacity adjustment strategies.**

10-5 **Explain the principles and logic of the Theory of Constraints.**

What do you think?

Have you ever experienced problems with a service because of inadequate labor or equipment capacity?

Comstock/Getty Images

In a general sense, *capacity* is a measure of the capability of a manufacturing or service system to perform its intended function. In practice, it is measured by the amount of output that can be produced in a particular time period—for example, the number of hamburgers made during a weekday lunch hour or the number of patients that can be handled during an emergency room shift. Having sufficient capacity to meet customer demand and provide high levels of customer service is vital to a successful business and long-term economic sustainability.

Capacity decisions cannot be taken lightly and can have profound impacts on business performance, as the introduction suggests. For example, Airbus has decided to produce the A380 with a much greater seating capacity than other aircraft, whereas Boeing's strategy is to make smaller planes. Clearly, more flights would be needed to achieve the same amount of passenger capacity over a fixed time period. Larger planes might result in better economies of scale, but reduce passenger choice and schedule flexibility. The decision of how much seating capacity to provide in new airplanes depends on

forecasts of demand along global air traffic routes, the planes' efficiencies and operating costs, how customers will accept them, and the operational implications of boarding, disembarking, and baggage retrieval.

10-1 Understanding Capacity

Capacity *is the capability of a manufacturing or service resource such as a facility, process, workstation, or piece of equipment to accomplish its purpose over a specified time period.* Capacity can be viewed in one of two ways:

Capacity is the capability of a manufacturing or service resource such as a facility, process, workstation, or piece of equipment to accomplish its purpose over a specified time period.

▼ *We've been very disciplined in making sure we've got the right level of capacity and not supplying over capacity, driving down pricing.*

Carlo Bollo/Alamy Limited

1. as the maximum rate of output per unit of time; or

2. as units of resource availability.

For example, the capacity of an automobile plant might be measured as the number of automobiles capable of being produced per week, and the capacity of a paper mill as the number of tons it can produce per year. As a resource availability measure, the capacity of a hospital would be measured by the number of beds available, and the capacity of "cloud" storage would be measured in gigabytes.

Operations managers must decide on the appropriate levels of capacity to meet current (short-term) and future (long-term) demand. Exhibit 10.1 provides examples of such capacity decisions. Short-term capacity decisions usually involve adjusting schedules or staffing levels. Longer-term decisions typically involve major capital investments. To satisfy customers in the long run, capacity must be at least as large as the average demand. However, demand for many goods and services typically varies over time. A process may not be capable of meeting peak demand at all times, resulting in either lost sales or customers who must wait until the good or service becomes available. At other periods of time, capacity may exceed demand, resulting in idle processes or facilities or buildups in physical inventories.

No Food for You!

McDonald's restaurants in Britain apologized to millions of unhappy customers for running out of Big Macs during a weekend 2-for-1 promotion to celebrate its 25th anniversary in Britain. The demand generated by the promotion far exceeded forecasts. The promotion caused many of the nation's 922 outlets to turn away long lines of customers.

Exhibit 10.1 *Examples of Short- and Long-Term Capacity Decisions*

Short-Term Capacity Decisions	Long-Term Capacity Decisions
• Amount of overtime scheduled for the next week	• Construction of a new manufacturing plant
• Number of emergency room nurses on call during a downtown festival weekend	• Expanding the size and number of beds in a hospital
• Number of call center workers to staff during the holiday season	• Number of branch banks to establish in a new market territory

© Cengage Learning 2013

Clogged Courts

Court systems in most major cities are strained past their capacity with case backlogs and long delays, often resulting in freeing criminals before they go to trial or incarcerating defendants who are subsequently acquitted for long periods of time. Civil cases, such as foreclosures, can be stuck in court systems for years. Some court systems are turning to technology and OM principles to address these capacity issues. For example, better computers and software for judges allow them to scan conviction and sentencing documents right from their courtrooms rather than recess to their chambers. Police departments are also scanning reports, allowing prosecutors faster access to information. Improved scheduling, such as blocking time for certain types of cases that are backlogged and hiring part-time retired judges, can help also. Can you think of other OM practices that might help?[2]

Andy Dean Photography/Shutterstock.com

10-1a Economies and Diseconomies of Scale

Capacity decisions are often influenced by economies and diseconomies of scale. **Economies of scale** *are achieved when the average unit cost of a good or service decreases as the capacity and/or volume of throughput increases.* For example, the design and construction cost per room of building a hotel decreases as the facility gets larger because the fixed cost is allocated over more rooms, resulting in a lower unit room cost. This lends support to building larger facilities with more capacity. **Diseconomies of scale** *occur when the average unit cost of the good or service begins to increase as the capacity and/or volume of throughput increases.* In the hotel example, as the number of rooms in a hotel continues to increase, the average cost per unit begins to increase, because of larger amounts of overhead and operating expenses required by higher levels of such amenities as restaurants, parking, and recreational facilities. This suggests that some optimal amount of capacity exists where costs are at a minimum. The pressure on global automakers for improving economies of scale is evident by Daimler and Nissan announcing plans to share the costs of developing small-car technology, including engines. They will swap 3.1 percent stakes in their companies with plans to generate $5.3 billion in savings over five years.[3]

As a single facility adds more and more goods and/or services to its portfolio, the facility can become too large and "unfocused." At some point, diseconomies of scale arise and unit costs increase because dissimilar product lines, processes, people skills, and technology exist in the same facility. In trying to manage a large facility with too many objectives and missions, key competitive priorities such as delivery, quality, customization, and cost performance can begin to deteriorate. This leads to the concept of a focused factory.

A **focused factory** *is a way to achieve economies of scale without extensive investments in facilities and capacity by focusing on a narrow range of goods or services, target market segments, and/or dedicated processes to maximize efficiency and effectiveness.* The focused factory argues to "divide and conquer" by adopting smaller, more focused facilities dedicated to (1) a few key products, (2) a specific technology, (3) a certain process design and capability, (4) a specific competitive priority objective such as next-day delivery, and (5) particular market segments or customers and associated volumes.

Solved Problem

An automobile transmission-assembly factory normally operates two shifts per day, five days per week. During each shift, 400 transmissions can be completed. What is the capacity of this factory?

$$\text{Capacity} = (2 \text{ shifts/day})(5 \text{ days/week}) \times \\ (400 \text{ transmissions/shift}) \times \\ (4 \text{ weeks/month}) \\ = 16,000 \text{ transmissions/month}$$

Economies of scale are achieved when the average unit cost of a good or service decreases as the capacity and/or volume of throughput increases.

Diseconomies of scale occur when the average unit cost of the good or service begins to increase as the capacity and/or volume of throughput increases.

A **focused factory** is a way to achieve economies of scale without extensive investments in facilities and capacity by focusing on a narrow range of goods or services, target market segments, and/or dedicated processes to maximize efficiency and effectiveness.

10-2 Capacity Measurement in Operations

Capacity measures are used in many ways in long-term planning and short-term management activities. For example, managers need to plan capacity contingencies for unanticipated demand and plan routine equipment and labor requirements. In this section we present several examples of how capacity measurements are used in OM.

10-2a Safety Capacity

The actual utilization rates at most facilities are not planned to be 100 percent of effective capacity. Unanticipated events such as equipment breakdowns, employee absences, or sudden short-term surges in demand will reduce the capability of planned capacity levels to meet demand and satisfy customers. This is evident in Exhibit 10.2. Therefore, some amount of **safety capacity** (*often called the* **capacity cushion**), *defined as an amount of capacity reserved for unanticipated events such as demand surges, materials shortages, and*

Safety capacity (often called the **capacity cushion**) is defined as an amount of capacity reserved for unanticipated events such as demand surges, materials shortages, and equipment breakdowns.

A work order is a specification of work to be performed for a customer or a client.

equipment breakdowns, is normally planned into a process or facility. In general, average safety capacity is defined by Equation 10.1.

Average safety capacity (%)
= 100% − Average resource utilization (%)   [10.1]

Note that Equation 10.1 is based on average resource utilizations over some time period. For a factory, average safety capacity might be computed over a year, whereas for an individual workstation, it might be updated monthly.

10-2b Capacity Measurement

A **work order** *is a specification of work to be performed for a customer or a client.* It generally includes the quantity to be produced, the processing requirements, and resources needed. Work orders may be defined for manufacturing (e.g., a job shop) or services (e.g., a patient at a dentist's office or room maintenance at a hotel). For any production situation, setup time can be a substantial part of total system capacity, and therefore must be included in evaluating capacity. Equation 10.2 provides a general expression for evaluating the capacity required to meet a given production volume for one work order, i.

Capacity required (C_i) = Setup time (S_i)
+ [Processing time (P_i)
× Order size (Q_i)]   [10.2]

where

C_i = capacity requirements in units of time (for instance, minutes, hours, days) for work order i.

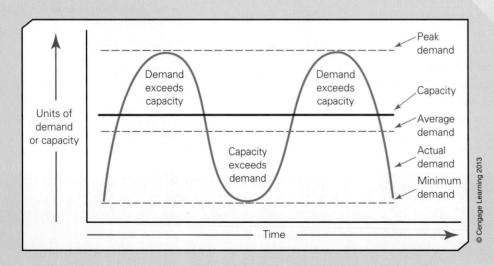

Exhibit 10.2
The Demand Versus Capacity Problem Structure

© Cengage Learning 2013

S_i = setup or changeover time for work order i as a fixed amount that does not vary with volume.

P_i = processing time for each unit of work order i (e.g., hours/part, minutes/transaction, and so on).

Q_i = size of order i in numbers of units.

If we sum the capacity requirements over all work orders, we can compute the total capacity required using Equation 10.3.

$$\Sigma C_i = \Sigma[S_i + (P_i \times Q_i)] \qquad [10.3]$$

Manufacturing work orders normally assume that one setup is necessary for each work order, and therefore, the setup time is spread over the single work order quantity. That is, setup time is independent of order size. Some services, such as hospital surgeries, may require a new setup for each unit (i.e., the order size is one). For example, setup time for a surgery might include sterilizing equipment, cleaning and disinfecting the surgical suite, and preparing equipment for the next procedure. It is important to understand these differences in goods-producing and service-providing applications so workload is correctly computed.

10-2c Using Capacity Measures for Operations Planning

Capacity needs must be translated into specific requirements for equipment and labor. To illustrate this, we present a simple example. Fast Burger, Inc. is building a new restaurant near a college football stadium. The restaurant will be open 16 hours per day, 360 days per year. Managers have concluded that the restaurant should have the capacity to handle a peak hourly demand of 100 customers. This peak hour of demand happens two hours before every home football game. The average customer purchase is

1 burger (4-ounce hamburger or cheeseburger)

1 bag of french fries (4 ounces)

1 soft drink (12 ounces)

Consequently, management would like to determine how many grills, deep fryers, and soft drink spouts are needed.

A 36 × 36-inch grill cooks 48 ounces of burgers every 10 minutes, and a single-basket deep fryer cooks 2 pounds of french fries in 6 minutes, or 20 pounds per hour. Finally, one soft drink spout dispenses 20 ounces of soft drink per minute, or 1,200 ounces per hour. These effective capacity estimates are based on the

Photodisc/Getty Imagess

equipment manufacturer's studies of actual use under normal operating conditions.

To determine the equipment needed to meet peak hourly demand, Fast Burger must translate expected demand in terms of customers per hour into needs for grills, deep fryers, and soft drink spouts. First note that the peak hourly demand for burgers, french fries, and soft drinks are as follow:

Product	Peak Hourly Demand (ounces)
Burgers	400
French fries	400
Soft drinks	1,200

Because the capacity of a grill is (48 oz/10 minutes) (60 minutes/hour) = 288 ounces/hour, the number of grills needed to satisfy a peak hourly demand of 400 ounces of burgers is

$$\text{Number of grills} = 400/288$$
$$= 1.39 \text{ grills}$$

To determine the number of single-basket deep fryers needed to meet a peak hourly demand of 400 ounces of french fries, we must first compute the hourly capacity of the deep fryer.

$$\text{Capacity of deep fryer} = (20 \text{ lb/hour})(16 \text{ oz/lb})$$
$$= 320 \text{ oz/hour}$$

Hence, the number of single-basket deep fryers needed is 400/320 = 1.25.

Finally, the number of soft drink spouts needed to satisfy peak demand of 1,200 ounces is

Number of soft drink spouts needed
= 1,200/1,200 = 1.0

After reviewing this analysis, the managers decided to purchase two 36 × 36-inch grills. Grill safety capacity is 2.0 − 1.39 = 0.61 grills or 175.7 oz/hour [(.61) × (48 oz/10 minutes) × (60 minutes/hour), or about 44 hamburgers per hour. Management decided this excess safety capacity was justified to handle demand surges and grill breakdowns. With two grills the managers reduced their risk of being unable to fill customer demand. If they installed two french fryer machines they would have 0.75 excess machines, and that was thought to be wasteful. However, they realized that if the one french fryer machine broke down they would not be able to cook enough fries, so they decided to purchase two deep fryers.

Management decided to go with a two-spout soft drink system. Although their analysis showed a need for only one soft drink spout, the managers wanted to provide some safety capacity, primarily because they felt the peak hourly demand for soft drinks might have been underestimated and customers tend to refill their drinks in this self-service situation.

The average expected equipment utilizations for the two grills, two fryers, and two soft drink spouts are as follows (refer to Equation 7.1 in Chapter 7):

Grill utilization (U) = Resources used/Resources available
= 1.39/2.0 = 69.5%

Fryer utilization (U) = Resources used/Resources available
= 1.25/2.0 = 62.5%

Soft drink spout utilization (U) = Resources used/Resources available
= 1.0/2.0 = 50.0%

The managers of Fast Burger, Inc. must also staff the new restaurant for peak demand of 100 customers/hour. Assume front-counter service personnel can take and assemble orders at the service rate of 15 customers per hour and the target labor utilization rate for this job is 85 percent. The number of front-service counter people that should be assigned to this peak demand period can be found using Equation 7.2 in Chapter 7:

Utilization (U) = Demand rate/
[Service rate × Number of servers]

Using the data for Fast Burger, we have

$$0.85 = \frac{(100 \text{ customers/hour})}{(15 \text{ customers/hour}) \times (\text{Number of servers})}$$

Solving this equation for the number of servers, we obtain

(12.75)(Number of servers) = 100
Number of servers = 7.8

Given these capacity computations, Fast Burger management decides to assign eight people to the front-service counter during this peak demand period. Safety capacity is included in this decision in two ways. First, the target utilization labor rate is 85 percent, so there is a 15 percent safety capacity according to Equation 10.1. Second, eight people are on duty when 7.8 are needed, so there is a safety capacity of 0.2 people. The management at Fast Burger now has an equipment and labor capacity plan for this peak-demand period. Notice that equipment capacity, which is difficult to increase in the short-term, is high, whereas labor is more easily changed. This equipment and labor capacity strategy must also be coupled with good forecasting of demand—the subject of the next chapter.

10-3 Long-Term Capacity Strategies

n developing a long-range capacity plan, a firm must make a basic economic trade-off between the cost of capacity and the opportunity cost of not having adequate capacity. Capacity costs include both the initial investment in facilities and equipment and the annual cost of operating and maintaining them, much of which are fixed costs.

The cost of not having sufficient capacity is the opportunity loss incurred from lost sales and reduced market share. Having too much capacity, particularly if demand falls, can be devastating. For example, International Paper recently closed its Franklin paper mill in Virginia. The mill had a capacity of 600,000 tons per year, but demand had fallen 30 percent and was forecasted to continue falling, much of it a result of new technologies such as e-mail, Kindles and iPads, and electronic transactions.[4] Too little capacity, on the other hand, can squeeze profit margins or leave a firm vulnerable to competitors if it cannot satisfy customer orders.

Solved Problem

A typical dentist's office has a complicated mix of dental procedures and significant setup times; thus, it is similar to a job shop. Suppose a dentist works a nine-hour day with one hour for lunch and breaks. During the first six months the practice is open, he does all the work,

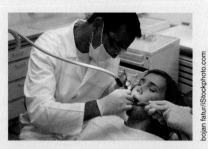

bojan fatur/iStockphoto.com

including cleaning and setting up for the next dental procedure. Setup and processing times for three procedures are shown in Exhibit 10.3. Also shown are the number of appointments and demand for each type.

Exhibit 10.3 *Dental Office Procedures and Times for Today*

Dental Procedure	Number of Appointments	Setup or Changeover Time (Minutes)	Processing Time (Minutes)	Demand (No. of Patients Scheduled)
Single tooth crown	1st	15	90	2
	2nd	10	30	1
Tooth whitening	1st	5	30	4
Partial denture	1st	20	30	3
	2nd	10	20	0
	3rd	5	30	2

© Cengage Learning 2013

Exhibit 10.4 *Dental Office Demand-Capacity Analysis Using the Excel Capacity Template**

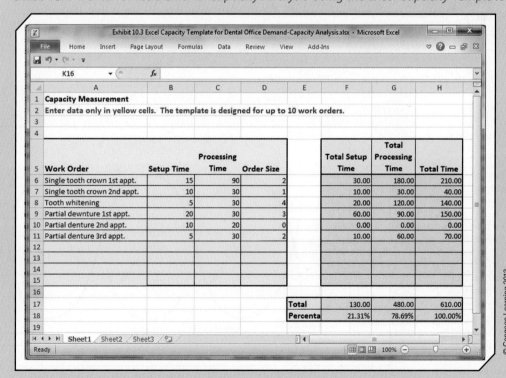

*Assumes one setup time per dental procedure to set up and clean the equipment and room before the next patient arrives.

On a particular day, there are two scheduled first appointments for single tooth crowns (see last column of Exhibit 10.3), one second appointment for a single tooth crown, four tooth-whitening appointments, three first appointments for a partial denture, and two third appointments for a partial denture. Is there sufficient capacity to perform all the work?

We may use Equation 10.3 to compute the capacity requirements. Exhibit 10.4 shows the results using the Excel Capacity template. We see that a total of 610 minutes of work are scheduled during a 480-minute workday. Therefore, there is a capacity shortage of 130 minutes. The dentist will either have to work two hours longer or reschedule some patients.

From this analysis, we see that 21.3 percent of his total capacity is used to set up and change over from one dental procedure to the next. If a dental assistant or technician is hired to do this work (assuming that this can be done off-line while the dentist continues to work on other patients), revenue would increase by about 20 percent. If setup times could be reduced by 50 percent, the total setup time would be 65 minutes instead of 130 minutes and the capacity shortage would only be 65 minutes, requiring only one hour of overtime.

David Lee/Alamy

Long-term capacity planning must be closely tied to the strategic direction of the organization—what products and services it offers. For example, many goods and services are seasonal, resulting in unused capacity during the off-season. Many firms offer **complementary goods and services,** *which are goods and services that can be produced or delivered using the same resources available to the firm, but whose seasonal demand patterns are out of phase with each other.* Complementary goods or services balance seasonal demand cycles and therefore use the excess capacity available, as illustrated in Exhibit 10.5. For instance, demand for lawnmowers peaks in the spring and summer; to balance manufacturing capacity,

Complementary goods and services are goods and services that can be produced or delivered using the same resources available to the firm, but whose seasonal demand patterns are out of phase with each other.

Exhibit 10.5 *Seasonal Demand and Complementary Goods or Services*

Units of demand or capacity

Lawnmower demand

Snowblower demand

Time

© Cengage Learning 2013

the producer might also produce leaf blowers and vacuums for the autumn season and snowblowers for the winter season.

10-3a Capacity Expansion

Capacity requirements are rarely static; changes in markets and product lines and competition will eventually require a firm to either plan to increase or reduce long-term capacity. Such strategies require determining the *amount*, *timing*, and *form* of capacity changes. To illustrate capacity expansion decisions, let us make two assumptions: (1) capacity is added in "chunks" or discrete increments, and (2) demand is steadily increasing.

Four basic strategies for expanding capacity over some fixed time horizon are shown in Exhibit 10.6 (these concepts can also be applied to capacity reduction):

1. One large capacity increase (Exhibit 10.6a)

2. Small capacity increases that match demand (Exhibit 10.6b)

3. Small capacity increases that lead demand (Exhibit 10.6c)

4. Small capacity increases that lag demand (Exhibit 10.6d)

The strategy in Exhibit 10.6a involves one large increase in capacity over a specified period. The advantage of one large capacity increase is that the fixed costs of construction and operating system setup needs to be incurred only once, and thus the firm can allocate these costs over one large project. However, if aggregate demand exhibits steady growth, the facility will be underutilized. The alternative is to view capacity expansion incrementally as in Exhibit 10.6b, c, and d.

Exhibit 10.6b illustrates the strategy of matching capacity additions with demand as closely as possible. This is often called a *capacity straddle strategy*. When capacity is above the demand curve, the firm has excess capacity; when it is below, there is a shortage of capacity to meet demand. In this situation, there will be short periods of over- and underutilization of resources. Exhibit 10.6c shows a capacity-expansion strategy with the goal of maintaining sufficient capacity to minimize the chances of not meeting demand. Here, capacity expansion leads or is ahead of demand, and hence is called a *capacity lead strategy*. Because there is always excess capacity, safety capacity to meet unexpected demand from large orders or new customers is provided.

Finally, Exhibit 10.6d illustrates a policy of a *capacity lag strategy* that results in constant capacity shortages. Such a strategy waits until demand has increased to a point where additional capacity is necessary. It requires less investment and provides for high capacity utilization and thus a higher rate of return on investment. However, it may also reduce long-term profitability through overtime, subcontracting, and productivity losses that occur as the firm scrambles to satisfy demand. In the long run, such a policy can lead to a permanent loss of market position.

BRIGGS & STRATTON: MANAGING CAPACITY

Briggs & Stratton is the world's largest producer of air-cooled gasoline engines for outdoor power equipment. The company designs, manufactures, markets, and services these products for original equipment manufacturers worldwide. These engines are primarily aluminum alloy gasoline engines ranging from 3 through 25 horsepower. Briggs & Stratton is a leading designer, manufacturer, and marketer of portable generators, lawnmowers, snow throwers, pressure washers, and related accessories. It also provides engines for manufacturers of other small engine-driven equipment such as snowmobiles, go-karts, and jet skis.

The complementary and diverse original equipment markets for Briggs & Stratton engines allows factory managers to plan equipment and labor capacities and schedules in a much more stable operating environment. This helps minimize manufacturing costs, stabilize workforce levels, and even out volumes so that assembly lines can be used in a more efficient fashion.[5]

Razvan Chirnoaga/Shutterstock.com

Exhibit 10.6 *Capacity Expansion Options*

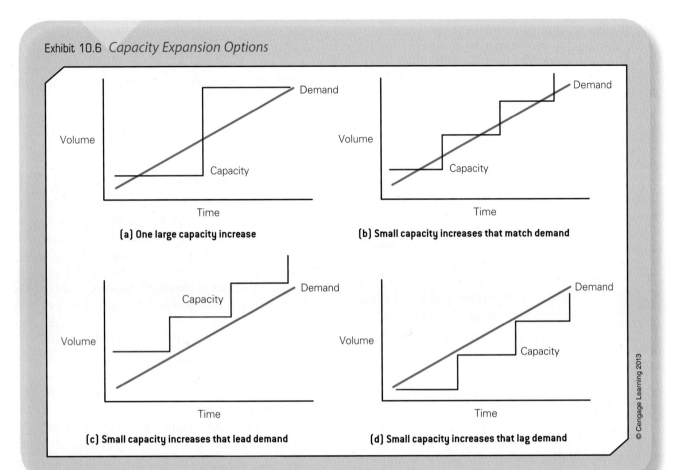

(a) One large capacity increase

(b) Small capacity increases that match demand

(c) Small capacity increases that lead demand

(d) Small capacity increases that lag demand

© Cengage Learning 2013

10-4 Short-Term Capacity Management

I f short-term demand is stable and sufficient capacity is available, then managing operations to ensure that demand is satisfied is generally easy. However, when demand fluctuates above and below average capacity levels as was illustrated in Exhibit 10.2, firms have two basic choices. First, they can adjust capacity to match the changes in demand by changing internal resources and capabilities. The second approach is to manage capacity by shifting and stimulating demand.

10-4a Managing Capacity by Adjusting Short-Term Capacity Levels

When short-term demand exceeds capacity, a firm must either temporarily increase its capacity or it will be unable to meet all of the demand. Similarly, if demand falls well below capacity, then idle resources reduce profits. Short-term adjustments to capacity can be done in a variety of ways and are summarized as follows:

- *Add or share equipment:* Capacity levels that are limited by machine and equipment availability are more difficult to change in the short run because of high capital expense. However, leasing equipment as needed can accomplish this in a cost-effective manner. Another way is through innovative partnership arrangements and capacity sharing. For example, a consortium of several hospitals might be set up in which each hospital focuses on a particular specialty and shares services.

- *Sell unused capacity:* Some firms might sell idle capacity, such as computer storage space and computing capacity, to outside buyers and even to competitors. For example, hotels often develop partnership arrangements to accommodate their competitors' guests when they are overbooked.

- *Change labor capacity and schedules:* Labor capacity can usually be managed easily through short-term changes in workforce levels and schedules. Overtime, extra shifts, temporary employees, and outsourcing are common ways of increasing capacity. Adjusting workforce schedules to better coincide with demand patterns is another. Many quick-service restaurants employ large numbers of part-time employees with varying work schedules.

- *Change labor skill mix:* Hiring the right people who can learn quickly and adjust to changing job requirements and cross-training them to perform different tasks provides the flexibility to meet fluctuating demand. In supermarkets, for example, it is common for employees to work as cashiers during busy periods and to assist with stocking shelves during slow periods.

- *Shift work to slack periods:* Another strategy is to shift work to slack periods. For example, hotel clerks prepare bills and perform other paperwork at night, when check-in and check out activity is light. This allows more time during the daytime hours to service customers. Manufacturers often build up inventory during slack periods and hold the goods for peak demand periods.

10-4b Managing Capacity by Shifting and Stimulating Demand

Some general approaches to influence customers to shift demand from periods without adequate capacity to periods with excess capacity, or to fill times with excess capacity, include the following:

- *Vary the price of goods or services:* Price is the most powerful way to influence demand. For example, hotels might offer cheaper rates on the weekend; airlines might offer better prices for midweek flights; a restaurant might cut its meal prices in half after 9:00 P.M. In a similar fashion, manufacturers typically offer sales and rebates of

Where Can I Park?

Finding a parking space in San Francisco is difficult because most spaces are privately owned—driveways, parking lots, carports. These same spaces are empty most of the day while the owners are at work or out of town. One company, Park Circa, asks these parking space owners to register their spaces, set a parking fee rate, and tell Park Circa when the spaces are free via a cell phone application. Customers hunting for parking spots also use the cell phone app to locate and find good parking spaces. Park Circa coordinates all parking space payments, requests, and reservations using its software. What general approaches to managing capacity by stimulating demand does this example demonstrate?

Martin Hospach/fStop/Jupiter Images

overstocks to stimulate demand, smooth production schedules and staffing requirements, and reduce inventories.

- *Provide customers with information:* Many call centers, for example, send notes to customers on their bills or provide an automated voice message recommending the best times to call. Amusement parks such as Disney World use signs and literature informing customers when certain rides are extremely busy.

- *Advertising and promotion:* After-holiday sales are heavily advertised in an attempt to draw customers to periods of traditionally low demand. Manufacturer or service coupons are strategically distributed to increase demand during periods of low sales or excess capacity.

- *Add peripheral goods and/or services:* Movie theaters offer rentals of their auditoriums for business meetings and special events at off-peak times. Fast-food chains offer birthday party planning services to fill up slow demand periods between peak meal times. Extended hours also represent a peripheral service; many supermarkets remain open 24/7 and encourage customers to shop during late-night hours to reduce demand during peak times.

- *Provide reservations: A* **reservation** *is a promise to provide a good or service at some future time and place.* Typical examples are reservations for hotel rooms, airline seats, and scheduled surgeries and operating rooms. Reservations reduce the uncertainty for both the good or service provider and the customer. With advance knowledge of when customer demand will occur, operations managers can better plan their equipment and workforce schedules and rely less on forecasts.

10-4c Revenue Management Systems (RMS)

Many types of organizations manage perishable assets, such as a hotel room, an airline seat, a rental car, a sporting event or concert seat, a room on a cruise line,

A **reservation** is a promise to provide a good or service at some future time and place.

A **revenue management system (RMS)** consists of dynamic methods to forecast demand, allocate perishable assets across market segments, decide when to overbook and by how much, and determine what price to charge different customer (price) classes.

the capacity of a restaurant catering service or electric power generation, or broadcast advertising space. For such assets, which essentially represent service capacity, high utilization is the key to financial success.

A **revenue management system (RMS)** *consists of dynamic methods to forecast demand, allocate perishable assets across market segments, decide when to overbook and by how much, and determine what price to charge different customer (price) classes.* These four components of RMS—forecasting, allocation, overbooking, and pricing—must work in unison if the objective is to maximize the revenue generated by a perishable asset. The ideas and methods surrounding RMS are often called yield management. Revenue management systems integrate a wide variety of decisions and data into a decision support system used mainly by service-providing businesses.

⌈"During the first year of RMS implementation, revenues at National Car Rental increased by $56 million."⌉

The earliest revenue management systems focused solely on overbooking—how many perishable assets to sell in excess of physical capacity to optimally trade off the cost of an unsold asset versus the loss of goodwill of having more arrivals than assets. Modern RMS software simultaneously makes changes in the forecast, allocation, overbooking, and pricing decisions in a real-time operating system. Forecasts are constantly being revised. Allocation involves segmenting the perishable asset into target market categories, such as first, business, and coach classes in an airline flight. Each class is defined by its size (number of seats), price, advance purchase restrictions, and booking policies. Allocation is a real-time, ongoing method that does not end until there is no more opportunity to maximize revenue (the night or concert is over, the airplane takes off). As happens with forecasts, bookings and time move forward,

If you don't sell or use the ticket, the revenue-generating opportunity for that seat cannot be recaptured—it is lost forever.

the target market categories are redefined, and prices change in an attempt to maximize revenue.

Many organizations have exploited RMS technology. Marriott improved its revenues by $25–$35 million by using RMS methods. Royal Caribbean Cruise Lines obtained a revenue increase in excess of $20 million for one year.[6] During the first year of RMS implementation, revenues at National Car Rental increased by $56 million.[7]

Theater seats provide another good example of managing a perishable asset. Revenue management systems are often used to manage theater, stadium, and concert seats. If you don't sell or use the ticket, the revenue-generating opportunity for that seat cannot be recaptured—it is lost forever.

10-5 Theory of Constraints

the **Theory of Constraints (TOC)** *is a set of principles that focuses on increasing total process throughput by maximizing the utilization of all bottleneck work activities and workstations.* The TOC was introduced in a fictional novel, *The Goal,* by Dr. Eliyahu M. Goldratt.[8] The philosophy and principles of the TOC are valuable in understanding demand and capacity management.

The traditional OM definition of throughput is the average number of goods or services completed per time period by a process. The TOC views throughput differently: **throughput** *is the amount of money generated per time period through actual sales.* For most business organizations the goal is to maximize throughput, thereby maximizing cash flow. Inherent in this definition is that it makes little sense to make a good or service until it can be sold, and that excess inventory is wasteful.

In the TOC, *a* **constraint** *is anything in an organization that limits it from moving toward or achieving its goal.* Constraints determine the throughput of a facility, because they limit production output to their own capacity. There are two basic types of constraints: physical and nonphysical.

Hemis.fr/SuperStock

A **physical constraint** *is associated with the capacity of a resource such as a machine, employee, or workstation.* Physical constraints result in process bottlenecks.

> The **Theory of Constraints (TOC)** is a set of principles that focuses on increasing total process throughput by maximizing the utilization of all bottleneck work activities and workstations.
>
> **Throughput** is the amount of money generated per time period through actual sales.
>
> A **constraint** is anything in an organization that limits it from moving toward or achieving its goal.
>
> A **physical constraint** is associated with the capacity of a resource such as a machine, employee, or workstation.

For most business organizations the goal is to maximize throughput, thereby maximizing cash flow.

A **bottleneck (BN) work activity** *is one that effectively limits the capacity of the entire process.* At a bottleneck, the input exceeds the capacity, restricting the total output that is capable of being produced. *A* **nonbottleneck (NBN) work activity** *is one in which idle capacity exists.*

A **nonphysical constraint** *is environmental or organizational, such as low product demand or an inefficient management policy or procedure.* Inflexible work rules, inadequate labor skills, and poor management are all forms of constraints. Removing nonphysical constraints is not always possible.

Because the number of constraints is typically small, the TOC focuses on identifying them; managing

A **bottleneck (BN) work activity** is one that effectively limits the capacity of the entire process.

A **nonbottleneck (NBN) work activity** is one in which idle capacity exists.

A **nonphysical constraint** is environmental or organizational, such as low product demand or an inefficient management policy or procedure.

BN and NBN work activities carefully; linking them to the market to ensure an appropriate product mix; and scheduling the NBN resources to enhance throughput. These principles are summarized in Exhibit 10.7.

In general, the TOC has been successful in many companies. As the TOC evolved, it has been applied not only to manufacturing but to other areas such as distribution, marketing, and human resource management. Binney and Smith, maker of Crayola crayons, and Procter & Gamble both use the TOC in their distribution efforts. Binney and Smith had high inventory levels yet poor customer service. By using the TOC to better position its distribution inventories, it was able to reduce inventories and improve service. Procter & Gamble reported $600 million in savings through inventory reduction and elimination of capital improvement through the TOC. A government organization that produces publications of labor statistics for the state of Pennsylvania used the TOC to better match work tasks to workers to reduce idle labor and overtime requirements, and to increase throughput, job stability, and profitability.[10]

KREISLER MANUFACTURING CORPORATION: USING THE TOC

Kreisler Manufacturing Corporation is a small, family-run company that makes metal components for airplanes. Its clients include Pratt & Whitney, General Electric, Rolls Royce, and Mitsubishi. After learning about the TOC, managers identified several areas of the factory, including the Internal Machine Shop and Supplier Deliveries, as bottlenecks, and began to focus on maximizing throughput at these bottlenecks. Setups were videotaped to see exactly what was happening. It was discovered that 60 percent of the time it took to complete a setup involved the worker looking for materials and tools. To remove this constraint, Kreisler assembled all the necessary materials and tools for setup into a prepackage "kit," thus cutting 60 percent off the setup time.

Kreisler also created a "visual factory" by installing red, yellow, and green lights on every machine. If a workstation is being starved or production stops, the operator turns on the red light. If there is a potential crisis or a risk of starving the constraint workstation, the worker turns on the yellow light. If all is running smoothly, the green light is on. Giving the machine operator control over these signals instilled a sense of ownership in the process and caught the attention and interest of everyone in the factory. In the early stages of implementing the TOC there were many red lights; today they are green. By applying the TOC, on-time deliveries increased to 97 percent from 65 percent, and 15 percent of the factory's "hidden capacity" was revealed and freed up. In addition, WIP inventory was reduced by 20 percent and is expected to be reduced by another 50 percent.[11]

Daniel Mihailescu/AFP/Getty Images

Exhibit 10.7 *Basic Principles of the Theory of Constraints*

Nonbottleneck Management Principles	Bottleneck Management Principles
Move jobs through nonbottleneck workstations as fast as possible until the job reaches the bottleneck workstation.	Only the bottleneck workstations are critical to achieving process and factory objectives and should be scheduled first.
At nonbottleneck workstations, idle time is acceptable if there is no work to do, and therefore resource utilizations may be low.	An hour lost at a bottleneck resource is an hour lost for the entire process or factory output.
Use smaller order (also called lot or transfer batches) sizes at nonbottleneck workstations to keep work flowing to the bottleneck resources and eventually to the marketplace to generate sales.	Work-in-process buffer inventory should be placed in front of bottlenecks to maximize resource utilization at the bottleneck.
An hour lost at a nonbottleneck resource has no effect on total process or factory output and incurs no real cost.	Use large order sizes at bottleneck workstations to minimize setup time and maximize resource utilization.
	Bottleneck workstations should work at all times to maximize throughput and resource utilization so as to generate cash from sales and achieve the company's goal.

Discussion Questions

1. Provide and discuss some examples of economies and diseconomies of scale in a college environment.

2. Define useful capacity measures for a(n)
   a. brewery.
   b. airline.
   c. movie theater.
   d. pizza restaurant.
   e. amusement park.

3. How might a college or university with growing enrollment use the capacity expansion strategies in Exhibit 10.6? Discuss the pros and cons of each of these.

4. Briefly describe a business you are familiar with and explain how it might use each of the five ways to adjust its short-term capacity levels.

5. How would you apply the Theory of Constraints to a quick-service automobile oil change service? Explain.

Problems and Activities

Note: an asterisk denotes problems for which a spreadsheet template on the CourseMate Web site may be used.

1. As the assistant manager of a restaurant, how many servers will you need given the following information for Saturday night's dinner menu?
   - Demand (dinners served) = 200 dinners per hour
   - Server target utilization = 85%
   - Service rate per server = 16 dinners/hour

   What does the service rate per server assume? Explain.

2. Research and write a short paper (two pages maximum) on organizations that have successfully used the focused factory concept.

3.* Medical Solutions, Inc. has the following claims it must complete in the next week. The jobs are as follows:

Claim Type	Number of Claims to Process	Setup Time per Claim Type (Hours)	Process-ing Time per Claim (Hours)
Cancer treatment	18	3	0.9
Spinal injury	12	4	1.1
Hip replacement	9	2	0.7

Given process claim capacity of 40 hours of work, can the workload be completed this week? Explain. If not, what short-term capacity solution would you recommend? Show all computations.

4.* Abbott Manufacturing produces plastic cases for solar photovoltaic panels and has decided to combine orders from customers to increase work order size, and thereby make one large production run per model type. Plastic injection molding machines are used to make these parts and it is time consuming to clean and re-setup the machines between production runs. Each molding machine and operator works one nine-hour shift with a one-hour lunch break and one-half hour for operator breaks.

Consolidated Work Orders	Work Order Quantity	Setup (Change-over) Time per Work Order (Minutes)	Processing Time per Panel (Seconds)
Model XVT-5 Case	11,500 panels	90	2.15
Model UYT-3 Case	6,500	60	1.78
Model KLY-6 Case	8,800	150	3.31

What is the total workload (demand) in hours for this work order mix? How many machines will it take to do this work in one, two, or three days? How might this process be improved?

5. Identify one example of a resource with a very low average utilization rate, and a second example with a very high average utilization rate. Consider both service and manufacturing organizations. Write a short (one-page typed) paper that describes these situations and their capacity implications.

6. Hickory Manufacturing Company forecasts the following demand for a product (in thousands of units) over the next five years:

Year	1	2	3	4	5
Forecast demand	60	79	81	84	84

Currently the manufacturer has seven machines that operate on a two-shift (eight hours each) basis. Twenty days per year are available for scheduled maintenance of equipment with no process output. Assume there are 250 workdays in a year. Each manufactured good takes 30 minutes to produce.

a. What is the capacity of the factory?

b. At what capacity levels (percentage of normal capacity) would the firm be operating over the next five years based on the forecasted demand? (Hint: Compute the ratio of demand to capacity for each year.)

c. Does the firm need to buy more machines? If so, how many? When? If not, justify.

7. The roller coaster at Treasure Island Amusement Park consists of 15 cars, each of which can carry up to three passengers. According to a time study, each run takes 1.5 minutes and the time to unload and load riders is 3.5 minutes. What is the maximum effective capacity of the system in number of passengers per hour?

8. Worthington Hills grocery store has five regular checkout lines and one express line (12 items or less). Based on a sampling study, it takes 11 minutes on the average for a customer to go through the regular line and 4 minutes to go through the express line. The store is open from 9 a.m. to 9 p.m. daily.

a. What is the store's maximum capacity (customers processed per day)?

b. What is the store's capacity by day of the week if the five regular checkout lines operate according to the following schedule? (The express line is always open.)

Hours/Day	Mon	Tue	Wed	Thur	Fri	Sat	Sun
9–12 a.m.	1	1	1	1	3	5	2
12–4 p.m.	2	2	2	2	3	5	4
4–6 p.m.	3*	3	3	3	5	3	2
6–9 p.m.	4	4	4	4	5	3	1

*A "3" means three regular checkout lines are open on Monday from 4 to 6 p.m.

9. Given the following data for Albert's fabricating production area:

Fixed costs for one shift	= $60,000
Unit variable cost	= $7
Selling price	= $12
Number of machines	= 5
Number of working days in year	= 340
Processing time per unit	= 40 minutes

a. What is the annual capacity with a single eight-hour shift?

b. What is the capacity with two shifts?

c. What is the break-even volume with a single-shift operation?

d. What is the maximum revenue with a single shift?

e. What is the break-even volume with a two-shift operation?

10. The process for renewing a driver's license at the Archer County Courthouse is as follows. First, the clerk fills out the application, then the clerk takes the driver's picture, and finally the typist types and processes the new license. It takes an average of five minutes to fill out an application, one minute to take a picture, and seven minutes to type and process the new license.

   a. If there are two clerks and three typists, where will the bottleneck in the system be? How many drivers can be processed in one hour if the clerks and typists work at an 80 percent utilization rate?

   b. If 40 drivers are to be processed each hour, how many clerks and typists should be hired assuming an 80 percent target utilization rate?

11. Due to county and state budget cuts, Archer County Courthouse (problem 10) now has only two clerks and two typists. All other information remains the same. What is the new labor utilization for each labor type, and where is the bottleneck in this three-stage process? What is the impact of your analysis on customer service? How might the job and process design be improved?

12. You have just been promoted to manage the process defined by the five stages A to E shown in the accompanying figure. After three months on the job you realize something is not right with process capacity because your employees experience big pile-ups of work, things take too long to be processed, the opportunity for error is increasing, and the entire process is approaching chaos. Do a capacity analysis of this process. The numbers in parentheses (#) are the time in minutes to complete one unit of work. Demand on the process averages 27 units per hour and each unit must be worked on by all five stages. Administrative clerks complete Stages A and B. The assistant manager completes Stages D and E. Processing times per stage can be combined when labor is assigned two or more stages (i.e., the resources are pooled). The coding specialist takes care of Stage C.

   a. How many administrative clerks should be hired, assuming a target utilization for them of 90 percent?

   b. What is the current labor utilization of the coders if two coding specialists are currently on duty?

   c. What is the total process (output) capacity in units per hour for the five-stage process A to E, assuming three administrative clerks, two coding specialists, and four assistant managers are on duty?

   d. Where do any bottlenecks exist, and what do you recommend to improve this process?

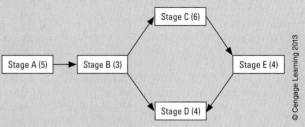

13. Perform a capacity analysis using the process structure defined in problem 12 with the following changes. Demand on the process has increased to 36 units per hour and each unit must be worked on by all five stages. The administrative clerk(s) complete Stages A, B, and D. The assistant manager completes Stage E. The coding specialist takes care of Stage C.

   a. How many administrative clerks should be hired, assuming a target utilization for them of 90 percent?

   b. What is the current labor utilization of the coders if four coding specialists are currently on duty?

   c. What is the total process (output) capacity in units per hour for the five-stage process A to E, assuming seven administrative clerks, four coding specialists, and three assistant managers are on duty?

   d. Where's the bottleneck(s) and what do you recommend to improve this process?

14. Research and write a short paper (two pages maximum) on two examples of revenue management applications not in the text and explain how they help organizations.

15. Research and write a short paper (two pages maximum) on how an organization has applied the Theory of Constraints.

Instructors may also want to consider the Greyhound Frequent Flyer Call Center Case Study at the end of Chapter 13 on staff capacity and scheduling.

David Christopher, Orthopedic Surgeon, Case Study

David Christopher received his medical degrees from the University of Kentucky and the University of Virginia. He did his residency and early surgeries at Duke University Medical Center. Eight years ago he set up his own orthopedic surgery clinic in Atlanta, Georgia. Today, one other doctor has joined his clinic in addition to 12 support personnel such as X-ray technicians, nurses, accounting, and office support. The medical practice specializes in all orthopedic surgery except it does not perform spinal surgery. The clinic has grown to the point where both orthopedic surgeons are working long hours and Dr. Christopher is wondering whether he needs to hire more surgeons.

Both surgeons are working long hours, and Dr. Christopher is wondering whether he needs to hire more surgeons.

Kiselev Andrey Valerevich/Shutterstock.com

An orthopedic surgeon is trained in the preservation, investigation, and restoration of the form and function of the extremities, spine, and associated structures by medical, surgical, and physical means. He or she is involved with the care of patients whose musculoskeletal problems include congenital deformities; trauma; infections; tumors; metabolic disturbances of the musculoskeletal system; deformities; injuries; and degenerative diseases of the spine, hands, feet, knee, hip, shoulder, and elbows in children and adults. An orthopedic surgeon is also concerned with primary and secondary muscular problems

Exhibit 10.8 *Orthopedic Surgeon One-Week Surgery Workload (This spreadsheet is available on the CourseMate Web site.)*

Orthopedic Surgery Procedure	Surgeon Changeover Time (Minutes)	Surgery Time (Minutes)	Surgeon Identity	Demand (No. of Patients Scheduled Weekly)
Rotator cuff repair	45	45	B	2
Cartilage knee repair	45	30	B	1
Fracture tibia/fibula	45	60	B	1
Achilles tendon repair	20	30	B	3
ACL ligament repair	20	60	B	4
Fractured hip	45	80	A	0
Fractured wrist	45	60	A	2
Fractured ankle	45	70	A	1
Hip replacement	60	150	A	2
Knee replacement	60	120	A	3
Shoulder replacement	120	180	B	1
Big toe replacement	45	90	B	0

© Cengage Learning 2013

and the effects of central or peripheral nervous system lesions of the musculoskeletal system. Osteoporosis, for example, results in fractures, especially in the hips, wrists, and spine. Treatments have been very successful in getting the fractures to heal.

Dr. Christopher collected the data in Exhibit 10.9 as an example of the clinic's typical workweek. Both surgeons work 11 hours each day with 1 hour off for lunch, or 10 effective hours. All surgeries are performed from 7:00 a.m. to 12:00 noon, four days a week. After lunch from noon to 1:00 p.m., the surgeons see patients in the hospital and at the clinic from 1:00 p.m. to 6:00 p.m. Over the weekend and on Fridays, the surgeons rest, attend conferences and professional meetings, and sometimes do guest lectures at a nearby medical school. The doctors want to leave a safety capacity each week of 10 percent for unexpected problems with scheduled surgeries and emergency patient arrivals.

The setup and changeover times in Exhibit 10.8 reflect time allowed between each surgery for the surgeons to clean themselves up, rest, review the next patient's medical record for any last-minute issues, and prepare for the next surgery. Dr. Christopher feels these changeover times help ensure the quality of their surgery by giving them time between operations. For example, standing on a concrete floor and bending over a patient in a state of concentration places great stress on the surgeon's legs and back. Dr. Christopher likes to sit down for a while between surgeries to relax. Some surgeons go quickly from one patient to the next; however, Dr. Christopher thinks this practice of rushing could lead to medical and surgical errors. Dr. Christopher wants answers to the following questions.

Case Questions for Discussion

1. What is the clinic's current weekly workload?
2. Should the clinic hire more surgeons, and if so, how many?
3. What other options and changes could be made to maximize patient throughput and surgeries, and therefore revenue, yet not compromise the quality of medical care?
4. What are your final recommendations? Explain your reasoning.

FORECASTING AND DEMAND PLANNING

he demand for rental cars in Florida and other warm climates peaks during college spring break season. Call centers and rental offices are flooded with customers wanting to rent a vehicle. National Car Rental took a unique approach by developing a customer-identification forecasting model, by which it identifies all customers who are young and rent cars only once or twice a year. These demand analysis models allow National to contact this target market segment in February, when call volumes are lower, to sign them up again. The proactive strategy is designed to both boost repeat rentals and smooth out the peaks and valleys in call center volumes.[1]

learning outcomes

After studying this chapter you should be able to:

11-1 **Describe the importance of forecasting to the value chain.**

11-2 **Explain basic concepts of forecasting and time series.**

11-3 **Explain how to apply simple moving average and exponential smoothing models.**

11-4 **Describe how to apply regression as a forecasting approach.**

11-5 **Explain the role of judgment in forecasting.**

11-6 **Describe how statistical and judgmental forecasting techniques are applied in practice.**

What do you think?

Think of a pizza delivery franchise located near a college campus. What factors that influence demand do you think should be included in trying to forecast demand for pizzas?

Lisa F. Young/iStockphoto.com

Forecasting *is the process of projecting the values of one or more variables into the future.* Good forecasts are needed in all organizations to drive analyses and decisions related to operations. Forecasting is a key component in many types of integrated operating systems, such as supply chain management, customer relationship management, and revenue management systems.

Poor forecasting can result in poor inventory and staffing decisions, resulting in part shortages, inadequate customer service, and many customer complaints. In the telecommunications industry, competition is fierce; and goods and services have very short life cycles. Changing technology, frequent price wars, and incentives for customers to switch services increase the difficulty of providing accurate forecasts.

Many firms integrate forecasting with value chain and capacity management systems to make better operational decisions. National Car Rental, for example, is using data analysis and forecasting methods in its value chain to improve service and reduce costs. Instead of accepting customer demand as it is and trying to plan resources to meet the peaks and valleys, its models help to shift demand to low-demand periods and better use its capacity. The proactive approach to spring break peak demand helps plan and coordinate rental office and call center staffing levels and schedules, vehicle availability, advertising campaigns, and vehicle maintenance and repair schedules. Many commercial software packages also tie forecasting modules into supply chain and operational planning systems.

> **Forecasting** is the process of projecting the values of one or more variables into the future.

▼ *National Car Rental developed a customer-identification forecasting model, by which it identifies all customers who are young and rent cars only once or twice a year.*

Jacobs Stock Photography/BananaStock/Jupiter Image

11-1 Forecasting and Demand Planning

Organizations make many different types of forecasts. Consider a consumer products company, such as Procter & Gamble, that makes many different goods in various sizes. Top managers need long-range forecasts expressed in total sales dollars for use in financial planning and for sizing and locating new facilities. At lower organizational levels, however, managers of the various product groups need aggregate forecasts of sales volume for their products in units that are more meaningful to them—for example, pounds of a certain type of soap—to establish production plans. Finally, managers of individual manufacturing facilities need forecasts by brand and size—for instance, the number of 64-ounce boxes of Tide detergent—to plan material usage and production schedules. Similarly, airlines need long-range forecasts of demand for air travel to plan their purchases of airplanes and short-term forecasts to develop seasonal routes and schedules; university administrators require enrollment forecasts; city planners need forecasts of population trends to plan highways and mass transit systems; and restaurants need forecasts to be able to plan for food purchases.

Accurate forecasts are needed throughout the value chain, as illustrated in Exhibit 11.1, and are used by all functional areas of an organization, such as accounting, finance, marketing, operations, and distribution. Forecasting is typically included in comprehensive value chain and demand-planning software systems. These systems integrate marketing, inventory, sales, operations planning, and financial data. For example, the SAP Demand Planning module enables companies to integrate planning information from different departments or organizations into a single demand plan. Some software vendors are beginning to use the words *demand planning*

DIRECTV: FORECASTING NEW TECHNOLOGY ADOPTION

When DIRECTV planned to launch its business in the early 1990s, it needed to forecast subscriptions of satellite television over a five-year horizon. As was noted, "The most critical forecast is the forecast prior to product launch." DIRECTV needed a forecast that would answer the following questions: how many of the homes in the United States would subscribe to satellite television, and when would they subscribe? The forecast was developed using a quantitative model that describes the adoption pattern of many new products and technologies.

DIRECTV's management made use of the forecast in several important ways:

- The forecast for the first year that indicated very rapid consumer acceptance of direct broadcast satellite systems supported DIRECTV's decision to launch a second million-dollar satellite sooner than originally planned. The second satellite permitted DIRECTV to carry a greater variety of programming.

- DIRECTV planned and budgeted for distribution arrangements and advertising expenditures to achieve the availability and awareness levels it had assumed as necessary in making the forecasts.

- DIRECTV management used the forecast to solicit funding and in developing partnerships with equipment manufacturers such as Sony, programming providers like Disney, and national retailers such as Radio Shack.

A comparison of the actual number of subscribers and the forecast over the first five years indicated that the forecast closely predicted the trends in actual values.[2]

Dennis MacDonald/Alamy

Exhibit 11.1 *The Need for Forecasts in a Value Chain*

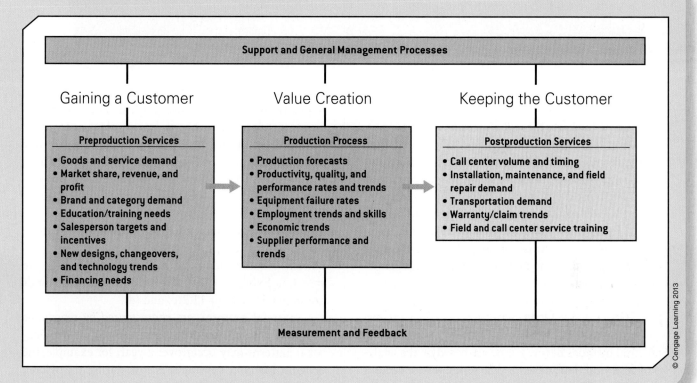

or *demand chain* instead of *supply chain*. This name change highlights the fact that customers' wants and needs define the customer benefit package and that customer demand pulls goods and services through the supply chain.

11-2 Basic Concepts in Forecasting

before diving into the process of developing forecasting models, it is important to understand some basic concepts that are used in model development. These concepts are independent of the type of model and provide a foundation for users to make better use of the models in operations decisions.

11-2a Forecast Planning Horizon

Forecasts of future demand are needed at all levels of organizational decision making. *The **planning horizon** is the length of time on which a forecast is based.* Long-range forecasts cover a planning horizon of 1 to 10 years and are necessary to plan for the expansion of facilities and to determine future needs for land, labor, and equipment. Intermediate-range forecasts over a 3- to 12-month period are needed to plan workforce levels, allocate budgets among divisions, schedule jobs and resources, and establish purchasing plans. Short-range forecasts focus on the planning horizon of up to three months and are used by operations managers to plan production schedules and assign workers to jobs, to determine short-term capacity requirements, and to aid

The **planning horizon** is the length of time on which a forecast is based.

Forecasts of future demand are needed at all levels of organizational decision making.

shipping departments in planning transportation needs and establishing delivery schedules.

The **time bucket** *is the unit of measure for the time period used in a forecast.* A time bucket might be a year, quarter, month, week, day, hour, or even a minute. For a long-term planning horizon, a firm might forecast in yearly time buckets; for a short-range planning horizon, the time bucket might be an hour or less. Customer call centers, for example, forecast customer demand in 5-, 6-, or 10-minute intervals. Selecting the right planning horizon length and time bucket size for the right situation is an important part of forecasting.

11-2b Data Patterns in Time Series

Statistical methods of forecasting are based on the analysis of historical data, called a time series. *A* **time series** *is a set of observations measured at successive points in time or over successive periods of time.* A time series provides the data for understanding how the variable that we wish to forecast has changed historically. For example, the daily ending Dow Jones stock index is one example of a time series; another is the monthly volume of sales for a product. To explain the pattern of data in a time series, it is often helpful to think in terms of five characteristics: *trend, seasonal, cyclical, random variation,* and *irregular (one-time) variation.* Different time series may exhibit one or more of these characteristics. Understanding these characteristics is vital to selecting the appropriate forecasting model or approach.

A **trend** *is the underlying pattern of growth or decline in* a time series. Although data generally exhibit random fluctuations, a trend shows gradual shifts or movements to relatively higher or lower values over a longer period of time. This gradual shifting over time is usually due to such long-term factors as changes in performance, technology, productivity, population, demographic characteristics, and customer preferences.

Trends can be increasing or decreasing and can be linear or nonlinear. Exhibit 11.2 shows various trend patterns. Linear increasing and decreasing trends are shown in Exhibit 11.2(a) and (b), and nonlinear trends are shown in Exhibit 11.2(c) and (d).

Seasonal patterns *are characterized by repeatable periods of ups and downs over short periods of time.* Seasonal patterns may occur over a year; for example, the demand for cold beverages is low during the winter, begins to rise during the spring, peaks during the summer months, and then begins to decline in the autumn. Manufacturers of coats and jackets, however, expect the opposite yearly pattern. Exhibit 11.3 shows an example of natural gas usage in a single-family home over a two-year period, which clearly exhibits a seasonal pattern.

We generally think of seasonal patterns occurring within one year, but similar repeatable patterns might occur over the weeks during a month, over days during a week, or hours during a day. For instance, pizza delivery peaks on the weekends, and grocery store traffic is higher during the evening hours. Likewise, customer call center volume might peak in the morning and taper off throughout the day. Different days of the week might have different seasonal patterns.

Cyclical patterns *are regular patterns in a data series that take place over long periods of time.* A common example of a cyclical pattern is the movement of stock market values during "bull" and "bear" market cycles.

Random variation *(sometimes called* **noise***) is the unexplained deviation of a time series from a predictable pattern, such as a trend, seasonal, or cyclical pattern.* Random variation is caused by short-term, unanticipated, and nonrecurring factors and is unpredictable. Because of random variation, forecasts are never 100 percent accurate.

The **time bucket** is the unit of measure for the time period used in a forecast.

A **time series** is a set of observations measured at successive points in time or over successive periods of time.

A **trend** is the underlying pattern of growth or decline in a time series.

Seasonal patterns are characterized by repeatable periods of ups and downs over short periods of time.

Cyclical patterns are regular patterns in a data series that take place over long periods of time.

Random variation (sometimes called **noise**) is the unexplained deviation of a time series from a predictable pattern, such as a trend, seasonal, or cyclical pattern.

Exhibit 11.2 *Example Linear and Nonlinear Trend Patterns*

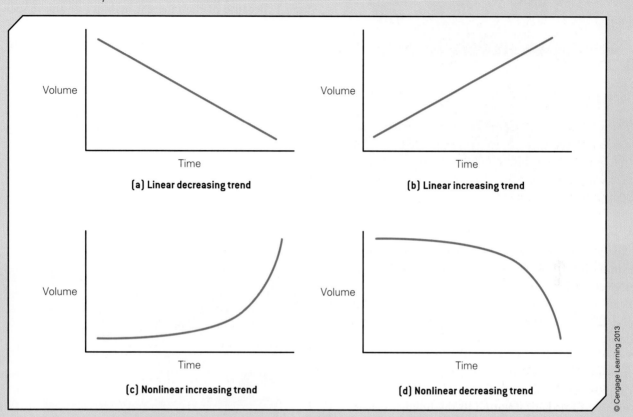

(a) Linear decreasing trend

(b) Linear increasing trend

(c) Nonlinear increasing trend

(d) Nonlinear decreasing trend

© Cengage Learning 2013

Exhibit 11.3 *Seasonal Pattern of Home Natural Gas Usage*

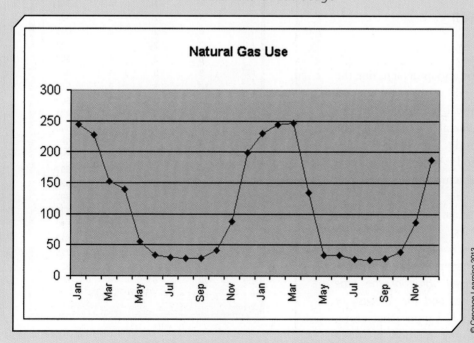

© Cengage Learning 2013

Irregular variation *is a one-time variation that is explainable.* For example, a hurricane can cause a surge in demand for building materials, food, and water. After the 9/11 terrorist attacks on the United States, many forecasts that predicted U.S. financial trends and airline passenger volumes had to be discarded due to the effects of this one-time event.

Irregular variation is a one-time variation that is explainable.

An example of a time series is given in the spreadsheet in Exhibit 11.4. These data represent the call volumes over 24 quarters from a call center at a major financial institution. The data are plotted on a chart in Exhibit 11.5. We can see both an increasing trend over the entire six years along with seasonal patterns within each of the years. For example, during the first three quarters of each year, call volumes increase, followed by a rapid decrease in the fourth quarter as customers presumably turn their attention to the holiday season. To develop a reliable forecast for the future, we would need to take into account both the long-term trend and the annual seasonal pattern.

11-2c Forecast Errors and Accuracy

All forecasts are subject to error, and understanding the nature and size of errors is important to making good decisions. We denote the historical values of a time series by $A_1, A_2, \ldots, A_t$. In general, A_t represents the value of the time series for period t. We will let F_t represent the forecast value for period t. When we make this forecast, we will not know the actual value of the time series in period t, A_t. However, once A_t becomes known, we can assess how well our forecast was able to predict the actual value of the time series.

Forecast error *is the difference between the observed value of the time series and the forecast, or* $A_t - F_t$. Suppose that a forecasting method provided the forecasts in column E

Forecast error is the difference between the observed value of the time series and the forecast, or $A_t - F_t$.

of Exhibit 11.6 for the call volume time series we discussed earlier. The forecast errors are computed in column F. Because of the inherent inability of any model to forecast accurately, we use quantitative measures of forecast accuracy to evaluate how well the forecasting model performs. Clearly, we want to use models that have small forecast errors. Generally, three types of forecast error metrics are used.

Mean square error, or MSE, is calculated by squaring the individual forecast errors and then averaging the results over all T periods of data in the time series.

$$\text{MSE} = \frac{\Sigma(A_t - F_t)^2}{T} \qquad [11.1]$$

For the call center data, this is computed in column H of Exhibit 11.6. The sum of the squared

Exhibit 11.4 *Call Center Volume (This Excel spreadsheet is available in the OM4 Data Workbook on the CourseMate Web site.)*

Period	Year	Quarter	Call Volume
1	1	1	362
2	1	2	385
3	1	3	432
4	1	4	341
5	2	1	382
6	2	2	409
7	2	3	498
8	2	4	387
9	3	1	473
10	3	2	513
11	3	3	582
12	3	4	474
13	4	1	544
14	4	2	582
15	4	3	681
16	4	4	557
17	5	1	628
18	5	2	707
19	5	3	773
20	5	4	592
21	6	1	627
22	6	2	725
23	6	3	854
24	6	4	661

errors is 87910.6, and therefore MSE is 87,910.6/24 = 3,662.94. MSE is probably the most commonly used measure of forecast accuracy. (Sometimes the square root of MSE is computed; this is called the *root mean square error, RMSE.*)

Another common measure of forecast accuracy is the mean absolute deviation (MAD), computed as

$$\text{MAD} = \frac{\Sigma|A_t - F_t|}{T} \quad [11.2]$$

This measure is simply the average of the sum of the absolute deviations for all the forecast errors. Using the information in column J of Exhibit 11.6, we compute MAD as 1,197/24 = 49.88.

Exhibit 11.5 *Chart of Call Volume*

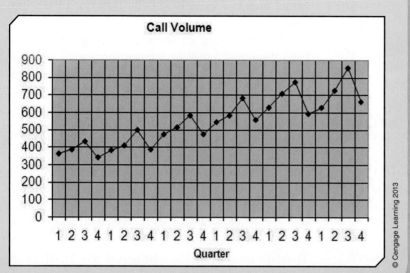

© Cengage Learning 2013

Exhibit 11.6 *Forecast Error of Example Time-Series Data (This spreadsheet is available in the OM4 Data Workbook on the CourseMate Web site.)*

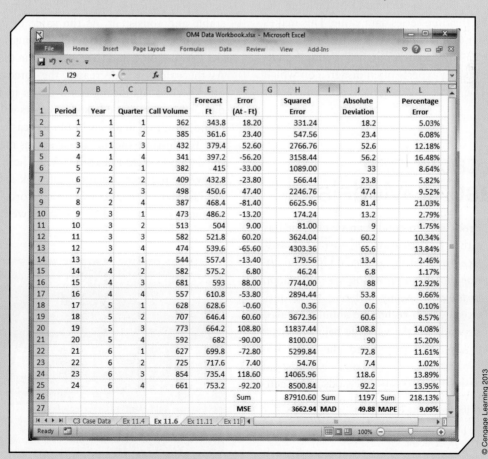

© Cengage Learning 2013

A third measure of forecast error is the mean absolute percentage error (MAPE):

$$\text{MAPE} = \frac{\Sigma |(A_t - F_t)/A_t| \times 100}{T} \quad [11.3]$$

This is simply the average of the percentage error for each forecast value in the time series. These calculations are shown in column L of Exhibit 11.6, resulting in MAPE = 218.13%/24 = 9.09 percent. Using MAPE, the forecast differs from actual call volume on average by plus or minus 9.09 percent.

A major difference between MSE and MAD is that MSE is influenced much more by large forecast errors than by small errors (because the errors are squared). The values of MAD and MSE depend on the measurement scale of the time-series data. For example, forecasting profit in the range of millions of dollars would result in very large values, even for accurate forecasting models. On the other hand, a variable like market share, which is measured as a fraction, will always have small values of MAD and MSE. Thus, the measures have no meaning except in comparison with other models used to forecast the same data. MAPE is different in that the measurement scale factor is eliminated by dividing the absolute error by the time-series data value. This makes the measure easier to interpret. The selection of the best measure of forecasting accuracy is not a simple matter; indeed, forecasting experts often disagree on which measure should be used; however, MSE generally is the most popular.

11-3 Statistical Forecasting Models

forecasting methods can be classified as either statistical or judgmental. **Statistical forecasting** *is based on the assumption that the future will be an extrapolation of the past.* Many different techniques exist; which technique should be used depends on the variable being forecast and the time horizon. Statistical methods can generally be categorized as *time-series methods*, which extrapolate historical time-series data,

Statistical forecasting is based on the assumption that the future will be an extrapolation of the past.

A moving average (MA) forecast is an average of the most recent "*k*" observations in a time series.

and *regression methods*, which extrapolate historical time-series data but can also include other potentially causal factors that influence the behavior of the time series.

Widely varying statistical forecasting models have been developed, and we cannot discuss all of them. However, we present some of the basic and more popular approaches used in OM applications.

11-3a Simple Moving Average

The simple moving average concept is based on the idea of averaging random fluctuations in a time series to identify the underlying direction in which the time series is changing. *A **moving average (MA) forecast** is an average of the most recent "k" observations in a time series.* Thus, the forecast for the next period ($t + 1$), which we denote as F_{t+1}, for a time series with t observations is

$$F_{t+1} = \Sigma(\text{most recent "}k\text{" observations})/k$$
$$= (A_t + A_{t-1} + A_{t-2} + \ldots + A_{t-k+1})/k \quad [11.4]$$

MA methods work best for short planning horizons when there is no major trend, seasonal, or business cycle patterns, that is, when demand is relatively stable and consistent. As the value of k increases, the forecast reacts slowly to recent changes in the time series because older data are included in the computation. As the value of k decreases, the forecast reacts more quickly. If a significant trend exists in the time-series data, moving-average-based forecasts will lag actual demand, resulting in a bias in the forecast.

To illustrate the moving averages method, consider the data presented in Exhibit 11.7. These data and chart show the number of gallons of milk sold each month at Gas-Mart, a local convenience store. To use moving averages to forecast the milk sales, we must first select

AP Photo/Al Behrman

Exhibit 11.7 *Summary of Three Month Moving Average Forecasts (This Excel Moving Average Template is available on the CourseMate Web site.)*

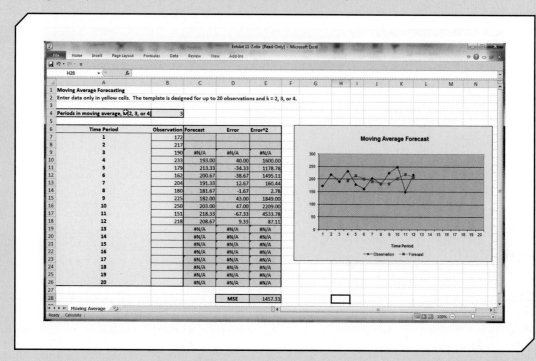

the number of data values to be included in the moving average. As an example, let us compute forecasts based on a three-month moving average ($k = 3$). The moving average calculation for the first three months of the milk-sales time series, and thus the forecast for month 4, is

$$F_4 = \frac{172 + 217 + 190}{3} = 193.00$$

Since the actual value observed in month 4 is 233, we see that the forecast error in month 4 is $233 - 193 = 40$. The calculation for the second three-month moving average (F_5) is

$$F_5 = \frac{217 + 190 + 233}{3} = 213.00$$

This provides a forecast for month 5. The error associated with this forecast is $179 - 213.33 = -34.33$. A complete summary of these moving average calculations is shown in Exhibit 11.8. The mean square error for these forecasts is 1,457.33.

The number of data values to be included in the moving average is often based on managerial insight and judgment. Thus, it should not be surprising that for

a particular time series, different values of k lead to different measures of forecast accuracy. One way to find the best number is to use trial and error to identify the value of k that minimizes MSE for the historical data.

11-3b Single Exponential Smoothing

Single exponential smoothing (SES) *is a forecasting technique that uses a weighted average of past time-series values to forecast the value of the time series in the next period.* SES forecasts are based on averages using and weighting the most recent actual demand more than older demand data. SES methods do not try to include trend or seasonal effects. The basic exponential smoothing model is

$$F_{t+1} = \alpha A_t + (1 - \alpha)F_t$$
$$= F_t + \alpha(A_t - F_t) \qquad [11.5]$$

Single exponential smoothing (SES) is a forecasting technique that uses a weighted average of past time-series values to forecast the value of the time series in the next period.

Exhibit 11.8 *Milk-Sales Forecast Error Analysis (This spreadsheet is available in the OM4 Data Workbook on the CourseMate Web site.)*

	A	B	C	D	E	F	G	H	I	J	K	L
1	Gas-Mart Monthly Milk Sales										Squared Errors	
2	Month	Sales	2-Month MA	Error	3-Month MA	Error	4-Month MA	Error		2-Month MA	3-Month MA	4-Month MA
3	1	172										
4	2	217										
5	3	190	194.5	-4.50						20.25		
6	4	233	203.5	29.50	193.00	40.00				870.25	1600.00	
7	5	179	211.5	-32.50	213.33	-34.33	203.00	-24.00		1056.25	1178.78	576.00
8	6	162	206	-44.00	200.67	-38.67	204.75	-42.75		1936.00	1495.11	1827.56
9	7	204	170.5	33.50	191.33	12.67	191.00	13.00		1122.25	160.44	169.00
10	8	180	183	-3.00	181.67	-1.67	194.50	-14.50		9.00	2.78	210.25
11	9	225	192	33.00	182.00	43.00	181.25	43.75		1089.00	1849.00	1914.06
12	10	250	202.5	47.50	203.00	47.00	192.75	57.25		2256.25	2209.00	3277.56
13	11	151	237.5	-86.50	218.33	-67.33	214.75	-63.75		7482.25	4533.78	4064.06
14	12	218	200.5	17.50	208.67	9.33	201.50	16.50		306.25	87.11	272.25
15										16147.75	13116.00	12310.75
16									MSE	1614.78	1457.33	1538.84
17												

where α is called the *smoothing constant* ($0 \leq \alpha \leq 1$). To use this model, set the forecast for period 1, F_1, equal to the actual observation for period 1, A_1. Note that F_2 will also have the same value.

Using the two preceding forms of the forecast equation, we can interpret the simple exponential smoothing model in two ways. In the first model shown in Equation 11.5, the forecast for the next period, F_{t+1}, is a weighted average of the forecast made for period t, F_t, and the actual observation in period t, A_t. The second form of the model in Equation 11.5, obtained by simply rearranging terms, states that the forecast for the next period, F_{t+1}, equals the forecast for the last period, F_t, plus a fraction, α, of the forecast error made in period t, $A_t - F_t$. Thus, to make a forecast once we have selected the smoothing constant, we need only know the previous forecast and the actual value.

To illustrate the exponential smoothing approach to forecasting, consider the milk-sales time series presented in Exhibit 11.9 using $\alpha = 0.2$. As we have said, the exponential smoothing forecast for period 2 is equal to the actual value of the time series in period 1. Thus, with $A_1 = 172$, we will set $F_1 = 172$ to get the computations started. Using Equation 11.5 for $t = 1$, we have

$$F_2 = 0.2A_1 + 0.8F_1$$
$$= 0.2(172) + 0.8(172) = 172.00$$

For period 3 we obtain

$$F_3 = 0.2A_2 + 0.8F_2$$
$$= 0.2(217) + 0.8(172) = 81.00$$

By continuing these calculations, we are able to determine the monthly forecast values and the corresponding forecast errors shown in Exhibit 11.9. The mean squared error is MSE $-$ 1285.28. Note that we have not shown an exponential smoothing forecast or the forecast error for period 1, because F_1 was set equal to A_1 to begin the smoothing computations. You could use this information to generate a forecast for month 13 as

$$F_{13} = 0.2A_{12} + 0.8F_{12}$$
$$= 0.2(218) + 0.8(194.59) = 199.27$$

Exhibit 11.9 also shows a plot of the actual and the forecast time-series values. Note in particular how the forecasts "smooth out" the random fluctuations in the time series.

By repeated substitution for F_t in the equation, it is easy to demonstrate that F_{t+1} is a decreasingly weighted average of all past time-series data. Thus, exponential smoothing models "never forget" past data as long as the smoothing constant is strictly between 0 and 1. In contrast, MA methods "completely forget" all the data older than k periods in the past.

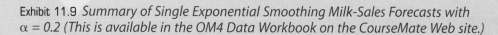

Exhibit 11.9 *Summary of Single Exponential Smoothing Milk-Sales Forecasts with α = 0.2 (This is available in the OM4 Data Workbook on the CourseMate Web site.)*

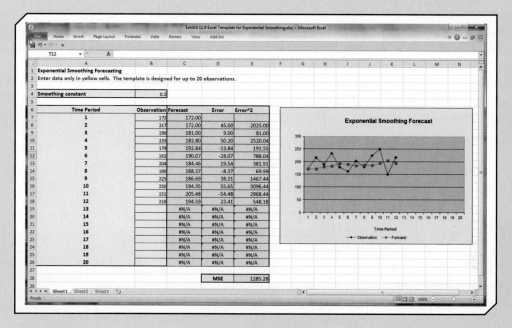

Typical values for α are in the range of 0.1 to 0.5. Larger values of α place more emphasis on recent data. If the time series is very volatile and contains substantial random variability, a small value of the smoothing constant is preferred. The reason for this choice is that since much of the forecast error is due to random variability, we do not want to overreact and adjust the forecasts too quickly. For a fairly stable time series with relatively little random variability, larger values of the smoothing constant have the advantage of quickly adjusting the forecasts when forecasting errors occur and therefore allowing the forecast to react faster to changing conditions.

Similar to the MA model, we can experiment to find the best value for the smoothing constant to minimize the mean square error or one of the other measures of forecast accuracy.

The smoothing constant is approximately related to the value of k in the moving average model by the following relationship:

$$\alpha = 2/(k + 1) \qquad [11.6]$$

Therefore, an exponential smoothing model with α = 0.5 is roughly equivalent to a moving average model with $k = 3$.

One disadvantage of exponential smoothing is that if the time series exhibits a positive trend, the forecast will lag the actual values and, similarly, will overshoot the actual values if a negative trend exists. It is good practice to analyze new data to see whether the smoothing constant should be revised to provide better forecasts. If values of α greater than 0.5 are needed to develop a good forecast, then other types of forecasting methods might be more appropriate.

11-4 Regression as a Forecasting Approach

egression analysis *is a method for building a statistical model that defines a relationship between a single dependent variable and one or more independent variables, all of which are numerical.* Regression analysis has wide applications in business; however, we will restrict our discussion to simple applications in forecasting. We will first consider only simple regression models

> **Regression analysis** is a method for building a statistical model that defines a relationship between a single dependent variable and one or more independent variables, all of which are numerical.

Solved Problem

A retail store records customer demand during each sales period. Use the following demand data to develop three-period and four-period moving average forecasts and single exponential smoothing forecasts with α = 0.5. Using MSE, which method provides the better forecast?

Period	Demand	Period	Demand
1	86	7	91
2	93	8	93
3	88	9	96
4	89	10	97
5	92	11	93
6	94	12	95

Using the Excel Moving Average and Exponential Smoothing templates, we find that the MSE for a three-period moving average is 5.98, the MSE for a four-period moving average is 6.21, and the MSE for the exponential-smoothing model is 9.65. Therefore, among these three models, the three-period moving average is best. Exhibit 11.10 shows the results for this model using the Excel template.

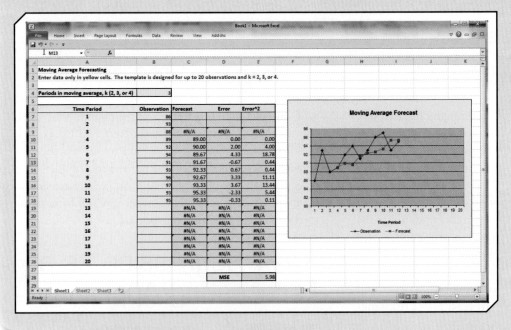

Exhibit 11.10 *Excel Moving Average Forecasting Template (This template is available on the OM4 CourseMate Web site.)*

in which the value of a time series (the dependent variable) is a function of a single independent variable, time.

Exhibit 11.11 shows total energy costs over the past 15 years at a manufacturing plant. The plant manager needs to forecast costs for the next year to prepare a budget for the VP of finance. The chart suggests that energy costs appear to be increasing in a fairly predictable linear fashion and that energy costs are related to time by a linear function

$$Y_t = a + bt \qquad [11.7]$$

where Y_t represents the estimate of the energy cost in year t. If we can identify the best values for a and b, which represent the intercept and slope of the straight line that best fits the time series, we can forecast cost for the next year by computing $Y_{16} = a + b(16)$.

Simple linear regression finds the best values of a and b using the *method of least squares*. The method of least squares minimizes the sum of the squared deviations between the actual time-series values (A_t) and the estimated values of the dependent variable (Y_t).

Exhibit 11.11 *Factory Energy Costs (This is available in the OM4 Data Workbook on the CourseMate Web site.)*

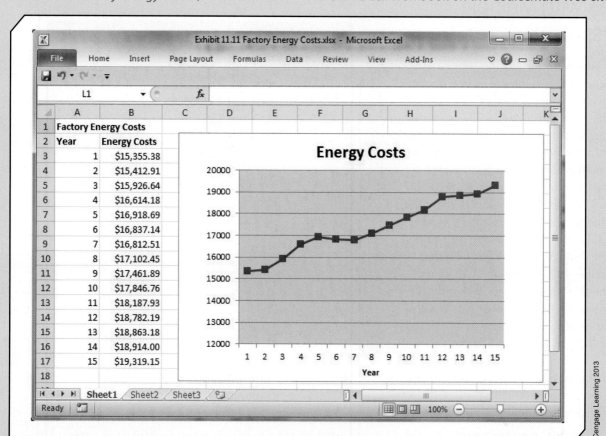

© Cengage Learning 2013

11-4a Excel's Add Trendline Option

Excel provides a very simple tool to find the best-fitting regression model for a time series. First, click the chart to which you wish to add a trendline to display the *Chart Tools* menu. The *Trendline* option is selected from the *Analysis* group under the *Layout* tab in the *Chart Tools* menu. Click the *Trendline* button and then *More Trendline Options*. . . . This brings up the *Format Trendline* dialog box shown in Exhibit 11.12. You may choose among a linear and a variety of nonlinear functional forms to fit the data. Selecting an appropriate nonlinear form requires some advanced knowledge of functions and mathematics, so we will restrict our discussion to the linear case. Check the boxes for *Display Equation on chart* and *Display R-squared value on chart*. Excel will display the results on the chart you have selected; you may move the equation and *R*-squared value for better readability by dragging them to a different location. For the linear trendline option only, you may simply click on the data series in the chart to select the series, and then add a trendline by clicking on the right mouse button (try it!).

Exhibit 11.13 shows the result. The model is

$$\text{Energy cost} = \$15,112 + 280.66(\text{Time})$$

Thus, to forecast the cost for the next year, we compute

$$\text{Energy cost} = \$15,112 + 280.66(16)$$
$$= \$19,602.56$$

We could forecast further out into the future if we wish, but realize that the uncertainty of the accuracy of the forecast will be higher. The R^2 value is a measure of how much variation in the dependent variable (energy cost) is explained by the independent variable (time). The maximum value for R^2 is 1.0; therefore, the high value of 0.97 suggests that the model will be a good predictor of cost.

11-4b Causal Forecasting Models with Multiple Regression

In more advanced forecasting applications, other independent variables such as economic indexes or demographic factors that may influence the time series can be incorporated into a regression model. *A linear regression model with more than one independent variable is called a* **multiple linear regression model.**

To illustrate the use of multiple linear regression for forecasting with causal variables, suppose that we wish to forecast gasoline sales. Exhibit 11.14 shows the sales over 10 weeks during June through August along with the average price per gallon. Exhibit 11.15 shows a chart of the gasoline-sales time series with a fitted regression line. During the summer months, it is not unusual to see an increase in sales as more people go on vacations. The chart shows that the sales appear to increase over time with a linear trend, making linear regression an appropriate forecasting technique.

The fitted regression line is

$$\text{Sales} = 6{,}382 + (1{,}084.7)(\text{Week})$$

The R^2 value of 0.6842 means that about 68 percent of the variation in the data is explained by time. Using the model, we would predict sales for week 11 as

$$\text{Sales} = 6{,}382 + (1{,}084.7)(11)$$
$$= 18{,}313.7$$

However, we also see that the average price per gallon changes each week, and this may influence consumer sales. Therefore, the sales trend might not simply be a factor of steadily increasing demand, but might also be influenced by the average price. Multiple

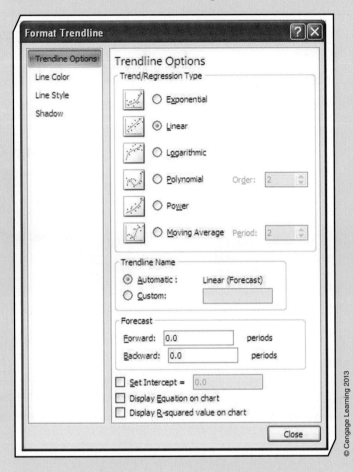

Exhibit 11.12 *Format Trendline Dialog Box*

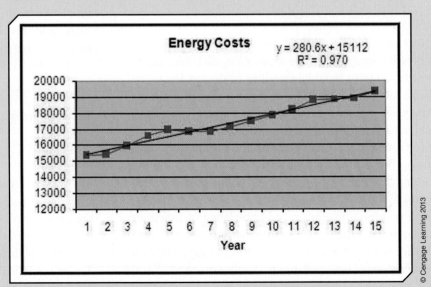

Exhibit 11.13 *Least-Squares Regression Model for Energy Cost Forecasting*

A linear regression model with more than one independent variable is called a **multiple linear regression model.**

Multiple regression provides a technique for building forecasting models that not only incorporate time but other potential causal variables.

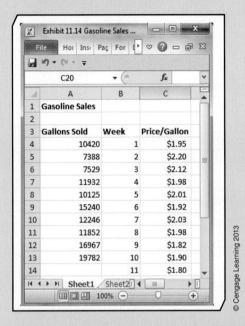

Exhibit 11.14 *Gasoline Sales Data (This is available in the OM4 Data Workbook on the CourseMate Web site.)*

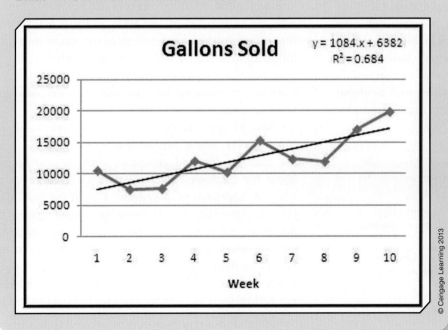

Exhibit 11.15 *Chart of Sales Versus Time*

regression provides a technique for building forecasting models that not only incorporate time, in this case, but other potential causal variables. Thus, to forecast gasoline sales (that is, the dependent variable) we propose a model using two independent variables (weeks and price):

$$\text{Sales} = \beta_0 + (\beta_1)(\text{Week}) + (\beta_2)(\text{Price})$$

Using the Excel Data Analysis tool for regression, we obtain the results shown in Exhibit 11.16. The regression model is

$$\text{Sales} = 47{,}747.81 + (640.71)(\text{Week}) - (19{,}550.6)(\text{Price})$$

This makes sense because as price increases, sales should decrease. Notice that the R^2 value is higher when both variables are included, explaining almost 86 percent of the variation in the data. The p-values for both variables are small, indicating that they are statistically significant variables in predicting sales.

Based on trends in crude oil prices, the company estimates that the average price for the next week will drop to $1.80. Then, using this model we would forecast the sales for week 11 as

$$\begin{aligned}\text{Sales} &= 47{,}747.81 + \\ &\quad (640.71)(11) - \\ &\quad (19{,}550.6)(\$1.80) \\ &= \$19{,}604.54\end{aligned}$$

Notice that this is higher than the pure time-series forecast because the price per gallon is estimated to fall in week 11 and result in a somewhat higher level of sales. The multiple regression model provides a more realistic and accurate forecast than simply extrapolating the historical time series. The theory of regression analysis is much more complex than presented here, so we caution you to consult more advanced books on the subject for a more complete treatment.

Exhibit 11.16 *Multiple Regression Results*

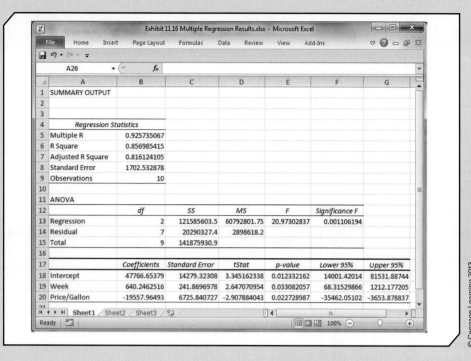

© Cengage Learning 2013

11-5 Judgmental Forecasting

Judgmental forecasting *relies upon opinions and expertise of people in developing forecasts.* When no historical data are available, only judgmental forecasting is possible. But even when historical data are available and appropriate, they cannot be the sole basis for prediction. The demand for goods and services is affected by a variety of factors, such as global markets and cultures, interest rates, disposable income, inflation, and technology. Competitors' actions and government regulations also have an impact. Thus, some element of judgmental forecasting is always necessary. One interesting example of the role of judgmental forecasting occurred during a national recession. All economic indicators pointed toward a future period of low demand for manufacturers of machine tools. However, the forecasters of one such company recognized that recent government regulations for automobile pollution control would require the auto industry to update its current technology by purchasing new tools. As a result, this machine tool company was prepared for the new business.

Several approaches are used in judgmental forecasts. **Grass Roots forecasting** *is asking those who are close to the end consumer, such as salespeople, about the customers' purchasing plans.* A more complicated approach is called the Delphi method. *The* **Delphi method** *consists of forecasting by expert opinion by gathering judgments and opinions of key personnel based on their experience and knowledge of the situation.* In the Delphi method, a group of people, possibly from both inside and outside the organization, is asked to make a prediction, such as industry sales for the next year. The

Judgmental forecasting relies upon opinions and expertise of people in developing forecasts.

Grass Roots forecasting is asking those who are close to the end consumer, such as salespeople, about the customers' purchasing plans.

The **Delphi method** consists of forecasting by expert opinion by gathering judgments and opinions of key personnel based on their experience and knowledge of the situation.

Simone van den Berg/Shutterstock.com

experts are not consulted as a group so as not to bias their predictions—for example, because of dominant personalities in the group—but make their predictions and justifications independently. The responses and supporting arguments of each individual are summarized by an outside party and returned to the experts along with further questions. Experts whose opinions fall in the midrange of estimates as well as those whose predictions are extremely high or low (that is, outliers) might be asked to explain their predictions. The process iterates until a consensus is reached by the group, which usually takes only a few rounds. Other common approaches to gathering data for judgmental forecasts are surveys using questionnaires, telephone contact, and personal interviews.

11-6 Forecasting in Practice

In practice, managers use a variety of judgmental and quantitative forecasting techniques. Statistical methods alone cannot account for such factors as sales promotions, competitive strategies, unusual economic or environmental disturbances, new product introductions, large one-time orders, labor union strikes, and so on.

Many managers begin with a statistical forecast and adjust it to account for such factors. Others may develop independent judgmental and statistical forecasts and then combine them, either objectively by averaging or in a subjective manner. It is impossible to provide universal guidance as to which approaches are best, for they depend on many things, such as the presence or absence of trends and seasonality, the number of data points available, length of the forecast time horizon, and the experience and knowledge of the forecaster.

The first step in developing a practical forecast is to understand its purpose. For instance, if financial personnel need a sales forecast to determine capital investment strategies, a long (two- to five-year) time horizon is necessary. For such forecasts, using aggregate groups of items is usually more accurate than using individual-item forecasts added together. These forecasts would probably be measured in dollars. In contrast, production personnel may need short-term forecasts for individual items as a basis for procurement of materials and scheduling. In this case, dollar values would not be appropriate; rather, forecasts should be made in terms of units of production. The level of aggregation often dictates the appropriate method. Forecasting the total amount of soap to produce over the next planning period is certainly different from forecasting the amount of each individual product to produce. Aggregate forecasts are generally much easier to develop, whereas detailed forecasts require more time and resources.

The choice of a forecasting method depends on other criteria as well. Among them are the time span for which the forecast is being made, the needed frequency of forecast updating, data requirements, the level of accuracy desired, and the quantitative skills needed. The time span is one of the most critical criteria. Different techniques are applicable for long-range, intermediate-range, and short-range forecasts. Also important is the frequency of updating that will be necessary. For example, the Delphi method takes considerable time to implement and thus would not be appropriate for forecasts that must be updated frequently.

Forecasters should also monitor a forecast to determine when it might be advantageous to change or update the model. *A tracking signal provides a method for doing this by quantifying* **bias**—*the tendency of forecasts to consistently be larger or smaller than the actual values of the time series.* The tracking method used most often is to compute the cumulative forecast error divided by the value of MAD at that point in time; that is,

$$\text{Tracking signal} = \frac{\Sigma(A_t - F_t)}{\text{MAD}} \qquad [11.8]$$

Typically, tracking signals between plus or minus 4 indicate that the forecast is performing adequately. Values outside this range indicate that you should reevaluate the model used.

A tracking signal provides a method for monitoring a forecast by quantifying **bias**—the tendency of forecasts to consistently be larger or smaller than the actual values of the time series.

Ten Practical Principles of Forecasting

A group of international experts published a set of principles to guide best practices in forecasting, yet it has been found that many organizations fall short in applying these principles.

1. *Use quantitative rather than qualitative methods.*
2. *Limit subjective adjustments of quantitative forecasts.*
3. *Adjust for events expected in the future.*
4. *Ask experts to justify their forecasts in writing.*
5. *Use structured procedures to integrate judgmental and quantitative methods.*
6. *Combine forecasts from approaches that differ.*
7. *If combining forecasts, begin with equal weights.*
8. *Compare past performance of various forecasting methods.*
9. *Seek feedback about forecasts.*
10. *Use multiple measures of forecast accuracy.*[4]

Discussion Questions

1. Discuss some forecasting issues that you encounter in your daily life. How do you make your forecasts?

2. Suppose that you were thinking about opening a new restaurant. How would you go about forecasting demand and sales?

3. Provide some examples of time series that exhibit
   a. trends
   b. seasonal patterns
   c. cyclical patterns

4. If a manager asked you whether to use time-series forecasting models or regression-based forecasting models, what would you tell him or her?

5. Looking back at the chapters you have studied so far, discuss how good forecasting can improve operations decisions in these areas.

Problems and Activities

Note: an asterisk denotes problems for which an Excel spreadsheet template on the CourseMate Web site may be used.

1. Search the Internet for some time-series data relating to sustainability, for example, environmental emissions. What types of patterns do these data exhibit? Apply forecasting techniques in this chapter to forecast 10 years into the future.

2. The historical demand for the Panasonic Model 304 Pencil Sharpener in units is: January, 60; February, 80; March, 75; April, 95; and May, 90. Using a two-month moving average, what is the forecast for June? If June experienced a demand of 100, what is the forecast for July?

3. In problem 2, suppose that the forecast for January was 70. Using single exponential smoothing with $\alpha = 0.2$, compute the exponential smoothing forecast for February through June.

4.* Forecasts and actual sales of MP3 players at Just Say Music are as follows:

Month	Forecast	Actual Sales
March	150	170
April	220	229
May	205	192
June	256	241
July	250	238
August	260	210
September	270	225
October	280	179

   a. Plot the data and provide insights about the time series.

   b. What is the forecast for November, using a two-period moving average?

   c. What is the forecast for November, using a three-period moving average?

   d. Compute MSE for the two- and three-period moving average models and compare your results.

   e. Find the best number of periods for the moving average model based on MSE.

5.* For the data in problem 4, find the best single exponential smoothing model by evaluating the MSE from 0.1 to 0.9, in increments of 0.1. How does this model compare with the best moving average model found in problem 4?

6.* A restaurant wants to forecast its weekly sales. Historical data (in dollars) for 15 weeks are shown below and can be found on worksheet C11P6 in the *OM4 Data Workbook on the CourseMate Web site*. (Note: you may copy the data from the worksheet to the appropriate Excel template.)

   a. Plot the data and provide insights about the time series.

   b. What is the forecast for week 16, using a two-period moving average?

   c. What is the forecast for week 16, using a three-period moving average?

   d. Compute MSE for the two- and three-period moving average models and compare your results.

   e. Find the best number of periods for the moving average model based on MSE.

Time Period	Observation
1	1486
2	1345
3	1455
4	1386
5	1209
6	1178
7	1581
8	1332
9	1245
10	1521
11	1544
12	1502
13	1856
14	1753
15	1789

7.* For the data in problem 6, find the best single exponential smoothing model by evaluating the MSE from 0.1 to 0.9, in increments of 0.1. How does this model compare with the best moving average model found in problem 6?

8.* The monthly sales of a new business software package at a local discount software store were as follows:

Week	1	2	3	4	5	6	7	8	9	10
Sales	460	415	432	450	488	512	475	502	449	486

a. Plot the data and provide insights about the time series.

b. Find the best number of weeks to use in a moving average forecast based on MSE.

c. Find the best single exponential smoothing model to forecast these data.

9.* Consider the quarterly sales data for Worthington Health Club shown here (also available on worksheet C11P9 in the *OM4 Data Workbook on the CourseMate Web site*):

	Quarter				Total
Year	1	2	3	4	Sales
1	4	2	1	5	12
2	6	4	4	14	28
3	10	3	5	16	34
4	12	9	7	22	50
5	18	10	13	35	76

a. Develop a four-period moving average model and compute MSE for your forecasts.

b. Find a good value of α for a single exponential smoothing model and compare your results to part (a).

10.* Using the factory energy cost data in Exhibit 11.11, find the best moving average and exponential smoothing models. Compare their forecasting ability with the regression model developed in the chapter. Which model would you choose and why?

11. The president of a small manufacturing firm is concerned about the continual growth in manufacturing costs in the past several years. The data series of the cost per unit for the firm's leading product over the past eight years is as follows:

Year	Cost/Unit ($)	Year	Cost/Unit ($)
1	20.00	5	26.60
2	24.50	6	30.00
3	28.20	7	31.00
4	27.50	8	36.00

a. Construct a chart for this time series. Does a linear trend appear to exist?

b. Develop a simple linear regression model for these data. What average cost increase has the firm been realizing per year?

12. Interview a current or previous employer about how he or she makes forecasts. Document in one page what you discovered, and describe it using the ideas discussed in this chapter.

13. Canton Supplies, Inc. is a service firm that employs approximately 100 people. Because of the necessity of meeting monthly cash obligations, the CFO wants to develop a forecast of monthly cash requirements. Because of a recent change in equipment and operating policy, only the past seven months of data are considered relevant.

Month	Cash Required ($1,000)	Month	Cash Required ($1,000)
1	205	5	230
2	212	6	240
3	218	7	246
4	224		

14.* Two experienced managers at Wilson Boat, Inc. are resisting the introduction of a computerized exponential smoothing system, claiming that their judgmental forecasts are much better than any computer could do. Their past record of predictions is as follows (these data can also be found on worksheet C11P14 in the *OM4 Data Workbook on the CourseMate Web site*):

Week	Actual Demand	Manager's Forecast
1	4,000	4,500
2	4,200	5,000
3	4,200	4,000
4	3,000	3,800
5	3,800	3,600
6	5,000	4,000
7	5,600	5,000
8	4,400	4,800
9	5,000	4,000
10	4,800	5,000

a. How would the manager's forecast compare to a single exponential smoothing forecast using $\alpha = 0.4$?

b. Based on whatever calculations you think appropriate, are the manager's judgmental forecasts performing satisfactorily?

c. What other criteria should be used to select a forecasting method for this company?

15. Research and write a short paper (two pages maximum) that summarizes the capabilities of commercial software available for forecasting. How does such software compare with using Excel?

BankUSA: Forecasting Help Desk Demand by Day Case Study

"Hello, is this the Investment Management Help Desk?" said a tired voice on the other end of the telephone line at 7:42 a.m. "Yes, how can I help you?" said Thomas Bourbon, customer service representative (CSR). "I've got a problem. My best customer, with assets of over $10 million in our bank, received his monthly trust account statement. He says we computed the market value of one of his stocks inaccurately by using the wrong share price, which makes his statement $42,000 too low. I assured him we would research the problem and get back to him by the end of the day. Also, do you realize that I waited over four minutes before you answered my call?" said the trust administrator, Chris Miami. "Mr. Miami, give me the customer's account number and the stock in question, and I'll get back to you within the hour. Let's solve the customer's problem first. I apologize for the long wait," said Bourbon in a positive and reassuring voice.

The Help Desk supports fiduciary operations activities worldwide by answering questions from company employees, such as portfolio managers, stock traders, backroom company process managers, branch bank managers, accountants, and trust account administrators. These internal customers originate over 98 percent of the volume of Help Desk inquiries. Over 50 different internal processes and organizational units call the Help Desk. Some external customers such as large estate and trust administrators are tied directly to their accounts via the Internet and occasionally call the Help Desk directly.

The Help Desk is the primary customer contact unit within fiduciary operations, employing 14 full-time customer service representatives (CSRs), 3 CSR support employees, and 3 managers, for a total of 20 people. The 3 CSR support employees work full-time on research in support of the CSRs answering the telephone.

The Help Desk handles about 2,000 calls a week, and the pressure to reduce unit cost is ongoing. Forecast accuracy is a key input to better staffing decisions that minimize costs and maximize service. The accompanying table shows the number of calls per day (Call Volume).

The senior manager of the Help Desk, Dot Gifford, established a team to try to evaluate short-term forecasting. The "Help Desk Staffing Team" consists of Gifford, Bourbon, Miami, and a new employee, David

Hamlet, who has an undergraduate major in operations management from a leading business school. This four-person team is charged with developing a long-term forecasting procedure for the Help Desk. Gifford asked the team to make an informal presentation of their analysis in 10 days. The primary job of analysis has fallen on Hamlet, the newly hired operations analyst. It's his chance to make a good first impression on his boss and colleagues.

Case Questions for Discussion

1. What are the service management characteristics of the CSR job?

2. Define the mission statement and strategy of the Help Desk. Why is the Help Desk important? Who are its customers?

The Help Desk handles about 2,000 calls a week, and the pressure to reduce unit cost is ongoing.

3. How would you handle the customer affected by the inaccurate stock price in the bank's trust account system? Would you take a passive or proactive approach? Justify your answer.

4. Using the data on call volume in the accompanying table, how would you forecast short-term demand?

Day	Call Volume
1	288
2	336
3	295
4	251
5	280
6	300
7	398
8	418
9	422
10	471
11	522
12	502
13	449
14	452
15	420
16	423

ONE APPROACH.
70 UNIQUE SOLUTIONS.

MANAGING INVENTORIES

anana Republic is a unit of San Francisco's Gap's, Inc., and accounts for about 13 percent of Gap's sales. As Gap shifted its product line to basics such as cropped pants, jeans, and khakis, Banana Republic had to move away from such staples and toward trends, trying to build a name for itself in fashion circles. But fashion items, which have a much shorter product life cycle and are riskier because their demand is more variable and uncertain, bring up a host of operations management issues. In one holiday season, the company had bet that blue would be the top-selling color in stretch merino wool sweaters. They were wrong. Marka Hansen, company president noted, "The No. 1 seller was moss green. We didn't have enough."[1]

learning outcomes

After studying this chapter you should be able to:

12-1 **Explain the importance of inventory, types of inventories, and key decisions and costs.**

12-2 **Describe the major characteristics that impact inventory decisions.**

12-3 **Describe how to conduct an ABC inventory analysis.**

12-4 **Explain how a fixed-order-quantity inventory system operates, and how to use the EOQ and safety stock models.**

12-5 **Explain how a fixed-period inventory system operates.**

12-6 **Describe how to apply the single-period inventory model.**

What do you think?

Can you cite any experiences in which the lack of appropriate inventory at a retail store has caused you as the customer to be dissatisfied?

AP Photo/David Goldman

Inventory *is any asset held for future use or sale.* Companies such as Banana Republic must order far in advance of the actual selling season with little information on which to base their inventory decisions. The wrong choices can easily lead to a mismatch between customer demand and availability, resulting in either lost opportunities for sales, or overstocks that might have to be sold at a loss or at least a minimal profit.

Simply maintaining large stocks of inventory is costly and wasteful. The old concept of keeping warehouses and stockrooms filled to capacity with inventory has been replaced with the idea of producing finished goods as late as possible prior to shipment to the customer. Better information technology and applications of quantitative tools and techniques for inventory management have allowed dramatic reductions in inventory.

The expenses associated with financing and maintaining inventories are a substantial part of the cost of doing business (i.e., cost of goods sold). Managers are faced with the dual challenges of maintaining sufficient inventories to meet demand while at the same time incurring the lowest possible cost. **Inventory management** *involves planning, coordinating, and controlling the acquisition, storage, handling, movement, distribution, and possible sale of raw materials, component parts and subassemblies, supplies and tools, replacement parts, and other assets that are needed to meet customer wants and needs.*

> **Inventory** is any asset held for future use or sale.
>
> **Inventory management** involves planning, coordinating, and controlling the acquisition, storage, handling, movement, distribution, and possible sale of raw materials, component parts and subassemblies, supplies and tools, replacement parts, and other assets that are needed to meet customer wants and needs.

▼ *Banana Republic moved away from staples and toward trends, trying to build a name for itself in fashion circles.*

12-1 Understanding Inventory

generally, inventories are physical goods used in operations and include raw materials, parts, subassemblies, supplies, tools, equipment or maintenance, and repair items. For example, a small pizza business must maintain inventories of dough, toppings, sauce, and cheese, as well as supplies such as boxes, napkins, and so on. Hospitals maintain inventories of blood and other consumables, and retail stores such as Best Buy maintain inventories of finished goods—televisions, appliances, and DVDs—for sale to customers. In some service organizations, inventories are not physical goods that customers take with them, but capacity available for serving customers, such as hotel rooms or airline seats.

One of the difficulties of inventory management is that every function in an organization generally views inventory objectives differently. Marketing and operations prefer high inventory levels to provide the best possible customer service and process efficiency, whereas financial personnel seek to minimize inventory investment and thus would prefer small inventories. Top management needs to understand the role that inventory plays in a company's financial performance, operational efficiency, and customer satisfaction and strike the proper balance in meeting strategic objectives.

Raw materials, component parts, subassemblies, and supplies are inputs to manufacturing and service-delivery processes.

Work-in-process (WIP) inventory consists of partially finished products in various stages of completion that are awaiting further processing.

Finished-goods inventory is completed products ready for distribution or sale to customers.

George Frey/Bloomberg/Getty Images

12-1a Key Definitions and Concepts

Many different types of inventories are maintained throughout the value chain—before, during, and after production—to support operations and meet customer demands (see Exhibit 12.1). **Raw materials, component parts, subassemblies, and supplies** *are inputs to manufacturing and service-delivery processes.* **Work-in-process (WIP) inventory** *consists of partially finished products in various stages of completion that are awaiting further processing.* For example, a pizza restaurant might prepare a batch of pizzas with only cheese and sauce and add other toppings when orders are placed. WIP inventory also acts as a buffer between workstations in flow shops or departments in job shops to enable the operating process to continue when equipment might fail at one stage or supplier shipments are late. **Finished-goods inventory** *is completed products ready for distribution or sale to customers.* Finished goods might be stored in a warehouse or at the point of sale in retail stores. Finished-goods inventories are necessary to satisfy customers' demands quickly without having to wait for a product to be made or ordered from the supplier.

Exhibit 12.1 *Role of Inventory in the Value Chain*

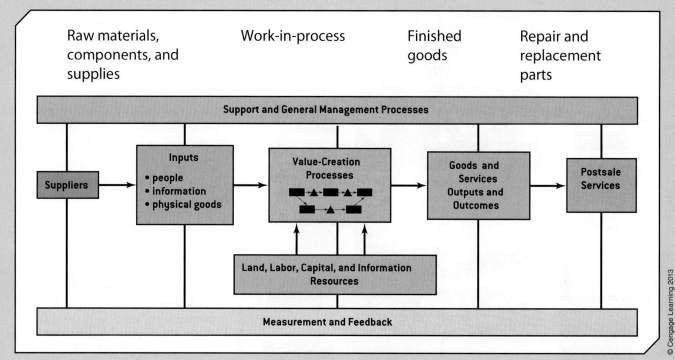

High levels of WIP and finished-goods inventories can be undesirable. Large WIP can hide such problems as unreliable machines, late supplier shipments, or defective parts; and large amounts of finished goods inventory can quickly become obsolete when technology changes or new products are introduced.

Customer demand is most often highly variable and uncertain. Lack of sufficient inventory can cause production lines to shut down or customers to become dissatisfied and purchase goods and services elsewhere. To reduce the risk associated with not having enough inventory, firms often maintain additional stock beyond their normal estimates. **Safety stock inventory** *is an additional amount that is kept over and above the average amount required to meet demand.*

12-1b Managing Inventories in Global Supply Chains

Today's global supply chains present significant challenges to inventory management. The components and materials used in nearly any product are often purchased from suppliers across the globe and shipped through complex supply chains. This is even more important for perishable goods. For example, a common cheeseburger at a fast-food restaurant may consist of wheat gluten from Poland, preservatives from the Netherlands, tomatoes from Latin America, lettuce from Mexico or New Zealand, mustard seeds from Canada, vinegar from Italy, garlic powder from Australia, and ground beef from more than 50 cows from several countries! Purchasing, tracking, and managing such a variety of items in global supply chains requires good technology, processes, and information technology (IT) support. Technology such as radio frequency identification (RFID) chips can increase inventory accuracy to better than 98 percent, much higher than the current industry average of 65 percent, and allow firms to track individual containers. With thousands of products and materials, hundreds of suppliers, and numerous orders and shippers, an accurate information system is essential. Enterprise resource planning (ERP) systems such as those sold by SAP and Oracle provide the infrastructure to effectively manage all of this information. Using cloud computing simplifies data management, improves the availability

Safety stock inventory is an additional amount that is kept over and above the average amount required to meet demand.

Yeast: Canada

Vitamin enrichments: China

Mold-inhibiting preservatives: Netherlands

Wheat gluten: Poland

Guatemala

Colombia

Mexico

Mostly Mexico

New Zealand

Sometimes Canada and Peru

Mustard seeds: Canada

One package of ground beef can contain meat from more than 50 cows from several countries

Vinegar: Italy

Garlic powder: Australia

redmonkey8/Getty Images

essential; and with the legal department, where contracts are reviewed.

Many firms (as well as consumers) subscribe to **Environmentally Preferable Purchasing (EPP)**, often referred to as **green purchasing**, *which is the affirmative selection and acquisition of products and services that most effectively minimize negative environmental impacts over their life cycle of manufacturing, transportation, use, and recycling or disposal.* Examples of environmentally preferable characteristics include products and services that conserve energy and water, and minimize generation of waste and releases of pollutants; products made from recycled materials and that can be reused or recycled; energy from renewable resources such as biobased fuels, solar power, and wind power; alternate fuel vehicles; and products using alternatives to hazardous or toxic chemicals, radioactive materials, and biohazardous agents. Not only does green purchasing conserve resources and the environment, but it improves safety,

and accessibility of data, and allows companies to share information among many suppliers.

The purchasing or procurement function is responsible for acquiring raw materials, component parts, tools, and other items required from outside suppliers. In the past, purchasing focused primarily on low-price acquisition. Today, however, purchasing must focus on global sourcing and total system cost; ensure quality, delivery performance, and technical support; and seek new suppliers and products and be able to evaluate their potential to the company. Accordingly, purchasing agents must maintain good relations and communication with global suppliers; with other departments, such as accounting and finance, where budgets are prepared; with product design and engineering, where material specifications are set; with production, where timely delivery is

Environmentally Preferable Purchasing (EPP), or **green purchasing,** is the affirmative selection and acquisition of products and services that most effectively minimize negative environmental impacts over their life cycle of manufacturing, transportation, use, and recycling or disposal.

Where Are the Animals?

Keeping up with the millions of SKUs in global food-supply chains is a monumental task.[3] Today, tiny RFID chips embedded in packaging or products allow scanners to track SKUs as they move throughout the store. RFID chips help companies locate items in stockrooms and identify where they should be placed in the store. An innovative use of RFIDs is to track and monitor food, livestock, and even trees. The technology also helps prevent crime, reduces disease, and provides proximity information on a real-time basis. China, for example, wants to use RFIDs to monitor 1.2 billion pigs in its Sichuan province, which is more than the total number of the pigs in the United States. An outbreak of pig disease in Sichuan in 2005 caused direct losses of $1.5 billion and indirect losses of $1.25 billion. New Zealand wants to pass a legal requirement that its 100 million pet dogs be RFID-tagged. Canada is tagging fish; Germany, trees; and Australia, cattle.

stimulates new markets for recycled materials, and provides potential cost savings.[2]

12-1c Inventory Management Decisions and Costs

Inventory managers deal with two fundamental decisions:

1. When to order items from a supplier or when to initiate production runs if the firm makes its own items
2. How much to order or produce each time a supplier or production order is placed

Inventory management is all about making trade-offs among the costs associated with these decisions.

Inventory costs can be classified into four major categories:

1. ordering or setup costs
2. inventory-holding costs
3. shortage costs
4. unit cost of the SKUs

Ordering costs or setup costs are incurred as a result of the work involved in placing orders with suppliers or configuring tools, equipment, and machines within a factory to produce an item. Order and setup costs do not depend on the number of items purchased or manufactured, but rather on the number of orders placed.

Inventory-holding or inventory-carrying costs are the expenses associated with carrying inventory. Holding costs are typically defined as a percentage of the dollar value of inventory per unit of time (generally one year). They include costs associated with maintaining storage facilities, such as gas and electricity, taxes, insurance, and labor and equipment necessary to handle, move, and retrieve inventory items, plus the opportunity cost of capital represented by holding inventory, normally for one year. However, from an accounting perspective, it is difficult to precisely allocate such costs to an individual stock-keeping unit (SKU). Essentially, holding costs reflect the opportunity cost associated with using the funds invested in inventory for alternative uses and investments.

> **Ordering costs** or **setup costs** are incurred as a result of the work involved in placing orders with suppliers or configuring tools, equipment, and machines within a factory to produce an item.
>
> **Inventory-holding** or **inventory-carrying costs** are the expenses associated with carrying inventory.

WEYERHAEUSER: REDUCING INVENTORY COSTS

In the pulp and paper industry, pulp mills use large outside storage facilities that store inventories of wood chips. These serve as buffers against differences between mill supply and demand to reduce stockout risk and also act as a hedge against changes in wood prices and allow timely buying when prices are low. However, aging of wood during storage can affect its properties, resulting in color deterioration, decreased pulp yield, lower quality, and higher processing costs. Weyerhaeuser developed a computer model called the Springfield Inventory Target model (SPRINT) to assist inventory managers in dealing with risk in inventory level decisions. The model projects chip inflows, outflows, and inventory levels by time period for any length of time in the future and helps managers to answer such questions as: How reliable are inventory projections? What is the stockout risk in each time period? What are the total inventory costs in each period? Given future projections, what is the optimal inventory level? SPRINT has taken a lot of the guesswork out of making inventory decisions by providing objective assessments of costs and risks. Its principal benefit has been to allow managers to reduce inventories and stay within acceptable risk levels, lowering annual inventory costs by at least $2 million.[4]

Josef Mohyla/Shutterstock.com

Shortage *or* stockout costs *are costs associated with inventory being unavailable when needed to meet demand.* These costs can reflect backorders, lost sales, or service interruptions for external customers, or costs associated with interruptions to manufacturing and assembly lines for internal customers. **Unit cost** *is the price paid for purchased goods or the internal cost of producing them.* In most situations, the unit cost is a "sunk cost" because the total purchase cost is not affected by the order quantity. However, the unit cost of SKUs is an important purchasing consideration when quantity discounts are offered; it may be more economical to purchase large quantities at a lower unit cost to reduce the other cost categories and thus minimize total costs.

12-2 Inventory Characteristics

Various inventory situations are possible.[5] For instance, a self-serve gasoline station maintains an inventory of only a few grades of gasoline, whereas a large appliance store may carry several hundred different items. Demand for gasoline is relatively constant, whereas the demand for air conditioners is highly seasonal and variable. If a gasoline station runs out of gas, a customer will go elsewhere. However, if an appliance store does not have a particular item in stock, the customer may be willing to order the item and wait for delivery or go to another appliance store. Since the demand and inventory characteristics of the gasoline station and appliance store differ significantly, the proper control of inventories requires different approaches.

One of the first steps in analyzing an inventory problem should be to describe the essential characteristics of the environment and inventory system that follow.

STEVE PARSONS/PA Photos/Landov

Number of Items

Most firms maintain inventories for a large number of items, often at multiple locations. To manage and control these inventories, each item is often assigned a unique identifier, called a stock-keeping unit, or SKU. *A* **stock-keeping unit (SKU)** *is a single item or asset stored at a particular location.* For example, each color and size of a man's dress shirt at a department store and each type of milk (whole, 2 percent, skim) at a grocery store would be a different SKU.

Nature of Demand

Demand can be classified as independent or dependent, constant or uncertain, and dynamic or static. **Independent demand** *is demand for an SKU that is unrelated to the demand for other SKUs and needs to be forecasted.* This type of demand is directly related to customer (market) demand. Inventories of finished goods such as toothpaste and electric fans have independent demand characteristics.

SKUs are said to have **dependent demand** *if their demand is directly related to the demand of other SKUs and can be calculated without needing to be forecasted.* For example, a chandelier may consist of a frame and six lightbulb sockets. The demand for chandeliers is an independent demand and would be forecasted, whereas the demand for sockets is dependent on the demand for chandeliers. That is, for a forecast of chandeliers we can calculate the number of sockets required.

Demand can either be constant over some period of time (or assumed to be constant), or we can assume that it is uncertain. Sometimes we might simply assume that demand is constant in order to make our models easier to solve and analyze, perhaps by using historical averages or statistical point estimates of forecasts. When such an assumption is unwarranted, we can characterize demand using a probability distribution. For example, we might assume that the daily demand for milk is constant at 100 gallons, or we might assume that it is normally distributed with a mean of 100 and a standard deviation of 10. Models that incorporate uncertainty are generally more difficult to build and analyze.

Demand, whether deterministic or stochastic, may also fluctuate or remain stable over time. *Stable demand is usually called* **static demand**, *and demand that varies over time is referred to as* **dynamic demand**. For example, the demand for milk might range from 90 to 110 gallons per day, every day of the year. This is an example of static demand because the parameters of the probability distribution do not change over time. However, the demand for airline flights to Orlando, Florida, will probably have different means and variances throughout the year, reaching peaks around Thanksgiving, Christmas, spring break, and in the summer, with lower demands at other times. This is an example of dynamic demand.

Number and Duration of Time Periods

In some cases, the selling season is relatively short, and any leftover items cannot be physically or economically stored until the next season. For example, Christmas trees that have been cut cannot be stored until the following year; similarly, other items such as seasonal fashions, are sold at a loss simply because there is no storage space or it is uneconomical to keep them for the next year. In other situations, firms are concerned with planning inventory requirements over an extended number of time periods, for example, monthly over a year, in which inventory is held from one time period to the next. The type of approach used to analyze "single-period" inventory problems is different from the approach needed for the "multiple-period" inventory situation.

Lead Time

The **lead time** *is the time between placement of an order and its receipt.* Lead time is affected by transportation carriers, buyer order frequency and size, and supplier production schedules and may be deterministic or stochastic (in which case it may be described by some probability distribution).

> A lost sale has an associated opportunity cost, which may include loss of goodwill and potential future revenue.

Stockouts

A **stockout** *is the inability to satisfy the demand for an item.* When stockouts occur, the item is either backordered or a sale is lost. *A* **backorder** *occurs when a customer is willing to wait for the item; a* **lost sale** *occurs when the customer is unwilling to wait and purchases the item elsewhere.* Backorders result in additional costs for transportation, expediting, or perhaps buying from another supplier at a higher price. A lost sale has an associated opportunity cost, which may include loss of goodwill and potential future revenue.

Stable demand is usually called **static demand,** and demand that varies over time is referred to as **dynamic demand.**

The **lead time** is the time between placement of an order and its receipt.

A **stockout** is the inability to satisfy the demand for an item.

A **backorder** occurs when a customer is willing to wait for the item; a **lost sale** occurs when the customer is unwilling to wait and purchases the item elsewhere.

Stockouts Matter

According to the Food Marketing Institute and Grocery Manufacturers of America, stock-outs in the fast-moving consumer goods sector are as high as 8.3%, with promotional products even higher. As a result, retailers lose around 4% of their sales because consumers will buy the item elsewhere, substitute the product with another brand, or just forget about it.[6]

12-3 ABC Inventory Analysis

ne useful method for defining inventory value is ABC analysis. It is an application of the *Pareto principle*, named after an Italian economist who studied the distribution of wealth in Milan during the 1800s. He found that a "vital few" controlled a high percentage of the wealth. ABC analysis consists of categorizing inventory items or SKUs into three groups according to their total annual dollar usage.

1. "A" items account for a large dollar value but a relatively small percentage of total items.
2. "C" items account for a small dollar value but a large percentage of total items.
3. "B" items are between A and C.

Typically, A items comprise 60 to 80 percent of the total dollar usage but only 10 to 30 percent of the items, whereas C items account for 5 to 15 percent of the total dollar value and about 50 percent of the items. There is no specific rule on where to make the division between A, B, and C items; the percentages used here simply serve as a guideline. Total dollar usage or value is computed by multiplying item usage (volume) times the item's dollar value (unit cost). Therefore, an A item could have a low volume but high unit cost, or a high volume and low unit cost.

ABC analysis gives managers useful information to identify the best methods to control each category of inventory. Class A items require close control by operations managers. Class C items need not be as closely controlled and can be managed using automated computer systems. Class B items are somewhere in the middle.

In a **fixed-quantity system (FQS)**, the order quantity or lot size is fixed; that is, the same amount, Q, is ordered every time.

Inventory position (IP) is defined as the on-hand quantity (OH) plus any orders placed but which have not arrived (called scheduled receipts, SR), minus any backorders (BO).

The **reorder point** is the value of the inventory position that triggers a new order.

12-4 Managing Fixed-Quantity Inventory Systems

n a **fixed-quantity system (FQS)**, *the order quantity or lot size is fixed; that is, the same amount, Q, is ordered every time.* The order quantity (Q) can be any quantity of product such as a box, pallet, or container as determined by the vendor or shipping standards; it does not have to be determined economically (see economic order quantity in the next section). FQSs are used extensively in the retail industry. For example, most department stores have cash registers that are tied into a computer system. When the clerk enters the SKU number, the computer recognizes that the item is sold, recalculates the inventory position, and determines whether a purchase order should be initiated to replenish the stock. If computers are not used in such systems, some form of manual system is necessary for monitoring daily usage. This requires substantial clerical effort and commitment by the users to fill out the proper forms when items are used and is often a source of errors, so it is not recommended.

A more appropriate way to manage an FQS is to continuously monitor the inventory level and place orders when the level reaches some "critical" value. The process of triggering an order is based on the inventory position. **Inventory position (IP)** *is defined as the on-hand quantity (OH) plus any orders placed but which have not arrived (called scheduled receipts, SR), minus any backorders (BO), or*

$$IP = OH + SR - BO \qquad [12.1]$$

When the inventory position falls at or below a certain value, *r*, called the *reorder point*, a new order is placed. *The* **reorder point** *is the value of the inventory position that triggers a new order.* Why not base the reordering decision on the physical inventory level, that is, just the on-hand quantity, instead of a more complex calculation? The answer is simple. When an order is placed but has not been received, the physical stock level will continue to fall below the reorder point before the order arrives. If the ordering process is automated, the computer logic will continue to place many unnecessary orders simply because it will see the stock level being less than *r*, even though the original order will soon arrive and replenish the stock. By including scheduled receipts, the inventory position will be larger than the reorder point, thus preventing duplicate orders.

Solved Problem

Consider the data for 20 inventoried items of a small company shown in columns A through C in the Excel ABC template shown in Exhibit 12.2. The projected annual dollar usage in column D in Exhibits 12.2 and 12.3 is found by multiplying the annual projected usage based on forecasts (in units) by the unit cost. We can sort these data easily in Microsoft Excel, where we have listed the cumulative percentage of items, cumulative dollar usage, and cumulative percent of total dollar usage. For column H in Exhibit 12.3 each item is 1/20th, or 5 percent, of the total number of items. Analysis of Exhibit 12.3 indicates that about 70 percent of the total dollar usage is accounted for by the first five items, that is, only 25 percent of the items. In addition, the lowest 50 percent of the items account for only about 5 percent of the total dollar usage. Exhibit 12.4 shows a simple histogram of the ABC analysis classification scheme for this set of data.

Exhibit 12.2 *Excel ABC Template Before Sorting*

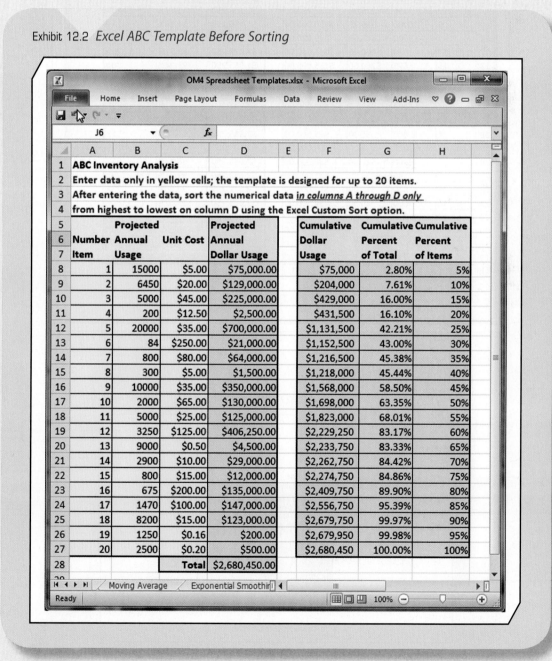

Item	Number Projected Annual Usage	Unit Cost	Projected Annual Dollar Usage	Cumulative Dollar Usage	Cumulative Percent of Total	Cumulative Percent of Items
1	15000	$5.00	$75,000.00	$75,000	2.80%	5%
2	6450	$20.00	$129,000.00	$204,000	7.61%	10%
3	5000	$45.00	$225,000.00	$429,000	16.00%	15%
4	200	$12.50	$2,500.00	$431,500	16.10%	20%
5	20000	$35.00	$700,000.00	$1,131,500	42.21%	25%
6	84	$250.00	$21,000.00	$1,152,500	43.00%	30%
7	800	$80.00	$64,000.00	$1,216,500	45.38%	35%
8	300	$5.00	$1,500.00	$1,218,000	45.44%	40%
9	10000	$35.00	$350,000.00	$1,568,000	58.50%	45%
10	2000	$65.00	$130,000.00	$1,698,000	63.35%	50%
11	5000	$25.00	$125,000.00	$1,823,000	68.01%	55%
12	3250	$125.00	$406,250.00	$2,229,250	83.17%	60%
13	9000	$0.50	$4,500.00	$2,233,750	83.33%	65%
14	2900	$10.00	$29,000.00	$2,262,750	84.42%	70%
15	800	$15.00	$12,000.00	$2,274,750	84.86%	75%
16	675	$200.00	$135,000.00	$2,409,750	89.90%	80%
17	1470	$100.00	$147,000.00	$2,556,750	95.39%	85%
18	8200	$15.00	$123,000.00	$2,679,750	99.97%	90%
19	1250	$0.16	$200.00	$2,679,950	99.98%	95%
20	2500	$0.20	$500.00	$2,680,450	100.00%	100%
		Total	$2,680,450.00			

Exhibit 12.3 *Excel ABC Template After Sorting*

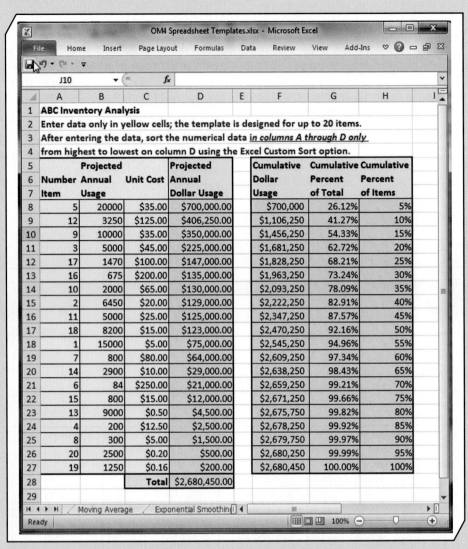

ABC Inventory Analysis
Enter data only in yellow cells; the template is designed for up to 20 items.
After entering the data, sort the numerical data *in columns A through D only*
from highest to lowest on column D using the Excel Custom Sort option.

Number Item	Projected Annual Usage	Unit Cost	Projected Annual Dollar Usage	Cumulative Dollar Usage	Cumulative Percent of Total	Cumulative Percent of Items
5	20000	$35.00	$700,000.00	$700,000	26.12%	5%
12	3250	$125.00	$406,250.00	$1,106,250	41.27%	10%
9	10000	$35.00	$350,000.00	$1,456,250	54.33%	15%
3	5000	$45.00	$225,000.00	$1,681,250	62.72%	20%
17	1470	$100.00	$147,000.00	$1,828,250	68.21%	25%
16	675	$200.00	$135,000.00	$1,963,250	73.24%	30%
10	2000	$65.00	$130,000.00	$2,093,250	78.09%	35%
2	6450	$20.00	$129,000.00	$2,222,250	82.91%	40%
11	5000	$25.00	$125,000.00	$2,347,250	87.57%	45%
18	8200	$15.00	$123,000.00	$2,470,250	92.16%	50%
1	15000	$5.00	$75,000.00	$2,545,250	94.96%	55%
7	800	$80.00	$64,000.00	$2,609,250	97.34%	60%
14	2900	$10.00	$29,000.00	$2,638,250	98.43%	65%
6	84	$250.00	$21,000.00	$2,659,250	99.21%	70%
15	800	$15.00	$12,000.00	$2,671,250	99.66%	75%
13	9000	$0.50	$4,500.00	$2,675,750	99.82%	80%
4	200	$12.50	$2,500.00	$2,678,250	99.92%	85%
8	300	$5.00	$1,500.00	$2,679,750	99.97%	90%
20	2500	$0.20	$500.00	$2,680,250	99.99%	95%
19	1250	$0.16	$200.00	$2,680,450	100.00%	100%
		Total	$2,680,450.00			

Exhibit 12.4 *ABC Histogram for the Results from Exhibit 12.3*

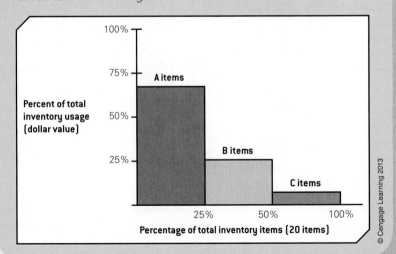

© Cengage Learning 2013

Once the order arrives and no scheduled receipts are outstanding, then the inventory position is the same as the physical inventory. Backorders are included in the inventory position calculation because these items have already been sold and are reserved for customers as soon as the order arrives.

A summary of fixed-quantity systems is given in Exhibit 12.5. Exhibits 12.6 and 12.7 contrast the performance of FQS when demand is relatively stable and highly variable. The dark lines in these exhibits track the actual inventory levels. In Exhibit 12.6, we see that the time between orders (TBO) is also constant in the deterministic and static case, and therefore the ordering cycle repeats itself exactly. Here, the TBO is constant because there is no uncertainty and average demand is assumed to be constant and continuous. Recall from our previous discussion that the reorder point should be based on the inventory position, not the physical inventory level. In Exhibit 12.6 you can see that the inventory position jumps by Q when the order is placed. With the highly variable demand rate, the TBO varies while Q is constant.

12-4a The EOQ Model

*The **economic order quantity (EOQ)** model is a classic economic model developed in the early 1900s that minimizes the total cost, which is the sum of the inventory-holding cost and the ordering cost.* Several key assumptions underlie the quantitative model we will develop:

- Only a single item (SKU) is considered.
- The entire order quantity (Q) arrives in the inventory at one time.
- Only two types of costs are relevant—order/setup and inventory-holding costs.

- No stockouts are allowed.
- The demand for the item is constant and continuous over time.
- Lead time is constant.

Under the assumptions of the model, the cycle inventory pattern is shown in Exhibit 12.8. Suppose that we begin with Q units in inventory. Because units are assumed to be withdrawn at a constant rate, the inventory level falls in a linear fashion until it hits zero. Because no stockouts are allowed, a new order can be planned to arrive when the inventory falls to zero; at this point, the inventory is replenished back up to Q. This cycle keeps repeating. This regular pattern allows us to compute the total cost as a function of the order quantity, Q.

Cycle inventory (*also called **order** or **lot size inventory***) *is inventory that results from purchasing or producing in larger lots than are needed for immediate consumption or sale.* From the constant demand assumption, the average cycle inventory can be easily computed as the average of the maximum and minimum inventory levels:

$$\text{Average cycle inventory} = (\text{Maximum inventory} + \text{Minimum inventory})/2 = Q/2 \qquad [12.2]$$

If the average inventory during each cycle is $Q/2$, then the average inventory level over any number of cycles is also $Q/2$.

The inventory-holding cost can be calculated by multiplying the average inventory by the cost of holding one item in inventory for the stated period (see Equation 12.5). The period of time selected for the model is up to the user; it can be a day, week, month, or year. However, because the inventory-holding costs for many industries and businesses are expressed as an annual

Exhibit 12.5 *Summary of Fixed-Quantity System (FQS)*

Managerial Decisions	Order Quantity (Q) and Reorder Point (r)
Ordering decision rule	A new order is triggered whenever the inventory position for the item drops to or past the reorder point. The size of each order is Q units.
Key characteristics	The order quantity Q is always fixed.
	The time between orders (TBO) is constant when the demand rate is stable.
	The TBO can vary when demand is variable.

© Cengage Learning 2013

The **economic order quantity (EOQ)** model is a classic economic model developed in the early 1900s that minimizes the total cost, which is the sum of the inventory-holding cost and the ordering cost.

Cycle inventory (also called **order** or **lot size inventory**) is inventory that results from purchasing or producing in larger lots than are needed for immediate consumption or sale.

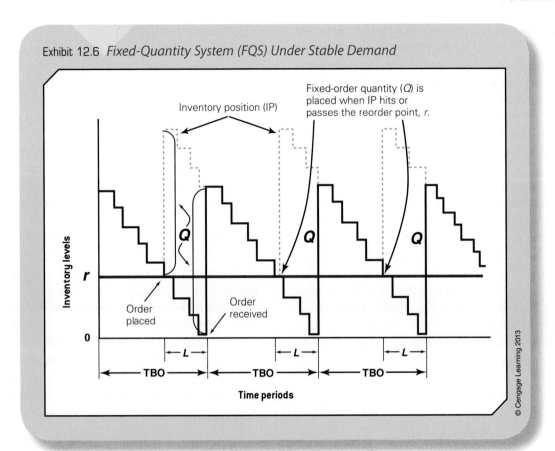

Exhibit 12.6 *Fixed-Quantity System (FQS) Under Stable Demand*

Inventory position (IP)

Fixed-order quantity (Q) is placed when IP hits or passes the reorder point, r.

Inventory levels

r

Q Q Q

Order placed   Order received

0

L L L

TBO   TBO   TBO

Time periods

© Cengage Learning 2013

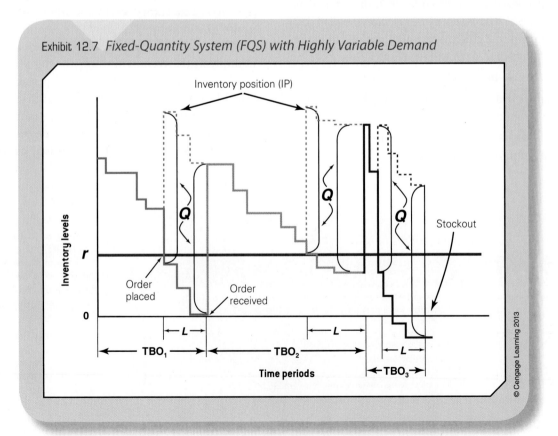

Exhibit 12.7 *Fixed-Quantity System (FQS) with Highly Variable Demand*

Inventory position (IP)

Inventory levels

r

Q Q Q

Stockout

Order placed   Order received

0

L L L

TBO_1 TBO_2 TBO_3

Time periods

© Cengage Learning 2013

percentage or rate, most inventory models are developed on an annual cost basis (see Equation 12.4). Let

I = annual inventory-holding charge expressed as a percent of unit cost

C = unit cost of the inventory item or SKU

I includes two types of costs—cost of capital (money) plus any inventory-handling and storage costs, both expressed as a percentage of the item cost. The cost of storing one unit in inventory for the year, denoted by C_h, is given by

$$C_h = (I)(C) \quad [12.3]$$

Thus, the general equation for annual inventory-holding cost is

$$\text{Annual inventory-holding cost} = \left(\begin{array}{c}\text{Average}\\\text{inventory}\end{array}\right)\left(\begin{array}{c}\text{Annual holding}\\\text{cost}\\\text{per unit}\end{array}\right)$$

$$= \frac{1}{2}QC_h \quad [12.4]$$

The second component of the total cost is the ordering cost. Because the inventory-holding cost is expressed on an annual basis, we need to express ordering costs as an annual cost also. Letting D denote the annual demand for the product, we know that by ordering Q items each time we order, we have to place D/Q orders per year. If C_o is the cost of placing one order, the general expression for the annual ordering cost is shown in Equation 12.5.

$$\text{Annual ordering cost} = \left(\begin{array}{c}\text{Number of}\\\text{orders}\\\text{per year}\end{array}\right)\left(\begin{array}{c}\text{Cost}\\\text{per}\\\text{order}\end{array}\right) = \frac{D}{Q}C_0 \quad [12.5]$$

Thus the total annual cost is the sum of the inventory-holding cost given by Equation 12.4 plus the order or setup cost given by Equation 12.5:

$$TC = \frac{1}{2}QC_h + \frac{D}{Q}C_0 \quad [12.6]$$

The next step is to find the order quantity, Q, that minimizes the total cost expressed in Equation 12.6. By using differential calculus, we can show that the quantity that minimizes the total cost, denoted by Q^*, is given by Equation 12.7. Q^* is referred to as the *economic order quantity*, or *EOQ*.

$$Q^* = \sqrt{\frac{2DC_0}{C_h}} \quad [12.7]$$

Finally, we need to determine *when* to place an order for Q^* units. The reorder point, r, depends on the lead time and the demand rate. Since we assume that demand is constant in the EOQ model, then the reorder point is found by multiplying the fixed demand rate, d (units/day, units/month, etc.), by the length of the lead time, L (in the same units, for example, days or months). Note that it is easy to convert the annual demand D (in units/year) to a demand rate, d, having the same time units as the lead time.

$$r = \text{Lead time demand}$$
$$= (\text{demand rate})(\text{lead time})$$
$$= (d)(L) \quad [12.8]$$

Because the EOQ model depends only on the order quantity, fixed costs associated with any ordering or inventory holding are irrelevant (in accounting language, these are *sunk costs*). Therefore, only variable costs of ordering and inventory holding are required for the model.

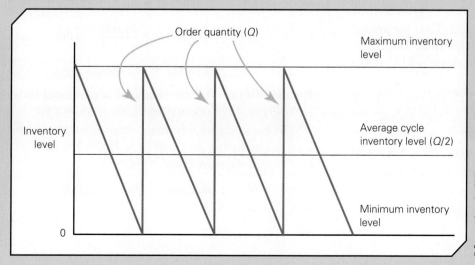

Exhibit 12.8 *Cycle Inventory Pattern for the EOQ Model*

Order quantity (Q)

Maximum inventory level

Inventory level

Average cycle inventory level (Q/2)

Minimum inventory level

0

© Cengage Learning 2013

12-4b Safety Stock and Uncertain Demand in a Fixed-Order-Quantity System

Stockouts occur whenever the lead-time demand exceeds the reorder point. When demand is uncertain, using EOQ based only on the average demand will result in a high probability of a stockout. One way to reduce this risk is to increase the reorder point by adding additional stock—called safety stock—to the average lead time demand. **Safety stock** *is additional planned on-hand inventory that acts as a buffer to reduce the risk of a stockout.*

To determine the appropriate reorder point, we first need to know the probability distribution of the lead-time demand, which we often assume to be normally distributed. The appropriate reorder point depends on the risk that management wants to take of incurring a stockout. *A* **service level** *is the desired probability of not having a stockout during a lead-time period.* For example, a 95 percent service level means that the probability of a stockout during the lead time is .05. Choosing a service level is a management policy decision.

When demand is uncertain, then the reorder point is the average demand during the lead time, μ_L plus the additional safety stock. The average demand during the lead time is found by multiplying the average demand per unit of time by the length of the lead time expressed in the same time units. When a normal probability distribution provides a good approximation of lead-time demand, the general expression for reorder point is

$$r = \mu_L + z\sigma_L \qquad [12.9]$$

where μ_L = average demand during the lead time

σ_L = standard deviation of demand during the lead time

z = the number of standard deviations necessary to achieve the acceptable service level

The term "$z\sigma_L$" represents the amount of safety stock.

> **Safety stock** is additional planned on-hand inventory that acts as a buffer to reduce the risk of a stockout.
>
> A **service level** is the desired probability of not having a stockout during a lead-time period.

Solved Problem

The sales of a popular mouthwash at Merkle Pharmacies over the past six months have averaged 2,000 cases per month, which is the current order quantity. Merkle's cost is $12.00 per case. The company estimates its cost of capital to be 12 percent. Insurance, taxes, breakage, handling, and pilferage are estimated to be approximately 6 percent of item cost. Thus the annual inventory-holding costs are estimated to be 18 percent of item cost. Because the cost of one case is $12.00, the cost of holding one case in inventory for one year using Equation 12.4 is $C_h = (IC) = 0.18(\$12.00) = \$2.16$ per case per year.

The cost of placing an order is estimated to be $38.00 per order regardless of the quantity requested in the order. From this information, we have

$$D = 24,000 \text{ cases per year.}$$
$$C_o = \$38 \text{ per order.}$$
$$I = 18 \text{ percent.}$$
$$C = \$12.00 \text{ per case.}$$
$$C_h = IC = \$2.16.$$

Thus, the minimum-cost economic order quantity (EOQ) as given by Equation 12.7 is

$$EOQ = \sqrt{\frac{2(24,000)(38)}{2.16}} = \begin{matrix} 919 \text{ cases rounded} \\ \text{to a whole number.} \end{matrix}$$

For the data used in this problem, the total-cost model based on Equation 12.6 is

$$TC = \frac{1}{2}Q(\$2.16) + \frac{24,000}{Q}(\$38.00)$$

$$= \$1.08Q + 912,000/Q$$

For the EOQ of 919, the total cost is calculated to be $(1.08)(919) + (24,000/919)(\$38.00) = \$1,984.90$.

We can compare this total cost using EOQ with the current purchasing policy of $Q = 2,000$. The total annual cost of the current order policy is

$$TC = 1.08(2,000) + 912,000/2,000$$
$$= \$2,616.00$$

Exhibit 12.9 *Excel Spreadsheet from EOQ Model Template*

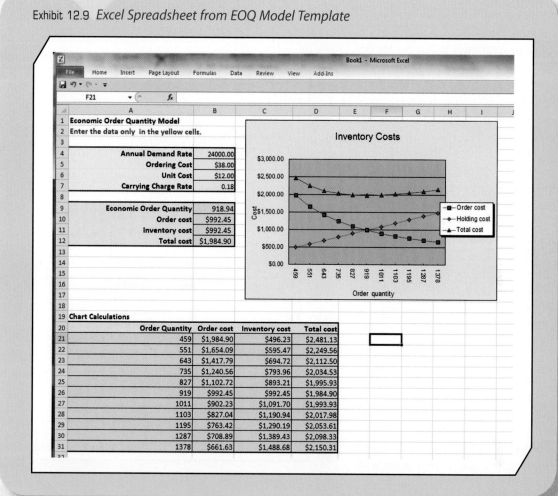

Thus, the EOQ analysis has resulted in a $2,616.00 − $1,984.90 = $631.10 savings, or 24.1 percent cost reduction. Notice also that the total ordering costs ($992) are equal to the total inventory-holding costs ($992) for the EOQ. In general, this will always be true for the EOQ model. Exhibit 12.9 shows the Excel EOQ Model template, which finds the EOQ and optimal costs, and charts the cost functions. You can see the curve is relatively flat around the minimum-total-cost solution.

To find the reorder point, suppose that the lead time to order a case of mouthwash from the manufacturer is $L = 3$ days. Considering weekends and holidays, Merkle operates 250 days per year. So, on a daily

basis, the deterministic annual demand of 24,000 cases corresponds to a daily demand of $d = 24,000/250 = 96$ cases per day. Thus, using Equation 12.8, we anticipate that $r = (d)(L) = 96 \times 3 = 288$ cases to be sold during the three-day lead time. Therefore, Merkle should order a new shipment from the manufacturer when the inventory level reaches 288 cases. Also note that the company will place $D/Q = 24,000/919 = 26.12$, or approximately 26 orders per year. With 250 working days per year, an order would be placed every (250 days per year)/(26.1 orders per year) = 9.6 days per order. This represents the average time between orders (TBO) of 9.6 days in Exhibit 12.6.

Solved Problem

Southern Office Supplies, Inc. distributes office supplies to customers in the Southeast. One popular SKU is laser printer paper. Ordering costs are $45.00 per order. One ream of paper costs $3.80, and Southern uses a 20 percent annual inventory-holding cost rate. Thus, the inventory-holding cost is $Ch = IC = 0.20(\$3.80) = \$0.76$ per ream per year. The average annual demand is 15,000 reams, or about $15,000/52 = 288.5$ per week, and historical data shows that the standard deviation of weekly demand is about 71. The lead time from the manufacturer is two weeks.

To determine the reorder point, begin by using Equations 12.10 and 12.11. The average demand during the lead time (μ_L) is $(288.5)(2) = 577$ reams, and the standard deviation of demand during the lead time (σ_L) is approximately $71\sqrt{2} = 100$ reams. If Southern's managers desire a service level of 95 percent, we use the normal distribution tables in Appendix A and find that a 5 percent upper tail area corresponds to a standard normal z-value of 1.645. Therefore, the reorder point with safety stock using Equation 12.9, r, is

$$r = \mu_L + z\sigma_L = 577 + 1.645(100)$$
$$= 742 \text{ reams}$$

If we apply the EOQ model using the average annual demand, we find that the optimal order quantity would be

$$Q^* = \sqrt{\frac{2DC_0}{C_h}} = \sqrt{\frac{2(15,000)(45)}{0.76}} = 1,333 \text{ reams}$$

Using this EOQ, Southern can anticipate placing approximately 11 orders per year ($D/Q = 15,000/1,333$),

Exhibit 12.10 *Excel FQS Safety Stock Template*

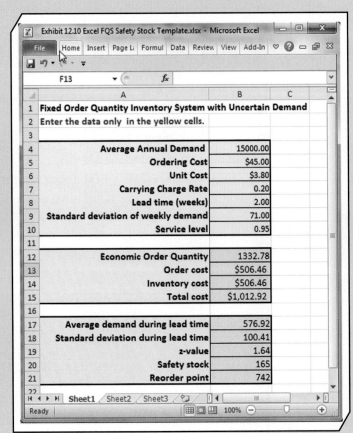

slightly more than a month apart. Using Equation 12.7, the total annual cost is $1,012.92.

The reorder point without any additional safety stock using Equation 12.2 is $2(288.5) = 577$. Considering safety stock, a policy of ordering 1,333 reams whenever the inventory position reaches the reorder point of 742 will minimize inventory costs and incur a risk of at most a 5 percent probability of stockout during a lead-time period. Exhibit 12.10 shows the Excel FQS Safety Stock template for performing these calculations.

HEWLETT-PACKARD: BALANCING INVENTORY AND SERVICE

The Hewlett-Packard (HP) Company has complex supply chains for its products. The Vancouver division manufactures one of HP's popular printers and ships them to distribution centers (DCs) in the United States, the Far East, and Europe. Because the printer industry is highly competitive, HP dealers like to carry as little inventory as possible, but must supply goods to end-users quickly. Consequently, HP operates under a lot of pressure to provide high levels of availability at the DCs for the dealers. DCs operate as inventory stocking points with large safety stocks to meet a target off-the-shelf fill rate, where replenishment of goods comes from manufacturing. HP developed a quantitative model to compute cost-effective target inventory levels considering safety stock to meet fill rate requirements. The model helped to improve inventory investment by over 20 percent. What would the HP chief financial officer think of this result?[7]

In many cases, we do not know the mean and standard deviation of demand during the lead time, but only for some other length of time, such as a day or week. Suppose that μ_t and σ_t are the mean and standard deviation of demand for some time interval t, and that the lead time L is expressed in the same units (days, weeks, and so on). If the distributions of demand for all time intervals are identical to and independent of each other, we can use some basic statistical results to find μ_L and σ_L based on μ_t and σ_t as follows:

$$\mu_L = \mu_t L \qquad [12.10]$$
$$\sigma_L = \sigma_t \sqrt{L} \qquad [12.11]$$

 12-5 Managing Fixed-Period Inventory Systems

an alternative to a fixed-order-quantity system is *a fixed-period system (FPS)—sometimes called a periodic review system—in which the inventory position is checked only at fixed intervals of time, T, rather than* on a continuous basis. At the time of review, an order is placed for sufficient stock to bring the inventory position up to a predetermined maximum inventory level, M, sometimes called the replenishment level, or "order-up-to" level.

There are two principal decisions in an FPS:

1. The time interval between reviews
2. The replenishment level

We can set the length of the review period judgmentally based on the importance of the item or the convenience of review. For example, management might select to review noncritical SKUs every month and more critical SKUs every week. We can also incorporate economics using the EOQ model.

The EOQ model provides the best "economic time interval" for establishing an optimal policy for an FPS system under the model assumptions. This is given by

$$T = Q^*/D \qquad [12.12]$$

where Q^* is the economic order quantity. The optimal replenishment level without any safety stock is computed by

$$M = d(T + L) \qquad [12.13]$$

where d = average demand per time period (days, weeks, months, etc.), L is the lead time in the same time units, and M is the demand during the lead time plus review period. When demand is stochastic, managers can add appropriate safety stock to the optimal replenishment level to ensure a target service level.

A **fixed-period system (FPS)**—sometimes called a periodic review system—is one in which the inventory position is checked only at fixed intervals of time, *T*, rather than on a continuous basis.

A summary of fixed-period systems is given in Exhibit 12.11. Exhibit 12.12 shows the system operation graphically. In Exhibit 12.12, at the time of the first review, a rather large amount of inventory (IP_1) is in stock, so the order quantity (Q_1) is relatively small. Demand during the lead time was small, and when the order arrived, a large amount of inventory was still available. At the third review cycle, the stock level is much closer to zero because the demand rate has increased (steeper slope). Thus, the order quantity (Q_3) is much larger and during the lead time, demand was high and some stockouts occurred. Note that when an order is placed at time T, it does not arrive until time $T + L$. Thus, in using an FPS, managers must cover the risk of a stockout over the time period $T + L$, and therefore, must carry more inventory.

To add safety stock to the replenishment level (M) in an FPS, we can use the same statistical principles as with the FQS. We must compute safety stock over the period $T + L$, so the replenishment level is computed as follows:

$$M = \mu_{T+L} + z\sigma_{T+L} \qquad [12.14]$$

$$\mu_{T+L} = \mu_t (T + L) \qquad [12.15]$$

$$\sigma_{T+L} = \sigma_t \sqrt{T + L} \qquad [12.16]$$

The choice of which system—FQS or FPS—to use depends on a variety of factors, such as how many total SKUs the firm must monitor, whether computer or

Exhibit 12.11 *Summary of Fixed-Period Inventory Systems*

Managerial Decisions	Review Period (*T*) and Replenishment Level (*M*)
Ordering decision rule	Place a new order every *T* periods, where the order quantity at time *t* is $Q_t = M - IP_t$, and IP_t is the inventory position at the time of review, *t*.
Key characteristics	The review period, *T*, is constant and placing an order is time-triggered.
	The order quantity, Q_t, varies at each review period.
	M is chosen to include the demand during the review period and lead time, plus any safety stock.
	Stockouts can occur when demand is stochastic and can be addressed by adding safety stock to the expected demand during time $T + L$.

© Cengage Learning 2013

Exhibit 12.12 *Operation of a Fixed-Period System (FPS)*

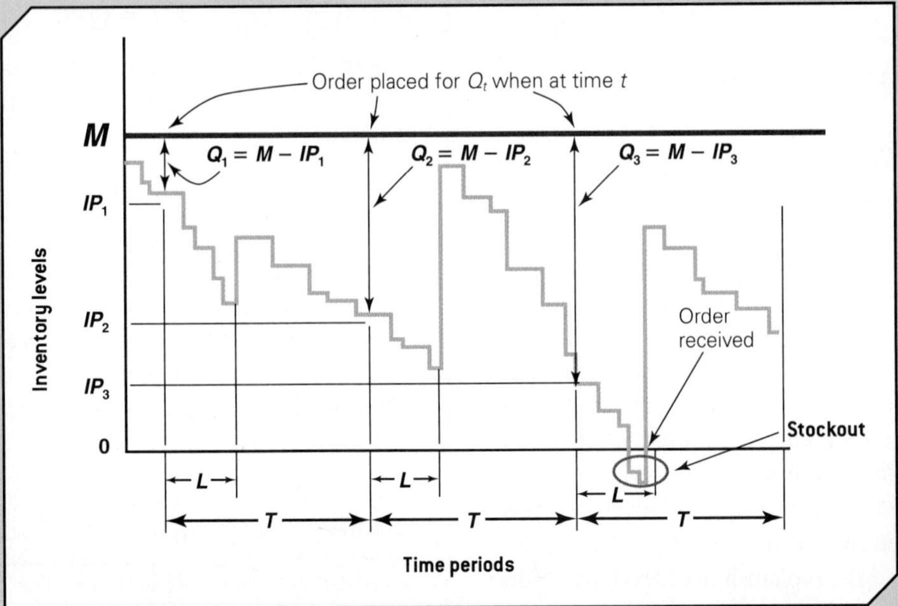

© Cengage Learning 2013

manual systems are used, availability of technology and human resources, the nature of the ABC profile, and the strategic focus of the organization, such as customer service or cost minimization. Thus, the ultimate decision is a combination of technical expertise and subjective managerial judgment. Many other advanced inventory models are available (see the box, "There's More to Inventory Modeling"), but the FQS and FPS provide the foundation for these.

12-6 Single-Period Inventory Model

The single-period inventory model applies to inventory situations in which one order is placed for a good in anticipation of a future selling season where demand is uncertain. At the end of the

Solved Problem

Refer back to the previous Solved Problem on Southern Office Supplies. Using the same information (ordering costs = $45.00 per order, inventory-holding cost = $0.76 per ream per year, and average annual demand = 15,000 reams), we can apply the EOQ model using the average annual demand, and find that the optimal order quantity would be

$$Q^* = \sqrt{\frac{2DC}{C_b}} = \sqrt{\frac{2(15,000)(45)}{0.76}} = 1,333 \text{ reams}$$

Data indicate that it usually takes two weeks ($L = 2$ weeks) for Southern to receive a new supply of paper from the manufacturer.

Using Equation 12.12 we compute the review period as

$$T = Q^*/D = 1,333/15,000 = .0889 \text{ years}$$

If we assume 52 weeks/year, then $T = 52(.0889) = 4.6$ weeks, which is approximately five weeks. Whether to round T up or down is a management decision. Because the average annual demand is 15,000 units, the average weekly demand is $15,000/52 = 288.46$. From Equation 12.13, the optimal replenishment level without safety stock is

$$M = (d)(T + L) = (288.46)(5 + 2) = 2,019.22 \text{ units}$$

Therefore, we review the inventory position every five weeks and place an order to replenish the inventory up to an M level of 2,019 units.

To add safety stock to the M level we compute the standard deviation of demand over the period $T + L$ using Equations 12.14 to 12.16 and the standard deviation of weekly demand of 71 reams as follows:

Exhibit 12.13 *Excel FPS Safety Stock Template*

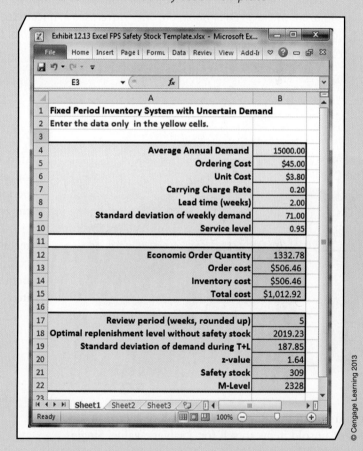

	A	B
1	**Fixed Period Inventory System with Uncertain Demand**	
2	Enter the data only in the yellow cells.	
3		
4	Average Annual Demand	15000.00
5	Ordering Cost	$45.00
6	Unit Cost	$3.80
7	Carrying Charge Rate	0.20
8	Lead time (weeks)	2.00
9	Standard deviation of weekly demand	71.00
10	Service level	0.95
11		
12	Economic Order Quantity	1332.78
13	Order cost	$506.46
14	Inventory cost	$506.46
15	Total cost	$1,012.92
16		
17	Review period (weeks, rounded up)	5
18	Optimal replenishment level without safety stock	2019.23
19	Standard deviation of demand during T+L	187.85
20	z-value	1.64
21	Safety stock	309
22	M-Level	2328

$$\sigma_{T+L} = 71\sqrt{5 + 2} = 187.8 \text{ reams}$$

and then the safety stock with a 95 percent service level is

$$z\sigma_{T+L} = 1.645(187.8) = 309 \text{ reams}$$

The M level with safety stock and a 95 percent service level is $M = 2,019 + 309 = 2,328$ reams. Exhibit 12.13 shows the Excel FPS Safety Stock template for performing these calculations.

There's More to Inventory Modeling

The inventory models we discussed are the basic models for managing inventories. Many other models have been developed to assist managers in other situations. For example, there are cases in which it may be desirable—from an economic point of view—to plan for and allow shortages. This situation is most common when the value per unit of the inventory is very high, and hence the inventory-holding cost is high. An example is a new-car dealer's inventory. Most customers do not find the specific car they want in stock, but are willing to backorder it. Another example is when suppliers offer discounts for purchasing larger quantities of goods.

David McNew/Getty Images

This often occurs because of economies of scale of shipping larger loads, from not having to break apart boxes of items, or simply as an incentive to increase total revenue. You might have noticed such incentives at stores like Amazon, where DVDs or books are often advertised in discounted bundles—for example, two DVDs by the same artist for a lower price than buying them individually. For both of these situations, quantitative models have been developed for finding optimal inventory order policies.

Sipa/AP Images

period the product has either sold out, or there is a surplus of unsold items to sell for a salvage value. Single-period models are used in situations involving seasonal or perishable items that cannot be carried in inventory and sold in future periods.

One example is the situation faced by Banana Republic at the beginning of the chapter; other examples would be ordering dough for a pizza restaurant, which stays fresh for only three days, and purchasing seasonal holiday items such as Christmas trees. In such a single-period inventory situation, the only inventory decision is how much of the product to order at the

start of the period. Because newspaper sales are a typical example of the single-period situation, the single-period inventory problem is sometimes referred to as the *newsvendor problem.*

The newsvendor problem can be solved using a technique called *marginal economic analysis,* which compares the cost or loss of ordering one additional item with the cost or loss of not ordering one additional item. The costs involved are defined as

c_s = the cost per item of overestimating demand (salvage cost); this cost represents the loss of ordering one additional item and finding that it cannot be sold.

c_u = the cost per item of underestimating demand (shortage cost); this cost represents the opportunity loss of not ordering one additional item and finding that it could have been sold.

The optimal order quantity is the value of Q^* that satisfies Equation 12.17:

$$P(\text{demand} \leq Q^*) = \frac{c_u}{c_u + c_s} \qquad [12.17]$$

This formula can be used for any probability distribution of demand, such as a uniform or a normal distribution.

Solved Problem

Let us consider a buyer for a department store who is ordering fashion swimwear about six months before the summer season. The store plans to hold an August clearance sale to sell any surplus goods by July 31. Each piece costs $40 per pair and sells for $60 per pair. At the sale price of $30 per pair, it is expected that any remaining stock can be sold during the August sale. We will assume that a uniform probability distribution ranging from 350 to 650 items, shown in Exhibit 12.14, describes the demand. The expected demand is 500.

The retailer will incur the cost of overestimating demand whenever it orders too much and has to sell the extra items available after July. Thus, the cost per item of overestimating demand is equal to the purchase cost per item minus the August sale price per item; that is, $C_s = \$40 - \$30 = \$10$. In other words, the retailer will lose $10 for each item that it orders over the quantity demanded. The cost of underestimating demand is the lost profit (opportunity loss) due to the fact that it could have been sold but was not available in inventory. Thus the per-item cost of underestimating demand is the difference between the regular selling price per item and the purchase cost per item; that is, $c_u = \$60 - \$40 = \$20$. The optimal order size Q must satisfy this condition:

$$P(\text{demand} \le Q^*) = \frac{c_u}{c_u + c_s} = \frac{20}{20 + 10} = \frac{20}{30} = \frac{2}{3}$$

Because the demand distribution is uniform, the value of Q^* is two-thirds of the way from 350 to 650. Thus, $Q^* = 550$ swimwear SKUs. Note that whenever $c_u \le c_s$, the formula leads to the choice of an order quantity more likely to be less than demand; hence a higher risk of a stockout is present. However, when $c_u > c_s$, as in the example, the optimal order quantity leads to a higher risk of a surplus. If the demand distribution were other than uniform, then the same process applies. The optimal order quantity, Q^*, must still satisfy the requirement that $P(\text{demand} \le Q^*) = 2/3$.

Exhibit 12.15 shows the Excel Single-Period Inventory template that can be used to find the optimal order quantity for either a uniform or a normal distribution for demand.

Exhibit 12.14 *Probability Distribution for Single-Period Model*

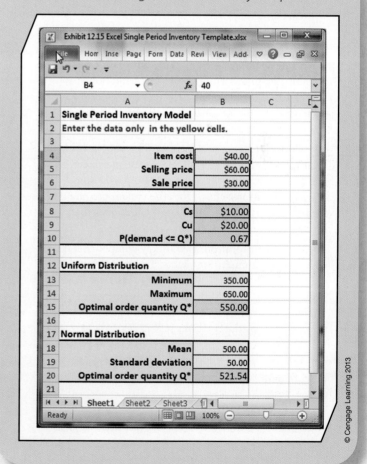

Exhibit 12.15 *Excel Single-Period Inventory Template*

© Cengage Learning 2013

Discussion Questions

1. Discuss some of the issues that a small pizza restaurant might face in inventory management. Would a pizza restaurant use a fixed-order-quantity or period system for fresh dough (purchased from a bakery on contract)? What would be the advantages and disadvantages of each in this situation?

2. List some products in your personal or family "inventory." How do you manage them? (For instance, do you constantly run to the store for milk? Do you throw out a lot of milk because of spoilage?) How might the ideas in this chapter change your way of managing these SKUs?

3. Does the EOQ increase or decrease if estimates of setup (order) costs include fixed, semi-variable, and pure variable costs while inventory-holding costs include only pure variable costs? Vice versa? What are the implications? Explain.

4. Find two examples of using RFID technology to monitor and control SKUs and explain the advantages and disadvantages of adopting such technology.

5. Identify at least two other practical examples of a single-period inventory model that differ from those in the book.

Problems and Activities

Note: an asterisk denotes problems for which an Excel spreadsheet template on the CourseMate Web site may be used.

1. Find, describe, and draw an organization's supply chain and identify the types of inventory in it and, if possible, the purpose of the inventory and how it is monitored and controlled. (The example could be a place you worked at, such as a call center, restaurant, factory, retail store, hotel, school, or medical office.)

2. Interview a manager at a local business about his or her inventory and materials-management system, and prepare a report (maximum two pages) summarizing its approaches. Does the system use any formal models? Why or why not? How does the manager determine inventory-related costs?

3.* The Welsh Corporation uses 10 key components in one of its manufacturing plants. The data are provided in worksheet C12P3 in the *OM4 Data Workbook* on the CourseMate Web site. Perform an ABC analysis. Explain your decisions and logic.

4.* Perform an ABC analysis for the data provided below and in worksheet C12P4 in the *OM4 Data Workbook* on the CourseMate Web site. Clearly explain why you classified items as A, B, or C.

Item	Annual Usage	Unit Value	Item	Annual Usage	Unit Value
1	8,800	$68.12	7	112,000	$7.59
2	9,800	$58.25	8	198,000	$3.19
3	23,600	$75.25	9	210,000	$2.98
4	40,000	$53.14	10	168,000	$4.27
5	60,000	$26.33	11	100,000	$9.00
6	165,000	$4.52	12	7,000	$13.57

5.* Perform an ABC analysis for the data provided below and in worksheet C12P5 in the *OM4 Data Workbook* on the CourseMate Web site. Clearly explain why you classified items as A, B, or C.

Item	Annual Usage	Unit Cost	Item	Annual Usage	Unit Cost
1	2,400	$19.51	11	500	$40.50
2	6,200	32.60	12	2,000	15.40
3	8,500	10.20	13	2,400	14.60
4	3,200	6.80	14	6,300	35.80
5	6,000	4.50	15	4,750	17.30
6	750	55.70	16	2,700	51.75
7	8,200	3.60	17	1,600	42.90
8	9,000	44.90	18	1,350	25.30
9	5,800	35.62	19	5,000	67.00
10	820	82.60	20	1,000	125.00

6.* MamaMia's Pizza purchases its pizza delivery boxes from a printing supplier. MamaMia's delivers on average 200 pizzas each month (assume deterministic demand). Boxes cost 20 cents each, and each order costs $10 to process. Because of limited storage space, the manager wants to charge inventory holding at 30 percent of the cost. The lead time is 7 days, and the restaurant is open 360 days per year, assuming 30 days per month. Determine the economic order quantity, reorder point assuming no safety stock, number of orders per year, and total annual cost.

7.* Refer to the situation in problem 6. Suppose the manager of MamaMia's current order quantity is 200 boxes. How much can be saved by adopting an EOQ versus the current $Q = 200$?

8.* Super K Beverage Company distributes a soft drink that has a constant annual demand rate of 4,600 cases. A 12-pack case of the soft drink costs Super K $2.25. Ordering costs are $20 per order, and inventory-holding costs are charged at 25 percent of the cost per unit. There are 250 working days per year, and the lead time is 4 days. Find the economic order quantity and total annual cost, and compute the reorder point.

9.* Environmental considerations, material losses, and waste disposal can be included in the EOQ model to improve inventory-management decisions. Assume that the annual demand for an industrial chemical is 1,200 lb, item cost is $5/lb, order cost is $40, and the inventory-holding cost rate (percent of item cost) is 18 percent.

   a. Find the EOQ and total cost, assuming no waste disposal.

   b. Now assume that 8 percent of the chemical is not used and is disposed of, with a disposal cost of $0.75/lb. Find the EOQ and total cost when disposal costs are incorporated into the model. (Hint: Add to the holding cost the disposal cost times the percent of product that is disposed of.)

   c. What implications do these results have for sustainability practices?

10.* High Tech, Inc. is a virtual store that stocks a variety of calculators in its warehouse. Customer orders are placed, the orders are picked and packaged, and then orders are shipped to the customers. A fixed-order-quantity inventory control system (FQS) helps monitor and control these SKUs. The following information is for one of the calculators that High Tech stocks, sells, and ships.

Average demand	12.5 calculators per week
Lead time	3 weeks
Order cost	$20/order
Unit cost	$8.00
Carrying charge rate	0.15
Number of weeks	52 weeks per year
Standard deviation of weekly demand	3.75 calculators
SKU service level	90 percent
Current on-hand inventory	35 calculators
Scheduled receipts	20 calculators
Backorders	2 calculators

   a. What are the economic order quantity?

   b. What are the total annual order and inventory-holding costs for the EOQ?

   c. What is the reorder point without safety stock?

   d. What is the reorder point with safety stock?

   e. Based on the previous information, should a fixed-order quantity be placed, and if so, for how many calculators?

11.* Crew Soccer Shoes Company is considering a change in its current inventory control system for soccer shoes. The information regarding the shoes is as follows:

Average demand = 200 pairs/week

Lead time = 3 weeks

Order cost = $65/order

Unit cost = $20

Carrying charge rate = 0.20

Desired service level = 95 percent

Standard deviation of weekly demand = 50

Number of weeks per year = 52

The company decides to use a fixed-order-quantity system. What is the economic order quantity? What should be the reorder point to have a 95 percent service level? Explain how the system will operate.

12.* Tune Football Helmets Company is considering changing its current inventory control system for football helmets. The information regarding the helmets is as follows:

Demand = 200 units/week

Lead time = 2 weeks

Order cost = $60/order

Unit cost = $20

Carrying charge rate = 0.075

Desired service level = 90 percent

Inventory position (IP) = 450

Standard deviation of weekly demand = 40

Number of weeks per year = 52

Compute T and M for a fixed-period inventory system model with and without safety stock. Explain how this system would operate.

13.* Suzie's Sweetshop makes special boxes of Valentine's Day chocolates. Each costs $10 in material and labor and sells for $15. After Valentine's Day, Suzie reduces the price to $9.00 and sells any remaining boxes. Historically, she has sold between 50 and 100 boxes. Determine the optimal number of boxes to make. How would her decision change if she can only sell all remaining boxes at a price of $6?

14.* For the Suzie's Sweetshop scenario in Problem 13, suppose that demand is normally distributed with a mean of 75 and a standard deviation of 8. How will her optimal order quantity change? (Hint: Note that for a normal distribution, the value of Q^* in Equation 12.17 can be found using Appendix A. Find the value of z that corresponds to the cumulative probability defined by Equation 12.17, and then find Q^* by converting back to the original normal distribution using the formula $z = (Q^* - \mu)/\sigma$.]) Verify your result using the Excel template.

15.* The J&B Card Shop sells calendars featuring a different colonial picture for each month. The once-a-year order for each year's calendar arrives in September. From past experience, the September-to-July demand for the calendars can be approximated by a normal distribution with $\mu = 500$ and standard deviation = 50. The calendars cost $4.50 each, and J&B sells them for $10 each.

a. Suppose that J&B throws out all unsold calendars at the end of July. Using marginal economic analysis, how many calendars should be ordered?

b. If J&B sells any surplus calendars for $1 at the end of July and can sell all of them at this price, how many calendars should be ordered?

Hardy Hospital Case Study

Caroline Highgrove, Hardy's Director of Materials Management, glanced at the papers spread across her desk. She wondered where the week had gone. On Monday, the Director of University Operations, Drew Paris, had asked Caroline to look into the purchasing and supplies systems for the hospital. Drew specifically wanted Caroline to evaluate the current materials-management system, identify ways to reduce costs, and recommend a final plan of action. Drew explained that the university was under pressure to cut expenses and hospital inventory did not seem to be under control.

As Caroline reviewed her notes, she was struck by the variations in order sizes and order frequencies for the hospital's stock-keeping units (SKUs). For some SKUs, inventory ran out before new orders came in, while for other SKUs, excessively high stock levels were being carried. The university and hospital's computerized materials-management system was about a decade old and generally worked well; however, employees often ignored, or did not update, key information. Thus, data integrity was a major problem in this information system.

Hospital and university supply orders were classified as either *regular stock* or *special order*. The hospital was the originator of almost all special orders. *Regular stock items,* such as bed sheets, uniforms, and syringes, were characterized by their long-standing and frequent use throughout the university and hospital, and by a low risk of obsolescence. When a department needed a regular stock item, that department generally ordered (requisitioned) the item. If the item is in stock, it would be delivered to the department by the next delivery date.

When the university did not normally stock an item, individual hospital departments could special-order them. Special-order items were supposed to be those of an experimental nature or critical to patient health care but not used frequently. Hospital departments requiring these special items bypassed the university purchasing system. Once a special order Hardy Hospital Case Study was placed, the hospital department informed university purchasing so that it could eventually authorize payment on the vendor's invoice. Hospital department coordinators, doctors, or head nurses were responsible for initiating and/or authorizing special orders. In total, these special orders required a significant amount of work that took department coordinators and head nurses away from their duties. University purchasing kept no records on the hospital's special-order inventories or for the 215 secondary hospital stocking points such as exam rooms and moveable carts.

One department's head nurse explained that many departments were afraid of running out of regular stock items. University purchasing didn't understand the importance and nature of hospital inventory, and they were slow to respond. The nurse cited the months-long period university purchasing process needed to place new items on the regular stock list, and the long lead times sometimes involved in receiving orders requisitioned from the university's approved vendor list.

Because the university was a state institution, strict bidding and purchasing procedures had to be followed for both regular stock and special orders. For example, three written bids were required for an individual order of $2,000 or more. The processing of these bids often took up to two months. For orders between $800 and

$1,999, three telephone bids were necessary. In these situations, purchases could be made only from the lowest bidder. Orders under $800, or items on the state contract list, could be ordered over the phone, without any bids. State contract list items were those for which statewide needs had been combined and one contract left to cover all of them.

Caroline had gathered information on the costs of ordering and storing hospital supplies. For order costs, she estimated that, on average, the purchasing, account payables, and receiving personnel spent three hours processing a single purchase order. A single purchase order typically included four SKUs (i.e., each SKU on a purchase order was called a line item). The average hospital storeroom's wage was $16 an hour; with employee benefits and associated overhead, the cost of one worker-hour came to $20.

For inventory-holding costs, the university warehouse and hospital storeroom used 36,750 square feet of storage space. The university stored an average of $4.15 million in hospital supplies in this space. Records indicated that the average annual variable and

Regular stock items were characterized by their long-standing and frequent use throughout the hospital.

semivariable cost for storage space this year would be $4.60 per square foot. Five warehouse workers and storeroom associates were required to handle the hospital's supplies. These individuals each earned $32,000 a year; benefits and overhead rates for these employees were the same as for other personnel of about 20 percent. Other warehouse costs, including obsolescence and taxes, were expected to reach $200,000 this year. The hospital operated 52 weeks per year. Also, the state recently had floated a bond issue at 8.9 percent, and Caroline thought that might be a good estimate of the cost of money to finance inventory but wasn't sure what other costs to include in inventory-holding cost.

After reviewing her notes on the hospital's materials-management situation, Caroline decided to take a closer look at some individual regular stock items. She sorted through the papers on her desk and found 30 SKUs of interest. She wanted to analyze all 30 SKUs but decided to begin with one SKU widely used in the hospital—Strike Disinfectant. Data on this SKU are shown in Exhibits 12.16 and 12.17.

Exhibit 12.16 *Hardy Hospital Strike Disinfectant Data**

		Case Size		Cost per Case	Order Lead Time
Strike Disinfectant+		4 gallons		$84.20	2 weeks
Beginning SKU Balance	96	Week	1		
Receipt	200	Week	7		
Ending Balance	110	Week	16		

*These inventory balances are for the central hospital storeroom only. The receipt is a reasonable estimate of the current order quantity (Q).
+In gallons, not cases.

© Cengage Learning 2013

AP Images/Tom Strattman

Exhibit 12.17 *Hardy Hospital Aggregate Strike Disinfectant Weekly Demand as Measured by Hospital Requisitions*

Week	Strike+
1	31
2	27
3	1
4	12
5	11
6	8
7	4
8	15
9	15
10	16
11	10
12	9
13	8
14	5
15	10
16	4
Total	186
Mean	11.63
Standard Deviation	8.02
Cycle Service Level	97%

+Strike Disinfectant demand is quoted in gallons.

© Cengage Learning 2013

Discussion Questions

1. What are good estimates of order cost and inventory-holding cost? (State all assumptions and show all computations.)

2. What is the EOQ and reorder point for Strike Disinfectant given your answer to question 1?

3. Compute the total order and inventory-holding costs for a fixed-quantity system (FQS) and compare to the current order *Q*'s. Can you save money by adopting an FQS?

4. What are your final recommendations, including what you would recommend regarding regular and special orders, the state bidding system, and overall control of the university materials-management system? Explain the reasoning for your recommendations.

4LTR Press solutions are designed for today's learners through the continuous feedback of students like you. Tell us what you think about **OM4** and help us improve the learning experience for future students.

YOUR FEEDBACK MATTERS.

Complete the Speak Up survey in CourseMate at www.cengagebrain.com

 Follow us at www.facebook.com/4ltrpress

RESOURCE MANAGEMENT

ill Carr, the manager of a retail pharmacy in a high-growth suburban location exclaimed, "The corporate office just doesn't get it! They set a budget and staffing level that doesn't fit this location. I can't do the work and ensure accuracy of the patients' prescriptions when the corporate office gives me an annual budget for only two pharmacists and two pharmacy technicians". The store was part of a national pharmaceutical chain with over 1,000 locations in the United States. The pharmacy was open 16 hours a day on Monday through Saturday and 10 hours on Sunday. Carr established two shifts for these professionals but they were now exhausted. The most senior pharmacist had already threatened to quit if something wasn't done to correct the problem soon. Carr also had considered reducing the time the store was open, but that would hurt store revenue.

 learning outcomes

After studying this chapter you should be able to:

13-1 **Describe the overall frameworks for resource planning in both goods-producing and service-providing organizations.**

13-2 **Explain options for aggregate planning.**

13-3 **Describe how to evaluate level production and chase demand strategies for aggregate planning.**

13-4 **Describe ways to disaggregate aggregate plans using master production scheduling and material requirements planning.**

13-5 **Explain the concept and application of capacity requirements planning.**

What do you think?

Think about planning a party or some student related function. What resources do you need to pull it off, and how might you plan to ensure that you have everything at the right time and in the right quantity?

AP Photo/*The Tribune-Star*, Joseph C. Garza

Resource management *deals with the planning, execution, and control of all the resources that are used to produce goods or provide services in a value chain.* Resources include materials, equipment, facilities, information, technical knowledge and skills, and of course, people. Typical objectives of resource management are to (1) maximize profits and customer satisfaction; (2) minimize costs; or (3) for not-for-profit organizations such as government and churches, maximize benefits to their stakeholders.

The preceding example highlights the difficulty service managers face when corporate budgets constrain their ability to grow and build market share. Here, a high-growth suburb with many new homeowners has created a situation where demand exceeds capacity. The pharmacy is constrained by too few pharmacists and technicians and therefore is confronted with options such as overtime, reduced store hours, and higher chance of errors. Clearly, resources must be matched better to the needs of customers and the level of demand.

> **Resource management** deals with the planning, execution, and control of all the resources that are used to produce goods or provide services in a value chain.

Resources include materials, equipment, facilities, information, technical knowledge and skills, and, of course, people.

Thomas Niedermueller/Getty Images

▼ *Accuracy in filling patients' prescriptions depends in part on adequate staffing.*

13-1 Resource Planning Framework for Goods and Services

a generic framework for resource planning is shown in Exhibit 13.1. This framework is broken down into three basic levels. Level 1 represents aggregate planning. **Aggregate planning** *is the development of a long-term output and resource plan in aggregate units of measure.* Aggregate plans define output levels over a planning horizon of one to two years, usually in monthly or quarterly time buckets. They normally focus on product families or total capacity requirements rather than individual products or specific capacity allocations. Aggregate plans also help to define budget allocations and associated resource requirements.

> **Aggregate planning** is the development of a long-term output and resource plan in aggregate units of measure.
>
> **Disaggregation** is the process of translating aggregate plans into short-term operational plans that provide the basis for weekly and daily schedules and detailed resource requirements.

Okea/iStockphoto.com

Aggregate planning is driven by demand forecasts. High-level forecasts are often developed for aggregate groups of items (see the Mayo Clinic box). For instance, a consumer-products company like Procter & Gamble might produce laundry soap in a variety of sizes. However, it might forecast the total demand for the soap in dollars over some future time horizon, regardless of product size. Aggregate planning would then translate these forecasts into monthly or quarterly production plans.

In Exhibit 13.1, Level 2 planning is called disaggregation. **Disaggregation** *is the process of translating aggregate plans into short-term operational plans that provide the basis for weekly and daily schedules and detailed resource requirements.* To disaggregate means to break up or separate into more detailed pieces. Disaggregation specifies more-detailed plans for the creation of individual goods and services or the allocation of capacity to specific time periods. For goods-producing firms, disaggregation takes Level 1 aggregate planning decisions and breaks them down into such details as order sizes and schedules for individual subassemblies and resources by week and day.

To illustrate aggregate planning and disaggregation, a producer of ice cream might use long-term forecasts to determine the total number of gallons of ice cream to produce each quarter over the next two years. This projection provides the basis for determining how many employees and other

MAYO CLINIC: AGGREGATE PLANNING BEGINS WITH THE FORECAST!

To allocate clinical resources efficiently and effectively, the Mayo Clinic in Rochester, Minnesota, needs annual forecasts of outpatient visits per year per clinic by week. Forecasting model variables included trends in disease, average length of stay per clinic, seasonal cycles including holidays and summer vacations, historical demand per clinic, and some consideration for possible flu epidemics and other irregular events. To determine patient appointment demand, staff capacity, schedules, and budgets, managers used these forecasts. Physician's calendars use a 12-week rolling planning horizon to enable advanced patient bookings and give patients time to make travel plans. The three most accurate patient forecasts per clinic were reported to the 23 clinic managers for their review and a final model selection decision. It all begins with an accurate forecast of patient demand by clinic.[1]

Ingram Publishing/Newscom

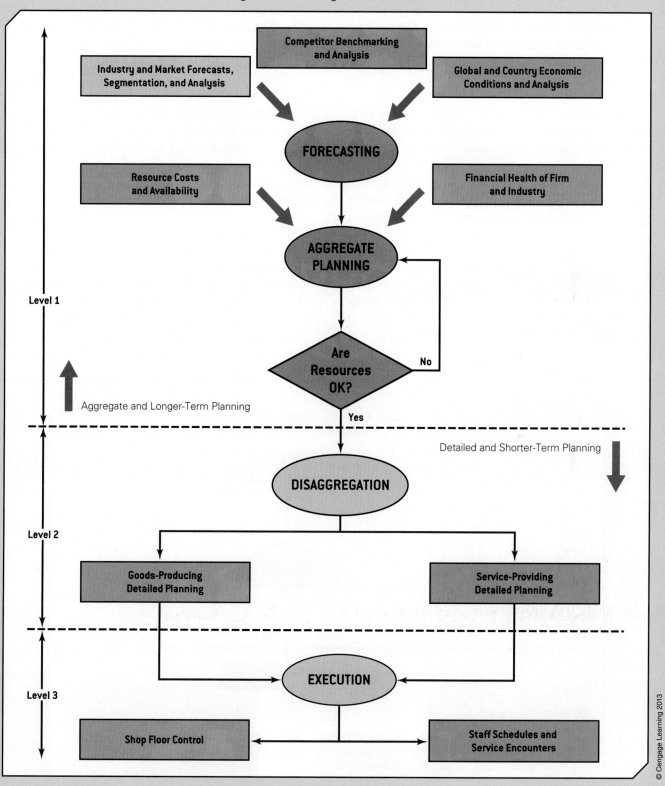

resources such as delivery trucks would be needed throughout the year to support this plan. Disaggregation of the plan would involve developing targets for the number of gallons of each flavor to produce (which would sum to the aggregate planned number for each quarter); purchasing requirements for cream, chocolate, and other ingredients; work schedules and overtime plans; and so on.

As another example, an airline might use long-term passenger forecasts to develop monthly aggregate plans based on the number of passenger miles each month. This aggregate plan would also specify the resource requirements in terms of total airline capacity, flight crews, and so on. Disaggregation would then create detailed point-to-point flight schedules, crew work assignments, food purchase plans, aircraft maintenance schedules, and other resource requirements.

Level 3 focuses on executing the detailed plans made at Level 2, creating detailed resource schedules and job sequences. **Execution** *refers to moving work from one workstation to another, assigning people to tasks, setting priorities for jobs, scheduling equipment, and controlling processes.* Level 3 planning and execution in manufacturing is sometimes called *shop floor control* and is addressed further in the next chapter.

Resource management for most service-providing organizations generally does not require as many intermediate levels of planning as it does for manufacturing. This is illustrated in Exhibit 13.2. Service firms frequently take their aggregate plans and disaggregate them down to the execution level as detailed front-line staff and resource schedules, job sequences, and service-encounter execution. There are several reasons for this:

Execution refers to moving work from one workstation to another, assigning people to tasks, setting priorities for jobs, scheduling equipment, and controlling processes.

- Most manufactured goods are discrete and are "built up" from many levels of raw materials, component parts, and subassemblies. However, many services, such as credit card authorizations, a telephone call, a movie, or arriving at a bank teller window, are instantaneous or continuous and are not discrete. Hence, there is no need for multiple levels of planning for some services.

Exhibit 13.2 *Two Levels of Disaggregation for Many Service Organizations*

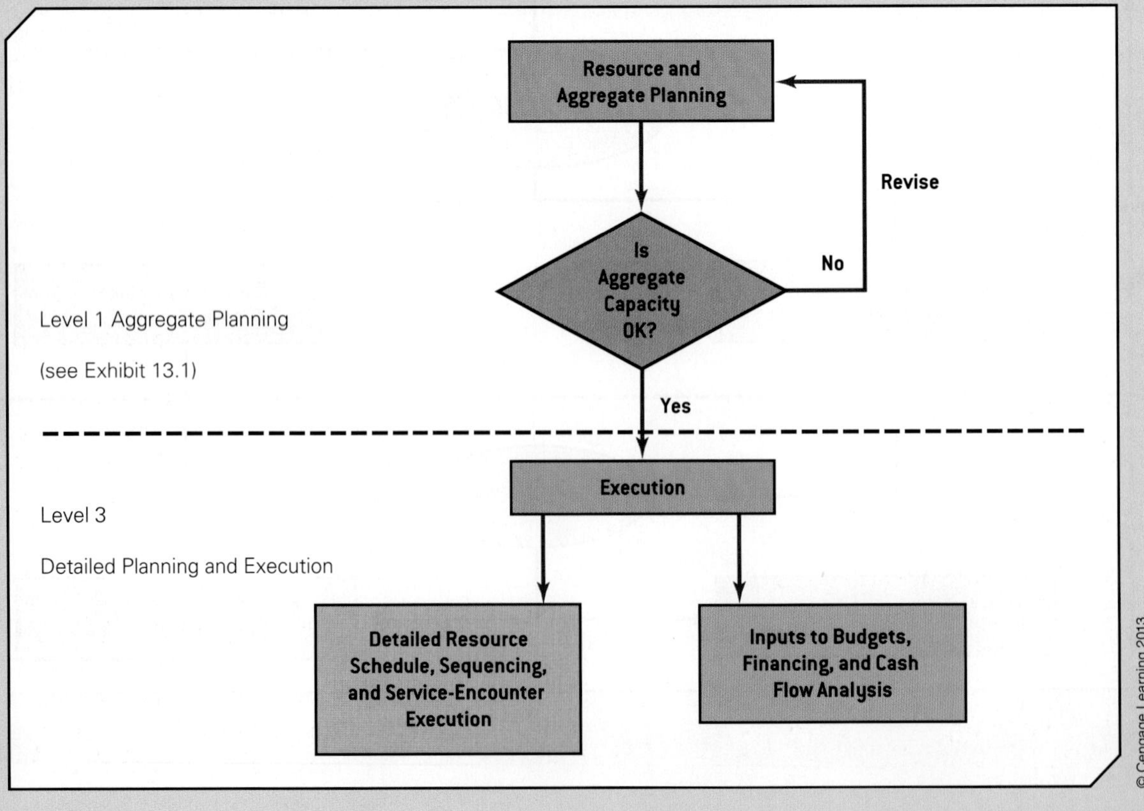

Level 1 Aggregate Planning

(see Exhibit 13.1)

Level 3

Detailed Planning and Execution

© Cengage Learning 2013

- Services do not have the advantage of physical inventory to buffer demand and supply uncertainty, so they must have sufficient service capacity on duty at the right time in the right place to provide good service to customers, making short-term demand forecasting and resource scheduling absolutely critical.

Some services, however, use the three levels of planning similar to manufacturing firms. For example, many service facilities, such as fast-food restaurants, need to be close to the customer, requiring them to be scattered within a geographical area. In these cases, the firm creates aggregate plans at the corporate level and then disaggregates them by region or district (geographically). This is similar to Level 2 intermediate planning in manufacturing. Regional and district offices further disaggregate these plans and budgets given the intermediate-level budgets and resource constraints. Level 3 resource planning and execution occurs at the store level, where local forecasts, food and other supply orders, staff work shifts and schedules, and service encounters are created.

13-2 Aggregate Planning Options

 anagers have a variety of options in developing aggregate plans in the face of fluctuating demand: workforce changes, inventory smoothing, and adjustments to facilities, equipment, and transportation. These are summarized in Exhibit 13.3. The choice of strategy depends on corporate policies, practical limitations, and cost factors.

Demand Management

Marketing strategies can be used to influence demand and to help create more feasible aggregate plans. For example, pricing and promotions can increase or decrease demand or shift it to other time periods. In services, recall that demand is time-dependent and there is no option to store the service. A hotel manager, for example, may advertise a low weekend rate to the local market in an attempt to increase short-term revenue and contribution to profit and overhead. Thus, demand management strategies are crucial for good aggregate planning and capacity utilization.

Production-Rate Changes

One means of increasing the output rate without changing existing resources is through planned overtime. Alternatively, hours can be reduced during slow periods through planned undertime. However, reduced overtime pay or sitting idle can seriously

Exhibit 13.3 *Example Aggregate Planning Variables and Revenue/Cost Implications*

Aggregate Planning Decision Options	Revenue/Cost Implications
Demand Management	
• Pricing strategies	• Increased revenue and lower unit costs
• Promotions and advertising	• Economies of scale
Production rate	
• Overtime	• Higher labor costs and premiums
• Undertime	• Idle time/lost opportunity costs
• Subcontracting	• Overhead costs and some loss of control
Workforce	
• Hiring	• Acquisition and training costs
• Layoffs	• Separation costs
• Full- and part-time labor mix	• Labor cost and productivity changes
Inventory	
• Anticipation (build) inventories	• Inventory-carrying costs
• Allow stockouts	• Lost sales (revenue) and customer loyalty costs
• Plan for backorders	• Backorder costs and customer waiting costs
Facilities, Equipment, and Transportation	
• Open/closed facilities and hours	• Variable and fixed costs
• Resource utilization	• Speed and reliability of service and delivery
• Carbon emissions	• Low- to high-utilization impact on unit costs
• Mode (truck, rail, ship, air)	• Inbound and outbound costs per mode
• Capacity and resource utilization	• Number of full or partial loads

© Cengage Learning 2013

Steve Cole/Digital Vision/Getty Images

affect employee morale. Subcontracting during periods of peak demand may also alter the output rate. This would probably not be a feasible alternative for some companies, but it is effective in industries that manufacture a large portion of their own parts, such as the machine-tool industry. When business is brisk, components can be subcontracted; when business is slow, the firm may act as a subcontractor to other industries that may be working at their capacity limit. In that way, a stable workforce is maintained.

Workforce Changes

Changing the size of the workforce is usually accomplished through hiring and layoffs. Both have disadvantages. Hiring additional labor usually results in higher costs for the personnel department and for training. Layoffs result in severance pay and additional unemployment insurance costs, as well as low employee morale.

In many industries, changing workforce levels is not a feasible alternative. In firms that consist primarily of jobs with low skill requirements, however, it may be cost-effective. The toy industry is a good example. Accurate forecasts for the winter holiday season cannot be made until wholesale buyers have placed orders, usually around midyear. Toy companies maintain a minimal number of employees until production is increased for the holidays. Then they hire a large number of part-time workers in order to operate at maximum capacity.

Inventory Changes

In planning for fluctuating demand, inventory is often built up during slack periods and held for peak periods. However, this increases carrying costs and may necessitate more warehouse space. A related strategy is to carry back orders or to tolerate lost sales during peak demand periods. But this may be unacceptable if profit margins are low and competition is high.

Facilities, Equipment, and Transportation

Facilities, equipment, and transportation generally represent long-term capital investments. Short-term changes in facilities and equipment are seldom used in traditional aggregate planning methods because of the capital costs involved. However, in some cases, it might be possible to rent additional equipment such as industrial forklifts, small machines, trucks, or warehouse space to accommodate periods of high demand.

13-3 Strategies for Aggregate Planning

To illustrate some of the major issues involved with aggregate planning, consider the situation faced by Golden Beverages, a producer of two major products—Old Fashioned and Foamy Delite root beers. The spreadsheet in Exhibit 13.4 shows a monthly aggregate demand forecast for the next year. Notice that demand is in barrels per month—an aggregate unit of measure for both products. Golden Beverages operates as a continuous flow factory and must plan future production for a demand forecast that fluctuates quite a bit over the year, with seasonal peaks in the summer and winter holiday season.

How should Golden Beverages plan its overall production for the next 12 months in the face of such fluctuating demand? Suppose that the company has a normal production capacity of 2,200 barrels per month and a current inventory of 1,000 barrels. If it produces at normal capacity each month, we have the aggregate plan shown in Exhibit 13.4. To calculate the ending inventory for each month, we use Equation 13.1.

Ending inventory = Beginning inventory
$$+ \text{Production} - \text{Demand} \quad [13.1]$$

For example, January is $1,000 + 2,200 - 1,500 = 1,700$ and February is $1,700 + 2,200 - 1,000 = 2,900$.

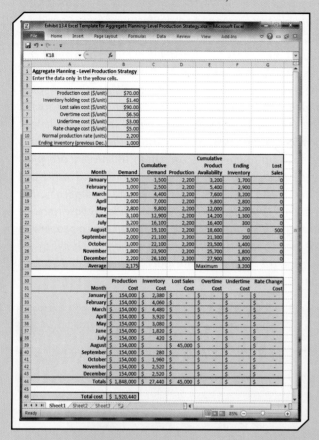

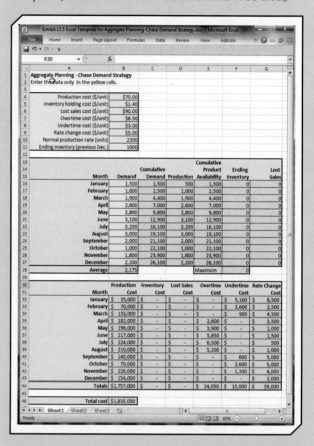

A **level production strategy** *plans for the same production rate in each time period.* The aggregate plan for Golden Beverages shown in Exhibit 13.4 is an example of a level production strategy with a constant production rate of 2,200 barrels per month. A level strategy avoids changes in the production rate, working within normal capacity restrictions. Labor and equipment schedules are stable and repetitive, making it easier to execute the plan. However, ending inventory builds up to a peak of 3,200 barrels in March and lost sales are 500 barrels in August due to inventory shortages.

An alternative to a level production strategy is to match production to demand every month. *A **chase demand strategy** sets the production rate equal to the demand in each time period.* While inventories will be reduced and lost sales will be eliminated, many production-rate changes will dramatically change resource levels (that is, the number of employees, machines, and so on). A chase demand strategy for Golden Beverages is shown in Exhibit 13.5 with a total cost of $1,835,050. As compared with the level production strategy documented in

A **level production strategy** plans for the same production rate in each time period.

A **chase demand strategy** sets the production rate equal to the demand in each time period.

Managers have a variety of options in developing aggregate plans when demand fluctuates.

NÉSTLÉ: AGGREGATE PLANNING FOR CANDY MANUFACTURING

Aggregate plans at a company that was acquired by Néstlé are focused on quality, personnel, capital, and customer service objectives.[2] It exports confectionery and grocery products (e.g., candy bars, boxed chocolates, cookies, and peanut butter) to over 120 countries.

One of its major brand items that has a highly seasonal demand is boxed chocolates. Boxed chocolates are produced in three types, with a total of nine distinct end items: Black Magic, in 2-lb., 1½-lb., 1-lb., and ½-lb. boxes; Rendezvous, in 14-oz. box; and Dairy Box, in the same four sizes as Black Magic. Forecasting is accomplished by dividing the year into 13 periods of four weeks each. Sales planning provides an item forecast, by period, for the full 13 periods. This estimate is updated every four weeks, reflecting the latest information on available inventories and estimated sales for the next 13 periods.

Aggregate planning is performed by first converting all items to a poundage figure. The planning task is to calculate levels of production that will best meet the quality, personnel, capital, and customer service restrictions. It is a stated company policy and practice to maintain a stable workforce. Short-term capacity can be increased with overtime and/or with part-time employees. The amount of inventory investment has become a major concern, and inventory levels must be kept low to meet restrictions on capital investment.

How Can We Use Aggregate Planning for a Tennis Club?

Services face many of the same issues in planning and managing resources as do manufacturing firms. Consider a 145-acre large oceanfront resort located in Myrtle Beach, South Carolina, that is owned and operated by a major corporation. The tennis club and four courts are located next to the Sport & Health Club. All courts are lighted for night play, and there is no more room to build additional tennis courts. The demand for tennis lessons is highly seasonal, with peak demand in June, July, and August. In the summer months when resort rooms are 98 percent to 100 percent occupied, requests for lesson time far exceed capacity, and owner and hotel guest complaints were increasing dramatically. The manager of the health club might consider a chase resource strategy with a base full-time tennis staff of two people and the use of part-time staff for much of the year. Or, she might consider a level strategy with four full-time staff and no part-time staff.

Kim Steele/Photodisc/Getty Images

Exhibit 13.4, the cost of the chase demand strategy is $1,920,440 − 1,835,050 = $85,390 less. Notice that no inventory carrying or lost sales costs are incurred, but substantial overtime, undertime, and rate-change costs are required.

Given the large number of aggregate planning decision variables with an infinite number of possible levels and combinations, countless alternative aggregate plans could be developed. Good solutions using spreadsheets can often be found by trial-and-error approaches. The Excel Aggregate Planning template allows you to experiment with production levels using trial-and-error methods to identify good options.

13-4 Disaggregation in Manufacturing

for manufacturing firms, Exhibit 13.6 shows a typical system for disaggregating aggregate plans into executable operations plans. Three important techniques in this process are master production scheduling (MPS), materials requirements planning (MRP), and capacity requirements planning (CRP).

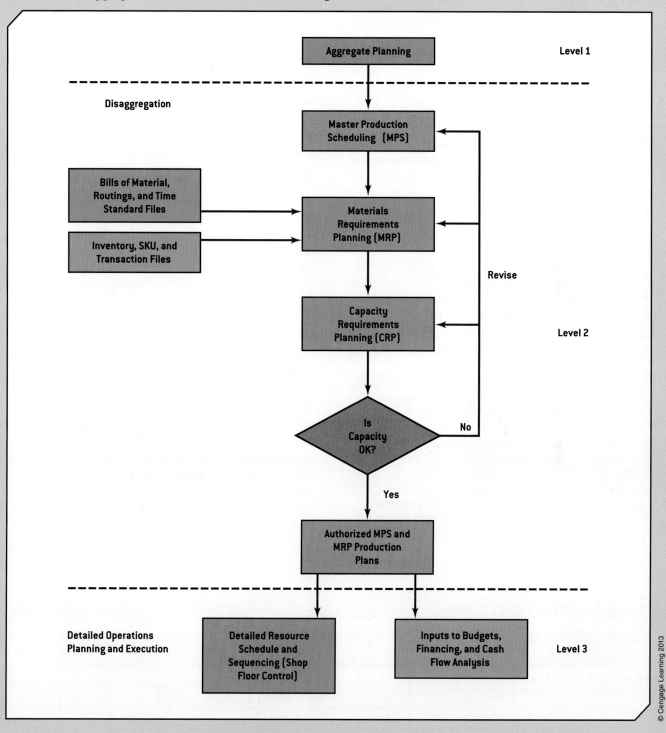

13-4a Master Production Scheduling

A **master production schedule (MPS)** *is a statement of how many finished items are to be produced and when they are to be produced.* An example of a portion of an MPS with an eight-week planning horizon is shown in Exhibit 13.7. Typically, the master schedule is developed for weekly time periods over a 6- to 12-month horizon. The purpose of the master schedule is to translate the aggregate plan into a separate plan for individual finished goods. It also provides a means for evaluating alternative schedules in terms of capacity requirements, provides input to the MRP system, and helps managers generate priorities for scheduling by setting due dates for the production of individual items.

For make-to-order industries, order backlogs provide the needed customer-demand information; thus the known customer orders (called *firm orders*) determine the MPS. In some industries where a few basic subassemblies and components are assembled in many different combinations to produce a large variety of end

A **master production schedule (MPS)** is a statement of how many finished items are to be produced and when they are to be produced.

A **final assembly schedule (FAS)** defines the quantity and timing for assembling subassemblies and component parts into a final finished good.

Materials requirements planning (MRP) is a forward-looking, demand-based approach for planning the production of manufactured goods and ordering materials and components to minimize unnecessary inventories and reduce costs.

products, the MPS is usually developed for the basic subassemblies and not for the ultimate finished goods. Therefore, a different plan and schedule are needed to assemble the final finished good. *A* **final assembly schedule (FAS)** *defines the quantity and timing for assembling subassemblies and component parts into a final finished good.*

13-4b Materials Requirements Planning

To produce a finished product, many individual parts or subassemblies must be manufactured or purchased and then assembled together. Fixed-order-quantity and fixed-period inventory systems (see Chapter 12) were used long ago for planning materials in manufacturing environments. However, these systems did not capture the dependent relationships between the demand for finished goods and their raw materials, components, and subassemblies. This insight led to the development of materials requirements planning.

Materials requirements planning (MRP) *is a forward-looking, demand-based approach for planning the production of manufactured goods and ordering materials and components to minimize unnecessary inventories and reduce costs.* MRP projects the requirements for the individual parts or subassemblies based on the demand for the finished goods as specified by the MPS. The primary output of an MRP system is a time-phased report that gives (1) the purchasing department a schedule for obtaining raw materials and purchased parts, (2) the production managers a detailed schedule for manufacturing the product and controlling manufacturing

Exhibit 13.7 *Eight-Week Master Production Schedule Example*

		\multicolumn{8}{c}{Week}	
		1	2	3	4	5	6	7	8
	Model A		200		200		350			← MPS Planned Quantities
	Model B	150	100		190			120		
	•	•	•	•	•	•	•	•	•
	•	•	•	•	•	•	•	•	•
	•	•	•	•	•	•	•	•	•
Totals Aggregate production plans (units)	X			75		75	75		60
		500	800	350	600	280	750	420	300

© Cengage Learning 2013

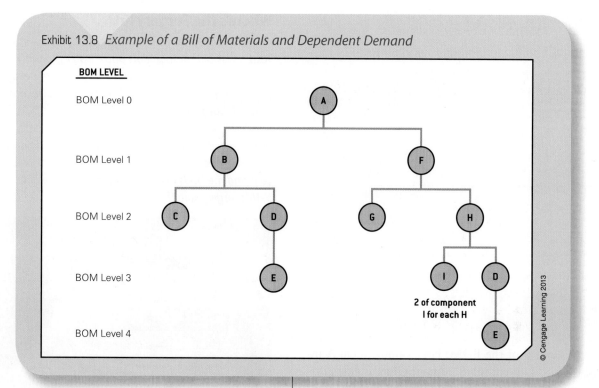

Exhibit 13.8 *Example of a Bill of Materials and Dependent Demand*

BOM LEVEL

BOM Level 0

BOM Level 1

BOM Level 2

BOM Level 3

**2 of component
I for each H**

BOM Level 4

© Cengage Learning 2013

inventories, and (3) accounting and financial functions production information that drives cash flow, budgets, and financial needs.

MRP depends on understanding three basic concepts: (1) the concept of dependent demand, (2) the concept of time phasing, and (3) lot sizing to gain economies of scale.

Dependent demand *is demand that is directly related to the demand of other SKUs and can be calculated without needing to be forecasted.* The concept of dependent demand is best understood by examining the bill of materials. A *bill of materials (BOM)* defines the hierarchical relationships between all items that comprise a finished good, such as subassemblies, purchased parts, and manufactured in-house parts. Some firms call the BOM the product structure. A BOM may also define standard times and alternative routings for each item.

For labor-intensive services, the analogy to the BOM is a bill of labor (BOL). **A bill of labor (BOL)** *is a*

hierarchical record analogous to a BOM that defines labor inputs necessary to create a good or service. For example, a BOL for surgery includes the doctors and supporting surgery technicians and nurses. A broader concept is a *bill of resources (BOR)*, where the labor, information (e.g., X rays, blood tests, and so on), equipment, instruments, and parts are all defined in a BOM format to support each specific type of surgery. Exhibit 13.8 shows the structure of a typical BOM.

End items *are finished goods scheduled in the MPS or FAS that must be forecasted.* These are the

MRP depends on understanding three basic concepts: (1) the concept of dependent demand, (2) the concept of time phasing, and (3) lot sizing to gain economies of scale.

Exhibit 13.9 *Dependent Demand Calculations*

Item	On-Hand Inventory	Dependent Demand Calculations
A	0	100 − 0 = 100
B	33	100 − 33 = 67
C	12	67 − 12 = 55
D	47	67 + 50 − 47 = 70
E	10	70 − 10 = 60
F	20	100 − 20 = 80
G	15	80 − 15 = 65
H	30	80 − 30 = 50
I	7	50 × 2 − 7 = 93

© Cengage Learning 2013

Where's the Surgery Kit?

A 374-bed hospital with nine operating rooms in Houston, Texas, uses bills of materials and master production scheduling to plan surgeries and the surgical kits needed for a seven-day planning horizon. Bills of labor (BOL) are used to schedule surgeons, nurses, and orderlies. The bill of materials (BOM) file contains the materials, instruments, and supplies needed for various surgical procedures. End items are specific surgery procedures with a lot size of one. The concept and methods of dependent demand are alive and well in this surgery suite![3]

Adam Radosavljevic/Shutterstock.com

items at Level 0 of the BOM. For example, item A in Exhibit 13.8 is an end item. *A **parent item** is manufactured from one or more components.* Items A, B, D, F, and H are parents in Exhibit 13.8. End items are composed of components and subassemblies. **Components** *are any item (raw materials, manufactured parts, purchased parts) other than an end item that goes into a higher-level parent item(s).* Items B, C, D, E, F, G, H, and I are all components in the BOM in Exhibit 13.8. *A **subassembly** always has at least one immediate parent and also has at least one immediate component.* Subassemblies (sometimes called *intermediate items*) reside in the middle of the BOM; items B, D, F, and H in Exhibit 13.8 are examples. BOMs for simple assemblies might be flat, having only two or three levels, whereas more complex BOMs may have up to 15 levels.

To understand the nature of dependent demand, assume that we wish to produce 100 units of end item A in Exhibit 13.8. Exhibit 13.9 shows the calculations for each of the items in the BOM, taking into account on-hand inventory. For each unit of A, we need one unit of items B and F. We have 33 units on hand for subassembly B, so we need to make only 100 − 33 = 67 units of B. Similarly, we have 20 units of F available and

A **parent item** is manufactured from one or more components.

Components are any item (raw materials, manufactured parts, purchased parts) other than an end item that goes into a higher-level parent item(s).

A **subassembly** always has at least one immediate parent and also has at least one immediate component.

therefore require an additional 100 − 20 = 80 units. Next, at Level 2 of the BOM, for each unit of B, we need one unit of components C and D; and for each F, we need one unit of components G and H. Because we need to produce only an additional 67 units of B, and we have 12 units of component C on hand, we need to produce an additional 67 − 12 = 55 units of C.

You should check the remaining calculations in Exhibit 13.9. Note that item D is a common subassembly that is used in both subassemblies B and H. Thus, we must include the requirements of item B (67 units) and item H (50 units) in computing the number of Ds to produce: 67 + 50 − 47 = 70 units.

Dependent demand also occurs in service businesses, but few managers recognize it. Many service organizations such as restaurants and retail stores offer repeatable and highly structured services and have high goods content of 50 percent or more. Therefore, the logic of dependent demand can be used to plan the goods-content portion of the customer benefit package. For example, meals in a restaurant can be thought of as end items. The service required to assemble an order can be defined in terms of the bill of materials (BOM) and lead times.

13-4c Time Phasing and Lot Sizing in MRP

Although the dependent demand calculations as described in the previous section provide the number of components or subassemblies needed in the BOM, they do not specify when orders should be placed or how much should be ordered. Because of the hierarchy of the BOM, there is no reason to order something until it is required to produce a parent item. Thus, all dependent demand requirements do not need to be ordered at the same time, but rather are *time-phased* as necessary. In addition, orders might be consolidated to take advantage of ordering economies of scale—this is called *lot sizing*. **MRP explosion** *is the process of using the logic of dependent demand to calculate the quantity and timing of orders for all subassemblies and components that go into and support the production of the end item(s).* In this section we will illustrate the process of time phasing.

Time buckets *are the time-period size used in the MRP explosion process and usually are one week in length.* Although small buckets such as one day are good for scheduling production over a short time horizon, they may be too precise for longer-range planning. Thus, larger buckets such as months are often used as the planning horizon gets longer. We assume that all time buckets are one week in length.

An MRP record consists of the following:

- **Gross requirements (GR)** *are the total demand for an item derived from all of its parents.* This is the quantity of the component needed to support production at the next-higher level of assembly. Gross requirements can also include maintenance, repair, and spare-part components that are added to the dependent demand requirements.

- **Scheduled or planned receipts (S/PR)** *are orders that are due or planned to be delivered.* A scheduled receipt was released to the vendor or shop in a previous time period and now shows up as a scheduled receipt. (In some of our examples we assume, for simplicity, that all scheduled receipts are zero.) A planned order receipt is defined later. If the order is for an outside vendor, it is a *purchase order*. If the order is produced in-house, it is a *shop or manufactured order.*

- *A* **planned order receipt (PORec)** *specifies the quantity and time an order is to be received.* When the order arrives it is recorded, checked into inventory, and available for use. It is assumed to be available for use at the beginning of the period.

- *A* **planned order release (PORel)** *specifies the planned quantity and time an order is to be released to the factory or a supplier.* It is a planned order receipt offset by the item's lead time. Planned order releases generate the gross requirements for all components in the MRP logic.

- **Projected on-hand inventory (POH)** *is the expected amount of inventory on hand at the beginning of the time period considering on-hand inventory from the previous period plus scheduled receipts or planned order receipts minus the gross requirements.* The formula for computing the projected on-hand inventory is defined by Equation 13.2 as follows:

$$\text{Projected on-hand in period } t \; (\text{POH}_t) = \text{On-hand inventory in period } t-1 \; (\text{OH}_{t-1})$$
$$+ \; \text{Scheduled or planned receipts in period } t \; (\text{S/PR}_t) - \text{Gross requirements in period } t \; (\text{GR}_t)$$

or

$$\text{POH}_t = \text{OH}_{t-1} + \text{S/PR}_t - \text{GR}_t \qquad [13.2]$$

Lot sizing *is the process of determining the appropriate amount and timing of ordering to reduce costs.* It can be uneconomical to set up a new production run or place a purchase order for the demand in each time bucket. Instead, it is usually better to aggregate orders and achieve economies of scale. Many different lot sizing rules have been proposed. Some are simple heuristic rules,

---

MRP explosion is the process of using the logic of dependent demand to calculate the quantity and timing of orders for all subassemblies and components that go into and support the production of the end item(s).

Time buckets are the time-period size used in the MRP explosion process and usually are one week in length.

Gross requirements (GR) are the total demand for an item derived from all of its parents.

Scheduled or planned receipts (S/PR) are orders that are due or planned to be delivered.

A planned order receipt (PORec) specifies the quantity and time an order is to be received.

A planned order release (PORel) specifies the planned quantity and time an order is to be released to the factory or a supplier.

Projected on-hand inventory (POH) is the expected amount of inventory on hand at the beginning of the time period considering on-hand inventory from the previous period plus scheduled receipts or planned order receipts minus the gross requirements.

Lot sizing is the process of determining the appropriate amount and timing of ordering to reduce costs.

Exhibit 13.10 Bill of Materials

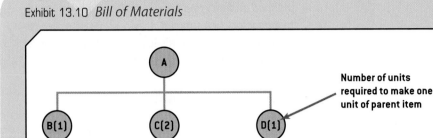

Number of units required to make one unit of parent item

© Cengage Learning 2013

Exhibit 13.11 Item Inventory File

Data category	Item B	Item C	Item D
Lead time (weeks)	1	2	1
Beginning (on-hand) inventory	100	10	40
Scheduled receipts	none	200 (week 2)	50 (week 3)

© Cengage Learning 2013

whereas others seek to find the best economic trade-off between the setup costs associated with production and the holding costs of carrying inventory. We discuss three common lot sizing methods for MRP—lot-for-lot (LFL), fixed-order quantity (FOQ), and periodic-order quantity (POQ).

To illustrate these, we will consider the production of a simple product (A) whose bill of materials and inventory records are given in Exhibits 13.10 and 13.11. Note that item B is a common component for both items A and C; therefore, we cannot compute the gross requirements for item B until the planned order releases for items A and C have been determined.

Suppose that the MPS calls for 150 units of product A to be completed in week 4; 300 units in week 5; 50 units in week 6; and 200 units in week 7. We assume that the lead time is one week. The MPS in Exhibit 13.12 shows the demand for product A. The planned order releases are offset by one week to account for the lead time.

> An ordering schedule that covers the gross requirements for each week is called **lot-for-lot (LFL)**.

First consider item C. The MRP explosion is given in Exhibit 13.13. Notice from the BOM in Exhibit 13.10 that two units of item C are needed to produce one unit of end item A. Therefore, the gross requirements for item C in Exhibit 13.13 are directly derived from the planned order releases in the MPS in Exhibit 13.12 (that is, $150 \times 2 = 300$ units in period 3; $300 \times 2 = 600$ units in period 4; and so on).

Lot-for-Lot Rule

*An ordering schedule that covers the gross requirements for each week is called **lot-for-lot (LFL)**.* In other words, we simply place orders each week to ensure that enough inventory is available to prevent shortages. If LFL is used for all dependent items, it clearly shows the true nature of dependent demand. Notice that LFL requires four planned orders and the average inventory during this planning horizon is $10 + 210 + 0 + 0 + 0 + 0 + 0 = 220/7 = 31.4$ units/week. The LFL rule minimizes the amount of inventory that needs to be carried; however, it ignores the costs associated with purchase orders or production setups. Thus, this rule is best applied when inventory-carrying costs are high and setup/order costs are low.

The projected on-hand quantity assumes the receipt of the planned order or scheduled receipt (S/PR_t) and is computed using Equation 13.2. LFL always tries to drive inventory levels to zero. We must compute the planned order release for item C before we can do the same for item B.

For example, using Equation 13.2 we compute the following:

$$POH_1 = OH_0 + S/PR_1 - GR_1 = 10 + 0 - 0 = 10$$
$$POH_2 = OH_1 + S/PR_2 - GR_2 = 10 + \blacksquare - 0 = 210$$
$$POH_3 = OH_2 + S/PR_3 - GR_3 = 210 + 90 - 300 = 0$$
$$POH_4 = OH_3 + S/PR_4 - GR_4 = 0 + 600 - 600 = 0$$
$$POH_5 = OH_4 + S/PR_5 - GR_5 = 0 + 100 - 100 = 0$$
$$POH_6 = OH_5 + S/PR_6 - GR_6 = 0 + 400 - 400 = 0$$
$$POH_7 = OH_6 + S/PR_7 - GR_7 = 0 + 0 - 0 = 0$$

Exhibit 13.12 Example MPS

MPS	Lead time = 1 week for assembly						
Week	1	2	3	4	5	6	7
Product A—end item	0	0	0	150	300	50	200
Planned order release	0	0	150	300	50	200	0

© Cengage Learning 2013

Exhibit 13.13 MRP Record for Item C Using the Lot-for-Lot (LFL) Rule

Item C (two units of C are needed for one unit of A) Description		Lot size: LFL Lead time: 2 weeks						
Week		1	2	3	4	5	6	7
Gross requirements		0	0	300	600	100	400	0
Scheduled receipts			800					
Projected OH inventory	10	10	210	0	0	0	0	0
Planned order receipts		0	0	90	600	100	400	0
Planned order releases		90	600	100	400			

© Cengage Learning 2013

The planned order releases in Exhibit 13.13 are planned but have not yet been released. *The **action bucket** is the current time period.* When a planned order release reaches the action bucket, analysts evaluate the situation and release the order to the appropriate provider—supplier or in-house work center. In Exhibit 13.13, for example, only the planned order of 90 units of item C is in the action bucket for current time period of week 1. Therefore, the planned order needs to be released in week 1 and will show up the next week in the scheduled receipts row. Clearly, the total number of MRP calculations is enormous in multiproduct situations with many components, making a computer essential. Action notices are usually computer-generated and provide a variety of information to help inventory planners make decisions about order releases delaying scheduled receipts, and expediting when necessary.

Fixed-Order-Quantity Rule

*The **fixed-order-quantity (FOQ)** rule uses a fixed order size for every order or production run.* This is similar to the fixed-order-quantity approach for independent demand items. The FOQ can be a standard-size container or pallet load or determined economically using the economic order quantity formula in Chapter 12. In the rare case where the FOQ does not cover the gross requirements, the order size is increased to equal the larger quantity, and FOQ defaults to LFL.

The rationale for the FOQ approach is that large lot sizes result in fewer orders and setups and therefore reduce the costs associated with ordering and setup. This allows the firm to take advantage of price breaks by suppliers and production economies of scale, and avoid less-than-truckload shipments (which are usually more expensive than full truckloads). However, this creates larger average inventory levels that must be held at a cost, and it can distort the true dependent demand gross requirements for lower-level components. Thus, the FOQ model is best applied when inventory-carrying costs are low and setup/order costs are high.

> The **action bucket** is the current time period.
>
> The **fixed-order-quantity (FOQ)** rule uses a fixed order size for every order or production run.

Exhibit 13.14 *Item B Fixed-Order-Quantity (FOQ) Lot Sizing and MRP Record*

Item B Description						Lot size: 800 units Lead time: 1 week		
Week		1	2	3	4	5	6	7
Gross requirements		90	600	250	700	50	200	0
Scheduled receipts								
Projected OH inventory	100	10	210	760	60	10	610	610
Planned order receipts		0	800	800	0	0	800	0
Planned order releases		800	800			800		

© Cengage Learning 2013

We will illustrate this rule for item B in Exhibit 13.10. Exhibit 13.14 shows the MRP explosion. Note that component part commonality increases the dependent demand requirements, as shown in the gross requirements row. For example, the 700-unit gross requirement in period 4 is due to the planned order release in the MPS for 300 units of item A in week 4 (see Exhibit 13.12) plus the planned order release for parent item C of 400 units in week 4 (see Exhibit 13.13).

Suppose that the FOQ is chosen using the EOQ as $\sqrt{2 \times 10,000 \text{ units} \times 864 / \$1} = \sqrt{640,000} = 800$ units Using Equation 13.2, we compute the following projected on-hand inventories for each period:

$$POH_1 = OH_0 + S/PR_1 - GR_1 = 100 + 0 - 90 = 10$$
$$POH_2 = OH_1 + S/PR_2 - GR_2 = 10 + 800 - 600 = 10$$
$$POH_3 = OH_2 + S/PR_3 - GR_3 = 210 + 800 - 250 = 760$$
$$POH_4 = OH_3 + S/PR_4 - GR_4 = 760 + 0 - 700 = 60$$
$$POH_5 = OH_4 + S/PR_5 - GR_5 = 60 + 0 - 50 = 10$$
$$POH_6 = OH_5 + S/PR_6 - GR_6 = 10 + 800 - 200 = 610$$
$$POH_7 = OH_6 + S/PR_7 - GR_7 = 610 + 0 - 0 = 610$$

The **periodic-order quantity (POQ)** orders a quantity equal to the gross requirement quantity in one or more predetermined time periods minus the projected on-hand quantity of the previous time period.

Notice that FOQ results in three planned orders, and an average inventory is 10 + 210 + 760 + 60 + 10 + 610 + 610 = 2,270/7 = 324.3 units/week. To understand the difference with LFL, we encourage you to compare these results to the LFL approach.

Periodic-Order-Quantity Rule

The **periodic-order quantity (POQ)** *orders a quantity equal to the gross requirement quantity in one or more predetermined time periods minus the projected on-hand quantity of the previous time period.* For example a POQ of two weeks orders exactly enough to cover demand during a two-week period, and therefore may result in a different quantity every order cycle. The POQ might be selected judgmentally—for example, "order every 10 days"—or be determined using an economic time interval, which is the EOQ divided by annual demand (D). For example, if EOQ/D = 0.1 of a year, and assuming 250 working days per year, then POQ = 25 days, or about every five weeks. A POQ for a one-week time period is equivalent to LFL. Using this rule, the projected on-hand inventory will equal zero at the end of the POQ time interval.

We illustrate this rule for item D using a POQ = 2 weeks. The result is shown in Exhibit 13.15. Using Equation 13.2, we compute the following:

Some MRP users only use the simple LFL rule; others apply other lot sizing approaches to take advantage of economies of scale and reduce costs.

Exhibit 13.15 *Item D Fixed-Period-Quantity (POQ) Lot Sizing and MRP Record*

Item D Description						Lot size: POQ = 2 weeks Lead time: 1 week		
Week		1	2	3	4	5	6	7
Gross requirements				150	300	50	200	
Scheduled receipts				50				
Projected OH inventory	40	40	40	300	0	200	0	0
Planned order receipts		0	0	360	0	250	0	0
Planned order releases			360		250			

© Cengage Learning 2013

$POH_1 = OH_0 + S/PR_1 - GR_1 = 40 + 0 - 0 = 40$

$POH_2 = OH_1 + S/PR_2 - GR_2 = 40 + 0 - 0 = 40$

$POH_3 = OH_2 + S/PR_3 - GR_3 = 40 + 50 + 360 - 150$
$\quad = 300$

$POH_4 = OH_3 + S/PR_4 - GR_4 = 300 + 0 - 300 = 0$

$POH_5 = OH_4 + S/PR_5 - GR_5 = 0 + 250 - 50 = 200$

$POH_6 = OH_5 + S/PR_6 - GR_6 = 200 + 0 - 200 = 0$

$POH_7 = OH_6 + S/PR_7 - GR_7 = 0 + 0 - 0 = 0$

The first time that POH becomes negative "without" a planned order receipt is in week 3 (40 + 50 − 150 = −60). Therefore, if we order 60 units to cover week 3 requirements plus 300 units to cover week 4 requirements, we have an order quantity of 360 units. The next time the POH is negative "without" a planned order receipt is week 5 (0 + 0 − 50 = −50). This requires us to order 50 units to cover week 5 requirements plus 200 units to cover week 6 requirements. For this example, POQ results in two planned orders of 360 and 250 units. The average inventory is 40 + 40 + 300 + 0 + 200 + 0 + 0 = 580/7 = 82.9 units/week.

The POQ approach results in moderate average inventory levels compared to FOQ because it matches order quantities to time buckets. Furthermore, it is easy to implement because inventory levels can be reviewed according to a fixed schedule. However, POQ creates high average inventory levels if the POQ becomes too long, and it can distort true dependent demand gross requirements for lower-level components. An economic-based POQ model is best applied when inventory-carrying costs and setup/order costs are moderate.

As you see, lot sizing rules affect not only the planned order releases for the particular item under consideration but also the gross requirements of all lower-level component items. Some MRP users only use the simple LFL rule; others apply other lot sizing approaches to take advantage of economies of scale and reduce costs. Exhibit 13.16 summarizes the MRP explosion for the BOM in Exhibit 13.10.

13-5 Capacity Requirements Planning

Capacity requirements planning (CRP) *is the process of determining the amount of labor and machine resources required to accomplish the tasks of production on a more detailed level, taking into account all component parts and end items in the materials plan.* For example, in anticipation of a big demand for pizzas on Super Bowl Sunday, one would have to ensure that sufficient capacity for dough making, pizza preparation, and delivery is available to handle the forecasted demand.

Capacity requirements are computed by multiplying the number of units scheduled for production at a work center by the unit resource requirements and then adding in the setup time. These requirements are then summarized by time period and work center. To

Capacity requirements planning (CRP) is the process of determining the amount of labor and machine resources required to accomplish the tasks of production on a more detailed level, taking into account all component parts and end items in the materials plan.

MPS

Lead time = 1 week for assembly

Week		1	2	3	4	5	6	7
Product A—end item		0	0	0	150	300	50	200
Planned order releases		0	0	150	300	50	200	0

Item C (two units of C are needed for one unit of A)
Description

Lot size: LFL
Lead time: 2 weeks

Week		1	2	3	4	5	6	7
Gross requirements		0	0	300	600	100	400	0
Scheduled receipts			200					
Projected OH inventory	10	10	210	0	0	0	0	0
Planned order receipts		0	0	90	600	100	400	0
Planned order releases		90	600	100	400			

Item B
Description

Lot size: 800 units
Lead time: 1 week

Week		1	2	3	4	5	6	7
Gross requirements		90	600	250	700	50	200	0
Scheduled receipts								
Projected OH inventory	100	10	210	760	60	10	610	610
Planned order receipts		0	800	800	0	0	800	0
Planned order releases		800	800			800		

Item D
Description

Lot size: POQ = 2 weeks
Lead time: 1 week

Week		1	2	3	4	5	6	7
Gross requirements				150	300	50	200	
Scheduled receipts				50				
Projected OH inventory	40	40	40	300	0	200	0	0
Planned order receipts		0	0	360	0	250	0	0
Planned order releases			360		250			

illustrate CRP calculations, suppose the planned order releases for a component are as follows:

Time period	1	2	3	4
Planned order release	30	20	40	40

Assume the component requires 1.10 hours of labor per unit in Work Center D and 1.5 hours of setup time. We can use Equation 10.2 from Chapter 10 to compute the total hours required (called *work center load*) on Work Center D:

Capacity required (C_i) = Setup time (S_i) + [Processing time (P_i) × Order size (Q_i)]

The capacity requirement in period 1 is 1.5 hours + (1.10 hours/unit)(30 units) = 34.5 hours. Similarly, in period 2 we have 1.5 hours + (1.10 hours/unit) (30 units) = 23.5 hours, and in periods 3 and 4 we have 1.5 hours + (1.10 hours/unit)(40 units) + 45.5 hours. The total load on Work Center D is 149 hours during these 4 weeks, or 37.25 hours per week if averaged.

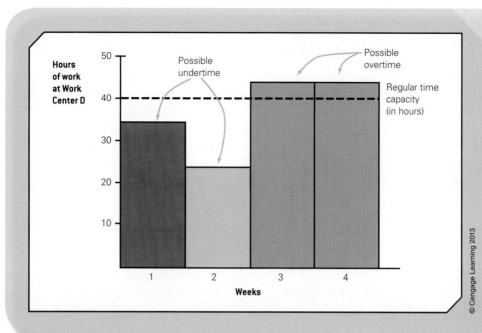

Exhibit 13.17 *Work Center D Example Load Report*

© Cengage Learning 2013

Radius Images/Photolibrary

Such information is usually provided in a *work center load report*, as illustrated in Exhibit 13.17.

If sufficient capacity is not available, decisions must be made about overtime, transfer of personnel between departments, subcontracting, and so on. The master production schedule may also have to be revised to meet available capacity by shifting certain end items to different time periods or changing the order quantities. For example, the workload in Exhibit 13.17 in periods 3 and 4 could be scheduled to period 2 to fill the idle time and avoid overtime in periods 3 and 4. However, additional inventory-carrying costs would be incurred. So, as you see, leveling out work center load involves many cost trade-offs. This closed-loop, iterative process provides a realistic deployment of the master schedule to the shop floor.

Discussion Questions

1. Identify a goods-producing or service-providing organization and discuss how it might make aggregate planning decisions using the variables described in Exhibit 13.3.

2. Provide an argument for or against adopting a chase strategy for a major airline call center.

3. Discuss some examples of real-life organizations that use demand management as a resource planning strategy.

4. How do the concepts of master production scheduling and material requirements planning translate to a service organization? Provide an example.

5. How should managers choose an appropriate lot sizing rule? Should it be chosen strictly on an economic basis, or should intangible factors be considered. Why?

Problems and Activities

Note: an asterisk denotes problems for which an Excel spreadsheet template on the CourseMate Web site may be used.

1. Interview a production manager at a nearby goods-producing company to determine how the company plans its production for fluctuating demand. What approaches does the company use?

2. Research and write a short paper (two pages maximum) describing how organizations use the aggregate planning options depicted in Exhibit 13.3.

3. The forecasted demand for fudge for the next four months is 140, 160, 90, and 70 pounds.

   a. What is the recommended production rate if a level strategy is adopted with no backorders or stockouts? What is the ending inventory for month 4 under this plan?

   b. What is the level production rate with no ending inventory in month 4?

4. *Use the Excel Aggregate Planning template to try to find the best production strategy for the Golden Beverages example to minimize the total cost. Note that the chase demand strategy has a total cost of $1,835,050, so you should seek a solution that has a lower cost.

5. *Chapman Pharmaceuticals, a large manufacturer of drugs, has this aggregate demand forecast for a liquid cold medicine:

Month	J	F	M	A	M	J	J	A	S	O	N	D
Liters (1,000s)	180	120	75	60	20	15	15	15	30	70	90	150

The firm has a capacity of 80,000 liters per month and the initial inventory is 120,000 liters. Inventory-holding costs are $25 per 1,000 liters per month, and regular-time production costs are $350 per 1,000 liters. Overtime costs an additional 20 percent, and undertime costs an additional 12 percent. Assume that there are no lost sales or rate change costs. Compute the costs of level and chase demand production plans.

6. *The Westerbeck Company manufactures several models of automatic washers and dryers. The projected requirements over the next year for its washers are as follows:

Month	J	F	M	A	M	J	J	A	S	O	N	D
Requirement	800	1,030	810	900	950	1,340	1,100	1,210	600	580	890	1,000

Current inventory is 100 units. Current capacity is 960 units per month. The average salary of production workers is $1,300 per month. Material costs $120/unit. Each production worker accounts for 30 units per month. Overtime is paid at time and a half. Any increase or decrease in the production rate costs $50/unit for tooling, setup, and line changes. This does not apply, however, to overtime. Inventory-holding costs are $25 per unit per month. Lost sales are valued at $75 per unit. Compare the costs of level and chase demand production plans.

7. The Silver Star Bicycle Company will be manufacturing men's and women's models of its Easy-Pedal 10-speed bicycle during the next two months, and the company would like a production schedule indicating how many bicycles of each model should be produced in each month. Current demand forecasts call for 150 men's and 125 women's models to be shipped during the first month and 200 men's and 150 women's models to be shipped during the second month. Additional data are shown in Exhibit 13.18. Last month Silver Star used a total of 4,000 hours of labor. Its labor relations policy will not allow the combined total hours of labor (manufacturing plus assembly) to increase or decrease by more than 500 hours from month to month. In addition, the company charges monthly inventory at the rate of 2 percent of the production cost based on the inventory levels at the end of the month. Silver Star would like to have at least 25 units of each model in inventory at the end of the two months. (This question is best approached using the linear programming techniques described in Supplementary Chapter SC C.)

a. Establish a production schedule that minimizes production and inventory costs and satisfies the labor-smoothing, demand, and inventory requirements. What inventories will be maintained, and what are the monthly labor requirements?

b. If the company changed the constraints so that monthly labor increases and decreases could not exceed 250 hours, what would happen to the production schedule? How much would the cost increase? What would you recommend?

8. Given the bill of materials for the printer cartridge (A) shown below, a gross requirement to build 170 units of A, on-hand inventory levels for each item as shown in the table below, and assuming zero lead-times for all items A, B, C, D, and E, compute the net requirements for each item.

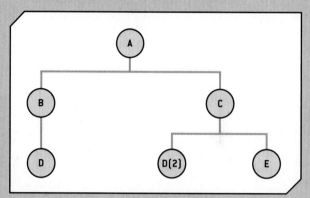

Item	On-Hand Inventory
A	50
B	50
C	90
D	70
E	15

9. Consider the same bill of material and information in problem 8 but change component part B(1) to B(2) and the gross requirements for A to 220 units. Compute the net requirements for each item assuming zero lead times.

10. Each bank teller workstation is forecasted to process 400 transactions (the end item) on Friday. The bank is open from 9:00 a.m. to 7:00 p.m. on Friday

Exhibit 13.18 *Silver Star Bicycle Data*

Model	Production Costs	Labor Required for Manufacturing (hours)	Labor Required for Assembly (hours)	Current Inventory
Men's	$40	10	3	20
Women's	$30	8	2	30

© Cengage Learning 2013

with 90 minutes for lunch and breaks. Three teller windows are open on Friday. A work-study analysis reveals that the breakdown of the transaction mix is 40 percent deposits, 45 percent withdrawals, and 15 percent transfers between accounts. A different form is used for each type of transaction, so there is one deposit slip per deposit, one withdrawal slip per withdrawal, and two transfer slips per transfer.

a. How many transfer slips are needed on Friday?

b. How many withdrawal slips are needed on Friday?

c. Deposit slips are delivered every second day. If the on-hand balance of deposit slips is 50 at this bank, how many deposit slips should be ordered?

d. What is the end item and what is the component part in this bank example?

e. What are the implications of having too many or too few deposit, withdrawal, and transfer slips? Explain.

11. The BOM for product A is shown next and data from the inventory records are shown in the table. In the master production schedule for product A, the MPS quantity row (showing completion dates) calls for 250 units in week 8. The lead time for production of A is two weeks. Develop the materials requirements plan for the next eight weeks for Items B, C, and D.

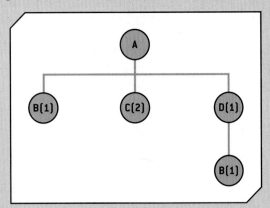

Data Category	B	C	D
Lot sizing rule	P = 2	FOQ = 1,000	LFL
Lead time	2 weeks	1 week	2 weeks
Scheduled receipts	100 (week 1)	0	0
Beginning (on-hand) inventory	0	100	0

12. David Christopher is an orthopedic surgeon who specializes in three types of surgery—hip, knee, and ankle replacements. The surgery mix is 40 percent hip replacement, 50 percent knee replacement, and 10 percent ankle replacement. Partial bills of materials for each type of surgery are shown in the following information.

Hip Replacement	Knee Replacement	Ankle Replacement
Surgical kits #203 & #428	Surgical kit #203	Surgical kit #108
Hip part package #A	Knee part package #V	Ankle part package #P
Patient's blood type—6 pints	Patient's blood type—4 pints	Patient's blood type—3 pints

a. Given that Dr. Christopher is scheduled to do five hip replacements, three knee replacements, and one ankle replacement next week, how many surgical kits and part packages of each type should the hospital have available next week?

b. How many total pints of blood are needed next week?

c. Design a "mistake-proof" system to ensure each patient gets the correct blood type.

d. What are the implications of a shortage (stock-out) of a surgical kit or part package discovered several hours before the operation? What if a part package has a missing part that is not discovered until surgery begins?

13. Consider the master production schedule, bills of materials, and inventory data shown below. Complete the MPS and MRP explosion and identify what actions, if any, you would take given this requirements plan.

Master Production Schedule

	Weeks							
	1	2	3	4	5	6	7	8
Customer req. "A"		5		8			10	
Customer req. "B"						5		10

Lead time for Product "A" is 1 week.
Lead time for Product "B" is 2 weeks.

Bills of Materials

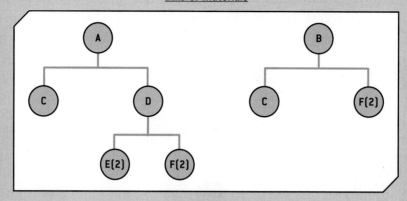

Item File

	Item			
	C	D	E	F
Lot sizing rule	LFL	LFL	FOQ (25)	POQ (P = 2)
Lead time (weeks)	3	1	3	1
Beginning (on-hand) inventory	5	8	19	3
Scheduled receipts	8 in week 1	None	25 in week 3	20 in week 1

14. The MPS for product A calls for 100 units to be completed in week 4 and 200 units in week 7 (the lead time is 1 week). Spare part demand for Item B is 10 units per week. The bill of materials for product A is shown on the right, and the inventory records are shown below.

Data category	Item B	Item C
Lot sizing rule	FOQ = 500	LFL
Lead time (weeks)	2	3
Beginning (on-hand) inventory	100	10
Scheduled receipts	none	200 (week 2)

a. Develop a materials requirements plan for the next 7 weeks for Items B and C.

b. Will any action notices be generated? If so, explain what they are and why they must be generated.

15. Garden Manufacturing is a small, family-owned garden tool manufacturer located in Florence, South Carolina. The bills of materials for models A and B of a popular garden tool are shown in Exhibit 13.19 and other additional component information is shown in Exhibit 13.20. There is considerable component part commonality between these two models, as shown by the BOM. The MPS calls for 100 units of Tool A to be completed in week 5 and 200 units of Tool A to be completed in week 7. End item A has a two-week lead time. The MPS calls for 300 units of Tool B to be completed in week 7. End item B has a one-week lead time. Do an MRP explosion for all items required to make these two garden tools. What actions, if any, should be taken immediately and what other potential problems do you see?

Bill of Materials for Problem 14

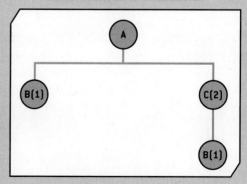

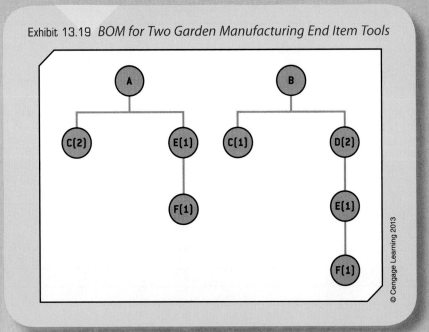

Exhibit 13.19 *BOM for Two Garden Manufacturing End Item Tools*

© Cengage Learning 2013

Exhibit 13.20 *Component Part Information*

Data Category	Item			
	C	D	E	F
Lot sizing rule	FOQ = 400	LFL	POQ = 4	LFL
Lead time	1 week	2 weeks	2 weeks	1 week
Scheduled receipts	450 (week 1)	50 (week 1)	None	None
Beginning inventory	100	70	50	900

© Cengage Learning 2013

Greyhound Frequent Flyer Call Center Case Study

"I'm an accounting major, not an operations expert," yelled just-promoted Bob Barthrow, the executive vice president of the Greyhound Frequent Flyer Call Center, during a senior-level management meeting. "Bob, Horizon Airlines (HA) is going to stop doing business with us if we don't provide better call center service. We need to maximize service and minimize costs! So, find a solution to HA's service problems or we are all out of a job," stated Adam Bishop, the CEO of Greyhound Call Center Services (GCCS).

Bob retreated to his office and closed the door. As he sat in his chair, he thought about the many meetings he had participated in where managers "promised great customer service but could not deliver it." Upon further reflection, he came to the conclusion that to promise great customer service you first must know how to analyze resource capacity and develop good schedules. He pulled out his old college operations management textbook and began reading. He also did a Google search on the topic and found several articles to read. He planned on building an electronic spreadsheet analysis of the situation.

Small and mid-sized airlines outsourced a variety of peripheral services to GCCS, such as billing and credit card management, baggage and customer flight claims management, reservations, loyalty programs, and call center management. HA accounted for 9 percent of GCCS revenues. HA customers had no idea the HA frequent flyer program was outsourced to GCCS. GCCS managed separate call centers for several airlines, each with its own dedicated staff and office space. GCCS customer service representatives (CSRs) who worked in the HA call center were trained by both GCCS and individual airlines such as HA. GCCS provided all CSRs with service management training and mentors, and CSR performance was electronically monitored. HA trained the CSRs by including airline tours and free flights so the CSRs would know the airline and its culture, and especially its frequent flyer program. HA CSRs were trained to handle 20 service upsets most likely to be described by incoming customer calls.

HA and GCCS categorized incoming calls into four categories as follows:

1. Redeem Calls: The customer wants to redeem frequent flyer points for future airline flights.

2. Problem Resolution: The customer wants to correct point debits and credits, flights, personal information, and so on.

3. Manage Accounts: The customer wants to split, combine, transfer, delete, rename, and/or update the frequent flyer account(s).

4. Travel Advice: The customer asks for travel advice. GCCS and HA provide "limited travel consulting service and advice." GCCS CSRs are trained to be nice yet tell the customer they do not provide full travel service, and refer customers to other travel agencies.

Average standard times for HA's call mix is shown in Exhibit 13.21. Bob wanted to get a standard service rate in the same units of measure used for other airlines, and that was calls per CSR per 30 minutes.

Exhibit 13.21 *Greyhound Frequent Flyer Call Mix*

Type of HA Call	Standard Time per Call (Seconds)	Percentage of Total Call (%)
Redeem	115	61%
Problem Resolution	175	25%
Manage Accounts	240	8%
Travel Advice	180	6%

© Cengage Learning 2013

Greyhound case data is also available in an Excel spreadsheet on CourseMate Web site.

Exhibit 13.22 *Greyhound Frequent Flyer Call Center Demand Data*

Time Period	Number of Calls Taken	Number of Abandon Calls by Customer+	Number of Busy Signal Calls Not Taken+	Total Calls
6:30	15	0	0	15
7:00	16	0	0	16
7:30	45	4	0	49
8:00	60	5	0	65
8:30	62	6	2	70
9:00	71	4	1	76
9:30	77	5	0	82
10:00	84	11	4	99
10:30	75	8	3	86
11:00	81	4	3	88
11:30	69	6	1	76
12:00	79	2	0	81
12:30	66	3	2	71
1:00	80	4	3	87
1:30	76	8	6	90
2:00	92	6	7	105
2:30	85	7	5	97
3:00	73	4	3	80
3:30	78	2	3	83
4:00	67	4	4	75
4:30	62	2	0	64
5:00	54	1	0	55
5:30	51	1	1	53
6:00	37	0	0	37
6:30	48	3	2	53
7:00	42	0	0	42
7:30	32	0	0	32
8:00	26	2	0	28
8:30	22	1	0	23
9:00	19	0	0	19
Totals	1,744	103	50	1,897
Average	58.1	3.4	1.7	63.2
Std Deviation	22.9	2.8	2.0	26.6
Minimum	15	0	0	15
Maximum	92	11	7	105

© Cengage Learning 2013

+ An abandon call means the customer gets into the GCCS call center system but then hangs up for some undetermined reason. A customer who gets a busy signal because all incoming trunk phone lines are busy cannot get into the GCCS system and therefore hangs up. What is true demand?

He planned to use a four-step analysis approach, with Step 1 being demand analysis. Exhibit 13.22 provided these data. Step 2 was to compute and explain the logic of setting a standard service time in calls/CSR/30 minutes. Step 3 involved analyzing staff (resource) capacity and using the following equation:

$$\text{Utilization (\%)} = \frac{\text{Demand rate per unit of time}}{(\text{Service rate per unit})(\text{Number of servers})}$$

If you know any three of the four variables in this equation, you can solve for the fourth variable. Step 4 required a revised detailed staff schedule to meet demand to be developed given the target number of CSRs per time period for a given service rate, and an assumption on the target labor utilization rate. He planned to explain and justify all of his logic and assumptions in a written report to be presented to other managers and his direct reports. (This case is similar to the service organization problem structure depicted in Exhibit 13.2, where there are fewer intermediate steps in the aggregate planning procedure to arrive at detailed resource schedules.)

Bob also found a year-old study on the cost of poor service for another airline serviced by GCCS, and it found the cost of an abandon (customer hangs up for undetermined reason) or busy signal call to be estimated at $21. This was his best estimate of the cost per call for poor customer service.

Decisions

Bob decides to answer the following questions and present answers to Adam next week. He knows his accounting principles, but if he is to be promoted, he must also demonstrate to management that he can "analyze a process and successfully manage it."

Average HA-GCCS call center demand rounded to the nearest integer for the last 10 Mondays is shown in Exhibit 13.22. Bob thought a planned (target) CSR labor utilization of 90 percent provided adequate safety capacity. The current HA-GCCS CSR staff schedule is shown in Exhibit 13.23. Full-time employee (FTE) policies require at least a 7-hour workday plus 1 hour for lunch or dinner and at least one 15-minute break per workday. Any workday less than FTE is consider part-time employment (PTE).

Case Questions for Discussion

1. Analyze the case data and *current* schedule, and answer the following "baseline" questions. What's labor utilization for each 30-minute period given the current staffing plan? Is the main problem lack of staff capacity or poor scheduling, or both? Can you support your answer with numerical analysis?

2. What is the cost of abandoned and busy signal calls for a typical Monday day? Annually? (Make and state assumptions as needed.)

3. Develop a better CSR staff schedule (see Excel current staff schedule in Exhibit 13.23) if needed and decide whether the company should hire more CSRs or lay off a abandoned. Will you use part-time employees? If so, explain why and justify.

4. What are your final recommendations? Explain and justify.

Note: This case can be used with OM 4 Chapters 7, 10, and 13 depending on the judgment and guidance of the instructor(s). Exhibits 13.22 and 13.23 are found as Excel files in the OM4 Data Workbook on the CourseMate web site.

Exhibit 13.23 *Greyhound Current CSR Staff Schedule*

Service Rep	6:30	7:00	7:30	8:00	8:30	9:00	9:30	10:00	10:30	11:00	11:30	12:00	12:30 PM	1:00	1:30	2:00
1	X---------	---------	---------	---------	---------	(----)	---------	---------	(Lunch)	(Lunch)	---------	---------	---------	(----)	---------	---------
2	X---------	---------	---------	---------	---------	---------	----(----)	---------	---------	(Lunch)	(Lunch)	---------	---------	---------	(----)	---------
3			X---------	---------	---------	(----)	---------	---------	---------	---------	(Lunch)	(Lunch)	---------	---------	(----)	---------
4				X---------	---------	---------	----(----)	---------	---------	---------	---------	(Lunch)	(Lunch)	---------	----(----)	---------
5				X---------	---------	---------	---------	---------	---------	(----)	---------	---------	(Lunch)	(Lunch)	---------	(----)
6						X---------	---------	---------	---------	---------	(----)	---------	(Lunch)	(Lunch)	---------	---------
7								X---------	---------	---------	---------	(----)	---------	(Lunch)	(Lunch)	---------
8								X---------	---------	---------	---------	(----)	---------	---------	(Lunch)	(Lunch)
9										X---------	---------	---------	(----)	---------	(Lunch)	(Lunch)
10																
11																
12																
13																
Avail CSR (Min)	60	60	90	150	150	150	150	180	210	210	180	180	180	150	135	180
Current # CSRs	2	2	3	5	5	5	5	6	7	7	6	6	6	5	4.5	6
Target # CSRs																
Short/Excess (-/+)																

Service Rep	2:30	3:00	3:30	4:00	4:30	5:00	5:30	6:00	6:30	7:00	7:30	8:00	8:30	9:00	Totals
1															
2															
3	---------	---------													
4	---------	---------	---------												
5	---------	---------	---------												
6	---------	---------	---------	---------	---------										
7	-----(----)	---------	---------	---------	---------										
8	---------	---------	---------	(----)	---------	---------	---------								
9	---------	---------	---------	-----(----)	---------	---------									
10	X---------	---------	---------	---------	---------	(Dinner)	(Dinner)	---------	---------	---------	(----)	---------	---------	---------	
11	X---------	---------	---------	(----)	---------	(Dinner)	(Dinner)	---------	---------	---------	-----(----)	---------	---------	---------	
12	X---------	---------	---------	-----(----)	---------	---------	---------	(Dinner)	(Dinner)	---------	---------	---------	---------	---------	
13	X---------	---------	---------	---------	(----)	---------	---------	(Dinner)	(Dinner)	---------	---------	---------	---------	---------	
Avail CSR (Min)	315	330	300	210	210	135	150	150	120	120	90	120	120	120	#REF!
Current # CSRs	10.5	11	10	7	7	4.5	5	5	4	4	3	4	4	4	#REF!
Target # CSRs															
Short/Excess (-/+)															

OPERATIONS SCHEDULING AND SEQUENCING

J ean Rowecamp, clinical coordinator of nursing services, was faced with a deluge of complaints by her nursing staff about their work schedules and complaints by floor supervisors about inadequate staffing. The nurses complained they were having too many shift changes each month. Supervisors said they had too many nurses during the days and not enough at night and on the weekends. It seemed that nothing she did would satisfy everyone. The nurses were unionized, so she couldn't schedule them for more than seven consecutive working days and the nurses required at least 16 hours between shift changes. Nurses were constantly making "special requests" for personal time off, despite the negotiated procedures for bidding for shifts and vacation times. Jean lamented that she became an administrator and longed for the days before she had these responsibilities.

learning outcomes

After studying this chapter you should be able to:

14-1 **Explain the concepts of scheduling and sequencing.**

14-2 **Describe staff scheduling and appointment system decisions.**

14-3 **Explain sequencing performance criteria and rules.**

14-4 **Describe how to solve single- and two-resource sequencing problems.**

14-5 **Explain the need for monitoring schedules using Gantt charts.**

What do you think?

As a student, how do you schedule your homework, school projects, and study activities? What criteria do you use?

Creating schedules is not easy. The chapter-opening nursing example highlights the complexity of scheduling. For example, union workforce rules and special requests can complicate the scheduling process. Nevertheless, good schedules have to be developed to provide high levels of patient care and to minimize costs.

Scheduling and sequencing are some of the more common activities that operations managers perform every day in every business. They are fundamental to all three levels of aggregation and disaggregation planning that we described in the previous chapter. Good schedules and sequences lead to efficient execution of manufacturing and service plans and better customer service. It's one thing to promise great customer service and another to actually achieve it. For example, having the right number of employees at a call center at different times of the day and week will ensure that customers do not have to wait long. Good scheduling of jobs in a factory will ensure that customers receive their orders as promised and increase productivity and efficiency.

14-1 Understanding Scheduling and Sequencing

Scheduling *refers to the assignment of start and completion times to particular jobs, people, or equipment.* For example, fast-food restaurants, hospitals, and call centers need to schedule employees for

Scheduling refers to the assignment of start and completion times to particular jobs, people, or equipment.

▼ *Scheduling is complicated by union regulations and "special requests" for personal time off.*

> It's one thing to promise great customer service and another to actually achieve it.

Javier Larrea/age fotostock/Photolibrary

work shifts; doctors, dentists, and stockbrokers need to schedule patients and customers; airlines must schedule crews and flight attendants; sports organizations must schedule teams and officials; court systems must schedule hearings and trials; factory managers need to schedule jobs on machines and preventive maintenance work; and salespersons need to schedule customer deliveries and visits to potential customers. Many schedules are repeatable over the long term, such as those for retail store staff and assembly-line employees. Others might change on a monthly, weekly, or even daily basis, as might be the case with call center employees, nurses, or salespeople.

A concept related to scheduling is sequencing. **Sequencing** *refers to determining the order in which jobs or tasks are processed.* For example, triage nurses must decide on the order in which emergency patients are treated; housekeepers in hotels must sequence the order of rooms to clean; operations managers who run an automobile assembly line must determine the sequence by which different models are produced; and airport managers must sequence outgoing flights on runways. Note that in all these situations, processing takes place using a common resource with limited capacity. Thus, the sequence will ultimately determine how well the resource is used to achieve some objective, such as meeting demand or customer due dates. Generally, a sequence specifies a schedule, and we will see this in various examples later in this chapter.

Scheduling and sequencing in back-office or low-contact service processes are similar to that for goods-producing processes. The same scheduling and sequencing concepts and methods used in manufacturing are beneficial in low-contact service processes.

It is not uncommon for a manufacturing facility to have hundreds of work stations or machine centers and to process thousands of different parts. Managers of such facilities also need daily or even hourly updates on the status of production to meet the information needs of supply chain managers, sales and marketing personnel, and customers. Similarly, service managers often manage dozens of part-time workers with varying work availability times (think of a fast-food restaurant manager near a college campus), or ever-changing workloads and demands (think of a hospital nurse administrator). The complexity of these situations dictates that effective scheduling systems be computerized, not only for generating schedules but also for retrieving information so that

Sequencing refers to determining the order in which jobs or tasks are processed.

Telling Umpires Where to Go

One of the authors of this book developed annual schedules for umpires in the American Baseball League for many years before this activity was merged with the National League. Some of the critical factors in developing these schedules were to ensure that umpire crews were not assigned to consecutive series with the same team if possible; that the number of times a crew was assigned to a team was balanced over the course of the season; that travel sequences be rational and realistic; and that a variety of constraints be met. For instance, it makes more sense to schedule a crew to several consecutive series out on the East Coast or West Coast and move the crew to nearby cities rather than shuttling back and forth across the country.

Various constraints limited the scheduling possibilities. For example, one could not schedule a crew for a day game in another city after working a night game on the previous day. In addition, crews need time to rest and travel between game assignments. All these factors needed to be considered in the context of the game schedule, which was created well in advance.

© Scott Boehm/Getty Images

a salesperson can check the status of a customer's order or project a delivery date. Thus, implementing scheduling systems requires good information technology support.

⌈ Scheduling applies to all aspects of the value chain—planning and releasing orders in a factory, determining work shifts for employees, and making deliveries to customers. ⌋

UPS: SUSTAINABLE SCHEDULING

Bob Stoffel has the longest title at UPS: Senior Vice President, Supply Chain, Strategy, Engineering, and Sustainability. The logic of the job title is that these functions fit together in a global economy where supply chains may be changing radically and UPS's customers must increasingly demonstrate sustainability to their own customers and investors. With 100,000 trucks, he is experimenting with virtually every green technology and reducing the company's carbon emissions by millions of tons annually. In addition to more efficient vehicles, better scheduling using GPS technology and telematics resulted in a reduction of 53,000 miles each day while delivering 350,000 more packages each day. Telematics involves sensors that monitor 200 different vehicle activities, such as braking, speeds, and even whether GPS coordinates match package addresses so that routes can be better planned and scheduled. UPS also developed software to provide routes that rely on right turns whenever possible to reduce fuel consumption as drivers wait to make a left turn.[1]

code6d/iStockphoto.com

Many organizations use spreadsheets, desktop software packages, or web-based tools for scheduling. Customized scheduling spreadsheets use readily available software such as Microsoft Excel, but may be rather expensive to develop. Commercial spreadsheet templates are simple to use and are generally inexpensive. One example is Simple Scheduler, which can be purchased from schedules.com for an annual fee of $39. Shiftschedules.com provides more sophisticated capabilities in its Template Scheduler, which starts at $79 per year.

Desktop and web-based software packages are more powerful and have optimization capabilities. Typical features include the ability to schedule days on and days off for both full- and part-time employees, create alternative schedules to compare costs, and handling multiple shifts. One product is SNAP Schedule, a $450 package available from www.bmscentral.com. Web-based scheduling systems have the advantage of being accessible anywhere but often cost more. Two popular systems are WhenToWork (www.whentowork.com) and Kronos (www.kronos.com).

Many software packages have been developed for specific industries, such as call centers, law enforcement, and health care. Each industry has unique problem structures and decision variables. Concerro (formerly known as BidShift), for example, is a web-based software package specifically designed for scheduling nurses. Over 170 hospitals have signed up to use this system; they estimate savings of $1 to $4 million per year, along with improved employee morale and quality of patient care.[2] In this section we present two common applications of scheduling that are prevalent in operations management.

14-2 Scheduling Applications and Approaches

Scheduling applies to all aspects of the value chain—planning and releasing orders in a factory, determining work shifts for employees, and making deliveries to customers. Many problems, such as staff scheduling, are similar across different organizations. Quite often, however (as with the baseball umpiring situation or scheduling classrooms and teachers at a university), unique situational factors require a unique solution approach.

14-2a Staff Scheduling

Staff scheduling problems are prevalent in service organizations because of high variability in customer demand. Examples include scheduling call center representatives, hotel housekeepers, tollbooth operators, nurses, airline reservation clerks, police officers, fast-food restaurant employees, and many others.

Staff scheduling attempts to match available personnel with the needs of the organization by

1. accurately forecasting demand and translating it into the quantity and timing of work to be done;
2. determining the staffing required to perform the work by time period;
3. determining the personnel available and the full- and part-time mix; and
4. matching capacity to demand requirements, and developing a work schedule that maximizes service and minimizes costs.

The first step requires converting demand to a capacity measure—that is, the number of staff required. For instance, we might determine that for every $400 of sales forecast, we need one additional full-time employee. The second step determines the quantity and timing of the work to be done in detail, usually by hour of the day, and sometimes in 5- to 10-minute time intervals. Determining the staffing required must take into account worker productivity factors, personal allowances, sickness, vacations, no-shows, and so on.

Step 4 focuses on the matching of capacity to demand requirements; this is the essence of scheduling. Different approaches are required for different situations because of the nature of constraints. If service demands are relatively level over time, as in the case of hotel housekeepers, it is usually easy to schedule personnel on standard weekly work shifts. If the workload varies greatly within a shift, as is the case for telephone customer service representatives, the problem becomes one of scheduling shifts to meet the varying demand. Let us examine a relatively simple problem of scheduling personnel with consecutive days off in the face of fluctuating requirements.[3]

T.R. Accounting Service is developing a workforce schedule for three weeks from now and has forecasted demand and translated it into the following minimum personnel requirements for the week:

Day	Mon.	Tue.	Wed.	Thur.	Fri.	Sat.	Sun.
Minimum personnel	8	6	6	6	9	5	3

The staff requirements are for full-time accountants who do accounting work such as end-of-month financial statements, tax record organization, and federal, state, and local tax payments. T.R., the owner of the accounting service, wants to schedule the employees so that each employee has two *consecutive* days off and all demand requirements are met.

The staffing procedure is as follows. First, we locate the *set of at least two consecutive days with the smallest requirements*. That is, we find the day with the smallest staff requirements, the next-smallest, and so on, until there are at least two consecutive days. Sunday and Saturday, for example, have requirements of 3 and 5, respectively, while all others are greater than 5. We then circle the requirements for those two consecutive days. Thus we have the following, for employee 1:

Day	Mon.	Tue.	Wed.	Thur.	Fri.	Sat.	Sun.
Requirements	8	6	6	6	9	(5)	(3)

We assign accountant 1 to work on all days that are not circled, that is, Monday through Friday. Then we subtract 1 from the requirement for each day that accountant will work. This gives us the following requirements that remain:

Day	Mon.	Tue.	Wed.	Thur.	Fri.	Sat.	Sun.
Requirements	7	5	5	5	8	5	3

The procedure is repeated with this new set of requirements for accountant 2.

Day	Mon.	Tue.	Wed.	Thur.	Fri.	Sat.	Sun.
Requirements	7	(5)	(5)	(5)	8	(5)	(3)

When there are several alternatives, as in this case, we do one of two things. First, we try to choose a pair of days with the lowest total requirement. If there are still ties, we are to choose the first available pair that makes the most sense to the scheduler. Hence, we again use Saturday and Sunday as days off for accountant 2, since this pair has the smallest total requirement of 8. We subtract 1 from each working day's requirement, yielding the following:

Day	Mon.	Tue.	Wed.	Thur.	Fri.	Sat.	Sun.
Requirements	6	4	4	4	7	5	3

Circling the smallest requirements until we obtain at least two consecutive days again yields the following for employee 3:

Day	Mon.	Tue.	Wed.	Thur.	Fri.	Sat.	Sun.
Requirements	6	(4)	(4)	(4)	7	5	(3)

Notice that Sunday is not adjacent to Tuesday, Wednesday, or Thursday, so we cannot use Sunday in the schedule. Remember we are looking for consecutive pairs of days. Let's choose the Tuesday-Wednesday pair. The remaining requirements are:

Day	Mon.	Tue.	Wed.	Thur.	Fri.	Sat.	Sun.
Requirements	5	4	4	3	6	4	2

Continuing with this procedure, we obtain the sequence of requirements shown in Exhibit 14.1 (with circled numbers representing the lowest-requirement pair selected). The final accountant schedule is shown in Exhibit 14.2. Even though some requirements are exceeded, such as Thursday with a demand for six accountants yet we schedule eight, the solution minimizes the number of employees required. A more difficult problem that we do not address is that of determining a schedule of rotating shifts so that employees do not always have the same two days off. Over a predetermined longer cycle such as a quarter, all employees rotate through all possible days off. This makes for a fair and more equitable staff schedule, but it is complicated and beyond the scope of this book.

Many software packages are available to help with staff scheduling. However, scheduling is so integrated with the practices and culture of the organization that these standardized software packages normally need to be modified to work well in specific operating environments. Accurate input data and the user's understanding of how the software techniques develop the schedules are other challenges when adopting off-the-shelf scheduling software.

Exhibit 14.1 *Scheduling Procedure for T.R. Accounting Service*

Employee Number	Mon.	Tue.	Wed.	Thur.	Fri.	Sat.	Sun.
4	5	4	4	3	6	④	②
5	4	3	③	②	5	4	2
6	3	2	3	2	4	③	①
7	②	①	2	1	3	3	1
8	2	1	①	⓪	2	2	0
9	①	⓪	1	0	1	1	0
10	1	⓪	⓪	0	0	0	0

© Cengage Learning 2013

Exhibit 14.2 *Final Accountant Schedule*

Employee Number	Mon.	Tue.	Wed.	Thur.	Fri.	Sat.	Sun.
1	X	X	X	X	X		
2	X	X	X	X	X		
3	X			X	X	X	X
4	X	X	X	X	X		
5	X	X				X	X	X
6	X	X	X	X	X		
7			X	X	X	X	X
8	X	X			X	X	X
9			X	X	X	X	X
10	X			X	X	X	X
Total	8	6	6	8	10	6	6

© Cengage Learning 2013

Using Spreadsheet Models to Schedule Medical Residents

The chief radiology resident from the University of Vermont's College of Medicine and a group of business students who were enrolled in a semester-long Master of Science course developed a spreadsheet model for creating a one-year schedule for a group of 15 medical residents in the radiology department. Demand for radiology services could occur at any time of the day; thus, they must ensure that adequate personnel are always available. The majority of demand occurs during the weekday working hours; approximately 20 to 25 certified radiologists and the residents serve this demand. Certified radiologists do not work on weeknights; however, a radiology resident is on call and is responsible for all radiology services at the hospital. The resident works the overnight shift alone and must be physically at the hospital, but is off during the next day shift. The radiology chief resident has the task of assigning each resident to these on-call and emergency room (ER) shifts. This scheduling task—to assign one resident to each on-call and ER assignment every day of the year—is incredibly complex because of many requirements and restrictions, such as having one and only one resident assigned to the ER schedule per four-week rotation block.

John Wood Photography/Stock Image/Getty Images

The student team used Microsoft Excel to create a spreadsheet that would allow them to measure the key metrics of the residents' assignments, such as the number of days worked in each category (e.g., Thursdays, Fridays, etc.). Then, they added an optimization model to find a feasible solution. The model was simple to use and increased the quality of the resulting resident assignments, and decreased the time required to obtain the assignments.[4]

14-2b Appointment Systems

Appointments can be viewed as a reservation of service time and capacity. Using appointments provides a means to maximize the use of time-dependent service capacity and reduce the risk of no-shows. Appointment systems are used in many businesses, such as consulting, tax preparation, music instruction, and medical, dental, and veterinarian practices. Indirectly, appointments reduce the cost of providing the service because the service provider is idle less each workday. An appointment system must try to accommodate customers and forecast their behavior, such as the no-show rate or a difficult customer who demands more processing time.

Four decisions to make regarding designing an appointment system are the following:

1. *Determine the appointment time interval,* such as 1 hour or 15 minutes. Some professional services such as dentists and physicians use smaller appointment intervals and then take multiples of it, depending on the type of procedure thought to be required by the patient.

2. Based on an analysis of each day's customer mix, *determine the length of each workday and the time off duty.* Once the on- and off-duty days for the year (annual capacity) are determined and assuming a certain customer mix and overbooking

rate (see step 3), the service provider can forecast expected total revenues for the year.

3. *Decide how to handle overbooking* for each day of the week. Often, customers do not show up as scheduled. If the no-show percentage is low, say 2 percent, then there may be no need to overbook. However, once the no-show percentage reaches 10 percent or more, overbooking is usually necessary to maximize revenue and make effective use of perishable and expensive time.

4. *Develop customer appointment rules* that maximize customer satisfaction. For example, some service providers leave one appointment interval open at the end of each workday. Others schedule a 60-minute lunch interval but can squeeze in a customer during lunch if necessary. Telephone and electronic appointment reminders are another way to help maximize service-provider utilization.

14-3 Sequencing

equencing is necessary when several activities (manufacturing goods, servicing customers, delivering packages, and so on) use a common resource. The resource might be a machine, a customer service representative, or a delivery truck. Sequencing can be planned, in which case it creates a schedule. For example, if a student plans to begin homework at 7:00 p.m. and estimates that it will take 60 minutes to complete an OM assignment, 45 minutes to read a psychology chapter, and 40 minutes to do statistics homework, then sequencing the work from most favorite to least favorite—OM, psychology, and statistics—creates the schedule:

Assignment	Start Time	End Time
OM	7:00	8:00
Psychology	8:00	8:45
Statistics	8:45	9:25

14-3a Sequencing Performance Criteria

In selecting a specific scheduling or sequencing rule, a manager must first consider the criteria on which to evaluate schedules. These criteria are often classified into three categories:

1. process-focused performance criteria,
2. customer-focused due date criteria, and
3. cost-based criteria.

The applicability of the various criteria depends on the availability of data. Later we will show how these performance measures are applied to various sequencing rules.

Process-focused performance criteria pertain only to information about the start and end times of jobs and focus on shop performance such as equipment utilization and work-in-process (WIP) inventory. Two common measures are flow time and makespan. **Flow time** *is the amount of time a job spent in the shop or factory.* Low flow times reduce WIP inventory. Flow time is computed using Equation 14.1.

$$F_i = \Sigma p_{ij} + \Sigma w_{ij} = C_i - R_i \qquad [14.1]$$

where

F_i = flow time of job i
Σp_{ij} = sum of all processing times of job i at work station or area j (run + setup times)

> **Flow time** is the amount of time a job spent in the shop or factory.

Software to Schedule Anywhere

One provider of small business software offers an online employee scheduling system called ScheduleAnywhere (ScheduleAnywhere.com). This service allows managers to schedule employees from any computer with Internet access, whether at work, at home, or on the road. "With over 70,000 users, we get a lot of feedback on what people really need in an employee scheduling system," said Jon Forknell, vice president and general manager of Atlas Business Solutions. "Many of our customers told us they needed an online solution that was affordable and easy to use." Small firms can use the online scheduling service for as little as $20 per month, while large organizations such as AT&T, Amazon.com, Bank of America, and the American Red Cross sign long-term contracts. ScheduleAnywhere gives users the power to do the following:

- *schedule employees from any computer with Internet access*
- *create schedules by position, department, location, and so on*
- *view schedule information in a 1-day, 7-day, 14-day, or 28-day format*
- *enter staffing requirements and view shift coverage*
- *see who's scheduled and who's available*
- *automatically rotate or copy employee schedules*
- *preschedule time-off requests*
- *avoid scheduling conflicts*
- *give employees read/write or read-only access to schedules[5]*

Σw_{ij} = sum of all waiting times of job i at work station or area j

C_i = completion time of job i

R_i = ready time for job i where all materials, specifications, and so on are available

Makespan *is the time needed to process a given set of jobs.* A short makespan aims to achieve high equipment utilization and resources by getting all jobs out of the shop quickly. Makespan is computed using Equation 14.2.

$$M = C - S \qquad [14.2]$$

where

M = makespan of a group of jobs

C = completion time of *last* job in the group

S = start time of *first* job in the group

Due-date criteria pertain to customers' required due dates or internally determined shipping dates. Common performance measures are lateness and tardiness, or the number of jobs tardy or late. **Lateness** *is the difference between the completion time and the due date (either positive or negative).* **Tardiness** *is the amount of time by which the completion time exceeds the due date.* (Tardiness is defined as zero if the job is completed before the due date, and therefore no credit is given for completing a job early.) In contrast to process-focused performance criteria, these measures focus externally on customer satisfaction and service. They are calculated using Equations 14.3 and 14.4.

$$L_i = C_i - D_i \qquad [14.3]$$

$$T_i = \text{Max}(0, L_i) \qquad [14.4]$$

where

L_i = lateness of job i

D_i = due date of job i

T_i = tardiness of job i

A third type of performance criteria is cost-based. Typical cost includes inventory, changeover or setup, processing or run, and material handling costs. This cost-based category might seem to be the most obvious criteria, but it is often difficult to identify the relevant cost categories, obtain accurate estimates of their values, and allocate costs to manufactured parts or services

correctly. In most cases, costs are considered implicitly in process performance and due-date criteria.

14-3b Sequencing Rules

Two of the most popular sequencing rules for prioritizing jobs are

- shortest processing time (SPT), and
- earliest due date (EDD).

In using one of these rules, a manager would compute the measure for all competing jobs and select them in the sequence according to the criterion. For example, suppose that the student we discussed earlier sequenced the homework according to SPT. The sequence would be statistics, psychology, and OM. These rules are often applied when a fixed set of jobs needs to be sequenced at one point in time.

In other situations, new jobs arrive in an intermittent fashion, resulting in a constantly changing mix of jobs needing to be sequenced. In this case, we assign priorities to whatever jobs are available at a specific time and then update the priorities when new jobs arrive. Some examples of these priority rules are

- first come, first served (FCFS),
- fewest number of operations remaining (FNO),
- least work remaining (LWR)—sum of all processing times for operations not yet performed, and
- least amount of work at the next process queue (LWNQ)—amount of work awaiting the next process in a job's sequence.

The SPT and EDD rules generally work well in the short term, but in most situations new orders and jobs arrive intermittently and the schedule must accommodate them. If SPT were used in a dynamic environment, a job with a large processing time might never get processed. In this case, some time-based exception rule (such as "if a job waits more than 40 hours, schedule it next") must be used to avoid this problem.

Different sequencing rules lead to very different results and performance. The SPT rule tends to minimize average flow time and WIP inventory and maximize resource utilization. The EDD rule minimizes the maximum of jobs past due but doesn't perform well on average flow time, WIP inventory, or resource utilization. The FCFS rule is used in many service-delivery systems and does not consider any job or customer criterion. FCFS focuses only on the time of arrival for the customer or job. The FNO rule does not consider the

---

Makespan is the time needed to process a given set of jobs.

Lateness is the difference between the completion time and the due date (either positive or negative).

Tardiness is the amount of time by which the completion time exceeds the due date.

length of time for each operation; for example, a job may have many small operations and be scheduled last. Generally, this is not a very good rule. The LWNQ rule tries to keep downstream work stations and associated resources busy.

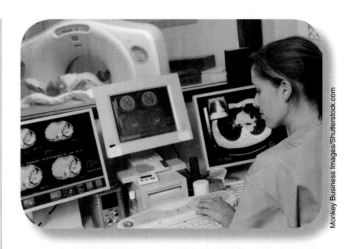

14-4 Applications of Sequencing Rules

Sequencing in a job shop, in which several different goods or services are processed, each of which may have a unique routing among process stages, is generally very complex, but some special cases lend themselves to simple solutions. These special cases provide understanding and insight into more complicated scheduling problems. One that we illustrate is scheduling on a single work station or processor.

14-4a Single-Resource Sequencing Problem

The simplest sequencing problem is that of processing a set of jobs on a single processor. This situation occurs in many firms. For example, in a serial manufacturing process, a bottleneck work station controls the output of the entire process. Thus, it is critical to schedule the bottleneck equipment efficiently. In other cases, such as in a chemical plant, the entire plant may be viewed as a single processor. Single processors for service situations include processing patients through an X-ray or CAT-scanning machine, trucks through a loading/unloading dock, or financial transactions through a control work station. For the single-processor sequencing problem, a very simple rule—shortest processing time—finds a minimal average flow-time sequence. An example of its use follows.

Consider a work station that has one maintenance mechanic to repair failed machines. We can think of the mechanic as the processor (scarce resource) and the machines awaiting repair as the jobs. Let us assume that six machines are down, with estimated repair times given here, and that no new jobs arrive.

Job (fix machine #)	1	2	3	4	5	6
Processing time (hours)	10	3	7	2	9	6

No matter which sequence is chosen, the makespan is the same, because the time to process all the jobs is the sum of the processing times, or in this example, 37 hours. Therefore, we use average flow time as the criterion to minimize the average time a job spends in the work station. The idea here is to get the most jobs done as soon as possible. Applying the SPT rule, we use the job sequence 4-2-6-3-5-1. We assume that all jobs are ready for processing at time zero (that is, $R_i = 0$ for all jobs i). Then the flow times (F_i) for the jobs are computed as follows:

Job Sequence	Flow Time
4	2 hours
2	2 + 3 = 5 hours
6	5 + 6 = 11 hours
3	11 + 7 = 18 hours
5	18 + 9 = 27 hours
1	27 + 10 = 37 hours

The average flow time for these six jobs is (2 + 5 + 11 + 18 + 27 + 37)/6 = 100/6 = 16.67 hours. This means that the average time a machine will be out of service is 16.7 hours. The SPT sequencing rule maximizes work station utilization and minimizes average job flow time and WIP inventory. For example, if you switch jobs 4 and 6 so the job sequence is 6-2-4-3-5-1, note that the average flow time increases to 18 hours. We encourage you to work through the calculations to show this. As long as no additional jobs enter the mix, all will eventually be processed. Of course, the job with the longest processing time will wait the longest (and this customer might not be very happy), but on average, SPT will reduce the average flow time.

When processing times are relatively equal, then most operating systems default to the first-come, first-served (FCFS) sequencing rule. There are, of course, exceptions to this rule. For example, a job for a firm's most important customer might be pushed to the front of the sequence, or the maître d' at a restaurant might seat a celebrity or VIP before other patrons.

In many situations, jobs have due dates that have been promised to customers. Although SPT provides the smallest average flow time and smallest average lateness of all scheduling rules that might be chosen, in a dynamic environment, jobs with long processing times are continually pushed back and may remain in the shop a long time. Thus it is advantageous to consider sequencing rules that take into account the due dates of jobs.

A popular and effective rule for scheduling on a single processor (resource) is the earliest-due-date (EDD) rule, which dictates sequencing jobs in order of earliest due date first. This rule minimizes the maximum job tardiness and job lateness. It does not minimize the average flow time or average lateness, as SPT

does, however. An example of how the EDD rule is used follows.

Suppose an insurance underwriting work area (that is, the single processor) has five commercial insurance jobs to quote that have these processing times and due dates:

Job	Processing Time (p_{ij})	Due Date (D_i)
1	4	15
2	7	16
3	2	8
4	6	21
5	3	9

If the jobs are sequenced "by the numbers" in the order 1-2-3-4-5, then the flow time, tardiness, and lateness for each job are calculated using Equations 14.1, 14.3, and 14.4, as shown in the table below.

Job	Flow Time (F_i)	Due Date	Lateness ($L_i = C_i - D_i$)	Tardiness [Max (0, L_i)]
1	4	15	−11	0
2	4 + 7 = 11	16	−5	0
3	11 + 2 = 13	8	5	5
4	13 + 6 = 19	21	−2	0
5	19 + 3 = 22	9	13	13
Average	69/5 = 13.8		0	3.6

Using Equation 14.2, the makespan is $M_t = C_t - S_t = 22 - 0 = 22$. If we use the SPT rule to schedule the

jobs, we obtain the sequence 3-5-1-4-2. The flow time, tardiness, and lateness are then given as follows:

Job	Flow Time (F_i)	Due Date	Lateness ($L_i = C_i - D_i$)	Tardiness [Max (0, L_i)]
3	2	8	−6	0
5	2 + 3 = 5	9	−4	0
1	5 + 4 = 9	15	−6	0
4	9 + 6 = 15	21	−6	0
2	15 + 7 = 22	16	6	6
Average	10.6		−3.2	1.2

Note that the makespan is 22 and that the maximum tardiness and the maximum lateness are both 6. Using the EDD rule, we obtain the sequence 3-5-1-2-4.

The flow time, tardiness, and lateness for this sequence are given in the following table:

Job	Flow Time (F_i)	Due Date	Lateness ($L_i = C_i - D_i$)	Tardiness [Max (0, L_i)]
3	2	8	−6	0
5	2 + 3 = 5	9	−4	0
1	5 + 4 = 9	15	−6	0
2	9 + 7 = 16	16	0	0
4	16 + 6 = 22	21	1	1
Average	10.8		−3.0	0.2

Exhibit 14.3 *Comparison of Three Ways to Sequence the Five Jobs*

Performance Criteria	Sequence 1-2-3-4-5	Sequence 3-5-1-4-2 (SPT)	Sequence 3-5-1-2-4 (EDD)
Average Flow Time	13.8	10.6	10.8
Average Lateness	0	−3.2	−3.0
Maximum Lateness	13	6	1
Average Tardiness	3.6	1.2	0.2
Maximum Tardiness	13	6	1

© Cengage Learning 2013

The results of applying three different sequencing rules to the five jobs are shown in Exhibit 14.3. Note that the SPT rule minimizes the average flow time and number of jobs in the system. The EDD rule minimizes the maximum lateness and tardiness. As previously noted, the SPT rule is internally focused, whereas the EDD rule is focused on external customers. Using a by-the-numbers sequencing rule, as in 1-2-3-4-5, results in very poor relative performance. This result helps illustrate that random or commonsense sequencing rules seldom give better results than the SPT or EDD rules for sequencing jobs over a single processor.

Solved Problem

Five tax analysis jobs are waiting to be processed by Martha at T.R. Accounting Service. Use the shortest-processing-time (SPT) and earliest-due-date (EDD) sequencing rules to sequence the jobs. Compute the flow time, tardiness, and lateness for each job, and the average flow time, average tardiness, and average lateness for all jobs. Which rule do you recommend? Why?

Job	Processing Time (days)	Due Date
1	7	11
2	3	10
3	5	8
4	2	5
5	6	17

Solution

The SPT sequence is 4-2-3-5-1.

Job	Flow Time (F_i)	Due Date (D_i)	Lateness ($L_i = C_i - D_i$)	Tardiness [Max (0, L_i)]
4	2	5	−3	0
2	2 + 3 = 5	10	−5	0
3	5 + 5 = 10	8	2	2
5	10 + 6 = 16	17	−1	0
1	16 + 7 = 23	11	12	12
Average	11.2		11.0	2.8

The EDD sequence is 4-3-2-1-5.

Job	Flow Time (F_i)	Due Date (D_i)	Lateness ($L_i = C_i - D_i$)	Tardiness [Max (0, L_i)]
4	2	5	−3	0
3	2 + 5 = 7	8	−1	0
2	7 + 3 = 10	10	0	0
1	10 + 7 = 17	11	6	6
5	17 + 6 = 23	17	6	6
Average	11.8		−1.6	2.4

Given the nature of the data, this is not an easy decision. The SPT rule minimizes average flow time and average lateness but job 1 is extremely late by 12 days. The EDD rule minimizes the maximum job tardiness and lateness. Jobs 1 and 5 are tardy by six days. If job 5 is a big client with significant revenue potential, then the EDD rule is probably best.

Exhibit 14.4 shows the Excel Sequencing template, which can be used to evaluate the performance of different sequences.

14-4b Two-Resource Sequencing Problem

In this section, we consider a flow shop with only two resources or work stations. We assume that each job must be processed first on Resource #1 and then on Resource #2. Processing times for each job on each resource are known. In contrast to sequencing jobs on a single resource, the makespan can vary for each different sequence. Therefore, for the two-resource sequencing problem, it makes sense to try to find a sequence with the smallest makespan.

S.M. Johnson developed the following algorithm in 1954 for finding a minimum makespan schedule.[6] The following algorithm (procedure) defines Johnson's sequencing rule for the two-resource problem structure.

1. List the jobs and their processing times on Resources #1 and #2.

2. Find the job with the shortest processing time (on either resource).

3. If this time corresponds to Resource #1, sequence the job first; if it corresponds to Resource #2, sequence the job last.

4. Repeat steps 2 and 3, using the next-shortest processing time and working inward from both ends of the sequence until all jobs have been scheduled.

Consider the two-resource sequencing problem posed by Hirsch Products. It manufactures certain custom parts that first require a shearing operation (Resource #1) and then a punch-press operation (Resource #2). Hirsch currently has orders for five jobs, which have processing times (days) estimated as follows:

Job	Shear (days)	Punch (days)
1	4	5
2	4	1
3	10	4
4	6	10
5	2	3

Roger Tully/Stone/Getty Images

The jobs can be sequenced in any order but they must be sheared first. Therefore, we have a flow shop situation where each job must first be sequenced on the shear operation and then on the punch operation.

Suppose the jobs are sequenced "by the numbers" in the order 1-2-3-4-5. This schedule can be represented by a simple Gantt chart showing the schedule of each job on each machine along a horizontal time axis (see Exhibit 14.5). This shows, for instance, that job 1 is scheduled on the shear for the first four days, job 2 for the next four days, and so on. We construct a Gantt chart for a given sequence by scheduling the first job

as early as possible on the first machine (shear). Then, as soon as the job is completed, it can be scheduled on the punch press, provided that no other job is currently in progress. First, note that all jobs follow each other on the shearing machine. Because of variations in processing times, however, the punch press, the second operation, is often idle while awaiting the next job. The makespan is 37 days, and the flow times in days for the jobs are as follows:

Job	1	2	3	4	5
Flow Time (days)	9	10	22	34	37

Applying Johnson's rule, we find that the shortest processing time is for job 2 on the punch press.

Job	Shear (days)	Punch (days)
1	4	5
2	4	①
3	10	4
4	6	10
5	2	3

Because the minimum time on either machine is on the second machine, job 2, with a one-day processing time, it is scheduled last.

$$\underline{\quad}\ \underline{\quad}\ \underline{\quad}\ \underline{\quad}\ \underline{\ 2\ }$$

Next, we find the second-shortest processing time. It is two days, for job 5 on machine 1. Therefore, job 5 is scheduled first.

$$\underline{\ 5\ }\ \underline{\quad}\ \underline{\quad}\ \underline{\quad}\ \underline{\ 2\ }$$

In the next step, we have a tie of four days between job 1 on the shear and job 3 on the punch press. When a tie occurs, either job can be chosen. If we pick job 1, we have the following sequence:

$$\underline{\ 5\ }\ \underline{\ 1\ }\ \underline{\quad}\ \underline{\quad}\ \underline{\ 2\ }$$

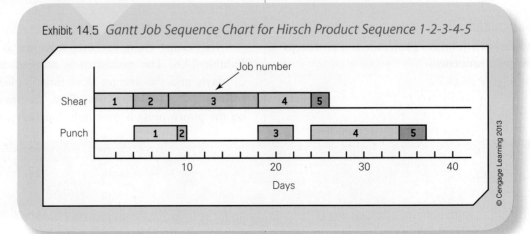

Exhibit 14.5 *Gantt Job Sequence Chart for Hirsch Product Sequence 1-2-3-4-5*

© Cengage Learning 2013

Solved Problem

A manufacturing process involving machined components consists of two operations done on two different machines. The status of the queue at the beginning of a particular week is as follows:

Job Number	Number of Components	Scheduled Time on Machine 1 (min. per piece)	Scheduled Time on Machine 2 (min. per piece)
101	200	2.5	2.5
176	150	1.5	0.5
184	250	1.0	2.0
185	125	2.5	1.0
201	100	1.2	2.4
213	100	1.2	2.2

The processing on machine 2 must follow processing on machine 1. Schedule these jobs to minimize the makespan. Illustrate the schedule you arrive at with a bar chart.

Solution

Because this is a two-machine flow shop problem, Johnson's rule is applicable. Total time in minutes on each machine is the product of the number of components and the unit times, as shown here.

Job	Machine 1	Machine 2	Job	Machine 1	Machine 2
101	500	500	185	312.5	125
176	225	75	201	120	240
184	250	500	213	120	220

The sequence specified by Johnson's rule is 201-213-184-101-185-176. The schedules are shown in the following two different versions of Gantt charts.

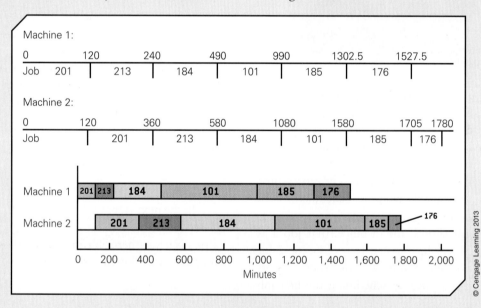

Continuing with Johnson's rule, the last two steps yield the complete sequence.

5	1		3	2
5	1	4	3	2

The Gantt chart for this sequence is shown in Exhibit 14.6. The makespan is reduced from 37 to 27 days, and the average flow time is also improved from 22.4 to 18.2 days. As noted, the total idle time on the punch press is now only four days, resulting in

Different sequencing rules lead to very different results and performance.

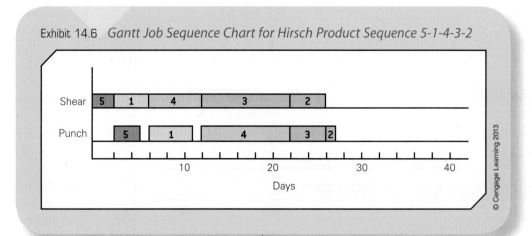

Exhibit 14.6 *Gantt Job Sequence Chart for Hirsch Product Sequence 5-1-4-3-2*

© Cengage Learning 2013

a punchpress resource utilization of 23/27, or 85.2 percent, and we gain 10 days to schedule other jobs. If the sequencing problem structure fits the assumptions of Johnson's rule, it is a powerful algorithm. Again, commonsense scheduling is seldom as good as Johnson's rule.

14-5 Schedule Monitoring and Control

urphy's Law states that if something can go wrong it will, and this is especially true with schedules. Thus, it is important that progress be monitored on a continuing basis. For example, in manufacturing, the master scheduler must know the status of orders that are ahead of schedule or behind schedule due to shortages of material, work stations that are backlogged, changes in inventory, labor turnover, and sales commitments. Schedules must be changed when these things occur. Therefore, reschedules are a normal part of scheduling.

Short-term capacity fluctuations also necessitate changes in schedules. Factors affecting short-term

⌈Murphy's Law states that if something can go wrong it will, and this is especially true with schedules.⌋

MOBIL OIL: COMPUTER-BASED SCHEDULING

Mobil Oil Corporation runs a nationwide system for dispatching and processing customer orders for gasoline and distillates. It is an integrated operating system that controls the flow of billions in annual sales from initial order entry to final delivery, confirmation, and billing. Although the entire dispatching process is overseen by a handful of people in a small office, it operates more efficiently than the old manual system in all respects: It provides better customer service; greatly improved credit, inventory, and operating cost control; and significantly reduced distribution costs. Central to this new system is computer-assisted dispatch (called CAD at Mobil), designed to assist schedulers in real time as they determine the means by which ordered products will be safely and efficiently delivered to customers.

Scheduling decisions include (1) assigning orders to terminals; (2) assigning orders to delivery trucks; (3) adjusting order quantities to fit truck compartments; (4) loading trucks to their maximum legal weight; and (5) routing trucks and sequencing deliveries. Annual net cost savings is in the millions of dollars.[7]

Fred Prouser/Reuters/Landov

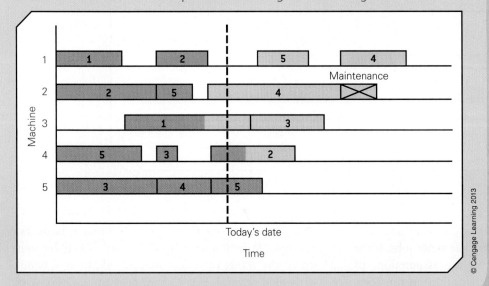

Exhibit 14.7 *Gantt Chart Example for Monitoring Schedule Progress*

are overtime, short-term subcontracting, alternate process routing, and re-allocations of the work-force, as described in the previous chapter.

Gantt (bar) charts are useful tools for monitoring schedules, and an example is shown in Exhibit 14.7. The dark shaded areas indicate completed work. This chart shows, for example, that job 4 has not yet started on machine 2, job 1 is currently behind schedule on machine 3, and jobs 2 and 5 are ahead of schedule. Perhaps needed material has not yet been delivered for job 4, or perhaps machine 3 has had a breakdown. In any event, it is up to production-control personnel to revise the schedule or to expedite jobs that are behind schedule. Many other types of graphical aids are useful and commercially available.

capacity include absenteeism, labor performance, equipment failures, tooling problems, labor turn-over, and material shortages. They are inevitable and unavoidable. Some alternatives available to operations managers for coping with capacity shortages

Discussion Questions

1. Discuss how you decide to schedule your school assignments. Do your informal scheduling rules correspond to any of the rules described in this chapter?

2. Explain why appointments are necessary for many professional services. (Hint: How do services differ from goods, as described in Chapter 1?) List and explain some key issues and decisions that must be addressed in designing appointment systems.

3. Scheduling and sequencing are typically viewed from a technical perspective; that is, they are focused on minimizing quantitative measures such as lateness or cost. However, schedules also have intangible effects on customers, employees, and the perception of service quality. Discuss what some of these intangible effects might be and how managers should consider them when constructing schedules.

4. Why is staff scheduling in a service environment a difficult task? What can managers do to ensure that staff schedules are effective and efficient?

5. Explain the advantages and disadvantages of SPT and EDD sequencing rules. Under what circumstances might you prefer one over the other?

Problems and Activities

Note: an asterisk denotes problems for which an Excel spreadsheet template on the CourseMate Web site may be used.

1. Write a short one-page paper listing the advantages and disadvantages of using part-time employees to help meet demand.

2. Research a desktop or web-based scheduling software system and write a short one-page paper describing its features and capabilities, and any

benefits obtained by real-world organizations that adopted the software.

3. Research and write a short paper (two pages maximum) on how efficient vehicle scheduling and routing can be accomplished. If possible, provide some examples of commercial software programs that are used for vehicle scheduling and routing and describe their capabilities.

4. Interview an operations manager at a nearby manufacturing or service company to find out about scheduling problems the company faces and how they are addressed.

5. A hospital emergency room needs the following numbers of nurses:

Day	M	T	W	T	F	S	S
Min. number	4	3	2	4	7	8	5

Each nurse should have two consecutive days off. How many full-time nurses are required and what is a good nurse schedule?

6. A supermarket has the following minimum personnel requirements during the week. Each employee is required to have two consecutive days off. How many regular employees are required, and what is a good schedule?

Day	Mon.	Tue.	Wed.	Thur.	Fri.	Sat.	Sun.
Min. personnel	4	4	5	6	6	5	4

7. These six jobs are to be scheduled on a single machine:

Job	1	2	3	4	5	6
Processing time (min.)	240	130	210	90	170	165

a. Suppose the jobs are processed in numerical order. Compute the average flowtime after each job is completed.

b. In what order would the jobs be processed using the SPT rule? Compute the average flowtime after each job is completed. Compare this answer with your answer to part a.

8.* An insurance claims work area has five claims waiting for processing as follows:

Job	Processing Time	Due Date (D_i)
1	22	35
2	18	40
3	20	32
4	15	28
5	17	30

Compute the average flow time, tardiness, and lateness for the following sequences: SPT sequence, EDD sequence, and the sequence 2-1-5-3-4. What sequencing rule do you recommend and why?

9.* Mike Reynolds has four assignments due in class tomorrow, and his class times are as follows:

Class	Time
Marketing 304	8 a.m.
OM 385	10 a.m.
Finance 216	1 p.m.
Psychology 200	3:30 p.m.

Each class lasts one hour, and Mike has no other classes. It is now midnight, and Mike estimates that the finance, OM, marketing, and psychology assignments will take him five, three, six, and two hours, respectively. How should he schedule the work? Can he complete all of it?

10.* Eight jobs have arrived in the following order:

Job	Processing Time	Due Date
1	7	21
2	3	7
3	5	8
4	2	5
5	6	17
6	9	16
7	14	38
8	4	12

Find and compare the average flowtime, lateness, and tardiness for the following sequencing rules:

a. Process in the order they have arrived

b. Shortest processing time

c. Earliest due date

11.* In this chapter we noted that the EDD rule minimizes the maximum job tardiness and maximum lateness, whereas the SPT rule minimizes the average flowtime. However, neither of these rules minimizes the average lateness or average tardiness. Use the data in problem 10 to do the following:

a. Try to find a sequence that minimizes the average lateness.

b. Try to find a sequence that minimizes the average tardiness.

c. Can you generalize your logic into a rule or procedure that will accomplish these objectives most of the time?

12. Monday morning Baxter Industries has the following jobs waiting for processing in two departments, milling and drilling, in that order:

Job	Time Required (hours)	
	Mill	Drill
216	7	4
327	6	10
462	10	3
519	5	6
258	3	9
617	7	2

Develop a minimum makespan schedule using Johnson's rule.

13. Graph the minimum makespan schedule in problem 12 on a Gantt chart.

14. Dan's Auto Detailing business performs two major activities: exterior cleanup and interior detailing. Based on the size of the car and its condition, time estimates for six cars on Monday morning are as follows:

	Car Number					
	1	2	3	4	5	6
Exterior	30	35	90	65	45	80
Interior	10	40	20	45	25	55

Sequence the cars so that all exterior detailing is done first and total completion time is minimized.

15. Draw a Gantt chart of your solution to problem 14. Evaluate the idle time, if any, for these two resources—exterior and interior cleaning capability.

Balloons Aloha Case Study

Susie Davis owns Balloons Aloha and must fill balloons with helium and assemble them into certain configurations today for six major parties. Her six customer jobs all need to use the same helium tank (that is, the single processor), and she was wondering what might be the best way to sequence these jobs. Client (job) number 5 is Balloons Aloha's top customer. Her assistant store man-

The company fills the balloons on the day of the party, so the workload is hectic.

ager, Lee Sailboat, wants to process them in sequential order (i.e., 1, 2, 3, 4, 5, and 6). Because the balloons lose air quickly, the company waits until the day of the parties to fill them and then the workload is hectic. Business is booming and growing about 15 percent per year in their new store location. The job processing time estimates are as follows:

Case Questions for Discussion

1. Compute the average flow time, lateness, and tardiness for this group of jobs using Mr. Sailboat's sequential order of 1 (first), 2, 3, 4, 5, and 6 (last).

2. In what order would the jobs be processed using the SPT rule? Compute the average flow time, lateness, and tardiness for this group of jobs.

3. Compare the answers in questions 1 and 2.

4. What are your short-term recommendations for this set of six jobs? Justify and explain.

5. What are your long-term recommendations with respect to sequencing jobs at Balloons Aloha? Justify and explain.

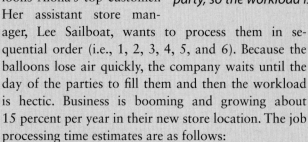

Job	1	2	3	4	5	6
Processing time (min.)	240	130	210	90	170	165
Due dates (6 a.m. to midnight in minutes from opening)	240	360	480	240	720	780

THE CROWD
IN-

Share your 4LTR Press story on Facebook at
www.facebook.com/4ltrpress for a chance to win.

To learn more about the
In-Crowd opportunity 'like'
us on Facebook.

QUALITY MANAGEMENT

t he importance of quality often makes headlines when things go wrong, especially when it involves consumer safety. A major news story in 2009 was the case of Peanut Corporation of America. At least 677 people were sickened and 9 died after eating salmonella-contaminated products made from peanut butter paste from the Peanut Corporation of America. It was found that at least 12 times, when one of the company's products tested positive for salmonella, the company shopped around for new tests until a laboratory certified that the product was clean. The company shipped the products and continued to use the same equipment, processes, and

learning outcomes

After studying this chapter you should be able to:

15-1 **Explain the concepts and definitions of quality.**

15-2 **Describe the quality philosophies and principles of Deming, Juran, and Crosby.**

15-3 **Explain the GAP model and its importance.**

15-4 **Describe the concepts and philosophy of ISO 9000:2000.**

15-5 **Describe the philosophy and methods of Six Sigma.**

15-6 **Explain the categories of cost-of-quality measurement.**

15-7 **Describe how to apply the Seven QC Tools.**

15-8 **Explain the concepts of kaizen and poka-yoke.**

What do you think?

What quality issues have you personally encountered or heard about regarding food?

Juanmonino/iStockphoto.com

global suppliers. Inspectors found roaches, mold, and a leaking roof in one of the company's factories. The salmonella outbreak led to more than 2,000 product recalls, one of the largest in U.S. history. On March 12, 2009, the company issued the following statement: "As you may know, certain recent events have made it necessary for Peanut Corporation of America to seek protection under the U.S. Bankruptcy Code. Effective immediately, all corporate operations will cease."[1]

High quality of goods and services provides an organization with a competitive edge; reduces costs due to returns, rework, scrap, and service upsets; increases productivity, profits, and other measures of success; and, most important, generates satisfied customers who reward the organization with continued patronage and favorable word-of-mouth advertising. And, as the introduction illustrates, high quality is vital to consumer safety in global food supply chains. High quality is

> Today, the high quality of goods and services is simply expected by consumers and business customers and is essential to survival and competitive success.

▼ *The Peanut Corporation of America continued using the same equipment and shipping their products, even after one of them tested positive for salmonella.*

TOYOTA: MANAGING QUALITY THROUGH DESIGN

Toyota has been known for high level of quality control in its production processes. However, Toyota lost a lot of credibility with consumers because of numerous recalls in 2010, which were traced to design defects in gas pedals, floor mats, and software used in braking systems that did not become apparent until consumers drove the cars. Plagued by recalls and fines from the U.S. government, Toyota set up a new division devoted to more quickly addressing customer concerns in the design process to improve quality. The company also promised to improve quality inspections, create regional research centers in which engineers can work on specific automotive systems, and use external consultants.

required in nearly every product, such as in banking, medical care, toys, cell phones, and automobiles.

Today, the high quality of goods and services is simply expected by consumers and business customers and is essential to survival and competitive success. Quality must be addressed throughout the value chain, beginning with suppliers and extending through operations and postsale services. **Quality management** *refers to systematic policies, methods, and procedures used to ensure that goods and services are produced with appropriate levels of quality to meet the needs of customers.* From the perspective of operations, quality management deals with key issues relating to how goods and services are designed, created, and delivered to meet customer expectations. The Malcolm Baldrige Award Criteria described in Chapter 3 provide a comprehensive framework for building quality into organizational processes and practices.

15-1 Understanding Quality

Why is there so much emphasis on quality today? It helps to review a bit of history. During the Industrial Revolution, the use of interchangeable parts and the separation of work into small tasks necessitated careful control of quality, leading to the dependence on inspection to identify and remove defects and reducing the role of the workers themselves in responsibility for quality. After World War II, two U.S. consultants, Dr. Joseph Juran and Dr. W. Edwards Deming, introduced statistical quality control techniques to the Japanese to aid them in their rebuilding efforts. While presenting to a group of Japanese industrialists (collectively representing about 80 percent of the nation's capital) in 1950, Deming emphasized the importance of consumers and suppliers, the interdependency of organizational processes, the usefulness of consumer research, and the necessity of continuous improvement of all elements of the production system.

Improvements in Japanese quality were slow and steady; some 20 years passed before the quality of Japanese products exceeded that of Western manufacturers. By the 1970s, primarily due to the higher quality levels of their products, Japanese companies had made significant penetration into Western markets. Most major U.S. companies answered the wake-up call by instituting extensive quality improvement campaigns, focused not only on conformance but also on improving design quality.

In recent years, a new interest in quality has emerged in corporate boardrooms under the concept of *Six Sigma*, a customer-focused and results-oriented approach to business improvement. Six Sigma integrates many quality tools and techniques that have been tested and validated over the years with a bottom-line orientation that has high appeal to senior managers.

What does quality mean? A study that asked managers of 86 firms in the eastern United States to define quality produced several dozen different responses, including

1. perfection,
2. consistency,
3. eliminating waste,
4. speed of delivery,
5. compliance with policies and procedures,
6. providing a good, usable product,

Quality management refers to systematic policies, methods, and procedures used to ensure that goods and services are produced with appropriate levels of quality to meet the needs of customers.

7. doing it right the first time,

8. delighting or pleasing customers, and

9. total customer service and satisfaction.[2]

Many of these perspectives relate to a good's or service's **fitness for use**—*the ability of a good or service to meet customer needs*. From an operations perspective, however, the most useful definition is how well the output of a manufacturing or service process conforms to the design specifications. **Quality of conformance** *is the extent to which a process is able to deliver output that conforms to the design specifications.* **Specifications** *are targets and tolerances determined by designers of goods and services.* Targets are the ideal values for which production is to strive; tolerances are the permissible variation. Specifications for physical goods are normally measured using some physical property such as length, weight, temperature, or pressure. For example, the specification for the diameter of a drilled hole might be 0.50 ± 0.02 cm. The target is 0.50 cm, and the tolerance is ± 0.02 cm; that is, the size of the hole is permitted to vary between 0.48 and 0.52 cm.

Service quality *is consistently meeting or exceeding customer expectations (external focus) and service-delivery system performance criteria (internal focus) during all service encounters.* Excellent service quality is achieved by the consistent delivery to the customer of a clearly defined customer benefit package, and associated process and service encounters, defined by many internal and external standards of performance. Performance standards are analogous to manufacturing specifications. For example, "on-time arrival" for an airplane might be specified as within 15 minutes of the scheduled arrival time. The target is the scheduled time, and the tolerance is specified to be 15 minutes.

An established instrument for measuring customer perceptions of service quality is SERVQUAL.[3] The initial instrument identified 10 dimensions of service quality performance: (1) reliability, (2) responsiveness, (3) competence, (4) access, (5) courtesy, (6) communication, (7) credibility, (8) security, (9) understanding/knowing the customer, and (10) tangibles. These were reduced to five dimensions based on further research: *tangibles, reliability, responsiveness, assurance,* and *empathy.* Tangibles are what the customer sees, such as physical facilities, equipment, and the appearance of service employees. Reliability is the ability to provide what was promised, dependably and accurately. Responsiveness is the willingness to help customers and provide prompt service. Assurance is the knowledge and courtesy of service providers and their ability to

convey trust and confidence. Finally, empathy is caring, individual attention the firm provides its customers. These five dimensions of service quality are normally measured using a survey instrument with ordinal scales such as yes or no or a 5- or 7-point Likert scale. A typical 5-point Likert scale is 1 = Strongly disagree; 2 = Disagree; 3 = Neither agree nor disagree; 4 = Agree, 5 = Strongly agree. SERVQUAL is designed to apply to all service industries; however, dimensions specific to a certain industry or business or process may provide more accurate measures.

Quality is more than simply ensuring that goods and services consistently conform to specifications. Achieving high-quality goods and services depends on the commitment and involvement of everyone in the entire value chain. The principles of total quality are simple:

1. a focus on customers and stakeholders,

2. a process focus supported by continuous improvement and learning, and

3. participation and teamwork by everyone in the organization.

There is considerable evidence that investment in quality—not only in goods, services, and processes but in the quality of management itself—yields numerous benefits. Specific operational and financial results that Baldrige recipients have achieved include the following:

- Nestlé Purina PetCare Co. (NPPC) manufactures, markets, and distributes pet food and snacks for dogs and cats, as well as cat litter. NPPC ranks first in market share for pet-care products in North America, has twice the market share of its closest competitor, and has grown its market share by almost 10 percent over 10 years in a mature industry. It is also recognized as best in the industry for its outstanding safety performance.

Fitness for use is the ability of a good or service to meet customer needs.

Quality of conformance is the extent to which a process is able to deliver output that conforms to the design specifications.

Specifications are targets and tolerances determined by designers of goods and services.

Service quality is consistently meeting or exceeding customer expectations (external focus) and service-delivery system performance criteria (internal focus) during all service encounters.

Charles Thatcher/Stone/Getty Images

- K&N Management is the licensed Austin,Texas–area developer for Rudy's "Country Store" & Bar-B-Q and the creator of Mighty Fine Burgers, Fries and Shakes, two fast-casual restaurant concepts. Guests rate their satisfaction with food quality, hospitality, cleanliness, and speed of service; overall customer satisfaction outperforms the best competitor. In 2010, the firm was named "the best place to work in Austin."

- Advocate Good Samaritan Hospital is an acute-care medical facility in Downers Grove, Illinois. Overall patient satisfaction levels for outpatient, emergency, ambulatory surgery, and convenient care exceed the top 10 percent nationally. Good Samaritan Hospital used Six Sigma methodology to pioneer improvement of "door-to-balloon" time, the critical period for assessing and diagnosing a heart attack and delivering the needed intervention, lowering the measure to 52 minutes, among the best in Illinois.

15-2 Influential Leaders in Modern Quality Management

many individuals have made substantial contributions to quality management thought and applications. However, three people—W. Edwards Deming, Joseph M. Juran, and Philip B. Crosby—are regarded as "management gurus" in the quality revolution.

15-2a W. Edwards Deming

Unlike other management gurus and consultants, Deming (pictured below) never defined or described quality precisely. In his last book, he stated, "A product or a service possesses quality if it helps somebody and enjoys a good and sustainable market."[4] The Deming philosophy focuses on bringing about improvements in product and service quality by reducing variability in goods and services design and associated processes. Deming professed that higher quality leads to higher productivity and lower costs, which in turn leads to improved market share and long-term competitive strength. In his early work in the United States, Deming preached his 14 Points. Although management practices today are vastly different than when Deming first began to preach his philosophy, the 14 Points still convey important insights for operations managers as well as every other manager in an organization.

Point 1: *Create a Vision and Demonstrate Commitment*

Point 2: *Learn the Philosophy*

Point 3: *Understand Inspection*

Point 4: *Stop Making Decisions Purely on the Basis of Cost*

Point 5: *Improve Constantly and Forever*

Point 6: *Institute Training*

Point 7: *Institute Leadership*

Point 8: *Drive Out Fear*

Point 9: *Optimize the Efforts of Teams*

Point 10: *Eliminate Exhortations*

Point 11: *Eliminate Numerical Quotas*

Point 12: *Remove Barriers to Pride in Work*

Point 13: *Encourage Education and Self-Improvement*

Point 14: *Take Action*

The 14 Points have become the basis for many organizations' quality approaches (see the feature on Hillerich & Bradsby Co. on the next page).

Deming also advocated a process to guide and motivate improvement activities, which has become known as the *Deming cycle*. The Deming cycle is composed

AP Photo/Richard Drew

HILLERICH & BRADSBY

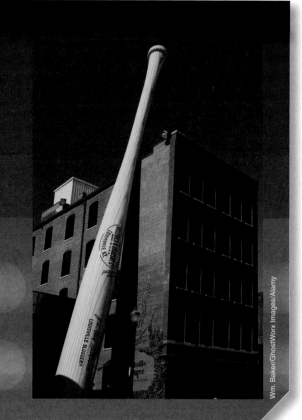

Hillerich & Bradsby Co. (H&B) has been making the Louisville Slugger brand of baseball bat for more than 115 years. When the company faced significant challenges from market changes and competition, CEO Jack Hillerich decided to apply the philosophy of Deming's 14 Points to change the company. Managers and union officials talked about building trust and changing the system "to make it something you want to work in."

One of the first changes was the elimination of work quotas that were tied to hourly salaries and a schedule of warnings and penalties for failures to meet quotas. Instead, a team-based approach was initiated. Although a few workers exploited the change, overall productivity actually improved as rework decreased because workers were taking pride in their work and producing things the right way the first time. H&B also eliminated performance appraisals and commission-based pay in sales. The company has also focused its efforts on training and education, resulting in an openness to change and a capacity for teamwork. Today, the Deming philosophy is still the core of H&B's guiding principles.[5]

of four stages: *plan*, *do*, *study*, and *act* (PDSA). PDSA guides teams to develop an improvement plan, try it out, examine the results, and institute changes that lead to improved results, and then repeat the process all over again.

15-2b Joseph Juran

Like Deming, Juran taught quality principles to the Japanese in the 1950s and was a principal force in their quality reorganization. Juran proposed a simple definition of quality: "fitness for use." Unlike Deming, however, Juran did not propose a major cultural change in the organization, but rather sought to improve quality by working within the system familiar to managers. He argued that employees at different levels of an organization speak in their own "languages." Juran stated that top management speaks in the language of dollars; workers speak in the language of things; and middle management must be able to speak both languages and translate between dollars and things. To get the attention of top managers, quality issues must be cast in the language they understand—dollars. Hence, Juran

advocated the use of quality cost measurement, discussed later in this chapter, to focus attention on quality problems. At the operational level, Juran focused on increasing conformance to specifications through elimination of defects, supported extensively by statistical tools for analysis. Thus, his philosophy fit well into existing management systems.

Juran's prescriptions focus on three major quality processes, called the Quality Trilogy: (1) quality planning—the process of preparing to meet quality goals; (2) quality control—the process of meeting quality goals during operations; and (3) quality improvement—the process of breaking through to unprecedented levels of performance. At the time he proposed this structure, few companies were engaging in any significant planning or improvement activities. Thus, Juran was promoting a major cultural shift in management thinking.

15-2c Philip B. Crosby

Philip B. Crosby authored several popular books. His first book, *Quality Is Free*, sold about 1 million copies and was greatly responsible for bringing quality to the attention of top corporate managers in the United States. The essence of Crosby's quality philosophy is embodied in what he calls the Absolutes of Quality Management and the Basic Elements of Improvement. Crosby's Absolutes of Quality Management include the following points:

- *Quality means conformance to requirements, not elegance.* Requirements must be clearly stated so that they cannot be misunderstood.

- *There is no such thing as a quality problem.* Problems are functional in nature. Thus, a firm may experience accounting problems, manufacturing problems, design problems, front-desk problems, and so on.

- *There is no such thing as the economics of quality; doing the job right the first time is always cheaper.* Quality is free. What costs money are all actions that involve not doing jobs right the first time.

- *The only performance measurement is the cost of quality, which is the expense of nonconformance.* Quality cost data are useful to call problems to management's attention, to select opportunities for corrective action, and to track quality improvement over time.

- *The only performance standard is "Zero Defects (ZD)."* This simply represents the philosophy of preventing defects in goods and services rather than finding them after the fact and fixing them.

15-3 The GAP Model

any people view quality by comparing features and characteristics of goods and services to a set of expectations, which may be promulgated by marketing efforts aimed at developing quality as an image variable in their minds. A framework for evaluating the quality of both goods and services and identifying where to focus design and improvement efforts is the GAP model.

The GAP model recognizes that there are several ways to mismanage the creation and delivery of high levels of quality. These "gaps" are shown in the model in Exhibit 15.1 and explained in the following list.

- *Gap 1 is the discrepancy between customer expectations and management perceptions of those expectations.* Managers may think they understand why customers buy a good or service, but if their perception is wrong, then all subsequent design and delivery activities may be misdirected. Some organizations, for example, require senior managers to work in front-line jobs a few days every year so they keep in contact with customers and front-line employees.

- *Gap 2 is the discrepancy between management perceptions of what features constitute a target level of quality and the task of translating these perceptions into executable specifications.* This represents a mismatch between management perceptions of what constitutes good performance and the actual job and process design specifications that we discussed in Chapter 6.

- *Gap 3 is the discrepancy between quality specifications documented in operating and training manuals and plans and their implementation.* Gap 3 recognizes that the manufacturing and service delivery systems must execute quality specifications well. One way to improve day-to-day execution, for example, is by doing a better job at service management training.

- *Gap 4 is the discrepancy between actual manufacturing and service-delivery system performance and external communications to the customers.* The customer should not be promised a certain type and level of quality unless the delivery system can achieve or exceed that level. Advertising, for example, can help establish customer expectations, and internal training and marketing materials can help set employee performance standards.

- *Gap 5 is the difference between the customer's expectations and perceptions.* Gap 5 is where the customer judges quality and makes future purchase decisions. The fifth gap depends on the other four gaps. The theory of the GAP model is that if gaps 1 to 4 are minimized, higher customer satisfaction will result.

Managers can use this model to analyze goods and services and the processes that make and deliver them to identify and close the largest gaps and improve performance. Failure to understand and minimize these gaps can seriously degrade the quality of a service and present the risk of losing customer loyalty.[6]

Exhibit 15.1 *GAP Model of Quality*

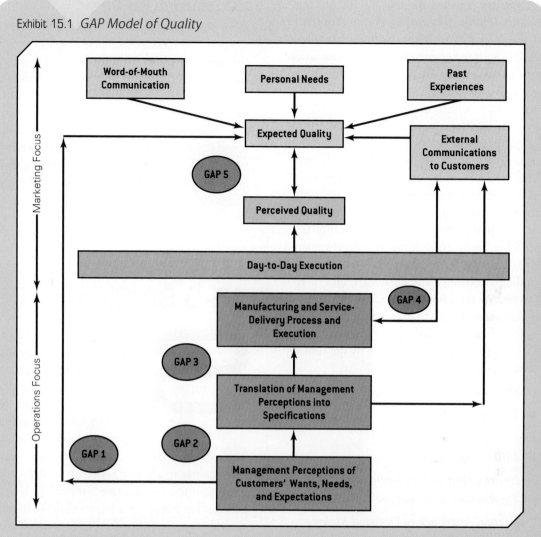

Source: A. Parasuraman, V. A. Zeithaml, and L. L. Berry, "A Conceptual Model of Service Quality and Its Implications for Future Research," *Journal of Marketing,* 49 (Fall 1985), pp. 41–50. Reprinted with permission from the American Marketing Association.

15-4 ISO 9000:2000

t o standardize quality requirements for European countries within the Common Market and those wishing to do business with those countries, a specialized agency for standardization, the International Organization for Standardization (ISO), founded in 1946 and composed of representatives from the national standards bodies of 91 nations, adopted a series of written quality standards in 1987. They were revised in 1994, and again (significantly) in 2000. The

PhotoLink/Photodisc/Getty Images

most recent version is called the ISO 9000:2000 family of standards. The standards have been adopted in the United States by the American National Standards Institute (ANSI) with the endorsement and cooperation of the American Society for Quality (ASQ) and are recognized by about 100 countries.

ISO 9000:2000 defines *quality system standards*, based on the premise that certain generic characteristics of management practices can be standardized and that a well-designed, well-implemented, and carefully managed quality system provides confidence that the outputs will meet customer expectations and requirements.

The standards prescribe documentation for all processes affecting quality and suggest that compliance through auditing leads to continuous improvement. The standards are intended to apply to all types of businesses, including electronics and chemicals, and to services such as health care, banking, and transportation. In some foreign markets, companies will not buy from suppliers who are not certified to the standards. The ISO 9000:2000 standards are supported by the following eight principles:

Principle 1—*Customer-Focused Organization*

Principle 2—*Leadership*

Principle 3—*Involvement of People*

Principle 4—*Process Approach*

Principle 5—*System Approach to Management*

Principle 6—*Continual Improvement*

Principle 7—*Factual Approach to Decision Making*

Principle 8—*Mutually Beneficial Supplier Relationships*

ISO 9000:2000 provides a set of good basic practices for initiating a basic quality management system and is an excellent starting point for companies with no formal quality assurance program. For companies in the early stages of developing a quality program, the standards enforce the discipline of control that is necessary before they can seriously pursue continuous improvement. The requirements of periodic audits reinforce the stated quality system until it becomes ingrained in the company.

Six Sigma is a business improvement approach that seeks to find and eliminate causes of defects and errors in manufacturing and service processes by focusing on outputs that are critical to customers, resulting in a clear financial return for the organization.

ISO Standards Pay Off

Many organizations have realized significant benefits from using the ISO 9000:2000 standards. At DuPont, for example, they have been been credited with increasing on-time delivery from 70 to 90 percent, decreasing cycle time from 15 days to 1.5 days, increasing first-pass yields from 72 to 92 percent, and reducing the number of test procedures by one-third. The first home builder to achieve registration, Michigan-based Delcor Homes, reduced its rate of correctable defects from 27.4 to 1.7 percent in two years and improved its building experience approval rating from the mid-60s to the mid-90s on a 100-point scale.[7]

15-5 Six Sigma

Six **Sigma** *is a business improvement approach that seeks to find and eliminate causes of defects and errors in manufacturing and service processes by focusing on outputs that are critical to customers, resulting in a clear financial return for the organization.*

The term "six sigma" is based on a statistical measure that equates to at most 3.4 errors or defects per million opportunities. An ultimate "stretch" goal of all organizations that adopt a Six Sigma philosophy is to have all critical processes, regardless of functional area, at a six-sigma level of capability—a level of near-zero defects. Robert Galvin, former Motorola CEO, stated back in 1987: "There is only one ultimate goal: zero defects—in everything we do." Six Sigma has garnered a significant amount of credibility over the last decade because of its acceptance at such major firms as Motorola, Allied Signal (now part of Honeywell), Texas Instruments, and General Electric. It is facilitated through use of basic and advanced quality improvement and control tools by individuals and teams whose members are trained to provide fact-based decision-making information.

⌈"There is only one ultimate goal: zero defects—in everything we do." —Robert Galvin, former Motorola CEO, 1987. ⌋

AP Photo/Ben Margot

In Six Sigma terminology, *a **defect** is any mistake or error that is passed on to the customer* (many people also use the term *nonconformance*). *A **unit of work** is the output of a process or an individual process step.* We can measure output quality by defects per unit (DPU), a popular quality measure that we introduced in Chapter 3:

$$\text{Defects per unit} = \frac{\text{Number of defects discovered}}{\text{Number of units produced}} \quad [15.1]$$

The Six Sigma concept characterizes quality performance by *defects per million opportunities (dpmo)*, computed as

$$\text{dpmo} = (\text{Number of defects discovered/opportunities for error}) \times 1,000,000 \quad [15.2]$$

In service applications, we often use the term *errors per million opportunities—epmo—*instead of dpmo. A "six-sigma" quality level corresponds to a dpmo or epmo equal to 3.4 (this is derived from some advanced statistical calculations), which represents almost perfect quality.

For example, suppose that an airline wishes to measure the effectiveness of its baggage handling system. A DPU measure might be lost bags per customer. However, customers may have different numbers of bags; thus, the number of opportunities for error is the total number of checked bags. The use of dpmo and epmo allows us to define quality broadly. In the airline case, we might expand the concept to mean every opportunity for a failure to meet customer expectations from initial ticketing until bags are retrieved.

We noted that a "six-sigma" process has a dpmo of 3.4. The sigma level can easily be calculated on an Excel spreadsheet using the cell formula:

$$= \text{NORMSINV}(1 - \text{Number of Defects/Number of Opportunities}) + 1.5$$

or equivalently,

$$= \text{NORMSINV}(1 - \text{dpmo}/1,000,000) + 1.5 \quad [15.3]$$

The value of 1.5 in this formula stems from the mathematical calculation of six sigma. The developers of this concept allowed a process to shift by as much as 1.5 standard deviations from the mean, recognizing that it is not possible to control a process perfectly. Using the formula in Equation 15.3, we can translate any value of dpmo into a "sigma measure." For example, while a six-sigma process has a dpmo of 3.4, we can also state that a three-sigma process has a dpmo of 66,807, a four-sigma process has dpmo = 6,210, and a five-sigma process has dpmo = 233. You can see that moving from a three- to a four-sigma level requires about a 10-fold improvement, and moving from a five- to a six-sigma level is almost a 70-fold improvement. It isn't easy to reach six-sigma quality levels!

Six Sigma has been applied in product development, new business acquisition, customer service, accounting, and many other business functions. For example, suppose that a bank tracks the number

A **defect** is any mistake or error that is passed on to the customer.

A **unit of work** is the output of a process or an individual process step.

Solved Problem

Suppose that the average number of bags checked by airline passengers is 1.6, and the airline recorded three lost bags for 8,000 passengers in one month. What is the epmo, and at what sigma level is this process operating?

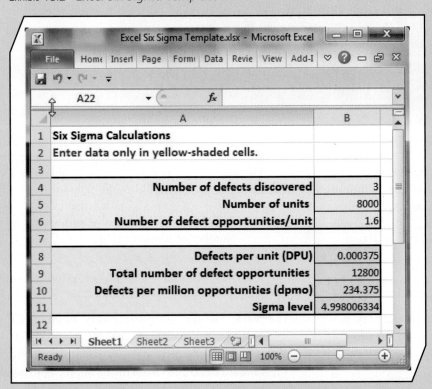

Exhibit 15.2 *Excel Six Sigma Template*

Solution

The three lost bags represent the number of defects discovered among 8,000 passengers (units). Therefore, using Equation 15.1, the number of defects per unit (i.e., passenger) is 3/8,000 = 0.000375. However, because each passenger checks an average of 1.6 bags, the total number of defect opportunities is (8,000 passengers) (1.6 bags/passenger) = 12,800. To find dpmo, we use Equation 15.2:

dpmo = (Number of errors discovered/opportunities for error) × 1,000,000 = (3/12,800) (1,000,000) = 234.375. Using the Excel formula in Equation 15.3, the sigma level is calculated as = NORMSINV(1 − 234.375/1000000) + 1.5 = 4.99828, or about a five-sigma level. Exhibit 15.2 shows the Excel Six Sigma template, which can be used to perform these calculations.

of errors reported in customers' checking account statements. If it finds 12 errors in 1,000 statements, this is equivalent to an epmo of (12/1,000) × 1,000,000 = 12,000 errors per million, (somewhere between 3.5- and 4-sigma levels).

15-5a Implementing Six Sigma

Six Sigma has developed from simply a way of measuring quality to an overall strategy to accelerate improvements and achieve unprecedented performance levels. An organization does this by finding and eliminating causes of errors or defects in processes by focusing on

characteristics that are critical to customers.[8] The core philosophy of Six Sigma is based on some key concepts:[9]

1. emphasizing dpmo or epmo as a standard metric that can be applied to all parts of an organization: manufacturing, engineering, administrative, software, and so on;

2. providing extensive training followed by project team deployment to improve profitability, reduce non-value-added activities, and achieve cycle time reduction;

3. focusing on corporate sponsors responsible for supporting team activities to help overcome

resistance to change, obtain resources, and focus the teams on overall strategic objectives;

4. creating highly qualified process improvement experts ("green belts," "black belts," and "master black belts") who can apply improvement tools and lead teams;

5. ensuring that appropriate metrics are identified early in the process and that they focus on business results; and

6. setting stretch objectives for improvement.

The recognized benchmark for Six Sigma implementation is General Electric. GE's Six Sigma problem-solving approach (DMAIC) employs five phases:

1. *Define (D)*
   - Identify customers and their priorities.
   - Identify a project suitable for Six Sigma efforts based on business objectives as well as customer needs and feedback.
   - Identify CTQs (*critical-to-quality characteristics*) that the customer considers to have the most impact on quality.

2. *Measure (M)*
   - Determine how to measure the process and how it is performing.
   - Identify the key internal processes that influence CTQs and measure the defects currently generated relative to those processes.

3. *Analyze (A)*
   - Determine the most likely causes of defects.
   - Understand why defects are generated by identifying the key variables that are most likely to create process variation.

4. *Improve (I)*
   - Identify means to remove the causes of the defects.
   - Confirm the key variables and quantify their effects on the CTQs.
   - Identify the maximum acceptable ranges of the key variables and a system for measuring deviations of the variables.
   - Modify the process to stay within the acceptable range.

5. *Control (C)*
   - Determine how to maintain the improvements.
   - Put tools in place to ensure that the key variables remain within the maximum acceptable ranges under the modified process.

Using a structured process like the DMAIC approach helps project teams ensure that Six Sigma is implemented effectively (see the box on American Express).

All Six Sigma projects have three key characteristics: a problem to be solved, a process in which the problem exists, and one or more measures that quantify the gap to be closed and can be used to monitor progress. These characteristics are present in all business processes; thus, Six Sigma can easily be applied to a wide variety of transactional, administrative, and service areas in both large and small firms.

The concepts and methods used in Six Sigma efforts have been around for a long time and may be categorized into seven general groups:

- *elementary statistical tools* (basic statistics, statistical thinking, hypothesis testing, correlation, simple regression);

- *advanced statistical tools* (design of experiments, analysis of variance, multiple regression);

- *product design and reliability* (quality function deployment, reliability analysis, failure mode and effects analysis);

- *measurement* (cost of quality, process capability, measurement systems analysis);

- *process control* (control plans, statistical process control, reducing variation);

- *process improvement* (process improvement planning, process mapping, mistake-proofing); and

- *implementation and teamwork* (organizational effectiveness, team assessment, facilitation tools, team development).

You may have covered some of these tools, such as statistics and teamwork, in other courses, and some, such as quality function deployment and statistical process control, are discussed in other chapters of this book.

In applying Six Sigma to services, there are four key measures of the performance: *accuracy*, as measured by correct financial figures, completeness of information, or freedom from data errors; *cycle time*, which is a measure of how long it takes to do

something, such as pay an invoice; *cost,* that is, the internal cost of process activities (in many cases, cost is largely determined by the accuracy and/or cycle time of the process—the longer it takes, and the more mistakes that have to be fixed, the higher the cost); and *customer satisfaction,* which is typically the primary measure of success.

15-6 Cost-of-Quality Measurement

he **cost of quality** *refers specifically to the costs associated with avoiding poor quality or those incurred as a result of poor quality.* Cost-of-quality analysis can help operations managers communicate with senior-level managers, identify and justify

> The **cost of quality** refers specifically to the costs associated with avoiding poor quality or those incurred as a result of poor quality.

Taking Six Sigma Out of the Factory

At DuPont, a Six Sigma project was applied to improve cycle time for an employee's application for long-term disability benefits.[11] Some examples of financial applications of Six Sigma include[12]

- *Reduce the average and variation of days outstanding of accounts receivable.*

- *Close the books faster.*

- *Improve the accuracy and speed of the audit process.*

- *Reduce variation in cash flow.*

- *Improve the accuracy of journal entries (most businesses have a 3–4 percent error rate).*

- *Improve the accuracy and cycle time of standard financial reports.*

major opportunities for process improvements, and evaluate the importance of quality and improvement in operations.

Quality costs can be organized into four major categories: prevention costs, appraisal costs, internal failure costs, and external failure costs.

Prevention costs *are those expended to keep noncon-forming goods and services from being made and reaching the customer.* They include

- *quality planning costs*—such as salaries of individuals associated with quality planning and problem-solving teams, the development of new procedures, new equipment design, and reliability studies;

- *process-control costs*—which include costs spent on analyzing processes and implementing process control plans;

- *information-systems costs*—which are expended to develop data requirements and measurements; and

- *training and general management costs*—which include internal and external training programs, clerical staff expenses, and miscellaneous supplies.

Appraisal costs *are those expended on ascertaining quality levels through measurement and analysis of data to detect and correct problems.* They include

- *test and inspection costs*—those associated with incoming materials, work-in-process, and finished goods, including equipment costs and salaries;

- *instrument maintenance costs*—those associated with the calibration and repair of measuring instruments; and

- *process-measurement and process-control costs*—which involve the time spent by workers to gather and analyze quality measurements.

Internal failure costs *are costs incurred as a result of unsatisfactory quality that is found before the delivery of a good or service to the customer.* Examples include

- *scrap and rework costs*—including material, labor, and overhead;

- *costs of corrective action*—arising from time spent determining the causes of failure and correcting problems;

- *downgrading costs*—such as revenue lost by selling a good or service at a lower price because it does not meet specifications; and

- *process failures*—such as unplanned equipment downtime or service upsets or unplanned equipment repair.

External failure costs *are incurred after poor-quality goods or services reach the customer.* They include

- *costs due to customer complaints and returns*—including rework on returned items, cancelled orders, discount coupons, and freight premiums;

- *goods and services recall costs and warranty and service guarantee claims*—including the cost of repair or replacement as well as associated administrative costs; and

- *product-liability costs*—resulting from legal actions and settlements.

By collecting and analyzing these costs, managers can identify the most important opportunities for improvement.

As the box on the Peanut Corporation of America illustrates, food supply chains are under increasing quality risks due to global sourcing. Thousands of global supply chains create and deliver food to your local supermarket or grocery store. For example, the ingredients in a Nutri-Grain bar includes citric acid from Europe, guar gum from India, carrageenan from the Philippines, malic acid from Italy, corn syrup from the USA, vitamin and mineral supplements (B_1, B_2, iron, folic acid) from China, and sodium alginate from Scotland. For operations management, an important challenge is to manage the flow of each raw material and ingredient from its source, such as a small farm, to factories to distributors to retailers and ultimately to consumers to ensure a safe food supply. This includes monitoring possible contamination from bacteria, pesticides, carcinogens, and heavy metals, as well as the cleanliness of food processing and storage facilities. "It's a global information management problem," says Mr. Blissett, head of consumer products for IBM.

Prevention costs are those expended to keep nonconforming goods and services from being made and reaching the customer.

Appraisal costs are those expended on ascertaining quality levels through measurement and analysis of data to detect and correct problems.

Internal failure costs are costs incurred as a result of unsatisfactory quality that is found before the delivery of a good or service to the customer.

External failure costs are incurred after poor-quality goods or services reach the customer.

When tainted food or ingredients enter supply chains, internal and external failure costs can increase dramatically. Monitoring requires increased appraisal. Suppliers, manufacturers, distributors, and retailers are adding more inspectors and inspection points in their supply chains. Many of these are a result of national laws and regulations; in the United States, for example, 12 federal agencies administer 35 different food safety laws. Nevertheless, better prevention through the design and control of food production processes can help to reduce such costs.[14]

15-7 The "Seven QC Tools"

Seven simple tools—flowcharts, checksheets, histograms, Pareto diagrams, cause-and-effect diagrams, scatter diagrams, and control charts—termed the *Seven QC (Quality Control) Tools* by the Japanese, support quality improvement problem-solving efforts.[15] The Seven QC Tools are designed to be simple and visual so that workers at all levels can use them easily and provide a means of communication that is particularly well suited in group problem-solving efforts.

Flowcharts

To understand a process, one must first determine how it works and what it is supposed to do. Flowcharting, or process mapping, identifies the sequence of activities or the flow of materials and information in a process. Once a flowchart is constructed, it can be used to identify quality problems as well as areas for productivity improvement. Questions such as "What work activities can be combined, simplified, or eliminated?" "Are process capacities well planned?" and "How is quality measured at points of customer contact?"

Run and Control Charts

A *run chart* is a line graph in which data are plotted over time. The vertical axis represents a measurement; the horizontal axis is the time scale. Run charts show the performance and the variation of a process or some quality or productivity indicator over time. They can be used to track such things as production volume, costs, and customer satisfaction indexes. Run charts summarize data in a graphical fashion that is easy to understand and interpret, identify process changes and trends over time, and show the effects of corrective actions.

A *control chart* is simply a run chart to which two horizontal lines, called *control limits*, are added: the *upper control limit (UCL)* and *lower control limit (LCL)*, as illustrated in Exhibit 15.3. Control limits are chosen statistically so that there is a high probability (generally greater than .99) that points will fall between these limits if the process is in control. Control limits make it easier to interpret patterns in a run chart and draw conclusions about the state of control. The next chapter addresses this topic in much more detail.

Checksheets

Checksheets are special types of data collection forms in which the results may be interpreted on the form directly without additional processing. For example, in the checksheet in Exhibit 15.4, one can easily identify the most frequent causes of defects.

Histograms

A histogram is a basic statistical tool that graphically shows the frequency or number of observations of a particular value or within a specified group. Histograms provide clues about the characteristics of the parent population from which a sample is taken. Patterns that would be difficult to see in an ordinary table of numbers become apparent. You are probably quite familiar with histograms from your statistics classes.

Pareto Diagrams

The *Pareto principle* was observed by Joseph Juran in 1950. Juran found that most effects resulted from only a few causes. He named this technique after Vilfredo Pareto (1848–1923), an Italian economist who

Exhibit 15.3 *The Structure of a Control Chart*

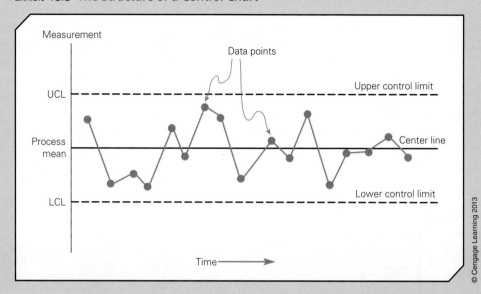

© Cengage Learning 2013

Exhibit 15.4 *Defective Item Checksheet*

Checksheet

Product: _____

Manufacturing stage: final insp. _____

Type of defect: scar, incomplete, misshapen _____

Total no. inspected: 2530 _____

Remarks: all items inspected _____

Date: _____
Factory: _____
Section: _____
Inspector's name: _____
Lot no. _____
Order no. _____

Type	Check	Subtotal
Surface scars	ℍ ℍ ℍ ℍ ℍ ℍ //	32
Cracks	ℍ ℍ ℍ ℍ ///	23
Incomplete	ℍ ℍ ℍ ℍ ℍ ℍ ℍ ℍ ℍ ///	48
Misshapen	////	4
Others	ℍ ///	8
	Grand total	115
Total rejects	ℍ ℍ ℍ ℍ ℍ ℍ ℍ ℍ ℍ ℍ ℍ ℍ ℍ ℍ ℍ ℍ ℍ /	86

Source: Ishikawa, Kaoru. "Defective Item Checksheet," *Guide to Quality Control*. Asian Productivity Organization, 1982, p. 33. Reprinted with permission.

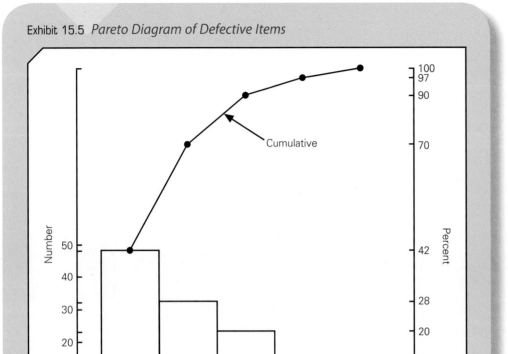

Exhibit 15.5 *Pareto Diagram of Defective Items*

Number

100
97
90

70

Cumulative

50

42

40

30

28

20

20

10

7
3

Percent

Incomplete | Surface scars | Cracks | Others | Misshapen

© Cengage Learning 2013

called a *fishbone diagram*. An example of a cause-and-effect diagram is shown in Exhibit 15.7. At the end of the horizontal line, a problem is listed. Each branch pointing into the main stem represents a possible cause. Branches pointing to the causes are contributors to those causes. The diagram identifies the most likely causes of a problem so that further data collection and analysis can be carried out.

Scatter Diagrams

Scatter diagrams are the graphical component of regression analysis. Although they do not provide rigorous statistical analysis, they often point to important relationships between variables, such as the percentage of an ingredient in an alloy and the hardness of the alloy. Scatter diagrams are often used to verify possible causes and effects obtained from cause-and-effect diagrams.

determined that 85 percent of the wealth in Milan was owned by only 15 percent of the people. Pareto analysis separates the vital few from the trivial many and provides direction for selecting projects for improvement.

An example of a Pareto diagram developed from the checksheet in Exhibit 15.4 is shown in Exhibit 15.5. The diagram shows that about 70 percent of defects result from the top two categories, Incomplete and Surface scars.

Pareto analysis is often used to analyze cost-of-quality data that we discussed in Section 6 of this chapter. The Solved Problem on page 343 illustrates how this can be applied.

Cause-and-Effect Diagrams

The cause-and-effect diagram is a simple, graphical method for presenting a chain of causes and effects and for sorting out causes and organizing relationships between variables. Because of its structure, it is often

15-7a Root Cause Analysis

The *root cause* is a term used to designate the source of a problem. Using the medical analogy, eliminating symptoms of problems provides only temporary relief; eliminating the root cause provides long-term relief. A useful approach to identify the root cause is called the *5-Why Technique*. This approach forces one to redefine a problem statement as a chain of causes and effects to identify the source of the symptoms by asking why, ideally five times. In a classic example at Toyota, a machine failed because a fuse blew. Replacing the fuse would have been the obvious solution; however, this action would have addressed only the symptom of the real problem. Why did the fuse blow? Because the bearing did not have adequate lubrication. Why? Because the lubrication pump was not

Solved Problem

D.B. Smith Company produces machine tools. The company conducted a cost-of-quality study and found the following:

Cost Category	Amount
Quality equipment design	$ 25,000
Scrap	330,000
Inspection and retest	340,000
Customer returns	90,000
Supplier quality surveys	8,000
Repair	80,000

What quality cost categories should each of these costs be associated with, and what does a Pareto analysis reveal?

Solution

Cost Category	Amount	Quality Cost Category
Equipment maintenance	$ 25,000	Prevention
Machine downtime	330,000	Internal failure

Product inspection	340,000	Appraisal
Customer field repairs	90,000	External failure
Supplier quality audits	8,000	Prevention
Equipment repair	80,000	Internal failure

The total costs in each category are:

Prevention: $25,000 + $8,000 = $33,000
Appraisal: $340,000
Internal failure: $330,000 + $80,000 = $410,000
External failure: $90,000

Exhibit 15.6 shows a Pareto chart using the Excel Pareto Chart template. This suggests that a very high amount of costs is spent on internal failure and appraisal. The company should probably invest more in activities focused on preventing internal failures, and seek to reduce the amount of inspection through better-quality processes.

Exhibit 15.6 *Cost-of-Quality Analysis Using the Excel Pareto Chart Template*

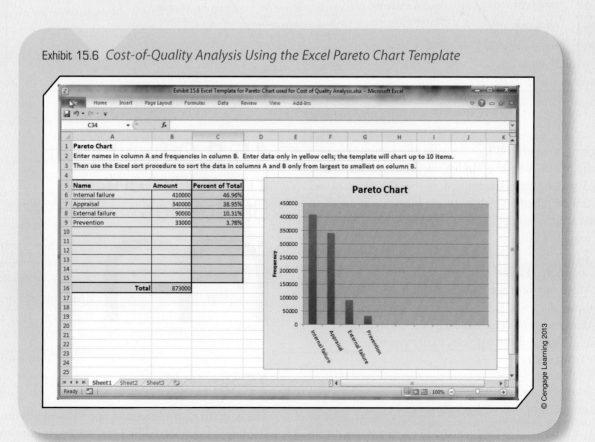

© Cengage Learning 2013

Exhibit 15.7 *Cause-and-Effect Diagram for Hospital Emergency Admission*

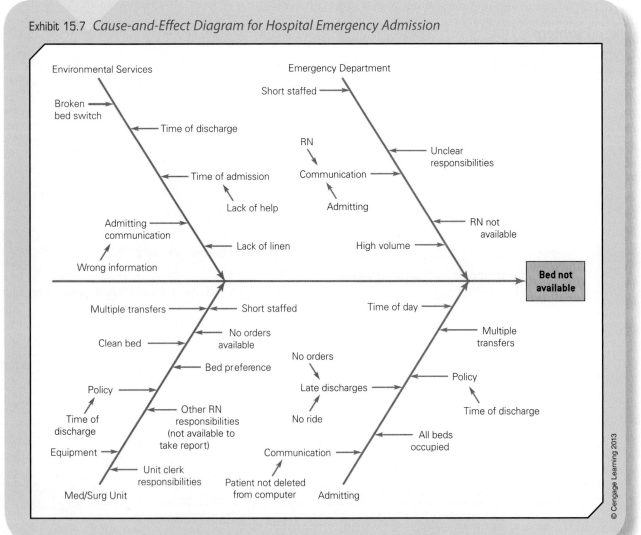

working properly. Why? Because the pump axle was worn. Why? Because sludge seeped into the pump axle, which was determined to be the root cause. Toyota attached a strainer to the lubricating pump to eliminate the sludge, thus correcting the problem of the machine failure.

Root cause analysis often uses the Seven QC Tools. For example, Pareto diagrams can also progressively help focus in on root causes. Exhibit 15.8 shows one example. At each step, the Pareto diagram stratifies the data to more detailed levels (or it may require additional data collection), eventually isolating the most significant issue.

Kaizen focuses on small, gradual, and frequent improvements over the long term with minimum financial investment and with participation by everyone in the organization.

15-8 Other Quality Improvement Strategies

many other approaches to quality improvement have been developed and refined over the years. Two powerful approaches are kaizen and poka-yoke.

15-8a Kaizen

The concept of continuous improvement advocated by Deming was embraced by Japanese organizations, leading to an approach known as *kaizen*. **Kaizen** *focuses on*

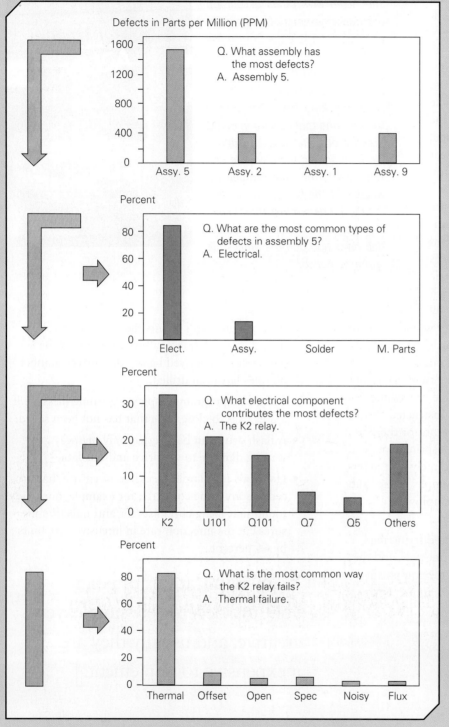

Exhibit 15.8 *Use of Pareto Diagrams for Root Cause Analysis*

Defects in Parts per Million (PPM)

Q. What assembly has the most defects?
A. Assembly 5.

Percent

Q. What are the most common types of defects in assembly 5?
A. Electrical.

Percent

Q. What electrical component contributes the most defects?
A. The K2 relay.

Percent

Q. What is the most common way the K2 relay fails?
A. Thermal failure.

Source: *Small Business Guidebook to Quality Management*, Office of the Secretary of Defense, Quality Management Office, Washington, DC (1988).

small, gradual, and frequent improvements over the long term with minimum financial investment and with participation by everyone in the organization. In the kaizen philosophy, improvement in all areas of business—cost, meeting delivery schedules, employee safety and skill development, supplier relations, new product development, or productivity—serve to enhance the quality of the firm. Thus, any activity directed toward improvement falls under the kaizen umbrella.

A **kaizen blitz** *is an intense and rapid improvement process in which a team or a department throws all its resources into an improvement project over a short time period, as opposed to traditional kaizen applications, which are performed on a part-time basis.* Blitz teams are generally comprised of employees from all areas involved in the process who understand it and can implement changes on the spot.[16]

15-8b Poka-Yoke (Mistake-Proofing)

Human beings tend to make mistakes inadvertently. Typical process-related mistakes include omitted processing

A **kaizen blitz** is an intense and rapid improvement process in which a team or a department throws all its resources into an improvement project over a short time period, as opposed to traditional kaizen applications, which are performed on a part-time basis.

steps, processing errors, setup or change-over errors, missing information or parts, not handling service upsets properly, wrong information or parts, and adjustment errors.

Poka-yoke *(POH-kah YOH-kay) is an approach for mistake-proofing processes using automatic devices or methods to avoid simple human error.* The poka-yoke concept was developed and refined in the early 1960s by the late Shigeo Shingo, a Japanese manufacturing engineer who developed the Toyota production system.[17]

Many applications of poka-yoke are deceptively simple, yet creative, and usually they are inexpensive to implement. One of Shingo's first poka-yoke devices involved a process at the Yamada Electric plant in which workers assemble a switch having two push buttons supported by two springs.[18] Occasionally, the worker would forget to insert a spring under each button, which led to a costly and embarrassing repair at the customer's facility. In the old method, the worker would take two springs out of a large parts box and then assemble the switch. To prevent this mistake, the worker was instructed first to place two springs in a small dish in front of the parts box, and then assemble the switch. If a spring remained in the dish, the operator knew immediately that an error had occurred. The solution was simple, cheap, and provided immediate feedback to the employee.

Many other examples can be cited:

- Fast-food restaurants use automated frying machines that can only be operated one way, and the french fries are prepackaged and the equipment automated to reduce the chance of human error.

> **Poka-yoke** (POH-kah YOH-kay) is an approach for mistake-proofing processes using automatic devices or methods to avoid simple human error.

Poka-Yoke for Auto Safety

The Acura ZDX offers a collision avoidance system that uses a radar unit located inside the front grille. It monitors the distance between the vehicle and the one ahead of it. If the radar indicates that the car is approaching the other vehicle too fast, and that a collision might occur, it activates a buzzer and a warning light. If the driver doesn't slow down, then the seatbelt retracts and the brakes are applied lightly. If it determines that a collision will occur, then both the seatbelt retraction and the brakes are strongly applied.[19]

- A device on a drill counts the number of holes drilled in a workpiece; a buzzer sounds if the workpiece is removed before the correct number of holes has been drilled.

- Computer programs display a warning message if a user tries to close a file that has not been saved.

- A flash drive can be inserted only one way, preventing damage to the drive and the data.

- Hospitals use simple checklists to ensure that procedures are done correctly; for example, one study found that using checklists for anti-infection measures cut the infection rate in intensive care units by 66 percent.

> Many applications of poka-yoke are deceptively simple, yet creative, and usually they are inexpensive to implement.

Discussion Questions

1. Select two of Deming's 14 Points and discuss the importance of them to operations managers (as well as all managers) in today's business environment.

2. How do you think that quality management concepts can support sustainability efforts? Find some sources or examples to support your beliefs.

3. What types of defects or errors might the following organizations measure and improve as part of a quality or Six Sigma initiative?
   a. a department store such as Walmart or Macy's
   b. Walt Disney World or a regional amusement park such as Six Flags
   c. your college or university

4. Explain how each of the 7 QC Tools would be used in the five phases of the Six Sigma DMAIC problem-solving approach. For example, in which phase(s) (Define, Measure, Analyze, Improve, or Control) would you expect to use flowcharts, checksheets, and so on?

5. Which of the Seven QC Tools would be most useful in addressing each of the following situations? Explain your reasoning. (You may decide more than one tool is useful.)

   a. A copy machine suffers frequent paper jams and users are often confused as to how to fix the problem.

   b. The publication team for an engineering department wants to improve the accuracy of its user documentation but is unsure of why documents are not error-free.

   c. A bank needs to determine how many teller positions, drive-through stations, and ATM machines it needs for a new branch bank in a certain busy location. Its information includes the average numbers and types of customers served by other similar facilities, as well as demographic information to suggest the level of customer traffic in the new facility.

   d. A contracting agency wants to investigate why it had so many changes in its contracts. The company believes that the number of changes may be related to the dollar value of the original contract or the days between the request for proposal and the contract award.

   e. A travel agency is interested in gaining a better understanding of how call volume varies by time of year in order to adjust staffing schedules.

Problems and Activities

Note: an asterisk denotes problems for which an Excel spreadsheet template on the CourseMate Web site may be used.

1. Find the Web sites for the W. Edwards Deming Institute, the Juran Institute, and Philip Crosby Associates. What services do they offer? How do these organizations maintain the philosophies and legacies of these quality leaders?

2. Identify an organization that has achieved ISO 9000 certification and write a short paper (one page maximum) that summarizes the benefits and results that the organization has achieved using ISO 9000. See if you can find a service organization rather than a traditional manufacturing company.

3. Identify an organization that uses the Six Sigma DMAIC improvement approach. Describe in a short paper (maximum of two pages) some of the ways that this organization has applied DMAIC and the results it has achieved.

4. Find two examples similar to the Intel box in this chapter that describe the economic consequences of poor quality.

5.* A bank has set a standard that mortgage applications be processed within a certain number of days of filing. If, out of a sample of 2,500 applications, 85 fail to meet this requirement, what is the epmo metric and what sigma level does it correspond to?

6.* Over the last year, 1,800 injections were administered at a clinic. Quality is measured by the proper amount of dosage as well as the correct drug. In six instances, the incorrect amount was given, and in three cases, the wrong drug was given. What is the epmo metric and what sigma level does it correspond to?

7. Provide some specific examples of quality costs in a fast-food operation or in the operation of your college or university. Classify the costs into the four major categories described in the chapter.

8. The following list gives the number of defects found in 30 samples of 100 electronic assemblies taken on a daily basis over one month. Plot these data on a run chart, computing the average value (center line). How do you interpret the chart?

1	6	5	5	4	3	2	2	4	6
2	1	3	1	4	5	4	1	6	15
12	6	3	4	3	3	2	5	7	4

9. Develop cause-and-effect diagrams for any one of the following problems:
   a. poor exam grade
   b. no job offers
   c. too many speeding tickets
   d. late for work or school

10. Find two examples (different from the ones in this chapter) of how checksheets have been applied in an organization.

11.* Analysis of customer complaints at an e-commerce retailer revealed the following:

   Billing errors 537

   Shipping errors 2,460

   Electronic charge errors 650

   Shipping delays 5,372

   Packing errors 752

   Construct a Pareto diagram and discuss the conclusions you may draw from it.

12.* Classify the following cost elements into the appropriate cost-of-quality categories, prepare a Pareto chart for the categories, interpret the results, and provide recommendations.

Cost Element	Amount
Customer complaint remakes	$ 28,000
Printing plate revisions	28,000
Quality improvement projects	14,000
Gauging	100,000
Other waste	39,000
Correction of typographical errors	210,000
Proofreading	450,000
Quality planning	57,000
Press downtime	285,000
Bindery waste	53,000
Checking and inspection	42,000

13.* The following cost-of-quality data were collected at the installment loan department of the Kenney Bank. Classify these data into the appropriate cost-of-quality categories and analyze the results. What suggestions would you make to management?

Loan Processing

1. Run credit checks:	$2,675.01
2. Review documents:	$3,000.63
3. Make document corrections; gather additional information:	$1,032.65
4. Prepare tickler file; review and follow up on titles, insurance, second meetings:	$ 155.75
5. Review all output:	$2,243.62
6. Correct rejects and incorrect output:	$425.00
7. Reconcile incomplete collateral report:	$78.34
8. Handle dealer problem calls; address associate problems; research and communicate information:	$2,500.00
9. Compensate for system downtime:	$519.01
10. Conduct training:	$1,500.00

Loan Payment

1. Receive, inspect, and process payments:	$800.00
2. Respond to inquiries when no coupon is presented with payments:	$829.65

Loan Payoff

1. Receive, inspect, and process payoff and release documents:	$224.99
2. Research payoff problems:	$15.35

14. Describe some examples of poka-yoke in consumer products or manufacturing or service processes different from the ones cited in the chapter.

15. Refer to the automobile repair flowchart in Exhibit 7.5 in Chapter 7. Identify three activities where a potentially serious service error may occur, suggest performance measures for each of these three activities in the flowchart, and describe poka-yokes that might prevent such errors from occurring.

"I think the waiter wrote in an extra $25 tip on my Sunshine Café bill after I received and signed my credit card receipt," Mr. Mark Otter said to the restaurant manager, Brad Gladiolus. "Mr. Otter, mail me a copy of the restaurant receipt and I'll investigate," responded Mr. Gladiolus. "I don't have the receipt—I lost it—but I have my monthly credit card statement," replied Mr. Otter. Mr. Gladiolus hesitated, then said, "Mr. Otter, I don't see any way to investigate your claim, so there's nothing I can do."

Mr. Gladiolus sat down at his desk and sketched out possible causes of this service upset as follows:

- The customer is responsible for adding the bill and tipping properly, writing legibly, retaining the second receipt, and drinking alcohol responsibly.

- The employee is responsible for typing the bill in the register/computer correctly, going back to the customer if the tip is unreadable and verifying the correct amount, and being honest.

- The restaurant manager is responsible for investigating the store's receipt history and finding this transaction, auditing the source of the error if possible such as a mistyped decimal or extra zero, and contacting the credit card company and customer to resolve the issue.

- The credit card company, a third-party provider in this value chain, is responsible for providing records of the electronic transaction, helping resolve the issue, and issuing a debit or credit to the customer and/or restaurant if needed.

Company Background

Abby Martin's parents came to Florida from Chicago in the 1960s. Her parents bought land in the Cape Coral area. Later they opened a hotel on Fort Myers Beach and Abby was part of the housekeeping staff, her first job. By 17, she was running the hotel on her own. Today, she owns and operates six

Sunshine restaurants average about one negative customer complaint per 100 customer comments.

Jochen Sand/Photodisc/Getty Images

restaurants and a by-the-sea hotel. The restaurants are located in shopping centers next to high-traffic facilities such as movie theaters, groups of retail stores, and other clusters of restaurants. Abby uses four different restaurant concepts (i.e., facility décor, size, and layout; prices, menus; music and bands; wine list, lounge areas, etc.) for these six restaurants, depending on the location and local market demographics.

Abby has other investments but loves the challenge of managing restaurants. "I have a great passion for finding a need and meeting it," she said. "The secret to our restaurant success is customizing the business to local needs and being very consistent. Offer good food and service at the most reasonable price you can afford. And know that even if you offer all those things you can still fail. The hospitality business is the hardest business, period. You can never sit back and coast."

In her spare time, she is a prominent community figure involved in activities such as helping build the Ronald McDonald House, fund-raising for the hospital cancer foundation, and serving as chairperson of the local board for the Salvation Army. She likes the Salvation Army because it runs a lean operation, with only six cents spent on management for every one dollar in donations.

Day-to-Day Service Management

Sunshine restaurants are normally open seven days a week from 11 a.m. to 10 p.m. Lunch prices are in the $10 to $20 range and include such entrees a wood-grilled hamburger, seafood salad croissant, and sesame-crusted yellow fin tuna. Dinner prices range from $20 to $30 per person and include dishes such as shrimp and scallop scampi, red snapper picatta, and wood-grilled filet mignon. Each restaurant keeps about 20 to 30 popular wines in stock, such as a Cakebread

Chardonnay. Wine, liquor, and some food items are ordered in bulk to take advantage of volume-price discounts and shipped directly from the suppliers to individual restaurants. All other items are ordered by the restaurant chef and general manager for each unique restaurant.

Abby, like most entrepreneurs, has her own approach to quality control. She notes that, "I visit my restaurants every few days and as I walk in I immediately begin to watch customer faces and behaviors. I try to see if they are happy, talking, smiling, and enjoying the food and surroundings. I look at their posture and facial expressions. I often talk with customers and ask if everything was to their liking. I ask my employees—waiters, bartenders, kitchen help, managers, and chef—if they have encountered any problems or service breakdowns. I look for untidy floors, tables, and restrooms. I try to learn from negative customer comments or complaints. My employees know that I will try to help them solve any problem—they trust me. I take the pulse of the restaurant in a short visit. I meet weekly with the restaurant chefs. I manage quality by observation and close contact with all of the people in the restaurant. At night I go over the financials and sales data."

A typical Sunshine restaurant has a core staff of about 12 employees consisting of a manager, an assistant manager, chef, assistant chef, four waiters, two bartenders, and two helpers in the kitchen. During peak season each restaurant hires about six to eight additional employees. Peak demand is when the "snow-birds" arrived in southwest Florida from November to April. During peak demand the populations of Lee and Collier counties double to almost 2 million people.

Abby's entrepreneurial approach to managing the business results in about one negative customer complaint per 100 customer comments. The complaints are nearly equal in focusing on food or service quality. Contribution to profit and overhead per restaurant is 35 percent. The typical customer averages one visit every two months, and the customer defection rate is in the 5 to 10 percent range, but is difficult to estimate given the seasonal nature of the business.

Long-Term Strategic Issues

Abby Martin has established a reputation in southwest Florida for superior service and food quality in her restaurants. She was considering expanding her restaurants to the Tampa and Orlando areas to leverage her expertise and grow the business for the family. She wondered whether she could maintain the proper financial and quality controls with more restaurants and whether to franchise or not. Due to the 2007–2009 credit crunch and high foreclosure rates, there were plenty of commercial properties in good locations for restaurants, and prices were at all-time lows. Abby thought it was now or never in terms of expanding up and down the west coast of Florida. She envisioned as many as 20 Sunshine restaurants in the next five years.

Decisions

Abby wondered when she would ever get the time to analyze these issues. It was not easy keeping up with her businesses. She knew that superior day-to-day food and service quality determines repeat business, so she had to successfully resolve this customer complaint about the waiter adding a $25 tip while trying to plan for the future. She happened to be at her hotel, so she sat down in a beach chair and watched the brilliant colors of a sunset over the Gulf of Mexico. She began to write down a number of questions she had to answer soon.

Case Questions for Discussion

1. Draw a cause-and-effect diagram for the possible causes of the $25 tip service upset. Select one possible root cause from your diagram and explain how you would investigate and fix it.

2. What is the average value of a loyal customer (VLC) at Abby's restaurants (see Chapter 3)? What is the best way to increase revenue given your VLC analysis?

3. Critique the current "informal" quality control system. What changes and improvements do you recommend if Sunshine expands to 20 restaurants?

4. What are your short- and long-term recommendations? Explain your rationale for these recommendations.

USE THE TOOLS.

- Rip out the Review Cards in the back of your book to study.

Or Visit CourseMate to:

- Read, search, highlight, and take notes in the Interactive eBook
- Review Flashcards (Print or Online) to master key terms
- Test yourself with Auto-Graded Quizzes
- Bring concepts to life with Games, Videos, and Animations!

Go to CourseMate for **OM4** to begin using these tools.
Access at **www.cengagebrain.com**

Complete the Speak Up
survey in CourseMate at
www.cengagebrain.com

Follow us at
www.facebook.com/4ltrpress

©iStockphoto.com/A-Digit | © Cengage Learning 2011

QUALITY CONTROL AND SPC

arriott has become infamous for its obsessively detailed standard operating procedures (SOPs), which result in hotels that travellers either love for their consistent good quality or hate for their bland uniformity. "This is a company that has more controls, more systems, and more procedural manuals than anyone—except the government," says one industry veteran. "And they actually comply with them." Housekeepers work with a 114-point checklist. One SOP: Server knocks three times. After knocking, the associate should immediately identify herself or himself in a clear voice, saying, "Room Service!" The guest's name is never mentioned outside the door. Although people love to make fun of such procedures, they are a serious part of Marriott's business, and SOPs are designed to protect the brand. Recently, Marriott has removed some of the rigid guidelines for owners of hotels it manages, empowering them to make some of their own decisions on details.[1]

 learning outcomes

After studying this chapter you should be able to:

16-1 **Describe quality control systems and key issues in manufacturing and service.**

16-2 **Explain types of variation and the role of statistical process control (SPC).**

16-3 **Describe how to construct and interpret simple control charts for both continuous and discrete data.**

16-4 **Describe practical issues in implementing SPC.**

16-5 **Explain process capability and calculate process capability indexes.**

What do you think?

What opportunities for improved quality control or use of SOPs can you think of at your college or university (e.g., bookstore, cafeteria)?

ZUMA Press/Newscom

Quality control is vital in ensuring consistent service experiences and creating customer satisfaction, as the Marriott example illustrates. Simple control mechanisms such as checklists and standard operating procedures provide cost-effective means of doing this. Contacting customers after a poor service experience only uncovers the damage that has already occurred, requires extraordinary measures for service recovery, and often results in lost customers.

*The task of **quality control** is to ensure that a good or service conforms to specifications and meets customer requirements by monitoring and measuring processes and making any necessary adjustments to maintain a specified level of performance.* The consequences of a lack of effective quality control systems and procedures can be serious and potentially cause large financial losses or affect a company's reputation. Health care is one industry that has been highly criticized for its lack of effective quality control systems. For instance, a hospital in Philadelphia promised to evaluate and redesign its laboratory procedures after state investigators confirmed that faulty lab tests led to dozens of patients receiving overdoses of a blood-thinning medication, resulting in the deaths of two patients.[2] Many health care organizations are using contemporary manufacturing quality control methods and other quality improvement approaches such as Six Sigma in an effort to minimize such errors.

> The task of **quality control** is to ensure that a good or service conforms to specifications and meets customer requirements by monitoring and measuring processes and making any necessary adjustments to maintain a specified level of performance.

▼ *Travelers may love the consistency that results from detailed standard operating procedures (SOPs) in hotel chains, or hate what they see as "bland uniformity."*

 16-1 Quality Control Systems

a ny control system has three components:

1. a performance standard or goal,
2. a means of measuring actual performance, and
3. comparison of actual performance with the standard to form the basis for corrective action.

Similar control measures are taken in services (we introduced service quality metrics in the previous chapter). Fast-food restaurants, for example, have carefully designed their processes for a high degree of accuracy and fast response time, using hands-free intercom systems, microphones that reduce ambient kitchen noise, and screens that display a customer's order. Timers at Wendy's count every segment of the order completion process to help managers control performance and identify problem areas.

Good control systems make economic sense. The importance of control is often explained by the *1:10:100 Rule:* If a defect or service error is identified and corrected at the design stage, it might cost $1 to fix. If it is first detected during the production process, it might cost $10 to fix. However, if the defect is not discovered until it reaches the customer, it might cost $100 to correct.

The dollar values and the exact ratios differ among firms and industries. However, the fact is that the cost of repair or service recovery grows dramatically the further that defects and errors move along the value chain. This rule clearly supports the need for control and a focus on prevention by building quality "at the source." **Quality at the source** *means the people responsible for the work control the quality of their processes by identifying and correcting any defects or errors when they first are recognized or occur.* This requires that employees have good data collection, observation, and analysis skills, as well as the proper tools, training, and support of management.

Quality at the source means the people responsible for the work control the quality of their processes by identifying and correcting any defects or errors when they first are recognized or occur.

Leveling the Playing Field in Golf

Golf balls must meet five standards to conform to the Rules of Golf: minimum size, maximum weight, spherical symmetry, maximum initial velocity, and overall distance.[3] Methods for measuring such quality characteristics may be automated or performed manually. For instance, golf balls are measured for size by trying to drop them through a metal ring—a conforming ball sticks to the ring while a nonconforming ball falls through; digital scales measure weight to one-thousandth of a gram; and initial velocity is measured in a special machine by finding the time it takes a ball struck at 98 mph to break a ballistic screen at the end of a tube exactly 6.28 feet away.

Bloomberg/Contributor/Getty Images

16-1a Quality Control Practices in Manufacturing

In manufacturing, control is generally applied at three key points in the supply chain: at the receiving stage from suppliers, during various production processes, and at the finished-goods stage.

Supplier Certification and Management

If incoming materials are of poor quality, then the final manufactured good will certainly be no better. Suppliers should be expected to provide documentation and statistical evidence that they are meeting required specifications. If supplier documentation is done properly, incoming inspection can be completely eliminated. Many companies have formal supplier certification programs to ensure the integrity of incoming materials.

In-Process Control

In-process quality control systems are needed to ensure that defective outputs do not leave the process and, more important, to prevent them in the first place. An organization must consider trade-offs between the explicit costs of detection, repair, or replacement and the implicit costs of allowing a nonconformity to continue through the production process. In-process control is typically performed by the people who run the processes on the front lines; this is an example of quality at the source.

Finished-Goods Control

Finished-goods control is often focused on verifying that the product meets customer requirements. For many consumer products, this consists of functional testing. For instance, a manufacturer of televisions might do a simple test on each unit to make sure it operates properly. Modern technology now allows for such tests to be conducted rapidly and cost-effectively. For example, imaging scanners along food packaging lines easily check for foreign particles.

16-1b Quality Control Practices in Services

Many of the same practices described in the previous section can be applied to quality control for back-office service operations such as check or medical insurance claim processing. Front-office services that involve substantial customer contact must be controlled differently. The day-to-day execution of thousands of service encounters is a challenge for any service-providing organization.

One way to control quality in services is to prevent sources of errors and mistakes in the first place by using the poka-yoke approach. Another way is to hire and

Quality Control in Call Centers

Maintaining quality is critical in every aspect of a company's operation, but in few areas is it more important than in the call center. The reason is simple: It is often the initial customer "touch point"—that is, one of the first areas of a business with which a customer makes contact. Accordingly, the call center carries the burden of providing a company's first impression; it is the gateway to your business. Consequently, managing quality in the call center has to be considered a top priority.

The most effective way to measure call center quality is call monitoring. By listening to a statistically valid sample of customer telephone interactions and scoring them against various criteria, companies can learn if their agents are performing up to standard while ensuring that the agents most in need of coaching actually get it. Call center monitoring is a discipline that is driven strongly by metrics. Virtually everything that happens in the call center is measured against a standard of some kind, whether it is quantitative (calls will be answered within a certain number of seconds) or qualitative (the customer's problem was resolved on the first call).

It's imperative that the criteria being measured are actually important to the customer transaction, thus ensuring that the process relates back to the primary goal: exceptional service quality.[4]

train service providers in service management skills as part of a prevention-based approach to quality control.

Customer satisfaction measurement can provide the basis for effective control systems in services. Customer satisfaction instruments often focus on service attributes such as attitude, lead time, on-time delivery, exception handling, accountability, and technical support; product attributes such as reliability and price; and overall satisfaction measures. At FedEx, customers are asked to rate everything from billing to the performance of couriers, package condition, tracking and tracing capabilities, complaint handling, and helpfulness of employees.

16-2 Statistical Process Control and Variation

Statistical process control (SPC) is a methodology for monitoring the quality of manufacturing and service-delivery processes to help identify and eliminate unwanted causes of variation. Variation occurs for many reasons, such as inconsistencies in material inputs; changes in environmental conditions (temperature,

> **Statistical process control (SPC)** is a methodology for monitoring the quality of manufacturing and service-delivery processes to help identify and eliminate unwanted causes of variation.

humidity); machine maintenance cycles; customer participation and self-service; tool wear; and human fatigue. Some variation is obvious, such as inconsistencies in meal delivery times or food quantity at a restaurant; other variation—such as minute differences in physical dimensions of machined parts—is barely perceptible, but can be determined through some type of measurement process.

Common cause variation *is the result of complex interactions of variations in materials, tools, machines, information, workers, and the environment.* Such variation is a natural part of the technology and process design and cannot be controlled; that is, we cannot influence each individual output of the process. It appears at random, and individual sources or causes cannot be identified or explained. However, their combined effect is usually stable and can be described statistically.

Common causes of variation generally account for about 80 to 95 percent of the observed variation in a process. They can be reduced only if better technology, process design, or training is provided. This clearly is the responsibility of management. **Special (or assignable) cause variation** *arises from external sources that are not inherent in the process, appear sporadically, and disrupt the random pattern of common causes.* Special cause variation occurs sporadically and can be prevented or at least explained and understood. For example, a tool might break during a process step, a worker might be distracted by a colleague, or a busload of tourists stops at a restaurant (resulting in unusual wait times). Special cause variation tends to be easily detectable using statistical methods because it disrupts the normal pattern of measurements. When special causes are identified, short-term corrective action generally should be taken by those who own the process and are responsible for doing the work, such as machine operators, order-fulfillment workers, and so on.

Keeping special cause variation from occurring is the essence of quality control. *If no special causes affect the output of a process, we say that the process is* **in control;** *when special causes are present, the process is said to be* **out of control.** A process that is in control does not need any changes or adjustments; an out-of-control process needs correction. However, employees often make two basic mistakes when attempting to control a process:

1. adjusting a process that is already in control, or
2. failing to correct a process that is out of control.

Although it is clear that a truly out-of-control process must be corrected, many workers mistakenly believe that whenever process output is off-target, some adjustment must be made. Actually, over adjusting a process that is in control will *increase* the variation in the output. Thus, employees must know when to leave a process alone to keep variation at a minimum.

16-3 Constructing Control Charts

Control charts are quite simple to use; they were developed in the early 20th century for use by shop floor workers (without computers or calculators!). Essentially, we take samples of output from a process at periodic intervals and measure the quality characteristic we wish to control, do some calculations, plot the data on a chart, and interpret the results.

The following is a summary of the steps required to develop and use control charts. Steps 1 through 4 focus on setting up an initial chart; in step 5, the charts are used for ongoing monitoring; and finally, in step 6, the data are used for process capability analysis.

1. Preparation
   a. Choose the metric to be monitored and controlled—for example, the diameter of a drilled hole, time to process an order, percentage of customer returns, or number of complaints/day.
   b. Determine the sample size (number of observations in each sample) and frequency of sampling (time between taking successive samples). We will discuss some practical issues related to these decisions in Section 4.
   c. Set up the control chart. This can be done on a sheet of paper or more efficiently on a computer using a spreadsheet or a commercial software package.

Common cause variation is the result of complex interactions of variations in materials, tools, machines, information, workers, and the environment.

Special (or assignable) cause variation arises from external sources that are not inherent in the process, appear sporadically, and disrupt the random pattern of common causes.

If no special causes affect the output of a process, we say that the process is **in control;** when special causes are present, the process is said to be **out of control.**

IZZY'S: MEASURING CUSTOMER SATISFACTION

Restaurants and hotels use simple satisfaction surveys. Izzy's, a small chain of restaurants specializing in reuben sandwiches and potato pancakes, seeks feedback about not only their food, but potential dissatisfiers such as cleanliness, service, and employee attitude. It also includes space for open-ended comments. Questions that are missing, however, are the likelihood of returning and referring others, which studies have shown are closely linked to customer loyalty.

IZZY'S CARES!

Pleasing you is our objective. We want our customers to enjoy the food and experience of Izzy's - your comments will help us in maintaining our high standards for service, quality, value & enjoyment. Kindly take a minute to complete this card. Please drop off at cash register, place in mail, or comment online at www.izzys.com. Thanks for your help and hurry back!

John Geisen - President

Location	Date	Time	AM/PM

☐Take-Out ☐Breakfast ☐Lunch   ☐Dinner
☐Eat-In   ☐PLATTERS/PARTY TRAY

Please rate the following:	Excellent	Good	Fair	Poor
Cleanliness	☐	☐	☐	☐
Service	☐	☐	☐	☐
Employee attitude	☐	☐	☐	☐
Portions	☐	☐	☐	☐
Taste	☐	☐	☐	☐
Value	☐	☐	☐	☐
Atmosphere	☐	☐	☐	☐

Are you a:
☐ First time person
☐ Occasional patron
☐ Regular patron

Travel time to IZZY'S:
☐ 1 to 10 minutes
☐ 11 to 20 minutes
☐ More than 20 minutes

WAS THE SERVICE PROMPT? _____
RESTROOMS CLEAN & SUPPLIED? _____
DINING AREA & UTENSILS CLEAN? _____

WHAT DID YOU HAVE TO EAT? _____
_____

COMMENTS: _____
_____
_____
_____

MORE QUESTIONS:
Do you have any suggestions for new menu items?
_____

Please send: Catering Info.☐ Take-out Menu☐ Party Tray Info☐

Optional:
Name: _____
Address: _____
City _____ State _____ Zip _____
Phone: _____
E-mail: _____

Source: www.izzys.com

> Variation occurs for many reasons, such as inconsistencies in material inputs, changes in environmental conditions, machine maintenance cycles, customer participation and self-service, tool wear, and human fatigue.

Quality Control for Medical Prescriptions

Estimates are that at least 7,000 patients die each year from medication errors. Better process management and quality control, such as streamlining processes, building quality checks into every stage of the process, and use technology to eliminate handwritten prescriptions can minimize such errors. Simple process changes such as scanning drug containers and double-checking for the correct drug, strength, and quantity, can avoid serious errors. Sloppy handwriting is a major cause of medication errors. Electronic prescriptions avoid handwriting altogether, but although more than 85 percent of pharmacies have the technology to receive electronic prescriptions, only one-third of the nation's prescribers use such systems. However, one study found that as many as 12 percent of prescriptions sent electronically to pharmacies contain errors, matching that of handwritten scrips.[5]

2. Data collection
   a. Record the data.
   b. Calculate relevant statistics: averages, ranges, proportions, and so on.
   c. Plot the statistics on the chart.

   These tasks may be done by hand or on a computer.

3. Determination of trial control limits
   a. Draw the center line (process average) on the chart.
   b. Compute the upper and lower control limits. Again, spreadsheets and computer software can automate these tasks.

4. Analysis and interpretation
   a. Investigate the chart for lack of control.
   b. Eliminate out-of-control points.
   c. Recompute control limits if necessary.

5. Use as a problem-solving tool
   a. Continue data collection and plotting.
   b. Identify out-of-control situations and take corrective action.

6. Determination of process capability using the control chart data

Many different types of control charts exist. All are similar in structure, but the specific formulas used to compute control limits for them differ. Moreover, different types of charts are used for different types of metrics.

> A **continuous metric** is one that is calculated from data that are measured as the degree of conformance to a specification on some continuous scale of measurement.
>
> A **discrete metric** is one that is calculated from data that are counted.

A **continuous metric** *is one that is calculated from data that are measured as the degree of conformance to a specification on some continuous scale of measurement.* Examples are length, weight, and time. Customer waiting time and order lead time are other examples. Continuous data usually require $\bar{x}$- ("x-bar") and R-charts.

A **discrete metric** *is one that is calculated from data that are counted.* A dimension on a machined part is either within tolerance or out of tolerance, an order is either complete or incomplete, or a customer made a complaint or not about a service experience. We can count the percentage or number of parts within tolerance, the percentage or number of complete orders, and the percentage or number of complaints. These are examples of discrete metrics and usually require control charts that we call p- or c-charts.

We will see examples of using both continuous and discrete metrics when we discuss how to construct different types of control charts.

16-3a Constructing $\bar{x}$- and R-Charts

The first step in developing $\bar{x}$- and R-charts is to gather data. Usually, about 25 to 30 samples are collected. Samples between size 3 and 10 are generally used, with 5 being the most common. The number of samples is indicated by k, and n denotes the sample size. For each sample i, the mean (denoted $\bar{x}_i$) and the range (R_i) are computed. These values are then plotted on their respective control charts. Next, the *overall mean* and *average range* calculations are made. These values specify the center lines for the $\bar{x}$- and R-charts, respectively. The

Solved Problem

The Goodman Tire and Rubber Company periodically tests its tires for tread wear under simulated road conditions. To study and control its manufacturing processes, the company uses $\bar{x}$- and R-charts. Twenty samples, each containing three radial tires, were chosen from different shifts over several days of operation. Because $n = 3$, the control limit factors for the R-chart are (see Exhibit 16.1) $D_3 = 0$ and $D_4 = 2.57$. Using Equations 16.1 and 16.2, $\bar{\bar{x}}$ is 31.88 and the average range is 10.8. The control limits are computed as follows:

$$UCL_R = D_4\bar{R} = 2.57(10.8) = 27.8$$

$$LCL_R = D_3\bar{R} = 0$$

For the $\bar{x}$-chart, $A_2 = 1.02$; thus the control limits are

$$UCL_{\bar{x}} = 31.88 + 1.02(10.8) = 42.9$$

$$LCL_{\bar{x}} = 31.88 - 1.02(10.8) = 20.8$$

Exhibit 16.1 shows the Excel $\bar{x}$- and R-Chart template, which calculates the control limits and plots the charts.

Exhibit 16.1 *Excel Template $\bar{x}$- and R-Chart Template for Solved Problem*

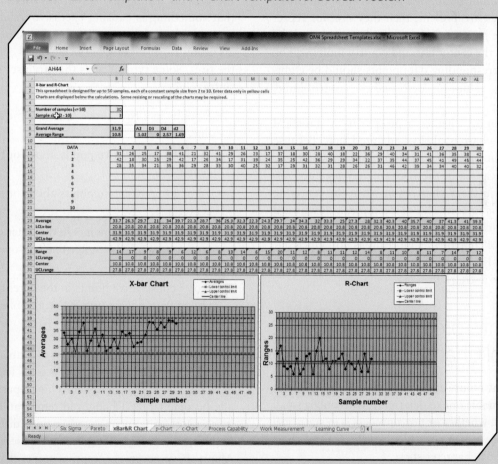

overall mean (denoted $\bar{\bar{x}}$) is the average of the sample means

$$\bar{\bar{x}} = \frac{\sum_{i=1}^{k} \bar{x}_i}{k} \qquad [16.1]$$

The average range $\bar{R}$ is similarly computed, using the formula

$$\bar{R} = \frac{\sum_{i=1}^{k} R_i}{k} \qquad [16.2]$$

The average range and average mean are used to compute upper and lower control limits (UCL and LCL) for the R- and $\bar{x}$-charts. Control limits are easily calculated using the following formulas:

$$\text{UCL}_R = D_4\bar{R} \qquad \text{UCL}_{\bar{x}} = \bar{\bar{x}} + A_2\bar{R}$$

$$\text{LCL}_R = D_3\bar{R} \qquad \text{LCL}_{\bar{x}} = \bar{\bar{x}} - A_2\bar{R} \qquad [16.3]$$

where the constants D_3, D_4, and A_2 depend on the sample size (see Appendix B).

The control limits represent the range between which all points are expected to fall if the process is in statistical control. If any points fall outside the control limits or if any unusual patterns are observed, then some special cause has probably affected the process. The process should be studied to determine the cause. If special causes are present, then they are *not* representative of the true state of statistical control, and the calculations of the center line and control limits will be biased. The corresponding data points should be eliminated, and new values for $\bar{\bar{x}}$, $\bar{R}$, and the control limits should be computed.

In determining whether a process is in statistical control, the R-chart is always analyzed first. Because the control limits in the $\bar{x}$-chart depend on the average range, special causes in the R-chart may produce unusual patterns in the $\bar{x}$-chart, even when the centering of the process is in control. For example, a downward trend in the R-chart can cause the data in the $\bar{x}$-chart to appear out of control when it really is not. Once statistical control is established for the R-chart, attention may turn to the $\bar{x}$-chart.

16-3b Interpreting Patterns in Control Charts

The location of points and the patterns of points in a control chart enable one to determine, with only a small chance of error, whether or not a process is in statistical control. A process is in control when the control chart has the following characteristics:

1. No points are outside control limits.
2. The number of points above and below the center line is about the same.
3. The points seem to fall randomly above and below the center line.
4. Most points, but not all, are near the center line, and only a few are close to the control limits.

You can see that these characteristics are evident in the R-chart in Exhibit 16.1. Therefore, we would conclude that the R-chart is in control.

When a process is out of control, we typically see some unusual characteristics. An obvious indication that a process may be out of control is a point that falls outside the control limits. If such a point is found, you should first check for the possibility that the control limits were miscalculated or that the point was plotted incorrectly. If neither is the case, this can indicate that the process average has changed.

Another indication of an out-of-control situation is a sudden shift in the average. For example, in Exhibit 16.1, we see that the last eight points in the $\bar{x}$-chart are all above the center line, suggesting that the process mean has increased. This might suggest that something is causing excessive tread wear in recent samples, perhaps a different batch of raw materials or improper mixing of the chemical composition of the tires. Some typical rules that are used to identify a shift include:

- 8 points in a row above or below the center line,
- 10 of 11 consecutive points above or below the center line,
- 12 of 14 consecutive points above or below the center line,
- 2 of 3 consecutive points in the outer one-third region between the center line and one of the control limits, and
- 4 of 5 consecutive points in the outer two-thirds region between the center line and one of the control limits.

A third thing to look for in a control chart is an increasing or decreasing trend. As tools wear down, for example, the diameter of a machined part will gradually become larger. Changes in temperature or humidity, general equipment deterioration, dirt buildup on fixtures, or operator fatigue may cause such a trend. About six or seven consecutive points that increase or decrease in value usually signify a gradual change. A wave or cycle pattern is also unusual and should be suspect. It might be a result of seasonal effects of material deliveries, temperature swings, maintenance cycles, or periodic rotation of operators. Whenever an unusual pattern in a control chart is identified, the process should be stopped until the problem has been identified and corrected.

16-3c Constructing *p*-Charts

Many quality characteristics assume only two values, such as good or bad, pass or fail, and so on. The proportion of nonconforming items can be monitored using a control chart called a *p-chart,* where *p* is the proportion of nonconforming items found in a sample. Often, it is also called a *fraction nonconforming* or *fraction defective* chart.

As with continuous data, a *p*-chart is constructed by first gathering 25 to 30 samples of the attribute being measured. The size of each sample should be large enough to have several nonconforming items. If the probability of finding a nonconforming item is small, a sample size of 100 or more items is usually necessary. Samples are chosen over time periods so that any special causes that are identified can be investigated.

Let us suppose that *k* samples, each of size *n*, are selected. If *y* represents the number nonconforming in a particular sample, the proportion nonconforming is *y/n*.

Let p_i be the fraction nonconforming in the *i*th sample; the average fraction nonconforming for the group of *k* samples, then, is

$$\bar{p} = \frac{p_1 + p_2 \cdots + p_k}{k} \qquad [16.4]$$

(Note that this formula applies only when all sample sizes are the same!) This statistic reflects the average performance of the process. One would expect a high percentage of samples to have a fraction nonconforming within 3 standard deviations of $\bar{p}$. An estimate of the standard deviation is given by

$$s_{\bar{p}} = \sqrt{\frac{\bar{p}(1 - \bar{p})}{n}} \qquad [16.5]$$

Therefore, upper and lower control limits are given by

$$\text{UCL}_p = \bar{p} + 3s_{\bar{p}}$$
$$\text{LCL}_p = \bar{p} - 3s_{\bar{p}} \qquad [16.6]$$

If LCL_p is less than zero, a value of zero is used.

Analysis of a *p*-chart is similar to that of an $\bar{x}$- or *R*-chart. Points outside the control limits signify an out-of-control situation. Patterns and trends should also be sought to identify special causes. However, a point on a *p*-chart below the lower control limit or the development of a trend below the center line indicates that the process might have improved, based on an ideal target of zero defectives. Caution is advised before such conclusions are drawn, because errors may have been made in computation.

Exhibit 16.2 shows the Excel *p*-Chart template spreadsheet, which allows you to enter data and then

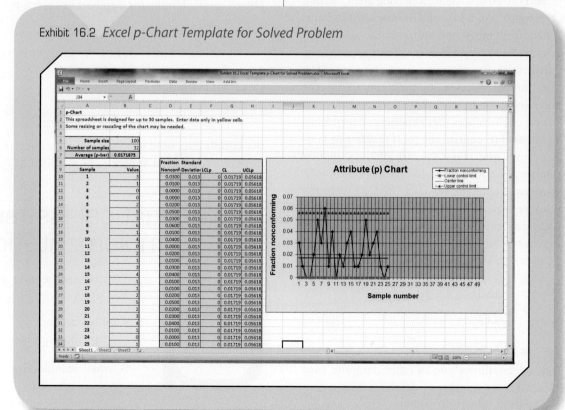

Exhibit 16.2 *Excel p-Chart Template for Solved Problem*

Solved Problem

The operators of automated sorting machines in a post office must read the ZIP code on letters and

Antoine Antonioli/Bloomberg via Getty Images

computes the proportion defective, control limits, and draws the control charts.

16-3d Constructing c-Charts

A p-chart monitors the proportion of nonconforming items, but a nonconforming item may have more than one nonconformance. For instance, a customer's order may have several errors, such as wrong item, wrong quantity, wrong price, and so on. To monitor the number of nonconformances per unit, we use a c-chart. These charts are used extensively in service applications because most managers of service processes are interested in the number of errors or problems that occur per customer (or patient, student, order), and not just the proportion of customers that experienced problems. The c-chart is used to control the *total number* of nonconformances per unit when the size of the sampling unit or number of opportunities for errors is constant.

To construct a c-chart, we must first estimate the average number of nonconformances per unit, $\bar{c}$. This is done by taking at least 25 samples of equal size, counting the number of nonconformances per sample, and finding the average. Then, control limits are given by

$$\text{UCL}_c = \bar{c} + 3\sqrt{\bar{c}}$$
$$\text{LCL}_c = \bar{c} - 3\sqrt{\bar{c}} \qquad [16.7]$$

Exhibit 16.3 shows the Excel c-Chart template spreadsheet, which allows you to enter data and then computes the average number of defects per unit, control limits, and draws the control charts. The c-chart for

divert the letters to the proper carrier routes. Over a month's time, 25 samples of 100 letters were chosen, and the number of errors was recorded. The average proportion defective, $\bar{p}$ is computed as 0.022.

The standard deviation is computed as

$$s_{\bar{p}} = \sqrt{\frac{0.022(1 - 0.022)}{100}} = 0.1467$$

Thus UCL = .022 + 3(.01467) = .066, and LCL = .022 − 3(.01467) = −.022. Because the LCL is negative and the actual proportion nonconforming cannot be less than zero, the LCL is set equal to zero. (See Exhibit 16.2.)

Solved Problem

The total number of machine failures over a 25-day period is 45. Therefore, the average number of failures per day is

$$\bar{c} = \frac{45}{25} = 1.8$$

Hence, control limits for a c-chart are given by

$$\text{UCL}_c = 1.8 + 3\sqrt{1.8} = 5.82$$
$$\text{LCL}_c = 1.8 - 3\sqrt{1.8} = -2.22, \text{ or zero}$$

(See Exhibit 16.3.)

the sample data used in solved problem above is shown in Exhibit 16.3, and appear to be in control.

16-4 Practical Issues in SPC Implementation

designing control charts involves two key issues:

1. sample size, and
2. sampling frequency.

A small sample size is desirable to keep the cost associated with sampling low. On the other

Exhibit 16.3 *Excel c-Chart Template for Solved Problem*

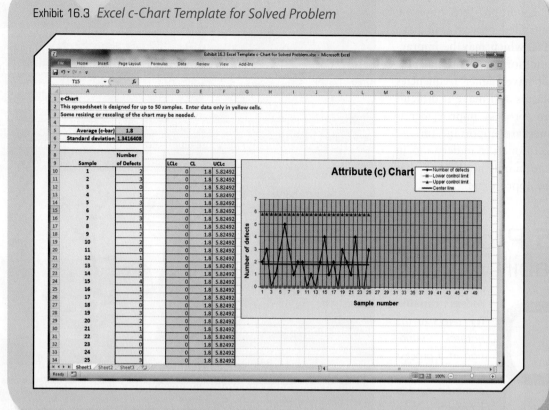

hand, large sample sizes provide greater degrees of statistical accuracy in estimating the true state of control. Large samples also allow smaller changes in process characteristics to be detected with higher probability. In practice, samples of about 5 have been found to work well in detecting process shifts of 2 standard deviations or larger. To detect smaller shifts in the process mean, larger sample sizes of 15 to 25 must be used.

For attributes data, too small of a sample size can make a *p*-chart meaningless. Even though many guidelines such as "use at least 100 observations" have been suggested, the proper sample size should be determined statistically, particularly when the true portion of nonconformances is small. If *p* is small, *n* should be large enough to have a high probability of detecting at least one nonconformance. For example, statistical calculations can show that if $p = .01$, then the sample size must be at least 300 to have at least a 95 percent chance of finding at least one nonconformance.

Managers must also consider the sampling frequency. Taking large samples on a frequent basis is desirable but clearly not economical. No hard-and-fast rules exist for the frequency of sampling. Samples should be close enough to provide an opportunity to detect changes in process characteristics as soon as possible

and reduce the chances of producing a large amount of nonconforming output. However, they should not be so close that the cost of sampling outweighs the benefits that can be realized. This decision depends on the individual application and volume of output.

16-4a Controlling Six Sigma Processes

SPC is a useful methodology for processes that operate at a low sigma level, for example the three sigma level or less. However, when the rate of defects is extremely low, standard control charts are not effective. For example, when using a *p*-chart for a process with a high sigma level, few defects will be discovered even with large sample sizes. For instance, if $p = .001$, a sample size of 500 will have an expected number of only $500(.001) = 0.5$ defects. Hence, most samples will have zero or only one defect, and the chart will provide little useful information for control. Using much larger sample sizes would only delay the timeliness of information and increase the chances that the process may have changed during the sampling interval. Small sample sizes will typically result in a conclusion that any observed defect indicates an out-of-control condition, thus implying that a controlled process will have zero defects, which may be impractical. In addition, conventional SPC charts will have higher frequencies of false alarms and make it difficult to evaluate process improvements. These issues are important for Six Sigma practitioners to understand, in order not to blindly apply tools that may not be appropriate.

16-5 Process Capability

Process capability *refers to the natural variation in a process that results from common causes.* Knowing process capability allows one to predict, quantitatively, how well a process will meet specifications and to specify equipment requirements and the level of control necessary. Process capability has no meaning if the process is not in statistical control because special causes will bias the mean or the standard deviation. Therefore, we should use control charts to first eliminate any special causes before computing the process capability.

A **process capability study** *is a carefully planned study designed to yield specific information about the performance of a process under specified operating conditions.* Typical questions that are asked in a process capability study are the following:

- Where is the process centered?
- How much variability exists in the process?
- Is the performance relative to specifications acceptable?

Process capability refers to the natural variation in a process that results from common causes.

A process capability study is a carefully planned study designed to yield specific information about the performance of a process under specified operating conditions.

IBM: Using SPC

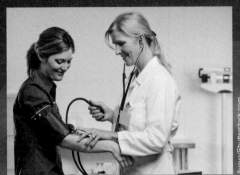

At one IBM branch, preemployment physical examinations took too long and taxed the medical staff assigned to conduct them. Such examinations are vital for ensuring that employees can perform certain jobs without excess stress and that they pose no health threat to other employees. Therefore, the challenge IBM faced was to maintain the quality of the exam while reducing the time needed to perform it by identifying and eliminating waiting periods between the various parts of it.

Preliminary control charts revealed that the average time required for the examination was 74 minutes, but the range varied greatly. New equipment and additional training of the medical staff were suggested as means of shortening the average time. Initial charts indicated that the process was out of control, but continued monitoring and process improvements lowered the average time to 40 minutes, and both the average and range were brought into statistical control with the help of $\bar{x}$- and R-charts.[6]

Avava/Shutterstock.com

- What proportion of output will be expected to meet specifications?

One of the properties of a normal distribution is that 99.73 percent of the observations will fall within 3 standard deviations from the mean. Thus, a process that is in control can be expected to produce a very large percentage of output between $\mu - 3\sigma$ and $\mu + 3\sigma$, where μ is the process average. Therefore, the natural variation of the process can be estimated by $\mu \pm 3\sigma$ and characterizes the capability of the process. One way of computing the standard deviation in this formula is to take a sample of data, compute the sample standard deviation, s, and use it as an estimate of σ. A second approach, often used in conjunction with an $\bar{x}$- and R-chart, is to estimate σ by dividing the average range by a constant, d_2, which can be found in Appendix B. That is,

$$\sigma = \frac{\bar{R}}{d_2} \qquad [16.8]$$

The process capability is usually compared to the design specifications to indicate the ability of the process to meet the specifications. Exhibit 16.4 illustrates four possible situations that can arise when the observed variability of a process is compared to design specifications. In part (a), the range of process variation is larger than the design specification; thus it will be impossible for the process to meet specifications a large percentage of the time. Managers can either scrap or rework nonconforming parts (100 percent inspection is necessary), invest in a better process with less variation, or change the design specifications. In part (b), the process is able to produce according to specification, although it will require close monitoring to ensure that it remains in that position. In part (c), the observed variation is tighter than the specifications; this is the ideal situation from a quality control viewpoint, as little inspection or control is necessary. Finally, in part (d), the observed variation is the same as the design specification, but the process is off-center; thus some nonconforming product can be expected.

16-5a Process Capability Index

*The relationship between the natural variation and specifications is often quantified by a measure known as the **process capability index**.* The process capability index, C_p, is defined as the ratio of the specification width to the natural variation of the process. C_p relates the natural variation of the process with the design specifications in a single, quantitative measure. In numerical terms, the formula is

$$C_p = \frac{USL - LSL}{6\sigma} \qquad [16.9]$$

where

USL = upper specification limit
LSL = lower specification limit
σ = standard deviation of the process (or an estimate based on the sample standard deviation, s)

C_p values less than 1 mean that a significant percentage of output (observed variation) will not conform

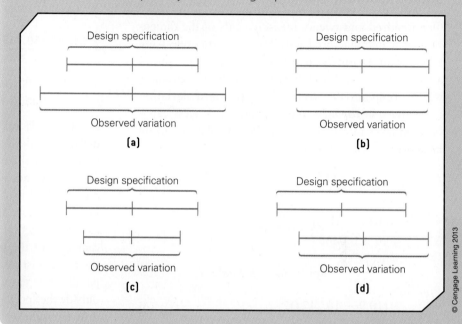

Exhibit 16.4 *Process Capability Versus Design Specifications*

Design specification

Observed variation

(a)

Design specification

Observed variation

(b)

Design specification

Observed variation

(c)

Design specification

Observed variation

(d)

© Cengage Learning 2013

to the design specifications (see Exhibit 16.4a). Note that when $C_p = 1$, the observed variation is the same as the design specification width, USL − LSL (as in Exhibit 16.4[b]). Values of C_p exceeding 1 indicate good capability (Exhibit 16.4[c]); in fact, many firms require that their suppliers demonstrate a high value of C_p.

The value of C_p does not depend on the mean of the process; thus, a process may be off-center such as in Exhibit 16.4(d) and still show an acceptable value of C_p. To account for the process centering, one-sided capability indexes are often used:

$$C_{pu} = \frac{USL - \mu}{3\sigma} \text{ (upper one-sided index)} \qquad [16.10]$$

$$C_{pl} = \frac{\mu - LSL}{3\sigma} \text{ (lower one-sided index)} \qquad [16.11]$$

$$C_{pk} = \min (C_{pl}, C_{pu}) \qquad [16.12]$$

For example, a high value of C_{pu} indicates that the process is very capable of meeting the upper specification. C_{pk} is the "worst case" and provides an indication of whether both the lower and upper specifications can

The relationship between the natural variation and specifications is often quantified by a measure known as the **process capability index**.

Solved Problem

One hundred and twenty measurements of the dimension of a manufactured part for an automobile were taken from a controlled process. Exhibit 16.5 shows a portion of the Excel Process Capability template, which computes the average and standard deviation of the data in rows 21 and 22, and the process capability indexes in cells G20:H23. We calculate C_p using Equation 16.9 as follows:

$$C_p = \frac{USL - LSL}{6\sigma} \qquad [16.9]$$

$$= \frac{(10.9 - 10.5)}{(6 \times 0.0868)} = 0.768$$

$$C_{pu} = \frac{USL - \mu}{3\sigma} \text{ (upper one-sided index)}$$

$$= \frac{(10.9 - 10.7171)}{(3 \times 0.0868)} = 0.702 \qquad [16.10]$$

$$C_{pl} = \frac{\mu - LSL}{3\sigma} \text{ (lower one-sided index)}$$

$$= \frac{(10.7171 - 10.5)}{(3 \times 0.0868)} = 0.833 \qquad [16.11]$$

$$C_{pk} = \min (C_{pl}, C_{pu})$$

$$= \min (0.833, 0.702) = 0.702 \qquad [16.12]$$

Because C_p is less than 1, the process is not capable of meeting the design specifications. The C_{pu} and C_{pl} analyses indicate that the process is not centered because C_{pl} and C_{pu} are not equal to C_p, and that the process has more difficulty in meeting the upper specification limit. Finally, the fact that $C_{pk} = 0.702$ is less than 1 tells us that the actual process capability (including the off-centering of the mean) is not very good. Exhibit 16.6 shows the histogram displayed in the Excel Process Capability template. Only a few data points are actually outside the specification limits, but if the process should drift from the nominal specification, more defects will be produced.

Exhibit 16.5 *Portion of the Excel Process Capability Template*

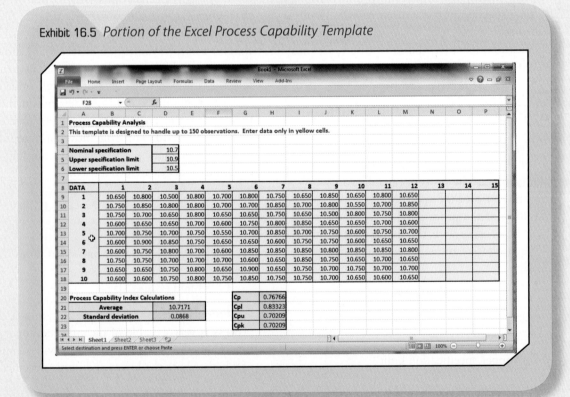

Exhibit 16.6 *Histogram Displayed in the Excel Process Capability Template*

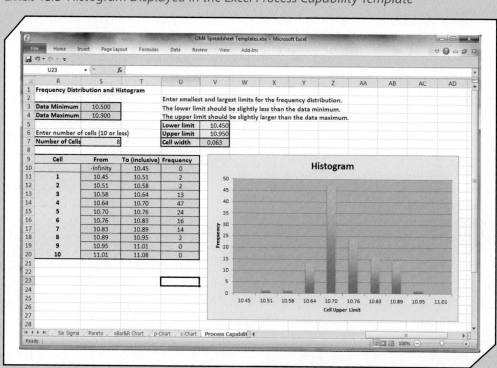

be met regardless of where the process is centered. This is the value that most managers pay attention to.

Process capability is important both to product designers and to process owners. If product specifications are too tight, the product will be difficult to manufacture. Employees who run the processes will be under pressure and will have to spend a lot of time adjusting the process and inspecting output.

Discussion Questions

1. Provide some examples in business or daily life in which a controlled process is erroneously adjusted and an out-of-control process is ignored. What implications do these errors have?

2. Discuss some examples of common and special causes of variation in your daily life (for example, at school or at home).

3. Hospital administrators wanted to understand and better control the waiting time of patients in the emergency room (ER) department. To do this, they constructed $\bar{x}$- and R-charts by sampling the waiting times of the first five patients admitted to the ER at the beginning of each shift (7 a.m., 3 p.m., and 11 p.m.). What do you think of this approach? Will it provide the information the hospital administrators seek? How might the sampling process be improved, and what would you recommend?

4. Suppose that you were monitoring the time it takes to complete order transactions at a call center. Discuss what might cause such out-of-control conditions as a trend, shift in the mean, or cycles in an $\bar{x}$-chart in this situation.

5. Would it make sense to draw specification limits on an $\bar{x}$-chart? Why or why not?

Problems and Activities

Note: an asterisk denotes problems for which an Excel spreadsheet template on the CourseMate Web site may be used.

1. Develop a "personal quality checklist" on which you tally nonconformances in your personal life (such as being late for work or school, not completing homework on time, not getting enough exercise, and so on). What type of chart would you use to monitor your performance?

2. Examine the questions in the satisfaction survey in the box "Izzy's: Measuring Customer Satisfaction." How do the questions relate to the five dimensions of service quality introduced in Chapter 3? Discuss how the survey results could be used to control quality. What types of quality control charts might be used?

3. Thirty samples of size 4 of the customer waiting time at a call center for a health insurance company resulted in an overall mean of 10.4 minutes and average range of 0.9 minutes. Compute the control limits for $\bar{x}$- and R-charts.

4.* Thirty samples of size 3, available in the C16P4 worksheet in the *OM4 Data Workbook*, were taken from a machining process over a 15-hour period. Construct control charts using the Excel $\bar{x}$- and R-Chart template. Verify the Excel calculations of the control limits by hand using the formulas in the chapter. Does the process appear to be in statistical control? Why or why not?

5.* Tri-State Bank is investigating the processing time for loan applications. Samples were taken for 25 random days from four branches. These data can be found in the C16P5 worksheet in the *OM4 Data Workbook*. Construct control charts using the Excel $\bar{x}$- and R-Chart template. Verify the Excel calculations of the control limits by hand using the formulas in the chapter. Does the process appear to be in statistical control? Why or why not?

6. Twenty-five samples of loan applications at a bank, each of size 150, resulted in a total of 22 errors. Compute the control limits for a p-chart.

7.* One hundred insurance claim forms are inspected daily for 25 working days, and the number of forms with errors is recorded in the C16P7 worksheet in the *OM4 Data Workbook*. Construct a p-chart using the Excel p-Chart template. Verify the Excel calculations of the control limits by hand using the formulas in the chapter. If any special causes are identified, remove them from the data and construct a revised control chart.

8.* An Internet service provider (ISP) measures the proportion of peak-period time when a customer is likely to receive busy signals. Data on the number of busy signals received from samples of 500 calls over a 30-day period can be found in the C16P8 worksheet in the *OM4 Data Workbook*. Construct and interpret a p-chart for these data.

9. A fast-food franchise tracked the number of errors that occurred in customers' orders. These included wrong menu item, wrong drink size, lack of condiments, wrong price total, and so on. Some orders have more than one error. In one week, 1,250 orders were filled, and a total of 30 errors was discovered. Find the control limits for a c-chart.

10.* Data showing the number of errors per thousand lines of code for a software development project are given in the C16P11 worksheet in the *OM4 Data Workbook*. Construct a c-chart and interpret the results.

11.* A mail-order prescription drug vendor measured the number of errors per standard order being picked in its distribution center. Data can be found in the C16P11 worksheet in the *OM4 Data Workbook*. Construct a c-chart and interpret the results.

12. The C16P12 worksheet in the *OM4 Data Workbook* provides five examples of control charts. Interpret the patterns in each and determine if the processes are in control. If not, state the type of out-of-control condition that you identify (for example, points outside of the control limits, shifts, trends, and so on.)

13. A specification for a spacer plate used in a machine tool has specifications LSL = 0.05 and USL = 0.10 cm in thickness. A sample of 100 parts found $\mu = 0.067$ and $\sigma = 0.011$. Compute and interpret the process capability indexes C_p, C_{pl}, C_{pu}, and C_{pk}.

14.* Use the data in problem 4 to calculate C_p, C_{pl}, C_{pu}, and C_{pk}, assuming that the specifications are 3.75 ± 1.30. Interpret the results for the manager of this process.

15.* The C16P15 worksheet in the *OM4 Data Workbook* provides sample times in hours for processing and shipping orders from a web-based retailer. The retailer advertises that orders are shipped within four hours of receipt. What is the capability of the process to achieve this standard? Explain your conclusions.

The Casey Company Case Study

The Casey Company is a distributor of electrical automation and power transmission products. When the company began to implement a total quality management process, one manager was eager to collect data about the organization's receiving process because of a decrease in the organization's on-time deliveries. The manager suspected that the data entry person in the purchasing department was not entering data in the computer in a timely fashion; consequently, packages could not be properly processed for subsequent shipping to the customer.

A preliminary analysis indicated that the manager's notion was inaccurate. In fact, the manager was able to see that the data entry person was doing an excellent job. The analysis showed that handling packages that were destined for a branch operation in the same fashion as other packages created significant delays. A simple process change of placing a branch designation letter in front of the purchase order number told the receiving clerk to place those packages on a separate skid for delivery to the branch.

One manager wanted to collect data on the company's receiving process because of a decrease in on-time deliveries.

Fancy/Veer/Corbis/Jupiter Images

However, this analysis revealed a variety of other problems. Packing slips were found to contain many errors in addition to the wrong destination designation that contributed to the delays. Errors included

A. Wrong quantity

B. Wrong parts

C. Parts do not match

D. Purchase order was entered incorrectly

E. Original order was not in the system

Many packing slips contained multiple errors. The data in the C16 Case worksheet in the *OM4 Data Workbook* show the number of packing slips and total errors identified for 50 samples of 275 of packing slips.

Case Questions for Discussion

1. Construct and interpret a control chart for the packing slip data.

2. Conduct a Pareto analysis of the errors.

3. What information might a separate chart for each error category provide? Conduct a more thorough analysis for each error category, and draw conclusions and suggest recommendations for improving the process.

LEAN OPERATING SYSTEMS

a Michigan hospital manager noted, "Our hospital pharmacy processes are out of control. Patient health is at stake," noted a Michigan hospital manager. A study of pharmacy outcomes revealed that technicians were spending 77.4 percent of their time locating products, medication errors were high, and the current 14-stage process had some unnecessary steps, resulting in a total lead time of 166 minutes to fill a hospital prescription. Teams with names like "Paper Pushers" and "Zip Scripts" were formed and trained in lean operating methods and principles. Their objective was to apply lean principles to enhance the ability to deliver medications safely to hospital patients. After redesigning the system, the pharmacy realized a 33 percent reduction in time to get medications to patients, and reduced the number of process steps from 14 to 9 simply by removing non-value-added steps. Patients have experienced a 40 percent reduction in pharmacy-related medication errors, and the severity of those errors has decreased.[1]

learning outcomes

After studying this chapter you should be able to:

17-1 **Explain the four principles of lean operating systems.**

17-2 **Describe the basic lean tools and approaches.**

17-3 **Explain the concept of Lean Six Sigma and how it is applied to improving operations performance.**

17-4 **Explain how lean principles are used in manufacturing and service organizations.**

17-5 **Describe the concepts and philosophy of just-in-time operating systems.**

What do **you** think?

Can you cite any personal experiences in your work or around your school where you have observed similar inefficiencies (how about your dorm or bedroom)?

Heath Korvola/UpperCut Images/Getty Images

Lean thinking *refers to approaches that focus on the elimination of waste in all forms, and smooth, efficient flow of materials and information throughout the value chain to obtain faster customer response, higher quality, and lower costs. Manufacturing and service operations that apply the principles of lean enterprise are often called* **lean operating systems.** Lean concepts were initially developed and implemented by the Toyota Motor Corporation, and lean operating systems are often benchmarked with "the Toyota Production System (TPS)."

In the opening scenario, the lean teams greatly improved hospital pharmacy processes, enhanced patient health, and reduced liability risk to the hospital. For example, with only one printer for prescription labels in the pharmacy, labels were not always printed in the same order that the physical goods were available. This created confusion, and pharmacy technicians occasionally placed labels on the wrong bottles and bags. After applying lean thinking and methods, processing time and quality were greatly improved.

Lean thinking is playing a large role in sustainability efforts. Lean thinking helps to drive a culture of waste elimination and environmental sustainability. At a recent conference of the Association for Manufacturing Excellence, Interface Americas, a LaGrange, Georgia, manufacturer of commercial carpet, tile, and

> **Lean thinking** refers to approaches that focus on the elimination of waste in all forms, and smooth, efficient flow of materials and information throughout the value chain to obtain faster customer response, higher quality, and lower costs.
>
> Manufacturing and service operations that apply the principles of lean enterprise are often called **lean operating systems.**

▼ *As a result of the application of lean principles to pharmacy systems, patients have experienced a 40 percent reduction in pharmacy-related medical errors.*

interior fabrics, cited numerous examples of waste elimination activities that resulted from lean thinking, including over $300 million in cost avoidance from waste elimination, a 70 percent reduction of manufacturing waste sent to landfills, a 60 percent reduction in greenhouse gas emissions, and over 1 million pounds of carpet diverted from landfills.[2]

17-1 Principles of Lean Operating Systems

Lean operating systems have four basic principles:

1. elimination of waste,
2. increased speed and response,
3. improved quality, and
4. reduced cost.

As simple as these may seem, organizations require disciplined thinking and application of good operations management tools and approaches to achieve them.

Eliminate Waste

Lean, by the very nature of the term, implies doing only what is necessary to get the job done. Any activity, material, or operation that does not add value in an organization is considered waste. The goal is zero waste in all value-creation and support processes in the entire value chain. Exhibit 17.1 shows a variety of specific examples. The Toyota Motor Company classified waste into seven major categories:

1. *Overproduction*: for example, making a batch of 100 when there are orders for only 50 in order to avoid an expensive setup, or making a batch of 52 instead of 50 in case there are rejects. Overproduction ties up production facilities, and the resulting excess inventory simply sits idle.

2. *Waiting time*: for instance, allowing queues to build up between operations, resulting in longer lead times and more work-in-process.

3. *Transportation*: the time and effort spent in moving products around the factory as a result of poor layout.

Exhibit 17.1 *Common Examples of Waste in Organizations*

Excess capacity	Excess inventory	Spoilage
Inaccurate information	Long changeover and setup times	Excessive energy use
Clutter		Unnecessary movement of materials, people, and information
Planned product obsolescence	Scrap	
	Rework and repair	
Excessive material handling	Long, unproductive meetings	Equipment breakdowns
Overproduction		Knowledge bottlenecks
Producing too early		
Long distance travelled	Poor communication	Non-value-added process steps
	Waiting time	Misrouting jobs
Retraining and relearning time and expense	Accidents	Wrong transportation mode
	Too much space	

4. *Processing*: the traditional notion of waste, as exemplified by scrap that often results from poor product or process design.

5. *Inventory*: waste associated with the expense of idle stock and extra storage and handling requirements needed to maintain it.

6. *Motion*: as a result of inefficient workplace design and location of tools and materials.

7. *Production defects*: the result of not performing work correctly the first time.

Increase Speed and Response

Lean operating systems focus on quick and efficient response in designing and getting goods and services to market, producing to customer demand and delivery requirements, responding to competitors' actions, collecting payments, and addressing customer inquiries or problems. Perhaps the most effective way of increasing speed and response is to synchronize the entire value chain. By this we mean that not only are all elements of the value chain focused on a common goal but that the transfer of all physical materials and information is coordinated to achieve a high level of efficiency. A champion of lean practices would argue "be fast or last" and "synchronize value chain operations."

Improve Quality

Lean operating systems cannot function if raw materials are bad, processing operations are not consistent, materials and tools are not located in the correct place, or machines break down. Poor quality disrupts work schedules and reduces yields, requiring extra inventory, processing time, and space for scrap and parts waiting for rework. All these are forms of waste and increase costs to the customer. Eliminating the sources of defects and errors in all processes in the value chain greatly improves speed, reduces variability, and supports the notion of continuous flow. All of the concepts and methods of quality management, such as product and process design simplification, root cause analysis, mistake-proofing, and statistical process control, are employed to improve quality.

Reduce Cost

Certainly, reducing cost is an important objective of lean enterprise. Anything that is done to reduce waste and improve quality often reduces cost at the same time. More efficient equipment, better preventive maintenance, and smaller inventories reduce costs in manufacturing firms. Simplifying processes, such as using customer labor via self-service in a fast-food restaurant, depositing a check using an automatic teller machine, and completing medical forms online before medical service, are ways for service businesses to become leaner and reduce costs.

Michael Dwyer/Alamy

17-2 Lean Tools and Approaches

meeting the objectives of lean enterprise requires disciplined approaches for designing and improving processes. Organizations use several tools and approaches to create a lean organization. We describe some of these here.

17-2a The 5Ss

Workers cannot be efficient if their workplaces are messy and disorganized. Efficient manufacturing plants are clean and well organized. Firms use the "5S" principles to create this work environment. *The 5Ss are derived from Japanese terms:* seiri *(sort),* seiton *(set in order),* seiso *(shine),* seiketsu *(standardize), and* shitsuke *(sustain).*

The **5Ss** are derived from Japanese terms: *seiri* (sort), *seiton* (set in order), *seiso* (shine), *seiketsu* (standardize), and *shitsuke* (sustain).

- *Sort* refers to ensuring that each item in a workplace is in its proper place or identified as unnecessary and removed.
- *Set in order* means to arrange materials and equipment so that they are easy to find and use.
- *Shine* refers to a clean work area. Not only is this important for safety, but as a work area is cleaned, maintenance problems such as oil leaks can be identified before they cause problems.
- *Standardize* means to formalize procedures and practices to create consistency and ensure that all steps are performed correctly.
- Finally, *sustain* means to keep the process going through training, communication, and organizational structures.

17-2b Visual Controls

Visual controls *are indicators for operating activities that are placed in plain sight of all employees so that everyone can quickly and easily understand the status and performance of the work system.* Visual signaling systems are known as *andon*, drawing from the Japanese term from which the concept first originated. For example, if a machine fails or a part is defective or manufactured incorrectly, a light might turn on or a buzzer might sound, indicating that immediate action should be taken. Many firms have cords that operators can pull that tell supervisors and other workers that a problem has occurred. Some firms, such as Honda (on the manufacturing floor) and JPMorgan Chase (at its call

centers), use electronic "scoreboards" to keep track of daily performance. These scoreboards are located where everyone can see them and report key metrics such as volume, quality levels, speed of service, and so on.

17-2c Single Minute Exchange of Dies (SMED)

Long setup times waste manufacturing resources. Short setup times, on the other hand, enable a manufacturer to have frequent changeovers and move toward single-piece flow, thus achieving high flexibility and product variety. Reducing setup time also frees up capacity for other productive uses. **Single Minute Exchange of Dies (SMED)** *refers to the quick setup or*

LEAN OPERATIONS FOR LUXURY BAGS

Louis Vuitton is one of the world's most recognizable luxury brands, and has grown significantly in recent years. When Louis Vuitton was building a new factory in Marsaz, France, it had to find other ways to increase production in its existing factories. One way was implementing lean thinking. Luxury bags are produced in low volume, but the production process can benefit from recognizing the common features across items and making sure that work is coordinated. By reorganizing teams of about 10 workers in U-shaped clusters, Vuitton was able to free up 10 percent more floor space in its factories and was able to hire 300 new people without increasing facility size. At Vuitton's shoe factory in Italy, robots now fetch the foot molds around which a shoe is made instead of workers walking back and forth from their workstations to the shelves, resulting in a considerable gain in time.[4]

Peter Horree/Alamy

changeover of tooling and fixtures in processes so that multiple products in smaller batches can be run on the same equipment. SMED was pioneered by Toyota and other Japanese manufacturers and has been adopted by companies around the world.

17-2d Small Batch and Single-Piece Flow

One of the practices that inhibits increasing speed and response in manufacturing or service processing of discrete parts such as a manufactured part, invoices, medical claims, or home loan mortgage approvals is **batching**—*the process of producing large quantities of items as a group before they are transferred to the next operation.* Batching is often necessary when producing a broad goods or service mix with diverse requirements on common equipment. When making different goods, manufacturers often need to change dies, tools, and fixtures on equipment, resulting in expensive and time-consuming setups and teardowns. For services, preprinted forms or software may have to be changed or modified. By running large batches, setups and teardowns are reduced, providing economies of scale. However, this often builds up inventory that might not match market demand, particularly in highly dynamic markets.

A better strategy would be to use small batches or single-piece flow. **Single-piece flow** *is the concept of ideally using batch sizes of one.* However, to do this economically requires the ability to change between products quickly and inexpensively.

17-2e Quality and Continuous Improvement

Quality at the source requires doing it right the first time, and therefore eliminates the opportunities for waste. Employees inspect, analyze, and control their own work to guarantee that the good or service passed on to the next process stage conforms to specifications. Continuous improvement initiatives are vital in lean environments, as is teamwork among all managers and employees.

An important synergy exists between quality improvement and lean thinking. Clearly as an organization continuously improves its processes, it eliminates rework and waste, thus making the processes leaner. Moreover, as an organization tries to make itself leaner

by eliminating non-value-added activities and simplifying processes, it reduces the number of opportunities for error, thus improving quality at the same time!

> Quality at the source requires doing it right the first time, and therefore eliminates the opportunities for waste.

17-2f Total Productive Maintenance

Total productive maintenance (TPM) *is focused on ensuring that operating systems will perform their intended function reliably.* The goal of TPM is to prevent equipment failures and downtime—ideally, to have "zero accidents, zero defects, and zero failures" in the entire life cycle of the operating system.[5] TPM seeks to

- maximize overall equipment effectiveness and eliminate unplanned downtime,
- create worker "ownership" of the equipment by involving them in maintenance activities, and
- foster continuous efforts to improve equipment operation through employee involvement activities.

Because of its importance in lean thinking, TPM has been called "lean

Batching is the process of producing large quantities of items as a group before they are transferred to the next operation.

Single-piece flow is the concept of ideally using batch sizes of one.

Total productive maintenance (TPM) is focused on ensuring that operating systems will perform their intended function reliably.

maintenance." Lean maintenance is more than preventing failures of equipment and processes; it now includes maintenance and backup systems for software and electronic network systems such as the Internet or wireless networks.

17-3 Lean Six Sigma

Six Sigma is a useful and complementary approach to lean production. For example, a cycle-time-reduction project might involve aspects of both. Lean tools might be applied to streamline an order entry process. This application leads to the discovery that significant rework occurs because of incorrect addresses, customer numbers, or shipping charges and results in high variation of processing time. Six Sigma tools might then be used to drill down to the root cause of the problems and identify a solution. Because of these similarities, many practitioners have begun to focus on *Lean Six Sigma*, drawing upon the best practices of both approaches. Both are driven by customer requirements, focus on real dollar savings, have the ability to make significant financial impacts on the organization, and can easily be used in nonmanufacturing environments. Both use basic root cause, process, and data analysis techniques.

However, some differences clearly exist between lean production and Six Sigma. First, they attack different types of problems. Lean production addresses visible problems in processes, for example, inventory, material flow, and safety. Six Sigma is more concerned with less visible problems, for example, variation in performance. In essence, lean is focused on efficiency by reducing waste and improving process flow, whereas Six Sigma is focused on effectiveness by reducing errors and defects. Another difference is that lean tools are more intuitive and easier to apply by anybody in the workplace, whereas many Six Sigma tools require advanced training and expertise of specialists, particularly in statistical analyses, commonly called Black Belts and Master Black Belts. For example, most workers can easily understand the concept of

the 5Ss, but may have more difficulty with statistical methods. Thus, organizations might be well advised to start with basic lean principles and evolve toward more sophisticated Six Sigma approaches. However, it is important to integrate both approaches with a common goal—improving business results. Often Lean Six Sigma is an important part of implementing a strategy built upon sustainability.

17-4 Lean Manufacturing and Service Tours

Lean manufacturing plants look significantly different from traditional plants. They are clean and organized, devoid of long and complex production lines and high levels of work-in-process, have efficient layouts and work area designs, use multiskilled workers who perform both direct and indirect work such as maintenance, and have no incoming or final inspection stations. Next, we "tour" a manufacturing firm to examine how it focuses on the four major lean objectives.

17-4a Timken Company

The Timken Company (www.timken.com) is a leading global manufacturer of highly engineered bearings and alloy steels and related products and services for three major markets—industrial, automotive, and steel. Timken employs about 18,000 employees in over 50 factories and more than 100 sales, design, and distribution centers located throughout the world. Timken places increasing emphasis on pre- and postproduction services, such as integrated engineering solutions to customer requirements.

Like most manufacturers, Timken faced intense, survival-threatening, global competition, and like many others, it placed itself on the leading edge of the U.S. industrial revival. In 1989, the company launched "Vision 2000," a program of lean production initiatives that developed throughout the 1990s. A key element was

PRNewsFoto/The Timken Company

increased productivity through lean manufacturing operating principles and technologies, some of which we highlight next.

Eliminate Waste

Timken's automotive business uses a "Boot Camp" in which a certain factory identifies several improvement opportunities, and Timken employees and managers from other sites then try to solve these specific problems at the host factory. The problems often focus on removing non-value-added steps from processes, reducing process and equipment variation, and eliminating waste. The boot camp approach allows "fresh eyes" to evaluate improvement opportunities and present solutions to host plant management.

Increase Speed and Response

Timken has focused on improving its product development process—a nonmanufacturing, information-intensive process—with the objective to radically reduce the total cycle time for new product development with fewer errors and to be more responsive to customer requests, competitor capabilities, and marketplace changes. Timken's objective of an integrated supply chain also focuses on agility to better meet customer wants and needs.

Timken exploited computer-aided design and computer-aided manufacturing (CAD/CAM) to better meet customer needs and improve design for manufacturability. It developed flexible manufacturing systems to facilitate rapid, cost-effective changeover from one product to another, combining the advantages of batch and mass production. Lean manufacturing's most distinguishing characteristic at Timken, however, was the authority and responsibility it gave to people on the shop floor. Initiatives aimed at empowering shop floor employees included more open communication, enhanced training, widespread adoption of a team approach to problem solving and decision making, and changes in measures of performance and rewards.

Improve Quality

Total quality and continuous improvement have long been areas of focus for Timken. Through programs like Breakthrough and Accelerated Continuous Improvement, thousands of improvement ideas have been implemented, saving millions of dollars. Quality standards are determined for all manufacturing processes, and worldwide quality audits make sure that these standards are being met. Each plant is certified to ISO 9000 or other quality certifications. Timken has applied Six Sigma tools to minimize process variation. One initiative was to improve machine operator efficiency and reduce variability. Workstation processes were standardized and machine operator walking and movement time were eliminated or reduced. The result was improved quality and reduced scrap.

Reduce Cost

Timken redefined its mission statement in 1993 to be "the best performing manufacturing company in the world as seen through the eyes of our customers and shareholders." Timken factories, suppliers, and customers share information using the Internet. Purchasing, order fulfillment, manufacturing strategy implementation, Lean Six Sigma, and logistics have been brought together to create an "integrated supply chain model." The purpose of this focus is to reduce asset intensity, improve customer service and systems support, respond faster to customer needs, and better manage inventory levels.

In the late 1990s, Timken decided to integrate its lean manufacturing practices and Six Sigma initiatives into one unified program, Lean Six Sigma. The objective of Timken's Lean Six Sigma program is "to identify and deliver value to our customers and shareholders by improving the flow of product and information through waste elimination and variation reduction." All manufacturing processes are flowcharted and the DMAIC problem-solving framework is used to generate process improvements. The automotive business achieved a net documented savings of $7 million from Lean Six Sigma projects in one year alone.

Service organizations can benefit significantly from applying lean principles. Lean principles are not always transferable to "front-office" services that involve high customer contact and service encounters. In these situations, the service provider and firm do not have complete control over creating the service. Different customers, service-encounter situations, and customer and employee behaviors cause the creation and delivery of the service to be much more variable and uncertain than producing a manufactured good in the confines of a factory. However, "back-office" service processes, such as hospital laboratory testing, check processing, and college application processing, are nearly identical to many manufacturing processes. Time, accuracy, and cost are all important to their performance, and therefore they can clearly benefit from the application of lean principles.

The following discussion shows how lean concepts have been used at Southwest Airlines.[6]

17-4b Southwest Airlines

Since its inception, Southwest Airlines has shown lean performance when compared to other major airlines. It has consistently been profitable while other major airlines have not. What is even more significant is that Southwest has historically operated small planes and short-distance flights and therefore cannot capitalize on the economies of scale available to larger airlines.

The vast majority of total airline cost focuses on operations management activities: traffic servicing (13 percent), aircraft servicing (7 percent), flight operations (47 percent), reservations and sales (10 percent), and passenger in-flight service (7 percent). Note that the first three are low-contact (back-office) operations, whereas passenger in-flight service and reservations and sales are high-contact service management functions. Therefore, taking a lean approach to all operations is vital to airline performance. Southwest is clearly a lean airline—it does more with less than any other airline competitor. Let us examine some of the reasons.

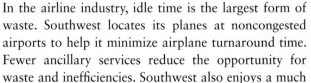
REUTERS/Jeff Haynes/Landov

Eliminate Waste

In the airline industry, idle time is the largest form of waste. Southwest locates its planes at noncongested airports to help it minimize airplane turnaround time. Fewer ancillary services reduce the opportunity for waste and inefficiencies. Southwest also enjoys a much lower employee turnover rate than its competitors, resulting in lower training costs.

All the resources at Southwest work to keep the airplanes in the air earning revenue—the primary focus of its strategy. The more time spent on the ground, the less revenue. It relies on motivated employees, a culture focused on the customer, and teamwork to accomplish this strategy. Southwest employees are cross-trained and organized into teams to accomplish all key operational activities. For example, all employees cooperate to ensure timely takeoffs and landings; it is not unusual to see pilots helping load baggage if this will get the plane off on time. This maintains smooth system schedules and reduces the need for reschedules and reticketing, both of which are a form of rework. As one example, in as little as 15 minutes, Southwest can change the flight crew; deplane and board 137 passengers; unload 97 bags, 1,000 pounds of mail, and 25 pieces of freight; load another 123 bags and 600 pounds of mail; and pump 4,500 pounds of jet fuel into the aircraft.[7]

Increase Speed and Response

Southwest uses a much simpler structure and operating system than its competitors. It uses only one type of aircraft—the Boeing 737—making it easier to schedule crews, perform maintenance, and standardize such activities as boarding, baggage storage and retrieval, and cabin operations. It books direct flights from point A to B and does not rely on the hub-and-spoke system used by competitors. This makes it easier for many customers to get to their destinations, instead of, for instance, flying from Orlando to Cincinnati or Detroit and then connecting back to Nashville. A simple operating structure reduces the time it takes to make decisions and allows employees to focus on the key drivers of airline performance such as turnaround time. For example, if Southwest can turn its planes around on average in at most ½ hour while competitors take 1 hour, then, assuming a 90-minute flight, approximately one to two more flights per day per plane can be made. This can be a significant economic and strategic advantage.

Southwest was the first airline to introduce ticketless travel. Customers simply get a confirmation number and show up on time. A significant proportion of customers book their flights directly on Southwest.com. No in-flight full-service meals are provided either, simplifying cabin operations and eliminating the need to stock meals, which increases the time to clean up from the previous flight and prepare for the next flight. Instead, Southwest was the first airline to offer continental breakfast in the gate area, and flight attendants serve drinks and peanuts using specially designed trays. If a customer misses a flight, he or she can use the ticket for a future flight with no penalty; this reduces paperwork and processing, contributing to a leaner operation.

Improve Quality

Simplified processes reduce variability in flight schedules, a major source of customer complaints, and therefore improve customers' perceptions of quality and satisfaction. Southwest encourages carry on baggage; hence, there is less opportunity for losing, misrouting, or damaging baggage. People-oriented employees are carefully chosen and empowered to both serve and entertain passengers.

Reduce Cost

Short setup and turnaround time translates into higher asset utilization and reduces the need for costly inventories of aircraft. Southwest does not have assigned seating; customers wait on a first-come, first-served basis and board in zones. This lowers costs, and only a few employees are needed to coordinate passenger boarding. In addition, rather than carry the high overhead costs of airplane maintenance and repair, Southwest outsources these tasks to third parties.

17-5 Just-in-Time Systems

Just-in-time (JIT) was introduced at Toyota during the 1950s and 1960s to address the challenge of coordinating successive production activities. An automobile, for instance, consists of thousands of parts. It is extremely difficult to coordinate the transfer of materials and components between production operations. Traditional factories use a **push system,** *which produces finished-goods inventory in advance of customer demand using a forecast of sales.* Parts and

subassemblies are "pushed" through the operating system based on a predefined schedule that is independent of actual customer demand. In a push system, a model that might not be selling well is still produced at the same predetermined production rate and held in finished-goods inventory for future sale, whereas enough units of a model in high demand might not get produced.

Another problem was that traditional automobile production systems relied on massive and expensive stamping press lines to produce car panels. The dies in the presses weighed many tons and specialists needed up to a full day to switch them for a new part. To compensate for long setup times, large batch sizes were produced so that machines could be kept busy while others were being set up. This resulted in high work-in-process inventories and high levels of indirect labor and overhead.

Toyota created a system based on a simple idea: produce the needed quantity of required parts each day. This concept characterizes a **pull system,** *in which employees at a given operation go to the source of required parts, such as machining or subassembly, and withdraw the units as they need them.* Then just enough new parts are manufactured or procured to replace those withdrawn. As the process from which parts were withdrawn replenishes the items it transferred out, it draws on the output of its preceding process, and so on. Finished goods are made to coincide

> A **push system** produces finished-goods inventory in advance of customer demand using a forecast of sales.
>
> A **pull system** is one in which employees at a given operation go to the source of required parts, such as machining or subassembly, and withdraw the units as they need them.

JIT for the Bookless Bookshelf

Traditionally, the supply chain for books has been a "push" system, physical goods produced and delivered to bookstores for sale to consumers. Despite the promulgation of eBooks and the demise of traditional bookstores such as Borders, many people still like to turn pages. As bookstores become leaner, many books are not available. For example, HarperCollins Publishers estimates that 25 to 80 percent of its paperback titles are not available in bookstores because of space considerations. However, the publisher is leveraging the JIT concept by using the Espresso Book Machine, distributed by On Demand Books LLC. This is a desk-sized machine that can custom print a book in only a few minutes. HarperCollins is using it to make about 5,000 paperback books available to bookstores using this technology.

with the actual rate of demand, resulting in minimal inventories and maximum responsiveness.

JIT systems are based on the concept of pull rather than push. In a JIT system, a key gateway workstation (such as final assembly) withdraws parts to meet demand and therefore provides real-time information to preceding workstations about how much to produce and when to produce to match the sales rate. By pulling parts from each preceding workstation, the entire manufacturing process is synchronized to the final assembly schedule. JIT operating systems prohibit all process workstations from pushing inventory forward only to wait idle if it is not needed.

A JIT system can produce a steady rate of output to meet the sales rate in small, consistent batch sizes to level loads and stabilize the operating system. This dramatically reduces the inventory required between stages of the production process, thus greatly reducing costs and physical capacity requirements (see the box on Conmed, Inc.).

Many suppliers are asked to provide materials on a JIT basis to reduce inventories. Arriving shipments are sent directly to production. To accomplish this, suppliers often locate their parts warehouses close to final assembly factories. At the other end of the supply chain, distribution centers and retail stores are located close to their customers to speed up delivery.

17-5a Operation of a JIT System

A simple generic JIT system with two process cycles—one for the customer and a second for the supply process—is shown in Exhibit 17.2. Conceptually, the customer can be an internal or external customer, and the customer-supply configuration in Exhibit 17.2 can be chained together to model a more complex sequence of production or assembly operations. In this process, the customer cycle withdraws what is needed at the time it is needed according to sales. The supply cycle creates the good to replenish only what has been withdrawn by the customer. The storage area is the interface and control point between the customer and supply cycles.

Slips, called Kanban cards (*Kanban* is a Japanese word that means "visual record" or "card"), are circulated within the system to initiate withdrawal and production items through the production process.

Exhibit 17.2 *A Two-Card Kanban JIT Operating System*

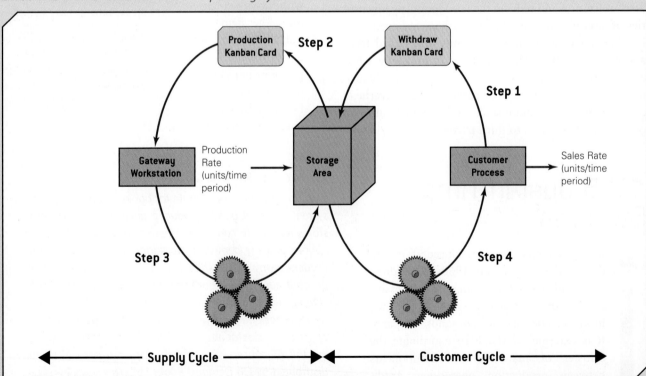

A **Kanban** is a flag or a piece of paper that contains all relevant information for an order: part number, description, process area used, time of delivery, quantity available, quantity delivered, production quantity, and so on. Because of this, a JIT system is sometimes called a Kanban system.

The Kanban system begins when the customer buys or uses the good and an empty container is created. The withdraw Kanban (step 1) authorizes the material handler to transfer empty containers to the storage area. Withdraw Kanbans trigger the movement of parts. The material handler detaches the withdraw-ordering Kanban that was attached to the empty container and places the Kanban card in the storage area or on the Kanban receiving post, leaving the empty container(s) (step 1). A material handler for the supply cycle places a production Kanban on the empty container and this authorizes the gateway workstation to produce parts (step 2). Production Kanbans trigger the production of parts. The container holds a small lot size of parts. Without the authorization of the production Kanban, the gateway workstation and all other workstations may be idle. The gateway workstation must be scheduled to meet the sales rate, and it pulls parts from all other workstations. The other workstations in the process do not need to be scheduled because they get their production orders from the production Kanban that pulls parts through the supply process. The supply process returns a full container of parts to the storage area with the production Kanban attached (step 3). The Kanban process is complete when the material handler for the customer process picks up a full container of parts and takes the production Kanban card off the container. Normally, the material handler drops off a withdrawal Kanban and empty container when picking up a full container of parts.

JIT practice is to set the lot size or container size equal to about 5 to 20 percent of a day's demand or between 20 to 90 minutes worth of demand. The number of containers in the system determines the average inventory levels. The following equation is used to calculate the number of Kanban cards (K) required:

$$K = \frac{\text{Average daily demand during lead time plus a safety stock}}{\text{Number of units per container}}$$
$$= \frac{d(p + w)(1 + \alpha)}{C} \qquad [17.1]$$

where K = the number of Kanban cards in the operating system.

d = the average daily production rate as determined from the master production schedule.

w = the waiting time of Kanban cards in decimal fractions of a day (that is, the waiting time of a part).

p = the processing time per part, in decimal fractions of a day.

C = the capacity of a standard container in the proper units of measure (parts, items, etc.).

α = a policy variable determined by the efficiency of the process and its workstations and the uncertainty of the workplace, and therefore a form of safety stock usually ranging from 0 to 1. However, technically, there is no upper limit on the value of α.

The number of Kanban cards is directly proportional to the amount of work-in-process inventory. Managers and employees strive to reduce the number of cards in the system through reduced lead time (p or w), lower α values, or through other improvements. The maximum authorized inventory in the operating system is $K \times C$.

CONMED, INC.: JIT AND LEAN KEEP JOBS IN THE USA

Conmed, Inc. was evaluating moving its surgical device manufacturing operations from New York to China. Instead, it overhauled its operating systems using JIT and lean practices. Conmed designed a JIT system to build only as many products as customers need based on actual demand, rather than a three- to six-month forecast. It calculated that every 90 seconds, hospitals worldwide use of one of its disposable surgical devices for inserting and removing fluids around joints during arthroscopic surgery. So that is exactly how long it takes one new device to roll off the assembly line. "The goal is to link our operations as closely as possible to the ultimate buyer of the product," says David Johnson, vice-president of global operations. The 600-worker Utica, New York, factory is now organized in a compact U-shaped set of workstations instead of one long assembly line. As a result, extensive piles of inventory have been replaced by just a few JIT containers, freeing up capital for other uses and reducing the need for financing.[8]

A **Kanban** is a flag or a piece of paper that contains all relevant information for an order: part number, description, process area used, time of delivery, quantity available, quantity delivered, production quantity, and so on.

Solved Problem

Babbitt Manufacturing uses a Kanban system for a component part. The daily demand is 800 brackets. Each container has a combined waiting and processing time of 0.34 days. The container size is 50 brackets and the safety factor (α) is 9 percent.

a. How many Kanban card sets should be authorized?

b. What is the maximum inventory of brackets in the system of brackets?

c. What are the answers to (a) and (b) if waiting and processing time is reduced by 25 percent?

d. If we assume one-half the containers are empty and one-half full at any given time, what is the average inventory in the system for the original problem?

Solution

a. Using Equation 17.1:

$$K = \frac{d(p + w)(1 + \alpha)}{C}$$

$$= \frac{(800\,\text{units})(0.34)(1 + 0.09)}{50} = 5.93$$

$$\cong 6 \text{ (rounded up to 6)}$$

Thus, six containers and six Kanban card sets are necessary to fulfill daily demand.

b. The maximum authorized inventory is $K \times C$ $= 6 \times 50 = 300$ brackets.

c. $$K = \frac{d(p + w)(1 + \alpha)}{C}$$

$$= \frac{(800\,\text{units})(0.255)(1 + 0.09)}{50} = 4.45$$

$$\cong 5 \text{ (rounded up to 5)}$$

Thus, five containers and five Kanban card sets are necessary to fulfill daily demand. The maximum authorized inventory is now $K \times C = 5 \times 50 = 250$ brackets.

d. The average inventory under this assumption is $300/2 = 150$ brackets. Many variables in the JIT system determine whether this assumption is valid or not. For example, for a given combination of daily demand, processing and waiting times, and other process inefficiencies and uncertainties, it is possible for more or fewer containers to be empty (full).

17-5b JIT in Service Organizations

Although JIT has had its biggest impact in manufacturing, many service organizations are increasingly applying it. At the Nashua Corporation, for example, a JIT-oriented study of administrative operations reduced order-cycle time from three days to one hour, office space requirements by 40 percent, and errors by 95 percent and increased productivity by 20 percent.[9] One overnight package-delivery service saw its inventory investment climb from $16 million to $34 million with conventional inventory management techniques.[10] Implementing JIT reduced its inventory investment, but the company's major objective was to increase profits by providing a 99.9 percent level of service to its customers. Before JIT implementation, its service level—computed by dividing the number of items filled weekly by the number of items requested—was 79 percent. After JIT, the level was 99 percent, and the firm looked forward to meeting its goal. Baxter International is another service company that has experienced the benefits of a JIT system.

Some of the characteristics of a well-designed JIT system are summarized in Exhibit 17.3.

However, lean principles can't be blindly implemented in services without considering their effects on customers, as Starbucks is discovering. Starbucks began to roll out "better way" initiatives—a series of process improvements using lean principles. Starbucks initiated a "lean team" that goes around the country with a Mr. Potato Head toy used in a lean training program for Starbuck managers. Managers learn how to assemble the toy in less than 45 seconds and apply the learnings to their store processes. However, customer service encounters may have suffered, as one customer wrote: "Customers come into Starbucks—at least they did—to experience something that could only happen without lean, friendly banter with the barista, sampling coffee or a pastry, etc. Lean is best suited to assembly lines and factories, not so for managing human interaction, which is never a repeatable routine."[11]

Mario Ruiz/Time Life Pictures/ Getty Images

Exhibit 17.3 *Example JIT Characteristics and Best Practices*

- Setup/changeover time minimized
- Excellent preventive maintenance
- Mistake-proof job and process design
- Stable, level, repetitive master production schedule
- Phantom bill of materials with zero lead time
- Fast processing times
- Clean and uncluttered workspaces
- Very little inventory to hide problems and inefficiencies
- Use production cells with no wasted motion
- May freeze the master production schedule
- Use reusable containers
- Outstanding communication and information sharing
- Keep it simple and use visual controls
- High quality approaching zero defects

- Small repetitive order/lot sizes
- Minimize the number of parts/items
- Minimize the number of bill of materials levels
- Facility layout that supports continuous or single-piece flow
- Minimize distance traveled and handling
- Clearly defined performance metrics
- Minimize the number of production, inventory, and accounting transactions
- Good calibration of all gauges and testing equipment
- Employees trained in quality management concepts and tools
- Excellent employee recognition and reward systems
- Employee cross-training and multiple skills
- Empowered and disciplined employees

Discussion Questions

1. Provide some examples of different types of waste in an organization with which you are familiar, such as an automobile repair shop or a fast-food restaurant.

2. Compare the lean service system of Southwest Airlines to a full-service airline such as United Airlines or British Airways on the following: (a) airplane boarding process, (b) cabin service, (c) ticket transfer to other Southwest flights, (d) frequent flyer program, (e) baggage handling, (f) seat assignment system, and (g) service encounters.

3. Recycle Technologies manufactures and sells recycled antifreeze that is 20 percent cheaper and has a carbon footprint about 80 percent smaller than new antifreeze made from original raw materials. The company is trying to reduce waste in the traditional antifreeze supply chain. Would you buy this recycled antifreeze and put it into your vehicle? Explain the pros and cons of your decision.

4. Do you think applying operations management concepts and methods such as Six Sigma and lean principles can reduce U.S. health care costs? Explain. Provide examples that show how OM can help the U.S. health care industry.

5. What types of "setups" do you perform in your work or school activities? How might you reduce the setup times?

Problems and Activities

1. Interview a manager at a local company that uses JIT. Report on how it is implemented and the benefits the company has realized.

2. Research JIT practices and how they impact purchasing. How do you think JIT systems affect purchasing functions and practices? Answer this question in a short paper of no more than two typed pages.

3. Research and briefly describe one or two lean initiatives in service organizations and then make an argument for or against adopting lean principles in service businesses. What is different about applying lean in a factory versus a service situation? Describe your findings in a two-page paper.

4. Research and write a short paper on the impact of global supply chains on JIT.

5. Choose one of the lean tools and approaches from Section 2 of this chapter and research and write a short paper (two pages maximum) on how organizations use this tool, and provide specific examples.

6. Search the Internet for manufacturing or service tours similar to the ones in this chapter. Classify a toured company's practices according to the four

lean principles in a manner similar to the examples in the chapter.

7. Search the Internet for images of visual controls. Select five of them and explain how they contribute to achieving one of the four principles of lean operating systems.

8. A catalog order-filling process can be described as follows.[12] Telephone orders are taken over a 12-hour period each day. Orders are collected from each person at the end of the day and checked for errors by the supervisor of the phone department, usually the following morning. The supervisor does not send each one-day batch of orders to the data processing department until after 1:00 p.m. In the next step—data processing—orders are invoiced in the one-day batches. Then they are printed and matched back to the original orders. At this point, if the order is from a new customer, it is sent to the person who did the customer verification and setup of new customer accounts. This process must be completed before the order can be invoiced. The next step—order verification and proofreading—occurs after invoicing is completed. The orders, with invoices attached, are given to a person who verifies that all required information is present and correct to permit typesetting. If the verifier has any questions, they are checked by computer or by calling the customer. Finally, the completed orders are sent to the typesetting department of the print shop.

    a. Develop a flowchart for this process (see Chapter 7).

    b. Identify opportunities for improving the process using lean principles.

9. A team at a hospital studied the process of performing a diagnostic CT scan. The current process can be described as follows.[13] The CT tech enters a "send for patient" request into a computer when the CT is available for the next patient. The computer prints a request for transport and an orderly is assigned to take the patient for the scan. The orderly walks to radiology and gets the ticket and patient information. The orderly takes the elevator to the patient's unit and goes to the nurse's station, locates the nurse in charge, and obtains the patient's chart. He or she signs out the patient and walks to the patient's room and waits for a nurse to help transfer the patient. The patient is transferred to a mobile bed and then taken to the elevator and brought to radiology. The chart is given to the CT technician while the patient waits in the hall. When the CT is ready, the patient is moved to the CT machine and the scan is performed. The orderly is called back to take the patient back to his or her room.

Draw a flowchart of this process, identify the value-added and non-value-added activities, and describe how lean thinking can be applied to shorten the throughput time to perform the CT scan.

10. Some companies use a technique called *heijunka*, which is a Japanese term that refers to production smoothing in which the total volume of parts and assemblies is kept as constant as possible. Research and write a short paper (two pages maximum) about this technique and how it relates to lean principles. Try to find a case study of a company that has used it.

11. Research and write a short paper (two pages maximum) on applications of the 5S principles in a service organization, such as a hospital. If possible, provide some pictures that illustrate the results of using the 5S principles.

12. Tooltron Manufacturing uses a Kanban system for a component. Daily demand is 800 units. Each container has a combined waiting and processing time of 1.2 days. If the container size is 50 and the alpha value (α) is 15 percent, how many Kanban card sets should be authorized? What is the maximum authorized inventory?

13. Lou's Bakery has established that JIT should be used for chocolate chips due to the high probability of the kitchen heat melting the chips. The average demand is 130 cups of chocolate chips per week. The average setup and processing time is $1/2$ day. Each container holds exactly 2 cups. The current safety stock factor is 5 percent. The baker operates six days per week.

    a. How many Kanbans are required for the bakery?

    b. What is the maximum authorized inventory?

    c. If the average setup and processing time is reduced to $3/8$ of a day due to better training and retention of experienced employees, what are the new answers to (a) and (b)?

14. Due to rapid changes in technology, a telecommunications manufacturer decides to produce a router using JIT methods. Daily demand for the router is 10 units per day. The routers are built on racks that hold four at a time (i.e., the container size). Total processing and waiting time is 3.75 days. The process manager wants a safety factor of only 5 percent.

    a. How many Kanbans are required?

    b. What is the maximum authorized router inventory?

    c. If you assume that one-half of the racks are empty and one-half are full at any given time, what is the average inventory of routers?

    d. What are the new answers to (a) through (c) if, due to process improvements, the total processing and waiting time is reduced from 3.75 to 2.75 days?

15. An automobile transmission manufacturer is considering using a JIT approach to replenishing its stock of transmissions. Daily demand for transmission #230 is 25 transmissions per day, and they are built in groups of six transmissions. Total assembly and waiting time is three days. The supervisor wants to use an alpha value (α) of 1, or 100 percent.

a. How many Kanbans are required?
b. What is the maximum authorized inventory?
c. What are the pros and cons of using such a high alpha (α) value?

Community Medical Associates Case Study

Community Medical Associates (CMA) is a large health care system with 2 hospitals, 25 satellite health centers, and 56 outpatient clinics. CMA had 1.5 million outpatient visits and 60,000 inpatient admissions the previous year. Just a few years ago, CMA's health care delivery system was having significant problems with quality of care. Long patient waiting times, uncoordinated clinical and patient information, and medical errors plagued the system. Doctors, nurses, lab technicians, managers, and medical students in training were very aggravated with the labyrinth of forms, databases, and communication links. Accounting and billing were in a situation of constant confusion and constantly correcting medical bills and insurance payments. The complexity of the CMA information and communication system overwhelmed its people.

Prior to redesigning its systems, physicians were faced with a complex array of appointments and schedules

Today, CMA uses an integrated operating system that consolidates over 50 CCMA databases into one.

in order to see patients in the hospital, centers, and clinics. For example, an elderly patient with shoulder pain would get an X ray at the clinic but have to set up an appointment for a CAT scan in the hospital. Furthermore, the patient's blood was sent to an off-site lab while physician notes were transcribed from tape recorders. Radiology would read and interpret the X rays and body scans in a consultant report. Past and present medication records were kept in the hospital and offsite pharmacies. Physicians would write paper prescriptions for each patient. Billing and patient insurance information was maintained in a separate database. The patient's medical chart was part paper-based and part electronic. The paper medical file could be stored at the hospital, centers, or clinics. Nurses handwrote their notes on each patient, but their notes were seldom input into the patient's medical records or chart.

"We must access one database for lab results, then log off and access another system for radiology, then log off and access the CMA pharmacy system to gain an integrated view of the patient's health. If I can't find the patient's records within five minutes or so, I have to abandon my search and tell the patient to wait or make another appointment," said one doctor. The doctor continued, "You have to abandon the patient because you have to move on to patients you truly can diagnose and help. If you don't abandon the patient, you might make clinical decisions about the patient's health without having a complete set of information. Not having all the medical information fast has a direct impact on quality of care and patient satisfaction."

Today, CMA uses an integrated operating system that consolidates over 50 CMA databases into one. Health care providers in the CMA system now have access to these records through 7,000 computer terminals. Using many levels of security and some restricted databases, all patient information is accessible in less than two minutes. For example, sensitive categories of patient records, such as psychiatric and AIDS problems, were kept in super-restricted databases. It cost CMA $4.46 to retrieve and transport a single patient's paper-based medical chart to the proper location, whereas the more complete and quickly updated electronic medical record costs $1.32 to electronically retrieve and transport once. A patient's medical records are retrieved on average 1.4 times for outpatient services and 4.8 times for inpatient admissions. In addition, CMA has spent more money on database security, although it has not been able to place a dollar value on this. Electronic security audit trails show who logs on, when, how long he or she views a specific file, and what information he or she has viewed.

The same doctor who made the previous comments two years ago now said, "The speed of the system is what I like. I can now make informed clinical decisions for my patients. Where it used to take several days and sometimes weeks to transcribe my patient medical notes, it now takes no more than 48 hours to see them pop up on the CMA system. Often my notes are up on the system the same day. I'd say we use about one-half the paper we used with the old system. I also find myself editing and correcting transcription errors in the database—so it is more accurate now."

The next phase in the development of CMA's integrated system is to connect it to suppliers, outside labs and pharmacies, other hospitals, and to doctors' home computers.

Case Questions for Discussion

1. Explain how CMA used the four principles of lean operating systems to improve performance.

2. Using the information from the case, sketch the original paper-based value chain and compare it to a sketch of the modern electronic value chain that uses a common database. Explain how the performance of both systems might compare.

3. What is the total annual record retrieval cost savings with the old (paper-based) versus new (electronic) systems?

4. Does this CMA improvement initiative have any effect on sustainability? If so, how? If not, why?

5. Using lean principles, can you simultaneously improve speed and quality while reducing waste and costs? What are the trade-offs? Explain your reasoning.

WHY CHOOSE?

Every 4LTR Press solution comes complete with a visually engaging textbook in addition to an interactive eBook. Go to CourseMate for **OM4** to begin using the eBook. Access at **www.cengagebrain.com**

Complete the Speak Up survey in CourseMate at
www.cengagebrain.com

 Follow us at
www.facebook.com/4ltrpress

PROJECT MANAGEMENT

t he Olympic Games were established over 2,500 years ago. Athens, Greece, was chosen in 1997 to host the 2004 Games, but organizers badly underestimated the cost and overestimated the city's ability to meet construction and preparation schedules. Organizers were plagued with construction delays and budget overruns, forcing them to complete seven years' worth of work in just four years. Delays in the main stadium's glass-and-steel room pushed back delivery of the entire complex to the end of July, immediately preceding the August 13, 2004, opening ceremonies. The International Olympic Committee had even considered asking the Athens organizers to cancel the Games.[1] Problems also occurred with other venues. Construction delays had consequences for Greece's own athletes, forcing them out of their own training centers. Even the famed Parthenon, which was to have been restored for the Games, was still shrouded with scaffolding when tourists began arriving. Despite all this, the venues were ready—although some at the last minute—and the Games were successfully completed.

learning outcomes

After studying this chapter you should be able to:

18-1 **Explain the key issues associated with project management.**

18-2 **Describe how to apply the Critical Path Method (CPM).**

18-3 **Explain how to make time/cost trade-off decisions in projects.**

18-4 **Describe how to calculate probabilities for project completion time using PERT.**

What do **you** think?

Think of a project in which you have been involved, perhaps at work or in some student activity. What factors made your project either difficult or easy to accomplish?

Vicki Reid/iStockphoto.com

A **project** *is a temporary and often customized initiative that consists of many smaller tasks and activities that must be coordinated and completed to finish the entire initiative on time and within budget.* Suppose that a small business is considering expanding its facility. Some of the major tasks in planning for expansion are hiring architects, designing a new facility, hiring contractors, building the facility, purchasing and installing equipment, and hiring and training employees. Each of these major tasks consists of numerous subtasks that must be performed in a particular sequence, on time, and on budget. Taken together, these activities constitute a project.

In many firms, projects are the major value-creation process, and the major activities in the value chain revolve around projects. Some examples are market research studies, construction, movie production, software development, book publishing, and wedding planning. In other firms, projects are used on an infrequent basis to implement new strategies and initiatives or for supporting value chain design and improvement activities. Some examples are preparation of annual reports, installing an automated materials-handling system, or training employees to learn a new computer support system. Even U.S. courts use projects to help resolve construction claim litigations. Exhibit 18.1 lists a variety of examples of projects in many different functional areas of business.

In all project situations, projects require systematic management. **Project management** *involves all activities associated with planning, scheduling, and controlling projects.* The 2004 Olympic Games provides a good example of the importance of project management. (The London 2012 Olympic Organizing Committee

A **project** is a temporary and often customized initiative that consists of many smaller tasks and activities that must be coordinated and completed to finish the entire initiative on time and within budget.

Project management involves all activities associated with planning, scheduling, and controlling projects.

▼ *Despite construction delays and budget overruns, the venues were ready for the 2004 Olympic Games in Athens, Greece.*

In many firms, projects are the major value-creation process, and the major activities in the value chain revolve around projects. Some examples are market research studies, construction, movie production, software development, book publishing, and wedding planning.

Exhibit 18.1 *Example Projects in Different Functional Areas That Impact the Value Chain*

Functional Areas	Example Projects
Marketing	Point-of-sale system installation
	New product introduction
	Market research studies
Accounting and Finance	Auditing a firm's accounting and financial systems
	Planning a firm's initial public offering (IPO)
	Auditing a firm's procedures and stock trading rules for compliance with the Securities & Exchange Commission
Information Systems	Software development
	Software upgrades throughout a firm
	Hardware installation
Human Resource Management	Launching and coordinating training programs
	Annual performance and compensation review
	Implementing new benefits plans
Engineering	Designing new manufactured parts
	Implementing a new computer-aided design system
	Installing factory automation
Logistics	Installing an automated warehouse system
	Implementing an order-tracking system
	Building a transportation hub
Operations	Planning preventive maintenance for an oil refinery
	Implementing enterprise resource planning (ERP) software and systems
	Installing a revenue management system

© Cengage Learning 2013

advertised for a variety of job opportunities, including project management, and a post at blogspot.com observed "Students of project management should train their binoculars on east London and watch what is going to be a lively and living case study. The London Olympics is a project that will unfold before our very eyes, and what we will see, at least for the project management geeks among us, is going to be a lot more amusing and instructive than the games themselves."[2]

Good project management ensures that an organization's resources are used efficiently and effectively. This is particularly important, as projects generally cut across organizational boundaries and require the coordination of many different departments and functions and sometimes companies. In addition, most projects

Justin Kasezfivez/Alamy

1. *Define:* Projects are implemented to satisfy some need; thus the first step in managing a project is to clearly define the goal of the project, its responsibilities and deliverables, and when it must be accomplished. A common way to capture this information is with a specific and measurable *statement of work*. For example, the goal of an accounting audit might be to "audit the firm's accounting and financial statements and submit a report by December 1 that determines statement accuracy in accordance with generally accepted accounting principles in the United States of America. The audit fee shall not exceed $200,000."

2. *Plan:* In this stage, the steps needed to execute a project are defined, it is determined who will perform these steps, and the start and completion dates are developed. Planning entails breaking down a project into smaller activities and developing a project schedule by estimating the time required for each activity and scheduling them so they meet the project due date.

3. *Organize:* Organizing involves such activities as forming a team, allocating resources, calculating costs, assessing risk, preparing project documentation, and ensuring good communications. It also requires identifying a project manager who provides the leadership to accomplish the project goal.

4. *Control:* This stage assesses how well a project meets its goals and objectives and makes adjustments as necessary. Controlling involves collecting and assessing status reports, managing changes to baselines, and responding to circumstances that can negatively impact the project participants.

5. *Close:* Closing a project involves compiling statistics, releasing and/or reassigning people, and preparing a "lessons learned" list.

are unique, requiring some customization and response to new challenges.

Project management is becoming more important in achieving environmental, social, and economic sustainability. New jobs are emerging, having titles such as environmental project manager, health and safety manager, environmental auditor, and sustainability compliance manager. Each of these requires project management skills. Green activities are becoming more common in construction, waste management, procurement, recycling, and energy conservation projects. Project management skills are also essential to coordinate the multiple project disciplines needed to successfully accomplish a project with complete or partial sustainability objectives and desired outcomes.

18-1 The Scope of Project Management

most projects go through similar stages from start to completion. These stages characterize the project life cycle and form the basis for effective project management.

18-1a Roles of the Project Manager and Team Members

Project managers have significant responsibilities. It is their job to build an effective team, motivate them, provide advice and support, align the project with the firm's strategy, and direct and supervise the conduct of the project from beginning to end. In addition to managing the project, they must manage the relationships

18-1b Organizational Structure

How a project fits into a firm's organizational structure impacts its effectiveness. Some organizations use a pure project organizational structure whereby team members are assigned exclusively to projects and report only to the project manager. This approach makes it easier to manage projects, because project teams can be designed for efficiency by including the right mix of skills. However, it can result in inefficiencies because of duplication of resources across the organization, for example, having a different information technology support person on each project.

A pure functional organizational structure charters projects exclusively within functional departments, such as manufacturing or research and development. Although this approach allows team members to work on different projects simultaneously and provides a "home" for the project, it ignores an important reality: In a typical functional organization, a project cuts across organizational boundaries. Assigning projects exclusively to functional areas makes communication across the organization difficult and can limit the effectiveness of projects that require a systems perspective.

among the project team, the parent organization, and the client. The project manager must also have sufficient technical expertise to resolve disputes among functional specialists.

Good project managers recognize that people issues are as important as technical issues. Several principles can help project managers be successful:[4]

- Manage people individually and as a project team.
- Reinforce the commitment and excitement of the project team.
- Keep everyone informed.
- Build agreements and consensus among the team.
- Empower the project team.

> In a typical functional organization, a project cuts across organizational boundaries.

Dan Lamont/Alamy

A practical solution to this dilemma is a matrix organizational structure, which "lends" resources to projects while still maintaining control over them. Project managers coordinate the work across the functions. This minimizes duplication of resources and facilitates communication across the organization but requires that resources be negotiated. Functional managers may be reluctant to provide the resources, and employees assigned to projects might relegate a project to a lower priority than their daily functional job, making it difficult for the project manager to control the project.

18-1c Factors for Successful Projects

Projects are not always successful. Information technology projects have a notorious rate of failure. One study in the United States found that over 30 percent of software projects are canceled before completion and more than half cost almost double their original estimates. Exhibit 18.2 summarizes the principal factors that help or hinder project management.

Exhibit 18.2 *Contributors and Impediments to Project Success*

Contributors to Project Success	Impediments to Project Success
Well-defined and agreed-upon objectives	Ill-defined project objectives
Top management support	Lack of executive champion
Strong project manager leadership	Inability to develop and motivate people
Well-defined project definition	Poorly defined project definition
Accurate time and cost estimates	Lack of data accuracy and integrity
Teamwork and cooperation	Poor interpersonal relations and teamwork
Effective use of project management tools	Ineffective use of project management tools
Clear channels of communication	Poor communication among stakeholders
Adequate resources and reasonable deadlines	Unreasonable time pressures and lack of resources
Constructive response to conflict	Inability to resolve conflicts

© Cengage Learning 2013

HERSHEY FOODS: HALLOWEEN NIGHTMARE

Some years ago, Hershey Foods Corp. decided to install an enterprise resource planning (ERP) system plus companion packages from two other vendors simultaneously during one of the busiest shipping seasons. What was envisioned originally as a four-year project was squeezed down into just 30 months, with disastrous consequences. When the system went live, retailers began ordering large amounts of candy for back-to-school and Halloween sales. Two months later, the company was still having trouble pushing orders through the new system, resulting in shipment delays and deliveries of incomplete orders. The new system required enormous changes in the way Hershey's workers did their jobs, which might not have been adequately addressed in the project management design. One analyst noted that most companies install ERP systems in a more staged manner, especially when applications from multiple vendors are involved.[5]

Philip Lewis/Alamy

Ensuring project success depends on having well-defined goals and objectives, clear reporting relationships and channels of communication, good procedures for estimating time and other resource requirements, cooperation and commitment among all project team members, realistic expectations, effective conflict resolution, and top management sponsorship.

18-2 Techniques for Planning, Scheduling, and Controlling Projects

ll project management decisions involve three factors: *time*, *resources*, and *cost*. Various techniques have long been used to help plan, schedule, and control projects. The key steps involved are the following:

1. *Project Definition:* Identifying the activities that must be completed and the sequence required to perform them.
2. *Resource Planning:* For each activity, determining the resource needs: personnel, time, money, equipment, materials, and so on.
3. *Project Scheduling:* Specifying a time schedule for the completion of each activity.
4. *Project Control:* Establishing the proper controls for determining progress and developing alternative plans in anticipation of problems in meeting the planned schedule.

Several software packages, such as Microsoft Project™, are available to help project managers plan and manage projects. Although we will not discuss such software in detail, we will introduce the underlying techniques that are used in modern project management software.

To illustrate how these steps are applied in project management, we will use a simple example. Wildcat Software Consulting, Inc. helps companies implement

---

Activities are discrete tasks that consume resources and time.

Immediate predecessors are those activities that must be completed immediately before an activity may start.

The work breakdown structure is a hierarchical tree of end items that will be accomplished by the project team during the project.

---

software integration projects. Raj Yazici has been named the project manager in charge of coordinating the design and installation of the new software system. In the following sections, we address the various tasks involved in project definition, resource planning, project scheduling, and project control that he will face in his role as project manager.

18-2a Project Definition

The first step is to define the project objectives and deliverables. Mr. Yazici and his project team decided on the following statements:

- **Project Objective:** To develop an integrative software package within a predetermined budget and promised project completion date that meets all system requirements while providing adequate interfaces with legacy systems.
- **Deliverables:** (1) new software package, (2) successful implementation of the package, (3) pretraining of sales force and PC system operators.

Next, Mr. Yazici needed to identify the specific activities required to complete the project and the sequence in which they must be performed. **Activities** *are discrete tasks that consume resources and time.* **Immediate predecessors** *are those activities that must be completed immediately before an activity may start.* Precedence relationships ensure that activities are performed in the proper sequence when they are scheduled.

The initial list of activities and precedence relationships associated with the software integration project is summarized in Exhibit 18.3. For instance, activities A and B can be started at any time because they do not depend on the completion of prior activities. However, activity C cannot be started until both activities A and B have been completed. Mr. Yazici and his team reviewed and discussed the list several times to be sure that no activities were omitted from the project definition.

Defining the list of activities in a project is often facilitated by creating a work breakdown structure, which breaks a project down into manageable pieces, or items, to help ensure that all of the work elements needed to complete the project are identified. *The* **work breakdown structure** *is a hierarchical tree of end items that will be accomplished by the project team during the project.*[6] A work breakdown structure allows project teams to drill down to the appropriate level of detail in defining activities. For example, activity A might be broken down into the individual tasks of defining the

Exhibit 18.3 *Project Activities and Precedence Relationships*

Activity	Activity Description	Immediate Predecessors
A	Define software project objectives, budget, due date, and possible staff	None
B	Inventory new and old software interfaces and features	None
C	Assemble teams and allocate work	A, B
D	Design and develop code from old to new databases	C
E	Design and develop code for PC network	C
F	Test and debug PC network code	E
G	Design and develop code for off-site sales force	C
H	New complete system test and debug	D, G, F
I	Train PC system and database operators	D, F
J	Train off-site sales force	H
K	Two-week beta test of new system with legacy backup system	I, J

© Cengage Learning 2013

objectives, developing the budget, determining the due date, and identifying staff. Deciding on the appropriate work breakdown structure depends on how responsibility and accountability for accomplishing the tasks are viewed, and the level at which the project team wants to control the project budget and collect cost data.

The activities and their sequence are usually represented graphically using a project network. *A project network consists of a set of circles or boxes called nodes, which represent activities, and a set of arrows called arcs, which define the precedence relationships between activities.* This is called an activity-on-node (AON) network representation. The project network for the software integration project is shown in Exhibit 18.4. You should be able to match the information in Exhibit 18.3 with the network.

18-2b Resource Planning

Resource planning includes developing time estimates for performing each activity, other resources that may be required, such as people and equipment, and a realistic budget. Activity times can be estimated from

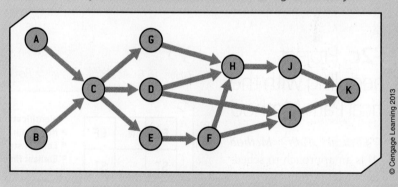

Exhibit 18.4 *Project Network for the Software Integration Project*

© Cengage Learning 2013

historical data of similar work tasks, or by the judgment and experience of managers and employees who perform the tasks. Cost control is a vital part of project management. This requires good budgeting, which in turn first requires estimating the costs of completing the activities. Exhibit 18.5 shows the estimated times and costs for the activities in the software integration project. We'll make use of these costs later in the chapter.

A **project network** consists of a set of circles or boxes called **nodes,** which represent activities, and a set of arrows called **arcs,** which define the precedence relationships between activities.

Exhibit 18.5 *Wildcat Software Consulting, Inc. Project Work Activities Times and Costs*

Activity Letter	Activity Description	Immediate Predecessors	Normal Time (in weeks)	Normal Cost Estimate ($)
A	Define software project objectives, budget, due date, and possible staff	None	3	1,200
B	Inventory new and old software interfaces and features	None	5	2,500
C	Assemble teams and allocate work	A, B	2	500
D	Design and develop code from old to new databases	C	6	300
E	Design and develop code for PC network	C	5	6,000
F	Test and debug PC network code	E	3	9,000
G	Design and develop code for off-site sales force	C	4	4,400
H	New complete system test and debug	D, G, F	3	3,000
I	Train PC system and database operators	D, F	4	4,000
J	Train off-site sales force	H	2	3,200
K	Two-week beta test of new system with legacy backup system	I, J	2	1,800

© Cengage Learning 2013

18-2c Project Scheduling with the Critical Path Method

The *Critical Path Method (CPM)* is an approach to scheduling and controlling project activities. *The* **critical path** *is the sequence of activities that takes the longest time and defines the total project completion time.* Understanding the critical path is vital to managing a project because any delays of activities on the critical path will delay the entire project. CPM assumes the following:

- The project network defines a correct sequence of work in terms of technology and workflow.

> The **critical path** is the sequence of activities that takes the longest time and defines the total project completion time.

- Activities are assumed to be independent of one another with clearly defined start and finish dates.

Exhibit 18.6 *Activity-on-Node Format and Definitions*

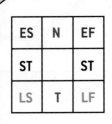

ES	N	EF
ST		ST
LS	T	LF

- Identification number (N) of the activity.
- Normal time (T) to complete the activity.
- Earliest start (ES) time
- Earliest finish (EF) time
- Latest start (LS) time
- Latest finish (LF) time
- Slack time (ST)—the length of time an activity can be delayed without affecting the competition date for the entire project, computed as $ST = LS - ES = LF - EF$

© Cengage Learning 2013

- The activity time estimates are accurate and stable.

- Once an activity is started it continues uninterrupted until it is completed.

To understand CPM, we need to define several terms. We will replace the simple circled nodes in the project network with boxes that provide other useful information, as shown in Exhibit 18.6.

Exhibit 18.7 *Wildcat Software Consulting Activity-on-Node Project Network*

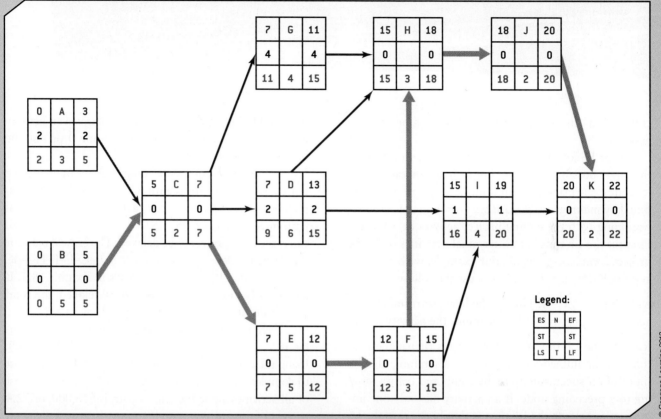

Exhibit 18.7 shows the software integration project network after all of this information has been computed. Use this figure to help follow the discussion of how these values are found in the project scheduling process.

For each activity we first compute the earliest possible times that the activity can start and finish without violating any precedence relationships. Earliest start (ES) and earliest finish (EF) times are computed by moving through the project network in a forward direction from start to finish, sometimes called the *forward pass*, through the network. We begin at the start of the project by assigning all nodes without any immediate predecessors an earliest starting time of 0. Two rules are used to guide the calculations of ES and EF during this step:

Rule 1: EF = ES + T. That is, the earliest time that an activity can be completed is equal to the earliest time it can begin plus the time to perform the activity.

Rule 2: The ES time for an activity equals the largest EF time of all immediate predecessors. Therefore,

whenever an activity is preceded by two or more activities, we must first compute the EF times of the preceding activities using Rule 1. Of course, if an activity has only one immediate predecessor, the ES time is simply equal to the EF time of the immediate predecessor.

To illustrate this process, note that in Exhibit 18.7, the EF time for activity A is 0 + 3 = 3 and the EF time for activity B is 0 + 5 = 5. Because both A and B are immediate predecessors to activity C, we use Rule 2 to find the EF time for activity C as the largest of 3 and 5, or 5. Then the EF time for activity C is computed using Rule 1 as EF = ES + T = 5 + 2 = 7. Activity G has only one immediate predecessor, so the EF time of activity C becomes the ES time of G. We suggest that you work through all calculations for the ES and EF times in the remainder of the network. The EF time of the last activity specifies the earliest time that the entire project can be completed. For our example, this is 22 weeks. If a project has more than one terminal activity, the earliest project

If you work on an activity on the critical path, it must be completed on time; otherwise, you and your team assigned to this work activity might receive some unwanted attention.

completion time is the largest EF time among these activities.

After ES and EF times are calculated, we compute the latest possible start and finish times for each activity. Latest start (LS) and latest finish (LF) times are computed by making a *backward pass* through the network, beginning with the ending project activity or activities. First set the LF time for all terminal activities to be the project completion time. In our example, we begin with activity K, setting LF = 22, and use the following rules:

Rule 3: LS = LF − T. That is, the latest start time for an activity is equal to its LF time minus the activity time.

Rule 4: The LF time for an activity is the smallest LS time of all immediate successors. Therefore, the LS times of all successors must be computed before moving to a preceding node. If an activity has only one immediate successor, the LF time is simply equal to the LS time of that immediate successor.

To illustrate this backward pass procedure, we first compute LS = LF − T for activity K as 22 − 2 = 20. Because activity K is the only successor to activities J and I, the LF times for both J and I are set equal to 20 and their LS times are computed using Rule 3. However, consider activity F. Activity F has two successors, H and I. The ES time for H is 15 and the ES time for I is 16. Using Rule 4, we set the EF time for activity F to be the smallest of the ES times for activities H and I, or 15. We encourage you to work through the remaining calculations of this backward pass procedure to better understand how to apply these rules.

After all ES, EF, LS, and LF times of all project activities are computed, we can compute slack time (ST) for each activity. Slack time is computed as ST = LS − ES = LF − EF (note that either one can be used). For example, the slack time for activity A is 5 − 3 = 2 − 0 = 2, and the slack time for activity B is 5 − 5 = 0 − 0 = 0. Note that although the earliest start time for activity A is 3, the activity need not begin until time LS = 5 and will not delay

A **schedule** specifies when activities are to be performed.

the completion of the entire project. However, activity B must start exactly on schedule at time 0 or else the project will be delayed.

After all slack times are computed, we may find the critical path. The critical path (CP) is the longest path(s) through the project network; activities on the critical path have zero slack time (ST = 0) and if delayed will cause the total project to be delayed. The critical path for the software development project is B–C–E–F–H–J–K, and is denoted by the heavy arrows in Exhibit 18.7. If any activity along the critical path is delayed, the total project duration will be longer than 22 weeks.

There are many ways to display the information in Exhibit 18.7; a summary is given in the table in Exhibit 18.8. Using the cost information in Exhibit 18.5, the total cost to complete the project in 22 weeks is $35,900. The cost of all activities along the critical path is $26,000, or 72.4 percent of total project cost. If you work on an activity on the critical path, it must be completed on time; otherwise, you and your team assigned to this work activity might receive some unwanted attention. If you were a "slacker," however, where would you want to work? Probably on activity G because it has four weeks of slack time!

18-2d Project Control

*A **schedule** specifies when activities are to be performed.* A schedule enables a manager to assign resources effectively and to monitor progress and take corrective action when necessary. Because of the uncertainty of task times, unavoidable delays, or other problems, projects rarely, if ever, progress on schedule. Managers must therefore monitor performance of the project and take corrective action when needed.

A useful tool for depicting a schedule graphically is a Gantt chart, named after Henry L. Gantt, a pioneer of scientific management. Gantt charts enable the project manager to know what activities should be performed at a given time and, more important, to monitor daily progress of the project so that corrective action can be taken when necessary.

Exhibit 18.8 *CPM Tabular Analysis for Wildcat Software Consulting Using Normal Time*

Activity Name	On Critical Path	Activity Time	Earliest Start	Earliest Finish	Latest Start	Latest Finish	Slack (LS − ES)
A	No	3	0	3	2	5	2
B	Yes	5	0	5	0	5	0
C	Yes	2	5	7	5	7	0
D	No	6	7	13	9	15	2
E	Yes	5	7	12	7	12	0
F	Yes	3	12	15	12	15	0
G	No	4	7	11	11	15	4
H	Yes	3	15	18	15	18	0
I	No	4	15	19	16	20	1
J	Yes	2	18	20	18	20	0
K	Yes	2	20	22	20	22	0

Project Completion Time = 22 weeks

Total Cost of Project = $35,900 (Cost on CP = $26,000)

Number of Critical Paths = 1

© Cengage Learning 2013

To construct a Gantt chart, we list the activities on a vertical axis and use a horizontal axis to represent time. The following symbols are commonly used in a Gantt chart:

Symbol	Description
⌐	Scheduled starting time for activity
⌐	Scheduled completion time for activity
▬	Completed work for an activity
⋈	Scheduled delay or maintenance
∨	Current date for progress review

Using the information in Exhibits 18.5 and 18.7 or 18.8, we will assume that each activity will be scheduled at its early start time, as shown in Exhibit 18.9. The resulting schedule will be an "early start" or "left-shifted" schedule. For instance, activities A and B can begin at time 0 and have durations of three and five weeks, respectively. Activity C cannot begin until A is completed; thus this activity is scheduled to begin at time 5. After activity C is completed at time 7, activities G, D, and E can then be scheduled. Activity D, for example, can start as early as week 7. Likewise, activity G can start as early as week 7. If you compare the Gantt chart in Exhibit 18.9 with the project network in Exhibit 18.7, you will see that they portray the same information, just in a different format.

Using this early start schedule, the project is scheduled to be completed in 22 weeks. What happens if an activity on the critical path is delayed? Suppose, for example, that activity E takes six weeks instead of five weeks. Because E is a predecessor of F and the starting time of F is the same as the completion time of E, F is forced to begin one week later. This forces a delay in activity H that is also on the critical path, and in turn delays activities J and K. In addition, activity I is also delayed one week. Now it would take 23 weeks to complete the project, as shown by the Gantt chart in Exhibit 18.10.

Gantt charts work well for small projects and subsets of larger projects because they are easy to read, visual, and provide a summary of project activities. However, for larger and more complex projects, Gantt charts are limited and do not clearly show the interdependencies among multiple activities, and other details such as activity slack and costs. In addition, they do not consider limited resources such as labor and equipment that must be shared among the activities. Determining how to allocate limited resources is often a very challenging task. Fortunately, project management software packages such as Microsoft Project™ provide these capabilities.

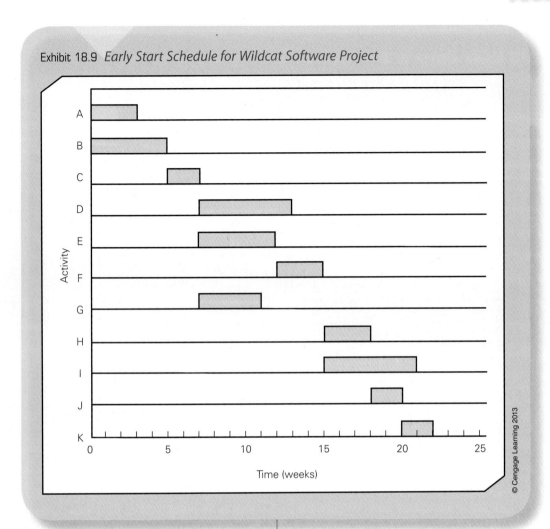

Exhibit 18.9 *Early Start Schedule for Wildcat Software Project*

18-3 Time/Cost Trade-Offs

One of the benefits of the Critical Path Method is the ability to consider shortening activity times by adding additional resources to selected activities and thereby reducing the overall project completion time. This is often referred to as "crashing." **Crashing a project** *refers to reducing the total time to complete the project to meet a revised due date.* However, doing so does not come without a cost. Therefore, it is necessary to evaluate the trade-offs between faster completion times and additional costs.

The first step is to determine the amount of time by which each activity may be reduced and its associated cost, as shown in Exhibit 18.11. **Crash time** *is the shortest possible time in which the activity can realistically be completed. The* **crash cost** *is the total additional cost associated with completing an activity in its crash time rather than in its normal time.* We assume that the normal times and costs are based on normal working conditions and work practices and therefore are accurate estimates. Some activities cannot be crashed because of the nature of the task. In Exhibit 18.11, this is evident when the normal and crash times as well as the normal and crash costs are equal. For example, activities F, H, J, and K cannot be crashed. If you examine the content of these activities, you see that activities H and K are related to testing and debugging the new system software, and activities I and J are related to training people to use this new software. In the judgment of the project managers, these

Crashing a project refers to reducing the total time to complete the project to meet a revised due date.

Crash time is the shortest possible time in which the activity can realistically be completed.

The **crash cost** is the total additional cost associated with completing an activity in its crash time rather than in its normal time.

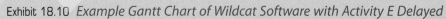

Exhibit 18.10 *Example Gantt Chart of Wildcat Software with Activity E Delayed*

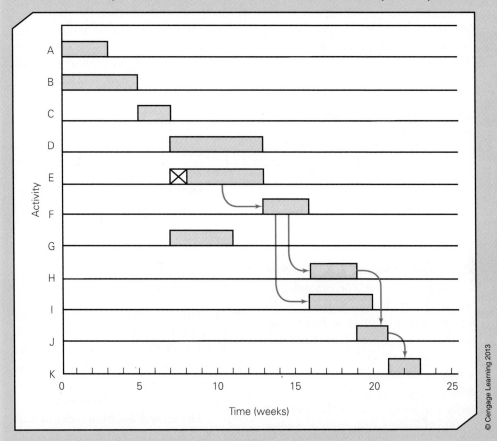

Exhibit 18.11 *Wildcat Software Project Data Including Crash Times and Costs*

Activity Letter	Activity Description	Immediate Predecessors	Normal Time (in weeks)	Crash Time (in weeks)	Normal Cost Estimate ($)	Crash Cost Estimate ($)
A	Define software project objectives, budget, due date, and possible staff	none	3	1	1,200	2,000
B	Inventory new and old software interfaces and features	none	5	3	2,500	3,500
C	Assemble teams and allocate work	A, B	2	1	500	750
D	Design and develop code from old to new databases	C	6	3	300	450
E	Design and develop code for PC network	C	5	3	6,000	8,400
F	Test and debug PC network code	E	3	3	9,000	9,000
G	Design and develop code for off-site sales force	C	4	3	4,400	5,500
H	New complete system test and debug	D, G, F	3	3	3,000	3,000
I	Train PC system and database operators	D, F	4	2	4,000	6,000
J	Train off-site sales force	H	2	2	3,200	3,200
K	Two-week beta test of new system with legacy backup system	I, J	2	2	1,800	1,800

work activities could not be expedited by adding any additional resources.

For example, in the software development project, activity A can be completed in one week at a cost of $2,000 instead of the normal time of three weeks at a cost of $1,200. A key assumption with crashing is that the time can be reduced to any proportion of the crash time at a proportional increase in cost; that is, the relationship between time and cost is linear, as shown in Exhibit 18.12 for activity A. The slope of this line is the crash cost per unit of time and is computed by Equation 18.1.

$$\text{Crash cost per unit of time} = \frac{\text{Crash cost} - \text{Normal cost}}{\text{Normal time} - \text{Crash time}}$$

[18.1]

Crashing an activity *refers to reducing its normal time, possibly up to its limit—the crash time.* For example, we can crash activity A from its normal time of three weeks down to one week or anywhere in between. Because the crash cost per unit of time for activity A is ($2,000 − $1,200)/(3 − 1) = $400 per week, crashing the activity from three weeks to two weeks will result in an additional cost of $400. Likewise, crashing from three to one and a half weeks will result in an additional cost of 1.5($400) = $600. Managers can crash a project and ignore the cost implications or they can search for the minimum cost crash schedule to meet the revised due date.

Suppose the client asks Wildcat Software Consulting, Inc. first how much it would cost to complete the project in 20 weeks instead of the current 22 weeks, and second how much it would cost to finish the project in the fastest possible time.

To address the first question, we need to determine the crash cost per unit of time for each activity using Equation 18.1. These are: A—$400 per week, B—$500 per week, C—$250 per week, D—$50 per week, E—$1,200 per week, G—$1,100 per week, and I—$1,000 per week. Activities F, H,

J, and K cannot be crashed. Note that the only way the project completion time can be reduced is by crashing activities on the critical path. When we do this, however, another path in the network might become critical, so this must be carefully watched.

In this example, several options exist for completing the project in 20 weeks:

Crashing Option #1

Crash B by one week =	$500
Crash C by one week =	$250
Additional cost =	$750

Crashing Option #2

Crash B by two weeks =	$1,000
Additional cost =	$1,000

Crashing Option #3

Crash C by one week =	$500
Crash E by one week =	$1,200
Additional cost =	$1,700

The least-expensive option is the first. The critical path remains the same, namely, B–C–E–F–H–J–K. Exhibit 18.13 summarizes the results for this option. Notice that although activity D costs only $50 per week to crash, it is not on the critical path—crashing it would not affect the completion time.

The second question seeks to find the crash schedule that minimizes the project completion time. Again, we will address this using a trial-and-error approach. From the previous crashing solution of 20 weeks, we

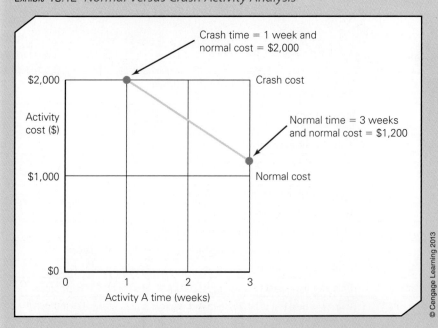

Exhibit 18.12 *Normal Versus Crash Activity Analysis*

© Cengage Learning 2013

Activity Name	On Critical Path	Activity Time	Earliest Start	Earliest Finish	Latest Start	Latest Finish	Slack (LS — ES)
A	No	3	0	3	1	4	1
B	Yes	4	0	4	0	4	0
C	Yes	1	4	5	4	5	0
D	No	6	5	11	7	13	2
E	Yes	5	5	10	5	10	0
F	Yes	3	10	13	10	13	0
G	No	4	5	9	9	13	4
H	Yes	3	13	16	13	16	0
I	No	4	13	17	14	18	1
J	Yes	2	16	18	16	18	0
K	Yes	2	18	20	18	20	0

© Cengage Learning 2013

Project completion time = 20 weeks

Total project cost = $36,650 (cost on CP = $26,750)

Number of Critical Paths = 1

can identify two crashing options to shorten the project to 19 weeks:

Crashing Option #4

Crash B by a second week = $500
Additional cost = $500

Crashing Option #5

Crash E by one week = $1,200
Additional cost = $1,200

The cheapest way to achieve a project completion date of 19 weeks is Option #4 by crashing B by two weeks and C by one week. The critical path for a 19-week project completion date is still B–C–E–F–H–J–K. The total project cost is now $37,150 ($35,900 + $1,000 + $250). Activities B and C have reached their crash time limits; therefore, to try to find an 18-week completion date we must examine other activities. Only one option is available because activities B, C, F, H, J, and K cannot be crashed further:

Crashing Option #6

Crash E by one week = $1,200
Additional cost = $1,200

At this point, there are two critical paths: A–C–E–F–H–J–K and B–C–E–F–H–J–K. All other paths through the network are less than 18 weeks. The total project cost is now $38,350 ($35,900 + $1,000 + $250 + $1,200).

The only way to achieve a 17-week project completion time is to crash activity E a second week. The total project cost for a 17-week completion time is now $39,550 ($35,900 + $1,000 + $250 + $1,200 + $1,200), and four critical paths now exist:

CP Path 1: B–C–E–F–H–J–K
CP Path 2: A–C–E–F–H–J–K
CP Path 3: A–C–D–H–J–K
CP Path 4: B–C–D–H–J–K

All other paths are not critical. Exhibit 18.14 summarizes the results for this 17-week minimum crash cost schedule. We cannot crash any other activities to reduce the project completion time further.

18-4 Uncertainty in Project Management

another approach to project management that was developed independently of CPM is called **PERT (Project Evaluation and Review Technique)**. PERT was introduced in the late 1950s specifically for planning, scheduling, and controlling the Polaris missile project. Because many activities associated with that project had never been attempted previously, it was difficult to predict the time needed to complete the various tasks. PERT was developed as a means of handling the uncertainties in activity completion times. In contrast, CPM assumes that activity times are constant.

⌈PERT was developed as a means of handling the uncertainties in activity completion times. In contrast, CPM assumes that activity times are constant.⌋

Any variation in critical path activities can cause variation in the project completion date. Also, if a non-critical activity is delayed long enough to expend all of its slack time, that activity will become part of a new critical path, and further delays there will extend the project completion date. The PERT procedure uses the variance in the critical path activities to understand the risk associated with completing the project on time.

When activity times are uncertain, they are often treated as random variables with associated probability

distributions. Usually three time estimates are obtained for each activity:

1. **Optimistic time** (*a*)—the activity time if everything progresses in an ideal manner;

2. **Most probable time** (*m*)—the most likely activity time under normal conditions; and

3. **Pessimistic time** (*b*)—the activity time if significant breakdowns and/or delays occur.

Exhibit 18.15 shows an assumed probability distribution for activity B. Note that this is a positively skewed distribution, allowing for a small chance of a large activity time. Different values of *a*, *m*, and *b* provide different shapes for the probability distribution of activity times. Technically, this characterizes a *beta probability distribution*. The beta distribution is usually assumed to describe the inherent variability in these three time estimates. This approach is quite practical because managers can usually identify the best case, worst case, and most likely case for activity times, and it provides much flexibility in characterizing the distribution of times, as opposed to forcing times to a symmetric

Solved Problem

The critical path calculations for a project network are shown in the accompanying figure. Using the information in Table 1, find the best crashing option to reduce the project completion time to 17 weeks.

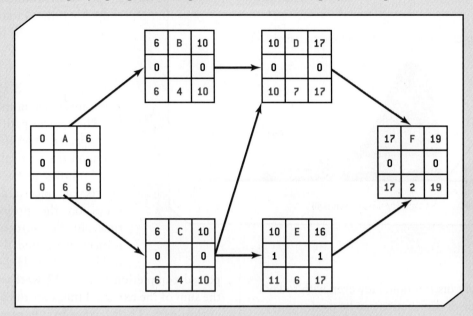

Table 1

Activity	Normal Duration	Normal Cost	Crash Duration	Total Crash Cost	Crash Cost Per Week
A	6	$ 500	4	$1,300	$400
B	4	300	2	1,000	350
C	4	900	3	1,200	300
D	7	1,600	5	2,000	200
E	6	200	4	300	50
F	2	400	1	900	500

One-Week Crash Options

We might first look at activities common to both critical paths (A–B–D–F and A–C–D–F), namely A and D, and consider crashing each of them individually. Other options are to crash activities B and C together, activity F, and activities A and D together. The lowest-cost option is to crash activity D by one week, costing $200. Now all three paths through the network are critical paths with a total duration of 18 weeks.

Crashing Option #1

Crash A by one week = $400

Crashing Option #2

Crash D by one week = $200

Crashing Option #3

Crash B by one week = $350
Crash C by one week = $300
Total cost = $650

Crashing Option #4

Crash F by one week = $500

Crashing Option #5

Crash A by one week = $400
Crash D by one week = $200
Total cost = $600

Second-Week Crash Options

All other crash options cost more than Option #2. Therefore, we should recommend that we crash D by a second week and E by one week, for a total cost of $250. All three network paths take 17 weeks to complete.

The total normal costs are $3,900 plus crashing D by two weeks (+$400) and E by one week (+$50), so the total cost of a 17-week project-completion schedule is $4,350.

Crashing Option #1

Crash A by one week = $400

Crashing Option #2

Crash D by one week = $200
Crash E by one week = $ 50
Total cost = $250

Crashing Option #3

Crash B by one week = $350
Crash C by one week = $300
Total cost = $650

Crashing Option #4

Crash F by one week = $500

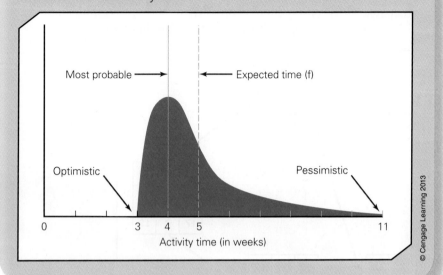

Exhibit 18.15 *Activity Time Distribution for Activity B of Wildcat Software Project*

Most probable ⟶ ⟵ Expected time (f)

Optimistic

Pessimistic

Activity time (in weeks)

0   3   4   5   11

© Cengage Learning 2013

normal probability distribution. However, with today's software, any type of distribution can be used.

For the Wildcat Software integration project, we will assume that the project manager has developed estimates for these times for each activity, as shown in Exhibit 18.16. The expected time is computed using the following formula:

$$\text{Expected time} = (a + 4m + b)/6 \quad [18.2]$$

Note that the expected times correspond to the normal times we used in the CPM example. We can also show that the variance of activity times is given by the following:

$$\text{Variance} = (b - a)^2/36 \quad [18.3]$$

Both the expected times and variances are shown in Exhibit 18.16.

The critical path is found using the expected times in the same fashion as in the Critical Path Method. PERT allows us to investigate the effects of uncertainty of activity times on the project completion time. In the software integration project, we found the critical path to be B–C–E–F–H–J–K with an expected completion time of 22 weeks. This is simply the sum of the expected times for the activities on the critical path. The variance (σ^2) in project duration is given by the sum of the variances of the critical path activities:

$$\sigma^2 = 1.78 + 0.11 + 0.44 + 0.11 + 0.11 + 0.11 + 0.11 = 2.77$$

Exhibit 18.16 *Activity Time Estimates for the Wildcat Software Integration Project*

Activity	Optimistic Time (*a*)	Most Probable Time (*m*)	Pessimistic Time (*b*)	Expected Time	Variance
A	2	3	4	3	0.11
B	3	4	11	5	1.78
C	1	2	3	2	0.11
D	4	5	12	6	1.78
E	3	5	7	5	0.44
F	2	3	4	3	0.11
G	2	3	10	4	1.78
H	2	3	4	3	0.11
I	2	3	10	4	1.78
J	1	2	3	2	0.11
K	1	2	3	2	0.11

© Cengage Learning 2013

This formula is based on the assumption that all the activity times are independent. With this assumption, we can also assume that the distribution of the project completion time is normally distributed. The use of the normal probability distribution as an approximation is based on the central limit theorem of statistics, which states that the sum of independent activity times follows a normal distribution as the number of activities becomes large. Therefore, we can say that the project completion time for the Wildcat example is normal with a mean of 22 weeks and a standard deviation of $\sqrt{2.77} = 1.66$.

Using this information, we can compute the probability of meeting a specified completion date. For example, suppose that the project manager has allotted 25 weeks for the project. Although completion in 22 weeks is expected, the manager wants to know the probability that the 25-week deadline will be met. This probability is shown graphically as the shaded area in Exhibit 18.17. The z-value for the normal distribution at $T = 25$ is given by

$$z = (25 - 22)/1.66 = 1.81$$

Using $z = 1.81$ and the tables for the standard normal distribution (see Appendix A), we find that the probability of the project meeting the 25-week deadline is $P(z \leq 1.81) = P(\text{completion time} \leq 25) = 0.96485$. Thus, while variability in the activity time may cause the project to exceed the 22-week expected duration, there is an excellent chance that the project will be completed before the 25-week deadline.

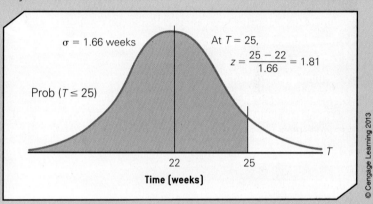

Exhibit 18.17 *Probability of Completing the Wildcat Software Project Within 25 Weeks*

© Cengage Learning 2013

Solved Problem

Consider the following simple PERT network used to remodel the kitchen at Rusty Buckets restaurant:

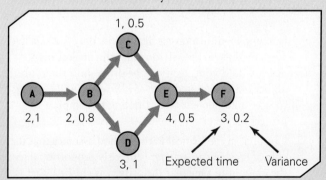

a. What is the expected completion time and variance for the project?

b. What is the probability that the project will meet a 12- and 15-day deadline?

Solution

a. There are two paths through the network—A–B–C–E–F with an expected completion time of 12 days,

and A–B–D–E–F with an expected completion time of 14 days. The critical path is A–B–D–E–F. The variance of the project time is the sum of the activity variances on the critical path, or $1 + 0.8 + 1 + 0.5 + 0.2 = 3.5$ days.

b. To find the probability of meeting a 12-day deadline, compute $z = (12 - 14)/\sqrt{3.5} = -2/1.871 = -1.07$. From Appendix A, the probability from $-\infty$ to $z = -1.07$ is $P(z \leq -1.07) = 0.14231$. Therefore, $P(\text{completion time} \leq 12) = 0.14231$. Also, note that there is only a 50 percent chance of completing the project within the expected time of 14 days (that is, $z = (14 - 14)/1.871 = 0$ and $P(\text{completion time} \leq 14) = 0.5000$.

The probability of meeting a 15-day completion time is found by computing $z = (15 - 14)/\sqrt{3.5} = 1/1.871 = +0.53$. From Appendix A, the probability from $-\infty$ to $z = 0.53 = P(z \leq 0.53) = 0.70194$, and therefore, $P(\text{completion time} \leq 15 \text{ days}) = 0.70194$.

XEROX GLOBAL SERVICES: PROJECT MANAGERS ARE CRITICAL!

Douglas Healey/AP Photo

Xerox Global Services is a consulting, integration, and outsourcing arm of Xerox Corporation with a vision "To provide the most comprehensive, most effective connections between people, knowledge, and documents that the world has ever seen." Central to Xerox Global Services' delivery of services is project management. The project manager manages a team that includes technical resource specialists, consultants, and project coordinators. The principal role of the project manager at Xerox Global Services is that of a customer advocate—to ensure that expectations are fully met. This requires careful understanding and documentation of customer expectations such as timeliness, meeting budget, system response, and security. As a manager in the project office notes, "Most projects fail because user requirements are not understood." These requirements are translated into a detailed work breakdown structure with specific tasks assigned to project team members. This also helps to prepare a budget and monitor progress. Finally, after each project is completed, the team conducts a review of "lessons learned"—What went right? and What went wrong?—to continuously improve the company's ability to meet its customer expectations.

Discussion Questions

1. Identify at least five additional examples of projects that are not cited in this chapter.

2. Exhibit 18.2 lists a number of impediments to project success. How might you minimize or eliminate these impediments?

3. The local chapter of the Project Management Institute is planning a dinner meeting with a nationally known speaker, and you are responsible for organizing it. How could the methodology discussed in this chapter help you?

4. The calculations in PERT allow you to determine the probability that a project will be completed. Suppose you calculate that the probability that a project will be completed by a target deadline is only 0.25. What steps might you take if you were the project manager? Would your decisions be different if the probability was calculated as 0.75? Would you be willing to take a 25 percent risk of failing to complete the project on time?

5. Crashing in the Critical Path Method assumes that the cost of crashing an activity is linearly proportional to the amount of time that the activity is crashed; that is, the rate of cost increase is constant (see Exhibit 18.12). Is this a reasonable assumption? Why or why not? How might the concepts of economies and diseconomies of scale help to address this issue?

Problems and Activities

1. Research and write a short paper (two pages maximum) on the skills needed to be a successful project manager.

2. Mary is planning her wedding and develops the following preliminary information.

Activity	Immediate Predecessors	Estimated Normal Time
A (select wedding date)	none	1 week
B (select wedding location)	none	4 weeks
C (guest list, who is attending)	A, B	3 weeks
D (select entertainment)	A	4 weeks
E (choose catering)	A, C	3 weeks
F (wedding day)	D, E	0 weeks

   a. Draw the network for this project.

   b. What are the critical path(s)?

   c. What is the project completion time?

   d. What activity has the most slack?

   e. What wedding activities did Mary leave out of her analysis? List them and now redraw the project network (but do NOT try to assign activity times or work out the new solution). What did you learn?

3. Perhaps the most well-known software for project management is Microsoft Project™. Investigate its capabilities and write a short paper (two pages maximum) that describes its features.

4. Develop a small example consisting of no more than 10 activities and illustrate the ideas, rules, and mechanics of forward and backward passes through the project network to compute the critical path.

5. Find an application of project management in your own life (for example, in your home, fraternity/sorority, or business organization). List the activities and events that comprise the project, and draw the precedence network. What problems did you encounter in doing this?

6. Rozales Manufacturing Co. is planning to install a new flexible manufacturing system. The activities that must be performed, their immediate predecessors, and estimated activity times follow. Draw the project network and find the critical path, computing early and late start days, early and late finish days, and activity slack.

Activity	Description	Immediate Predecessors	Estimated Activity Time (days)
A	Analyze current performance	—	2
B	Identify goals	A	2
C	Conduct study of existing operation	A	6
D	Define new system capabilities	B	7
E	Study existing technologies	B	8
F	Determine specifications	D	7
G	Conduct equipment analyses	C, F	10
H	Identify implementation activities	C	9
I	Determine organizational impacts	H	4
J	Prepare report	E, G, I	2
K	Establish audit procedure	H	3
L	Dummy ending activity	J, K	0

7. A computer-system installation project consists of eight activities. The immediate predecessors and activity times in weeks are as follows:

Activity	Immediate Predecessors	Activity Time
A	—	3
B	—	6
C	A	2
D	B, C	5
E	D	4
F	E	3
G	B, C	9
H	F, G	3

a. Draw the network for this project.

b. What are the critical path activities?

c. What is the project completion time?

8. Environment Recycling, Inc. must clean up a large automobile tire dump under a state environmental cleanup contract. The tasks, durations (in weeks), costs, and predecessor relationships are as follows:

Activity	Immediate Predecessors	Activity Time
A	—	5
B	A	8
C	A	7
D	—	6
E	B, D, C	8
F	D	3
G	D	3
H	E	4
I	F, G, H	6

a. Draw the project network.

b. Identify the critical path(s).

c. What is the total project completion time and total cost?

9. Two international banks are integrating two financial processing software systems as a result of their merger. Preliminary analysis and interviews with all parties involved resulted in the following project information. The "systems integration team" for this project plans to define and manage the project on two levels. The following activities represent an aggregate view, and within each activity is a more detailed view with sub-tasks and project networks defined. All times are in weeks.

Activity	Immediate Predecessors	Activity Time
A	—	3
B	A	1
C	A	2
D	B, C	3
E	C	5
F	C	3
G	E	7
H	E, F	5
I	D, G, H	8

a. Draw the project network.

b. Identify the critical path.

c. What is the total project completion time and total cost?

10. A competitor of Kozar International, Inc. has begun marketing a new instant-developing film project. Kozar has had a similar product under study in its research and development (R&D) department but has not yet been able to begin production. Because of the competitor's action, top managers have asked for a speedup of R&D activities so that Kozar can produce and market instant film at the earliest possible date. The predecessor information and activity time estimates in months are as follows:

Activity	Immediate Predecessors	Optimistic Time	Most Probable Time	Pessimistic Time
A	—	1	1.5	5
B	A	3	4	5
C	A	1	2	3
D	B, C	3.5	5	6.5
E	B	4	5	12
F	C, D, E	6.5	7.5	11.5
G	E	5	9	13

a. Draw the project network.

b. Develop an activity schedule for this project using early and late start and finish times, compute activity slack time, and define the critical activities.

11. Construct an early-start-date Gantt chart for the computer-system installation project described in problem 7. As a project manager, where would you focus your attention, given your analysis?

12. Suppose that some of the activities in the Environment Recycling, Inc. situation in problem 8 can be crashed. The following table shows the crash times and costs associated with performing the activities at their original (normal) times and also for the crash times. Find the total project completion time and lowest-cost solution if the state wants to complete the project three weeks early.

Activity	Immediate Predecessors	Normal Time	Crash Time	Normal Cost	Crash Cost
A	—	5	4	$ 400	$ 750
B	A	8	6	1,800	2,200
C	A	7	6	800	1,100
D	—	6	5	600	1,000
E	B, D, C	8	6	1,700	2,200
F	D	3	2	800	1,000
G	D	3	2	500	650
H	E	4	3	400	600
I	F, G, H	6	5	900	1,300

13. The following table shows the crash times and normal and crash costs for the international bank systems integration project described in problem 9.

What is the total project completion time and lowest-cost solution if the bank wants to complete the project two weeks early?

Activity	Immediate Predecessors	Normal Time	Crash Time	Normal Cost	Crash Cost
A	—	3	1	$1,000	$ 8,000
B	A	1	1	4,000	4,000
C	A	2	2	2,000	2,000
D	B, C	3	1	5,000	6,000
E	C	5	4	2,500	3,800
F	C	3	2	1,500	3,000
G	E	7	4	4,500	8,100
H	E, F	5	4	3,000	3,600
I	D, G, H	8	5	8,000	18,000

14. The following table shows estimates of activity times (weeks) for a project:

Activity	Immediate Predecessors	Optimistic Time	Most Probable Time	Pessimistic Time
A	—	4	5	6
B	A	2.5	3	3.5
C	A	6	7	8
D	B, C	5	5.5	9
E	D	5	7	9
F	D	2	3	4
G	E, F	8	10	12

Suppose that the critical path is A–C–D–E–G. What is the probability that the project will be completed within

a. 34.5 weeks?

b. 33 weeks?

c. 35 weeks?

15. The following table shows estimates of the optimistic, most probable, and pessimistic times for the situation described in problem 10. What is the probability that the project will be completed in time for Kozar to begin marketing the new product within 27 months?

Activity	Immediate Predecessors	Optimistic Time	Most Probable Time	Pessimistic Time
A	—	1	1.5	5
B	A	3	4	5
C	A	1	2	3
D	B, C	3.5	5	6.5
E	B	4	5	12
F	C, D, E	6.5	7.5	11.5
G	E	5	9	13

Alternative Water Supply—Single Project Case Study

Gordon Rivers, the City Manager of Saratoga, Florida, pitched the proposed design schedule back at Jay Andrews. Jay Andrews is the project manager for Major Design Corporation (MDC). The city of Saratoga selected MDC for this project. As project manager, it is Jay's responsibility to assemble the technical team necessary to complete the project, develop and track the budget, establish and maintain the schedule, allocate resources as required, and manage the project until completion.

"We need the intake and transmission main designed, bid, and completed in 35 weeks. The city of Saratoga has a future $2 million dollar federal grant riding on the project getting done on time," Mr. Rivers said. Jay nodded in agreement. Mr. Rivers continued by saying, "Jay, the project needs to come in on schedule and within the budget. Now take this schedule back and figure out how we are going to do it."

Background

Major Design Corporation (MDC) is a 3,500-employee firm with annual revenues of more than $1 billion. The firm is divided into five geographically based global sales divisions, an engineering/technical services division based in the United States, and a wholly owned construction company. MDC offers full services—consulting, engineering, construction, and operations—across the "project life cycle" for water, environment, transportation, energy, and facility resources.

MDC was selected by the city of Saratoga to design a new 10-million-gallon-per-day surface water intake and transmission main. The intake withdraws water from a canal and pumps the water more than two miles to the city's wastewater treatment plant. There, the canal water is blended with reclaimed water (i.e., treated sewage water) and distributed back to customers for irrigation purposes. This project is touted as an "alternative" water supply project because the water source is not a historically used source. The project will increase the long-term sustainability of the city because it will diversify the city's water supply portfolio and recycle water. The project will also minimize the need for additional withdrawals from historic water sources, which have become less productive and more highly regulated in the past 10 years, as the city's population continues to grow. Other green benefits of the project include reduced environmental impacts on the historic water sources and a reduced carbon footprint, as the irrigation water requires less energy-intensive treatment than the city's other drinkable water sources.

Project Description

The objective of the project is to design a fully functional surface water intake that is protective of the environment, will last at least 30 years, and will have a low life-cycle cost (i.e., capital, maintenance, and energy consumption). For this type of project, engineering design accounts for 20 percent of total project cost. The design stage is also important because the decisions made during design lock in 80 percent or more of the life-cycle costs of the project. As a result, engineers take a holistic approach when selecting equipment and features for projects. A piece of equipment, for example, that is inexpensive upfront may have significant long-term maintenance costs.

The following narrative describes the main activities required to complete the AWS project. Exhibit 18.18

Exhibit 18.18 *Alternative Water Supply (AWS)—Single Project*

Activity ID	Description	Immediate Predecessors	Regular Time (weeks)	Crash Time (weeks)	Normal Cost Estimate	Crash Cost Estimate
A	Conceptual design	none	4	3	$ 30,000	$ 33,500
B	Preliminary design	A	12	10	$ 52,000	$ 58,000
C	Final design	B	19	16	$ 59,000	$ 76,000
D	Environmental permit application preparation	B	8	5	$ 48,000	$ 58,200
E	Environmental permit review and approval	D	4	4	$ 38,000	$ 38,000
F	Building permit application preparation	E	2	1	$ 35,000	$ 38,000
G	Building permit review and approval	F	4	4	$ 6,000	$ 6,000
H	Property acquisition	B	20	18	$ 90,000	$115,000
I	Bid project	C, H	4	4	$ 6,000	$ 6,000
J	Construction start (dummy activity)	G, I	0	0	$ 0	$ 0

© Cengage Learning 2013

provides project work activities, precedence relationships, and costs.

The project will begin with the development of a conceptual design (activity A). During the conceptual design, engineers confirm the applicable regulations and laws for the project, including sustainability criteria; perform evaluations of alternative equipment; identify site conditions and constraints; and develop initial facility and equipment layouts.

Once the conceptual design is complete and MDC has received feedback on it from the city of Saratoga, preliminary design (B) begins. Preliminary design expands the design based on the preferences and constraints identified during the conceptual design. The preliminary design finalizes the project design criteria (e.g., sizing, operational capacity, reliability, sustainability) and incorporates them (along with additional geotechnical, survey, and environmental findings) into preliminary drawings and written specifications. Drawings and specifications are the key information-intensive products that come out of this work. The drawings show in graphical form how the project will look when constructed and the specifications provide detailed guidance and criteria by which the construction is to proceed.

For this project, the completion of the preliminary design allows three other parallel tasks to begin: final design (C), environmental permit application preparation (D), and property acquisition (H). Final design is a continuation of the preliminary design stage. In final design, additional information is added to the specifications.

Environmental permit application preparation (D) involves taking certain drawings from the preliminary design and modifying them to illustrate what controls are included in the project to minimize environmental impacts. The engineers must demonstrate that the project will have little to no impact on the environment and be constructed in accordance with applicable laws to receive a permit. Typical impacts engineers try to prevent include: storm water runoff from the site, pollutant discharges from the site, uncontrolled emissions from equipment, destruction of natural habitats, and displacement of endangered species. Once the environmental permit application is complete, it is submitted to a regulatory agency for review. This activity, identified as environmental permit review and approval (E), does not require any work on the part of the MDC engineers, but cannot be crashed because another outside entity is responsible for it.

Property acquisition (H) starts with the identification of all properties on which the project sits or passes through. For the properties identified that the city doesn't currently own, the city must acquire rights to use the properties. There are two ways the city can obtain these rights. The first is to find a willing seller, which is a property owner who, for a price, will turn over certain property rights to the city. The second is through condemnation. Condemnation is a lengthy legal process by which the city can take the property rights from the owner by demonstrating to a court that the project serves the public good and that there are no other viable alternatives.

Upon approval of the environmental permit, the engineers can begin work on preparing the building permit application (F). This task involves filling out the application form and compiling the necessary sheets from the drawing set to illustrate that the project will be constructed to the latest local, state, and federal building codes. When the application has been completed it is submitted to the appropriate government entities for building permit review and approval (G). During the review, the MDC engineer is not required to do any work, but, similar to the environmental permit, nothing can be done to make the review go quicker because it is done by an outside party.

When the final design is complete and the building permit issued, the city can bid the project (I). Bidding the project involves advertising the project in the local newspaper and online. Contractors interested in building the project obtain a copy of the project drawings and specifications from the city. Based on what they see in the drawings and how they interpret the specifications, each interested contractor then develops a bid that will be low enough to win the project while still allowing for a reasonable profit. During the bidding stage, MDC will assist the city by responding to contractor questions, holding a meeting to discuss the project with potential contractors (known as pre-bid meetings), and holding site visits of the actual construction site so the contractors can get a better understanding of the conditions they will face if they win the job. At the end of the bidding period, the contractors submit their bids in sealed envelopes to the city of Saratoga.

MDC was selected by the City of Saratoga to design a new 10-million-gallon per day surface water intake and transmission main.

The city opens the bids and compares the submissions. The apparent low bid will be sent to MDC for review. MDC will review both the dollar amount of the bid and the other documents (e.g., drawings, references, insurance, specifications, and bonds) included in the submittal. If a low bidder has not completed the other documents properly, it is deemed nonresponsive and the engineer begins review of the next lowest bid. This process continues until the lowest responsive bidder is identified. The bid phase ends with MDC's recommendation to the city of which qualified contractor to award the job.

Immediately following the bid phase, as long as the building permit has been issued, construction can start (J). This dummy activity has an activity time of zero. The construction start is a milestone that designates the end of the engineering design phase of the project and the beginning of the construction phase (another project).

Decisions

Jay manages about a half dozen engineering projects at any one time, so he asks you to analyze this project for ways to complete it in 35 weeks. Jay would like to meet with you tomorrow to discuss the results of your analysis.

Case Questions for Discussion

1. Draw the project network diagram and determine the normal time to complete the project, activity slack times, the critical path(s), and total project costs (i.e., baseline your project) using the Critical Path Method.

2. Determine the best way to crash the project to complete it in 35 weeks with *revised* activity slack times, critical path(s), and total project costs. Provide reasoning as to how all crashing decisions were made.

3. Activity times with the greatest uncertainty are activities D, E, and H. Describe conceptually how you could model this uncertainty in activity times. (You do not have the necessary data to actually do this numerically.)

4. What are your final recommendations?

Appendix A

Areas for the Cumulative Standard Normal Distribution

Entries in the table give the area under the standard normal distribution less than z. For example, for $z = -1.25$, the area below z is 0.10565. The first half of the table applies to negative values of z.

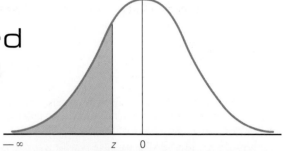

z	0	0.01	0.02	0.03	0.04	0.05	0.06	0.07	0.08	0.09
−3.9	0.00005	0.00005	0.00004	0.00004	0.00004	0.00004	0.00004	0.00004	0.00003	0.00003
−3.8	0.00007	0.00007	0.00007	0.00006	0.00006	0.00006	0.00006	0.00005	0.00005	0.00005
−3.7	0.00011	0.00010	0.00010	0.00010	0.00009	0.00009	0.00008	0.00008	0.00008	0.00008
−3.6	0.00016	0.00015	0.00015	0.00014	0.00014	0.00013	0.00013	0.00012	0.00012	0.00011
−3.5	0.00023	0.00022	0.00022	0.00021	0.00020	0.00019	0.00019	0.00018	0.00017	0.00017
−3.4	0.00034	0.00032	0.00031	0.00030	0.00029	0.00028	0.00027	0.00026	0.00025	0.00024
−3.3	0.00048	0.00047	0.00045	0.00043	0.00042	0.00040	0.00039	0.00038	0.00036	0.00035
−3.2	0.00069	0.00066	0.00064	0.00062	0.00060	0.00058	0.00056	0.00054	0.00052	0.00050
−3.1	0.00097	0.00094	0.00090	0.00087	0.00084	0.00082	0.00079	0.00076	0.00074	0.00071
−3	0.00135	0.00131	0.00126	0.00122	0.00118	0.00114	0.00111	0.00107	0.00104	0.00100
−2.9	0.00187	0.00181	0.00175	0.00169	0.00164	0.00159	0.00154	0.00149	0.00144	0.00139
−2.8	0.00256	0.00248	0.00240	0.00233	0.00226	0.00219	0.00212	0.00205	0.00199	0.00193
−2.7	0.00347	0.00336	0.00326	0.00317	0.00307	0.00298	0.00289	0.00280	0.00272	0.00264
−2.6	0.00466	0.00453	0.00440	0.00427	0.00415	0.00402	0.00391	0.00379	0.00368	0.00357
−2.5	0.00621	0.00604	0.00587	0.00570	0.00554	0.00539	0.00523	0.00508	0.00494	0.00480
−2.4	0.00820	0.00798	0.00776	0.00755	0.00734	0.00714	0.00695	0.00676	0.00657	0.00639
−2.3	0.01072	0.01044	0.01017	0.00990	0.00964	0.00939	0.00914	0.00889	0.00866	0.00842
−2.2	0.01390	0.01355	0.01321	0.01287	0.01255	0.01222	0.01191	0.01160	0.01130	0.01101
−2.1	0.01786	0.01743	0.01700	0.01659	0.01618	0.01578	0.01539	0.01500	0.01463	0.01426
−2	0.02275	0.02222	0.02169	0.02118	0.02068	0.02018	0.01970	0.01923	0.01876	0.01831
−1.9	0.02872	0.02807	0.02743	0.02680	0.02619	0.02559	0.02500	0.02442	0.02385	0.02330
−1.8	0.03593	0.03515	0.03438	0.03362	0.03288	0.03216	0.03144	0.03074	0.03005	0.02938
−1.7	0.04457	0.04363	0.04272	0.04182	0.04093	0.04006	0.03920	0.03836	0.03754	0.03673
−1.6	0.05480	0.05370	0.05262	0.05155	0.05050	0.04947	0.04846	0.04746	0.04648	0.04551
−1.5	0.06681	0.06552	0.06426	0.06301	0.06178	0.06057	0.05938	0.05821	0.05705	0.05592
−1.4	0.08076	0.07927	0.07780	0.07636	0.07493	0.07353	0.07215	0.07078	0.06944	0.06811
−1.3	0.09680	0.09510	0.09342	0.09176	0.09012	0.08851	0.08691	0.08534	0.08379	0.08226
−1.2	0.11507	0.11314	0.11123	0.10935	0.10749	0.10565	0.10383	0.10204	0.10027	0.09853
−1.1	0.13567	0.13350	0.13136	0.12924	0.12714	0.12507	0.12302	0.12100	0.11900	0.11702
−1	0.15866	0.15625	0.15386	0.15151	0.14917	0.14686	0.14457	0.14231	0.14007	0.13786
−0.9	0.18406	0.18141	0.17879	0.17619	0.17361	0.17106	0.16853	0.16602	0.16354	0.16109
−0.8	0.21186	0.20897	0.20611	0.20327	0.20045	0.19766	0.19489	0.19215	0.18943	0.18673
−0.7	0.24196	0.23885	0.23576	0.23270	0.22965	0.22663	0.22363	0.22065	0.21770	0.21476
−0.6	0.27425	0.27093	0.26763	0.26435	0.26109	0.25785	0.25463	0.25143	0.24825	0.24510
−0.5	0.30854	0.30503	0.30153	0.29806	0.29460	0.29116	0.28774	0.28434	0.28096	0.27760
−0.4	0.34458	0.34090	0.33724	0.33360	0.32997	0.32636	0.32276	0.31918	0.31561	0.31207
−0.3	0.38209	0.37828	0.37448	0.37070	0.36693	0.36317	0.35942	0.35569	0.35197	0.34827
−0.2	0.42074	0.41683	0.41294	0.40905	0.40517	0.40129	0.39743	0.39358	0.38974	0.38591
−0.1	0.46017	0.45620	0.45224	0.44828	0.44433	0.44038	0.43644	0.43251	0.42858	0.42465
0	0.50000	0.49601	0.49202	0.48803	0.48405	0.48006	0.47608	0.47210	0.46812	0.46414

Entries in the table give the area under the standard normal distribution less than z. The second half of the table applies to positive values of z. For example, for z = 2.33, the area below z is 0.99010.

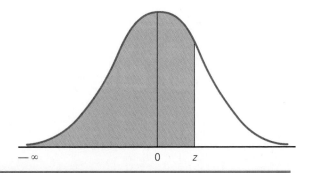

z	0	0.01	0.02	0.03	0.04	0.05	0.06	0.07	0.08	0.09
0	0.50000	0.50399	0.50798	0.51197	0.51595	0.51994	0.52392	0.52790	0.53188	0.53586
0.1	0.53983	0.54380	0.54776	0.55172	0.55567	0.55962	0.56356	0.56749	0.57142	0.57535
0.2	0.57926	0.58317	0.58706	0.59095	0.59483	0.59871	0.60257	0.60642	0.61026	0.61409
0.3	0.61791	0.62172	0.62552	0.62930	0.63307	0.63683	0.64058	0.64431	0.64803	0.65173
0.4	0.65542	0.65910	0.66276	0.66640	0.67003	0.67364	0.67724	0.68082	0.68439	0.68793
0.5	0.69146	0.69497	0.69847	0.70194	0.70540	0.70884	0.71226	0.71566	0.71904	0.72240
0.6	0.72575	0.72907	0.73237	0.73565	0.73891	0.74215	0.74537	0.74857	0.75175	0.75490
0.7	0.75804	0.76115	0.76424	0.76730	0.77035	0.77337	0.77637	0.77935	0.78230	0.78524
0.8	0.78814	0.79103	0.79389	0.79673	0.79955	0.80234	0.80511	0.80785	0.81057	0.81327
0.9	0.81594	0.81859	0.82121	0.82381	0.82639	0.82894	0.83147	0.83398	0.83646	0.83891
1	0.84134	0.84375	0.84614	0.84849	0.85083	0.85314	0.85543	0.85769	0.85993	0.86214
1.1	0.86433	0.86650	0.86864	0.87076	0.87286	0.87493	0.87698	0.87900	0.88100	0.88298
1.2	0.88493	0.88686	0.88877	0.89065	0.89251	0.89435	0.89617	0.89796	0.89973	0.90147
1.3	0.90320	0.90490	0.90658	0.90824	0.90988	0.91149	0.91309	0.91466	0.91621	0.91774
1.4	0.91924	0.92073	0.92220	0.92364	0.92507	0.92647	0.92785	0.92922	0.93056	0.93189
1.5	0.93319	0.93448	0.93574	0.93699	0.93822	0.93943	0.94062	0.94179	0.94295	0.94408
1.6	0.94520	0.94630	0.94738	0.94845	0.94950	0.95053	0.95154	0.95254	0.95352	0.95449
1.7	0.95543	0.95637	0.95728	0.95818	0.95907	0.95994	0.96080	0.96164	0.96246	0.96327
1.8	0.96407	0.96485	0.96562	0.96638	0.96712	0.96784	0.96856	0.96926	0.96995	0.97062
1.9	0.97128	0.97193	0.97257	0.97320	0.97381	0.97441	0.97500	0.97558	0.97615	0.97670
2	0.97725	0.97778	0.97831	0.97882	0.97932	0.97982	0.98030	0.98077	0.98124	0.98169
2.1	0.98214	0.98257	0.98300	0.98341	0.98382	0.98422	0.98461	0.98500	0.98537	0.98574
2.2	0.98610	0.98645	0.98679	0.98713	0.98745	0.98778	0.98809	0.98840	0.98870	0.98899
2.3	0.98928	0.98956	0.98983	0.99010	0.99036	0.99061	0.99086	0.99111	0.99134	0.99158
2.4	0.99180	0.99202	0.99224	0.99245	0.99266	0.99286	0.99305	0.99324	0.99343	0.99361
2.5	0.99379	0.99396	0.99413	0.99430	0.99446	0.99461	0.99477	0.99492	0.99506	0.99520
2.6	0.99534	0.99547	0.99560	0.99573	0.99585	0.99598	0.99609	0.99621	0.99632	0.99643
2.7	0.99653	0.99664	0.99674	0.99683	0.99693	0.99702	0.99711	0.99720	0.99728	0.99736
2.8	0.99744	0.99752	0.99760	0.99767	0.99774	0.99781	0.99788	0.99795	0.99801	0.99807
2.9	0.99813	0.99819	0.99825	0.99831	0.99836	0.99841	0.99846	0.99851	0.99856	0.99861
3	0.99865	0.99869	0.99874	0.99878	0.99882	0.99886	0.99889	0.99893	0.99896	0.99900
3.1	0.99903	0.99906	0.99910	0.99913	0.99916	0.99918	0.99921	0.99924	0.99926	0.99929
3.2	0.99931	0.99934	0.99936	0.99938	0.99940	0.99942	0.99944	0.99946	0.99948	0.99950
3.3	0.99952	0.99953	0.99955	0.99957	0.99958	0.99960	0.99961	0.99962	0.99964	0.99965
3.4	0.99966	0.99968	0.99969	0.99970	0.99971	0.99972	0.99973	0.99974	0.99975	0.99976
3.5	0.99977	0.99978	0.99978	0.99979	0.99980	0.99981	0.99981	0.99982	0.99983	0.99983
3.6	0.99984	0.99985	0.99985	0.99986	0.99986	0.99987	0.99987	0.99988	0.99988	0.99989
3.7	0.99989	0.99990	0.99990	0.99990	0.99991	0.99991	0.99992	0.99992	0.99992	0.99992
3.8	0.99993	0.99993	0.99993	0.99994	0.99994	0.99994	0.99994	0.99995	0.99995	0.99995
3.9	0.99995	0.99995	0.99996	0.99996	0.99996	0.99996	0.99996	0.99996	0.99997	0.99997

Factors for Control Charts

	x-charts				s-charts				R-charts					
n	A	A_2	A_3	c_4	B_3	B_4	B_5	B_6	d_2	d_3	D_1	D_2	D_3	D_4
2	2.121	1.880	2.659	0.7979	0	3.267	0	2.606	1.128	0.853	0	3.686	0	3.267
3	1.732	1.023	1.954	0.8862	0	2.568	0	2.276	1.693	0.888	0	4.358	0	2.574
4	1.500	0.729	1.628	0.9213	0	2.266	0	2.088	2.059	0.880	0	4.698	0	2.282
5	1.342	0.577	1.427	0.9400	0	2.089	0	1.964	2.326	0.864	0	4.918	0	2.114
6	1.225	0.483	1.287	0.9515	0.030	1.970	0.029	1.874	2.534	0.848	0	5.078	0	2.004
7	1.134	0.419	1.182	0.9594	0.118	1.882	0.113	1.806	2.704	0.833	0.204	5.204	0.076	1.924
8	1.061	0.373	1.099	0.9650	0.185	1.815	0.179	1.751	2.847	0.820	0.388	5.306	0.136	1.864
9	1.000	0.337	1.032	0.9690	0.239	1.761	0.232	1.707	2.970	0.808	0.547	5.393	0.184	1.816
10	0.949	0.308	0.975	0.9727	0.284	1.716	0.276	1.669	3.078	0.797	0.687	5.469	0.223	1.777
11	0.905	0.285	0.927	0.9754	0.321	1.679	0.313	1.637	3.173	0.787	0.811	5.535	0.256	1.744
12	0.866	0.266	0.886	0.9776	0.354	1.646	0.346	1.610	3.258	0.778	0.922	5.594	0.283	1.717
13	0.832	0.249	0.850	0.9794	0.382	1.618	0.374	1.585	3.336	0.770	1.025	5.647	0.307	1.693
14	0.802	0.235	0.817	0.9810	0.406	1.594	0.399	1.563	3.407	0.763	1.118	5.696	0.328	1.672
15	0.775	0.223	0.789	0.9823	0.428	1.572	0.421	1.544	3.472	0.756	1.203	5.741	0.347	1.653
16	0.750	0.212	0.763	0.9835	0.448	1.552	0.440	1.526	3.532	0.750	1.282	5.782	0.363	1.637
17	0.728	0.203	0.739	0.9845	0.466	1.534	0.458	1.511	3.588	0.744	1.356	5.820	0.378	1.622
18	0.707	0.194	0.718	0.9854	0.482	1.518	0.475	1.496	3.640	0.739	1.424	5.856	0.391	1.608
19	0.688	0.187	0.698	0.9862	0.497	1.503	0.490	1.483	3.689	0.734	1.487	5.891	0.403	1.597
20	0.671	0.180	0.680	0.9869	0.510	1.490	0.504	1.470	3.735	0.729	1.549	5.921	0.415	1.585
21	0.655	0.173	0.663	0.9876	0.523	1.477	0.516	1.459	3.778	0.724	1.605	5.951	0.425	1.575
22	0.640	0.167	0.647	0.9882	0.534	1.466	0.528	1.448	3.819	0.720	1.659	5.979	0.434	1.566
23	0.626	0.162	0.633	0.9887	0.545	1.455	0.539	1.438	3.858	0.716	1.710	6.006	0.443	1.557
24	0.612	0.157	0.619	0.9892	0.555	1.445	0.549	1.429	3.895	0.712	1.759	6.031	0.451	1.548
25	0.600	0.153	0.606	0.9896	0.565	1.435	0.559	1.420	3.931	0.708	1.806	6.056	0.459	1.541

Source: Adapted from Table 27 of ASTM STP 15D ASTM Manual on Presentation of Data and Control Chart Analysis. © 1976 American Society for Testing and Materials, Philadelphia, PA.

Random Digits

Row										
1	63271	59986	71744	51102	64895	72728	87305	46260	81351	74102
2	64909	23335	73532	81757	21965	65453	23760	66868	67868	56503
3	76396	63407	14768	68665	63302	72754	62437	64619	27648	05504
4	89313	37253	00742	13710	69577	30698	54103	29052	82553	16881
5	48804	42723	07009	10147	48459	76311	77025	43345	66641	02539
6	78305	78150	86853	79058	50031	85448	38960	63251	21470	76644
7	60960	89864	82258	19432	15131	39909	32768	42182	89962	80139
8	18325	72128	03830	27902	07961	28358	49966	61630	54400	25216
9	48518	91563	40764	34192	79970	83471	16365	21223	86587	33442
10	81628	36100	39254	56835	37636	02421	98063	43962	28698	85165
11	56996	66664	29222	10459	71904	78070	62169	20475	42256	07934
12	14801	87412	32615	15290	30120	31865	97614	70509	44171	67206
13	13515	72370	29664	58918	96665	72001	10876	12133	69366	53122
14	31811	01367	34615	47476	48372	47065	42298	14670	23842	67511
15	85501	22581	46211	74733	82948	53980	14905	06808	44448	26285
16	45145	48148	98342	19389	05991	05741	38675	84803	47245	46244
17	42923	06140	84104	25756	33761	12122	59210	39412	48327	89606
18	55791	06180	85084	93868	18804	20985	53991	98457	44282	35188
19	34177	55939	62570	31834	22395	84396	42960	93073	10989	38134
20	42751	51425	41471	16448	05700	06745	93800	10113	78598	17518
21	75679	69889	49966	88109	19138	43983	36837	74278	32107	26215
22	07012	71369	05388	33673	81374	25132	83751	10559	16565	54461
23	41797	13982	14715	54171	85056	21248	80983	92462	08870	23547
24	42741	56932	55818	39790	08742	60991	33612	80408	94023	81026
25	74763	93765	14810	13042	05167	00035	44131	79938	91757	24321
26	33026	36895	46066	09820	73383	44718	27830	66960	40855	18465
27	80670	08848	25084	09735	82975	14712	21282	70310	61714	15275
28	54249	17912	35709	74157	84685	15494	17791	82553	15074	46060
29	76252	12353	82111	29597	27189	16592	17333	09792	98693	10587
30	92813	89047	21866	23882	37345	25823	59942	77750	94198	81737
31	13450	28129	78826	34886	08080	98012	82670	31089	88271	89921
32	73918	75366	04676	04973	59311	43384	43641	87084	64475	46868
33	21604	24978	62263	81498	34041	89035	74592	44386	34638	02829
34	12580	24572	43453	01447	22171	54106	46354	25529	49410	64609
35	06791	38556	93195	59284	39210	95865	76737	92130	87237	26860
36	57315	71086	01471	78161	08100	78305	19330	52629	27742	64925
37	19391	60110	82258	13773	83517	91922	14493	90092	61110	22804
38	24879	11362	04464	37579	21294	94067	21636	21986	96220	49244
39	64443	33916	76511	96896	01013	68986	35418	13819	91897	54944
40	91522	07959	31675	18205	33956	53845	80047	88198	74219	89035

Endnotes

Chapter 1

1. D. A. Collier, *The Service/Quality Solution: Using Service Management to Gain Competitive Advantage*, Milwaukee, WI: ASQC Quality Press and Burr Ridge, IL: Irwin Professional Publishing, 1994, pp. 16, 63–64, 167.

2. These differences between goods and services were first defined by W. E. Sasser, R. P. Olsen, and D. D. Wyckoff, *Management of Service Operations*, Boston: Allyn and Bacon, 1978, pp. 8–21, and later improved and expanded by Fitzsimmons, J. A. and Sullivan, R. S. *Service Operations Management*, New York: McGraw-Hill, 1982; and D. A. Collier, "Managing a Service Firm: A Different Management Game" *National Productivity Review*, Winter 1983–84, pp. 36–45.

3. D. A. Collier, "New Orleans Hilton & Hilton Towers," *Service Management: Operating Decisions*, Englewood Cliffs, NJ: Prentice-Hall, Inc., 1987, p. 120.

4. Jan Carlzon, CEO of Scandinavian Airlines Systems, first defined a moment of trust or truth. See T. J. Peters and N. Austin, *A Passion for Excellence: The Leadership Difference*, New York: Warner Books, 1985, pp. 58 and 78.

5. "iPhone a Short-Term Loss for Verizon," *The New-Press*, January 25, 2012, p. B9.

6. D. A. Collier, *The Service/Quality Solution: Using Service Management to Gain Competitive Advantage*, Milwaukee, WI: ASQC Quality Press and Burr Ridge, IL: Irwin Professional Publishing, 1994, Chapter 4, pp. 63–96.

7. *AT&T's Total Quality Approach*, AT&T Corporate Quality Office, 1992, p. 6.

8. Reprinted from *Business Horizons*, "Using 'biztainment' to gain competitive advantage," by Mi Kyong Newsom, David A. Collier, and Eric O. Olsen, 52:2, 167–176, 2009 with permission from Elsevier.

9. Matthew J. Liberatore and Wenhong Luo, "The Analytics Movement: Implications for Operations Research," *Interfaces*, 40, 4 (July–August 2010), pp. 313–324.

10. Mike Boyer, "Manufacturing Enters a New Age," *The Cincinnati Enquirer*, September 5, 2010, pp. F1, F4; and http://www.smartplanet.com/blog/ business-brains/half-of-employers-cannot-fill-open-positions-survey/15930.

11. A more comprehensive perspective of the threats to manufacturing can be found in Kaj Grichnik and Conrad Winkler, "Manufacturing's 'Make or Break' Moment," *Strategy + Business*, Winter 2007, pp. 8–10; and Joseph A. De Feo and Matt Barney, "The Future of Manufacturing," *Quality Digest*, February 2008, pp. 34–37.

12. Facts in this case adapted from Jeffrey M. O'Brien, "Zappos Knows How to Kick It," *Fortune*, January 15, 2009, http://www.fortune.com; and "Zappos," *Fast Company*, March 2009, pp. 75–76.

Chapter 2

1. Thomas Wailbum, "Study: Apple, Nokia, Dell Tops Among Global Supply Chains," May 29, 2008, http://www.cio.com/article/373563/Study_Apple_Nokia_Dell_Tops_Among_Global_Supply_Chains; Adam Satariano and Peter Burrows, "Apple's Supply-Chain Secret? Hoard Lasers," *Business Week Technology*, November 03, 2011, http://www.businessweek.com/magazine/apples-supplychain-secret-hoard-lasers-11032011.html.

2. K. O'Sullivan and D. Durfee, "Offshoring by the Numbers," *CFO Magazine*, June 2004, p. 53.

3. Larry Selden and Geoffrey Colvin, "What Customers Want," *Fortune*, July 3, 2003, pp. 122–128.

4. S. Davis, *Future Perfect*, New York: Addison-Wesley, 1987, p. 108.

5. http://www.dell.com/content/topics/global.aspx/casestudies/en/emea/eu/fy2009_q2_id916?c=us&l=en&s=corp, July 12, 2010.

6. "Is Your Job Next?" *Business Week*, February 3, 2003, pp. 50–60.

7. "It's All About the Shoes," *Fast Company*, 2004, p. 85, http://pf.fastcompany.com/magazine/86/stollenwerk.html.

8. http://www.allenedmonds.com. Read about the company history.

9. Brad Kane, "Outsourced Manufacturing Coming Back?" Hartford Business.com, October 3, 2011.

10. R. Price, "Rocky Clocks Out," *The Columbus Dispatch*, Columbus, Ohio, April 28, 2002, pp. A1, A8–A9 and April 29, pp. A1, A4–A5.

11. J. L. Graham and N. M. Lam, "The Chinese Negotiation," *Harvard Business Review*, October, 2003, pp. 19–28. We highly recommend reading this article.

12. "Toyota Goes with Standard Approach to Globalization," *The International Herald Tribune*, February 25, 2008.

13. "Quake Stirs Unease About Global Supply Chain," *Associated Press*, March 31, 2011; Chang-Ran Kim, "Toyota Aims for Quake-Proof Supply Chain," baltimoresun.com, September 6, 2011.

14. "Volcano Delays Parts to BMW Factory," *USA Today*, April 20, 2010, p. 5B.

15. U.S. Environmental Protection Agency, "The Lean and Environment Toolkit," http://www.epa.gov/lean/environment/toolkits/environment/.

Chapter 3

1. Robert S. Kaplan and David P. Norton, *The Balanced Scorecard*, Boston, MA: Harvard Business School Press, 1996, p. 1.

2. Private communication from Stephen D. Webb, manager of quality control, ground operations, American Airlines.

3. Adapted from Lashinsky, Adam, "Meg and the Machine," *Fortune*, September 1, 2003, pp. 68–78.

4. A. Parasuraman, V. A. Zeithaml, and L. L. Berry, "SERVQUAL: A Multiple-Item Scale for Measuring Consumer Perceptions of Service Quality," *Journal of Retailing, 64*, Spring 1988, pp. 12–40.

5. "Are You Built for Speed?" *Fast Company*, June 2003, p. 85.

6. "It's the Latest Thing—Really," *Business Week*, March 27, 2006, pp. 70–71. Used with permission of Bloomberg L.P. Copyright © 2012. All rights reserved.

7. David A. Collier, *The Service/Quality Solution*, Milwaukee, WI: ASQC Quality Press, and Burr Ridge, IL: Irwin Professional Publishing, pp. 235–260. Also, see for example, D. A. Collier, "A Service Quality Process Map for Credit Card Processing," *Decision Sciences*, 22, 2, 1991, pp. 406–20; or D. D. Wilson and D. A. Collier, "The Role of Automation and Labor in Determining Customer Satisfaction in a Telephone Repair Service," *Decision Sciences*, 28, 3, 1997, pp. 1–21.

8. 2007 Malcolm Baldrige Application Summary.

9. J. L. Heskett, T. O. Jones, et al., "Putting the Service-Profit Chain to Work," *Harvard Business Review*, 72, 1994, pp. 164–174.

Chapter 4

1. Tim Laseter, Anton Ovchinnikov, and Gal Raz, "Reduce, Reuse, Recycle . . . or Rethink," *Strategy + Business,* 61, Winter 2010, pp. 30–34.

2. "How I Got Started: Papa John's John Schnatter," *Fortune*, September 28, 2009, p. 12.

3. Daniel H. Pink, "Out of the Box," *Fast Company*, October 2003, pp. 104–106; Patricia Sellers, "Gap's New Guy Upstairs," *Fortune*, April 14, 2003, pp. 110–116; and "How to Listen to Consumers," *Fortune*, January 11, 1993, p. 77.

4. V. A. Zeithaml, "How Consumer Evaluation Processes Differ Between Goods and Services," in J. H. Donnelly and W. R. George, eds., *Marketing in Services*, Chicago, IL: American Marketing Association, 1981, pp. 186–199.

5. "Southwest Sets Standards on Costs," *The Wall Street Journal*, October 9, 2002, p. A2.

6. *The PIMS Letter on Business Strategy*, Cambridge, MA: The Strategic Planning Institute, Number 4, 1986.

7. "Small Businesses Make Square Deals," *USA Today*, December 6, 2011, p. 1B.

8. G. Berton Lafamore, "The Burden of Choice," *APICS— The Performance Advantage*, January 2001, pp. 40–43.

9. James Brian Quinn, *Strategies for Change: Logical Incrementalism*, Homewood IL: Richard D. Irwin, 1980.

10. http://www.freewheelchairmission.org/site/c.fgLFIXOJKtF/b.4916275/k.BE91/Home.htm.

11. Adapted in part from Rich Kauffeld, Abhishek Malhotra, and Susan Higgins "Green Is a Strategy: Five Steps to 'Differentiated' Sustainability for a Full Embrace of Environmentalism," *Strategy + Business*, December 21, 2009, http://www.strategy-business.com/article/00013?pg=all.

12. T. Hill, *Manufacturing Strategy: Text and Cases*, 2nd ed., Burr Ridge, IL: Irwin Publishers, 1994.

13. http://www.mcdonalds.com/corporate/info/vision/index.html. This example is the book author's interpretation of McDonald's public information with the objective of illustrating Professor Terry Hill's generic strategy development framework. It may or may not be perfectly accurate and it is only partially complete due to space limitations.

Chapter 5

1. *Award, The Newsletter of Baldrigeplus*, May 7, 2000, http://www.baldrigeplus.com.

2. Mike Dusharme, "RFID Tunes into Supply Chain Management," *Quality Digest*, October 18, 2007, http://www.qualitydigest.com.

3. *BusinessWeek* Online Extra: "The Quickening at Nissan," March 27, 2006.

4. "Honda All Set to Grow," *The Columbus Dispatch*, Columbus, Ohio, September 18, 2002, pp. B1–B2.

5. Laura Braverman, "Kroger Testing Faster Self-Checkout Machine," *The Cincinnati Enquirer*, September 30, 2010, pp. B1, B2.

6. Michael Garry, "Stop & Shop Completes Rollout of Portable EasyShop Shopping Device," *Supermarket News*, Dec. 12, 2007, http://supermarketnews.com/technology_logistics/stopshop_easyshop/.

7. Neil McManus, "Robots at Your Service," *Wired*, January 2003, pp. 58–59.

8. Amazon.com, Inc.

9. http://phx.corporate-ir.net/phoenix.zhtml?c=176060&p=irolnewsArticle&ID=1430365&highlight=, June 3, 2010.

10. Thomas H. Davenport and Jeanne G. Harris, *Competing on Analytics: The New Science of Winning*, Boston, MA: Harvard Business School Press, 2007.

11. Michael V. Copeland, "Reed Hastings: Leader of the Pack," *Fortune*, December 6, 2010, pp. 121–130; Netflix Consumer Press Kit; Netflix Investor Press Kit.

12. Talha Omer, "From Business Intelligence to Analytics," *Analytics*, January/February, 2011, p. 20, analyticsmagazine.com.

13. "Florida Courses on Leading Edge of Water Conservation Technology," http://www.visitflorida.com/experts/golf/action.blog/id.1977, April 26, 2010.

14. "Advancing Global Sustainability Through Technology," Intel White Paper, 2007.

15. Paraphrased from a news item reported at http://www.autofieldguide.com.

16. "Why WebVan Went Bust," *The Wall Street Journal*, July 16, 2001, p. A22.

Chapter 6

1. Adapted and reprinted with permission from "Building Cars by Design" by Vikas Sehgal, Robert Reppa, and Kazutoshi Tominaga from the strategy+business website, published by Booz & Company, Inc. (http://www.strategy-business.com/article/li00107?gko=7b465) Copyright © 2009. All rights reserved.

2. Charles Fishman, "To The Moon! (In a Minivan)," *Fast Company*, December 2007/January 2008.

3. http://www.adidasgolf.com; http://www.adidas-group.com; Ralph Irvin, "Interview with Dave Ortley," video clip, "The Golf Spotlight: Adidas Golf Footwear 2008," http://www.youtube.com/watch?v=s4AyrLXyKT8.

4. Eric Fish, "Rapid Prototyping: How It's Done at GM," *Automotive Design and Production*, 123(5), September/October 2011, pp. 46–47.

5. Douglas Daetz, "The Effect of Product Design on Product Quality and Product Cost," *Quality Progress*, June 1987, 63–67.

6. "Venza Revealed," *Automotive Design and Production*, December 2008, pp. 30–32.

7. *BusinessWeek: Quality 1991* (special issue), October 25, 1991, p. 73.

8. Early discussions of this topic can be found in Bruce Nussbaum and John Templeton, "Built to Last—Until It's Time to Take It Apart," *BusinessWeek*, September 17, 1990, pp. 102–106. A more recent reference is Michael Lenox, Andrew King, and John Ehrenfeld, "An Assessment of Design-for-Environment Practices in Leading US Electronics Firms," *Interfaces* 30, 3, May–June 2000, pp. 83–94.

9. "Pepsi Makes Bottles from Plants," *USAToday*, Money, March 16, 2011, p. 1B; "Pepsi Bottles: No More Plastic," *The Christian Science Monitor*, http://www.csmonitor.com/Business/Latest-News-Wires/2011/0315/Pepsi-bottles-no-more-plastic.

10. http://www.energystar.gov, April 19, 2010.

11. M. J. Bitner, "Servicescapes: The Impact of Physical Surroundings on Customers and Employees," *Journal of Marketing*, 56, 2, 1994, pp. 57–71; M. J. Bitner, "Managing the Evidence of Service," in F. F. Scheuing and W. F. Christopher, eds., *The Service Quality Handbook*, New York: American Management Association (AMACOM), 1993, pp. 358–370.

12. Ibid.

13. Ibid.

14. Sarah Anne Wright, "Putting Fast-Food to the Test," *The Cincinnati Enquirer*, July 9, 2000, pp. F1, 2.

15. Laura Layden, "21st Century Clean," http://www.naplesnews.com, Naples, FL, October 21, 2007.

16. R. B. Chase, "Where Does the Customer Fit in a Service Operation?" *Harvard Business Review*, November–December 1978, pp. 137–142.

17. R. B. Chase, 1983, op. cit., pp. 1037–1050. "The Customer Contact Model for Organizational Design," *Management Science*, 29, 9, 1983, pp. 1037–1050.

18. The Disney Institute, *Be Our Guest*, Disney Enterprises, Inc., 2001, p. 86.

19. http://www.llbean.com/customerService/aboutLLBean/guarantee.html, June 6, 2010.

20. D. A. Collier and T. K. Baker, "The Economic Payout Model for Service Guarantees," *Decision Science*, 36, 2, 2005, pp. 197–220. Also, see D. A. Collier, "Process Moments of Trust: Analysis and Strategy," *The Service Industry Journal*, 9, 2, April 1989, pp. 205–222.

21. http://www.lenscrafter.com/al_mission.html, December 2, 2002.

22. http://www.lenscrafters.com/eyeglasses/6/30-day-unconditional-return-guarantee, June 6 2010.

Chapter 7

1. Chris Woodyard, "Ford Focuses on Flexibility at Its Factories," http://www.usatoday.com/cleanprint/?1298911481142; "Flexibility, Quality in Focus at New Ford Plant," *Targeted News Service*, March 18, 2011, http://asq.org/qualitynews/qnt/execute/displaySetup?newsID=10869. Copyright © 2005–2008 American Society for Quality.

2. Alfa Laval Business Principles Progress Report, 2009, published March 31, 2010, p. 4, http://www.alfalaval.com/about-us/sustainability/reports/Documents/Progress_report_2009.pdf.

3. This discussion is adapted from Charles A. Horne, "Product Strategy and the Competitive Advantage," P&IM Review with *APICS News*, 7, 12, December 1987, pp. 38–41.

4. Nancy Keates, "Custom Bikes for the Masses," *The Wall Street Journal OnLine*, September 28, 2007, http://online.wsj.com; Bela Gold, "CAM Sets New Rules for Production," *Harvard Business Review*, November–December 1982, p. 169.

5. R. H. Hayes and S. C. Wheelwright, "Linking Manufacturing Process and Product Life Cycles," *Harvard Business Review* 57, 1, 1979, pp. 133–140; R. H. Hayes and S. C. Wheelwright, "The Dynamics of Process-Product Life Cycles," *Harvard Business Review* 57, 2, 1979, pp. 127–136; and R. H. Hayes and S. C. Wheelwright, *Restoring Our Competitive Edge*, New York: John Wiley & Sons, 1984.

6. H. Noori, *Managing the Dynamics of New Technology: Issues in Manufacturing Management*, Englewood Cliffs, NJ: Prentice-Hall, 1989.

7. D. A. Collier and S. M. Meyer, "A Service Positioning Matrix," *International Journal of Production and Operations Management*, 18, 12, 1998, pp. 1123–1244.

8. D. A. Collier and S. Meyer, "An Empirical Comparison of Service Matrices," *International Journal of Operations and Production Management*, 20, 5–6, 2000, pp. 705–729.

9. Prince McLean, "Apple Details New MacBook Manufacturing Process, *AppleInsider*, October 14, 2008, http://www.appleinsider.com/articles/08/10/14/.

10. http://en.wikipedia.org/wiki/Ringling_Brothers_Circus and http://en.wikipedia.org/wiki/Circus_train, June 8, 2010.

11. Michael Hammer and James Champy, *Reengineering the Corporation*, New York: HarperBusiness, 1993, pp. 177–178.

12. Patricia Houghton, "Improving Pharmacy Service," *Quality Digest*, October 18, 2007.

13. J. D. C. Little, "A Proof for the Queuing Formula: $L = \lambda W$," *Operations Research*, no. X, 1961, pp. 383–387.

Chapter 8

1. P. C. Bell and J. Van Brenk, "Vytec Corporation: Warehouse Layout Planning," *The European Case Clearing House*, England, Case # 9B03E013. (http://www.ecch.cranfield.ac.uk).

2. "Green Grow the Ballparks," *BusinessWeek*, April 20, 2009, p. 74.

3. "GM Plans to Lay Off 1,600 Workers," *The News-Press*, Fort Myers, FL, October 17, 2008, p. D2.

4. Sue Shellenbarger, "Does Your Chair Have Your Back?" *The Wall Street Journal*, September 21, 2011, pp. D1 and D4 or on web at http://online.wsj.com/article/SB10001424053111903374004576582673310637998.html.

5. "Dilbert Is Right, Says Gallup Study," *Gallup Management Journal*, April 13, 2006.

6. Profiles of Winners, Malcolm Baldrige National Quality Award, and Sunny Fresh Foods Baldrige Application Summary, 1999.

7. P. Johnson, V. Heimann, and K. O'Neill, "The Wonderland of Virtual Teams," *Journal of Workplace Learning*, 13, 1, 2001, pp. 24–29.

Chapter 9

1. http://www.gapinc.com.

2. Hallie Forcinio, "Supply Chain Mastery: HP," *Managing Automation*, November 3, 2006, http://www.managingautomation.com/maonline/magazine/read/view/Supply_Chain_Mastery_HP_2588698.

3. The Supply-Chain Council was formed in 1996–1997 as a grassroots initiative by firms including AMR Research, Bayer, Compaq Computer, Pittiglio Rabin Todd & McGrath (PRTM), Procter & Gamble,

Lockheed Martin, Nortel, Rockwell Semiconductor, and Texas Instruments. See http://www.supply-chain.org/ for information on the Supply Chain council and development of the SCOR model.

4. "Boeing Again Delays Dreamliner's Debut," *USA Today*, January 1, 2008, p. 3B; and "Turbulence in Supply Chain Could Lead to Another Boeing Delay," *Seattle Post-Intelligencer*, March 12, 2008.

5. http://content.dell.com/us/en/gen/d/press-releases/2009-05-20-TBR-Green-Report.aspx.

6. *Dell Fiscal 2003 Report*, http://www.dell.com. Also see "Dell Knows His Niche and He'll Stick with It," *USA Today*, April 5, 2004, p. 3B.

7. "A Key Link in the Supply Chain," advertisement in *Fortune* magazine, September 6, 2010, http://www.fortune.com/adsections.

8. "The UPS Green Dream," *Fortune*, December 27, 2010, pp. 44–51.

9. Charles Dominick, "Green Procurement: Let's Get Started," April 18, 2010, http://www.nextlevelpurchasing.com/articles/green-procurement.html.

10. Patrick Penfield, "The Green Supply Chain: Sustainability Can Be a Competitive Advantage," August 7, 2007, http://www.mhia.org/news/industry/7056/ the-green-supply-chain.

11. D. C. Esty and A. S. Winston, *Green to Gold*, (New Haven, CT, and London: Yale University Press, 2006).

12. http://www.ups.com/content/us/en/bussol/browse/leadership-environment.html?srch_pos=1&srch_phr=environmental+impact.

13. http://about.van.fedex.com/conservation.

14. Chuck Salter, "Surprise Package," *Fast Company*, February 2004, pp. 62–66.

15. Larry Kishpaugh, "Process Management and Business Results," presentation at the 1996 Regional Malcolm Baldrige Award Conference, Boston, MA.

16. Texas Instruments Defense Systems & Electronics Group, *Malcolm Baldrige Application Summary*, 1992.

17. Adapted from "Wal-Mart Takes Next Step in RFID Tagging," *Dallas Morning News*, January 31, 2008.

Chapter 10

1. *Fortune*, April 19, 2011, http://money.cnn.com/2011/04/19/news/companies/jeff_smisek_united_continental.fortune/index.htm.

2. http://articles.baltimoresun.com/2000-07-14/news/0007140079_1_district-court-criminal-justice-system-indigent-defendants.

3. "Strategy: European Auto Union," *Bloomberg BusinessWeek*, April 19, 2010, p. 8.

4. Philip Walzer, "Analysts: Slumping Demand Why Franklin Paper Mill Closing," *The Virginian-Pilot*, April 11, 2010.

5. http://www.briggsandstratton.com.

6. W. Liberman, "Implementing Yield Management," ORSA/TIMS National Meeting Presentation, San Francisco, November 1992.

7. M. Geraghty and M. Johnson, "Revenue Management Saves National Car Rental," *Interfaces*, 12, 7, 1997, pp. 107–127.

8. Eliyahu M. Goldratt and Jeff Cox, *The Goal*, 2nd rev. ed. Croton-on-Hudson, NY: North River Press, 1992; and Eliyahu M. Goldratt, *The Theory of Constraints*, Croton-on-Hudson, NY: North River Press, 1990.

9. "Disney Restaurant No-Shows Will Pay," *USA Today*, October 21, 2011, p. 4D.

10. Jeremy Pastore, Sekar Sundararajan, and Emory W. Zimmers, "Innovative Application," *APICS—The Performance Advantage*, 14, 3, March 2004, pp. 32–35.

11. http://www.goldratt.com/kreisler.htm.

Chapter 11

1. "Holding Patterns," *CIO Magazine*, http://www.cio.com/archive, May 15, 1999.

2. Frank M. Bass, Kent Gordon, Teresa L. Ferguson, and Mary Lou Githens, "DIRECTV: Forecasting Diffusion of a New Technology Prior to Product Launch," *Interfaces*, 31, 3, Part 2 of 2, May–June 2001, pp. S82–S93.

3. Srinivas Bollapragada, Salil Gupta, Brett Hurwitz, Paul Miles, and Rajesh Tyagi, "NBC-Universal Uses a Novel Qualitative Forecasting Technique to Predict Advertising Demand," *Interfaces*, 38, 2, March–April 2008, pp. 103–111.

4. Robert Fildes and Paul Goodwin, "Against Your Better Judgment? How Organizations Can Improve Their Use of Management Judgment in Forecasting," *Interfaces*, 37, 6, November–December 2007, pp. 570–576.

Chapter 12

1. Louise Lee, "Yes, We Have a New Banana," *BusinessWeek*, May 31, 2004, pp. 70–72.

2. http://orf.od.nih.gov/Environmental+Protection/Green+Purchasing/.

3. "RFID for Animals, Food and Farming—the Largest Market of All," IDTechEx, October 19, 2007, http://www.idtechex.com.

4. Gary Finke, "Determining Target Inventories of Wood Chips Using Risk Analysis," *Interfaces*, 14, 5, September–October 1984, pp. 53–58.

5. A more complete technical classification and survey of inventory problems is given in E. A. Silver, "Operations Research in Inventory Management," *Operations Research*, 29, 1981, pp. 628–645.

6. http://www.themanager.org/Strategy/Out-Of-Stock_Situations.htm.

7. Hau L. Lee, Corey Billington, and Brent Carter, "Hewlett-Packard Gains Control of Inventory and Service Through Design for Localization," *Interfaces*, 23, 4, July–August, 1993, pp. 1–11.

Chapter 13

1. S. Delurgio, B. Denton, R. Cabanela, S. Bruggeman, N. Groves, A. Williams, S. Ward, and J. Osborn, "Planning and Forecasting Weekly Outpatient Demands for a Large Medical Center," *Production & Inventory Management*, 45, 2, 2009, pp. 35–46 an pp. 44–51.

2. Adapted from Martin S. Visagie, "Production Control on a Flow Production Plant" *APICS 1975 Conference Proceedings*, pp. 161–166.

3. E. Steinberg, B. Khumawala, and R. Scamell, "Requirements Planning Systems in the Healthcare Environment," *Journal of Operations Management* 2, 4, 1982, pp. 251–259.

Chapter 14

1. "The UPS Green Dream," *Fortune*, December 27, 2010, p. 44–51; Tricia Bisoux, "The Connected Capitalists, *BizEd*, May/June 2010, pp. 24–28 and pp. 44–51.

2. G. M. Campbell, "Overview of Workforce Scheduling Software," *Production and Inventory Management*, 45, 2, pp. 7–22.

3. This approach is suggested in R. Tibrewala, D. Phillippe, and J. Browne, "Optimal Scheduling of Two Consecutive Idle Periods," *Management Science*, 19, 1, September 1972, pp. 71–75.

4. Anton Ovchinnikov and Joseph Milner, "Spreadsheet Model Helps to Assign Medical Residents at the University of Vermont's College of Medicine," *Interfaces*, 38, 4, July–August 2008, pp. 311–323.

5. http://www.abs-usa.com.

6. S. M. Johnson, "Optimal Two- and Three-Stage Production Schedules with Setup Times Included," *Naval Research Logistics Quarterly*, 1, 1, March 1954, pp. 61–68.

7. Gerald G. Brown, Carol J. Ellis, Glenn W. Graves, and David Ronen, "Real-Time, Wide-Area Dispatch of Mobil Tank Trucks," *Interfaces*, 17, 1, 1987, pp. 107–120.

Chapter 15

1. "The peanut peril," *Chicago Tribune*, March 7, 2009 (www.chicagotribune.com); "Peanut firm files for bankruptcy," The News-Press, Fort Myers, FL, February 14, 2009, p. A14.

2. Nabil Tamimi and Rose Sebastianelli, "How Firms Define and Measure Quality," *Production and Inventory Management Journal*, 37, 3, Third Quarter 1996, pp. 34–39.

3. A. Parasuraman, V. Zeithaml, and L. Berry, "A Conceptual Model of Service Quality and Its Implications for Future Research," *Journal of Marketing*, 49, 4, 1985, pp. 41–50; A. Parasuraman, V. Zeithaml, and L. Berry, "SERVQUAL: A Multiple-Item Scale for Measuring Consumer Perceptions of Service Quality," *Journal of Retailing*, 64, 1, 1988, pp. 29–40; A. Parasuraman, V. A. Zeithaml, and L. L. Berry, "Refinement and Reassessment of the SERVQUAL instrument," *Journal of Retailing*, 67, 4, 1991, pp. 420–450.

4. W. Edwards Deming, *The New Economics for Industry, Government, Education*, Cambridge, MA: MIT Center for Advanced Engineering Study, 1993.

5. Adapted from March Laree Jacques, "Big League Quality," *Quality Progress*, August 2001, pp. 27–34.

6. A. Parasuraman, V. A. Zeithaml, and L. L. Berry, "A Conceptual Model of Service Quality and Its Implications for Future Research," *Journal of Marketing*, 49, Fall 1985, pp. 41–50.

7. "Home Builder Constructs Quality with ISO 9000," *Quality Digest*, February 2000, p. 13.

8. Ronald D. Snee, "Why Should Statisticians Pay Attention to Six Sigma?" *Quality Progress*, September 1999, pp. 100–103.

9. Stanley A. Marash, "Six Sigma: Business Results Through Innovation," in *ASQ's 54th Annual Quality Congress Proceedings*, 2000, pp. 627–630.

10. Chris Bot, Elizabeth Keim, Sai Kim, and Lisa Palser, "Service Quality Six Sigma Case Studies," in *ASQ's 54th Annual Congress Proceedings*, 2000, pp. 225–231.

11. Lisa Palser, "Cycle Time Improvement for a Human Resources Process," in *ASQ's 54th Annual Quality Congress Proceedings*, 2000 (CD-ROM).

12. Roger Hoerl, "An Inside Look at Six Sigma at GE," *Six Sigma Forum Magazine*, 1, 3, May 2002, pp. 35–44.

13. "Intel Finds Design Flaw in Chip," *USA Today*, February 1, 2011, p. 1B.

14. A. V. Roth, A. A. Tsay, M. E. Pullman, and J. V. Gray, "Unraveling the Food Supply Chain: Strategic Insights from China and the 2007 Recalls," *Journal of Supply Chain Management*, 44, 1, January 2008, pp. 22–39.

15. *Reports of Statistical Application Research, Japanese Union of Scientists and Engineers*, 33, 2, June 1986.

16. Davis R. Bothe, "Improve Service and Administration," *Quality Progress*, September 2003, pp. 53–57.

17. Massaki Imai, *KAIZEN—The Key to Japan's Competitive Success*, New York: McGraw-Hill, 1986.

18. Harry Robinson, "Using Poka Yoke Techniques for Early Defect Detection," paper presented at the Sixth International Conference on Software Testing and Analysis and Review (STAR '97).

19. http://www.autofieldguide.com.

Chapter 16

1. Eryn Brown, "Heartbreak Hotel?" *Fortune*, November 26, 2001, pp. 161–165.

2. "Hospital to Revise Lab Procedures After Faulty Tests Kill 2," *The Columbus Dispatch*, Columbus, OH, August 16, 2001, p. A2.

3. "Testing for Conformity: An Inside Job," *Golf Journal*, May 1998, pp. 20–25.

4. *Quality Digest* Copyright 2008 by *Quality Digest*. Reproduced with permission of *Quality Digest* in the format Textbook via Copyright Clearance Center.

5. http://www.kevinmd.com/blog/2010/12/medical-errors-involve-handwritten-prescriptions.html and http://www.pharmalot.com/2011/07/e-prescribing-handwritten-error-rates-are-similar/.

6. W. J. McCabe, "Improving Quality and Cutting Costs in a Service Organization," *Quality Progress*, June 1985, pp. 85–89.

Chapter 17

1. Patricia Houghton, "Improving Pharmacy Service," *Quality Digest*, October 18, 2007.

2. "Lean + Sustainability = Good Business," http://leaninsider.productivitypress.com/2007/12/leansustainability-good-business.html.

3. Damian Joseph, "Score Two for Sustainability," *FastCompany*, November 2010, p. 54.

4. Marty Lariviere, "Lean Operations for Luxury Bags," The Operations Room, June 28, 2011, http://operationsroom.wordpress.com/2011/06/28/lean-operation; "At Vuitton, Growth in Small Batches," *The Wall Street Journal*, June 27, 2011.

5. Seiichi Nakajima, "Explanation of New TPM Definition," *Plant Engineer*, 16, 1, pp. 33–40.

6. R. Ellis and K. Hankins, "The Timken Journey for Excellence," presentation for the Center of Excellence in Manufacturing Management, Fisher College of Business, The Ohio State University, Columbus, OH, August 22, 2003. Also see Timken's 2003 Annual Report and "From Missouri to Mars—A Century of Leadership in Manufacturing," http://www.timken.com.

7. "Lean and Pharmacies," *Quality Digest*, October 2006, http://www.qualitydigest.com.

8. P. Engardio, "Lean and Mean Gets Extreme," *BusinessWeek*, March 23 & 30, 2009, pp. 60–62.

9. Paul E. Dickinson, Earl C. Dodge, and Charles S. Marshall, "Administrative Functions in a Just-in-Time Setting," *Target*, Fall 1988, pp. 12–17.

10. R. Inman and S. Mehra, "JIT Implementation Within a Service Industry: A Case Study," *International Journal of Service Industry Management*, 1, 3, 1990, pp. 53–61.

11. http://www.qualitydigest.com/print/8704, August 11, 2009.

12. Modeled after an example in Soren Bisgaard and Johannes Freiesleben, "Six Sigma and the Bottom Line," *Quality Progress*, 37, 9, September 2004, pp. 57–62.

13. Adapted and modified from Nancy B. Riebling, Angelo Pellicone, Antz Joseph, and Charles Winterfeldt, "CT Scan Throughput," *iSixSigma Magazine*, January/February 2010.

Chapter 18

1. http://sportsillustrated.cnn.com/2004/olympics/2004/06/28/bc.oly.athensnotebook.ap/index.html.

2. http://ijourneys.blogspot.com/2008/01/london-olympics-is-live-project.html.

3. Baldrige Award Recipient Profile, Custom Research Inc., National Institute of Standards and Technology, 1996, http://baldrige.nist.gov/Custom_Research_96.htm.

4. W. Alan Randolph and Barry Z. Posner, "What Every Manager Needs to Know About Project Management," *Sloan Management Review*, Summer 1988, pp. 65–73.

5. Craig Stedman, "Failed ERP Gamble Haunts Hershey," *Computerworld*, November 1, 1999, http://www.computerworld.com/news/1999.

6. Jack Gido and James P. Clements, *Successful Project Management*, 2nd ed., Mason, OH: Thomson South-Western 2003, p. 103.

Supplementary Chapter A

1. S. M. Genovese, "Work Measurement and Process Improvement Study of Roller Coaster Preventive Maintenance," March 23, 2003, http://www.theroadscholars.com.

2. City of Phoenix, Arizona, Job Description, Operations Analyst, http://www.ci.phoenix.az.us/JOBSPECS/05260.html.

3. Paul S. Adler, "Time-and-Motion Regained," *Harvard Business Review*, January–February 1993, pp. 97–108.

4. Copyright © 2004, David A. Collier. All rights reserved.

Supplementary Chapter B

1. D. Brady, "Why Service Stinks," *Business Week* October 23, 2000, pp. 118–128. This episode is partially based on this article.

2. Adapted from Quinn et al., "Allocating Telecommunications Resources at L.L. Bean, Inc," *Interfaces*, 21, 1, January/February, 1991, pp. 75–91.

3. D. Machalaba, "Taking the Slow Train: Amtrak Delays Rise Sharply," *The Wall Street Journal*, August 10, 2004, pp. D1–D2.

4. A. Schatz, "Airport Security-Checkpoint Wait Times Go Online," *The Wall Street Journal*, August 10, 2004, p. D2.

Supplementary Chapter C

1. William M. Makuch, Jeffrey L. Dodge, Joseph E. Ecker, Donna C. Granfors, and Gerald J. Hahn, "Managing Consumer Credit Delinquency in the U.S. Economy: A Multi-Billion Dollar Management Science Application," *Interfaces*, 22, 1, January–February 1992, pp. 90–109.

Supplementary Chapter D

1. "Simulation Dynamics Puts Power into SCM," reprinted from the June 2001 *IIE Solutions*, http://www.simulationdynamics.com.

2. "A Picture Is Worth a Thousand Words—Takes on New Meaning for Kodak," *Simulation Success*, July 1999, http://www.processmodel.com/Kodak.pdf.

3. Adapted from David O. Willis, Jerald R. Smith, and Peggy Golden, "A Computerized Business Simulation for Dental Practice Management," *Journal of Dental Education*, 61, 10, October 1997, pp. 821–828.

Supplementary Chapter E

1. William E. Balson, Justin L. Welsh, and Donald S. Wilson, "Using Decision Analysis and Risk Analysis to Manage Utility Environmental Risk," *Interfaces*, 22, 6, November–December 1992, pp. 126–139.

2. Virgil Carter and Robert E. Machol, "Optimal Strategies on Fourth Down," *Management Science*, 24, 16, December 1978, pp. 1758–1762.

3. Bruce F. Baird, *Managerial Decisions Under Uncertainty*, New York: John Wiley & Sons, 1989, p. 6; and Ralph L. Keeney, "Decision Analysis: An Overview," *Operations Research*, 30, 5, September–October 1982, pp. 803–838.

4. Nancy A. Nichols, "Scientific Management at Merck: An Interview with CFO Judy Lewent," *Harvard Business Review*, January–February 1994, pp. 89–99.

5. Adapted from Charles D. Feinstein, "Deciding Whether to Test Student Athletes for Drug Use," *Interfaces*, 20, 3, May–June 1990, pp. 80–87.

Note: Pages beginning with the letters A through E represent topics in the on-line supplementary chapters.

reviewcard

Learning Outcomes

1-1   Explain the concept and importance of operations management.

Effective operations management is essential to providing high-quality goods and services that customers demand, motivating and developing the skills of the people who actually do the work, maintaining efficient operations to ensure an adequate return on investment, and protecting the environment.

1-2   Describe what operations managers do.

Everyone who manages a process or some business activity should process a set of basic OM skills. OM is an integrative and interdisciplinary body of knowledge. OM skills are needed in all functional areas _____ re, education, lodging, consulting, and manufacturing _____ ctions managers do include

- Translating mar_____ and manage goods, services, and processes.
- Helping organiz_____
- Ensuring that re_____ nd information) and operations are coordinated
- Exploiting tech_____
- Building quality_____
- Determining res_____
- Creating a high_____
- Continually lear_____ global and environmental changes.

How to use this Card:

1. Look over the card to preview the new concepts you'll be introduced to in the chapter.

2. Read the chapter to fully understand the material.

3. Go to class (and pay attention).

4. Review the card one more time to make sure you've registered the key concepts.

5. Don't forget—this card is only one of many OM learning tools available to help you succeed in your operations management course.

1-3   Explain th_____ services.

- Goods are tang_____
- Customers parti_____ ities, and transactions.
- The demand for _____ an the demand for goods.
- Services cannot _____
- Service management skills are paramount to a successful service encounter.
- Service facilities typically need to be in close proximity to the customer.
- Patents do not protect services.

1-4   Describe a customer benefit package.

A CBP consists of a primary good or service, coupled with peripheral goods and/or services (see Exhibit 1.2).

Each good or service in the CBP requires a process to create and deliver it, and that is why OM skills are so important.

1-5   Explain the role of processes in OM and identify three general types of processes.

A process is how work gets done and creates value for customers.

1. *Value creation processes, focused on primary goods or services.*

Key Terms

 1-1

Opera_____
science _____
services _____
fully to _____

 1__

A **good** _____
see, touch, or possibly consume.

A **durable good** is a product that typically lasts at least three years.

A **nondurable good** is perishable and generally lasts for less than three years.

A **service** is any primary or complementary activity that does not directly produce a physical product.

A **service encounter** is an interaction between the customer and the service provider.

Moments of truth are any episode, transaction, or experience in which a customer comes into contact with any aspect of the delivery system, however remote, and thereby has an opportunity to form an impression.

Service management integrates marketing, human resources, and operations functions to plan, create, and deliver goods and services, and their associated service encounters.

 1-4

A **customer benefit package (CBP)** is a clearly defined set of tangible (goods-content) and intangible (service-content) features that the customer recognizes, pays for, uses, or experiences.

Exhibit **1.2** *A CBP Example for Purchasing a Vehicle*

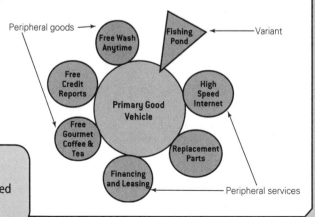

A **primary good or service** is the "core" offering that attracts customers and responds to their basic needs.

Peripheral goods or services are those that are not essential to the primary good or service, but enhance it.

A **variant** is a CBP feature that departs from the standard CBP and is normally location- or firm-specific.

 1-5

A **process** is a sequence of activities that is intended to create a certain result.

 1-6

Sustainability refers to an organization's ability to strategically address current business needs and successfully develop a long-term strategy that embraces opportunities and manages risk for all products, systems, supply chains, and processes to preserve resources for future generations.

Environmental sustainability is an organization's commitment to the long-term quality of our environment.

Social sustainability is an organization's commitment to maintain healthy communities and a society that improves the quality of life.

Economic sustainability is an organization's commitment to address current business needs and economic vitality, and to have the agility and strategic management to prepare successfully for future business, markets, and operating environments.

Business analytics is a process of transforming data into actions through analysis and insights in the context of organizational decision making and problem solving.

3. *General management processes*, including accounting and information systems, human resource management, and marketing.

1-6 Summarize the historical development of OM.

OM has evolved historically along several key themes: a focus on efficiency, quality, customization and design, time-based competition, service, and sustainability (see Exhibit 1.4).

Exhibit 1.4 *Seven Eras of Operations Management*

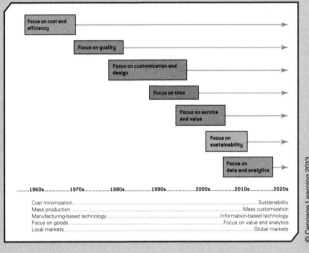

© Cengage Learning 2013

1-7 Describe current challenges facing OM.

Current challenges in OM include technology, globalization, changing customer expectations, and a changing workforce.

- Technology was one of the most important influences on the growth and development of OM during the second half of the 20th century. Advances in design and fabrication of goods as well as in information technology have provided the ability to develop products and enhance services that one could only dream of a few decades ago. They also enable managers to more effectively manage and control extremely complex operations.

- Globalization has changed the way companies do business and must manage their operations. With advances in communications and transportation, we have passed from the era of huge regional factories with large labor forces and tight community ties to an era of the "borderless marketplace." No longer are "American" or "Japanese" products manufactured exclusively in America or Japan.

- Consumers' expectations have risen dramatically. They demand an increasing variety of products with new and improved features that meet their changing needs—products that are defect-free, have high performance, are reliable and durable, and are easy to repair; with rapid and excellent service. Companies must now compete on all these dimensions.

- Today's workers demand increasing levels of empowerment and more meaningful work. Service plays a much greater role within organizations. Finally, we live in a global business environment without boundaries.

- Today, manufacturing is truly a global management challenge in which OM plays a vital role. Companies that are persistent innovators of their global operations and supply chains create a huge competitive advantage. For such industries as recycling, genetic engineering, nanotechnology, green manufacturing, space technology, new ways of energy generation, and robotic medical equipment, new and exciting opportunities emerge for manufacturers. To compete, manufacturers must stay ahead of consumers' needs by increasing product innovation, speeding up time-to-market, and operating highly effective global supply chains.

Buying More Than a Car

People usually think that when they buy a new car, they are simply purchasing the vehicle. Far from it. Most automobiles, for example, bundle a good, the auto ... *vices. Such services might include the* ... *insurance, warranty programs, loaner* ... *ir is needed, free car washes at the deal* ... *anufacturer's driving school, monthly ne* ... *-based scheduling of oil changes and ot* ... *dling is described by the customer benefit package framework.*

Boxed Features

These examples will help you connect what you are learning in class to the real world.

Source: D.A. Collier, The Service/Quality Solution: Using Service Management to Gain Competitive Advantage (jointly published by ASQC Quality Press, Milwaukee, Wisconsin and Irwin Professional Publishing, Burr Ridge, Illinois, Chapter 4, pp. 63–96).

Learning Outcomes

1-1 Explain the concept and importance of operations management.

Effective operations management is essential to providing high-quality goods and services that customers demand, motivating and developing the skills of the people who actually do the work, maintaining efficient operations to ensure an adequate return on investment, and protecting the environment.

1-2 Describe what operations managers do.

Everyone who manages a process or some business activity should process a set of basic OM skills. OM is an integrative and interdisciplinary body of knowledge. OM skills are needed in all functional areas and industries as diverse as health care, education, lodging, consulting, and manufacturing. Some of the key activities that operations managers do include

- Translating market knowledge of customers to design and manage goods, services, and processes.
- Helping organizations do more with less.
- Ensuring that resources (labor, equipment, materials, and information) and operations are coordinated.
- Exploiting technology to improve productivity.
- Building quality into goods, services, and processes.
- Determining resource capacity and schedules.
- Creating a high performance workplace.
- Continually learning and adapting the organization to global and environmental changes.

1-3 Explain the differences between goods and services.

- Goods are tangible while services are intangible.
- Customers participate in many service processes, activities, and transactions.
- The demand for services is more difficult to predict than the demand for goods.
- Services cannot be stored as physical inventory.
- Service management skills are paramount to a successful service encounter.
- Service facilities typically need to be in close proximity to the customer.
- Patents do not protect services.

1-4 Describe a customer benefit package.

A CBP consists of a primary good or service, coupled with peripheral goods and/or services (see Exhibit 1.2).

Each good or service in the CBP requires a process to create and deliver it, and that is why OM skills are so important.

1-5 Explain the role of processes in OM and identify three general types of processes.

A process is how work gets done and creates value for customers.

1. *Value creation processes*, focused on primary goods or services, such as assembling dishwashers or providing a home mortgage;

2. *Support processes*, such as purchasing materials and supplies, managing inventory, installation, customer support, technology acquisition, and research and development; and

Key Terms

 1-1

Operations management (OM) is the science and art of ensuring that goods and services are created and delivered successfully to customers.

 1-3

A **good** is a physical product that you can see, touch, or possibly consume.

A **durable good** is a product that does not quickly wear out and typically lasts at least three years.

A **nondurable good** is no longer useful once it's used, or lasts for less than three years.

A **service** is any primary or complementary activity that does not directly produce a physical product.

A **service encounter** is an interaction between the customer and the service provider.

Moments of truth are any episodes, transactions, or experiences in which a customer comes into contact with any aspect of the delivery system, however remote, and thereby has an opportunity to form an impression.

Service management integrates marketing, human resources, and operations functions to plan, create, and deliver goods and services, and their associated service encounters.

1-4

A **customer benefit package (CBP)** is a clearly defined set of tangible (goods-content) and intangible (service-content) features that the customer recognizes, pays for, uses, or experiences.

Exhibit 1.2 *A CBP Example for Purchasing a Vehicle*

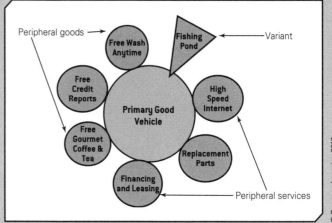

© Cengage Learning 2013

3. *General management processes*, including accounting and information systems, human resource management, and marketing.

1-6 Summarize the historical development of OM.

OM has evolved historically along several key themes: a focus on efficiency, quality, customization and design, time-based competition, service, sustainability, and recently, data and analytics (see Exhibit 1.4).

Exhibit 1.4 *Seven Eras of Operations Management*

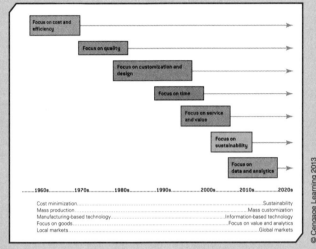

© Cengage Learning 2013

1-7 Describe current challenges facing OM.

Current challenges in OM include technology, globalization, changing customer expectations, and a changing workforce.

- Technology was one of the most important influences on the growth and development of OM during the second half of the 20th century. Advances in design and fabrication of goods as well as in information technology have provided the ability to develop products and enhance services that one could only dream of a few decades ago. They also enable managers to more effectively manage and control extremely complex operations.

- Globalization has changed the way companies do business and must manage their operations. With advances in communications and transportation, we have passed from the era of huge regional factories with large labor forces and tight community ties to an era of the "borderless marketplace." No longer are "American" or "Japanese" products manufactured exclusively in America or Japan.

- Consumers' expectations have risen dramatically. They demand an increasing variety of products with new and improved features that meet their changing needs—products that are defect-free, have high performance, are reliable and durable, and are easy to repair; with rapid and excellent service. Companies must now compete on all these dimensions.

- Today's workers demand increasing levels of empowerment and more meaningful work. Service plays a much greater role within organizations. Finally, we live in a global business environment without boundaries.

- Today, manufacturing is truly a global management challenge in which OM plays a vital role. Companies that are persistent innovators of their global operations and supply chains create a huge competitive advantage. For such industries as recycling, genetic engineering, nanotechnology, green manufacturing, space technology, new ways of energy generation, and robotic medical equipment, new and exciting opportunities emerge for manufacturers. To compete, manufacturers must stay ahead of consumers' needs by increasing product innovation, speeding up time-to-market, and operating highly effective global supply chains.

Buying More Than a Car

People usually think that when they buy a new car, they are simply purchasing the vehicle. Far from it. Most automobiles, for example, bundle a good, the automobile, with many peripheral services. Such services might include the sales process, customized leasing, insurance, warranty programs, loaner cars when a major service or repair is needed, free car washes at the dealership, opportunities to attend a manufacturer's driving school, monthly newsletters sent by e-mail, and Web-based scheduling of oil changes and other service requirements. Such bundling is described by the customer benefit package framework.

Source: D.A. Collier, The Service/Quality Solution: Using Service Management to Gain Competitive Advantage (jointly published by ASQC Quality Press, Milwaukee, Wisconsin and Irwin Professional Publishing, Burr Ridge, Illinois, Chapter 4, pp. 63–96).

Learning Outcomes

2-1 Explain the concept of value and how it can be increased.

The decision to purchase a good or service or a customer benefit package is based on an assessment by the customer of the perceived benefits in relation to its price. One of the simplest functional forms of value is

$$Value = Perceived\ benefits/Price\ (cost)\ to\ the\ customer$$

To increase value, an organization must (a) increase perceived benefits while holding price or cost constant, (b) increase perceived benefits while reducing price or cost, or (c) decrease price or cost while holding perceived benefits constant.

2-2 Describe a value chain and the two major perspectives that characterize it.

The value chain begins with suppliers. Inputs are transformed into value-added goods and services through processes or networks of work activities. The value chain outputs—goods and services—are delivered or provided to customers and targeted market segments.

The first perspective of a value chain is input/output model of operations in which suppliers provide inputs to a goods-producing or service-providing process or network of processes (see Exhibit 2.1).

The second perspective is the pre- and postproduction service view that focuses on gaining the customer, value creation, and keeping the customer (see Exhibit 2.4).

2-3 Explain outsourcing and vertical integration in value chains.

Vertical integration refers to the process of acquiring and consolidating elements of a value chain to achieve more control, and outsourcing is the process of having suppliers provide goods and services that were previously provided internally. Companies must decide whether to integrate backward (acquiring suppliers) or forward (acquiring distributors), or both. Backward integration refers to acquiring capabilities toward suppliers, whereas forward integration refers to acquiring capabilities toward distribution or even customers. The decision on whether to outsource is usually based on economics, and break-even analysis can be used to provide insight into the best decision.

Key Terms

 2-1

A **value chain** is a network of facilities and processes that describes the flow of materials, finished goods, services, information, and financial transactions from suppliers, through the facilities and processes that create goods and services, and that those deliver them to the customer.

A **supply chain** is the portion of the value chain that focuses primarily on the physical movement of goods and materials, and supporting flows of information and financial transactions through the supply, production, and distribution processes.

Value is the perception of the benefits associated with a good, service, or bundle of goods and services (i.e., the customer benefit package) in relation to what buyers are willing to pay for them.

A competitively dominant customer experience is often called a **value proposition.**

 2-3

The **operational structure** of a value chain is the configuration of resources, such as suppliers, factories, warehouses, distributors, technical support centers, engineering design and sales offices, and communication links.

Vertical integration refers to the process of acquiring and consolidating elements of a value chain to achieve more control.

Exhibit 2.1 *An Input-Output Perspective of a Value Chain*

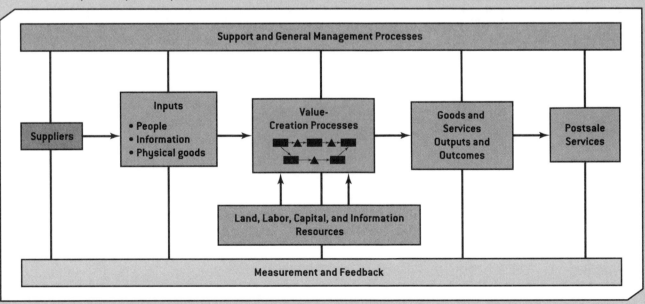

Exhibit 2.4 *Pre- and Postservice View of the Value Chain*

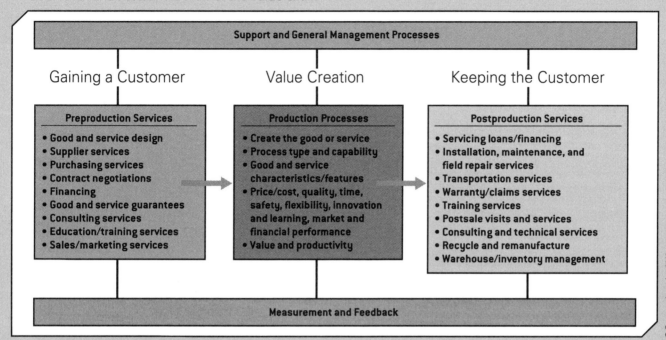

Support and General Management Processes

Gaining a Customer · Value Creation · Keeping the Customer

Preproduction Services
- Good and service design
- Supplier services
- Purchasing services
- Contract negotiations
- Financing
- Good and service guarantees
- Consulting services
- Education/training services
- Sales/marketing services

Production Processes
- Create the good or service
- Process type and capability
- Good and service characteristics/features
- Price/cost, quality, time, safety, flexibility, innovation and learning, market and financial performance
- Value and productivity

Postproduction Services
- Servicing loans/financing
- Installation, maintenance, and field repair services
- Transportation services
- Warranty/claims services
- Training services
- Postsale visits and services
- Consulting and technical services
- Recycle and remanufacture
- Warehouse/inventory management

Measurement and Feedback

© Cengage Learning 2013

2-4 **Explain offshoring and issues that managers must consider in offshoring decisions.**

Offshoring is the building, acquiring, or moving of process capabilities from a domestic location to another country location while maintaining ownership and control. The decision to offshore or outsource involves a variety of economic and noneconomic issues (see Exhibit 2.7).

2-5 **Identify important issues associated with value chains in a global business environment.**

- Global supply chains face higher levels of risk and uncertainty, requiring more inventory and day-to-day monitoring to prevent product shortages.

- Transportation is more complex in global value chains, as they often involve more than one mode and foreign company.

- The transportation infrastructure may vary considerably in foreign countries.

- Global purchasing can be a difficult process to manage when sources of supply, regional economies, and even governments change.

- International purchasing can lead to disputes and legal challenges relating to such things as price fixing and quality defects.

- Cultural differences must be understood in designing, implementing, and managing operations and logistics.

- Privatizing companies and property affects trade and regulatory issues.

- The preplanning, response, and recovery from natural or man-made disasters, often called disaster or emergency management, is another important part of value chain management.

2-6 **Describe how sustainability plays an important role in value chains.**

Sustainability is vital to long-term business survival. It not only improves the organization's perception among consumers, but it also improves the bottom line through reduced costs. In addition, sustainable practices can lead to increased revenues.

Learning Outcomes

3-1 **Describe the types of measures used for decision making.**

Performance measures can be classified into several key categories:

- Financial
- Customer and Market
- Quality
- Time
- Flexibility
- Innovation and Learning
- Productivity and Operational Efficiency
- Sustainability

$$\text{Productivity} = \text{Quantity of Output}/\text{Quantity of Input} \qquad [3.1]$$

As output increases for a constant level of input, or as the amount of input decreases for a constant level of output, productivity increases. Thus, a productivity measure describes how well the resources of an organization are being used to produce output. Productivity measures are often used to track trends over time.

3-2 **Explain the use of analytics in OM and how internal and external measures are related.**

Cause-and-effect linkages between key measures of performance often explain the impact of (internal) operational performance on external results, such as profitability, market share, or customer satisfaction. For example, how do goods- and service-quality improvements impact revenue growth? How do improvements in complaint handling affect customer retention? How do increases or decreases in processing time affect customer satisfaction? How do changes in customer satisfaction affect costs and revenues?

Exhibit 3.1 *The Scope of Business and Operations Performance Measurement*

Performance Measurement Category	Typical Organizational-Level Performance Measures	Typical Operational-Level Performance Measures
Financial	Revenue and profit Return on assets Earnings per share	Labor and material costs Cost of quality Budget variance
Customer and market	Customer satisfaction Customer retention Market share	Customer claims and complaints Type of warranty failure/upset Sales forecast accuracy
Quality	Customer ratings of goods and services Product recalls	Defects/unit or errors/opportunity Service representative courtesy
Time	Speed Reliability	Flow processing or cycle time Percent of time meeting promised due date
Flexibility	Design flexibility Volume flexibility	Number of engineering changes Assembly-line changeover time
Innovation and learning	New product development rates Employee satisfaction Employee turnover	Number of patent applications Number of improvement suggestions implemented Percent of workers trained on statistical process control
Productivity and operational efficiency	Labor productivity Equipment utilization	Manufacturing yield Order fulfillment time
Sustainability	Environmental and regulatory compliance Product-related litigation Financial audits	Toxic waste discharge rate Workplace safety violations Percent of employees with emergency preparedness training

© Cengage Learning 2013

Key Terms

 3-1

Measurement is the act of quantifying the performance of organizational units, goods and services, processes, people, and other business activities.

A **customer-satisfaction measurement system** provides a company with customer ratings of specific goods and service features and indicates the relationship between those ratings and the customer's likely future buying behavior.

Quality measures the degree to which the output of a process meets customer requirements.

Goods quality relates to the physical performance and characteristics of a good.

Service quality is consistently meeting or exceeding customer expectations (external focus) and service-delivery system performance (internal focus) for all service encounters.

Errors in service creation and delivery are sometimes called **service upsets** or **service failures.**

Processing time is the time it takes to perform some task.

Queue time is a fancy word for **wait time**—the time spent waiting.

Flexibility is the ability to adapt quickly and effectively to changing requirements.

Goods and service design flexibility is the ability to develop a wide range of customized goods or services to meet different or changing customer needs.

Volume flexibility is the ability to respond quickly to changes in the volume and type of demand.

Innovation refers to the ability to create new and unique goods and services that delight customers and create competitive advantage.

Learning refers to creating, acquiring, and transferring knowledge, and modifying the behavior of employees in response to internal and external change.

Productivity is the ratio of the output of a process to the input.

Operational efficiency is the ability to provide goods and services to customers with minimum waste and maximum utilization of resources.

The **triple bottom line (TBL or 3BL)** refers to the measurement of environmental, social, and economic sustainability.

 3-2

The quantitative modeling of cause-and-effect relationships between external and internal performance criteria is called **interlinking.**

The **value of a loyal customer (VLC)** quantifies the total revenue or profit each target market customer generates over the buyer's life cycle.

 3-3

Actionable measures provide the basis for decisions at the level at which they are applied.

The value of a loyal customer (VLC) also provides an understanding of how customer satisfaction and loyalty affect the bottom line. Understanding the effects of operational decisions on revenue and customer retention can help organizations more appropriately use their resources. VLC is computed using the following formula:

$$VLC = (P)(CM)(RF)(BLC) \tag{3.2}$$

where

P = the revenue per unit

CM = contribution margin to profit and overhead expressed as a fraction (i.e., 0.45, 0.5, and so on).

RF = repurchase frequency = number of purchases per year

BLC = buyer's life cycle, computed as 1/defection rate, expressed as a fraction (1/0.2 = 5 years, 1/0.1 = 10 years, and so on).

By multiplying the VLC times the absolute number of customers gained or lost, the total market value can be found and used to justify product and process improvements initiatives.

3-3 **Explain how to design a good performance measurement system.**

Good performance measures are actionable. They should be meaningful to the user, timely, and reflect how the organization generates value to customers. Performance measures should support, not conflict with, customer requirements. IBM Rochester, for example, asks the following questions:

- Does the measurement support our mission?
- Will the measurement be used to manage change?
- Is it important to our customers?
- Is it effective in measuring performance?
- Is it effective in forecasting results?
- Is it easy to understand/simple?
- Are the data easy/cost-efficient to collect?
- Does the measurement have validity, integrity, and timeliness?
- Does the measure have an owner?

3-4 **Describe four models of organizational performance.**

Four models of organizational performance—the Malcolm Baldrige Award framework, the balanced scorecard, the value chain model, and the Service-Profit Chain—provide popular frameworks for thinking about designing, monitoring, and evaluating performance. The first two models provide more of a "big picture" of organizational performance, whereas the last two provide more detailed frameworks for operations managers.

Exhibit 3.4 *Baldrige Model of Organizational Performance*

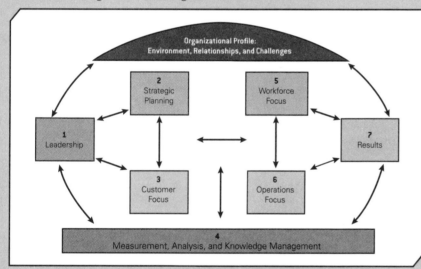

Source: 2011–12 Baldrige Criteria for Performance Excellence, U.S. Dept of Commerce.

Exhibit 3.7 *The Service-Profit Chain Model*

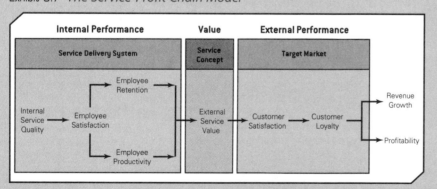

Adapted from J. L. Heskett, T. O. Jones, G. W. Loveman, W. E. Sasser, Jr., and L. A. Schlesinger, "Putting the Service-Profit Chain to Work," *Harvard Business Review*, March–April 1994, pp. 164–174. Copyright © 1994 by the Harvard Business School Publishing Corporation. Reprinted by permission.

Learning Outcomes

4-1 Explain how organizations seek to gain competitive advantage.

Creating a competitive advantage requires a fundamental understanding of two things. First, management must understand customer wants and needs—and how the value chain can best meet these needs through the design and delivery of customer benefit packages that are attractive to customers. Second, management must build and leverage operational capabilities to support desired competitive priorities.

4-2 Explain approaches for understanding customer wants and needs.

To correctly identify what customers expect requires being "close to the customer." There are many ways to do this, such as having employees visit and talk to customers, having managers talk to customers, and doing formal marketing research. The Kano model helps to differentiate between basic customer needs, expressed needs, and the "wow" features that can often be order winners.

4-3 Describe how customers evaluate goods and services.

Research suggests that customers use three types of attributes in evaluating the quality of goods and services: search, experience, and credence. This classification has several important implications for operations. For example, the most important search and experience attributes should be evaluated during design, measured during manufacturing, and drive key operational controls to ensure that they are built into the good with high quality. Credence attributes stem from the nature of services, the design of the service system, and the training and expertise of the service providers.

Exhibit 4.1 *How Customers Evaluate Goods and Services*

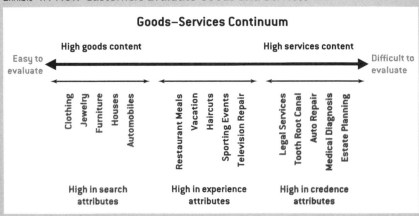

4-4 Explain the five key competitive priorities.

Five key competitive priorities are the following:

1. Cost—Many firms gain competitive advantage by establishing themselves as the low-cost leader in an industry.

2. Quality—Quality is positively and significantly related to a higher return on investment for almost all kinds of market situations.

3. Time—Customers demand quick response, short waiting times, and consistency in performance.

4. Flexibility—Success in globally competitive markets requires a capacity for both design and demand flexibility.

5. Innovation—Many firms focus on research and development for innovation as a core component of their strategy.

Key Terms

 4-1

Competitive advantage denotes a firm's ability to achieve market and financial superiority over its competitors.

 4-2

Basic customer expectations are generally considered the minimum performance level required to stay in business and are often called **order qualifiers.**

Order winners are goods and services features and performance characteristics that differentiate one customer benefit package from another, and win the customer's business.

 4-3

Search attributes are those that a customer can determine prior to purchasing the goods and/or services.

Experience attributes are those that can be discerned only after purchase or during consumption or use.

Credence attributes are any aspects of a good or service that the customer must believe in, but cannot personally evaluate even after purchase and consumption.

 4-4

Competitive priorities represent the strategic emphasis that a firm places on certain performance measures and operational capabilities within a value chain.

Mass customization is being able to make whatever goods and services the customer wants, at any volume, at any time for anybody, and for a global organization, from any place in the world.

Innovation is the discovery and practical application or commercialization of a device, method, or idea that differs from existing norms.

 4-5

Strategy is a pattern or plan that integrates an organization's major goals, policies, and action sequences into a cohesive whole.

Core competencies are the strengths that are unique to an organization.

An **operations strategy** defines how an organization will execute its chosen business strategies.

Key Terms

Operations design choices are the decisions management must make as to what type of process structure is best suited to produce goods or create services.

Infrastructure focuses on the nonprocess features and capabilities of the organization and includes the workforce, operating plans and control systems, quality control, organizational structure, compensation systems, learning and innovation systems, and support services.

4-5 Explain the role of OM, sustainability, and operations in strategic planning.

Developing an operations strategy involves translating competitive priorities into operational capabilities by making a variety of choices and trade-offs in design and operating decisions. That is, operating decisions must be aligned with achieving the desired competitive priorities. For example, if corporate objectives are to be the low-cost and mass-market producer of a good, then adopting an assembly-line type of process is how operations can help achieve this corporate objective. How operations are designed and implemented can have a dramatic effect on business performance and achievement of the strategy. Therefore, operations require close coordination with functional strategies in other areas of the firm, such as marketing and finance. An operations strategy should exploit an organization's core competencies, such as a particularly skilled or creative workforce, customer relationship management, clever bundling of goods and services, strong supply chain networks, extraordinary service, marketing expertise, or the ability to rapidly develop new products or change production-output rates.

Many companies view sustainability as a corporate strategy. A majority of global consumers believes that it is their responsibility to contribute to a better environment and would pay more for brands that support this aim. Likewise, retailers and manufacturers are demanding greener products and supply chains. Companies that have embraced sustainability pursue this strategy throughout their operations.

Exhibit 4.3 *Hill's Strategy Development Framework*

Corporate Objectives	Marketing Strategy	How Do Goods and Services Qualify and Win Orders in the Marketplace?	Operations Strategy	
			Operations Design Choices	Infrastructure
• Growth	• Goods and services markets and segments	• Safety	• Type of processes and alternative designs	• Workforce
• Economic sustainability (survival)⁺	• Range	• Price (cost)	• Supply chain integration and outsourcing	• Operating plans and control system(s)
• Profit	• Mix	• Range	• Technology	• Quality control
• Return on investment	• Volumes	• Flexibility	• Capacity and facilities (size, timing, location)	• Organizational structure
• Other market and financial measures	• Standardization versus customization	• Demand	• Inventory	• Compensation system
• Social (welfare) sustainability⁺	• Level of innovation	• Goods and service design	• Trade-off analysis	• Learning and innovation systems
• Environmental sustainability⁺	• Leader versus follower alternatives	• Quality		• Support services
		• Service		
		• Goods		
		• Environment		
		• Social (community)		
		• Brand image		
		• Delivery		
		• Speed		
		• Variability		
		• Technical support		
		• Pre- and postservice support		

⁺Note: We have added sustainability criteria to Professor Hill's original framework.

Sources: T. Hill, *Manufacturing Strategy: Text and Cases*, 3rd ed., Burr Ridge, IL: McGraw-Hill, 2000, p. 32; T. Hill, *Operations Management: Strategic Context and Managerial Analysis*, 2nd ed., Prigrame MacMillan, 2005, p. 50. Reprinted with permission from the McGraw-Hill Companies.

Exhibit 4.4 *Four Key Decision Loops in Terry Hill's Generic Strategy Framework*

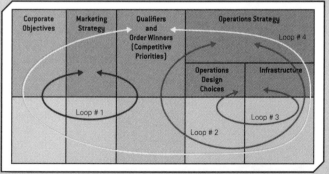

4-6 Describe Hill's framework for operations strategy.

Hill's framework defines the essential elements of an effective operations strategy in the last two columns—operations design choices and building the right infrastructure. A key feature of this framework is the link between operations and corporate and marketing strategies. This linkage is described by the four major decision loops that link together the elements of the framework (see Exhibit 4.4).

© Cengage Learning 2013

review card/ OM4 CHAPTER 5
TECHNOLOGY AND OPERATIONS MANAGEMENT

Learning Outcomes

5-1 Describe different types of technology and their role in manufacturing and service operations.

Some examples of hard technology are computers, computer chips and microprocessors, optical switches and communication lines, satellites, sensors, robots, automated machines, and RFID tags. Some examples of soft technology are database systems, artificial intelligence programs, and voice-recognition software. Computer integrated manufacturing systems (CIMSs) play an important role in modern manufacturing.

All organizations face common issues regarding technology:

- The right technology must be selected for the goods that are produced.

- Process resources such as machines and employees must be set up and configured in a logical fashion to support production efficiency.

- Labor must be trained to operate the equipment.

- Process performance must be continually improved.

- Work must be scheduled to meet shipping commitments/customer promise dates.

- Quality must be ensured.

5-2 Explain how manufacturing and service technology and analytics strengthen the value chain.

With all the new technology that has evolved, a new perspective and capability for the value chain has emerged—the *e-commerce view of the value chain*. This includes business-to-business (B2B), business-to-customer (B2C), customer-to-customer (C2C), and government-to-customer (G2C) value chains; some examples are GE Plastics, Federal Express, and eBay, respectively.

Exhibit 5.1 *E-Commerce View of the Value Chain*

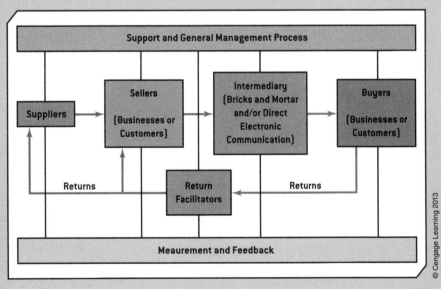

© Cengage Learning 2013

Key Terms

⊘ 5-1

Hard technology refers to equipment and devices that perform a variety of tasks in the creation and delivery of goods and services.

Soft technology refers to the application of the Internet, computer software, and information systems to provide data, information, and analysis and to facilitate the accomplishment of creating and delivering goods and services.

Computer-integrated manufacturing systems (CIMSs) represent the union of hardware, software, database management, and communications to automate and control production activities, from planning and design to manufacturing and distribution.

Numerical control (NC) machine tools enable the machinist's skills to be duplicated by a programmable device (originally punched paper tape) that controls the movements of a tool used to make complex shapes.

Computer numerical control (CNC) machines are NC machines whose operations are driven by a computer.

A **robot** is a programmable machine designed to handle materials or tools in the performance of a variety of tasks.

Computer-aided design/computer-aided engineering (CAD/CAE) enables engineers to design, analyze, test, simulate, and "manufacture" products before they physically exist, thus ensuring that a product can be manufactured to specifications when it is released to the shop floor.

Computer-aided manufacturing (CAM) involves computer control of the manufacturing process, such as determining tool movements and cutting speeds.

Flexible manufacturing systems (FMSs) consist of two or more computer controlled machines or robots linked by automated handling devices such as transfer machines, conveyors, and transport systems. Computers direct the overall sequence of operations and route the work to the appropriate machine, select and load the proper tools, and control the operations performed by the machine.

E-service refers to using the Internet and technology to provide services that create and deliver time, place, information, entertainment, and exchange value to customers and/or support the sale of goods.

Key Terms

 5-2

An **intermediary** is any entity—real or virtual—that coordinates and shares information between buyers and sellers.

Return facilitators specialize in handling all aspects of customers returning a manufactured good or delivered service and requesting their money back, repairing the manufactured good and returning it to the customer, and/or invoking the service guarantee.

Enterprise resource planning (ERP) systems integrate all aspects of a business—accounting, customer relationship management, supply chain management, manufacturing, sales, human resources—into a unified information system and provide more timely analysis and reporting of sales, customer, inventory, manufacturing, human resource, and accounting data.

Customer relationship management (CRM) is a business strategy designed to learn more about customers' wants, needs, and behaviors in order to build customer relationships and loyalty and ultimately enhance revenues and profits.

 5-4

Scalability is a measure of the contribution margin (revenue minus variable costs) required to deliver a good or service as the business grows and volumes increase.

High scalability is the capability to serve additional customers at zero or extremely low incremental costs.

Low scalability implies that serving additional customers requires high incremental variable costs.

5-3   Explain the benefits and challenges of using technology.

Benefits and challenges are summarized in Exhibit 5.2.

5-4   Describe key technology decisions.

Scalability is also a key issue in whether chains succeed or fail. OM decisions affect the ability to handle changes in demand and variable costs, and therefore the scalability of a firm's processes and value chain. Monster.com and the failed WebVan are examples of high and low scalability.

Exhibit **5.2** *Example Benefits and Challenges of Adopting Technology*

Benefits	Challenges
Creates new industries and job opportunities	Higher employee skill levels required, such as information technology and service management skills
Restructures old and less productive industries	Integration of old (legacy) and new technology and systems
Integrates supply and value chain players	Job shift and displacement
Increases marketplace competitiveness and maintains the survival of the firm	Less opportunity for employee creativity and empowerment
Provides the capability to focus on smaller target market segments through mass customization	Protecting the employee's and customer's privacy and security
Improves/increases productivity, quality, customer satisfaction, speed, safety, and flexibility/customization—does more with less	Fewer human service providers, resulting in customer ownership not being assigned, nonhuman service encounters, and inability of the customer to change decisions and return goods easily
Lowers cost	Information overload
Raises world's standard of living	Global outsourcing and impact on domestic job opportunities
Monitors the environment and health of the planet	Enforcement of regulations and laws to support sustainability goals

© Cengage Learning 2013

WebVan: A Value Chain Failure

One dot.com company, WebVan, focused on customers' ordering their groceries online and then the company picking up the orders in a warehouse and delivering them to the customers' homes. The idea was to support the order-pick-pack-deliver process of acquiring groceries through an e-service at the front end of the value chain and with delivery vans at the back end of the value chain. This service made several assumptions about customer wants and needs; for example, that customers have perfect knowledge of what they want when they surf the online catalogs; that customers would be home when the delivery arrived; that what the e-catalogue shows is what the customer will get; that the customer doesn't make mistakes when selecting the items; and that time-starved customers are willing to pay a high premium for home delivery. Unfortunately, this was a very high-cost process. The $30 to $40 delivery charge for complex and heterogeneous customer orders and the many opportunities for error doomed WebVan. The founders of WebVan did not clearly define their strategy and target market and properly evaluate the operational and logistical issues associated with their value chain design. WebVan designed its system with low scalability and limited growth potential.[17]

Learning Outcomes

6-1 **Describe the steps involved in designing goods and services.**

Exhibit 6.1 *An Integrated Framework for Goods and Service Design*

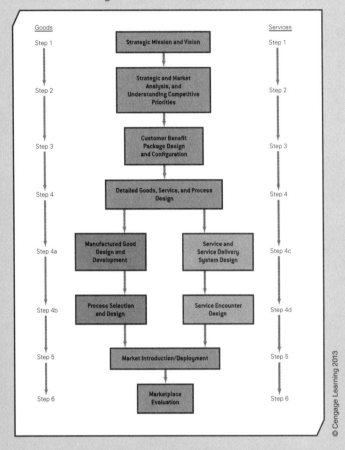

© Cengage Learning 2013

6-2 **Explain the concept and application of quality function deployment.**

QFD focuses on turning the voice of the customer into specific technical requirements that characterize a design and provide the "blueprint" for manufacturing or service delivery.

The process is initiated with a matrix, which because of its structure is often called the House of Quality (see Exhibit 6.2).

Building a House of Quality begins by identifying the voice of the customer and technical features of the design. The roof of the House of Quality shows the interrelationships between any pair of technical features, and these relationships help in answering questions such as "How does a change in one product characteristic affect others?" Next, a relationship matrix between the customer requirements and the technical features is developed. The next step is to add market evaluation and key selling points. Next, technical features of competitive products are evaluated and targets are developed. The final step is to select technical features that have a strong relationship to customer needs, have poor competitive performance, or are strong selling points. Those characteristics will need to be "deployed," or translated into the language of each function in the design and process, so that proper actions and controls are taken to ensure that the voice of the customer is maintained. Characteristics that are not identified as critical do not need such rigorous attention.

Key Terms

 6-1

Prototype testing is the process by which a model (real or simulated) is constructed to test the product's performance under actual operating conditions, as well as consumer reactions to the prototypes.

 6-2

Customer requirements, as expressed in the customer's own words, are called the **voice of the customer.**

Quality function deployment (QFD) is an approach to guide the design, creation, and marketing of goods and services by integrating the voice of the customer into all decisions.

6-3

Reliability is the probability that a manufactured good, piece of equipment, or system performs its intended function for a stated period of time under specified operating conditions.

Design for manufacturability (DFM) is the process of designing a product for efficient production at the highest level of quality.

Product simplification is the process of trying to simplify designs to reduce complexity and costs and thus improve productivity, quality, flexibility, and customer satisfaction.

Design for Environment (DfE) is the explicit consideration of environmental concerns during the design of goods, services, and processes and includes such practices as designing for recycling and disassembly.

 6-4

Service-delivery system design includes facility location and layout, the servicescape, service process and job design, technology and information support systems, and organizational structure.

The **servicescape** is all the physical evidence a customer might use to form an impression. The servicescape also provides the behavioral setting where service encounters take place.

Lean servicescape environments provide service using simple designs (for example, Ticketron outlets or FedEx kiosks).

Elaborate servicescape environments provide service using more complicated designs and service systems (for example, hospitals, airports, and universities).

Service process design is the activity of developing an efficient sequence of activities to satisfy both internal and external customer requirements.

 6-5

Service-encounter design focuses on the interaction, directly or indirectly, between the service provider(s) and the customer.

Customer contact refers to the physical or virtual presence of the customer in the service-delivery system during a service experience.

Systems in which the percentage of customer contact is high are called **high-contact systems;** those in which it is low are called **low-contact systems.**

Customer-contact requirements are measurable performance levels or expectations that define the quality of customer contact with representatives of an organization.

Empowerment simply means giving people authority to make decisions based on what they feel is right, to have control over their work, to take risks and learn from mistakes, and to promote change.

A **service upset** is any problem a customer has—real or perceived—with the service-delivery system and includes terms such as *service failure, error, defect, mistake,* and *crisis.*

A **service guarantee** is a promise to reward and compensate a customer if a service upset occurs during the service experience.

Service recovery is the process of correcting a service upset and satisfying the customer.

6-3 **Describe how the Taguchi loss function, reliability, design for manufacturability, and design for sustainability are used for designing manufactured goods.**

The Taguchi loss function is a reaction to the *goal-post model of* conforming to specifications. Taguchi's approach assumes that the smaller the variation about the nominal specification, the better is the quality. In turn, products are more consistent, and total costs are less. Taguchi measured quality as the variation from the target value of a design specification and then translated that variation into an economic "loss function" that expresses the cost of variation in monetary terms. The loss function is represented by

$$L(x) = k(x - T)^2 \qquad [6.1]$$

Reliability is the probability that a manufactured good, piece of equipment, or system performs its intended function for a stated period of time under specified operating conditions. Many goods are configured using a series of components, parallel (redundant) components, or a combination of these. If the individual reliabilities are denoted by $p_1, p_2, p_3, \ldots, p_n$ and the system reliability is denoted by R_s, then for a series system,

$$R_s = (p_1)\,(p_2)(p_3) \ldots (p_n) \qquad [6.2]$$

The system reliability of an n-component parallel system is computed as

$$R_p = 1 - (1 - p_1)\,(1 - p_2)\,(1 - p_3) \ldots (1 - p_n) \qquad [6.3]$$

To compute the reliability of systems that include combinations of series and parallel components, *first* compute the reliability of the parallel components and treat the result as a single series component; *then* use the series reliability formula to compute the reliability of the resulting series system.

One way to improve reliability during design is to anticipate any product failures that may occur and then design the product to prevent such failures. Another useful approach is DFM, or design for manufacturability, which is intended to prevent product designs that simplify assembly operations but require more complex and expensive components, designs that simplify component manufacture while complicating the assembly process, and designs that are simple and inexpensive to produce but difficult or expensive to service or support. Sustainability concerns are being addressed through approaches called Design for Environment (DfE), which often includes designing goods that can be repaired or recycled.

6-4 **Explain the five elements of service-delivery system design.**

Service-delivery system design includes facility location and layout, the servicescape, service process and job design, technology and information support systems, and organizational structure. A servicescape has three principal dimensions:

1. *Ambient conditions,* which are manifest by sight, sound, smell, touch, and temperature.
2. *Spatial layout and functionality*—how furniture, equipment, and office spaces are arranged.
3. *Signs, symbols, and artifacts*—the more explicit signals that communicate an image about a firm.

Service process designers must concentrate on developing procedures to ensure that things are done right the first time, that interactions are simple and quick, and that human error is avoided.

6-5 **Describe the four elements of service-encounter design.**

The principal elements of service-encounter design are customer-contact behavior and skills; service-provider selection, development, and empowerment; recognition and reward; and service guarantees and recovery.

Service guarantees are offered prior to the customer buying or experiencing the service and help to minimize the risk to the customer. Service recovery normally occurs after a service upset and may require free meals, discount coupons, or a simple apology.

6-6 **Explain how goods and service design concepts are integrated at LensCrafters.**

Managers at LensCrafters must understand both the goods and service sides of the business to be successful. Complex customer benefit packages require complex operating systems. To design and manage LensCrafters' processes, an understanding of OM is a critical skill.

Learning Outcomes

7-1 Describe the four types of processes used to produce goods and services.

Four principal types of processes are used to produce goods and services (see Exhibit 7.1):

1. projects,
2. job shop processes,
3. flow shop processes, and
4. continuous flow processes.

7-2 Explain the logic and use of the product-process matrix.

The most appropriate match between type of product and type of process occurs along the diagonal in the product-process matrix (see Exhibit 7.2). As one moves down the diagonal, the emphasis on both product and process structure shifts from low volume and high flexibility to higher volumes and more standardization.

7-3 Explain the logic and use of the service-positioning matrix.

The SPM focuses on the service-encounter level and helps management design a service system that best meets the technical and behavioral needs of customers (see Exhibit 7.3). The position along the horizontal axis is described by the sequence of service encounters. The SPM is similar to the product-process matrix in that it suggests that the nature of the customer's desired service-encounter activity sequence should lead to the most appropriate service system design and that superior performance results from generally staying along the diagonal of the matrix. As in the product-process matrix, organizations that venture too far off the diagonal create a mismatch between service system characteristics and desired activity sequence characteristics. As we move down the diagonal of the SPM, the service-encounter activity sequence becomes less unique and more repeatable with fewer pathways. Like the product-process matrix, the midrange portion of the matrix contains a broad range of intermediate design choices.

7-4 Describe how to apply process and value stream mapping for process design.

Designing a goods-producing or service-providing process requires six major activities:

1. Define the purpose and objectives of the process.
2. Create a detailed process or value stream map that describes how the process is currently performed.
3. Evaluate alternative process designs.
4. Identify and define appropriate performance measures for the process.
5. Select the appropriate equipment and technology.
6. Develop an implementation plan to introduce the new or revised process design.

A process map documents how work either is, or should be, accomplished and how the transformation process creates value. We usually first develop a "baseline" map of how the current process operates in order to understand it and identify improvements for redesign. In service applications, flowcharts generally highlight the points of contact with the customer and are often called *service blueprints or service maps*. Such flowcharts often show the separation between the back office and the front office with a "line of customer visibility." A value stream map (VSM) shows the process flows in a manner similar to an ordinary process map; however, the difference lies in that value stream maps highlight value-added versus non-value-added activities and include costs associated with work activities for both value- and non-value-added activities (see Exhibits 7.4 to 7.7).

Key Terms

 7-1

Custom, or **make-to-order, goods and services** are generally produced and delivered as one-of-a-kind or in small quantities, and are designed to meet specific customers' specifications.

Option, or **assemble-to-order, goods and services** are configurations of standard parts, subassemblies, or services that can be selected by customers from a limited set.

Standard, or **make-to-stock, goods and services** are made according to a fixed design, and the customer has no options from which to choose.

Projects are large-scale, customized initiatives that consist of many smaller tasks and activities that must be coordinated and completed to finish on time and within budget.

Job shop processes are organized around particular types of general-purpose equipment that are flexible and capable of customizing work for individual customers.

Flow shop processes are organized around a fixed sequence of activities and process steps, such as an assembly line, to produce a limited variety of similar goods or services.

Continuous flow processes create highly standardized goods or services, usually around the clock in very high volumes.

A **product life cycle** is a characterization of product growth, maturity, and decline over time.

 7-2

The **product-process matrix** is a model that describes the alignment of process choice with the characteristics of the manufactured good.

 7-3

A **pathway** is a unique route through a service system.

Customer-routed services are those that offer customers broad freedom to select the pathways that are best suited for their immediate needs and wants from many possible pathways through the service-delivery system.

Provider-routed services constrain customers to follow a very small number of possible and predefined pathways through the service system.

Key Terms

The **service-encounter activity sequence** consists of all the process steps and associated service encounters necessary to complete a service transaction and fulfill a customer's wants and needs.

 7-4

A **task** is a specific unit of work required to create an output.

An **activity** is a group of tasks needed to create and deliver an intermediate or final output.

A **process** consists of a group of activities.

A **value chain** is a network of processes.

A **process map (flowchart)** describes the sequence of all process activities and tasks necessary to create and deliver a desired output or outcome.

A **process boundary** is the beginning or end of a process.

The **value stream** refers to all value-added activities involved in designing, producing, and delivering goods and services to customers.

 7-5

Reengineering has been defined as "the fundamental rethinking and radical redesign of business processes to achieve dramatic improvements in critical, contemporary measures of performance, such as cost, quality, service, and speed."

 7-6

Utilization is the fraction of time a workstation or individual is busy over the long run.

The average number of entities completed per unit time—the output rate—from a process is called **throughput.**

A **bottleneck** is the work activity that effectively limits the throughput of the entire process.

Flow time, or **cycle time,** is the average time it takes to complete one cycle of a process.

7-5 Explain how to improve process designs and analyze process maps.

Management strategies to improve process designs usually focus on one or more of the following:

- *increasing revenue* by improving process efficiency in creating goods and services and delivery of the customer benefit package;

- *increasing agility* by improving flexibility and response to changes in demand and customer expectations;

- *increasing product and/or service quality* by reducing defects, mistakes, failures, or service upsets;

- *decreasing costs* through better technology or elimination of non-value-added activities;

- *decreasing process flow time* by reducing waiting time or speeding up movement through the process and value chain.

Key improvement questions include the following:

- Are the steps in the process arranged in logical sequence?

- Do all steps add value? Can some steps be eliminated and should others be added in order to improve quality or operational performance? Can some be combined? Should some be reordered?

- Are capacities of each step in balance; that is, do bottlenecks exist for which customers will incur excessive waiting time?

- What skills, equipment, and tools are required at each step of the process? Should some steps be automated?

- At which points in the system might errors occur that would result in customer dissatisfaction, and how might these errors be corrected?

- At which point or points should performance be measured?

- Where interaction with the customer occurs, what procedures and guidelines should employees follow that will present a positive image?

7-6 Describe how to compute resource utilization and apply Little's Law.

Two ways of computing resource utilization are defined by Equations 7.1 and 7.2:

$$\text{Utilization (U)} = \text{Resources Used/Resources Available} \qquad [7.1]$$

$$\text{Utilization (U)} = \text{Demand Rate/[Service Rate} \times \text{Number of Servers]} \qquad [7.2]$$

Little's Law is a simple formula defined by Equation 7.3 that explains the relationship among flow time (T), throughput (R), and work-in-process (WIP):

$$\text{Work-in-process} = \text{Throughput} \times \text{Flow time}$$

or

$$WIP = R \times T \qquad [7.3]$$

If we know any two of the three variables, we can compute the third using Little's Law.

For example, if a voting facility processes an average of 50 people per hour and it takes an average of 10 minutes (1/6 hour) for each person to vote, then we would expect $WIP = R \times T = 50 \times (1/6) = 8.33$ voters inside the facility. If a loan department of a bank takes an average of 6 days (0.2 months) to process an application and about 100 applications are in process at any one time, then the throughput of the department is $R = WIP/T = 100/0.2 = 500$ applications per month. If a restaurant uses 200 pounds of dough per week and maintains an inventory of 70 pounds, then the average flow time is $T = WIP/R = 70/200 = 0.35$ weeks.

Learning Outcomes

8-1 Describe four layout patterns and when they should be used.

Four major layout patterns are commonly used in designing and building processes: product layout, process layout, cellular layout, and fixed-position layout. Product layouts support a smooth and logical flow where all goods or services move in a continuous path from one process stage to the next using the same sequence of work tasks and activities. Job shops are an example of firms that use process layouts to provide flexibility in the products that can be made and the utilization of equipment and labor. Cellular layouts facilitate the processing of families of parts with similar processing requirements. The production of large items such as heavy machine tools, airplanes, buildings, locomotives, and ships is usually accomplished in a fixed-position layout. This fixed-position layout is synonymous with the "project" classification of processes.

Exhibit 8.1 *Product Layout for Wine Manufacturer*

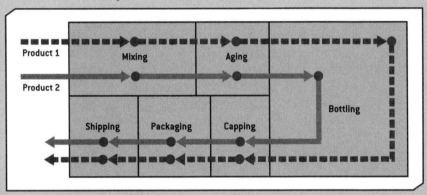

© Cengage Learning 2013

Service organizations use product, process, cellular, and fixed-position layouts to organize different types of work. Those that need the ability to provide a wide variety of services to customers with differing requirements usually use a process layout. Service organizations that provide highly standardized services tend to use product layouts.

Exhibit 8.4 *Comparison of Basic Layout Patterns*

Characteristic	Product Layout	Process Layout	Cellular Layout	Fixed-Position Layout
Demand volume	High	Low	Moderate	Very low
Equipment utilization	High	Low	High	Moderate
Automation potential	High	Moderate	High	Moderate
Setup/changover requirements	High	Moderate	Low	High
Flexibility	Low	High	Moderate	Moderate
Type of equipment	Highly specialized	General purpose	Moderate specialization	Moderate specialization

© Cengage Learning 2013

8-2 Explain how to design product layouts using assembly-line balancing.

Assembly-line balancing seeks to achieve the throughput necessary to meet sales commitments and minimize the cost of operations. Typically, one either minimizes the number of workstations for a given production rate or maximizes the production rate for a given number of workstations.

Key Terms

8-1

Facility layout refers to the specific arrangement of physical facilities.

A **product layout** is an arrangement based on the sequence of operations that is performed during the manufacturing of a good or delivery of a service.

A **process layout** consists of a functional grouping of equipment or activities that do similar work.

In a **cellular layout,** the design is not according to the functional characteristics of equipment, but rather by self-contained groups of equipment (called cells) needed for producing a particular set of goods or services.

A **fixed-position layout** consolidates the resources necessary to manufacture a good or deliver a service, such as people, materials, and equipment, in one physical location.

8-2

Flow-blocking delay occurs when a work center completes a unit but cannot release it because the in-process storage at the next stage is full.

Lack-of-work delay occurs whenever one stage completes work and no units from the previous stage are awaiting processing.

An **assembly line** is a product layout dedicated to combining the components of a good or service that has been created previously.

Assembly-line balancing is a technique to group tasks among workstations so that each workstation has—in the ideal case—the same amount of work.

Cycle time is the interval between successive outputs coming off the assembly line.

8-4

Ergonomics is concerned with improving productivity and safety by designing workplaces, equipment, instruments, computers, workstations, and so on that take into account the physical capabilities of people.

A **job** is the set of tasks an individual performs.

Job design involves determining the specific job tasks and responsibilities, the work environment, and the methods by which the tasks will be carried out to meet the goals of operations.

Job enlargement is the horizontal expansion of the job to give the worker more variety—although not necessarily more responsibility.

Job enrichment is vertical expansion of job duties to give the worker more responsibility.

To begin, we need to know three types of information:

1. the set of tasks to be performed and the time required to perform each task;

2. the precedence relations among the tasks—that is, the sequence in which tasks must be performed; and

3. the desired output rate or forecast of demand for the assembly line.

The cycle time (*CT*) must satisfy:

maximum operation time $\leq CT \leq$ sum of operation times [8.1]

Cycle time (*CT*) is related to the output required to be produced in some period of time (*R*) by the following equation:

$$CT = A/R \qquad [8.2]$$

where A = available time to produce the output and R = demand forecast. For a given cycle time:

Minimum number of workstations required = Sum of task times/Cycle time = $\sum t/CT$ [8.3]

Additional formulas for assembly line performance:

Total time available = (Number workstations)(Cycle time)
= $(N)(CT)$ [8.4]

Total idle time = $(N)(CT) - \sum t$ [8.5]

Assembly-line efficiency = $\sum t/(N \times CT)$ [8.6]

Balance delay = $1 -$ Assembly-line efficiency [8.7]

One line-balancing decision rule example is to assign the task with the *longest task time first* to a workstation if the cycle time would not be exceeded. The longest-task-time-first decision rule assigns tasks with long task times first, because shorter task times are easier to fit in the line balance later in the procedure. In the real world, assembly-line balancing is quite complicated, because of the size of practical problems as well as constraints that mechanization or tooling place on work tasks.

8-3 Explain the concepts of process layout.

In designing process layouts, we are concerned with the arrangement of departments or work centers relative to each other. Costs associated with moving materials or the inconvenience that customers might experience in moving between physical locations are usually the principal design criteria for process layouts. In general, work centers with a large number of moves between them should be located close to one another.

8-4 Describe issues related to workplace design.

Key questions that must be addressed at the workstation level include the following:

1. Who will use the workplace? Will the workstation be shared? How much space is required?

2. How will the work be performed? What tasks are required? How much time does each task take? How much time is required to set up for the workday or for a particular job?

How might the tasks be grouped into work activities most effectively?

3. What technology is needed?

4. What must the employee be able to see?

5. What must the employee be able to hear?

6. What environmental and safety issues need to be addressed? What protective clothing or gear should the employee wear?

The objective of ergonomics is to reduce fatigue, the cost of training, human errors, the cost of doing the job, and energy requirements while increasing accuracy, speed, reliability, and flexibility. Although ergonomics has traditionally focused on manufacturing workers and service providers, it is also important in designing the servicescape to improve customer interaction in high-contact environments.

8-5 Describe the human issues related to workplace design.

Two broad objectives must be satisfied in job design. One is to meet the firm's competitive priorities—cost, efficiency, flexibility, quality, and so on; the other is to make the job safe, satisfying, and motivating for the worker. Resolving conflicts between the need for technical and economic efficiency and the need for employee satisfaction is the challenge that faces operations managers in designing jobs. The relationships between the technology of operations and the social/psychological aspects of work has been understood since the 1950s and is known as the *sociotechnical approach* to job design and provides useful ideas for operations managers. Sociotechnical approaches to work design provide opportunities for continual learning and personal growth for all employees.

Some of the more common approaches to job enrichment are

- natural work teams, which perform entire jobs, rather than specialized, assembly-line work;

- virtual teams, in which members communicate by computer, take turns as leaders, and join and leave the team as necessary; and

- self-managed teams (SMTs), which are empowered work teams that also assume many traditional management responsibilities.

Virtual teams, in particular, have taken on increased importance in today's business world.

Learning Outcomes

9-1 Explain the concept of supply chain management.

The basic purpose of a supply chain is to coordinate the flow of materials, services, and information among the elements of the supply chain to maximize customer value. The key functions generally include sales and order processing, transportation and distribution, operations, inventory and materials management, finance, and customer service. A goods producing supply chain generally consists of suppliers, manufacturers, distributors, retailers, and customers. Raw materials and components are ordered from suppliers and must be transported to manufacturing facilities for production and assembly into finished goods. Finished goods are shipped to distributors that operate distribution centers.

The **Supply Chain Operations Reference (SCOR) model** is based on five basic functions: plan, source, make, deliver, and return.

Exhibit 9.1 *Typical Goods-Producing Supply Chain Structure*

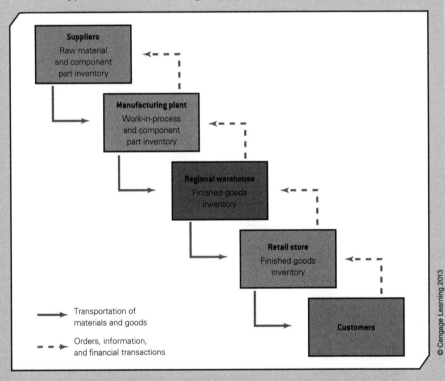

© Cengage Learning 2013

9-2 Describe the key issues in designing supply chains.

Supply chains should support an organization's strategy, mission, and competitive priorities. Many supply chains use contract manufacturing. Outsourcing to contract manufacturers can offer significant competitive advantages, such as access to advanced manufacturing technologies, faster product time-to-market, customization of goods in regional markets, and lower total costs resulting from economies of scale.

Supply chains can be designed from two strategic perspectives—providing high efficiency and low cost or providing agile response. A focus on efficiency works best for goods and services with highly predictable demand, stable product lines with long life cycles that do not change frequently, and low contribution margins. A focus on flexibility and response is best when demand is unpredictable, product life cycles are short and change often because of product innovations, fast response is the main competitive priority, customers require customization, and contribution margins are high.

Key Terms

9-1

Distribution centers (DCs) are warehouses that act as intermediaries between factories and customers, shipping directly to customers or to retail stores where products are made available to customers.

Inventory refers to raw materials, work-in-process, or finished goods that are maintained to support production or satisfy customer demand.

The **Supply Chain Operations Reference (SCOR) model** is a framework for understanding the scope of supply chain management (SCM) based on five basic functions involved in managing a supply chain: plan, source, make, deliver, and return.

Supply chain management (SCM) is the management of all activities that facilitate the fulfillment of a customer order for a manufactured good to achieve satisfied customers at reasonable cost.

9-2

A **contract manufacturer** is a firm that specializes in certain types of goods-producing activities, such as customized design, manufacturing, assembly, and packaging, and works under contract for end users.

Third-party logistics (3PL) providers provide integrated services that might include packaging, warehousing, inventory management, and transportation.

Efficient supply chains are designed for efficiency and low cost by minimizing inventory and maximizing efficiencies in process flow.

Responsive supply chains focus on flexibility and responsive service and are able to react quickly to changing market demand and requirements.

A **push system** produces goods in advance of customer demand using a forecast of sales and moves them through the supply chain to points of sale, where they are stored as finished-goods inventory.

A **pull system** produces only what is needed at upstream stages in the supply chain in response to customer demand signals from downstream stages.

The point in the supply chain that separates the push system from the pull system is called the **push-pull boundary.**

Postponement is the process of delaying product customization until the product is closer to the customer at the end of the supply chain.

A **green sustainable supply chain** can be defined as "the process of using environmentally friendly inputs and transforming these inputs through change agents—whose by-products can improve or be recycled within the existing environment."

Reverse logistics refers to managing the flow of finished goods, materials, or components that may be unusable or discarded through the supply chain from customers toward either suppliers, distributors, or manufacturers for the purpose of reuse, resale, or disposal.

Multisite management is the process of managing geographically dispersed service-providing facilities.

The **center-of-gravity method** determines the *x* and *y* coordinates (location) for a single facility.

Vendor-managed inventory (VMI) is where the vendor (a consumer goods manufacturer, for example) monitors and manages inventory for the customer (a grocery store, for example).

Two ways to configure and run a supply chain are as a push or pull system. Push systems work best when sales patterns are consistent and when there are small numbers of distribution centers and products. Pull systems are more effective when there are many production facilities, many points of distribution, and a large number of products.

9-3 **Define metrics used in evaluating supply chain performance.**

Supply chain managers use numerous metrics to evaluate performance and identify improvements to the design and operation of their supply chains. These include delivery reliability, responsiveness, customer-related measures, supply chain efficiency, and financial measures.

9-4 **Explain important factors and decisions in locating facilities.**

Location decisions in supply and value chains are based on both economic and noneconomic factors.

Facility location is typically conducted hierarchically and involves the following four basic decisions where appropriate: global location decision, regional location decision, community location decision, and local site location decision.

The center-of-gravity method takes into account the locations of the facility and markets, demand, and transportation costs in arriving at the best location for a single facility.

9-5 **Describe the role of transportation, supplier evaluation, technology, and inventory in supply chain management.**

The selection of transportation services is a complex decision, as varied services are available—rail, motor carrier, air, water, and pipeline. Many companies are moving toward third-party logistics providers.

Many companies segment suppliers into categories based on their importance to the business and manage them accordingly.

SCM has benefited greatly from information technology, particularly bar coding and radio frequency identification (RFID) tags, to have accurate receipt information identifying goods that have been received, reduce the time spent in staging (between receipt and storage) at distribution centers, update inventory records, route customer orders for picking, generate bills of lading, and provide various managerial reports.

Careful management of inventory is critical to supply chain time-based performance in order to respond effectively to customers. VMI essentially outsources the inventory management function in supply chains to suppliers. VMI allows the vendor to view inventory needs from the customer's perspective and use this information to optimize its own production operations, better control inventory and capacity, and reduce total supply chain costs.

Exhibit 9.3 *Example of a Manufactured Goods Recovery (Reverse Logistics) Supply Chain*

Source: "Example of a Manufactured Good Recovery (Reverse Logistics) Supply Chain," in Martijn Thierry et al., "Strategic Issues in Product Recovery Management," in *California Management Review* vol. 37, no. 2 (Winter 1995), pp. 114–135. © 1995 by the Regents of the University of California. Reprinted by permission of the University of California Press.

review card/ OM4 CHAPTER 10
CAPACITY MANAGEMENT

Learning Outcomes

10-1 Explain the concept of capacity.

Capacity can be viewed in one of two ways:

1. as the maximum rate of output per unit of time, or

2. as units of resource availability.

Operations managers must decide on the appropriate levels of capacity to meet current (short-term) and future (long-term) demand.

As a single facility adds more and more goods and/or services to its portfolio, the facility can become too large and "unfocused." At some point, diseconomies of scale arise and unit cost increases because dissimilar product lines, processes, people skills, and technology exist in the same facility. The focused factory argues to "divide and conquer" by adopting smaller, more focused facilities dedicated to a (1) few key products, (2) a specific technology, (3) a certain process design and capability, (4) a specific competitive priority objective such as next-day delivery, and (5) particular market segments or customers and associate volumes.

Exhibit 10.1 *Examples of Short- and Long-Term Capacity Decisions*

Short-Term Capacity Decisions	Long-Term Capacity Decisions
• Amount of overtime scheduled for the next week	• Construction of a new manufacturing plant
• Number of emergency room nurses on call during a downtown festival weekend	• Expanding the size and number of beds in a hospital
• Number of call center workers to staff during the holiday season	• Number of branch banks to establish in a new market territory

© Cengage Learning 2013

10-2 Describe how to compute and use capacity measures.

Average safety capacity is defined by

$$\text{Average safety capacity (\%)} = 100\% - \text{Average resource utilization (\%)} \quad [10.1]$$

In a job shop, setup time can be a substantial part of total system capacity, and therefore must be included in evaluating capacity. A general expression for evaluating the capacity required to meet a given production volume for one work order, i, is

$$\text{Capacity required } (C_i) = \text{Setup time } (S_i) + [\text{Processing time } (P_i) \times \text{Order size } (Q_i)] \quad [10.2]$$

where

C_i = capacity requirements in units of time (for instance, minutes, hours, days) for work order i.

S_i = setup or changeover time for work order i as a fixed amount that does not vary with volume.

P_i = processing time for each unit of work order i (e.g., hours/part, minutes/transaction, and so on).

Q_i = size of order i in numbers of units.

If we sum the capacity requirements over all work orders, we can compute the total capacity required:

$$C = \Sigma C_i = \Sigma[S_i + (P_i \times Q_i)] \quad [10.3]$$

10-3 Describe long-term capacity expansion strategies.

In developing a long-range capacity plan, a firm must make a basic economic trade-off between the cost of capacity and the opportunity cost of not having adequate capacity. Capacity costs include both the initial investment in facilities and equipment, and the

Key Terms

 10-1

Capacity is the capability of a manufacturing or service resource such as a facility, process, workstation, or piece of equipment to accomplish its purpose over a specified time period.

Economies of scale are achieved when the average unit cost of a good or service decreases as the capacity and/or volume of throughput increases.

Diseconomies of scale occur when the average unit cost of the good or service begins to increase as the capacity and/or volume of throughput increases.

A **focused factory** is a way to achieve economies of scale without extensive investments in facilities and capacity by focusing on a narrow range of goods or services, target market segments, and/or dedicated processes to maximize efficiency and effectiveness.

 10-2

Safety capacity (often called the **capacity cushion**), is defined as an amount of capacity reserved for unanticipated events such as demand surges, materials shortages, and equipment breakdowns.

A **work order** is a specification of work to be performed for a customer or a client.

 10-3

Complementary goods and services are goods and services that can be produced or delivered using the same resources available to the firm, but whose seasonal demand patterns are out of phase with each other.

 10-4

A **reservation** is a promise to provide a good or service at some future time and place.

A **revenue management system (RMS)** consists of dynamic methods to forecast demand, allocate perishable assets across market segments, decide when to overbook and by how much, and determine what price to charge different customer (price) classes.

 10-5

The **Theory of Constraints (TOC)** is a set of principles that focuses on increasing total process throughput by maximizing the utilization of all bottleneck work activities and workstations.

Key Terms

Throughput is the amount of money generated per time period through actual sales.

A **constraint** is anything in an organization that limits it from moving toward or achieving its goal.

A **physical constraint** is associated with the capacity of a resource such as a machine, employee, or workstation.

A **bottleneck (BN) work activity** is one that effectively limits the capacity of the entire process.

A **nonbottleneck (NBN) work activity** is one in which idle capacity exists.

A **nonphysical constraint** is environmental or organizational, such as low product demand or an inefficient management policy or procedure.

annual cost of operating and maintaining them. The cost of not having sufficient capacity is the opportunity loss incurred from lost sales and reduced market share.

Four basic strategies for expanding capacity over some fixed time horizon are: one large capacity increase, small capacity increases that match average demand, small capacity increases that lead demand, and small capacity increases that lag demand (see Exhibit 10.6).

10-4 Describe short-term capacity adjustment strategies.

When demand fluctuates above and below average capacity levels, then firms can adjust capacity to match the changes in demand by changing internal resources and capabilities, or manage capacity by shifting and stimulating demand. Short-term adjustments to capacity can be done in a variety of ways, such as adding or sharing equipment, selling unused capacity, changing labor capacity and schedules, changing labor skill mix, and shifting work to slack periods. Some general approaches to influence customers to shift demand are varying the price of goods or services, providing customers with information, advertising and promotion, adding peripheral goods and/or services, and providing reservations. Revenue management systems help organizations maximize revenue by adjusting prices to influence demand.

10-5 Explain the principles and logic of the Theory of Constraints.

The TOC focuses on identifying bottlenecks (BN) and nonbottlenecks (NBN), managing BN and NBN work activities carefully, linking them to the market to ensure an appropriate product mix, and scheduling the NBN resources to enhance throughput.

Exhibit 10.6 *Capacity Expansion Options*

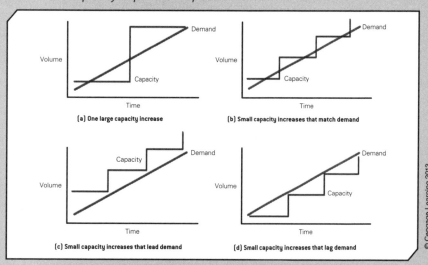

(a) One large capacity increase

(b) Small capacity increases that match demand

(c) Small capacity increases that lead demand

(d) Small capacity increases that lag demand

© Cengage Learning 2013

See Exhibit 10.7 for the basic principles of the TOC. For most business organizations the goal is to maximize throughput, thereby maximizing cash flow. Inherent in this definition is that it makes little sense to make a good or service until it can be sold, and that excess inventory is wasteful.

Constraints determine the throughput of a facility, because they limit production output to their own capacity. There are two basic types of constraints: physical and nonphysical. Physical constraints result in process bottlenecks. Inflexible work rules, inadequate labor skills, and poor management are all forms of constraints. Removing nonphysical constraints is not always possible.

Exhibit 10.7 *Basic Principles of the Theory of Constraints*

Nonbottleneck Management Principles	Bottleneck Management Principles
Move jobs through nonbottleneck workstations as fast as possible until the job reaches the bottleneck workstation.	Only the bottleneck workstations are critical to achieving process and factory objectives and should be scheduled first.
At nonbottleneck workstations, idle time is acceptable if there is no work to do, and therefore resource utilizations may be low.	An hour lost at a bottleneck resource is an hour lost for the entire process or factory output.
Use smaller order (also called lot or transfer batches) sizes at nonbottleneck workstations to keep work flowing to the bottleneck resources and eventually to the marketplace to generate sales.	Work-in-process buffer inventory should be placed in front of bottlenecks to maximize resource utilization at the bottleneck.
	Use large order sizes at bottleneck workstations to minimize setup time and maximize resource utilization.
An hour lost at a nonbottleneck resource has no effect on total process or factory output and incurs no real cost.	Bottleneck workstations should work at all times to maximize throughput and resource utilization so as to generate cash from sales and achieve the company's goal.

© Cengage Learning 2013

Learning Outcomes

11-1 Describe the importance of forecasting to the value chain.

Accurate forecasts are needed throughout the value chain, and are used by all functional areas of an organization, such as accounting, finance, marketing, operations, and distribution. Poor forecasting can result in poor inventory and staffing decisions, resulting in part shortages, inadequate customer service, and many customer complaints. In the telecommunications industry, competition is fierce, and goods and services have very short life cycles. Forecasting is typically included in comprehensive value chain and demand-planning software systems. These systems integrate marketing, inventory, sales, operations planning, and financial data.

Exhibit 11.1 *The Need for Forecasts in a Value Chain*

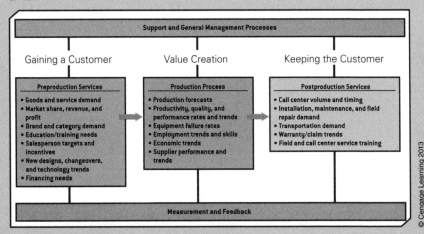

© Cengage Learning 2013

11-2 Explain basic concepts of forecasting and time series.

Long-range forecasts cover a planning horizon of 1 to 10 years and are necessary to plan for the expansion of facilities and to determine future needs for land, labor, and equipment. Intermediate-range forecasts over a 3- to 12-month period are needed to plan workforce levels, allocate budgets among divisions, schedule jobs and resources, and establish purchasing plans. Short-range forecasts focus on the planning horizon of up to three months and are used by operations managers to plan production schedules and assign workers to jobs, to determine short-term capacity requirements, and to aid shipping departments in planning transportation needs and establishing delivery schedules.

Different time series may exhibit one or more of the following characteristics: *trend, seasonal, cyclical, random variation,* and *irregular (one-time) variation.*

All forecasts are subject to error, and understanding the nature and size of errors is important to making good decisions. Generally, three types of forecast error metrics are used:

1. Mean square error, or MSE

$$\text{MSE} = \frac{\Sigma (A_t - F_t)^2}{T} \qquad [11.1]$$

2. Mean absolute deviation (MAD)

$$\text{MAD} = \frac{\Sigma |A_t - F_t|}{T} \qquad [11.2]$$

3. Mean absolute percentage error (MAPE)

$$\text{MAPE} = \frac{\Sigma |(A_t - F_t) / A_t| \times 100}{T} \qquad [11.3]$$

Key Terms

11-1

Forecasting is the process of projecting the values of one or more variables into the future.

11-2

The **planning horizon** is the length of time on which a forecast is based.

The **time bucket** is the unit of measure for the time period used in a forecast.

A **time series** is a set of observations measured at successive points in time or over successive periods of time.

A **trend** is the underlying pattern of growth or decline in a time series.

Seasonal patterns are characterized by repeatable periods of ups and downs over short periods of time.

Cyclical patterns are regular patterns in a data series that take place over long periods of time.

Random variation (sometimes called **noise**) is the unexplained deviation of a time series from a predictable pattern, such as a trend, seasonal, or cyclical pattern.

Irregular variation is a one-time variation that is explainable.

Forecast error is the difference between the observed value of the time series and the forecast, or $A_t - F_t$.

11-3

Statistical forecasting is based on the assumption that the future will be an extrapolation of the past.

A **moving average (MA) forecast** is an average of the most recent "*k*" observations in a time series.

Single exponential smoothing (SES) is a forecasting technique that uses a weighted average of past time-series values to forecast the value of the time series in the next period.

11-4

Regression analysis is a method for building a statistical model that defines a relationship between a single dependent variable and one or more independent variables, all of which are numerical.

A linear regression model with more than one independent variable is called a **multiple linear regression model**.

11-5

Judgmental forecasting relies upon opinions and expertise of people in developing forecasts.

Grass Roots forecasting is asking those who are close to the end consumer, such as salespeople, about the customers' purchasing plans.

The **Delphi method** consists of forecasting by expert opinion by gathering judgments and opinions of key personnel based on their experience and knowledge of the situation.

11-6

A tracking signal provides a method for monitoring a forecast by quantifying **bias**—the tendency of forecasts to consistently be larger or smaller than the actual values of the time series.

11-3 Explain how to apply simple moving average and exponential smoothing models.

The simple moving average concept is based on the idea of averaging random fluctuations in a time series to identify the underlying direction in which the time series is changing.

$$F_{t+1} = \Sigma(\text{most recent "}k\text{" observations}/k$$
$$= (A_t + A_{t-1} + A_{t-2} + \ldots + A_{t-k+1})/k \qquad [11.4]$$

MA methods work best for short planning horizons when there are no major trend, seasonal, or business cycle patterns, that is, when demand is relatively stable and consistent. As the value of k increases, the forecast reacts slowly to recent changes in the time series because older data are included in the computation. As the value of k decreases, the forecast reacts more quickly. If a significant trend exists in the time-series data, moving-average-based forecasts will lag actual demand, resulting in a bias in the forecast.

Single exponential smoothing (SES) forecasts are based on averages using and weighting the most recent actual demand more than older demand data. SES methods do not try to include trend or seasonal effects. The basic exponential smoothing model is

$$F_{t+1} = \alpha A_t + (1 - \alpha)F_t$$
$$= F_t + \alpha(A_t - F_t) \qquad [11.5]$$

Typical values for α are in the range of 0.1 to 0.5. Larger values of α place more emphasis on recent data. If the time series is very volatile and contains substantial random variability, a small value of the smoothing constant is preferred. The reason for this choice is that because much of the forecast error is due to random variability, we do not want to over-react and adjust the forecasts too quickly. For a fairly stable time series with relatively little random variability, larger values of the smoothing constant have the advantage of quickly adjusting the forecasts when forecasting errors occur and therefore allowing the forecast to react faster to changing conditions.

11-4 Describe how to apply regression as a forecasting approach.

Simple regression models forecast the value of a time series (the dependent variable) as a function of a single independent variable, time.

$$Y_t = a + bt \qquad [11.7]$$

In more advanced forecasting applications, other independent variables such as economic indexes or demographic factors that may influence the time series can be incorporated into a regression model. An example is

$$\text{Sales} = \beta_0 + (\beta_1)(\text{Week}) + (\beta_2)(\text{Price})$$

Multiple regression models often provide a more realistic and accurate forecast than simply extrapolating the historical time series.

11-5 Explain the role of judgment in forecasting.

When no historical data are available, only judgmental forecasting is possible. The demand for goods and services is affected by a variety of factors, such as global markets and cultures, interest rates, disposable income, inflation, and technology. Competitors' actions and government regulations also have an impact. Thus, some element of judgmental forecasting is always necessary.

The major reasons given for using judgmental methods rather than quantitative methods are (1) greater accuracy, (2) ability to incorporate unusual or one-time events, and (3) the difficulty of obtaining the data necessary for quantitative techniques. Also, judgmental methods seem to create a feeling of "ownership" and add a commonsense dimension.

11-6 Describe how statistical and judgmental forecasting techniques are applied in practice.

In practice, managers use a variety of judgmental and quantitative forecasting techniques. Statistical methods alone cannot account for such factors as sales promotions, competitive strategies, unusual economic or environmental disturbances, new product introductions, large one-time orders, labor union strikes, and so on. Many managers begin with a statistical forecast and adjust it to account for such factors. Others may develop independent judgmental and statistical forecasts and then combine them, either objectively by averaging or in a subjective manner.

The choice of a forecasting method depends on other criteria, such as the time span for which the forecast is being made, the needed frequency of forecast updating, data requirements, the level of accuracy desired, and the quantitative skills needed.

Forecasters should also monitor a forecast to determine when it might be advantageous to change or update the model. The tracking method used most often is to compute the cumulative forecast error divided by the value of MAD at that point in time; that is,

$$\text{Tracking signal} = \Sigma(A_t - F_t)/\text{MAD} \qquad [11.8]$$

Typically, tracking signals between plus or minus 4 indicate that the forecast is performing adequately. Values outside this range indicate that you should reevaluate the model used.

Learning Outcomes

12-1 Explain the importance of inventory, types of inventories, and key decisions and costs.

Inventories may be physical goods used in operations, and include raw materials, parts, subassemblies, supplies, tools, equipment or maintenance, and repair items. In some service organizations, such as airlines and hotels, inventories are not physical goods that customers take with them, but provide capacity available for serving customers.

Inventory managers deal with two fundamental decisions:

1. When to order items from a supplier or when to initiate production runs if the firm makes its own items; and

2. How much to order or produce each time a supplier or production order is placed.

Inventory management is all about making trade-offs among the costs associated with these decisions.

Inventory costs can be classified into four major categories: ordering or setup costs, inventory-holding costs, shortage costs, and unit cost of the SKUs.

12-2 Describe the major characteristics that impact inventory decisions.

One of the first steps in analyzing an inventory problem should be to describe the essential characteristics of the environment and inventory system:

1. *Number of items.* To manage and control these inventories, each item is often assigned a unique identifier, called a stock-keeping unit, or SKU.

2. *Nature of demand.* Demand can be classified as independent or dependent, deterministic or stochastic, and dynamic or static.

3. *Number and size of time periods.* The type of approach used to analyze "single-period" inventory problems is different from the approach needed for the "multiple-period" inventory situation.

4. *Lead time.* Lead time is affected by transportation carriers, buyer order frequency and size, and supplier production schedules and may be deterministic or stochastic (in which case it may be described by some probability distribution).

5. *Stockouts.* Backorders result in additional costs for transportation, expediting, or perhaps buying from another supplier at a higher price. A lost sale has an associated opportunity cost, which may include loss of goodwill and potential future revenue.

12-3 Describe how to conduct an ABC inventory analysis.

ABC analysis consists of categorizing inventory items or SKUs into three groups according to their total annual dollar usage.

1. "A" items account for a large dollar value but a relatively small percentage of total items.

2. "C" items account for a small dollar value but a large percentage of total items.

3. "B" items are between A and C.

Class A items require close control by operations managers. Class C items need not be as closely controlled and can be managed using automated computer systems. Class B items are somewhere in the middle.

12-4 Explain how a fixed-order-quantity inventory system operates, and how to use the EOQ and safety stock models.

A way to manage a fixed-order-quantity system (FQS) is to continuously monitor the inventory level and place orders when the level reaches some "critical" value. The process of triggering an order is based on the inventory position. When the inventory position falls at

Key Terms

12-1

Inventory is any asset held for future use or sale.

Inventory management involves planning, coordinating, and controlling the acquisition, storage, handling, movement, distribution, and possible sale of raw materials, component parts and subassemblies, supplies and tools, replacement parts, and other assets that are needed to meet customer wants and needs.

Raw materials, component parts, subassemblies, and supplies are inputs to manufacturing and service-delivery processes.

Work-in-process (WIP) inventory consists of partially finished products in various stages of completion that are awaiting further processing.

Finished-goods inventory is completed products ready for distribution or sale to customers.

Safety stock inventory is an additional amount that is kept over and above the average amount required to meet demand.

Environmentally Preferable Purchasing (EPP), often referred to as **green purchasing,** is the affirmative selection and acquisition of products and services that most effectively minimize negative environmental impacts over their life cycle of manufacturing, transportation, use, and recycling or disposal.

Ordering costs or **setup costs** are incurred as a result of the work involved in placing orders with suppliers or configuring tools, equipment, and machines within a factory to produce an item.

Inventory-holding or **inventory-carrying costs** are the expenses associated with carrying inventory.

Shortage or **stockout costs** are costs associated with inventory being unavailable when needed to meet demand.

Unit cost is the price paid for purchased goods or the internal cost of producing them.

12-2

A **stock-keeping unit (SKU)** is a single item or asset stored at a particular location.

Independent demand is demand for an SKU that is unrelated to the demand for other SKUs and needs to be forecasted.

SKUs are said to have **dependent demand** if their demand is directly related to the demand of other SKUs and can be calculated without needing to be forecasted.

Stable demand is usually called **static demand,** and demand that varies over time is referred to as **dynamic demand.**

The **lead time** is the time between placement of an order and its receipt.

A **stockout** is the inability to satisfy the demand for an item.

A **backorder** occurs when a customer is willing to wait for the item; a **lost sale** occurs when the customer is unwilling to wait and purchases the item elsewhere.

 12-4

In a **fixed-quantity system (FQS)**, the order quantity or lot size is fixed; that is, the same amount, Q, is ordered every time.

Inventory position (IP) is defined as the on-hand quantity (OH) plus any orders placed but which have not arrived (called scheduled receipts, SR), minus any backorders (BO).

The **reorder point** is the value of the inventory position that triggers a new order.

The **economic order quantity (EOQ)** model is a classic economic model developed in the early 1900s that minimizes the total cost, which is the sum of the inventory-holding cost and the ordering cost.

Cycle inventory (also called **order** or **lot size inventory**) is inventory that results from purchasing or producing in larger lots than are needed for immediate consumption or sale.

Safety stock is additional planned on-hand inventory that acts as a buffer to reduce the risk of a stockout.

A **service level** is the desired probability of not having a stockout during a lead-time period.

 12-5

A **fixed-period system (FPS)**—sometimes called a periodic review system—is one in which the inventory position is checked only at fixed intervals of time, T, rather than on a continuous basis.

or below a certain value, r, called the *reorder point*, a new order is placed (see Exhibits 12.5 and 12.6).

The EOQ model is based on the following assumptions:

- Only a single item (SKU) is considered.
- The entire order quantity (Q) arrives in the inventory at one time.
- Only two types of costs are relevant—order/setup and inventory-holding costs.
- No stockouts are allowed.
- The demand for the item is deterministic and continuous over time.
- Lead time is constant.

Thus the total annual cost is $TC = \frac{1}{2} QC_h + \frac{D}{Q} C_0$.

The order quantity that minimizes the total cost, denoted by Q^*, is $Q^* = \sqrt{\dfrac{2DC_0}{C_h}}$.

The reorder point depends on the lead time and the demand rate. One approach to choosing the reorder point is to use the *average demand during the lead time* (μL). If d is the demand per unit of time (day, week, and so on), and L is the lead time expressed in the same units of time, then the demand during the lead time is calculated as $r = (d)(L)$.

When demand is uncertain, we may reduce the risk of a stockout by adding additional stock—called safety stock—to the average lead-time demand, thus increasing the reorder point. Choosing the appropriate amount of safety stock depends on the risk that management wants to take of incurring a stockout. This is specified by the service level—the probability of not having a stockout during a lead-time period. For normally distributed demand, the reorder point is $r = \mu_L + z\sigma_L$, where μ_L = average demand during the lead time, σ_L = standard deviation of demand during the lead time, and z = the number of standard deviations necessary to achieve the acceptable service level.

12-5 **Explain how a fixed-period inventory system operates.**

For a fixed-period inventory system, at the time of review, an order is placed for sufficient stock to bring the inventory position up to a predetermined maximum inventory level, M, sometimes called the *replenishment level*, or *"order-up-to"* level. We can set the length of the review period judgmentally based on the importance of the item or the convenience of review. The EOQ model provides the best "economic time interval" for establishing an optimal policy for an FPS system under the model assumptions. This is given by $T = Q^*/D$. The optimal replenishment level is computed by $M = d(T = L)$, where d = average demand per time period, L is the lead time, and M is the demand during the lead time plus review period (see Exhibits 12.11 and 12.12). Safety stock can also be added to M, if desired.

12-6 **Describe how to apply the single-period inventory model.**

The single-period inventory model applies to inventory situations in which one order is placed for a good in anticipation of a future selling season where demand is uncertain. At the end of the period the product has either sold out or there is a surplus of unsold items to sell for a salvage value.

The news-vendor problem can be solved using a technique called *marginal economic analysis*, which compares the cost or loss of ordering one additional item with the cost or loss of not ordering one additional item. The costs involved are defined as

- c_s = the cost per item of overestimating demand (salvage cost); this cost represents the loss of ordering one additional item and finding that it cannot be sold.
- c_u = the cost per item of underestimating demand (shortage cost); this cost represents the opportunity loss of not ordering one additional item and finding that it could have been sold.

The optimal order quantity is the value of Q^* that satisfies

$$P(\text{demand} \leq Q^*) = \frac{c_u}{c_u + c_s} \qquad [12.17]$$

Learning Outcomes

13-1 Describe the overall frameworks for resource planning in both goods-producing and service-providing organizations.

Level 1 represents aggregate planning. Aggregate plans define output levels over a planning horizon of one to two years, usually in monthly or quarterly time buckets. They normally focus on product families or total capacity requirements rather than individual products or specific capacity allocations. Aggregate plans also help to define budget allocations and associated resource requirements.

Level 2 planning is called disaggregation. To disaggregate means to break up or separate into more detailed pieces. Disaggregation specifies more detailed plans for the creation of individual goods and services or the allocation of capacity to specific time periods. For goods producing firms, disaggregation takes Level 1 aggregate planning decisions and breaks them down into such details as order sizes and schedules for individual subassemblies and resources by week and day.

Level 3 focuses on executing the detailed plans made at Level 2, creating detailed resource schedules and job sequences. Level 3 planning and execution in manufacturing is sometimes called *shop floor control*.

Resource management for most service-providing organizations generally does not require as many intermediate levels of planning as it does for manufacturing.

13-2 Explain options for aggregate planning.

Managers have a variety of options in developing aggregate plans in the face of fluctuating demand:

- **Demand Management** Marketing strategies can be used to influence demand and to help create more feasible aggregate plans.
- **Production-Rate Changes** One means of increasing the output rate without changing existing resources is through planned overtime. Alternatively, hours can be reduced during slow periods through planned undertime.
- **Workforce Changes** Changing the size of the workforce is usually accomplished through hiring and layoffs.
- **Inventory Changes** In planning for fluctuating demand, inventory is often built up during slack periods and held for peak periods. A related strategy is to carry back orders or to tolerate lost sales during peak-demand periods.
- **Facilities, Equipment, and Transportation** Short-term changes in facilities and equipment are seldom used in traditional aggregate planning methods because of the capital costs involved.

13-3 Describe how to evaluate level production and chase demand strategies for aggregate planning.

A level strategy avoids changes in the production rate, working within normal capacity restrictions. Labor and equipment schedules are stable and repetitive, making it easier to execute the plan. An alternative to a level production strategy is to match production to demand every month (chase demand strategy). Although inventories will be reduced and lost sales will be eliminated, many production rate changes will dramatically change resource levels (that is, the number of employees, machines, and so on). Both strategies can easily be evaluated using a spreadsheet.

13-4 Describe ways to disaggregate aggregate plans using master production scheduling and material requirements planning.

The purpose of the master schedule is to translate the aggregate plan into a separate plan for individual finished goods. It also provides a means for evaluating alternative schedules in terms

Key Terms

 13-1

Resource management deals with the planning, execution, and control of all the resources that are used to produce goods or provide services in a value chain.

Aggregate planning is the development of a long-term output and resource plan in aggregate units of measure.

Disaggregation is the process of translating aggregate plans into short-term operational plans that provide the basis for weekly and daily schedules and detailed resource requirements.

Execution refers to moving work from one workstation to another, assigning people to tasks, setting priorities for jobs, scheduling equipment, and controlling processes.

 13-3

A **level production strategy** plans for the same production rate in each time period.

A **chase demand strategy** sets the production rate equal to the demand in each time period.

 13-4

A **master production schedule (MPS)** is a statement of how many finished items are to be produced and when they are to be produced.

A **final assembly schedule (FAS)** defines the quantity and timing for assembling subassemblies and component parts into a final finished good.

Materials requirements planning (MRP) is a forward-looking, demand-based approach for planning the production of manufactured goods and ordering materials and components to minimize unnecessary inventories and reduce costs.

Dependent demand is demand that is directly related to the demand of other SKUs and can be calculated without needing to be forecasted.

A **bill of labor (BOL)** is a hierarchical record analogous to a BOM that defines labor inputs necessary to create a good or service.

End items are finished goods scheduled in the MPS or FAS that must be forecasted.

A **parent item** is manufactured from one or more components.

Components are any item (raw materials, manufactured parts, purchased parts) other than an end item that go into a higher-level parent item(s).

A **subassembly** always has at least one immediate parent and also has at least one immediate component.

MRP explosion is the process of using the logic of dependent demand to calculate the quantity and timing of orders for all subassemblies and components that go into and support the production of the end item(s).

Time buckets are the time-period size used in the MRP explosion process and usually are one week in length.

Gross requirements (GR) are the total demand for an item derived from all of its parents.

Scheduled or planned receipts (S/PR) are orders that are due or planned to be delivered.

A **planned order receipt (PORec)** specifies the quantity and time an order is to be received.

A **planned order release (PORel)** specifies the planned quantity and time an order is to be released to the factory or a supplier.

Projected on-hand inventory (POH) is the expected amount of inventory on hand at the beginning of the time period considering on-hand inventory from the previous period plus scheduled receipts or planned order receipts minus the gross requirements.

Lot sizing is the process of determining the appropriate amount and timing of ordering to reduce costs.

An ordering schedule that covers the gross requirements for each week is called **lot for-lot (LFL)**.

The **action bucket** is the current time period.

The **fixed-order-quantity (FOQ)** rule uses a fixed order size for every order or production run.

The **periodic-order quantity (POQ)** orders a quantity equal to the gross requirement quantity in one or more predetermined time periods minus the projected on-hand quantity of the previous time period.

 13-5

Capacity requirements planning (CRP) is the process of determining the amount of labor and machine resources required to accomplish the tasks of production on a more detailed level, taking into account all component parts and end items in the materials plan.

of capacity requirements, provides input to the MRP system, and helps managers generate priorities for scheduling by setting due dates for the production of individual items.

MRP projects the requirements for the individual parts or subassemblies based on the demand for the finished goods as specified by the MPS. The primary output of an MRP system is a time-phased report that gives (1) the purchasing department a schedule for obtaining raw materials and purchased parts, (2) the production managers a detailed schedule for manufacturing the product and controlling manufacturing inventories, and (3) accounting and financial functions production information that drives cash flow, budgets, and financial needs. MRP depends on understanding three basic concepts: (1) the concept of dependent demand, (2) the concept of time phasing, and (3) lot sizing to gain economies of scale.

The concept of dependent demand is best understood by examining the bill of materials. Because of the hierarchy of the BOM, there is no reason to order something until it is required to produce a parent item. Thus, all dependent demand requirements do not need to be ordered at the same time, but rather are *time phased* as necessary (see LFL MRP time-phased record as an example). In addition, orders might be consolidated to take advantage of ordering economies of scale—this is called *lot sizing*.

An MRP record (see Exhibit 13.13) consists of the following:

- **Gross requirements (GR)**
- **Scheduled or planned receipts (S/PR)**
- **Projected on-hand inventory (POH)**
- **Planned order receipt (PORec)**
- **Planned order release (PORel)**

There are three common lot sizing methods for MRP—lot-for-lot (LFL), fixed-order quantity (FOQ), and periodic-order quantity (POQ). Lot sizing rules affect not only the planned order releases for the particular item under consideration, but also the gross requirements of all lower-level component items. Some MRP users only use the simple LFL rule; others apply other lot sizing approaches to take advantage of economies of scale and reduce costs.

13-5 **Explain the concept and application of capacity requirements planning.**

Capacity requirements are computed by multiplying the number of units scheduled for production at a work center by the unit resource requirements and then adding in the setup time. These requirements are then summarized by time period and work center. Such information is usually provided in a **work center load report**. If sufficient capacity is not available, decisions must be made about overtime, transfer of personnel between departments, subcontracting, and so on. The master production schedule may also have to be revised to meet available capacity by shifting certain end items to different time periods or changing the order quantities.

Exhibit 13.13 *MRP Record for Item C Using the Lot-for-Lot (LFL) Rule*

Item C (two units of C are needed for one unit of A) Description		Lot size: LFL Lead time: 2 weeks						
Week		1	2	3	4	5	6	7
Gross requirements		0	0	300	600	100	400	0
Scheduled receipts			200					
Projected OH inventory	10	10	210	0	0	0	0	0
Planned order receipts		0	0	90	600	100	400	0
Planned order releases		90	600	100	400			

© Cengage Learning 2013

reviewcard/ OM4 CHAPTER 14
OPERATIONS SCHEDULING AND SEQUENCING

Learning Outcomes

14-1 Explain the concepts of scheduling and sequencing.

Scheduling and sequencing are some of the more common activities that operations managers perform every day in every business. They are fundamental to all three levels of aggregation and disaggregation planning that we described in the previous chapter. Good schedules and sequences lead to efficient execution of manufacturing and service plans. Some examples of scheduling: fast-food restaurants, hospitals, and call centers need to schedule employees for work shifts; doctors, dentists, and stockbrokers need to schedule patients and customers; airlines must schedule crews and flight attendants; sports organizations must schedule teams and officials; court systems must schedule hearings and trials; factory managers need to schedule jobs on machines and preventive maintenance work; and salespersons need to schedule customer deliveries and visits to potential customers. Some examples of sequencing: triage nurses must decide on the order in which emergency patients are treated; housekeepers in hotels must sequence the order of rooms to clean; operations managers who run an automobile assembly line must determine the sequence by which different models are produced; and airport managers must sequence outgoing flights on runways.

14-2 Describe staff scheduling and appointment system decisions.

Staff scheduling problems are also prevalent in service organizations because of high variability in customer demand. Examples include scheduling call center representatives, hotel housekeepers, tollbooth operators, nurses, airline reservation clerks, police officers, fast-food restaurant employees, and many others.

Staff scheduling attempts to match available personnel with the needs of the organization by

1. accurately forecasting demand and translating it into the quantity and timing of work to be done;

2. determining the staffing required to perform the work by time period;

3. determining the personnel available and the full- and part-time mix; and

4. matching capacity to demand requirements, and developing a work schedule that maximizes service and minimizes costs.

The first step requires converting demand to a capacity measure, that is, the number of staff required. The second step determines the quantity and timing of the work to be done in detail, usually by hour of the day, and sometimes in 5- to 10-minute time intervals. Determining the staffing required must take into account worker productivity factors, personal allowances, sickness, vacations, no-shows, and so on. Step 4 focuses on the matching of capacity to demand requirements; this is the essence of scheduling.

A simple problem of scheduling personnel with consecutive days off in the face of fluctuating requirements can be solved as follows. First, locate the *set of at least two consecutive days with*

Key Terms

 14-1

Scheduling refers to the assignment of start and completion times to particular jobs, people, or equipment.

Sequencing refers to determining the order in which jobs or tasks are processed.

 14-3

Flow time is the amount of time a job spent in the shop or factory.

Makespan is the time needed to process a given set of jobs.

Lateness is the difference between the completion time and the due date (either positive or negative).

Tardiness is the amount of time by which the completion time exceeds the due date.

the smallest requirements. Circle the requirements for those two consecutive days. Assign staff to work on all days not circled and update the remaining requirements. When there are several alternatives, do one of two things. First, try to choose a pair of days with the lowest total requirement. If there are still ties, choose the first available pair that makes the most sense to the scheduler. Continue circling the smallest requirements until you obtain at least two consecutive days and repeat the procedure until all requirements are scheduled.

Appointments can be viewed as a reservation of service time and capacity. Using appointments provides a means to maximize the use of time-dependent service capacity and reduce the risk of no shows. Appointment systems are used in many businesses, such as consulting, tax preparation, music instruction, and medical, dental, and veterinarian practices. Indirectly, appointments reduce the cost of providing the service because the service provider is idle less each workday. An appointment system must try to accommodate customers and forecast their behavior, such as the no-show rate or a difficult customer who demands more processing time.

Four decisions to make regarding designing an appointment system are the following:

1. *Determine the appointment time interval,* such as 1 hour or 15 minutes.

2. Based on an analysis of each day's customer mix, *determine the length of each workday and the time off duty.*

3. *Decide how to handle overbooking* for each day of the week.

4. *Develop customer appointment rules* that maximize customer satisfaction.

14-3 Explain sequencing performance criteria and rules.

Sequencing criteria are often classified into three categories:

1. process-focused performance criteria,
2. customer-focused due date criteria, and
3. cost-based criteria.

Process-focused performance criteria pertain only to information about the start and end times of jobs and focus on shop performance such as equipment utilization and WIP inventory. Two common measures are flow time and makespan.

Due date criteria pertain to customers' required due dates or internally determined shipping dates. Common performance measures are lateness and tardiness, or the number of jobs tardy or late.

Cost-based performance criteria include inventory, changeover or setup, processing or run, and material-handling costs. In most cases, costs are considered implicitly in process performance and due-date criteria.

Two of the most popular sequencing rules for prioritizing jobs are the following:

- Shortest processing time (SPT)
- Earliest due date (EDD)

In other situations, new jobs arrive in an intermittent fashion, resulting in a constantly changing mix of jobs needing to be sequenced. In this case, we assign priorities to whatever jobs are available at a specific time and then update the priorities when new jobs arrive. Some examples of these priority rules are the following:

- First come, first served (FCFS)
- Fewest number of operations remaining (FNO)
- Least work remaining (LWR)—sum of all processing times for operations not yet performed
- Least amount of work at the next process queue (LWNQ)—amount of work awaiting the next process in a job's sequence

The SPT rule tends to minimize average flow time and WIP inventory and maximize resource utilization. The EDD rule minimizes the maximum of jobs past due but doesn't perform well on average flow time, WIP inventory, or resource utilization. The FCFS rule is used in many service-delivery systems and does not consider any job or customer criterion. FCFS focuses only on the time of arrival for the customer or job. The FNO rule does not consider the length of time for each operation; for example, a job may have many small operations and be scheduled last. Generally, this is not a very good rule. The LWNQ rule tries to keep downstream work stations and associated resources busy.

14-4 Describe how to solve single- and two-resource sequencing problems.

The simplest sequencing problem is that of processing a set of jobs on a single processor. For the single-processor sequencing problem, a very simple rule—shortest processing time—finds a minimal average flow time sequence. The EDD, which dictates sequencing jobs in order of earliest due date first, minimizes the

maximum job tardiness and job lateness. It does not minimize the average flow time or average lateness, as SPT does, however.

S.M. Johnson developed an algorithm for finding a minimum makespan schedule for a two-resource sequencing problem.

1. List the jobs and their processing times on Resources #1 and #2.
2. Find the job with the shortest processing time (on either resource).
3. If this time corresponds to Resource #1, sequence the job first; if it corresponds to Resource #2, sequence the job last.
4. Repeat steps 2 and 3, using the next-shortest processing time and working inward from both ends of the sequence until all jobs have been scheduled.

Gantt charts are often used to display the results, such as those shown in Exhibit 14.5.

14-5 Explain the need for monitoring schedules using Gantt charts.

Murphy's Law states that if something can go wrong it will, and this is especially true with schedules. Thus, it is important that progress be monitored on a continuing basis. Reschedules are a normal part of scheduling.

Short-term capacity fluctuations also necessitate changes in schedules. Factors affecting short-term capacity include absenteeism, labor performance, equipment failures, tooling problems, labor turnover, and material shortages. They are inevitable and unavoidable. Gantt (bar) charts are useful tools for monitoring schedules (see Exhibit 14.7).

Exhibit 14.5 *Gantt Job Sequence Chart for Hirsch Product Sequence 1-2-3-4-5*

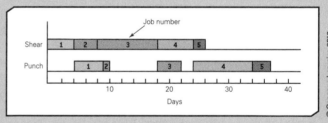

Exhibit 14.7 *Gantt Chart Example for Monitoring Schedule Progress*

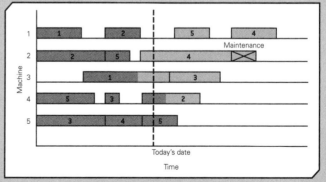

Learning Outcomes

15-1 Explain the concepts and definitions of quality.

Many perspectives on quality relate to a good or service's fitness for use. From an operations perspective, however, the most useful definition is how well the output of a manufacturing or service process conforms to the design specifications. Excellent service quality is achieved by the consistent delivery to the customer of a clearly defined customer benefit package and associated process and service encounters, defined by many internal and external standards of performance.

An established instrument for measuring the external customer perceptions of service quality is SERVQUAL, which identifies five key dimensions: tangibles, reliability, responsiveness, assurance, and empathy.

The principles of total quality are simple:

- a focus on customers and stakeholders,
- a process focus supported by continuous improvement and learning, and
- participation and teamwork by everyone in the organization.

15-2 Describe the quality philosophies and principles of Deming, Juran, and Crosby.

The Deming philosophy focuses on bringing about improvements in product and service quality by reducing variability in goods and services design and associated processes. Deming professed that higher quality leads to higher productivity and lower costs, which in turn leads to improved market share and long-term competitive strength. In his early work in the United States, Deming preached his 14 Points:

Point 1: *Create a Vision and Demonstrate Commitment*

Point 2: *Learn the Philosophy*

Point 3: *Understand Inspection*

Point 4: *Stop Making Decisions Purely on the Basis of Cost*

Point 5: *Improve Constantly and Forever*

Point 6: *Institute Training*

Point 7: *Institute Leadership*

Point 8: *Drive Out Fear*

Point 9: *Optimize the Efforts of Teams*

Point 10: *Eliminate Exhortations*

Point 11: *Eliminate Numerical Quotas*

Point 12: *Remove Barriers to Pride in Work*

Point 13: *Encourage Education and Self-Improvement*

Point 14: *Take Action*

Juran proposed a simple definition of quality: "fitness for use." Unlike Deming, however, Juran did not propose a major cultural change in the organization, but rather sought to improve quality by working within the system familiar to managers. Juran stated that top management speaks in the language of dollars; workers speak in the language of things; and middle management must be able to speak both languages and translate between dollars and things. Thus, to get the attention of top managers, quality issues must be cast in the language they understand—dollars.

Crosby's Absolutes of Quality Management include the following points:

- *Quality means conformance to requirements, not elegance.*
- *There is no such thing as a quality problem.*

Key Terms

 15-1

Quality management refers to systematic policies, methods, and procedures used to ensure that goods and services are produced with appropriate levels of quality to meet the needs of customers.

Fitness for use is the ability of a good or service to meet customer needs.

Quality of conformance is the extent to which a process is able to deliver output that conforms to the design specifications.

Specifications are targets and tolerances determined by designers of goods and services.

Service quality is consistently meeting or exceeding customer expectations (external focus) and service-delivery system performance criteria (internal focus) during all service encounters.

 15-5

Six Sigma is a business improvement approach that seeks to find and eliminate causes of defects and errors in manufacturing and service processes by focusing on outputs that are critical to customers, resulting in a clear financial return for the organization.

A **defect** is any mistake or error that is passed on to the customer.

A **unit of work** is the output of a process or an individual process step.

 15-6

The **cost of quality** refers specifically to the costs associated with avoiding poor quality or those incurred as a result of poor quality.

Prevention costs are those expended to keep nonconforming goods and services from being made and reaching the customer.

Appraisal costs are those expended on ascertaining quality levels through measurement and analysis of data to detect and correct problems.

Internal failure costs are costs incurred as a result of unsatisfactory quality that is found before the delivery of a good or service to the customer.

External failure costs are incurred after poor-quality goods or services reach the customer.

Key Terms

Kaizen focuses on small, gradual, and frequent improvements over the long term with minimum financial investment and with participation by everyone in the organization.

A **kaizen blitz** is an intense and rapid improvement process in which a team or a department throws all its resources into an improvement project over a short time period, as opposed to traditional kaizen applications, which are performed on a part-time basis.

Poka-yoke (POH-kah YOH-kay) is an approach for mistake-proofing processes using automatic devices or methods to avoid simple human error.

- *There is no such thing as the economics of quality; doing the job right the first time is always cheaper.*
- *The only performance measurement is the cost of quality, which is the expense of nonconformance.*
- *The only performance standard is "Zero Defects (ZD)."*

15-3 Explain the GAP model and its importance.

The GAP model (see Exhibit 15.1) recognizes that there are several ways to misspecify and mismanage the creation and delivery of high levels of quality.

- **Gap 1** *is the discrepancy between customer expectations and management perceptions of those expectations.*
- **Gap 2** *is the discrepancy between management perceptions of what features constitute a target level of quality and the task of translating these perceptions into executable specifications.*
- **Gap 3** *is the discrepancy between quality specifications documented in operating and training manuals and plans and their implementation.*

- **Gap 4** *is the discrepancy between actual manufacturing and service-delivery system performance and external communications to the customers.*
- **Gap 5** *is the difference between the customer's expectations and perceptions.*

15-4 Describe the concepts and philosophy of ISO 9000:2000.

ISO 9000 defines *quality system standards*. The ISO 9000:2000 standards are supported by the following eight principles:

Principle 1—Customer-Focused Organization

Principle 2—Leadership

Principle 3—Involvement of People

Principle 4—Process Approach

Principle 5—System Approach to Management

Principle 6—Continual Improvement

Principle 7—Factual Approach to Decision Making

Principle 8—Mutually Beneficial Supplier Relationships

15-5 Describe the philosophy and methods of Six Sigma.

The term *Six Sigma* is based on a statistical measure that equates to at most 3.4 errors or defects per million opportunities.

The core philosophy of Six Sigma is based on some key concepts:

- emphasizing dpmo or epmo as a standard metric that can be applied to all parts of an organization: manufacturing, engineering, administrative, software, and so on;
- providing extensive training followed by project team deployment to improve profitability, reduce non-value-added activities, and achieve cycle time reduction;
- focusing on corporate sponsors responsible for supporting team activities to help overcome resistance to change, obtain resources, and focus the teams on overall strategic objectives;
- creating highly qualified process improvement experts ("green belts," "black belts," and "master black belts") who can apply improvement tools and lead teams;

- ensuring that appropriate metrics are identified early in the process and that they focus on business results; and
- setting stretch objectives for improvement.

The Six Sigma problem-solving approach is Define, Measure, Analyze, Improve, and Control (DMAIC).

15-6 Explain the categories of cost-of-quality measurement.

Quality costs can be organized into four major categories: prevention costs, appraisal costs, internal failure costs, and external failure costs. By collecting and analyzing these costs, managers can identify the most important opportunities for improvement.

15-7 Describe how to apply the Seven QC Tools.

Seven simple tools—flowcharts, checksheets, histograms, Pareto diagrams, cause-and-effect diagrams, scatter diagrams, and control charts—termed the *Seven QC* (Quality Control) *Tools* by the Japanese, support quality improvement problem-solving efforts. The Seven QC Tools are designed to be simple and visual so that workers at all levels can use them easily and provide a means of communication that is particularly well suited in group problem-solving efforts. Root cause analysis often uses the Seven QC Tools. The root cause is a term used to designate the source of a problem.

15-8 Explain the concepts of kaizen and poka-yoke.

The concept of continuous improvement is known as *kaizen*. In the kaizen philosophy, improvement in all areas of business—cost, meeting delivery schedules, employee safety and skill development, supplier relations, new product development, productivity—serve to enhance the quality of the firm.

Human beings tend to make mistakes inadvertently. Typical process-related mistakes include omitted processing steps, processing errors, setup or changeover errors, missing information or parts, not handling service upsets properly, wrong information or parts, and adjustment errors. Poka-yoke is designed to prevent such errors from occurring.

Learning Outcomes

16-1 Describe quality control systems and key issues in manufacturing and service.

Any control system has three components:

1. a performance standard or goal,
2. a means of measuring actual performance, and
3. comparison of actual performance with the standard to form the basis for corrective action.

The importance of control is often explained by the *1:10:100 Rule:*

If a defect or service error is identified and corrected at the design stage, it might cost $1 to fix. If it is first detected during the production process, it might cost $10 to fix. However, if the defect is not discovered until it reaches the customer, it might cost $100 to correct.

In manufacturing, control is generally applied at three key points in the supply chain: at the receiving stage from suppliers, during various production processes, and at the finished-goods stage.

One way to control quality in services is to prevent sources of errors and mistakes in the first place by using the poka-yoke approaches. Another way is to hire and train service providers in service management skills as part of a prevention-based approach to quality control.

16-2 Explain types of variation and the role of statistical process control (SPC).

Variation occurs for many reasons, such as inconsistencies in material inputs; changes in environmental conditions (temperature, humidity); machine maintenance cycles; customer participation and self-service; tool wear; and human fatigue. Common cause variation is the responsibility of management while front-line employees focus more on special cause variation.

16-3 Describe how to construct and interpret simple control charts for both continuous and discrete data.

The five steps required to develop and construct control charts are (1) preparation such as choose the metric to be monitored and determine sample size and the frequency; (2) collect the data and calculate basic statistics; (3) determine trial upper and lower control limits and center line; (4) investigate and interpret the control chart, eliminate out-of-control points, and recompute the control limits; and (5) use problem-solving tools and take corrective action(s).

Key formulas for an $\bar{x}$- and R-chart are

$$\bar{\bar{x}} = \frac{\sum_{i=1}^{k} \bar{x}_i}{k} \qquad [16.1]$$

$$\bar{R} = \frac{\sum_{i=1}^{k} R_i}{k} \qquad [16.2]$$

$$UCL_R = D_4\bar{R} \qquad UCL_{\bar{x}} = \bar{\bar{x}} + A_2\bar{R}$$

$$LCL_R = D_3\bar{R} \qquad LCL_{\bar{x}} = \bar{\bar{x}} - A_2\bar{R} \qquad [16.3]$$

where $\bar{x}$ is the average of the *i*th sample.

Key formulas for a *p*-chart are

$$\bar{p} = \frac{p_1 + p_2 + \ldots + p_k}{k} \qquad [16.4]$$

Key Terms

 16-1

The task of **quality control** is to ensure that a good or service conforms to specifications and meets customer requirements by monitoring and measuring processes and making any necessary adjustments to maintain a specified level of performance.

Quality at the source means the people responsible for the work control the quality of their processes by identifying and correcting any defects or errors when they first are recognized or occur.

 16-2

Statistical process control (SPC) is a methodology for monitoring the quality of manufacturing and service-delivery processes to help identify and eliminate unwanted causes of variation.

Common cause variation is the result of complex interactions of variations in materials, tools, machines, information, workers, and the environment.

Special (or assignable) cause variation arises from external sources that are not inherent in the process, appear sporadically, and disrupt the random pattern of common causes.

If no special causes affect the output of a process, we say that the process is **in control;** when special causes are present, the process is said to be **out of control.**

 16-3

A **continuous metric** is one that is calculated from data that are measured as the degree of conformance to a specification on some continuous scale of measurement.

A **discrete metric** is one that is calculated from data that are counted.

 16-5

Process capability refers to the natural variation in a process that results from common causes.

A **process capability study** is a carefully planned study designed to yield specific information about the performance of a process under specified operating conditions.

The relationship between the natural variation and specifications is often quantified by a measure known as the **process capability index.**

$$S_{\bar{p}} = \sqrt{\frac{\bar{p}(1-\bar{p})}{n}}$$ [16.5]

$$UCL_p = \bar{p} + 3s_{\bar{p}}$$

$$LCL_p = \bar{p} - 3s_{\bar{p}}$$ [16.6]

where p_i is the fraction nonconforming in the ith sample.

Key formulas for a c-chart are

$$UCL_c = \bar{c} + 3\sqrt{\bar{c}}$$

$$LCL_c = \bar{c} - 3\sqrt{\bar{c}}$$ [16.7]

where $\bar{c}$ is the average number of nonconformances per unit.

A process is in control when the control chart has the following characteristics:

1. No points are outside control limits.

2. The number of points above and below the center line is about the same.

3. The points seem to fall randomly above and below the center line.

4. Most points, but not all, are near the center line, and only a few are close to the control limits.

16-4 Describe practical issues in implementing SPC.

Designing control charts involves two key issues:

1. sample size, and

2. sampling frequency.

A small sample size is desirable to keep the cost associated with sampling low. On the other hand, large sample sizes provide greater degrees of statistical accuracy in estimating the true state of control. Large samples also allow smaller changes in process characteristics to be detected with higher probability. In practice, samples of about 5 have been found to work well in detecting process shifts of 2 standard deviations or larger. To detect smaller shifts in the process mean, larger sample sizes of 15 to 25 must be used.

Taking large samples on a frequent basis is desirable but clearly not economical. No hard-and-fast rules exist for the frequency of sampling. Samples should be close enough to provide an opportunity to detect changes in process characteristics as soon as possible and reduce the chances of producing a large amount of nonconforming output. However, they should not be so close that the cost of sampling outweighs the benefits that can be realized.

SPC is a useful methodology for processes that operate at a low sigma level—for example, the three-sigma level or less. However, when the rate of defects is extremely low, standard control charts are not effective.

Example Problem

A controlled process shows an overall mean of 2.50 and an average range of 0.42. Samples of size 4 were used to construct the control charts. What is the process capability? If specifications are 2.60 ± 0.25, how well can this process meet them?

From Appendix B, $d_2 = 2.059$ and $\sigma = \bar{R}/d_2 = 0.42 / 2.059 = 0.20$. Thus, the process capability is $2.50 \pm 3(0.020)$, or 1.90 to 3.10. Because the specification range is 2.35 to 2.85 with a target of 2.60, we may conclude that the observed natural variation exceeds the specifications by a large amount. In addition, the process is off-center (see the exhibit below).

Comparison of Observed Variation and Design Specifications

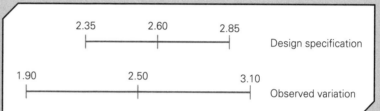

© Cengage Learning 2013

16-5 Explain process capability and calculate process capability indexes.

Knowing process capability allows one to predict, quantitatively, how well a process will meet specifications and to specify equipment requirements and the level of control necessary. Process capability has no meaning if the process is not in statistical control because special causes will bias the mean or the standard deviation. Therefore, we should use control charts to first eliminate any special causes before computing the process capability.

Typical questions that are asked in a process capability study are the following:

• Where is the process centered?

• How much variability exists in the process?

• Is the performance relative to specifications acceptable?

• What proportion of output will be expected to meet specifications?

The process capability index, C_p, is defined as the ratio of the specification width to the natural tolerance of the process.

$$C_p = \frac{USL - LSL}{6\sigma}$$ [16.9]

Values of C_p exceeding 1 indicate good capability. To account for the process centering, one-sided capability indexes are often used:

$$C_{pu} = \frac{USL - \mu}{3\sigma} \text{ (upper one-sided index)}$$ [16.10]

$$C_{pl} = \frac{\mu - LSL}{3\sigma} \text{ (lower one-sided index)}$$ [16.11]

$$C_{pk} = \min(C_{pl}, C_{pu})$$ [16.12]

Learning Outcomes

17-1 Explain the four principles of lean operating systems.

Lean operating systems have four basic principles:

1. elimination of waste,
2. increased speed and response,
3. improved quality, and
4. reduced cost

The Toyota Motor Company classified waste into seven major categories:

1. *Overproduction*: for example, making a batch of 100 when there are orders for only 50 in order to avoid an expensive setup, or making a batch of 52 instead of 50 in case there are rejects. Overproduction ties up production facilities, and the resulting excess inventory simply sits idle.

2. *Waiting time*: for instance, allowing queues to build up between operations, resulting in longer lead times and more work-in-process.

3. *Transportation*: the time and effort spent in moving products around the factory as a result of poor layout.

4. *Processing*: the traditional notion of waste, as exemplified by scrap that often results from poor product or process design.

5. *Inventory*: waste associated with the expense of idle stock and extra storage and handling requirements needed to maintain it.

6. *Motion*: as a result of inefficient workplace design and location of tools and materials.

7. *Production defects*: the result of not performing work correctly the first time.

Lean operating systems focus on quick and efficient response in designing and getting goods and services to market, producing to customer demand and delivery requirements, responding to competitors' actions, collecting payments, and addressing customer inquiries or problems.

17-2 Describe the basic lean tools and approaches.

The 5Ss are derived from Japanese terms: seiri *(sort),* seiton *(set in order),* seiso *(shine),* seiketsu *(standardize), and* shitsuke *(sustain).*

- *Sort* refers to ensuring that each item in a workplace is in its proper place or identified as unnecessary and removed.

- *Set in order* means to arrange materials and equipment so that they are easy to find and use.

- *Shine* refers to a clean work area. Not only is this important for safety, but as a work area is cleaned, maintenance problems such as oil leaks can be identified before they cause problems.

- *Standardize* means to formalize procedures and practices to create consistency and ensure that all steps are performed correctly.

- Finally, *sustain* means to keep the process going through training, communication, and organizational structures.

Visual signaling systems are known as *andon*, drawing from the Japanese term from which the concept first originated. For example, if a machine fails or a part is defective or manufactured incorrectly, a light might turn on or a buzzer might sound, indicating that immediate action should be taken. Many firms have cords that operators can pull that tell supervisors and other workers that a problem has occurred.

Key Terms

 17-1

Lean thinking refers to approaches that focus on the elimination of waste in all forms, and smooth, efficient flow of materials and information throughout the value chain to obtain faster customer response, higher quality, and lower costs.

Manufacturing and service operations that apply the principles of lean enterprise are often called **lean operating systems.**

 17-2

The **5Ss** are derived from Japanese terms: *seiri* (sort), *seiton* (set in order), *seiso* (shine), *seiketsu* (standardize), and *shitsuke* (sustain).

Visual controls are indicators for operating activities that are placed in plain sight of all employees so that everyone can quickly and easily understand the status and performance of the work system.

Single Minute Exchange of Dies (SMED) refers to the quick setup or changeover of tooling and fixtures in processes so that multiple products in smaller batches can be run on the same equipment.

Batching is the process of producing large quantities of items as a group before they are transferred to the next operation.

Single-piece flow is the concept of ideally using batch sizes of one.

Total productive maintenance (TPM) is focused on ensuring that operating systems will perform their intended function reliably.

 17-5

A **push system** produces finished-goods inventory in advance of customer demand using a forecast of sales.

A **pull system** is one in which employees at a given operation go to the source of required parts, such as machining or subassembly, and withdraw the units as they need them.

A **Kanban** is a flag or a piece of paper that contains all relevant information for an order: part number, description, process area used, time of delivery, quantity available, quantity delivered, production quantity, and so on.

Single Minute Exchange of Dies (SMED), pioneered by Toyota and other Japanese manufacturers, refers to quickly changing tooling and fixtures to reduce setup time and achieve higher flexibility and productivity.

Batching is often necessary when producing a broad goods or service mix with diverse requirements on common equipment. By running large batches, setups and teardowns are reduced, providing economies of scale. However, this often builds up inventory that might not match market demand, particularly in highly dynamic markets. A better strategy would be to use small batches or single-piece flow. However, to do this economically requires the ability to change between products quickly and inexpensively.

Quality at the source eliminates opportunities for waste and is a fundamental approach in lean thinking.

The goal of total productive maintenance is to prevent equipment failures and downtime—ideally, to have "zero accidents, zero defects, and zero failures" in the entire life cycle of the operating system.

Many companies are actively recovering and recycling parts (sometimes called *green manufacturing*).

17-3 Explain the concept of Lean Six Sigma and how it is applied to improving operations performance.

Six Sigma is a useful and complementary approach to lean production. Lean Six Sigma draws upon the best practices of both approaches; however, they attack different types of problems. Lean production addresses visible problems in processes, for example, inventory, material flow, and safety. Six Sigma is more concerned with less visible problems, for example, variation in performance.

17-4 Explain how lean principles are used in manufacturing and service organizations.

Lean manufacturing plants look significantly different from traditional plants. They are clean and organized, devoid of long and complex production lines and high levels of work-in-process, have efficient layouts and work area designs, use multiskilled workers that perform both direct and indirect work such as maintenance, and have no incoming or final inspection stations.

Lean principles are not always transferable to "front-office" services that involve high customer contact and service encounters. Different customers, service-encounter situations, and customer and employee behaviors cause the creation and delivery of the service to be much more variable and uncertain than producing a manufactured good in the confines of a factory. However, "back-office" service processes, such as hospital laboratory testing, check processing, and college application processing, are nearly identical to many manufacturing processes.

17-5 Describe the concepts and philosophy of just-in-time operating systems.

Just-in-time (JIT) was introduced at Toyota during the 1950s and 1960s to address the challenge of coordinating successive production activities. Toyota created a system based on a simple idea: Produce the needed quantity of required parts each day. Then just enough new parts are manufactured or procured to replace those withdrawn. As the process from which parts were withdrawn replenishes the items it transferred out, it draws on the output of its preceding process, and so on. Finished goods are made to coincide with the actual rate of demand, resulting in minimal inventories and maximum responsiveness.

A JIT system can produce a steady rate of output to meet the sales rate in small, consistent batch sizes to level loads and stabilize the operating system. This dramatically reduces the inventory required between stages of the production process, thus greatly reducing costs and physical capacity requirements. In a JIT process, the customer cycle withdraws what is needed at the time it is needed according to sales. The supply cycle creates the good to replenish only what has been withdrawn by the customer. The storage area is the interface and control point between the customer and supply cycles.

Slips, called Kanban cards (*Kanban* is a Japanese word that means "visual record" or "card"), are circulated within the system to initiate withdrawal and production items through the production process. The number of Kanban cards is directly proportional to the amount of work-in-process inventory. Exhibit 17.3 summarizes key characteristics and best practices for JIT systems.

Exhibit 17.3 *Example JIT Characteristics and Best Practices*

- Setup/changeover time minimized
- Excellent preventive maintenance
- Mistake-proof job and process design
- Stable, level, repetitive master production schedule
- Phantom bill of materials with zero lead time
- Fast processing times
- Clean and uncluttered workspaces
- Very little inventory to hide problems and inefficiencies
- Use production cells with no wasted motion
- May freeze the master production schedule
- Use reusable containers
- Outstanding communication and information sharing
- Keep it simple and use visual controls
- High quality approaching zero defects

- Small repetitive order/lot sizes
- Minimize the number of parts/items
- Minimize the number of bill of materials levels
- Facility layout that supports continuous or single-piece flow
- Minimize distance traveled and handling
- Clearly defined performance metrics
- Minimize the number of production, inventory, and accounting transactions
- Good calibration of all gauges and testing equipment
- Employees trained in quality management concepts and tools
- Excellent employee recognition and reward systems
- Employee cross-training and multiple skills
- Empowered and disciplined employees

Learning Outcomes

18-1 **Explain the key issues associated with project management**

In many firms, projects are the major value-creation process, and the major activities in the value chain revolve around projects. In other firms, projects are used on an infrequent basis to implement new strategies and initiatives or for supporting value chain design and improvement activities.

Most projects go through similar stages from start to completion:

1. *Define:* The first step in managing a project is to clearly define the goal of the project, responsibilities, deliverables, and when it must be accomplished.

2. *Plan:* In this stage, the steps needed to execute a project are defined, it is determined who will perform these steps, and the start and completion dates are developed.

3. *Organize:* Organizing involves such activities as identifying a project manager, forming a team, allocating resources, calculating costs, assessing risk, preparing project documentation, and ensuring good communications.

4. *Control:* This stage assesses how well a project meets its goals and objectives and makes adjustments as necessary.

5. *Close:* Closing a project involves compiling statistics, releasing and/or reassigning people, and preparing "lessons learned."

The job of project managers is to build an effective team, motivate team members, provide advice and support, align the project with the firm's strategy, and direct and supervise the conduct of the project from beginning to end. In addition to managing the project, they must manage the relationships among the project team, the parent organization, and the client. The project manager must also have sufficient technical expertise to resolve disputes among functional specialists.

A matrix organizational structure that "lends" resources to projects while still maintaining control over them is an effective structure for projects. Project managers coordinate the work across the functions. This minimizes duplication of resources and facilitates communication across the organization but requires that resources be negotiated. Ensuring project success depends on having well-defined goals and objectives, clear reporting relationships and channels of communication, good procedures for estimating time and other resource requirements, cooperation and commitment among all project team members, realistic expectations, effective conflict resolution, and top management sponsorship.

Exhibit 18.2 *Contributors and Impediments to Project Success*

Contributors to Project Success	Impediments to Project Success
Well-defined and agreed-upon objectives	Ill-defined project objectives
Top management support	Lack of executive champion
Strong project manager leadership	Inability to develop and motivate people
Well-defined project definition	Poorly defined project definition
Accurate time and cost estimates	Lack of data accuracy and integrity
Teamwork and cooperation	Poor interpersonal relations and teamwork
Effective use of project management tools	Ineffective use of project management tools
Clear channels of communication	Poor communication among stakeholders
Adequate resources and reasonable deadlines	Unreasonable time pressures and lack of resources
Constructive response to conflict	Inability to resolve conflicts

Key Terms

 18-1

A **project** is a temporary and often customized initiative that consists of many smaller tasks and activities that must be coordinated and completed to finish the entire initiative on time and within budget.

Project management involves all activities associated with planning, scheduling, and controlling projects.

 18-2

Activities are discrete tasks that consume resources and time.

Immediate predecessors are those activities that must be completed immediately before an activity may start.

The **work breakdown structure** is a hierarchical tree of end items that will be accomplished by the project team during the project.

A **project network** consists of a set of circles or boxes, called **nodes,** which represent activities, and a set of arrows, called **arcs,** which define the precedence relationships between activities.

The **critical path** is the sequence of activities that takes the longest time and defines the total project completion time.

A **schedule** specifies when activities are to be performed.

 18-3

Crashing a project refers to reducing the total time to complete the project to meet a revised due date.

Crash time is the shortest possible time in which the activity can realistically be completed.

The **crash cost** is the total additional cost associated with completing an activity in its crash time rather than in its normal time.

Crashing an activity refers to reducing its normal time, possibly up to its limit—the crash time.

18-2 Describe how to apply the Critical Path Method (CPM).

All project management decisions involve three factors: *time, resources*, and *cost*. Various techniques have long been used to help plan, schedule, and control projects. The key steps involved are the following:

1. *Project Definition:* Identifying the activities that must be completed and the sequence required to perform them.

2. *Resource Planning:* For each activity, determining the resource needs: personnel, time, money, equipment, materials, and so on.

3. *Project Scheduling:* Specifying a time schedule for the completion of each activity.

4. *Project Control:* Establishing the proper controls for determining progress and developing alternative plans in anticipation of problems in meeting the planned schedule.

The **Critical Path Method (CPM)** is an approach to scheduling and controlling project activities. CPM assumes:

- The project network defines a correct sequence of work in terms of technology and workflow.

- Activities are assumed to be independent of one another with clearly defined start and finish dates.

- The activity time estimates are accurate and stable.

- Once an activity is started it continues uninterrupted until it is completed.

Earliest start (ES) and earliest finish (EF) times are computed by moving through the project network in a forward direction from start to finish, sometimes called the *forward pass*, through the network.

Rule 1: The earliest time that an activity can be completed is equal to the earliest time it can begin plus the time to perform the activity.

Rule 2: The ES time for an activity equals the largest EF time of all immediate predecessors.

Latest start (LS) and latest finish (LF) times are computed by making a *backward pass* through the network, beginning with the ending project activity or activities.

Rule 3: The latest start time for an activity is equal to its LF time minus the activity time.

Rule 4: The LF time for an activity is the smallest LS time of all immediate successors.

Slack time is computed as $ST = LS - ES$ or $LF - EF$.

The critical path (CP) is the longest path(s) through the project network; activities on the critical path have zero slack time $(ST = 0)$ and if delayed will cause the total project to be delayed.

Because of the uncertainty of task times, unavoidable delays, or other problems, projects rarely, if ever, progress on schedule. Managers must therefore monitor performance of the project and take corrective action when needed. Gantt charts are often used for this purpose.

18-3 Explain how to make time/cost trade-off decisions in projects.

The first step is to determine the amount of time by which each activity may be reduced and its associated cost. Then determine the crash cost per unit of time for each activity. To find the crash schedule that minimizes the project completion time, use a trial-and-error approach.

18-4 Describe how to calculate probabilities for project completion time using PERT.

PERT (Project Evaluation and Review Technique) was developed as a means of handling the uncertainties in activity completion times. The PERT procedure uses the variance in the critical path activities to understand the risk associated with completing the project on time.

When activity times are uncertain, they are often treated as random variables with associated probability distributions. Usually three time estimates are obtained for each activity: optimistic, most probable, and pessimistic times.

The expected project completion time is the sum of the expected times for the activities on the critical path. The variance in project duration is given by the sum of the variances of the critical path activities.

$$\text{Expected time} = (a + 4m + b)/6 \qquad [18.2]$$

$$\text{Variance} = (b - a)^2/36 \qquad [18.3]$$

Using this information, we can compute the probability of meeting a specified completion date.

XEROX GLOBAL SERVICES: PROJECT MANAGERS ARE CRITICAL!

Xerox Global Services is a consulting, integration, and outsourcing arm of Xerox Corporation with a vision "To provide the most comprehensive, most effective connections between people, knowledge, and documents that the world has ever seen." Central to Xerox Global Services' delivery of services is project management. The project manager manages a team that includes technical resource specialists, consultants, and project coordinators. The principal role of the project manager at Xerox Global Services is that of a customer advocate—to ensure that expectations are fully met. This requires careful understanding and documentation of customer expectations such as timeliness, meeting budget, system response, and security. As a manager in the project office notes, "Most projects fail because user requirements are not understood." These requirements are translated into a detailed work breakdown structure with specific tasks assigned to project team members. This also helps to prepare a budget and monitor progress. Finally, after each project is completed, the team conducts a review of "lessons learned"—What went right? and What went wrong?—to continuously improve the company's ability to meet its customer expectations.

Break-even quantity for outsourcing

$$Q^* = \frac{FC}{VC_2 - VC_1}$$ [2.1]

Productivity

$$\text{Productivity} = \frac{\text{Quantity of output}}{\text{Quantity of input}}$$ [3.1]

Value of a loyal customer

$$VLC = (P)(CM)(RF)(BLC)$$ [3.2]

Taguchi loss function

$$L(x) = k(x - T)^2$$ [6.1]

System reliability of an *n*-component series system

$$R_s = (p_1)(p_2)(p_3) \dots (p_n)$$ [6.2]

System reliability of an *n*-component parallel system

$$R_p = 1 - (1 - p_1)(1 - p_2)(1 - p_3) \dots (1 - p_n)$$ [6.3]

Resource utilization

$$\text{Utilization (U)} = \frac{\text{Resources used}}{\text{Resources available}}$$ [7.1]

$$\text{Utilization (U)} = \frac{\text{Demand rate}}{[\text{Service rate} \times \text{Number of servers}]}$$ [7.2]

Little's Law

$$WIP = R \times T$$ [7.3]

Feasible range of cycle times

$$\text{Maximum operation time} \leq CT \leq \text{Sum of operation times}$$ [8.1]

Cycle time

$$CT = A/R$$ [8.2]

Theoretical minimum number of workstations

Minimum number of workstations required =
Sum of task times/Cycle time $= \Sigma t / CT$ [8.3]
Total time available
$= (\text{Number of workstations})(\text{Cycle time})$
$= (N)(CT)$ [8.4]
Total idle time $= (N)(CT) - \Sigma t$ [8.5]
Assembly-line efficiency $= \Sigma t / (N \times CT)$ [8.6]
Balance delay $= 1 - \text{Assembly-line efficiency}$ [8.7]

Center of gravity

$$C_x = \Sigma X_i W_i / \Sigma W_i$$ [9.1]
$$C_y = \Sigma Y_i W_i / \Sigma W_i$$ [9.2]

Average safety capacity

Average safety capacity (%) =
100% − Average resource utilization (%) [10.1]

Capacity required to meet a given production volume for one work order (*i*)

Capacity required $(C_i) =$
Setup time $(S_i) + [\text{Processing time } (P_i) \times \text{Order size } (Q_i)]$ [10.2]

Total capacity required over all work orders

$$\Sigma C_i = \Sigma [S_i + (P_i \times Q_i)]$$ [10.3]

Mean square error (MSE)

$$MSE = \frac{\Sigma (A_t - F_t)^2}{T}$$ [11.1]

Mean absolute deviation (MAD)

$$MAD = \frac{\Sigma |A_t - F_t|}{T}$$ [11.2]

Mean absolute percentage error

$$MAPE = \frac{\Sigma |(A_t - F_t)/A_t| \times 100}{T}$$ [11.3]

Moving average (MA) forecast

$$F_{t+1} = \Sigma(\text{most recent "}k\text{" observations})/k$$
$$= (A_t + A_{t-1} + A_{t-2} + \dots + A_{t-k+1})/k$$ [11.4]

Exponential-smoothing forecasting model

$$F_{t+1} = \alpha A_t + (1 - \alpha)F_t = F_t + \alpha (A_t - F_t)$$ [11.5]

Smoothing constant approximate relationship to the value of *k* in the moving average model

$$\alpha = 2/(k + 1)$$ [11.6]

Linear regression forecasting model

$$Y_t = a + bt$$ [11.7]

Tracking signal

$$\text{Tracking signal} = \Sigma(A_t - F_t)/MAD$$ [11.8]

Inventory position (IP)

$$IP = OH + SR - BO$$ [12.1]

Average cycle inventory

Average cycle inventory = (Maximum inventory + Minimum inventory)/2 $= Q/2$ [12.2]

Holding cost

$$C_h = (I)(C)$$ [12.3]

Annual inventory holding cost

$$\begin{pmatrix} \text{Annual} \\ \text{inventory} \\ \text{holding cost} \end{pmatrix} = \begin{pmatrix} \text{Average} \\ \text{inventory} \end{pmatrix} \begin{pmatrix} \text{Annual} \\ \text{holding cost} \\ \text{per unit} \end{pmatrix} = \frac{1}{2}QC_h$$ [12.4]

Annual ordering cost

$$\begin{pmatrix} \text{Annual} \\ \text{ordering} \\ \text{cost} \end{pmatrix} = \begin{pmatrix} \text{Number} \\ \text{of orders} \\ \text{per year} \end{pmatrix} \begin{pmatrix} \text{Cost} \\ \text{per} \\ \text{order} \end{pmatrix} = \frac{D}{Q}C_0$$ [12.5]

Total annual cost

$$TC = \frac{1}{2}QC_h + \frac{D}{Q}C_0$$ [12.6]

Economic order quantity

$$Q^* = \sqrt{\frac{2DC_0}{C_h}} \qquad [12.7]$$

Reorder point

r = Lead time demand = (Demand rate)(Lead time)

$$= (d)(L) \qquad [12.8]$$

Reorder point with safety stock

$$r = \mu_L + z\sigma_L \qquad [12.9]$$

Mean demand during lead time with uncertain demand

$$\mu_L = \mu_t L \qquad [12.10]$$

Standard deviation of demand during lead time with uncertain demand

$$\sigma_L = \sigma_t \sqrt{L} \qquad [12.11]$$

Economic time interval

$$T = Q^*/D \qquad [12.12]$$

Replenishment level without safety stock (FPS)

$$M = d(T + L) \qquad [12.13]$$

Replenishment level with safety stock (FPS)

$$M = \mu_{T+L} = z\sigma_{T+L} \qquad [12.14]$$
$$\mu_{T+L} = \mu_t(T + L) \qquad [12.15]$$
$$\sigma_{T+L} = \sigma_t \sqrt{T + L} \qquad [12.16]$$

Marginal economic analysis for a single-period inventory model

$$P(\text{demand} \leq Q^*) = \frac{c_u}{c_u + c_s} \qquad [12.17]$$

Projected on-hand inventory

Ending inventory = Beginning inventory
$$+ \text{Production} - \text{Demand} \qquad [13.1]$$

Projected on-hand in period t (POH$_t$) = On-hand inventory in period $t - 1$ (OH$_{t-1}$)

or

$$\text{POH}_t = \text{OH}_{t-1} + \text{S/PR}_t - \text{GR}_t \qquad [13.2]$$

Flow time

$$F_i = \Sigma p_{ij} + \Sigma w_{ij} = C_i - R_i \qquad [14.1]$$

Makespan

$$M = C - S \qquad [14.2]$$

Lateness (L)

$$L_i = C_i - D_i \qquad [14.3]$$

Tardiness (T)

$$T_i = \text{Max}\,(0, L_i) \qquad [14.4]$$

Overall mean

$$\bar{\bar{x}} = \frac{\sum\limits_{i=1}^{k} \bar{x}_i}{k} \qquad [16.1]$$

Average range

$$\bar{R} = \frac{\sum\limits_{i=1}^{k} R_i}{k} \qquad [16.2]$$

Upper and lower control limits

$$UCL_R = D_4\bar{R} \qquad UCL_{\bar{x}} = \bar{\bar{x}} + A_2\bar{R}$$
$$LCL_R = D_3\bar{R} \qquad LCL_{\bar{x}} = \bar{\bar{x}} - A_2\bar{R} \qquad [16.3]$$

Average fraction nonconforming for p-chart

$$\bar{p} = \frac{p_1 + p_2 \cdots + p_k}{k} \qquad [16.4]$$

Standard deviation of fraction nonconforming for p-chart

$$s_{\bar{p}} = \sqrt{\frac{\bar{p}(1 - \bar{p})}{n}} \qquad [16.5]$$

Upper and lower control limits for p-charts

$$UCL_p = \bar{p} + 3s_{\bar{p}}$$
$$LCL_p = \bar{p} - 3s_{\bar{p}} \qquad [16.6]$$

Upper and lower control limits for c-charts

$$UCL_c = \bar{c} + 3\sqrt{\bar{c}}$$
$$LCL_c = \bar{c} - 3\sqrt{\bar{c}} \qquad [16.7]$$

Approximation of standard deviation with x- and R-charts

$$\sigma = \frac{\bar{R}}{d_2} \qquad [16.8]$$

Process capability index

$$C_p = \frac{USL - LSL}{6\sigma} \qquad [16.9]$$

One-sided capability index

$$C_{pu} = \frac{USL - \mu}{3\sigma} \quad \text{(upper one-sided index)} \qquad [16.10]$$

$$C_{pl} = \frac{\mu - LSL}{3\sigma} \quad \text{(lower one-sided index)} \qquad [16.11]$$

$$C_{pk} = \min\,(C_{pl}, C_{pu}) \qquad [16.12]$$

Number of Kanban cards required

$$K = \frac{\text{Average daily demand during lead time plus a safety stock}}{\text{Number of units per container}}$$

$$= \frac{d(p + w)(1 + \alpha)}{C} \qquad [17.1]$$

Crash cost per unit of time

$$\text{Crash cost per unit of time} = \frac{\text{Crash cost} - \text{Normal cost}}{\text{Normal time} - \text{Crash time}} \qquad [18.1]$$

Expected time

$$\text{Expected time} = (a + 4m + b)/6 \qquad [18.2]$$

Variance of activity times

$$\text{Variance} = (b - a)^2/36 \qquad [18.3]$$